SPARKNOTES®

★ ★ ★ ★ ★ ★ ★ ★ ★ ★ ★ ★ ★

283 GREAT COLLEGES

★ ★ ★ ★ ★ ★ ★ ★ ★ ★ ★ ★ ★

SPARK PUBLISHING

Spark Publishing
120 Fifth Avenue
New York, NY 10011
www.sparknotes.com

Library of Congress Cataloging-in-Publication Data

283 Great Colleges. p. cm.
"SparkCollege."
ISBN-13: 978-1-4114-0938-5
ISBN-10: 1-4114-0938-8
1. Universities and colleges—United States. I. Title: Two hundred eighty-three great colleges.
LA226.A13 2008
378.73—dc22

2008004295

Please submit changes or report errors to www.sparknotes.com/errors.

Printed and bound in Canada

10 9 8 7 6 5 4 3 2 1

CONTENTS

CONTENTS

CONTENTS

CONTENTS

CONTENTS

Acknowledgments

SparkNotes would like to thank the following writers and contributors: Josh Cracraft, Oriane Delfosse, Katherine Gopteke, Laura Jeanne Hammond, Erwin Montgomery, Laura Nathan, Justine E. Schroeder, and Andrew Wilson.

We would also like to thank the following education experts: David S. Bonner, director of college counseling at King & Low-Heywood Thomas School, CT; Ralph Burrelle, department chair, counseling, at North Medford (OR) High School; David P. Coates, school counselor, Kenmore East High School, NY, and NYSACAC high school delegate; Donnamarie Hehn, director of college guidance at Canterbury School of Florida; Greg McCandless, assistant director of college counseling at Sage Hill School, CA; Carl Peterson, counselor at Forest Hills Eastern High School, MI, and board of directors for the National Association for College Admission Counseling; Bill Pruden, head of upper school and college counselor for Ravenscroft School, NC; Bruce M. Richardson, director of guidance at Plano Senior High School, and Plano Independent School District, TX; Mary Ellen Setlock, director of guidance at Pottsville Area High School, PA; and Lindsey Waite, assistant director of college counseling at Ravenscroft School, NC.

Finally, we would like to thank the following students, parents, and educators at Freehold Township and Manalapan High Schools for generously donating their time to the SparkNotes guides: Cyndee Baumgartner, English supervisor; Leanne Dinverno, high school graduate; Elizabeth Higley, principal; Lida Nagel, guidance counselor; Kim Parks, high school student; Jan Peterson, parent; Maggie Rogers, parent; Dani Rosen, high school student; and Jacqueline Thomas, head guidance counselor.

Introduction

Higher education is no longer a cookie-cutter, one-size-fits-all enterprise. Terms like *best* and *top tier* have lost their relevance. And those all-important rankings that you hear so much about aren't as useful as you've been led to believe. Rankings may provide great publicity for the few schools hovering at the top of the list, but the truth is, those rankings rely on a narrow range of statistics. The average SAT score of the incoming class is an interesting figure, but it isn't going to tell you much about what a college is really like.

And we're sure you've heard the familiar phrases "small liberal arts college," "big state school," and so on. Guess what: You can forget those too. They're mostly outdated and inaccurate. These days, a small college in Maine might have a great engineering program in addition to its excellent humanities offerings, and a giant state school might create (for students who want it) a small private college experience.

So how are you supposed to find the right school? By using a method that reflects what colleges are really like today.

"Great" Colleges

We've assembled a team of experts to help us identify criteria for measuring *great* (not "best") colleges. Our team includes teachers and guidance counselors—experts who know the schools in their regions inside and out. We've also enlisted the help of students—high school students, college students, and recent college graduates.

Our team talked. And talked. And eventually they defined the qualities that characterize great colleges. According to our experts, all great colleges:

- Provide innovative and unique programs of study—not just impressive endowments
- Offer a real community—not just a photogenic campus
- Arm students with strong writing and speaking skills—not just inflated grades
- Attract bright and diverse students—not just those who score well on standardized tests
- Give students the skills they need to thrive in the working world or grad school—not just a fancy diploma

With our team's guidance and expertise, we narrowed down the thousands of colleges and universities out there to the 283 you'll find profiled in this book. Our colleges come in all shapes and sizes and include Ivy League schools, public universities, small colleges, art schools, military academies, and more.

Our Icons

To help you navigate through the 283 colleges and universities, we've come up with an icon system that will make it easier for you to find your college matches. Each icon captures the unique ways in which schools approach academics and their students' future careers. And because no college neatly fits into one category, you'll see that most schools are assigned two or three icons.

Here's what the icons mean:

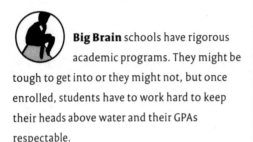 **Big Brain** schools have rigorous academic programs. They might be tough to get into or they might not, but once enrolled, students have to work hard to keep their heads above water and their GPAs respectable.

 Big Idea schools take an outside-the-box approach to academics. Professors might write evaluations instead of giving grades, students might design their own programs of study, or a Great Books program may make up the focus of the curricula, to name just three possibilities.

Big Plan schools offer a specialized program of study designed to train students for a specific job or field. These schools are great for students who know exactly what they want to pursue after graduation, whether it's performing ballet or flying jets.

 Big Perspective schools emphasize interdisciplinary thinking.

They provide a solid grounding in the liberal arts and sciences and may require students to complete a substantial series of core classes.

 Big Choice schools give their students a multitude of academic options. They offer at least five or six distinct programs of study and dozens of majors.

 Big Research schools boast excellent, well-funded research programs that undergrads may access, whether by assisting professors with research or by working on projects of their own.

 Big Hand schools give their students a little extra support. This attention might come in the form of an encouraging academic environment, inventive orientation programs, attentive professors, small classes, or some combination of these elements.

 Big Job schools make it a priority to help their students prepare for the working world. They offer co-op programs, require internships, or take other steps to help their students lay the groundwork for successful careers.

 Big World schools emphasize experiential learning. Rather than confining students to the classroom, they encourage travel abroad, community projects, and other service learning initiatives.

Finding Your Best College Match

As our icons suggest, there are many kinds of schools out there. Which are the best ones? Well, our premise is this: The best school is nothing more or less than the best school for you. We'll say it one more time, with feeling:

The best school is nothing more or less than the best school for you.

A school might be best for you because of one or several factors, including location, facilities, major, reputation, size, philosophy, faculty, student body, extracurricular options, admissions standards, and financial considerations. We've come up with a little self-assessment to get you thinking about these factors.

Set aside an hour or two, find a quiet place free of distractions, and answer the following questions. The most important thing here is to *be honest with yourself.*

- **The big picture:** What are you looking to get out of college? Where do you see yourself in five years? Ten years?
- **Types of programs:** Do pre-professional programs, such as business, nursing, or engineering programs, appeal to you? Or do you favor the idea of a more broad-based liberal arts education?
- **Majors:** Do you have a specific major in mind? Or would you like to explore different academic options before settling on one major?
- **Academic climate:** Does a competitive academic environment appeal to you, or would you prefer one that's more laid-back?
- **Class size:** Can you see yourself in large, lecture-style classes? Or are small, seminar classes more your style?
- **Core requirements:** Some schools ask their students to take a strict regimen of required classes. Does this appeal to you, or do you prefer to have more freedom in planning your own course of study?
- **Activities:** Do you love playing sports—or watching other people play them? Does Greek life appeal to you? Are there particular student organizations that interest you?
- **Students:** Is the on-campus political climate, whether liberal or conservative, important to you? What about the religious climate? Do you dream of being surrounded by artists and musicians? Dorky-and-proud engineering students? People of your gender? A broad spectrum of students from every country, ethnicity, race, and economic class?
- **Location:** Do you want to be close to home or far away? In (or near) a big city or in a more rural location? Do you want mountains, beaches, grasslands, forests, cement?

You may have noticed that cost isn't included in that list. While we'd never pretend that money isn't an issue for most students beginning their college search, we also have to say (and we mean this): *Look into every school that interests you—and don't be put off by the price tag.* If you find a school you really love, even a pricey one, you absolutely should investigate its financial aid offerings and see what outside scholarships and aid you qualify for. You'll be surprised by what's out there.

College Match Quiz

Fortunately, unlike those quizzes your chemistry teacher loves to spring on you whenever you're least pre-pared, our quiz is short and highly unscientific. Best of all, it requires absolutely no advance preparation. Its purpose is to help match your interests to the academic programs represented by our icons. In fact, each question in the quiz corresponds to one of our icons.

Ready to get started? Sharpen up that No. 2 pencil and dig in.

1. The library is:

a) Your home away from home

b) A nice place to visit, but you wouldn't want to live there

c) A great place to hang out with your friends—sort of like a bar without beer

d) What's a library?

2. A professor just handed you a packet of written remarks in lieu of a grade. You feel:

a) Pleased. These personalized comments are far more meaningful than a letter grade.

b) Neutral. Remarks, grades, it's all the same to you.

c) Irritated. How will grad schools and potential employers be able to measure you against other candidates if you don't have a GPA?

d) Enraged. Written remarks are for neo-hippy drum-circle participants.

3. What do you want to do after you graduate?

a) Since the fourth grade, you've known you want to be a _____ (pilot, singer, business mogul—you fill in the blank).

b) You're not sure, but you have a few vague possibilities in mind.

c) Maybe travel for a few years?

d) You have no idea. After all, you're still in high school. The real world is *years* away. And isn't college the time to figure this stuff out, anyway?

4. You got into an excellent school that offers a well-rounded, interdisciplinary course of study. Your reaction:

a) Sweet. I'm excited about studying across the disciplines and being well rounded.

b) Sure, sounds fine.

c) I'm not crazy about the idea of core requirements.

d) Shoot. I really wanted total freedom to choose my own classes.

5. Pick the option that sounds most appealing:

a) A LAAARGE university. We're talking two hundred or more programs, from a School of the Arts to a degree in zoology.

b) A university (a school with undergrads and

grad students) that's not too big, not too small, and has just the right number of academic programs.

c) A *college* (a school with just undergrads) that's not too big, not too small, and has just the right number of academic programs.

d) A small college that specializes in a select few programs.

6. **You got into a great school that offers tons of research opportunities for undergrads. Your reaction:**

a) Hooray! All I wanted was the chance to work with professors in a research setting and maybe get my name on some papers!

b) Doing research might be a good option for me.

c) I'm not too interested in research.

d) I cannot think of a worse fate than being cooped up in a lab with a bunch of professors and grad students.

7. **You've matriculated at a school that is *not* known for babying students. How do you feel about that?**

a) Nervous. College is so different from high school, and you could use a helping hand in making the transition.

b) Neutral. You don't mind forging your own path.

c) Fine. You get all the babying you need from your mom.

d) Relieved. The last thing you want is hectoring advisors and smothering RAs. You're an independent person, after all.

8. **Would you like to be an intern?**

a) Of course. Internships are a necessity for anyone who actually wants to get a job after graduation. Real-world working experience should blend seamlessly with your studies.

b) Sure. You'd like to try out different fields and get some experience to put on your resume.

c) No. You're here to study, first and foremost. A required internship would only distract you from your pursuit of higher knowledge.

d) You're kidding, right? What kind of moron volunteers to make photocopies and bad coffee for no pay?

9. **Which most nearly describes your feelings?**

a) You can't learn everything in the classroom. Traveling, volunteering, and serving the community are crucial aspects of the college learning experience.

b) Outside-the-classroom learning is enlightening, but only in small doses, and only when it doesn't take you away from your studies.

c) You're fine with just going to class, hitting the stacks, and reading on the quad on nice days.

d) You dislike leaving campus for any reason.

$a = 3$
$b = 5$
$c = 1$
$d = 0$

Answer Key

Look over your answers. Are any of your answers A's? Or are most of your answers B's or C's? Are there a few D's sprinkled in for good measure?

As we mentioned earlier, each question on this quiz corresponds to a specific icon:

Question number . . .	corresponds to . . .	
1	the Big Brain icon.	
2	the Big Idea icon.	
3	the Big Plan icon.	
4	the Big Perspective icon.	
5	the Big Choice icon.	
6	the Big Research icon.	
7	the Big Hand icon.	
8	the Big Job icon.	
9	the Big World icon.	

If you answered A for one of the questions, it means schools with the corresponding icon *will probably* interest you. If you answered B, schools with that icon *might* interest you. If you chose C, schools with that icon *might not* interest you. And if you answered D, schools with that icon *probably won't* interest you.

See which icons your A's match up with, and hone in on schools with those icons. In the back of this book, you'll find a list showing you which pages these schools can be found on. If you're not a strong match with any of the icons, that simply means that you're someone who will do well at a broad variety of schools.

That's All, Folks!

Well, not quite. You still have a lot of work to do—visit colleges, write application essays, and so on. Think of this guide as a starting point. We hope to get you a little closer to starting the college search process and moving on to what will probably be one of the most exciting experiences of your life.

For more information on choosing colleges and lots of great tips and advice, go to *www.sparknotes. com/college.*

If you've got something to say about this book, tell us! Your input makes us better. Go to the "comments" section of our website and give us the straight story. We can't wait to hear your opinion!

A note about our data: Each profile is accompanied by data, including admissions info, demographics, and figures on tuition and financial aid. On occasion, you'll see a dash instead of a number. A dash means either that the information has not been provided or that the information is not applicable to that school. For more information, visit the school's website.

The Great Colleges

Allegheny College

520 North Main Street
Meadville, PA 16335

(814) 332-3100
http://www.allegheny.edu/

BIG PERSPECTIVE

Study (real) hard in a (real) small town.

5 REASONS IT'S COOL

1. Allegheny **produces more business leaders than** 90 percent of liberal arts colleges.

2. The Allegheny College Center for Experiential Learning is a one-stop shop for internships, community service, and other **out-of-the-classroom enrichment.**

3. The college has extra-ordinary success **sending its students on to top graduate programs** in medicine, law, and the sciences.

4. The **283-acre nature preserve** inspires students to venture outdoors.

5. This **jock-friendly school** gives basketball nuts and Pilates addicts alike all the sweat space they need.

The Basics

Public / private: private nonprofit
Total enrollment / undergrads: 2,095 / 2,095
Campus setting: small town
Students call it: Allegheny
Students are called: Gators
Notable alums: Robert Dowling (heart transplant pioneer), Ida Tarbell (journalist), William McKinley (U.S. president), Richard Murphy (photographer)

A High-Octane Blend

Allegheny's academic programs are the main draw for many students, and, by all indications, these young scholars get what they've come for. Students speak highly of their professors—leaders in their fields who reward committed pupils with loads of personal attention. Approximately 95 percent of faculty members have PhDs or the terminal degree in their areas of study, and the average class size is only sixteen. The overarching aim of the Allegheny undergraduate program is to produce well-rounded critical thinkers who are comfortable in more than one mode of inquiry. To this end, students are required to select not only majors but also minors. From art to dance to the college's strong science programs, students have more than 900 major-minor combinations from which to choose. Biology and English, political science and geology, and economics and physics are typical combinations. Outside of the classroom, the Center for Experiential Learning helps students incorporate volunteer work, internships, and laboratory research into their academic programs.

From Prankster to President

When William McKinley was an Allegheny student, he lured a cow up to the bell tower at Bentley Hall and left it there. An (probably apocryphal) addendum to the story holds that the cow refused to walk back down and had to be butchered at the top of the stairs. McKinley did not return to Allegheny the next semester, and some believe he was unofficially expelled. The cow-shaped sign at the campus's McKinley Food Court memorializes the incident.

A Strong Community

Students report that, despite the intense focus on academics, Gators generally avoid the antisocial behaviors—for example, hoarding library books, holing up in dorm rooms—that sometimes poison campuses. In fact, studying frequently becomes a social event in itself. So, too, does binge drinking, which is just as common here as anyplace else. About 25 percent of students belong to fraternities, meaning that Greek life is an important, but not overwhelming, component of the Allegheny scene. A similar percentage of students are involved in intercollegiate athletics, and about half the others participate in intramurals. There's a real sense of community at Allegheny, as all students are required to live in university housing for at least three years. Lack of diversity is consistently cited as the biggest downside to life at Allegheny: About 90 percent of students are white.

Small-Town Life: It Is What It Is

If the charm and safety of small-town living sound like a dream come true, Meadville might be your kind of place. If subpar nightlife, quiet streets, and a conservative and homogenous population sound like a nightmare, consider visiting the home of Allegheny before sending in your deposit. Meadville apologists point to the town's growing punk scene as evidence of its fun quirkiness, but skeptics counter that the punks and their music are noticeable only because everything else in town is so dull. Nature-loving Gators appreciate the surrounding forests, particularly in the fall, and students suffering urban withdrawal can head to Pittsburgh or Cleveland, both ninety miles away, on the weekends. Either way, having a car helps a lot, as public transport in Meadville is paltry at best.

Admissions

Average high school GPA:	3.76
Average freshman SAT verbal / math score:	612 / 610
Average freshman ACT score:	24
Application fee:	$35
Application deadlines: 2/15 (freshmen) 7/1 (transfer) 11/15 (early decision)	
Total applicants:	3,668
Total accepted:	2,314 (63%)
Total accepted who enrolled:	570
Notification dates: 4/1 (freshmen) 8/1 (transfer) 12/15 (early decision)	
Acceptance rate for early decision applicants:	77%

Students

Percentage of male / female students:	46% / 54%
Percentage of students from out of state:	36%
Percentage of students graduating in 4 years / 6 years:	66% / 73%

Money

Total endowment:	$135,551,800
Total tuition:	$29,680
Total cost with fees & expenses:	$37,500
Average financial aid package:	$22,400
Percentage of students who sought aid and received it:	91%
Percentage of students receiving financial aid:	66%

Also Check Out

Cornell University

Dickinson College

Juniata College

Muhlenberg College

Skidmore College

American University

4400 Massachusetts Avenue, NW
Washington, DC 20016

(202) 885-1000
http://www.american.edu/

 BIG JOB

 **BIG WORLD**

Where eagles fly high

5 REASONS IT'S COOL

1. American cultivates **a truly global perspective.**

2. **Political discussions are lively and frequent** inside and outside the classroom.

3. **Washington, D.C., offers plentiful internship opportunities** and as much art and culture as students can cram into their schedules.

4. The first-rate resources include **campuswide wireless Internet access.**

5. Future professionals of all stripes **prepare themselves for lives of service and success.**

The Basics

Public / private: private religious
Total enrollment / undergrads: 11,279 / 5,921
Campus setting: suburban
Students call it: AU
Students are called: Eagles
Notable alums: Goldie Hawn (actress), Star Jones (lawyer, TV personality), General Barry McCaffrey (U.S. Army), Nancy Myers (writer, director)

Public Affairs

American offers some of the nation's strongest programs in the social sciences and humanities. The university has over sixty majors and pre-professional programs, all of which emphasize global perspectives and intercultural experience. The most popular major is international studies, followed closely by business administration, political science, journalism, and public communication. The College of Arts and Sciences also has strong programs in creative writing, theater, history, and economics. The number of students entering the School of International Service has also skyrocketed in recent years, especially since AU Abroad offers more than a hundred study abroad options. This program, combined with the university's commitment to social service, speaks to the importance AU places on getting out into the world. The other schools of business, public affairs, and communication, meanwhile, give budding professionals the skills they need to succeed in the international community. It's no surprise that AU's alumni include ambassadors, politicians, lawyers, and communications professionals—many of whom

Taking Their Sweet Time

The idea of creating American University began in the late 1700s, but it wasn't until the 1890s that construction actually began. The school didn't grant its first degrees until 1916 and didn't begin its undergraduate program until 1925. The university may have gotten off to a slow start, but it has since excelled in its mission to educate future generations of young public leaders.

are at the top of their fields. If you're interested in a career in law, government, and public service, this is the place to be.

Proud to Be at American

Flags fly and the eagles soar at this school in the nation's capital. Many of AU's exceptional students intern at the city's best political, cultural, and research institutions. Life in the capital also offers students access to some of the country's best museums, parks, and national monuments. AU's NCAA Division I athletics teams are in the Patriot League, so there's a lot of red, white, and blue there too, especially since the school mascot is none other than a bird named Clawed Z. Eagle. Just fewer than 70 percent of students live on campus, and about 17 percent go Greek. For grub, on-campus freshmen have to enroll in the 200 Block Plan, which provides a combination of meals and EagleBuck$ for grabbing food when it's convenient.

A Capital Idea

AU's campus was designed by none other than Frederick Law Olmstead, the landscape architect who also created New York City's Central Park. The seventy-six acre main campus begins at Ward Circle at the top of Embassy Row and spans the entire residential neighborhood of Tenleytown in Northwest D.C. Like Central Park, the AU campus features many idyllic spots. In fact, the main campus has been designated a national arboretum. Students tend to congregate at the Bender Library for studying and the Mary Graydon Center for hanging out. The stunning Katzen Arts Center, meanwhile, serves as a multidisciplinary arts space and is designed to accommodate performances, instruction, and exhibitions. Wireless Internet access throughout campus makes it easy for students to do work wherever they are. And when the work is finally done, students can easily explore downtown D.C. via shuttles and the Metro.

Admissions

Average high school GPA:	3.5
Average freshman SAT verbal / math score:	656 / 632
Average freshman ACT score:	26
Application fee:	$45
Application deadlines: 1/15 (freshmen) 7/1 (transfer) 11/15 (early decision)	
Total applicants:	13,583
Total accepted:	6,973 (51%)
Total accepted who enrolled:	1,221
Notification dates: 4/1 (freshmen) continuous (transfer) 12/31 (early decision)	
Acceptance rate for early decision applicants:	61%

Students

Percentage of male / female students:	38% / 62%
Percentage of students from out of state:	99%
Percentage of students graduating in 4 years / 6 years:	64% / 71%

Money

Total endowment:	$318,000,000
Total tuition:	$29,206
Total cost with fees & expenses:	$41,843
Average financial aid package:	$26,453
Percentage of students who sought aid and received it:	75%
Percentage of students receiving financial aid:	47%

Also Check Out

The George Washington University

Georgetown University

Syracuse University

University of Maryland–College Park

University of Virginia

Amherst College

PO Box 5000
Amherst, MA 01002

(413) 542-2000
http://www.amherst.edu/

 BIG BRAIN

 BIG PERSPECTIVE

The complete package: smart, pretty, and fun

5 REASONS IT'S COOL

1. **Professors enthusiastically engage with students** outside the classroom.

2. You can count the **easygoing distribution requirements** on one finger!

3. With **four other prestigious colleges nearby**, students can find hundreds more courses and thousands more potential friends . . . or dates.

4. It won't necessarily put you in debt for twenty years. Amherst has a **well-funded, need-blind financial aid program.**

5. With a student body that's 35 percent nonwhite, Amherst's campus is **one of the most diverse** patches of New England.

The Basics

Public / private: private nonprofit
Total enrollment / undergrads: 1,648 / 1,648
Campus setting: small town
Students call it: Amherst
Students are called: Lord Jeffs, Lady Jeffs
Notable alums: Calvin Coolidge (U.S. president), Susannah Grant (screenwriter), Scott Turow (novelist), Jeffrey Wright (actor)

They Pick One, You Pick Thirty-One

Academics at Amherst are top rate, and admission is cutthroat. You could form an awe-inspiring freshman class from the pool of applicants who *don't* get in every year. The college is deeply committed to the ideals of liberal education, with an unusual twist: Only one of the thirty-two courses you'll need to graduate is required. Even this course—a freshman seminar introduction to liberal study, critical thinking, and writing— comes in more than a dozen flavors. Each department has its own requirements for majors, but aside from those, the entire course catalogue is fair game. Amherst trusts its students to be disciplined enough to explore, on their own, the breadth of the school's offerings. And so, since there aren't any distribution requirements to force students into courses, you can assume every classroom is full of people who actually want to be there. The same goes for the professors, who are known for taking passionate interest in their students' success—and for expecting everyone to have done the previous night's reading assignment. Amherst is a member of the Five Colleges Consortium. This means

A War of Books

In 1821, Zephaniah Swift Moore resigned as president of Williams College and founded Amherst. Some say that Moore, who took a number of Williams's students and faculty to his newly opened school, also stole a sizeable portion of the Williams library. In 1995, the president of Williams declared this rumor false. Despite this gesture of goodwill, the rivalry between the two schools remains fierce.

that students have access to thousands of additional courses (at no additional cost) at neighboring institutions Smith, Hampshire, Mount Holyoke, and the University of Massachusetts, Amherst.

The Other 8 Percent Just Didn't Like the Food

Life as a Lord or Lady Jeff must be pretty good, because in a recent survey, 92 percent of alumni said they would attend Amherst a second time if they had to "do it all over again." Students credit the cohesiveness of the campus community for improving their academic and personal lives, and it's worth noting that the line between studying and socializing is often blurred. With 98 percent of the student body living on campus, it's easy to find someone down the hall or across the street who's willing to continue a class discussion over a beer. Or several. Amherst, books aside, has a vibrant party scene, and shuttle buses connect students to the other colleges in the Five Colleges Consortium. Amherst students keep 110 extracurricular organizations running—an impressive figure for such a small school. A cappella is popular, as are student newspapers, magazines, and literary journals. Athletics, both varsity and intramural, benefit from high-quality, modern sports facilities. In fact, the only consistently cited problem with life on campus is the cafeteria's pathetic offerings.

Small, Safe, and Friendly

Many Amherst students consider locking their front doors unnecessary. Whether you're a chronic fate tempter or not, there's no denying this place has all the hominess of classic New England. Town-gown relations are healthy, and it's not unusual for students to form friendships with neighbors who don't have anything to do with the college. On weekends, 95 percent of students remain in Amherst. Optimists say that's because there's more than enough to do on campus and in town. Others point out that it's hard to get anywhere else. Nearby Northampton, the comparatively large and lively home of Smith College, provides a destination for weekend trips, but Boston, ninety miles to the east, is the nearest big city. You'll need to drive considerably further than that to escape the New England winters.

Admissions

Average high school GPA:	—
Average freshman SAT verbal / math score:	705 / 705
Average freshman ACT score:	26
Application fee:	$55
Application deadlines:	
1/1 (freshmen)	
2/1 (transfer)	
11/15 (early decision)	
Total applicants:	6,142
Total accepted:	1,144 (19%)
Total accepted who enrolled:	433
Notification dates:	
4/5 (freshmen)	
6/1 (transfer)	
12/15 (early decision)	
Acceptance rate for early decision applicants:	38%

Students

Percentage of male / female students:	50% / 50%
Percentage of students from out of state:	88%
Percentage of students graduating in 4 years / 6 years:	89% / 96%

Money

Total endowment:	$1,337,158,000
Total tuition:	$34,280
Total cost with fees & expenses:	$44,946
Average financial aid package:	$32,041
Percentage of students who sought aid and received it:	100%
Percentage of students receiving financial aid:	47%

Also Check Out

Dartmouth College

Kenyon College

Swarthmore College

Wesleyan University

Williams College

zona State University

P.O. Box 870112
Tempe, AZ 85287

(480) 965-9011
http://www.asu.edu/

 **BIG CHOICE**

 **BIG RESEARCH**

Raising Arizona, one graduate at a time

5 REASONS IT'S COOL

1. With over 45,000 undergraduates and more than 250 degree programs, ASU is **one of the largest universities in the nation**.

2. Fascinating facilities, new construction, and signature public art displays create an **atmosphere of opportunity and potential.**

3. The school sits in the heart of the **gorgeous Southwest.**

4. The **highly selective Barrett Honors College** offers promising students enhanced academic challenges.

5. The successful Sun Devils offer some of the **best college sports action in the country.**

The Basics

Public / private: public state
Total enrollment / undergrads: 51,234 / 41,815
Campus setting: suburban
Students call it: ASU
Students are called: Sun Devils
Notable alums: Steve Allen (comedian), Jimmy Kimmel (TV personality), David Spade (actor), Kate Spade (designer), Reggie Jackson (pro baseball player), Pat Tillman (pro football player), Brenda Strong (actress)

AS U Like It

With hundreds of programs and tens of thousands of potential friends, the opportunities at ASU are endless. Students, including those in the affiliated Barrett Honors College, are sure to find their niche with over 250 different majors to choose from. Most students choose a major within the Business or Liberal Arts & Sciences colleges. Standout majors include creative writing, journalism, psychology, and business. If none of the available majors is quite right for you, you have the chance to combine two different majors via the popular interdisciplinary studies program to create your own academic blend. Despite its massive size, ASU keeps its focus on the individual with a modest 22:1 student-to-faculty ratio. The Freshman Year Residential Experience (FYRE) program, which provides social and academic support to new undergrads, is an invaluable resource at a school so large.

Light the Way to Homecoming

Homecoming at ASU is not just about pigskin and school spirit. As part of the festivities, the campus engages in a Lantern Walk to "A" Mountain (the *A* stands for Arizona, naturally). Students and alumni alike gather at the base of the mountain, candles in hand, and glow with devilish pride.

Devilish Fun

There's a lot that's sunny about ASU. Sun Devils Stadium draws hundreds of thousands of spectators a year for Pac 10 football, which imbues the campus with a hefty dose of Sun Devil pride. Racial and ethnic diversity is excellent, as are the number of out-of-state students, which fosters a mix of perspectives and cultures. And while Greek life is pretty low key, the 450 clubs and student groups on campus offer more than a little something for everyone. The arts take center stage at ASU, which sponsors numerous art exhibits and cultural performances every year in the world-famous Grammage Auditorium, designed by none other than renowned architect Frank Lloyd Wright. The Percent-for-Art Program, meanwhile, channels half of 1 percent of the construction costs of all new buildings toward the production of public art. That might not sound like much, but given the rapid development of the campus, it's a significant contribution. So while Sun Devils superfans will love life here, so will the more artistically inclined.

Phoenix on the Rise

ASU's four campuses stretch throughout the greater Phoenix area. The Tempe campus anchors this sprawling center of learning. While the straight lines and right angles of most of the buildings on the Tempe campus might leave you begging for a little variety, you'll find relief in additions such as the newly built Lattie F. Coor Hall's public art displays, which appeal to even the most demanding sense of aesthetics. When campus life pales, students head to the hills for a little R & R in the great outdoors. Nearby Tempe Town Lake offers fishing, swimming, boat racing, and the opportunity to perfect that characteristic ASU tan. Vegas, San Diego, and the Colorado Rockies aren't too far away either.

Admissions

Average high school GPA:	3.27
Average freshman SAT verbal / math score:	544 / 560
Average freshman ACT score:	22
Application fee:	$25
Application deadlines: continuous (freshmen) continuous (transfer) — (early action)	
Total applicants:	20,702
Total accepted:	19,133 (92%)
Total accepted who enrolled:	7,076
Notification dates: continuous (freshmen) continuous (transfer) — (early action)	
Acceptance rate for early action applicants:	—

Students

Percentage of male / female students:	50% / 50%
Percentage of students from out of state:	25%
Percentage of students graduating in 4 years / 6 years:	27% / 55%

Money

Total endowment:	$394,796,000
Total in-state tuition, fees & expenses:	$12,538
Total out-of-state tuition, fees & expenses:	$23,697
Average financial aid package:	$8,649
Percentage of students who sought aid and received it:	64%
Percentage of students receiving financial aid:	32%

Also Check Out

Northern Arizona University

San Diego State University

The University of Arizona

University of California–Los Angeles

The University of Texas at Austin

Auburn University

108 Mary Martin Hall
Auburn University, AL 36849

(334) 844-4000
http://www.auburn.edu/

 **BIG CHOICE**

 **BIG RESEARCH**

Southern comfort

5 REASONS IT'S COOL

1. Auburn is one of the country's few **land-, sea-, and space-grant research institutions.**

2. **Econ-minded libertarians** can take advantage of courses at the Ludwig von Mises Institute.

3. **Tigers football brings beer-fueled bonhomie** to fans of every class and walk of life.

4. Recent university enhancements include a **new science lab center and an airport terminal for aviation students.**

5. The co-op program allows students to **earn credit and money** in several professional fields.

The Basics

Public / private: public state
Total enrollment / undergrads: 23,547 / 19,367
Campus setting: small town
Students call it: Auburn
Students are called: Tigers
Notable alums: Bo Jackson (pro football and baseball player), General Richard Myers (U.S. Air Force), Chuck Person (pro basketball player), Anne Rivers Siddons (novelist), Toni Tennille (singer)

Practical, if Not Liberal, Arts

Auburn has weathered some tough times. Its fiscal fortunes have fluctuated, and a parade of university presidents has passed through its administration. But in recent years, the university has bounced back with a renewed focus on its curriculum. While some professors object to the diminished importance of liberal arts, others feel the general education curriculum has retained a sufficient liberal arts component. The majority of students pursue studies in business, education, or engineering, three of the university's strongest programs. The Economics Department, part of the College of Business, is loaded with some of the best and brightest faculty in the nation. Students who elect not to go the economics route can opt for studies in agriculture, forestry, conservation, and related fields, all of which Auburn has devoted more resources to developing in recent years. Literary and artsy types might be happier at another school, but for devotees of practical arts, Auburn has quite a bit to offer.

Please, Drape the Charmin

The intersection known as Toomer's Corner has been the site of mischief among Auburn students for decades, as students have taken to draping its oak trees in toilet paper. Originally, this decorative frenzy commemorated away-game victories, but in recent years, it has been used to celebrate any good news.

Tiger Balm

Tigers have an air of propriety and southern gentility. While keggers are frequently part of football game fever, the decadence doesn't go much further than that. The Greek presence is strong, with roughly a quarter of the student population participating, but it doesn't dominate the social scene. Nearly 70 percent of students are native Alabamians, and legacies reach back two and three generations. While a campus-wide spirit of community exists and is a source of pride among Tigers, ethnic diversity is somewhat lacking. African Americans are the only significant minority, representing less than 10 percent of the student body. Most Auburn students are conservative, but for those who find a niche, the atmosphere is friendly and easygoing.

Plain Livin'

Campus is a sprawling 1,700 acres of beautiful southern grace. Housing shortages are notorious, and under a quarter of students live on campus. Most head instead for one of the many apartment complexes that have sprung up in neighboring areas to accommodate the university's growth. For those remaining on the grounds, residence halls vary from the serviceable, Depression-era Quad to recently renovated buildings. The university is by far the biggest action in the town of Auburn, which markets itself as "The Loveliest Village on the Plains." Auburn has recently become one of the fastest-growing U.S. cities, but urbanites shouldn't expect cosmopolitan living. The town is closely tied to the university—historically, economically, and culturally—and relations between the two are strong, particularly during football season. For students needing a break from the picnic-and-pie pace, the hopping college hub of Atlanta is just two hours away.

Admissions

Average high school GPA:	3.56
Average freshman SAT verbal / math score:	561 / 581
Average freshman ACT score:	23
Application fee:	$25
Application deadlines: 8/1 (freshmen) continuous (transfer)	
Total applicants:	15,919
Total accepted:	11,538 (72%)
Total accepted who enrolled:	4,069
Notification dates: continuous (freshmen) continuous (transfer)	

Students

Percentage of male / female students:	50% / 50%
Percentage of students from out of state:	39%
Percentage of students graduating in 4 years / 6 years:	32% / 62%

Money

Total endowment:	$378,570,463
Total in-state tuition, fees & expenses:	$14,060
Total out-of-state tuition, fees & expenses:	$24,060
Average financial aid package:	$7,614
Percentage of students who sought aid and received it:	47%
Percentage of students receiving financial aid:	30%

Also Check Out

Clemson University

Louisiana State University– Baton Rouge

University of Florida

University of Georgia

The University of Mississippi

Austin College

900 North Grand Avenue
Sherman, TX 75090

(903) 813-2000
http://www.austincollege.edu/

BIG PERSPECTIVE

BIG WORLD

A small school with a big heart

5 REASONS IT'S COOL

1. **AC offers competitive merit-based scholarships** for academics, leadership, religious affiliation, and the creative arts, among others.

2. **Nearly half the students graduated in the top 10 percent** of their high school class.

3. During the three-week January term, students can **study in far-flung places** such as Costa Rica, West Africa, and New Zealand.

4. Looking for a **cozy and close-knit campus community?** You'll find it at AC.

5. The Posey Leadership Institute gives select students **hands-on leadership and service experience**, plus a hefty annual scholarship.

The Basics

Public / private: private religious
Total enrollment / undergrads: 1,354 / 1,321
Campus setting: suburban
Students call it: AC
Students are called: Kangaroos
Notable alums: Robert Johnson (film producer), Ron Kirk (mayor, Dallas), Candace Kita (actress, model), Kim Powers (writer), Bill Wilson (film producer)

Looking for a Student-Centered Education?

AC offers challenging academics along with student friendly amenities. There are just over 1,300 students, and few classes exceed 25. TAs are few and far between; most of the teaching and attention comes straight from profs. Freshmen take a required communication/inquiry (or "C/I") seminar, which covers topics such as children's lit, studio art, and food and culture. Professors mentor the students in their C/I seminars from the first day of classes until graduation. During the month-long credit-bearing January term, students can take classes in quirky topics such as comic books or the philosophy of mythological archetypes. Alternatively, they can spend this term studying in NYC, D.C., or overseas. About 70 percent of Kangaroos study abroad. Of the twenty-eight possible majors, business administration and psychology are the most popular. AC is also known for its teaching program, as well as pre-med, pre-law, and international studies programs. Those looking for something a little different have the option of designing their own major.

Who's That Kangaroo?

AC adopted the Kangaroo nickname in 1915 after abolishing its Kangaroo Kourt (mock trials in which upperclassmen "tried" unlucky freshmen). The class of 1923 bought a kangaroo from a California zoo, named him Pat, and took him to home football games and bonfires on a leash. Pat died within two years. After the second of Pat's successors died in 1960, the school handed the roo role over to a costumed student. There hasn't been a fatality since.

Love Thy Neighbor

Many students plan and lead youth missions as members of the ACtivators student group. And despite AC's Presbyterian affiliation, the school has a reputation for being liberal, particularly compared to other Texas institutions. Diversity is a strong suit; 24 percent of AC students belong to ethnic or racial minorities. The sense of community is strong, thanks in part to a requirement that students live on campus for their first three years. In the Jordan Family Language House, residents study a common language and live together (and earn credits for it!). Popular extracurriculars include competing for one of AC's Division III athletic teams, singing in the a cappella group, playing alongside local musicians in the Sherman Symphony Orchestra, contributing to student publications, or performing community service. More than half of students go Greek through one of the school's exclusive frats and sororities, which are separate from any nationally chartered organizations and are open only to students in good standing.

My Campus, My Home

Life at AC starts and ends on campus. Students spend their time with the Greeks or organizations such as Christian Intervarsity, which sponsors activities including video scavenger hunts, Ultimate Frisbee, and box-sledding. There are also intramural sports, local dance halls, free movies, art exhibits, theater, music, and spectator sports. AC recently invested $1 million in campus beautification and renovation. Along with more color, the tree-lined campus is gaining a new esplanade, pedestrian mall, and studio art building, and the baseball field is getting a facelift. Students needing an escape from campus and the small town of Sherman can make the sixty-mile drive to Dallas–Fort Worth, where big-city options such as good restaurants, bars, and professional sports await. Closer to campus lies Lake Texoma, where students spend free time swimming, boating, camping, and fishing.

Admissions

Average high school GPA:	—
Average freshman SAT verbal / math score:	621 / 625
Average freshman ACT score:	24
Application fee:	$35

Application deadlines:
5/1 (freshmen)
5/1 (transfer)
12/1 (early decision)
1/15 (early action)

Total applicants:	1,385
Total accepted:	1,051 (76%)
Total accepted who enrolled:	340

Notification dates:
— (freshmen)
— (transfer)
1/10 (early decision)
3/1 (early action)

Acceptance rate for early action/early decision applicants:	77% / 84%

Students

Percentage of male / female students:	46% / 54%
Percentage of students from out of state:	8%
Percentage of students graduating in 4 years / 6 years:	69% / 75%

Money

Total endowment:	$120,221,782
Total tuition:	$24,760
Total cost with fees & expenses:	$33,179
Average financial aid package:	$22,532
Percentage of students who sought aid and received it:	99%
Percentage of students receiving financial aid:	58%

Also Check Out

Baylor University

Southern Methodist University

Southwestern University

Trinity University

Babson College

231 Forest Street
Babson Park, MA 02457

(781) 235-1200
http://www.babson.edu/

 BIG JOB

Where innovation is tradition

5 REASONS IT'S COOL

1. Every year, Babson is named **the #1 college for entrepreneurship** by just about everyone.

2. Located **just outside the thriving metropolis of Boston,** this school is close to the job action—and one of the best college cities in the United States.

3. A whopping **50 percent of students receive financial aid** directly from the college.

4. The innovative **undergraduate business education programs** are world-renowned.

5. With an astounding **97 percent job placement rate,** this school truly puts its grads on the fast track to success.

The Basics

Public / private: private nonprofit
Total enrollment / undergrads: 3,359 / 1,776
Campus setting: suburban
Students call it: Babson
Students are called: Beavers
Notable alums: Arthur Blank (owner, Atlanta Falcons), Edsel Ford (director, Ford Motor Company), Daniel Gerber (founder, Gerber Baby Foods), Stephen Spinelli Jr. (founder, Jiffy Lube)

They *Really* Mean Business

Babson's dedication to innovation is clear. The highly respected Arthur M. Blank Center for Entrepreneurship is just one of the ways the college takes a novel approach to learning. In fact, Babson has to be one of the few colleges in America where students are encouraged to be entrepreneurs—while they're still in school! The Foundation Management Experience, or FME, gives students the skills they need to launch their own companies straight out of their dorm rooms. The student-to-faculty ratio is 13:1, which means that every student has the ability to work alongside his or her instructors. Faculty members here had successful careers in the business world before becoming professors, so they offer real-world expertise in addition to scholarly wisdom. Co-op programs allow students to mix job experience with their classes. Babson is known for its international business program and its unique management curriculum, which offers an integrated curriculum covering accounting, marketing, finance, management, information

The Other Mascot

Since 1955, the twenty-five-ton Babson Globe has served as an unusual landmark for students. In its early years, the Globe rotated on an axis as a symbol of time's progression. After the Globe succumbed to rust and deterioration, administrators decided to destroy it in the late 1980s. It was saved, however, by the passionate advocacy of students, alumni, and faculty, who raised money to restore the Globe to its rightful place on campus.

technology, and economics. Upperclassmen generally plan their own curricula, mixing liberal arts, out-of-classroom opportunities, and management studies.

Food for the Body, Food for the Mind

Students may be gearing up for future mogul-dom, but despite their hard work and ambition, they still know how to have fun. There are eight hundred student activities on offer, which means even the most specific hobbies and interests have an associated group. The arts are particularly well represented on campus, between the Babson Players, TheaterWorks, Improv Comedy Troupe, and Dance Ensemble, not to mention the Sorenson Visual Arts Center. Babson also has a strong community of international students, who come from thirty-five different countries. The Webster Center bursts with facilities to keep students in shape, including an indoor track, three basketball courts, squash and racquetball courts, a fitness center, a pool, and its own ice skating center. With so much to do both inside and outside of class, there'll never be a dull moment.

Travel . . . without Going Anywhere

Located fourteen miles outside of Boston, Babson is just close enough to the big city that it offers all the advantages of an urban environment with none of the disadvantages. The campus is surrounded by 370 acres of rolling hills and woods, which creates a rustic mood. Students can feel they are getting away from it all simply by stepping outside their dorms. Many students head to the city for eating, drinking, art viewing, and mingling with the 250,000 other students from the sixty colleges in the greater Boston area. It goes without saying that at a school this career oriented, the job opportunities and internships Boston provides are a major selling point.

Admissions

Average high school GPA:	—
Average freshman SAT verbal / math score:	588 / 649
Average freshman ACT score:	25
Application fee:	$60

Application deadlines:
1/15 (freshmen)
4/1 (transfer)
11/15 (early decision)
11/15 (early action)

Total applicants:	3,436
Total accepted:	1,265 (37%)
Total accepted who enrolled:	443

Notification dates:
4/1 (freshmen)
5/15 (transfer)
12/15 (early decision)
1/1 (early action)

Acceptance rate for early action/early decision applicants:	50% / 52%

Students

Percentage of male / female students:	61% / 39%
Percentage of students from out of state:	70%
Percentage of students graduating in 4 years / 6 years:	80% / 85%

Money

Total endowment:	$179,152,232
Total tuition:	$34,112
Total cost with fees & expenses:	$45,782
Average financial aid package:	$27,453
Percentage of students who sought aid and received it:	97%
Percentage of students receiving financial aid:	41%

Also Check Out

Bentley College

Drexel University

Indiana University–Bloomington

Northeastern University

Bard College

PO Box 5000
Annandale-on-Hudson, NY 12504

(845) 758-6822
http://www.bard.edu/

BIG PERSPECTIVE

Over the river and through the woods . . . to leftyland we go!

5 REASONS IT'S COOL

1. **Nonconformity is the norm.** Here, you're not expected to be like everyone else—or, for that matter, like *anyone* else.

2. **Want to save the world?** Community service, including the renowned Bard Prison Initiative, is big here.

3. **Science is no longer the ugly stepchild.** Administrators are working hard to strengthen Bard's nonarts and nonhumanities offerings.

4. Are those the **Catskills outside your dorm-room window**? Yep.

5. **A workshop on language and critical thinking** prepares incoming freshmen for their two-semester first-year seminar.

The Basics

Public / private: private nonprofit
Total enrollment / undergrads: 2,012 / 1,735
Campus setting: rural
Students call it: Bard
Students are called: Raptors
Notable alums: Chevy Chase (actor), Blythe Danner (actress), Christopher Guest (actor, filmmaker), Daniel Pinkwater (writer, NPR commentator)

Broadening Your Horizons and Its Own

Bard has struggled with a reputation for catering solely to artists and performers. Recently, however, the administration has developed a scholarship program for students who intend to major in science or math. They have also invested in new science facilities and collaborated with Rockefeller University for a class in New York City on human disease. There's no denying that Bard's greatest strengths lie in its excellent English and arts departments. Students of all kinds, whether scientists or dramaturges, encounter a rigorous and highly structured academic program that emphasizes individualized research and writing. The first-year seminar exposes students to many fields of knowledge and analytical traditions. Distribution requirements in the sciences and humanities add further structure to the course selection process. The Senior Project, a capstone to the four-year academic program, is also a unique opportunity for extended one-on-one interactions with professors.

Crossing Toward—*gulp*—the Mainstream?

For many years, it was a tradition for Bard students of all stripes to cross-dress during Parent's Weekend, as a sort of nose-thumbing welcome to the parents. This practice is fading. In related news, the annual Drag Race party was recently cancelled, causing serious concern among some that Bard's affinity for (though certainly not tolerance of) gender-bending is fading.

Lefties Welcome

Life at Bard is lively, infused with arts and culture, and tolerant of every lifestyle imaginable—as long as that lifestyle isn't Republican, of course. Some complain that aggressively liberal students discourage their conservative peers from voicing their opinions or feeling like a part of the community. Bard does not have fraternities, sororities, or theme houses, which means that the social scene is relatively diffuse. Still, because about 80 percent of students live on campus, it's not exactly an onerous task to find someone else looking to kick back. Housing here runs the gamut from old mansions to standard dorms, from modern apartments to FEMA-style trailers. That's right: Bard sometimes faces a housing shortage so severe that students end up in double-wides. Fortunately, the rest of the facilities are top-notch. The student recreational and exercise complex is well-appointed, with a big pool and nearby Nordic ski trails. Organized athletics are mostly a low-key affair. The Bard Music Festival is a huge annual event, and every week of the year there are performances by students and visiting professionals.

Welcome to the Boonies

Bard is situated in Annandale-on-Hudson, a tiny village two and a half hours from New York City. Translation: Having a car is a good thing. Red Hook and Tivoli, two nearby towns, are popular destinations for weekend trips, and although the college operates free bus shuttles to both places, it's nice to control your itinerary. There are a few things to do in Annandale other than leave. The town is nestled between the Catskill Mountains and the Hudson River, and outdoor enthusiasts have an easy time taking advantage of both. The surrounding forests are veined with hiking and biking trails, and organizations on campus frequently organize outings.

Admissions

Average high school GPA:	3.5
Average freshman SAT writing / math / critical reading score:	669 / 645 / —
Average freshman ACT score:	—
Application fee:	$50
Application deadlines:	
1/15 (freshmen)	
3/15 (transfer)	
11/1 (early action)	
Total applicants:	4,828
Total accepted:	1,382 (29%)
Total accepted who enrolled:	498
Notification dates:	
4/1 (freshmen)	
5/15 (transfer)	
1/1 (early action)	
Acceptance rate for early action applicants:	66%

Students

Percentage of male / female students:	43% / 57%
Percentage of students from out of state:	69%
Percentage of students graduating in 4 years / 6 years:	59% / 72%

Money

Total endowment:	—
Total tuition:	$34,080
Total cost with fees & expenses:	$43,930
Average financial aid package:	$25,147
Percentage of students who sought aid and received it:	88%
Percentage of students receiving financial aid:	56%

Also Check Out

New York University

Oberlin College

Reed College

Sarah Lawrence College

Wesleyan University

Barnard College

3009 Broadway
New York, NY 10027

(212) 854-5262
http://www.barnard.edu/

 **BIG BRAIN**

 **BIG PERSPECTIVE**

Wanted: a few ambitious women

5 REASONS IT'S COOL

1. Barnard students choose from more than **2,500 internship opportunities.**

2. About 70 percent of profs at this **all-women's college** are women.

3. Attend a small liberal arts college and **get an Ivy League diploma.** Barnard students not only attend classes at Columbia University, but also graduate with Columbia degrees.

4. **Get two degrees for the price of one.** Barnard students can earn both a bachelor's degree and a master's degree or a law degree through special five- and six-year programs.

5. **New York, New York!** Need we say more?

The Basics

Public / private: private nonprofit
Total enrollment / undergrads: 2,350 / 2,350
Campus setting: urban
Students call it: Barnard
Students are called: Bears
Notable alums: Lauren Graham (actress), Jhumpa Lahiri (writer), Margaret Mead (cultural anthropologist), Cynthia Nixon (actress), Joan Rivers (TV personality)

Small School, Big Opportunities

Barnard, the sister college of Columbia in that school's pre-coed days, is now an all-women's college within the Columbia University system. Barnard is an academic powerhouse in its own right. With a faculty-to-student ratio of 1:7, Barnard employs profs who are accessible and know their stuff. You'll discover this during your first semester in the required Ways of Knowing courses, which focus on different ways of understanding the world. The college offers more than fifty majors and over three hundred study-abroad programs in seventy countries. Among the many strong departments is English; a remarkable number of renowned writers have graduated from this school. And if there's anything Barnard students want that their school doesn't have, they can walk across the street to Columbia, where they can take classes, use the library, live in dorms, and join student organizations. There are also opportunities to earn dual or joint degrees, including law degrees and master's degrees from some of Columbia's other renowned schools.

Feast on Some Midnight Oil

Even the brightest minds need fuel. At midnight on the evening before finals begin each fall and spring, Barnard staff and faculty—academic heads, trustees, college deans, and president included—don aprons and dish out eggs, pancakes, hash browns, and plenty of coffee to hundreds of exhausted students. Columbia students often head across the street to grab some grub, and it's not uncommon to find nearly two thousand people happily waiting in line for Midnight Breakfast.

My Dorm, My Home

Few generalizations can be made about Barnard students, but here are two: They devote considerable time to their schoolwork, and they are a very diverse bunch. Barnard's nearly 2,400 students hail from all over the world and include members of every race, ethnicity, religion, and economic class imaginable. And there tends to be plenty of intermingling among these groups. That's because the residence halls unite neighboring students and encourage them to partake in cultural events, social activities, and educational programs. About 90 percent of students live on campus in one of Barnard's eleven residence halls or one of four Columbia residence halls, although some complain that Barnard's aging student housing and classrooms could use some remodeling. When they're not in the dorms, at the library, in class, or on the streets of New York, Barnard students can usually be found in the McIntosh Student Center, which is home to a snack bar, an art exhibit area, lounges, music rehearsal rooms, student mailboxes, a bowling alley, and meeting places for the college's more than eighty clubs.

Big City Love

Barnard's Manhattan locale is one of its biggest selling points. The city has many of the best museums, internships, restaurants, theaters, sporting events, shops, bars, and nightclubs in the world. And with Columbia right across the street and the Manhattan School of Music, Teachers College, Bank Street College of Education, Union Theological Seminary, and Jewish Theological Seminary all nearby, Barnard's neighborhood, Morningside Heights, is bustling with college students. That's good news for Barnard women, who are popular with the area's business owners. Most students feel that the collegiate neighborhood more than makes up for the lack of a sprawling campus—although Barnard's campus does boast a small quad and a lawn. Of course, city living isn't for everyone, and some students find Manhattan a distraction from their schoolwork.

Admissions

Average high school GPA:	3.91
Average freshman SAT writing / math / critical reading score:	685 / 672 / 683
Average freshman ACT score:	26
Application fee:	$55
Application deadlines:	
1/1 (freshmen)	
4/1 (transfer)	
11/15 (early decision)	
Total applicants:	4,599
Total accepted:	1,177 (26%)
Total accepted who enrolled:	550
Notification dates:	
4/1 (freshmen)	
5/15 (transfer)	
12/15 (early decision)	
Acceptance rate for early decision applicants:	41%

Students

Percentage of male / female students:	— / 100%
Percentage of students from out of state:	64%
Percentage of students graduating in 4 years / 6 years:	82% / 89%

Money

Total endowment:	$171,141,000
Total tuition:	$31,714
Total cost with fees & expenses:	$45,550
Average financial aid package:	$30,664
Percentage of students who sought aid and received it:	100%
Percentage of students receiving financial aid:	42%

Also Check Out

Brown University

Columbia University

New York University

Sarah Lawrence College

Wellesley University

Bates College

Andrews Road
Lewiston, ME 04240

(207) 786-6255
http://www.bates.edu/

BIG PERSPECTIVE

Where the weather's chilly and the students are chill

5 REASONS IT'S COOL

1. Bates's **top-notch study-abroad programs** send students packing to more than seventy destinations.

2. Bates offers **ten interdisciplinary majors** out of thirty-two majors overall.

3. **Student-professor relationships are tight,** strengthened by the fact that most students complete a semester- or year-long thesis or project their senior year.

4. Fun times lie ahead: The Bates community is **close-knit, tolerant, inclusive,** and known for throwing rockin' parties.

5. **Ain't it quaint?** Surrounding areas, especially along the Maine coast, are picturesque.

The Basics

Public / private: private nonprofit
Total enrollment / undergrads: 1,744 / 1,744
Campus setting: small town
Students call it: Bates
Students are called: Batesies, Bobcats
Notable alums: Bryant Gumbel (broadcast journalist), Paul Kazarian (businessman, philanthropist), Benjamin Mays (educator, scholar), Edmund Muskie (senator), Daniel Stedman (filmmaker), William Stringfellow (activist, theologian), Dorothy Clarke Wilson (author)

Pioneering Spirit

Bates has long been on the forefront of academic change. When it was founded in 1855 by Maine abolitionists, it was New England's first coed college, and it was one of the first colleges in the nation to stop requiring standardized tests for admission. Bates's most popular and prestigious majors are social sciences, such as economics and political science, and English. Distributional requirements include three sciences and a physical education class. The academic calendar is divided into two four-month terms and one five-week spring term, which many students use to pursue individual interests off campus. These five-week projects can range from marine biology study along the Maine coastline to music studies in New York City. Students also keep busy through faculty-directed summer research projects, internships, and a mandatory senior thesis project. Aspiring engineers take advantage of Bates's Combined Plan programs, which allow students to pursue a liberal arts degree at

Puddle Jumpin'

Bates's hardiest tradition is the annual "Puddle jump." Students cut a hole in frozen Lake Andrew (known to students as the "Puddle"), strip down to their skivvies, and courageously brave the frigid waters.

Bates for three years and then finish their studies at an affiliated engineering school. Very small class sizes (most with fewer than twenty students) and close faculty-student interaction are icing on the cake.

Keeping Warm

Despite the cold and snowy conditions that characterize the winter months in Maine, Bates students generate plenty of heat through fun parties and a close-knit social scene. On the annual Newman Day (a tradition shared by Princeton), students down twenty-four beers in twenty-four hours while going about normal daytime activities. Students also enjoy the yearly Winter Carnival, the nation's second oldest four-day festival, replete with torch lighting, concerts, and snow sculpting. Bates guarantees housing to students for all four years, and more than 90 percent of students live on campus. There are no Greek organizations, as dictated by an official policy that all campus organizations be open to all students. Varsity sports at Bates are somewhat popular, and interest surges when teams compete against neighboring rivals Bowdoin and Colby. Students must purchase an unlimited meal plan, but students report that dining hall food is decent and veggie friendly.

I Love L-A

The Bates campus mixes old-style New England architecture with an increasing number of modern additions. The oldest building, Hathorn Hall, has earned a spot on the National Register of Historic Places. One of the newer buildings, Pettengill Hall, features a three-story glass atrium overlooking Lake Andrew (which is actually the campus pond). Bates students are by and large content to stay on or near campus, and some are wary of venturing into Lewiston-Auburn, as town and gown relations have been tense in the past. The Lewiston-Auburn region makes up the second largest metropolitan area in Maine. The cities of Boston and Portland are within easy reach by car, as are the outdoor splendors of Acadia National Park and the Maine coastline.

Admissions

Average high school GPA:	—
Average freshman SAT verbal / math score:	671 / 672
Average freshman ACT score:	—
Application fee:	$60
Application deadlines:	
1/1 (freshmen)	
3/1 (transfer)	
11/15 (early decision)	
Total applicants:	4,305
Total accepted:	1,363 (32%)
Total accepted who enrolled:	492
Notification dates:	
3/31 (freshmen)	
4/1 (transfer)	
12/20 (early decision)	
Acceptance rate for early decision applicants:	54%

Students

Percentage of male / female students:	48% / 52%
Percentage of students from out of state:	90%
Percentage of students graduating in 4 years / 6 years:	84% / 89%

Money

Total endowment:	$234,268,076
Total tuition:	—
Total cost with fees & expenses:	$46,400
Average financial aid package:	$27,428
Percentage of students who sought aid and received it:	100%
Percentage of students receiving financial aid:	39%

Also Check Out

Bowdoin College

Colby College

College of Wooster

Hamilton College

Middlebury College

Baylor University

One Bear Place #97056
Waco, TX 76798

(254) 710-1011
http://www.baylor.edu/

 **BIG CHOICE**

 **BIG JOB**

 **BIG WORLD**

Close-knit, close to God

5 REASONS IT'S COOL

1. Tap into your spiritual side: Baylor is the **world's largest Baptist university**.

2. Students **volunteer more than 150,000 hours a year**, including the annual Steppin' Out volunteer Saturday.

3. Baylor 2012, a bold new campuswide plan, means that facilities and programs will see **many improvements in the upcoming years.**

4. Intern for the top dogs: Corporate recruiters include Exxon/Mobil, the Houston Astros, Dell, and AT&T.

5. **Want to run the state?** No school has graduated more Texas governors.

The Basics

Public / private: private religious
Total enrollment / undergrads: 14,040 / 11,831
Campus setting: urban
Students call it: Baylor
Students are called: Bears
Notable alums: John Baugh (founder, Sysco Corp.), Thomas Harris (author), Jim Hillin (visual effects artist), Michael Johnson (sprinter), Ann Richards (governor, Texas), Mike Singletary (pro football player), Mark White (governor, Texas), Trey Wingo (sports broadcaster)

A Faith-Based Education

Baylor is a big place, but thanks to the 16:1 student-to-faculty ratio and average class size of twenty-nine, students receive plenty of personal attention. And with more than one hundred majors to choose from, including unusual offerings such as ancient Near Eastern and biblical languages, entrepreneurship, and museum studies, Baylor offers something for everyone. Marketing and psychology are the most popular majors. Also hard to beat are the seminary, pre-med, pre-dental, nursing, engineering, business, and pre-law programs. Students are required to take two religion courses and attend chapel twice a week for the first two semesters. Nearly all professors impart Christian values to their students in class, but the aim is to inspire discussion rather than to evangelize. The university also encourages students to participate in service learning and study-abroad programs, and the school takes pride in its involvement in the Model Organization of American States.

Spring Fling

Spring fever runs especially high at Baylor. Since 1934, the university has cancelled one day of classes each spring. The Baylor University Chamber of Commerce also organizes a popular spring festival, known as Diadeloso ("The Day of the Bear"). The day's entertainment options include sand sculpting, hypnotists, gospel choirs, and a schoolwide dance.

The Bear Necessities

Religion is integral to the Baylor community, and many students participate in activities such as ministry, community outreach, and service. Seminary grad students serve as chaplains in the residence halls, where they provide spiritual guidance to undergrads and organize Bible studies, retreats, and missions. About 30 percent of students participate in extracurriculars, including debate, student government, intramural sports, anime clubs and arts organizations, student publications, or Greek life. Partying is prevalent despite a strict ban on alcohol. The student body is not the most diverse—about 70 percent of students are white, and most are Christian with conservative leanings—but an abundant number of special-interest organizations serve minority populations. Housing availability is tight, and only about 30 percent of students live on campus, but the Baylor 2012 improvement plan includes provisions to increase these options.

Home Sweet Home

Baylor is surrounded by some of Waco's poorest neighborhoods. But thanks to the university's lovely architecture and pedestrian-friendly landscape, most students get stuck in the Baylor Bubble and rarely leave campus. The university sponsors numerous social events as well as concerts, symposia, theater, opera, and a lecture series that has featured such luminaries as Bill Cosby, John Updike, Archbishop Desmond Tutu, and Margaret Thatcher. The state-of-the-art student center houses a comprehensive fitness facility, health and wellness clinics, and a freestanding climbing rock. The Baylor Marina rents canoes, kayaks, and sailboats for use on the Brazos River. For those looking to break the bubble, Austin and Dallas are both an hour-and-a-half drive away. Many students prefer these big cities to the local nightlife, which consists of three movie theaters, several restaurant chains, and a couple of malls.

Admissions

Average high school GPA:	—
Average freshman SAT verbal / math score:	602 / 619
Average freshman ACT score:	24
Application fee:	$50
Application deadlines: 2/1 (freshmen) continuous (transfer)	
Total applicants:	21,393
Total accepted:	9,097 (43%)
Total accepted who enrolled:	2,782
Notification dates: 3/15 (freshmen) continuous (transfer)	

Students

Percentage of male / female students:	40% / 60%
Percentage of students from out of state:	17%
Percentage of students graduating in 4 years / 6 years:	45% / 72%

Money

Total endowment:	$870,000,000
Total tuition:	$22,220
Total cost with fees & expenses:	$32,016
Average financial aid package:	$15,882
Percentage of students who sought aid and received it:	63%
Percentage of students receiving financial aid:	47%

Also Check Out

Austin College

Texas A&M University–College Station

Texas Christian University

Trinity University

The University of Texas at Austin

Beloit College

700 College Street
Beloit, WI 53511

(608) 363-2000
http://www.beloit.edu/

BIG PERSPECTIVE

Birkenstocks recommended (but not required)

5 REASONS IT'S COOL

1. Beloit's open curriculum means you can **steer your own academic course.**

2. **Get cozy with your professors!** The student-to-faculty ratio hovers around 11:1, and faculty members serve as students' mentors and advisors.

3. Beloit provides **lavish funding for student activities,** and there are more of these than you can shake a stick at!

4. Ultimate Frisbee inspires cultlike fervor in students, and **a Frisbee golf course graces the campus.**

5. The small size and middle-of-nowhere location encourage a **supportive and close-knit campus social scene.**

The Basics

Public/private: private nonprofit
Total enrollment/undergrads: 1,432 / 1,432
Campus setting: small town
Students call it: Beloit
Students are called: Buccaneers
Notable alums: James Arness (actor), Tom Hulce (actor, producer), Evan Montvel Cohen (cofounder, Air America Radio), Lorine Niedecker (poet), Jameson Parker (actor)

Open Curriculum for Open Minds

Latitude and flexibility are the hallmarks of Beloit's open curriculum, which blends work, study abroad, and other off-campus opportunities with traditional class time. Students are required to enroll in two classes from each of three major academic areas, along with writing courses. Beloit has strong programs in the natural sciences and social sciences, as well as humanities, geology, economics, anthropology, English, and theater arts. Close relations with faculty members are ensured through the First Year Initiative program, which teams freshmen with faculty members to help ease the transition to college life. After spending another year in the "Sophomore Year Program" students embark on their own interests with a self-devised Comprehensive Academic plan as a guide.

Mindset List

At the beginning of each academic year, Beloit publishes its trademark Mindset List for the year's incoming freshman class. This annual rundown of pop-culture data is intended to offer a quick summary of the world as seen through the eyes of Beloit students. For instance, according to a recent list, the Class of 2011 has never known the Berlin Wall, never rolled down a car window, and never watched MTV when it actually played music videos in high rotation. While it's anyone's guess how effective a measure the Mindset List actually is, it sure is funny.

Small Campus, Small Town

Beloit is small; there's no way around it. If you don't mind a parade of familiar faces every day, you can enjoy an active and varied social life. Festivities, activities, and clubs abound, thanks to the resourcefulness of students who refuse to succumb to boredom in the boondocks. Administrators for the most part adopt a laissez-faire attitude toward alcohol consumption, provided students demonstrate they can drink responsibly. Students are required to live on campus for three out of the four years. Beloit offers recently refurbished residence halls, and upperclassmen have the option of campus apartments. Having a car, however, can definitely boost your status among your fellow students by putting the nearby (and considerably larger) college town Madison within reach. Milwaukee and Chicago are also potential places for students to get their parties on.

Front Porch Living

Beloit's hometown, also named Beloit, sits just north of the Illinois state line in Rock County, Wisconsin. Known as "Wisconsin's front porch" (which may give you an insight into the pace of life), Rock County has considerably more to offer to outdoor types than to would-be urban movers and shakers. This relative isolation means that, for most students, Beloit's cozy, forty-acre campus serves as the center of the universe. The state capital, Madison, is a short jaunt (fifty miles) away, and the cities of Milwaukee and Chicago can be reached in about two hours' time.

Admissions

Average high school GPA:	3.46
Average freshman SAT verbal / math score:	640 / 604
Average freshman ACT score:	25
Application fee:	$35

Application deadlines:
1/15 (freshmen)
continuous (transfer)
12/15 (early action)

Total applicants:	2,048
Total accepted:	1,375 (67%)
Total accepted who enrolled:	347

Notification dates:
4/1 (freshmen)
continuous (transfer)
1/15 (early action)

Acceptance rate for early action applicants:	88%

Students

Percentage of male / female students:	41% / 59%
Percentage of students from out of state:	82%
Percentage of students graduating in 4 years / 6 years:	62% / 72%

Money

Total endowment:	$109,550,786
Total tuition:	$28,130
Total cost with fees & expenses:	$35,012
Average financial aid package:	$22,781
Percentage of students who sought aid and received it:	100%
Percentage of students receiving financial aid:	55%

Also Check Out

Grinnell College

Kenyon College

Macalester College

Oberlin College

Bennington College

One College Drive
Bennington, VT 05201

(802) 442-5401
http://www.bennington.edu/

 BIG IDEA

 **BIG WORLD**

A very rare gem

5 REASONS IT'S COOL

1. With **no SAT requirement and no letter grades,** you know your profs are treating you like people, not numbers.

2. The yearly seven-week fieldwork term gives students great **professional experience in the real world.**

3. Despite the hefty price tag, Bennington offers some form of **financial aid to 80 percent of students.**

4. There are no required courses, and students work with their faculty advisers to **design their own curriculum.**

5. Professors in the writing, dance, visual arts, and theater programs are **some of the best artists in their fields.**

The Basics

Public / private: private nonprofit
Total enrollment / undergrads: 657 / 523
Campus setting: small town
Students call it: Bennington
Notable alums: Alan Arkin (actor), Kiran Desai (writer), Bret Easton Ellis (writer), Jonathan Lethem (writer), Donna Tartt (writer), Justin Theroux (actor)

Whatever Works for You

If you're self-motivated, creative, and unwilling to slog through curriculum requirements, Bennington may be the college for you. Founded on the belief that "the most valuable education is one you create yourself," this college gives students the reins. Rather than selecting a major, students work closely with faculty advisers to devise their own independent plan of study. Creative programs are the norm here and include dance, drama, video and media studies, and foreign language arts. Potential students shouldn't stress about the burden of committing to an academic path; professors typically urge freshmen to take a potpourri of courses so they can see what's out there before settling down. If they like, students can request grades for two years rather than written critiques, so that they have GPAs to produce for potential employers or grads schools. Some students find their niche while participating in their required Field Work Term, when they spend two winter months off campus—and sometimes abroad—volunteering, interning, or working in their field of interest.

Don't Mess with My Dancing Shoes

In the 1930s, before the first class graduated, Bennington faculty initially decided not to hold graduation ceremonies. But when the students protested, the college gave in but decided to have a nontraditional ceremony, one that felt like a party. Today that tradition continues with upbeat bongo music that faculty, students, and guests often dance to as they're walking in or out of the ceremony.

Get Creative

It's not uncommon for Bennington's five-hundred-plus students to devote most of their waking hours to some project or performance they're working on. These students love what they do and often get caught up in intense discussions with friends and professors after class and in the dorms. Student housing is cozy; each building houses about thirty students. When they're not working or hanging out with friends at the student center or around the fireplaces in the dorms, students may be volunteering in the community or participating in one of the many campus organizations, ranging from the *Bennington Free Press* and intramural sports to the Knitting Club and the Legal Aliens, a group for international students. They won't be found participating in Greek life or cheering on one of the school's athletics teams—this creative campus has neither.

Think Small, Very Small

The towns of Bennington and North Bennington are quintessential New England. Nestled at the foot of the Taconic Mountains and overlooking Vermont's Green Mountains, they enjoy the full sweep of Northeast seasons: verdant springs, blissful summers, multicolored falls, and snow white winters. The surroundings make for tons of opportunities for the outdoorsy types, ranging from swimming and hiking in the warmer months to skiing in the winter. The campus itself is lined in an odd combination of Georgian-style architecture and more contemporary buildings, including several new modern dorms and the Student Center, which is home to the campus bar, a convenience store, dance parties, food, and more. If students want to get off campus, there are a few charming little restaurants and bars in Bennington, but little else. For the wilder nights out, students trek down to nearby Boston and New York City.

Admissions

Average high school GPA:	3.45
Average freshman SAT writing / math / critical reading score:	632 / 576 / 645
Average freshman ACT score:	25
Application fee:	$60

Application deadlines:
1/3 (freshmen)
3/15 (transfer)
11/15 (early decision)

Total applicants:	798
Total accepted:	525 (66%)
Total accepted who enrolled:	127

Notification dates:
4/1 (freshmen)
5/1 (transfer)
12/15 (early decision)

Acceptance rate for early decision applicants:	69%

Students

Percentage of male / female students:	34% / 66%
Percentage of students from out of state:	96%
Percentage of students graduating in 4 years / 6 years:	45% / 60%

Money

Total endowment:	$12,817,766
Total tuition:	$35,850
Total cost with fees & expenses:	$46,180
Average financial aid package:	$26,894
Percentage of students who sought aid and received it:	78%
Percentage of students receiving financial aid:	66%

Also Check Out

Bard College

Brown University

Hampshire College

Sarah Lawrence College

Bentley College

175 Forest Street
Waltham, MA 02452

(781) 891-2000
http://www.bentley.edu

 BIG JOB

Where business *is* pleasure

The Basics

Public / private: private nonprofit
Total enrollment / undergrads: 5,497 / 4,241
Campus setting: suburban
Students call it: Bentley
Students are called: Falcons
Notable alums: Elkin B. McCallum (CEO, Joann Fabrics), Robert F. Smith (CEO, American Express Bank), Charles Taylor (president, Liberia), Richard F. Zannino (CEO, Dow Jones & Company)

Where Opportunities Abound

With a student-to-teacher ratio of 12:1 and an average class size of twenty-four, students get lots of personal attention at Bentley. Although students sometimes resent the core curriculum and required classes that take up most of their first two years, they tend to find professors helpful, knowledgeable, and student focused. Bentley is known for its business majors, such as finance, accounting, and marketing, but in recent years it has increased its effort to produce more well-rounded graduates. Students may choose from a wide variety of nonbusiness majors such as philosophy, English, and public policy studies. The college is a leader in integrating information technology studies into the core business curriculum. Bentley also offers a variety of study-abroad opportunities in Australia, Belgium, China, Singapore, and other business hot spots around the globe.

Perks: from Computers to Donuts

There's no doubt that Bentley's outstanding job placement rate has something to do with its strong reputation in the business world. In fact, businesses in need of advice often seek out the help of Bentley profs and students. In 2002, for example, the Bentley Marketing Department did some work for HP. In appreciation, the company rewarded students involved with free tablet computers.

Not Strictly Business

Since Bentley is chock-full of future leaders, it's not surprising that there are more than eighty student associations on campus. An eclectic range of cultural, religious, sporting, and student government groups sponsor yearly events such as comedy nights, fashion shows, and scavenger hunts. Particularly popular events include Breakfast by Moonlight, during which faculty and staff members serve students a late-night meal before final exams, and the Festival of Colors, when international students showcase the fashions, dances, and food from their home countries. The Festival of Colors testifies to an increasing level of diversity at Bentley: a healthy 20 percent of students are from minority groups. There is a fledgling Greek presence on campus, but none of the students live in fraternity or sorority houses. Campus housing gets nicer and newer as students get closer to graduating. And for the 20 percent or so of students who live off campus, the Commuter Association puts on bowling nights, pool outings, movie watching, and Boston excursions.

Share and Share Alike

Bentley is located in the New England town of Waltham, which also houses neighboring Brandeis University. Many of Bentley's buildings date back to 1968, when the school moved from Boston to the 'burbs, and the campus architecture alongside the pristine, trim lawns reflects the college's contemporary feel. Most buildings are equipped with computerized, high-tech amenities, especially the newly built Student Center, which features a dining hall, game rooms, a chapel, and work space. While many students love the campus and the city of Waltham, most find nearby Cambridge and Boston much bigger draws. With more than eighty colleges in the greater Boston area, students can party and connect with people from almost everywhere.

Admissions

Average high school GPA:	—
Average freshman SAT writing / math / critical reading score:	588 / 637 / 580
Average freshman ACT score:	25
Application fee:	$50

Application deadlines:
2/1 (freshmen)
continuous (transfer)
11/15 (early decision)
12/1 (early action)

Total applicants:	6,156
Total accepted:	2,402 (39%)
Total accepted who enrolled:	888

Notification dates:
4/1 (freshmen)
continuous (transfer)
12/22 (early decision)
1/30 (early action)

Acceptance rate for early action/early decision applicants:	60% / 63%

Students

Percentage of male / female students:	60% / 40%
Percentage of students from out of state:	49%
Percentage of students graduating in 4 years / 6 years:	71% / 81%

Money

Total endowment:	$217,986,000
Total tuition:	$29,810
Total cost with fees & expenses:	$41,534
Average financial aid package:	$23,305
Percentage of students who sought aid and received it:	91%
Percentage of students receiving financial aid:	48%

Also Check Out

Babson College

Boston College

Northeastern University

University of Pennsylvania

Birmingham-Southern College

900 Arkadelphia Road
Birmingham, AL 35254

(205) 226-4600
http://www.bsc.edu/

 **BIG PERSPECTIVE**

 **BIG WORLD**

Grow in intellect, spirit, and heart.

5 REASONS IT'S COOL

1. BSC is a Methodist college where **spiritual growth mingles with strong academics** and a highly Greek party scene.

2. Interim Term, an intensive four-week session, gives students time to **concentrate on one area of study.**

3. The Foundations curriculum means that students attend at least thirty **on-campus cultural or intellectual events.**

4. Leadership studies and Service Learning programs are mainstays at this civic-minded university.

5. The cozy campus is just **three miles from downtown Birmingham.**

The Basics

Public / private: private religious
Total enrollment / undergrads: 1,256 / 1,207
Campus setting: urban
Students call it: BSC
Students are called: Panthers
Notable alums: Marguerite Johnston Barnes (journalist), Howell Heflin (senator), Hugh Martin (songwriter), Howell Raines (Pulitzer Prize winning journalist), Elton B. Stephens (founder, EBSCO Industries)

How Will You Spend the Interim?

Students choose from among fifty majors. Business, biology, and English are some the college's strongest and most popular programs. Interdisciplinary majors are available, and students are even encouraged to work with professors to design their own course of study. In addition, 3-2 Bridge programs in environmental studies, engineering, and nursing allow students to earn a dual BA/MA in five years. BSC aims to give students a well-rounded liberal arts education. Key to this approach is Interim Term, a yearly four-week experiential learning session in January, during which students explore one area of interest in depth. This can take the form of a creative writing project, a specialized science class, or an internship. During Interim Term, classes such as Discovering the Pacific Northwest or Culture in Prague, Vienna, and Budapest allow students to travel the world. All students must also take courses in the six areas that make up the Foundations program. With a 12:1 student-to-faculty ratio, students have an easy time connecting with their profs.

My Owl Is the Ugliest!

Given the strong presence of the frats and sororities, it's no surprise that Greek life accounts for many of BSC's traditions. Here's a wise one: To welcome new sisters each year, the Chi Omega sorority engages in an (nonlive) owl swap. The catch? These sisters are trading *ugly* owls, so everyone walks away with a hideous feathered friend.

Faith and Fraternities

True to the Methodist tradition, BSC students are service-oriented and involved in their campus community. Thirty-five percent are Methodist, while 65 percent observe another religion of some kind. Religious life is important on campus, and the school offers pre-professional guidance in church-related vocations. Although most students are in-staters staying close to their Alabama roots, minorities and international students constitute 12 percent of the student body. All students are required to live on campus until junior year, and students enjoy a close sense of community. Most of the residence halls are grouped on the residence hall quad, which includes six sorority townhouses and the ever-popular Fraternity Row. About half the student body goes Greek, and frats and sororities account for much of the campus social scene. Though BSC's twenty NCAA Division III sports aren't as popular as teams on other 'Bama campuses, they still enjoy a good deal of support. A football program kicked off in 2007, and construction of a new state-of-the-art athletic facility is underway.

Folks up Here Know What They've Got

As its nickname, "The Hilltop," might suggest, BSC's 192-acre campus is situated high on a hilltop. The facilities on campus are modern, and a new environmental park and lake area near the residence quad is being constructed. Prospective students will benefit from a new Admission Welcome Center, which is soon to be completed. Students love the proximity of campus to Birmingham, the largest city in Alabama. From museum visits to sporting events to the many student-friendly bars and restaurants, Birmingham offers plenty to amuse college kids. Plus, you'll get to experience classic southern culture—sweet tea and grits, oh my!

Admissions

Average high school GPA:	3.34
Average freshman SAT verbal / math score:	600 / 581
Average freshman ACT score:	24
Application fee:	$25

Application deadlines:
continuous (freshmen)
continuous (transfer)
specific (early action)

Total applicants:	2,198
Total accepted:	1,253 (57%)
Total accepted who enrolled:	292

Notification dates:
continuous (freshmen)
continuous (transfer)
specific (early action)

Acceptance rate for early action applicants:	—

Students

Percentage of male / female students:	41% / 59%
Percentage of students from out of state:	27%
Percentage of students graduating in 4 years / 6 years:	62% / 70%

Money

Total endowment:	$122,404,527
Total tuition:	$23,600
Total cost with fees & expenses:	$32,362
Average financial aid package:	$22,166
Percentage of students who sought aid and received it:	87%
Percentage of students receiving financial aid:	38%

Also Check Out

Baylor University

Hendrix College

Rollins College

Vanderbilt University

Boston College

140 Commonwealth Avenue
Chestnut Hill, MA 02467

(617) 552-8000
http://www.bc.edu/

BIG PERSPECTIVE

Where Eagles Excel

5 REASONS IT'S COOL

1. **Jesuit ideals define life at BC**, where the focus is on educating the whole person and where community service is a value shared by all.

2. **Sports are such a huge deal at BC** that fans aren't content being called just fans—they're known as *Superfans*.

3. Oh, the options. BC has **strong academic programs** in the liberal arts, business, nursing, and education.

4. Boston (just six miles away) is an **ideal home base** that's loaded with students and student-friendly establishments.

5. BC's gorgeous, Gothic-style campus give students that **classic East Coast college experience.**

The Basics

Public / private: private religious
Total enrollment / undergrads: 13,652 / 9,020
Campus setting: suburban
Student call it: BC
Students are called: Eagles
Notable alums: Leonard Nimoy (actor), Chris O'Donnell (actor), Tip O'Neill (congressman), Amy Poehler (actress, comedienne)

Whole Grain Students

BC's academics are shaped largely by the college's Jesuit history. The college has a fairly extensive core curriculum, which students must complete during their freshman and sophomore years. Students take courses in liberal arts subjects such as art, history, literature, mathematics, natural science, social science, and the study of a non-European culture. Students in the College of Arts and Sciences must also be proficient in a foreign language; students in the Carroll School of Management add business-related courses; and nursing students boost up the number of science courses. Faculty advisors are available to students to help puzzle out these requirements. BC's Capstone Program helps seniors and second-semester juniors cap off their undergraduate experience with courses that encourage introspection and personal development. The Jesuit value of community service is incorporated into many classes. For example, the two-semester PULSE program fulfills the philosophy and theology core requirement, and it puts students in touch with those suffering from social injustice.

You Can't Just Middlemarch In

BC's legendary Middlemarch costume party is an annual event that comes with an interesting price. Tickets are so highly coveted—and so limited in number—that students compete for the chance to have their names entered into the ticket lottery. Usually, lengthy scavenger hunts stand in the way. And in some years, students have had to correctly answer trivia questions about BC history. The party is reportedly worth all the trouble: A recent year's party had a *Charlie and the Chocolate Factory* theme and came complete with a chocolate fountain.

Not Just Fans, Superfans

Better get your vocal chords primed and ready for some serious cheering. Sports are a big deal at BC, where the Eagles compete at the NCAA Division I-A level in the Atlantic Coast Conference. BC fans are known as "Superfans," and they wear gold (BC's school color) and cheer so loud that they shake the foundations of the Conte Forum (during basketball season) and Alumni Stadium (during football season). Sports madness reaches its peak on campus during the annual "Holy War" football game with rival Notre Dame. BC's student body of nine thousand is large enough that students from many diverse cultures are represented. Minority students receive support through the campus's AHANA office, which stands for African American, Hispanic, Asian, and Native American. On-campus parties consist mostly of small gatherings, and there are no Greek organizations. As is the Jesuit tradition, community service plays a big role in student life. The Appalachia Volunteers, the country's biggest student-run service program, sends students on projects throughout the country.

Beantown and Beyond

BC's main campus, known as the "Heights," is located in suburban Chestnut Hill, just six miles west of bustling Boston. The tree-lined Linen Lane leads to the hilltop campus, where St. Mary's Hall, Devlin Hall, and Bapst Library are all stunning examples of Collegiate Gothic architecture. A wide variety of modern buildings now commingle with the older buildings, including the cool, prefab "Mods," the student apartments on the lower campus. The nearby town of Newton is home to BC's law school as well as freshman housing. Boston, the consummate college city, is just a short T-ride away, and New England's natural wonders (such as skiing!) are easy to get to by car.

Admissions

Average high school GPA:	—
Average freshman SAT writing / math / critical reading score:	662 / 675 / 654
Average freshman ACT score:	—
Application fee:	$70
Application deadlines:	
1/1 (freshmen)	
4/1 (transfer)	
11/1 (early action)	
Total applicants:	26,584
Total accepted:	7,736 (29%)
Total accepted who enrolled:	2,284
Notification dates:	
4/15 (freshmen)	
6/1 (transfer)	
12/25 (early action)	
Acceptance rate for early action applicants:	43%

Students

Percentage of male / female students:	48% / 52%
Percentage of students from out of state:	72%
Percentage of students graduating in 4 years / 6 years:	87% / 89%

Money

Total endowment:	$1,355,600,795
Total tuition:	$33,000
Total cost with fees & expenses:	$45,594
Average financial aid package:	$25,967
Percentage of students who sought aid and received it:	100%
Percentage of students receiving financial aid:	42%

Also Check Out

College of the Holy Cross

Fordham University

Georgetown University

Providence College

Syracuse University

Boston University

One Sherborn Street
Boston, MA 02215

(617) 353-2000
http://www.bu.edu/

BIG CHOICE

Make Beantown your campus!

5 REASONS IT'S COOL

1. BU is **one of the nation's largest private universities;** from friends to classes to clubs, you'll find what you want.

2. The system of separate undergraduate schools allows you to **focus your academic program and form close ties** with students who have similar interests.

3. The highly regarded and interdisciplinary Theology department counts **Nobel laureate Elie Wiesel** among its faculty.

4. Experience-hungry Terriers can hook into the network of **local businesses and media outlets starving for college interns.**

5. If you want **Boston as your front yard,** BU is the ticket.

The Basics

Public / private: private nonprofit
Total enrollment / undergrads: 31,574 / 18,000
Campus setting: urban
Students call it: BU
Students are called: Terriers
Notable alums: Chris Drury (pro hockey player), Olympia Dukakis (actress), Rick Pitino (pro basketball coach), Steven Untracht (Nobel Laureate, Peace; Doctors Without Frontiers)

The Light at the End of the Bureaucracy

Students who already know what they want to study enroll in one of BU's eleven different schools, including the College of Arts & Sciences, the School of Management, and the School of Hospitality Administration. Undecided students spend their first few semesters in the College of General Studies and then join one of the specialized schools. Each school has a different feel, with its own faculty and buildings, and many students say that compartmentalization is helpful at a university as big as this one. Others complain that for students with unusual combinations of interests, the need to choose a school can be overwhelming. Fortunately, once you've picked your course of study, you'll be able to take advantage of some world-class facilities. The School of Music has its own concert hall, and the College of Communication is one of the best-equipped in the country. BU's most valuable resource is its faculty, which includes a number of Pulitzer and Nobel Prize winners. These high-profile teachers constitute the backbone of the University

All Aboard

BU and Boston are so intertwined that the Green Line on the T (the public transportation system) is informally known as the BU Shuttle. Seven aboveground stations service the university, including three in front of just one—admittedly sprawling—building. Trains are notoriously overcrowded, and student are notorious for overcrowding them by insisting on taking one- and two-stop rides that cover no more than a few hundred yards.

Professors program, a prestigious liberal arts curriculum that concludes with a two-year, self-designed, interdisciplinary course of study.

You're on Your Own

With 15,000 undergraduates and 450 student organizations, BU presents a menu of social options that can be inspiring or overwhelming, depending on your perspective. About 70 percent of the student body lives on campus, but at BU, the on-campus/off-campus distinction is mostly technical. There *is* no "campus" in the traditional sense; most of the university's buildings are side by side with privately owned stores, residences, and offices. Students report feeling safe, even at night. Because of strict and rigorously enforced rules regarding alcohol and social gatherings, BU students often spend their weekend nights at one of Boston's many clubs, bars, or other colleges, rather than throwing their own parties. To the extent that school spirit exists, it revolves around the varsity hockey team, a perennially competitive source of Terrier pride that has produced a great number of professional hockey players.

City Mice Welcome

The relative thinness of BU's campus culture is balanced by the richness of Boston life, which literally washes up to the doors of the dorms and classroom buildings. Fenway Park is within walking distance, and Harvard lies just across the Charles River, which runs alongside the northern cluster of BU's buildings. Internships and jobs are easily gained, and there are all manner of watering holes and concert venues right outside the dorm doors. Those who come expecting to find a genuine campus nestled away in a corner of the city will be disappointed, but the vast majority of Terriers consider Boston *the* major advantage of life at BU. In all respects, it helps to be a little aggressive here and to have an idea of what you're looking for.

Admissions

Average high school GPA:	3.46
Average freshman SAT writing / math / critical reading score:	637 / 647 / 631
Average freshman ACT score:	26
Application fee:	$75

Application deadlines:
1/1 (freshmen)
4/1 (transfer)
11/1 (early decision)

Total applicants:	31,851
Total accepted:	18,578 (58%)
Total accepted who enrolled:	4,124

Notification dates:
4/15 (freshmen)
— (transfer)
12/15 (early decision)

Acceptance rate for early decision applicants:	47%

Students

Percentage of male / female students:	40% / 60%
Percentage of students from out of state:	77%
Percentage of students graduating in 4 years / 6 years:	65% / 77%

Money

Total endowment:	$946,400,000
Total tuition:	$33,330
Total cost with fees & expenses:	$45,064
Average financial aid package:	$27,633
Percentage of students who sought aid and received it:	90%
Percentage of students receiving financial aid:	40%

Also Check Out

American University

Boston College

The George Washington University

Northeastern University

Syracuse University

Bowdoin College

5000 College Station Brunswick, ME 04011	(207) 725-3000 http://www.bowdoin.edu/

BIG PERSPECTIVE

Tradition and innovation, oceanside

5 REASONS IT'S COOL

1. Bowdoin offers world-class academics in a **quaint, unusually beautiful Maine setting.**

2. **Seventy percent of freshmen participate in pre-orientation activities,** including hiking, canoeing, kayaking, and—for the less outdoorsy—community service programs.

3. You can leave your knife at home: Bowdoin is **far less cutthroat academically** than many of its fellow top-ranked colleges.

4. **The nearby Atlantic Ocean** stands at the ready to aid your studying and sporting.

5. The **SAT I is optional!**

The Basics

Public / private: private nonprofit
Total enrollment / undergrads: 1,734 / 1,734
Campus setting: small town
Students call it: Bowdoin
Students are called: Polar bears
Notable alums: Joshua Chamberlain (Civil War hero; governor, Maine; president, Bowdoin), William Cohen (U.S. secretary of defense), Nathaniel Hawthorne (writer), Alfred Kinsey (sex researcher), Henry Wadsworth Longfellow (poet), DJ Spooky (musician)

Classic Liberal Arts with a Few Surprises

Bowdoin's distribution requirements cover the usual math-to-literature spectrum, but with a little twist: Students must take at least one course with a "non-Eurocentric" focus. Students seem to enjoy, or at least tolerate, fulfilling these requirements. Freshman seminars, which examine everything from art to economics to the economics of art, emphasize reading and writing to prepare students for the work they'll do in their majors. Bowdoin offers a selection of forty-two majors and thirty-eight minors. The most popular concentrations are political science, economics, and English, and new interdisciplinary offerings in Latin American studies and gay and lesbian studies are gaining attention. Science majors join rigorous and well-respected programs boasting opportunities for undergraduate research in Labrador and Kent Island. Budding scientists are not the only ones who get to travel; the college offers programs in over a hundred countries, and 60 percent of

Sign on the Line for Tradition

During the first week of every academic year, the matriculation books, bearing the signatures of past students, are laid out in the president's office. Freshmen add their names to the rolls, introduce themselves to the leader of their school, and examine past volumes, opened to the signatures of such illustrious alums as Nathaniel Hawthorne.

Bowdoin students study abroad for at least a semester. Closer to home, more than half of students get involved in service learning, incorporating their academic program with experiences at local mentoring programs or Habitat for Humanity.

A Warm Place for Polar Bears

From the get-go, Bowdoin cultivates a sense of community among its students. There are lots of upper-middle-class white kids, but 22 percent of students are minorities, a relatively high proportion for a small liberal arts school. Bowdoin's fraternities and sororities have been disbanded, and the old Greek houses have been turned into social houses inhabited by upperclassmen who organize the college's social life. Most of the rest of the students live on campus—90 percent—and housing can be hit-or-miss. Several of the dorm buildings are new, with comfortable facilities, but many are older. The cafeteria food is reported to be very good, and Bowdoin makes an effort to pacify foodies with a campuswide lobster bake now and then. Aside from free shellfish, sports are the activity most likely to draw students together. The rivalry with Colby College needs no stoking, and over half the Polar Bears participate in either varsity or club sports.

We Hope You Like Saltwater

Brunswick is a town of 21,000 people, many of whom are affiliated with the college. If you think you'd enjoy hanging out at a local pub with lobster boat pilots and professors alike, this might be your kind of place. Bowdoin owns 118 acres of wetlands and forest along the coast eight miles from campus, and these holdings greatly enhance field studies in science classes. The college provides a shuttle to Boston, which is three hours away, and Portland is close enough for a day trip or a night on the town. And then there's Freeport, fifteen minutes away by car and home to L. L. Bean's 24-hour factory store, which students traditionally visit in the wee small hours of the morning.

Admissions

Average high school GPA:	—
Average freshman SAT verbal / math score:	692 / 694
Average freshman ACT score:	—
Application fee:	$60

Application deadlines:
1/1 (freshmen)
3/1 (transfer)
11/15 (early decision)

Total applicants:	5,401
Total accepted:	1,165 (22%)
Total accepted who enrolled:	474

Notification dates:
4/5 (freshmen)
4/1 (transfer)
12/31 (early decision)

Acceptance rate for early decision applicants:	30%

Students

Percentage of male / female students:	49% / 51%
Percentage of students from out of state:	88%
Percentage of students graduating in 4 years / 6 years:	90% / 94%

Money

Total endowment:	$673,440,000
Total tuition:	$34,280
Total cost with fees & expenses:	$44,750
Average financial aid package:	$29,641
Percentage of students who sought aid and received it:	100%
Percentage of students receiving financial aid:	42%

Also Check Out

Amherst College

Brown University

Wesleyan University

Williams College

Yale University

Brandeis University

415 South Street
Waltham, MA 02454

(781) 736-2000
http://www.brandeis.edu/

BIG RESEARCH

Para-deis in the Boston suburbs

5 REASONS IT'S COOL

1. At the youthful age of sixty, Brandeis has already become a **world-famous research university**.

2. **The student body is very political**, with an active student government and 257 student organizations.

3. Although professors tend to be experts, they still give students **lots of individualized attention**.

4. The **architecture is as innovative and distinct** as the school itself: A replica Scottish castle houses upperclassmen, the theater is shaped like a top hat, and the music center exterior resembles a grand piano.

5. It's **hard to get bored** when Boston and Cambridge are just a free shuttle ride away.

The Basics

Public / private: private nonprofit
Total enrollment / undergrads: 5,313 / 3,304
Campus setting: suburban
Students call it: Brandeis
Students are called: Owls
Notable alums: Kathy Acker (novelist), Sidney Blumenthal (journalist), Thomas Friedman (journalist), Abbie Hoffman (political activist), Debra Messing (actress)

Devotion to Research and Teaching

Brandeis has attracted the cream of the crop since its founding in 1948. Back then it reeled in the likes of Eleanor Roosevelt and composer-maestro Leonard Bernstein, who now lends his name to full-tuition scholarships for talented musicians. Now it attracts equally stellar professors and very serious students. The 9:1 student-to-faculty ratio creates an intimate learning environment in which students focus intently on academics. Although a secular institution, Brandeis is funded in large part by the Jewish community and therefore boasts a large number of Judaic studies scholars. In addition to economics, biology, and history, students can also major in Yiddish and Eastern European Jewish culture, along with an increasing number of interdisciplinary topics such as environmental, peace, and Latin American studies. Most students double or even triple major, and roughly a third of students spend a semester or two studying abroad in one of the school's 250 programs in seventy different countries.

Bestselling Lessons

Brandeis graduate Mitch Albom wrote about his favorite Brandeis professor in his hugely popular bestseller *Tuesdays with Morrie*. In his inspirational book, Albom writes lovingly of his aging sociology professor and the life lessons the man imparted to him as he lay dying from ALS, or Lou Gehrig's Disease.

Come One, Come All

While Brandeis has had a high percentage of Jewish students since its inception, the school has always sought and recruited top students from all religious backgrounds. Reflecting the school's founding ideals of inclusion and acceptance, the student body comes from a variety of economic backgrounds as well. Most students live on campus, and those that don't reside just minutes away. Most students agree that the food at Brandeis is better than average, since there is a wide range of options (including kosher and nonkosher dishes) and flexible meal plans. Greek life does not exist, and nor does a university football team, which some students feel contributes to a flagging sense of school spirit and general lack of interest in sports. Students have other, equally strong interests, though, including the Festival of Creative Arts, a five-day artistic extravaganza featuring over a hundred exhibitions and performances from both local and international artists. Bronstein Weekend, held before spring finals, provides students with a lively concert break, while the Tropics Night dance requires revelers to don beach gear in the dead of Boston winter.

An Eclectic, Innovative Mix

Before Brandeis was founded in 1948, the hilltop on which it sits was home to a medical and veterinary school. The pioneering planners transformed the rustic, decaying vestiges of the defunct school into a vibrant campus. Architectural styles encompass an eclectic mix, but tend to be mostly modern, brick-and-glass constructions. A Scottish castle left over from the previous school is a registered historical landmark and represents the oldest architectural style on campus. Brandeis's first master planner, renowned modern architect Euro Saarinen, designed Brandeis buildings to align closely with the contemporary, innovative educational endeavor of the school itself. Although many of Saarinen's plans were too expensive to build, he left his mark in the orange-toned brick and mortar that dominates the campus. And even though the elongated campus was originally designed to accommodate cars, most students prefer to take the free Brandeis shuttle bus down the hill to Waltham or into Cambridge and Boston, where thousands of other college students can be found.

Admissions

Average high school GPA:	3.83
Average freshman SAT verbal / math score:	674 / 680
Average freshman ACT score:	26
Application fee:	$55
Application deadlines: 1/15 (freshmen) 4/1 (transfer) 11/15 (early decision)	
Total applicants:	7,640
Total accepted:	2,776 (36%)
Total accepted who enrolled:	765
Notification dates: 4/1 (freshmen) 5/25 (transfer) 12/15 (early decision)	
Acceptance rate for early decision applicants:	67%

Students

Percentage of male / female students:	44% / 56%
Percentage of students from out of state:	73%
Percentage of students graduating in 4 years / 6 years:	84% / 88%

Money

Total endowment:	$580,000,000
Total tuition:	$32,951
Total cost with fees & expenses:	$44,198
Average financial aid package:	$25,928
Percentage of students who sought aid and received it:	85%
Percentage of students receiving financial aid:	47%

Also Check Out

Boston College

Brown University

Emory University

Lehigh University

New York University

Brigham Young University

150 East Bulldog Boulevard
Provo, UT 84602

(801) 422-1211
http://www.byu.edu/

 **BIG CHOICE**

 **BIG WORLD**

Education to lift you higher

5 REASONS IT'S COOL

1. BYU is affiliated with the Mormon church, and **about 98% of students are Mormons.**

2. Take off for Paris, Jerusalem, or other exotic locales: BYU has **the largest study-abroad program in the country.**

3. Become a future business leader at the **world-renowned Marriott School of Management.**

4. Find your step with one of the **nationally ranked dance teams,** such as the Cougaretts or the Ballroom Dance Company.

5. Get to know the first-rate faculty with the Freshmen Academy program, which provides smaller classes and **fosters close faculty-student relationships.**

The Basics

Public / private: private religious
Total enrollment / undergrads: 34,185 / 30,480
Campus setting: suburban
Students call it: BYU
Students are called: Cougars
Notable alums: Jon Heder (actor), Neil LaBute (director, playwright), Mitt Romney (governor, Massachusetts), Steve Young (pro football quarterback)

They Really Speak Your Lingo

While BYU is a big school, it is invested in giving its students a personalized experience. A special program for first-year students helps newbies feel at home, and a competitive honors program provides opportunities for more personal interaction between faculty and students. The school also boasts one of the most active and rigorous language learning programs in the country. Students can choose from over seventy languages. Everything from Spanish and French to Welsh and Zulu is on offer. In fact, foreign languages are so popular that about a third of the student body is enrolled in a language course during any given semester. Perhaps the most intense and difficult general course requirement at BYU is religious in nature. Students must take no fewer than fourteen religious courses. The extensive list of core requirements also includes classes in American heritage, physical and biological sciences, math, and three physical activity courses. The most popular majors are business/marketing and education, and the business and law majors are among the most prestigious.

Clean Parties, Clean Living . . . Clean Protests?

BYU students are known for their conservative views and love of the status quo. It therefore came as a shock when the College Democrats circulated petitions and organized a protest following the school's decision to allow Vice President Dick Cheney to address the 2007 graduating class. BYU allowed the dissenters to protest on campus—albeit without any speeches, offensive signs, marching, or criticism of BYU or the LDS Church. Former presidential candidate Ralph Nader gave an alternative commencement speech.

You Don't Have to Be a Saint . . . But It Helps

BYU is affiliated with the Church of Jesus Christ of Latter-day Saints (LDS or Mormon Church), and 98 percent of students are Mormon. Almost all students live in school-owned on- and off-campus housing. The dorms and apartments are single sex, except for the units reserved for married couples. The school honor code prohibits the use of drugs, alcohol, and tobacco. Students are notable for their friendliness and cheery dispositions, and they take deep pride in their school. After taking a look at the school's long list of professional sports alums, you won't be surprised to learn that both varsity and intramural sports are a big part of campus life. Football games are particularly huge campus events, especially when BYU plays its bitter rival, Utah. Church-sponsored events and community service projects are also popular. The flexible meal plans allow students to spend their dining dollars anywhere—including at Provo's many Mexican restaurants, which are local dating hotspots.

Natural Beauty

Nestled between the waters of Utah Lake and Mount Timpanogos, the main campus in Provo lies in close proximity to some of the nation's most awesome natural attractions. The Rocky Mountain range is a short car ride away, and students particularly love to hike through the range branded with a Y for Brigham Young, the school's namesake and founder. Nearby Provo Canyon is another popular outdoor spot, and students often lug projectors and sleeping bags to camp and watch movies. The rapidly growing metropolis of Salt Lake City is just a forty-five-minute drive away. Construction sites are a perennial feature of the landscape, as buildings undergo refurbishing and earthquake retrofitting. The recently constructed Joseph F. Smith Building—an airy, modern building with a glass-enclosed gallery, courtyard, and fountain—houses the two largest undergrad schools on campus, including the Humanities College, and a family history and genealogy center for ancestral research.

Admissions

Average high school GPA:	3.76
Average freshman SAT verbal / math score:	618 / 634
Average freshman ACT score:	26
Application fee:	$30
Application deadlines:	
2/1 (freshmen)	
3/1 (transfer)	
Total applicants:	9,737
Total accepted:	6,827 (70%)
Total accepted who enrolled:	4,553
Notification dates:	
continuous (freshmen)	
continuous (transfer)	

Students

Percentage of male / female students:	51% / 49%
Percentage of students from out of state:	68%
Percentage of students graduating in 4 years / 6 years:	22% / 57%

Money

Total endowment:	—
Total tuition:	$7,680
Total cost with fees & expenses:	$14,140
Average financial aid package:	$4,067
Percentage of students who sought aid and received it:	31%
Percentage of students receiving financial aid:	40%

Also Check Out

University of Denver

University of Idaho

University of Utah

Brown University

Box 1876, 45 Prospect Street
Providence, RI 02912

(401) 863-1000
http://www.brown.edu/

 **BIG BRAIN**

 **BIG IDEA**

Not your ordinary Ivy

5 REASONS IT'S COOL

1. Brown's open curriculum lets **students shape their own academic destinies.**

2. **Students go wild for the food service,** which offers tasty morsels well into the wee hours.

3. Annual events SexPowerGod and Spring Weekend are **big-league bacchanals.**

4. The **need-blind admission** means that students are accepted because of their merits, not because of how much they can pony up for tuition.

5. Brown guarantees it will fully meet students' tuition needs, which means **generous financial aid packages.**

The Basics

Public / private: private nonprofit
Total enrollment / undergrads: 8,125 / 6,010
Campus setting: urban
Students call it: Brown
Students are called: Bears
Notable alums: John F. Kennedy Jr. (publisher), Laura Linney (actress), Lisa Loeb (musician), Joe Paterno (football coach), Alison Stewart (journalist), Nathanael West (writer)

A League of Its Own

Brown's open curriculum, in which major courses are the only required ones, makes Brown by far the most avant-garde of the Ivies. Once considered a safety school for underachieving country-clubbers, Brown has turned into a competitive but quirky place where students can let their freak flags fly—a reputation The O. C. only enhanced. Brown's free-and-easy approach to matriculation doesn't please everyone. Self-motivated students flourish in this milieu, though, and express great appreciation for Brown's educational philosophy of liberty and personal growth. Such highly individualized learning experiences mean that Brown is not terribly cutthroat, so those who perform best in pressure-cooker situations should probably look elsewhere. When students are ready to knuckle down, they may choose such academic programs as computer science, engineering, history, international relations, and writing, which are among the university's strongest.

Naked Came the Stranger

Brown has many kooky traditions, but only one requires public nudity. In the days before final exams every semester, some students disrobe and bring donuts to stressed-out crammers in the various campus libraries. How they offer these doughy delights to their fellow students is best left to the imagination.

What Cheer?

Brown's liberal curriculum means its students find plenty of time for fun. Brown has no Greek scene to speak of, so party hosting duties fall to students with off-campus digs. Brown students also hit up the bars, particularly Viva and Fish Co. Brown's own Graduate Center Bar, which admits of-age undergrads, pours liquid cheer at reasonable prices for the budget minded. Revelers with the munchies can satisfy their cravings late into the night with treats from the campus food service. For those who want something more exotic, Providence has plenty of great restaurants. When not eating, drinking, or attending class, students hang around in their dorms. The residence halls may not be spectacular, but they're clean and serviceable—with the exception of New Pembroke Hall, which earns a collective thumbs down from Brown students.

An Enviable Prospect

Brown's stately campus sits on the summit of College Hill in Providence's historic east side. This choice piece of real estate gives students wonderful views of the city, especially at sunset. Nearby Thayer Street offers boutiques, bars, coffee houses, and eclectic eateries, and downhill has Providence Place, a mall famous for its wall-to-wall carpeting. The maze of city roads, coupled with the Darwinian parking situation, doesn't exactly make Providence an auto-friendly town, but Brown's Safe Ride shuttle and the eastside trolley offer low- or no-cost transportation alternatives to hoofing it or driving. Convenient bus and train lines are popular, cheap means of day-tripping to Boston or weekending in New York. Most student residents of Providence, the self-proclaimed Renaissance City, find it pedestrian friendly and full of cultural attractions and local color.

Admissions

Average high school GPA:	—
Average freshman SAT verbal / math score:	705 / 712
Average freshman ACT score:	26
Application fee:	$70

Application deadlines:
1/1 (freshmen)
3/1 (transfer)
11/1 (early decision)

Total applicants:	18,316
Total accepted:	2,573 (14%)
Total accepted who enrolled:	1,466

Notification dates:
4/1 (freshmen)
5/25 (transfer)
12/15 (early decision)

Acceptance rate for early decision applicants:	29%

Students

Percentage of male / female students:	48% / 52%
Percentage of students from out of state:	96%
Percentage of students graduating in 4 years / 6 years:	83% / 95%

Money

Total endowment:	—
Total tuition:	$33,888
Total cost with fees & expenses:	$44,882
Average financial aid package:	$26,477
Percentage of students who sought aid and received it:	100%
Percentage of students receiving financial aid:	41%

Also Check Out

New York University

Northwestern University

Tufts University

University of Pennsylvania

Yale University

Bryn Mawr College

101 North Merion Avenue
Bryn Mawr, PA 19010

(610) 526-5000
http://www.brynmawr.edu/

 BIG HAND

 BIG PERSPECTIVE

Sisterly community in the City of Brotherly Love

5 REASONS IT'S COOL

1. **Professors get high marks** not just for teaching but also for showing students why the material is exciting.

2. The honor code dignifies academic pursuits and **fosters collegial relationships among students** and between students and faculty.

3. You'll hold the past in your hands: The night before May Day, **seniors pass down to younger students gifts** they received the previous year.

4. **The campus is straight out of central casting:** lots of green, lots of brick, lots of quiet.

5. You can **run the Rocky Steps in Philadelphia**—and then check out the art museum at the top.

The Basics

Public / private: private nonprofit
Total enrollment / undergrads: 1,799 / 1,378
Campus setting: suburban
Students call it: Bryn Mawr
Students are called: Mawrtyrs
Notable alums: Emily Greene Balch (Nobel Laureate, Peace), A. S. Byatt (novelist), H. D. (poet), Katharine Hepburn (actress), Edith Hamilton (scholar, writer), Sari Horwitz (journalist), Marianne Moore (poet), Jeannette Picard (teacher, priest, balloonist)

For the Love of Learning

Bryn Mawr has respected programs in fields as diverse as physics, art history, and the "growth and structure of cities," but what links all the school's departments is the expectation that students will immerse themselves deeply, every day, in whatever they've chosen to study. The student body is a group of talented and diverse young women who share a willingness to work hard. Bryn Mawr encourages serious commitment to every course, in the belief that all learning is valuable. To fulfill distribution requirements, students must do work in social sciences, natural sciences, humanities, and a foreign language. All students must also complete coursework in quantitative fields. Students have to participate in physical education for half of their semesters and must pass a swim test before graduation. The honor code is a distinguishing aspect of academic life at Bryn Mawr.

Kiss Here, Not There

The list of Bryn Mawr superstitions deserves its own guidebook, but here's one you need to know before you visit: Legend has it that no one who walks down the Senior Steps will ever graduate from Bryn Mawr. Other superstitions have it that kissing on the Moon Bench will doom a couple, while kissing under the Rock Arch will help them find happiness. And those needing extra help with schoolwork will be happy to learn that the statue of Athena fields requests for general academic problems twenty-four hours a day.

Traditions and Tolerance

Bryn Mawr students are independent and often nonconformist, but they also love tradition. Various festivals and unofficial holidays brighten up the year. Lantern Night celebrates the assignment of class colors to the incoming first-years, while the Elizabethan May Day celebration includes the donning of white dresses, the staging of Greek plays, and the singing of traditional songs (plus some skinny-dipping). Year-round, tolerance is the name of the game at Bryn Mawr, and students generally report a strong sense of community. In part, this is due to the fact that most students take advantage of all four years of their guaranteed housing. The residences here are high quality, with some of the dorms boasting hardwood floors and fireplaces. The food service has won several national awards. Between study sessions, Mawrtyrs participate in performance and literary clubs, as well as a relatively high number of intramural athletic leagues. The campus doesn't have much of a party scene, but there are plenty of other universities in and around Philadelphia that do.

Pretty As a Picture

Bryan Mawr's campus—leafy, idyllic, and dotted with gothic buildings—sits in the wealthy suburban town of Bryn Mawr. There are coffee shops, bookstores, and restaurants aplenty, many of them (sigh) national chains. The commuter train to Philadelphia stops two blocks from campus, and it's just a twenty-minute ride to Center City. Some students say they wish their lives had a little more grit, but many find the school's location ideal, with the city near enough for spur-of-the-moment visits but far enough away that campus retains the feel of a genuine retreat from urban hustle and bustle. New York and the Jersey Shore are popular weekend destinations, as is Hersheypark, the only outdoors location in the world that actually smells like chocolate.

Admissions

Average high school GPA:	—
Average freshman SAT writing / math / critical reading score:	673 / 632 / 673
Average freshman ACT score:	26
Application fee:	$50
Application deadlines:	
1/15 (freshmen)	
3/15 (transfer)	
11/15 (early decision)	
Total applicants:	2,133
Total accepted:	940 (44%)
Total accepted who enrolled:	358
Notification dates:	
4/15 (freshmen)	
6/1 (transfer)	
12/15 (early decision)	
Acceptance rate for early decision applicants:	73%

Students

Percentage of male / female students:	— / 100%
Percentage of students from out of state:	83%
Percentage of students graduating in 4 years / 6 years:	80% / 86%

Money

Total endowment:	$557,843,000
Total tuition:	$32,230
Total cost with fees & expenses:	$43,560
Average financial aid package:	$29,169
Percentage of students who sought aid and received it:	100%
Percentage of students receiving financial aid:	52%

Also Check Out

Smith College

Swarthmore College

University of Pennsylvania

Vassar College

Wellesley College

Bucknell University

701 Moore Avenue
Lewisburg, PA 17837

(570) 577-2000
http://www.bucknell.edu/

BIG RESEARCH

A big-city education in a small-town environment

5 REASONS IT'S COOL

1. Bucknell's **School of Engineering is consistently ranked among the top 10** in its category in the country.

2. For those times when you're craving a jolt of urbanity, the university offers **free shuttles to several metropolitan areas.**

3. Tell that loan officer to take a hike: Bucknell's **average financial aid award is around $20,000.**

4. *All* undergrads are eligible to **participate in summer research projects with faculty mentors.**

5. The Susquehanna River Valley offers plenty of opportunities for **hiking, camping, kayaking, and biking.**

The Basics

Public / private: private nonprofit
Total enrollment / undergrads: 3,706 / 3,550
Campus setting: small town
Students call it: Bucknell
Students are called: Bisons, Bucknellians
Notable alums: Diane Allen (senator), Philip Roth (writer), Rob Andrews (congressman), Les Moonves (CEO, CBS), Christy Mathewson (pro baseball player)

Personal Attention and Maybe a Coauthor Credit

Among Bucknell's many highly rated academic programs, the Engineering School and Biology Department are standouts. Students provide varying reports on the rigor of the education. Some say the curriculum is tough but inspiring, while others say they're not sufficiently challenged by the faculty or their fellow students. With a student-to-faculty ratio of just 11:1, no one complains about getting lost in the crowd. Overall, students are highly satisfied: 96 percent of first-years return as sophomores. Bucknell grads are well prepared for graduate and professional study, in part thanks to the summer research project program. Students earn a modest stipend for their summer labors and are required to present work at an annual symposium. It's not unusual for students to receive coauthor credit on papers published in top-flight academic journals. Bucknell students also value travel; 42 percent of undergraduates spend at least one semester studying abroad.

A Tradition of Service

Bucknell's tradition of service reaches back to the university's early days. During the famous Battle of Gettysburg during the Civil War, Bucknell saw so many students and faculty members (including the university's President) enlist to serve the Union cause that it shut down shop temporarily.

Go Greek, or Science, or Music, or . . .

The rural Pennsylvanian setting of Bucknell's campus means that Greek life is a big deal. Still, plenty of students say that the frats and sororities aren't the only social game in town. Bucknell has over 150 clubs and organizations, and the town of Lewisburg is a safe and scenic place to hang out. Students can root for Bucknell's twenty-seven NCAA Division I teams or go out for any of seventeen club sports. The recent successes of the basketball team have helped to intensify spirit. A world-class athletic facility, named for alumnus and former CEO of Home Depot Kenneth Langone, was completed in 2003. Although the campus is regularly called one of the most beautiful in the country, the university's administration isn't resting on its laurels. New construction is always going on, and many key buildings have been built or rebuilt.

The Bucknell Bubble

Bucknell's 450-acre campus is an important part of Lewiston, a small town in the Susquehanna River Valley of Pennsylvania. While Lewiston is a pretty and historic place, prospective students looking for a small town near a big city should look elsewhere. Nestled in central Pennsylvania, Lewisburg offers all of the advantages and disadvantages of distance from the hustle and bustle of Philadelphia, New York, and Boston. Trips to Philly, New York, and D.C. take about three hours. Students both complain about the lack of social and cultural options in Lewiston and admit that the insular location helps them concentrate on their studies.

Admissions

Average high school GPA:	—
Average freshman SAT verbal / math score:	641 / 674
Average freshman ACT score:	26
Application fee:	$60
Application deadlines: 1/1 (freshmen) 3/15 (transfer) 11/15 (early decision)	
Total applicants:	9,021
Total accepted:	2,990 (33%)
Total accepted who enrolled:	923
Notification dates: 4/1 (freshmen) 5/1 (transfer) 12/15 (early decision)	
Acceptance rate for early decision applicants:	49%

Students

Percentage of male / female students:	49% / 51%
Percentage of students from out of state:	73%
Percentage of students graduating in 4 years / 6 years:	85% / 90%

Money

Total endowment:	$522,059,000
Total tuition:	$37,934
Total cost with fees & expenses:	$46,186
Average financial aid package:	$23,400
Percentage of students who sought aid and received it:	100%
Percentage of students receiving financial aid:	47%

Also Check Out

Amherst College

Brandeis University

Lafayette College

Lehigh University

Villanova University

California Institute of Technology

1200 East California Boulevard
Pasadena, CA 91125

(626) 395-6811
http://www.caltech.edu/

 **BIG BRAIN**

 **BIG PLAN**

 **BIG RESEARCH**

They've got this college thing down to a science.

5 REASONS IT'S COOL

1. **Love science?** Caltech is *the* place to study.

2. At this **prank-happy institute**, students have transformed the Hollywood sign so that it read "Caltech."

3. **Nobels, MacArthurs, National Medals of Science** . . . alums and professors have won a staggering number.

4. At the Jet Propulsion Laboratory (JPL), a **NASA laboratory managed by Caltech,** undergrads can collaborate with researchers.

5. This most prestigious of schools gives its students **amazing research opportunities** and lots of access to labs and equipment.

The Basics

Public / private: private nonprofit
Total enrollment / undergrads: 2,086 / 864
Campus setting: suburban
Students call it: Caltech
Students are called: Techers
Notable alums: Sabeer Bhatia (cofounder, Hotmail), Frank Capra (film-maker), Richard Feynman (Nobel Laureate, Physics), Gordon Moore (cofounder, Intel), Linus Pauling (Nobel Laureate, Chemistry and Peace), Kenneth Pitzer (winner, National Medal of Science), Harrison Schmitt (astronaut, geologist, senator)

Purely Science, Totally Stellar

One of the top schools in the nation, Caltech offers an undergraduate experience unlike any other. Caltech has a reputation as one of the best (if not *the* best) school for pure sciences. Required courses include five terms each of mathematics and physics, along with chemistry, biology, and a hefty dose of humanities. The student-to-faculty ratio is an awe-inspiring 3:1. Students work closely with faculty on their research, which has been some of the most innovative in the scientific community. Academics are rigorous, and grading is harsh. The first two terms are graded pass/fail, and all students declare an "option" (or major) at the end of their first year. Fully 40 percent of Caltech grads go on to earn PhDs—the highest percentage of any school in the nation. Although most students dive in rather than branch out, the institute has several exchange agreements, including with Cambridge and the University of Edinburgh.

Tech Trickery

Techers are notorious pranksters. The pranks, like scientific innovations, tend to build on previous achievements. Every year on Ditch Day, seniors leave elaborate "stacks" or puzzles designed to keep underclassmen from entering their rooms. In one of many pranks pulled against MIT, Caltech students went to one of their rival's preview events and handed out T-shirts that read "MIT" on the front and " . . . because not everyone can go to Caltech" on the back.

Work Hard . . . uh, Work Hard

"Play hard" is a phrase that doesn't really apply at Caltech, where "nose to the grindstone" is a more applicable cliché. When students do have a free moment or two, they find Pasadena a great city full of wonderful restaurants, lively pedestrian zones such as Old Town, and plenty of places to take a date. Unfortunately (or fortunately, depending on your perspective), the male-to-female ratio is severely imbalanced. Other aspects of life win almost universal praise. Students have lots of access to labs and facilities, and the provisions of the honor code allow them to take exams without supervision. Students join one of six residential houses during their freshman year. This system, modeled on Cambridge's and Oxford's, gives students a social base, not to mention dining companions—no small matter at a school that provides waiters and table service during evening meals. Lunches at Chandler also win raves. And competition doesn't stop in the classroom: Caltech's Division III and club teams are open to all students.

Pasadena Plus

Caltech is situated in the lovely city of Pasadena, home of the Rose Parade, stunning mansions, and the Jet Propulsion Laboratory (JPL). You would be hard pressed to find a prettier place to slice atoms or study the stars. Students aren't limited to the small campus, as the institute operates several other off-campus research facilities, including the W. M. Keck Observatory in Hawaii, the Palomar Observatory in San Diego, and many others throughout the West. Some of the school's buildings are in the Southern California mission style, while newer buildings have cleaner lines and modern shapes. Pasadena is just northeast of downtown Los Angeles, so students with cars have endless activity options in the area. For those without wheels, the Metro Gold Line, which stops about a mile from campus, is a cheap way to get around town.

Admissions

Average high school GPA:	—
Average freshman SAT verbal / math score:	717 / 750
Average freshman ACT score:	—
Application fee:	$60

Application deadlines:
1/1 (freshmen)
2/15 (transfer)
11/1 (early action)

Total applicants:	3,330
Total accepted:	573 (17%)
Total accepted who enrolled:	214

Notification dates:
4/1 (freshmen)
6/1 (transfer)
12/15 (early action)

Acceptance rate for early action applicants:	28%

Students

Percentage of male / female students:	71% / 29%
Percentage of students from out of state:	69%
Percentage of students graduating in 4 years / 6 years:	79% / 89%

Money

Total endowment:	$1,154,540,000
Total tuition:	$29,940
Total cost with fees & expenses:	$42,375
Average financial aid package:	$25,923
Percentage of students who sought aid and received it:	100%
Percentage of students receiving financial aid:	58%

Also Check Out

Carnegie Mellon University

Harvey Mudd College

Massachusetts Institute of Technology

Stanford University

University of California–Berkeley

California Polytechnic State University–San Luis Obispo

I Grand Avenue
San Luis Obispo, CA 93407

(805) 756-IIII
http://www.calpoly.edu/

 **BIG CHOICE**

 **BIG JOB**

 **BIG RESEARCH**

Learn by doing.

5 REASONS IT'S COOL

1. **"Learn by doing"** is the driving philosophy behind this top-ranked public university.

2. Cal Poly students enjoy a **ninety-percent job placement rate** upon graduation.

3. Whatever their major, students acquire **real-world professional skills**.

4. Students love the **laid-back lifestyle** of the California coast, where beaches and wide-open countryside abound.

5. **Project-based learning** helps students develop a passion for their fields of interest.

The Basics

Public / private: public state
Total enrollment / undergrads: 18,722 / 17,777
Campus setting: small town
Students call it: Cal Poly, Cal Poly SLO
Students are called: Mustangs
Notable alums: Robert L. Gibson (astronaut), John Madden (pro football coach, sports broadcaster), Ozzie Smith (pro baseball player), William H. Swanson (CEO, Raytheon), "Weird Al" Yankovic (musician)

Real Hands-On Experience

Cal Poly is a steal for the practical minded student who wants a hands-on education. In fact, the university prides itself on its "learn by doing" approach, and students can feel confident knowing they'll have the skills they need when they graduate and enter the workforce. Not surprisingly, the most popular majors at Cal Poly are very practical, such as agricultural business, architecture, business administration, and mechanical engineering. A large number of students study abroad through the California State University system's International Programs, while others choose to pursue their own research interests to help solve real world problems. All majors, however, emphasize fieldwork and lab work over book learning, and professors work closely with their students. With so much attention and hands-on experience, students often develop a deep passion for their majors that goes well beyond the desire to get good grades.

Float On

Every year, Cal Poly SLO teams up with its sister campus, Cal Poly Pomona, to produce an all-student-built float for the Rose Parade in Pasadena, California. The two universities have collaborated on many award-winning floats since 1949. Each university focuses on a specific part of the float: SLO spearheads the drive system, while Pomona is in charge of the animation. In the weeks leading up to the big day, SLO students head down to Pomona to decorate the float's all-flower surface.

Job Offers Galore

With its low in-state tuition, it's no wonder that over ninety percent of Cal Poly students hail from the state of California. Many students choose to live on campus in one of the campus's four dormitory clusters, although the university plans to add a new on-campus apartment complex soon. Students in the dorms tend to live with people of the same grade, major, and interests, which allows them to make friends easily. Many students lament that Cal Poly's alcohol ban and San Luis Obispo's paucity of bars and clubs can make the campus a little boring on evenings and weekends, but other students find that there's always plenty of partying to be found on campus, and cheering on the school's NCAA Division I sports teams remains a popular pastime. All students agree that Cal Poly's major draw is its ninety percent job placement rate; in fact, sixty percent of students have lucrative job offers before they even graduate!

Take It SLO

Cal Poly owns over nine thousand acres of land in California, which means it has plenty of room to grow. The university plans to increase its student enrollment over the next twelve years and expand its campus facilities as well. Current facilities on the thirteen hundred acre main campus include a state-of-the-art recreation center; the peaceful Leaning Pine Arboretum; a well-equipped library; and the Dexter Lawn, where students stretch out, study, and socialize. The old Spanish mission town of San Luis Obispo holds a Farmers' Market each Thursday night, and there are lots of student-friendly shops and restaurants too. West of the main campus, meanwhile, are miles of gorgeous California coastline with camping, surfing, and hiking options galore. Monterey and Santa Barbara are not far away, and just a few more hours will take you to San Francisco and L.A.

Admissions

Average high school GPA:	3.7
Average freshman SAT verbal / math score:	576 / 621
Average freshman ACT score:	25
Application fee:	$55

Application deadlines:
11/30 (freshmen)
11/30 (transfer)
10/31 (early decision)

Total applicants:	26,724
Total accepted:	12,453 (47%)
Total accepted who enrolled:	3,610

Notification dates:
continuous (freshmen)
3/1 (transfer)
12/15 (early decision)

Acceptance rate for early decision applicants: 24%

Students

Percentage of male / female students:	56% / 44%
Percentage of students from out of state:	7%
Percentage of students graduating in 4 years / 6 years:	21% / 69%

Money

Total endowment:	—
Total in-state tuition, fees & expenses:	$14,153
Total out-of-state tuition, fees & expenses:	$28,673
Average financial aid package:	$7,456
Percentage of students who sought aid and received it:	64%
Percentage of students receiving financial aid:	30%

Also Check Out

Harvey Mudd College

Rice University

University of California–Berkeley

University of California–Davis

University of California–San Diego

California State University–Chico

400 West First Street
Chico, CA 95929

(530) 898-6116
http://www.csuchico.edu/

 **BIG CHOICE**

 BIG JOB

Where it's easy being green

5 REASONS IT'S COOL

1. Environmental awareness is a priority here, as the **new, sustainable construction** proves.

2. Chico State offers a range of professional degrees, including construction management and liberal studies for teachers, **for students who want to jump-start their careers.**

3. **Optional tracks customize the curriculum** and enhance the educational experiences.

4. The *Orion*, the **award-winning student newspaper**, breaks the news across campus every week.

5. **From parties to parades,** Wildcats make their own fun.

The Basics

Public / private: public state
Total enrollment / undergrads: 16,250 / 14,927
Campus setting: small town
Students call it: CSU Chico, Chico State, CSUC
Students are called: Wildcats
Notable alums: Raymond Carver (writer), Sandra Lerner (founder, Cisco Systems), Mat Kearney (musician), Matt Olmstead (writer, *NYPD Blue* and *Prison Break*), Carolyn Shoemaker (astronomer)

Lots of Learning in a Small Town

Chico State has over a hundred majors and thousands of students, but still manages to replicate its hometown's cozy vibe on campus. While the student-to-faculty ratio of 21:1 is typical of larger state schools, this university makes it easy for students to customize their educations. For high achievers, the University Honors Program intensifies the undergrad experience and offers a slew of enhancements. For future educators, the innovative Integrated Teacher Core brings together liberal studies and a multiple-subject credential. The university also offers introductory honors courses in business and other disciplines, major-based classes, and honors housing. The General Studies Thematic allows students to complete their general education coursework through a yearlong integrated studies program. The most popular majors are business administration, liberal studies (for elementary school teachers), psychology, nursing, and construction management, which posts amazing job placement rates for its grads. The university

Don't Rain on Their Parade

Since the early 1900s, the university has held a yearly parade. It was banned temporarily in the 1980s and '90s due to dangerously boisterous parade watchers and then reincarnated as Rancho Chico Days and then Celebration of the People. In its current incarnation, it's called the Pioneer Days Parade.

also has unique programs in forensic anthropology, music industry, and applied computer graphics.

The Chico State of Things

The *Orion*, CSU Chico's award-winning newspaper, has drawn many national accolades, and students check its pages for local news, commentary, and events listings. When the weather gets hot, throngs flock to the Feather River for tubing, merriment, and libations. Chico State has a reputation as a party school (*Playboy* magazine named it the number 2 party school in 2002), and house parties and barhopping are popular nighttime diversions. There are thirteen Wildcats athletic teams, which play in Division II of the NCAA. In particular, the men's and women's soccer and basketball teams make the crowds growl. Chico State is a popular choice for Latino and Latina students, and fraternities and sororities include multicultural groups. About 90 percent of students live off campus, and the city of Chico has lots of boutiques, shops, and eateries catering to student tastes. When it's time to bid adieu to the undergraduate years, students can turn to their school's excellent career placement services, or interview with the major companies that regularly recruit on campus.

A Green Statement

Unlike many of California's public universities, Chico State has a remarkably pleasant and green campus. It shares an arboretum with Bidwell Mansion State Park, and the Rose Garden, near the Meriam Library, has been blooming since 1957. New construction places an emphasis on sustainability and green technology. The university boasts the first LEED (Leadership in Energy and Environmental Design) gold-certified building in the California State University System, and a retrofitted dorm, renamed the Sustainability House, is the first of its kind in the nation. The Northern California Museum of Natural History, which is currently under construction, will be affiliated with the university's College of Natural Sciences. The town of Chico is about 160 miles from San Francisco and 90 miles from Sacramento.

Admissions

Average high school GPA:	3.15
Average freshman SAT verbal / math score:	511 / 522
Average freshman ACT score:	21
Application fee:	$55
Application deadlines: 11/30 (freshmen) 11/30 (transfer)	
Total applicants:	12,733
Total accepted:	11,509 (90%)
Total accepted who enrolled:	2,430
Notification dates: 3/1 (freshmen) 3/1 (transfer)	

Students

Percentage of male / female students:	48% / 52%
Percentage of students from out of state:	3%
Percentage of students graduating in 4 years / 6 years:	16% / 51%

Money

Total endowment:	$31,029,308
Total in-state tuition, fees & expenses:	$12,945
Total out-of-state tuition, fees & expenses:	$25,635
Average financial aid package:	$8,508
Percentage of students who sought aid and received it:	78%
Percentage of students receiving financial aid:	45%

Also Check Out

California Polytechnic State University–San Luis Obispo

San Diego State University

University of California–Davis

University of California–Santa Cruz

Carleton College

One North College Street
Northfield, MN 55057

(507) 646-4000
http://www.carleton.edu/

 **BIG BRAIN**

 **BIG PERSPECTIVE**

Where the elite meet sleet

5 REASONS IT'S COOL

1. Get on a **first-name basis with your profs.** At Carleton, teaching is a big deal to both students and professors.

2. Students of all stripes thrive in the campus's "learning for learning's sake" environment.

3. Considering its small size and out-of-the-way location, Carleton is **a surprisingly diverse place.**

4. Carleton offers **wacky traditions-a-plenty,** from the campuswide scream during finals to the day-long softball game to . . .

5. If you like doing anything—*anything*—in **the great outdoors**, chances are there's a group of students already doing it.

The Basics

Public / private: private nonprofit
Total enrollment / undergrads: 1,980 / 1,980
Campus setting: small town
Students call it: Carleton, Carls
Students are called: Knights
Notable alums: Pierce Butler (founding father), Jane Hamilton (novelist), Melvin Laird (politician, writer), James Loewen (historian)

Bread and Butter Liberal Arts

Carleton makes no bones about the fact that its students are expected to dive deeply—very deeply—into all of their classes. To facilitate such intense study, the college runs on a trimester system, meaning that students typically take only three courses at a time. Professors are firmly focused on teaching and receive praise for both their accessibility and passion about their fields. Seventy percent of Carleton students pursue a postgraduate degree within five years of graduation. The college, in fact, prides itself on preparing its students for graduate work, particularly in the sciences. Engineers can enroll in a 3-2 program with Columbia University or with Washington University in St. Louis; geology majors do field work in Death Valley; and ecology specialists use the on-campus arboretum to liven up their classroom work. The English, history, and fine arts programs are also strong. Every department expects a comprehensive senior project, and the collegewide distribution requirements mandate at least one course focusing on non-Western cultures.

Stick 'Em Up!

In an apparent attempt to give **Carleton** students a run for their money in the wacky traditions department, the local residents of Northfield stage an annual reenactment of a Wild West bank robbery. The performance is meant to evoke the mystique of Jesse James, whose gang committed their final heist here.

Calling All Class Clowns

If you're concerned that student life at Carleton will be snowed under, don't worry. Just consider such "make the best of the cold weather" activities as the winter carnival featuring human bowling and the popular wintertime naked runs. Social life at Carleton is often an informal affair—the closest things to a Greek system are the upperclassmen theme houses—but informality seems to suit most students just fine. The college's relaxed enforcement of its alcohol policy means that parties are easy to come by, though nondrinkers also find plenty to do. Carleton students revel in their healthy prank culture; for instance, on the eve of finals, students join in a campuswide 10 P.M. scream. Annual events include a big spring concert and a party on a lake island. Two-thirds of students participate in either varsity or intramural leagues, and the new indoor recreation and athletics center allows running, mini-golfing, rock climbing, and broomball (we're not sure what that is, either) to continue right through the winter.

Bring Your Boots

Northfield is not considered a particularly exciting place—which may explain Carleton's thriving on-campus activity scene. Northfield is home to seventeen thousand residents who are generally considered to be friendly and welcoming to neighboring students. To escape the doldrums of small-town life, students have the twin cities of Minneapolis and St. Paul, thirty-five miles to the north, as escape options. Carleton students aren't allowed to keep cars on campus, so you'll probably get to know the weekend charter bus schedule fairly well. Most students consider the best aspect of Carleton's location to be the vast wilderness stretching away from campus and into the distance. You'd need way more than four years to exhaust all the hiking, camping, and fishing options in the region, and it's a fair question which is the most beautiful local site: spring's lilacs, autumn's foliage, or winter's snowdrifts.

Admissions

Average high school GPA:	—
Average freshman SAT writing / math / critical reading score:	690 / 700 / 701
Average freshman ACT score:	26
Application fee:	$30
Application deadlines: 1/15 (freshmen) 3/31 (transfer) 11/15 (early decision)	
Total applicants:	4,450
Total accepted:	1,405 (32%)
Total accepted who enrolled:	504
Notification dates: 4/15 (freshmen) 5/15 (transfer) 12/15 (early decision)	
Acceptance rate for early decision applicants:	44%

Students

Percentage of male / female students:	47% / 53%
Percentage of students from out of state:	73%
Percentage of students graduating in 4 years / 6 years:	81% / 86%

Money

Total endowment:	$540,039,151
Total tuition:	$34,083
Total cost with fees & expenses:	$43,464
Average financial aid package:	$29,116
Percentage of students who sought aid and received it:	100%
Percentage of students receiving financial aid:	55%

Also Check Out

Grinnell College

Kalamazoo College

Macalester College

University of Chicago

Williams College

Carnegie Mellon University

5000 Forbes Avenue
Pittsburgh, PA 15213

(412) 268-2000
http://www.cmu.edu/

 **BIG BRAIN**

 **BIG RESEARCH**

From Gamma Rays to Grammys

5 REASONS IT'S COOL

1. Carnegie Mellon offers **top-tier programs in the hard sciences and fine arts**.

2. The Institute of Technology offers one of the **top-ranked engineering degrees** in the nation.

3. Enjoy the **newly renovated and state-of-the-art** buildings on campus, which range in style from Renaissance to space-age contemporary.

4. This is one of the few schools that **matches financial aid offers from competing universities** in an effort to attract the best of the best.

5. Toot your own horn by choosing the only university in America with **a major in bagpiping**.

The Basics

Public / private: private nonprofit
Total enrollment / undergrads: 10,120 / 5,669
Campus setting: urban
Students call it: Carnegie Mellon
Notable alums: Ted Danson (actor), Judith Light (actress), Judith Resnik (astronaut), Joshua Schachter (creator, del.icio.us), Andy Warhol (artist)

Where the Left Brain Meets the Right

Each of the six undergraduate colleges at Carnegie Mellon is distinct, with its own strengths and emphases. But the core mission of the university—to broaden students' academic horizons with a well-rounded education—is central to all the colleges. And across the board, students are smart, hard workers. Engineering majors can select from humanities and social science courses, while social science majors can combine traditional disciplinary studies with work in such fields as artificial intelligence. The university has smaller satellite campuses around the globe, at which students may want to study depending on their particular interests. The campus in Qatar is run by renowned robotics scholar Charles Thorpe, and there are a variety of exchange programs in Australia, China, and many European countries. On the main campus, the student-to-faculty ratio is 10:1, and the majority of classes are fewer than twenty students. A few popular lecture courses do attract upwards of two hundred students, though. In most courses, students appreciate professors' engaged and willing-to-help attitudes. Engineering, business, and the arts are among the most popular programs.

Robot Love

Computers feature big in this university's history. In fact, Carnegie Mellon researchers built one of the first large computers that could do more than simply store data or solve math problems. Twenty years later, the school's robotics center amazed the world again when it created robots to help clean up nuclear waste from the fallout of the Three Mile Island disaster in 1979. Carnegie Mellon continues this strong tradition of innovation today.

Freaks, Geeks, and Greeks

Carnegie Mellon's student body reflects the school's unique strengths in both the arts and hard sciences. A majority of students are well-off, and at 2:1, the male-to-female ratio is pretty lopsided. Carnegie Mellon attracts a laudably diverse crowd: 35 percent of undergraduates are minorities, the largest of those being of Asian/Pacific Islander descent. Almost a tenth of students take part in fraternities and sororities, which are a visible part of campus culture. Aside from Greek life, the University Center offers $1 movies five nights a week, and the drama club productions are also a big draw. The most widely anticipated event is the Spring Carnival, which is held every April. To prepare for this one-day break from classes, science students construct alloyed pushcarts for racing, theater majors rehearse original shows, and other students channel their energies into designing themed booths. Most students find the on-campus food selection expensive and disappointing, but off-campus choices provide alternatives. Intramural sports are much bigger at Carnegie Mellon than varsity sports, which are Division III.

Living It Up Downtown

Carnegie Mellon's self-contained campus is located three miles from downtown Pittsburgh, near the city's wealthier neighborhoods and bordering the University of Pittsburgh. A museum named after the school's founder, Andrew Carnegie, along with city's largest park, lies next door. A twenty-minute bus ride takes students to Pittsburgh opera, ballet, and sports events. Like the varied architecture of the city, the buildings on campus range in design from Renaissance style, in sedate cream or yellow, to strikingly airy, bright, window-filled buildings. The school frequently renovates its dorms and academic buildings, and it boasts the nation's first green residence hall. Washington, D.C. is 190 miles away, and Philadelphia is a little further a field.

Admissions

Average high school GPA:	3.61
Average freshman SAT writing / math / critical reading score:	659 / 722 / 659
Average freshman ACT score:	26
Application fee:	$65

Application deadlines:
1/1 (freshmen)
3/1 (transfer)
11/1 (early decision)

Total applicants:	18,864
Total accepted:	6,357 (34%)
Total accepted who enrolled:	1,424

Notification dates:
4/15 (freshmen)
6/30 (transfer)
12/15 (early decision)

Acceptance rate for early decision applicants:	53%

Students

Percentage of male / female students:	61% / 39%
Percentage of students from out of state:	76%
Percentage of students graduating in 4 years / 6 years:	66% / 86%

Money

Total endowment:	$941,525,000
Total tuition:	$34,180
Total cost with fees & expenses:	$43,858
Average financial aid package:	$22,143
Percentage of students who sought aid and received it:	81%
Percentage of students receiving financial aid:	48%

Also Check Out

Cornell University

Lehigh University

Massachusetts Institute of Technology

Princeton University

University of Pennsylvania

Case Western Reserve University

10900 Euclid Avenue
Cleveland, OH 44106

(216) 368-2000
http://www.case.edu/

BIG RESEARCH

The crème de la Cleveland

5 REASONS IT'S COOL

1. Case Western students enjoy the perks of **a small campus that offers proximity to Cleveland.**

2. Three residential colleges for freshmen **ease the transition to college life.**

3. The university's **broadminded housing policy** allows students to live in coed suites.

4. Students enjoy the **freedom to study practically anything** they want.

5. The hi-tech campus features more than a thousand wireless hotspots and **a computer lab devoted entirely to video games.**

The Basics

Public / private: private nonprofit
Total enrollment / undergrads: 9,592 / 4,080
Campus setting: urban
Student call it: Case Western, Case
Students are called: Spartans, Case Westerners
Notable alums: Alene B. Duerk (first female Navy admiral), Michael McCaskey (chairman, Chicago Bears), M. Scott Peck (psychiatrist, author)

Experiential Learning from the Best of the Best

Case Western has 2,030 full-time faculty members, 95 percent of whom hold terminal degrees in their fields. With a student-to-faculty ratio of 8:1, students are working in close contact with these luminaries. Half of all Case Western courses have fewer than twenty students. Administrators and faculty members believe firmly in the value of experiential, innovative learning, which means opportunities abound to do hands-on research, study abroad, or participate in, say, a nursing clinical, a sailing expedition, or a theatrical production. The new Seminar Approach to General Education and Scholarship (SAGES) program, which spans the undergraduate years, offers out-of-classroom learning experiences, small-group interaction with professors, and the ability to network beyond campus. Students can choose from sixty different majors in engineering, management, nursing, and the arts and sciences.

Just in Case

Although the university is commonly referred to as Case Western, its full name is actually Case Western Reserve University. The lengthy, somewhat confusing name was the result of a merger of the Case Institute of Technology with Western Reserve University. In 2003, the administration created a new university logo that emphasized *Case*, which went over like a lead balloon. The school abandoned the project and decided to revert to good old Case Western Reserve University.

Building Community

Residential life and extracurricular activities unite the student body. For the first couple of years, students are required to live on campus, which fosters a deep sense of community across the disciplines. Greek life has a strong presence on campus too, and nearly a third of Case Westerners belong to a fraternity or sorority. You'll find plenty of varsity men's and women's sports teams here, several of which compete in NCAA Division III. There's also a spate of annual traditions that students can look forward to, including the twenty-six-mile Hudson Relays, Springfest, and the Science Fiction Film Marathon, to name just a few. And of course, Case Western offers the traditional gamut of club activities that emphasize academics, community service, foreign languages, and media.

A Diamond in the Rough

Case Western sits on 155 acres of tree-lined space smack dab in the middle of Cleveland, one of America's loveliest cities. The city in which *A Christmas Story* takes place is packed full of things to do, from museums to sports to the Rock and Roll Hall of Fame. An afternoon stroll downtown will take you to the Cleveland Museum of Art, which boasts one of the finest art collections on the continent. The Cleveland Playhouse, Little Italy, and the Museum of Natural History are all nearby too and well worth the visit. And don't forget the beaches on Lake Erie, which are perfect for boating, swimming, picnicking, and taking romantic strolls as the sun sets.

Admissions

Average high school GPA:	—
Average freshman SAT writing / math / critical reading score:	641 / 677 / 650
Average freshman ACT score:	26
Application fee:	—
Application deadlines:	
1/15 (freshmen)	
5/15 (transfer)	
11/1 (early action)	
Total applicants:	7,508
Total accepted:	5,002 (67%)
Total accepted who enrolled:	1,014
Notification dates:	
4/1 (freshmen)	
6/15 (transfer)	
1/1 (early action)	
Acceptance rate for early action applicants:	95%

Students

Percentage of male / female students:	59% / 41%
Percentage of students from out of state:	44%
Percentage of students graduating in 4 years / 6 years:	57% / 77%

Money

Total endowment:	$1,622,000,000
Total tuition:	$31,090
Total cost with fees & expenses:	$42,058
Average financial aid package:	$32,131
Percentage of students who sought aid and received it:	94%
Percentage of students receiving financial aid:	57%

Also Check Out

The Ohio State University

Rensselaer Polytechnic Institute

Rose-Hulman Institute of Technology

The University of Pittsburgh

Claremont McKenna College

500 East 9th Street
Claremont, CA 91711

(909) 621-8000
http://www.claremontmckenna.edu/

BIG PERSPECTIVE

Attention future world leaders

5 REASONS IT'S COOL

1. Ready to lead? CMC is a great place for **career-minded students ready for professional leadership**— especially in fields like law, business, and government.

2. CMC offers small-school perks along with the resources that come with being **one of the five schools in the Claremont Colleges consortium**.

3. Inspiration visits the campus every week through CMC's **Athenaeum series of big-name speakers**.

4. CMC is known for **emphasizing real-world issues and current events** in the classroom.

5. Sports fans will **dig the sporty vibe** on campus.

The Basics

Public / private: private nonprofit
Total enrollment / undergrads: 1,153 / 1,153
Campus setting: small town
Students call it: Claremont McKenna, CMC
Students are called: Stags, Athenas, CMCers
Notable alums: Joel Appel (CEO, Orange Glo), Diane Halpern (psychologist), Tom Leppert (politician, businessman), Harry T. McMahon (vice chairman, Merrill Lynch), Ashwin Navin (cofounder, BitTorrent)

Lead the Pack!

CMC's core curriculum mixes liberal arts disciplines with more practical courses. Limited to just 1,100 or so enrollees, the college specializes in business- and public policy–related degree programs; 70 percent of students go on to pursue advanced degrees. The most popular majors are economics, government, international relations, and psychology. Small classes (the average class size is about nineteen) and a low student-to-faculty ratio ensure that each and every student receives personal attention from his or her professors. CMC is a contributing member to the Claremont Colleges consortium, which spreads the academic programs and resources of a larger university over five smaller schools. While it's a bit unusual for students to major outside of the main professional disciplines, it's certainly done, often by enrolling in courses at other member schools of the consortium. Each year, about 10 percent of students venture off campus to study abroad and for internships through the school's Washington, D.C., program. All of this

What Is Wassail, Anyways?

Every year during Christmastime, CMC students take part in the annual medieval-themed Madrigal Feast. Student "wenches" serve hungry guests a five-course meal in the Marian Miner Cook Athenaeum. Diners imbibe either wassail or eggnog poured into a souvenir mug. The Claremont Colleges Chamber Choir fills the air with tunes of old. Guests pass the "kissing orange" along with a kiss on the cheek for each recipient.

intellectual activity culminates in a required senior thesis, which can be a research paper or a creative project.

Get Ready for Late-Night Dorm Room Debates

CMC is filled with high achievers who study, intern, and discuss their way to professional success. Students are known for their penchant for discussing politics, public affairs, and current affairs both in the classroom and the dorm rooms. Freshman year kicks off with the Wilderness Orientation Adventure for incoming students, which includes camping and hiking trips led by current students, alumni, and faculty. Dorms are divided between North Quad, Mid Quad, and South Quad and the senior apartments, each area with its own distinct personality. The Athenaeum speaker series, running Monday through Thursday, brings leaders in their fields to campus to inspire and stimulate students. Student athletes complete in NCAA Division III sports along with students from Harvey Mudd and Scripps, and the rivalry is heated with the Pitzer-Pomona teams that represent the other schools in the Claremont Colleges consortium. The majority of students live on campus, where activities outweigh the ho-hum city of Claremont, and the great majority of students live on campus.

Comfy, Cozy Claremont

CMC sits on fifty acres in the quiet college city of Claremont, where's it lies within one square mile of the five other schools in the Claremont Colleges consortium. Scripps, Pitzer, and CMC share the spiffy Keck Science Center. Comfy is a good way to describe the buildings on campus—the administration even takes up residence in the former home of CMC's first president. The Emmett Student Center, also known as the Hub, offers eats, games, computers, and places to gather. Dorms in the North Quad open to the outside, rather than into a hallway—not unlike a motel. Off campus, Claremont Village is just about a ten-minute walk. It offers shops and cafés, and a movie theater has recently opened, much to the delight of students. Los Angeles is located about 35 miles to the east.

Admissions

Average high school GPA:	3.91
Average freshman SAT verbal / math score:	683 / 694
Average freshman ACT score:	—
Application fee:	$60
Application deadlines: 1/2 (freshmen) 4/1 (transfer) 11/15 (early decision)	
Total applicants:	3,593
Total accepted:	805 (22%)
Total accepted who enrolled:	296
Notification dates: 4/1 (freshmen) 5/15 (transfer) 12/15 (early decision)	
Acceptance rate for early decision applicants:	29%

Students

Percentage of male / female students:	54% / 46%
Percentage of students from out of state:	56%
Percentage of students graduating in 4 years / 6 years:	82% / 87%

Money

Total endowment:	$316,000,000
Total tuition:	$33,000
Total cost with fees & expenses:	$47,440
Average financial aid package:	$28,191
Percentage of students who sought aid and received it:	100%
Percentage of students receiving financial aid:	46%

Also Check Out

The George Washington University

Princeton University

Stanford University

University of California–Los Angeles

University of Southern California

Clark University

950 Main Street
Worcester, MA 01610

(508) 793-7711
http://www.clarku.edu/

 **BIG PERSPECTIVE**

 **BIG RESEARCH**

Calling all science nerds!

5 REASONS IT'S COOL

1. Clark is rated among the country's "hottest schools for student research."

2. The **BA/MA Fifth-Year-Free Program** allows you to earn your bachelor's and master's degrees in five years—and as the name suggests, the fifth year is free!

3. The **optional four-year Career Exploration Program** will help you define your career goals and hit the ground running come graduation.

4. With 2,200 undergrads, the school is **small—but not *too* small.**

5. True, the city of Worcester isn't the coolest place to spend four years. But bustling **Boston is just forty miles away.**

The Basics

Public / private: private nonprofit
Total enrollment / undergrads: 3,071 / 2,262
Campus setting: urban
Students call it: Clark
Students are called: Clarkies, Cougars
Notable alums: Beth Edmonds (senator), John Heard (actor), Padma Lakshmi (model, TV personality)

From Geography to Psychology

Clark offers twenty-eight majors, twenty-three minors, and eleven interdisciplinary concentrations. The most popular majors include psychology and government/international relations, while programs in geography and urban teacher training are also notable. The university offers a well-rounded liberal-arts-based curriculum combined with loads of research and career opportunities. Classes average twenty or so students, and the student-to-faculty ratio is 10:1. There are 172 full-time faculty members, 96 percent of whom have doctorates or terminal degrees in their fields. One of the university's big draws is its BA/MA Fifth-Year-Free Program, which allows select students to complete a master's degree during a free fifth year of study. More than twenty study-abroad programs are offered in countries ranging from Namibia to Japan to Costa Rica. To assist the impoverished neighborhoods surrounding campus, Clark established the University Park Campus School, a well-respected public high school.

Get Psyched!

In 1909, Sigmund Freud, the founder of modern psychology, gave his famous "Clark Lectures" at the university. These lectures introduced Freud and his theories of psychoanalysis to American audiences, truly making him a household name. In commemoration of the visit, a life-size statue of Freud was erected at the center of the campus.

Good Times in Main South

Students are required to live on campus through sophomore year, and many continue to do so as juniors and seniors. The university offers approximately 90 student organizations. Popular groups include Hillel, the Pub Entertainment Committee, the Massachusetts PIRG (Public Interest Research Group), and the Student Activities Board. Among the seventeen Cougar varsity sports teams are baseball, basketball, lacrosse, soccer, and volleyball. Cougars compete at the Division III level. Students come from about forty-five states and sixty countries, and 10 percent represent minority groups. More than 50 percent volunteer in community service activities on campus and in the Worcester area. Once a year on Spree Day, classes are cancelled and an annual student carnival takes over the campus. Festivities include daylong parties, performances by bands, outdoor movie screening, and other opportunities for students to unwind.

Safety First

Clark is located in Worcester, a city with about 170,000 residents. While the campus is located in a somewhat rough part of town, most students agree that safety is prioritized. The university provides security officers who patrol the campus around the clock, as well as shuttle escorts throughout the night hours. Clark is home to four libraries and research buildings, including a center for geographic analysis. Worcester is situated about forty-five minutes west of Boston, so students have easy access to nightlife, music venues, and loads of restaurants—not to mention fifty-five other colleges and universities. State parks, lakes, and ski mountains are all within an easy reach of campus. Be sure to pack a winter coat: Worcester gets an average of sixty-seven inches of snow annually!

Admissions

Average high school GPA:	3.45
Average freshman SAT verbal / math score:	616 / 598
Average freshman ACT score:	25
Application fee:	$50

Application deadlines:
1/15 (freshmen)
4/15 (transfer)
11/15 (early decision)

Total applicants:	4,726
Total accepted:	2,826 (60%)
Total accepted who enrolled:	563

Notification dates:
4/1 (freshmen)
6/1 (transfer)
12/15 (early decision)

Acceptance rate for early decision applicants:	83%

Students

Percentage of male / female students:	40% / 60%
Percentage of students from out of state:	62%
Percentage of students graduating in 4 years / 6 years:	63% / 70%

Money

Total endowment:	$233,795,000
Total tuition:	$31,200
Total cost with fees & expenses:	$38,165
Average financial aid package:	$24,072
Percentage of students who sought aid and received it:	94%
Percentage of students receiving financial aid:	54%

Also Check Out

American University

Skidmore College

University of Vermont

Wheaton College

Clemson University

105 Sikes Hall, Box 345124
Clemson, SC 29634

(864) 656-3311
http://www.clemson.edu/

 **BIG RESEARCH**

 **BIG WORLD**

Did somebody say . . . football?!

5 REASONS IT'S COOL

1. Jock alert! **Football is kind of a big deal here**—as are the tailgating, pep rallies, and partying that goes along with it.

2. Clemson stresses service learning and **the integration of community service into academics.**

3. This up-and-comer aims to become one of the **top twenty public research institutions by 2011.**

4. A former military college, the university still **offers strong ROTC programs.**

5. The small southern town of Clemson, South Carolina, is located right **near the Blue Ridge Mountains.**

The Basics

Public / private: public state
Total enrollment / undergrads: 17,165 / 14,096
Campus setting: small town
Students call it: CU
Students are called: Tigers
Notable alums: Robert H. Brooks (president, Hooters), Bobby Johnson (college football coach), Nancy O'Dell (host, *Access Hollywood*), George Ross (Trump advisor, *The Apprentice*), Strom Thurmond (senator)

Do-Gooders, Take Note

Volunteering is a watchword at Clemson, where community service is often a course requirement. Don't be surprised if your health course involves educating elementary school students about the dangers of tobacco, or your class on landscape architecture requires planning public parks. The average class size is about thirty students, but more than 50 percent of classes have fewer than twenty. There are over seventy degree programs, including agronomy, wildlife and fisheries biology, experimental statistics, and a well-regarded engineering program. Science and humanities students can get credit for student research through the Creative Inquiry project. Recent project topics have included analyzing the competition of South Carolina coastal tourist outfits, studying older adults in communal living, and developing tools for rural health clinics. All Clemson freshmen are required to participate in the summer reading program, which culminates in a lecture from the chosen author at Freshman Convocation.

Welcome, Estrogen

Clemson started as an all-male military school, but after World War II, veterans brought their wives and families to the university. After pressing to attend classes, the wives were eventually admitted as commuter students in 1955. No coed dorms were allowed, and one woman who lived in a neighboring town had to hitchhike to school. That hitchhiker earned a degree in chemistry and was Clemson's first female graduate.

Lovin' the Pigskin

Football is big here, and there's no escaping the tide of school spirit that washes over the town before home games. Students flock to watch the Tigers play at Death Valley (more formally known as Clemson Memorial Stadium), so named for the number of teams the Tigers have "killed" on their turf. Students don't hesitate to raise a glass to their team. First Friday Parade, a huge pep rally and float display before the first home football game, is a major event, and tailgating is the norm. Health-minded freshmen can join the learning community, Tiger Fitness, which places members in a dorm with gyms in or close to the building. Dorms also house sororities and fraternities, but these coveted spots are generally reserved for upperclassmen. About 20 percent of the student body goes Greek. True to its roots as military college, Clemson also offers strong ROTC programs for the Army and Air Force.

Small Town, Bigger College

There can be no doubt that Clemson, SC, is a college town through and through. With a population of just twelve thousand, the town is smaller than the university it hosts. The much larger cities of Atlanta, GA, and Charlotte, NC, are two hours away. Foot travel is the norm, as campus is just a fifteen-minute walk to downtown. If you have the walking blues, the CAT (Clemson Area Transit) will transport you to the grocery store, around town, and even to neighboring towns. For outdoor enthusiasts, Lake Hartwell and the foothills of the Blue Ridge Mountains are nearby. You can also stretch your legs by hiking through Clemson's lovely Experimental Forest.

Admissions

Average high school GPA:	3.9
Average freshman SAT verbal / math score:	606 / 630
Average freshman ACT score:	25
Application fee:	$50
Application deadlines: 5/1 (freshmen) 8/1 (transfer)	
Total applicants:	12,463
Total accepted:	7,154 (57%)
Total accepted who enrolled:	2,893
Notification dates: continuous (freshmen) continuous (transfer)	

Students

Percentage of male / female students:	54% / 46%
Percentage of students from out of state:	32%
Percentage of students graduating in 4 years / 6 years:	44% / 75%

Money

Total endowment:	$301,213,410
Total in-state tuition, fees & expenses:	$16,590
Total out-of-state tuition, fees & expenses:	$27,014
Average financial aid package:	$9,743
Percentage of students who sought aid and received it:	62%
Percentage of students receiving financial aid:	35%

Also Check Out

College of Charleston

North Carolina State University

University of Georgia

University of North Carolina at Chapel Hill

University of South Carolina–Columbia

Colby College

4000 Mayflower Hill	(207) 872-3000
Waterville, ME 04901	http://www.colby.edu/

BIG PERSPECTIVE

Start with Maine. Add books.

5 REASONS IT'S COOL

1. Colby's January Plan helps **students design a short "extra semester"** dedicated to one in-depth independent study.

2. Innovative academics emphasize **project-based learning** and interdisciplinary classes.

3. Environmental studies students are literally **a hop, skip, and jump away from the wilderness** they want to study.

4. Ivy, brick, and white columns: the **campus is the sort of place film directors dream of** when they want to shoot a college movie.

5. Live your ideals: The college has won a number of awards for its **excellent campus environmental practices.**

The Basics

Public / private: private nonprofit
Total enrollment / undergrads: 1,865 / 1,865
Campus setting: small town
Students call it: Colby
Students are called: Mules
Notable alums: Benjamin F. Butler (Civil War general; governor, Massachusetts), Doris Kearns Goodwin (historian), Elijah P. Lovejoy (abolitionist), Annie Proulx (writer), Richard Russo (writer), Margaret Chase Smith (congresswoman, senator)

A Family Affair

Colby faculty members take a genuine and long-lasting interest in their students; it's not uncommon to remain in close contact with one's first-year professors for four full years. Many students rave about the nurturing, supportive environment, although some say it's stifling. If you're looking to blend into a crowd, academically or otherwise, this might not be the school for you, but you'd have a decent shot at anonymity in the biology, economics, and English programs, which post the highest enrollments. Natural sciences, in particular, have been gaining popularity and prestige. The recently completed Olin Science Center, replete with equipment and facilities usually available only at large-scale research universities, is expected to draw increasingly high-caliber students and professors. Another major current in Colby academics is internationalism. The Goldfarb Center for Public Affairs and the Oak Institute for the Study of International Human Rights help students

Doors Getting Wider and Wider

Colby has some problems with diversity, but don't fault the place for lack of trying. Its founders guaranteed religious freedom in the college charter; the nation's first anti-slavery campus association formed here in 1833; and women were first admitted in 1871, years before any other all-male New England college welcomed both sexes.

connect their classroom work with real-world political and diplomatic challenges. On a broader scale, Colby was recently recognized for "internationalizing" its program by facilitating study abroad, enriching curricular offerings, and cultivating diversity among the student body and faculty.

Sports Make Us Thirsty

The two most important and inextricably linked traditions at the heart of Colby campus life are sports and beer drinking. Over half the student body is either a varsity or intramural athlete, and, of those who aren't, many root for the school's various Division III teams with the intensity of Olympians. Students at all levels of physical fitness take advantage of Colby's "outdoor clubs," which organize camping, hiking, biking, and skiing expeditions. Especially since the elimination of the fraternity system, these sports teams and clubs have come to play an important role in the social scene. Athletes practice, compete, and then kick back together, and a large proportion of Colby's open parties are hosted by teams. What these parties hold in common with Colby academics is that pretty much everyone knows everybody else. Do something stupid—or, yes, brilliant—and you'll hear about it till you graduate.

Middle of Nowhere, Connected to Everything

Colby's campus is beautiful, and many students recall that they "just knew" this was the place for them when they first visited. Town-gown relations, meanwhile, are poor, although not entirely negative. For example, a campus volunteer center lets students work with and learn from community members through public service projects. The all-around efficacy of such programs is reflected in the high number of Colby grads who are inspired to join the Peace Corps, AmeriCorps, and similar organizations after graduation. Beyond town, of course, there's the great outdoors, which Colby students get to experience even before cracking their first book. The COOT (Colby Outdoor Orientation Trip) Program teams ten first-years with two upperclassmen in hiking and biking expeditions at the start of the fall semester. Meanwhile, Colby's significant IT investments—it has been named one of the country's "most wired" colleges—keep it in close contact with the world outside Maine.

Admissions

Average high school GPA:	—
Average freshman SAT writing / math / critical reading score:	667 / 681 / 667
Average freshman ACT score:	26
Application fee:	$65
Application deadlines: 1/1 (freshmen) 3/1 (transfer) 11/15 (early decision)	
Total applicants:	4,242
Total accepted:	1,411 (33%)
Total accepted who enrolled:	475
Notification dates: 4/1 (freshmen) 5/15 (transfer) 12/15 (early decision)	
Acceptance rate for early decision applicants:	40%

Students

Percentage of male / female students:	46% / 54%
Percentage of students from out of state:	91%
Percentage of students graduating in 4 years / 6 years:	84% / 89%

Money

Total endowment:	$482,019,000
Total tuition:	—
Total cost with fees & expenses:	$44,780
Average financial aid package:	$29,908
Percentage of students who sought aid and received it:	100%
Percentage of students receiving financial aid:	37%

Also Check Out

Amherst College

Bates College

Bowdoin College

Hamilton College

Middlebury College

Colgate University

13 Oak Drive
Hamilton, NY 13346

(315) 228-1000
http://www.colgate.edu/

 **BIG PERSPECTIVE**

 **BIG WORLD**

Recommended by dentists (and guidance counselors)

5 REASONS IT'S COOL

1. Want to know your profs? Colgate offers small classes and a **stellar student-to-faculty ratio**.

2. Pack your pom-poms: you'll want to cheer on the **Division I hockey and lacrosse teams**.

3. Upperclassmen host pre-orientation activities such as Wilderness Adventure, **a canoeing and hiking trip through the Adirondacks**.

4. The **515-acre campus boasts Taylor Lake,** the site of an annual Torchlight Ceremony that welcomes freshman in and escorts seniors out.

5. Get outta town with one of one of the **popular off-campus study programs**.

The Basics

Public / private: private nonprofit
Total enrollment / undergrads: 2,788 / 2,782
Campus setting: rural
Students call it: Colgate
Students are called: Raiders
Notable alums: Andy Rooney (journalist), Monica Crowley (media commentator), Bob Woodruff (journalist), Andy McDonald (pro hockey player)

Good Things Come in Small Packages

When it comes to academics, the only diminutive thing about Colgate is its class size: There are consistently fewer than twenty students per class. One hundred percent of classes are taught by professors, and with an impressive 10:1 student-faculty ratio, students are guaranteed personal attention. Colgate's approach to academics emphasizes an interdisciplinary education that extends beyond the boundaries of the classroom. Every summer, over a hundred students work as research assistants for professors who are often leading scholars in their field. Half the student body participates in one of the many faculty-led off-campus study programs in places such as Beijing and Zambia. Colgate students also have the chance to vie for a one-of-a-kind internship at the National Institutes of Health in Maryland. Students must complete a liberal arts core curriculum. There are over fifty-one possible concentrations, the most popular of which are economics, English, history, and political science.

Got Triskaidekaphobia? Not Here, You Don't!

Think the number 13 is unlucky? Think again. Back in 1819, Colgate was founded by thirteen men with thirteen dollars and thirteen prayers. Since then, the number thirteen has taken on a mystical quality: The address is 13 Oak Drive, the ZIP code is 13346 (add up those last three numbers and see what happens), there are thirteen letters in Colgate's motto . . . you get the idea.

Happy on the Hill

Colgate students make up an insular community of bright, future-minded, and fun-loving people. Many incoming freshmen were student body president or captain of a sports team in high school, and the supportive atmosphere on campus allows them to continue finding leadership roles. There's an extracurricular for everyone, whether it's intramural sports or the debate team, and COVE—Colgate's Center for Outreach, Volunteerism, and Education—offers many opportunities for community service. Partying tends to take place at fraternities or "theme houses," on-campus housing for upperclassmen. Freshmen live in dorms on the hill, and they tend to stick around after their first year; 80 percent of the student body lives on the lovely tree-lined campus. The general atmosphere is relaxed and inclusive, but don't go to Colgate looking for diversity; most of the students are white, preppy, and from upper-class backgrounds. In his off-time, the typical Raider can be found running along the trails around campus, sailing on Lake Moraine, rock climbing at the quarry, or golfing at the first-rate course nearby. Sports are a big deal here, especially the Division I ranked lacrosse and hockey teams. School spirit doesn't end with graduation; the alumni network is 28,000 strong.

Middle of Nowhere: Just the Right Place

Colgate sits on a hill that overlooks the small town of Hamilton, which is a short walk or free bus ride from campus. Most would consider Hamilton to be in the middle of nowhere, but Colgate students don't seem to mind. If anything, they're grateful for the beauty of the rolling hills, the safety of campus, and the great town-gown relationship. Hamilton welcomes the college students—its population doubles when they arrive each fall—but it doesn't offer more than the bare bones: bar, club, coffee shop, and movie theater. When cabin fever sets in (those Upstate New York winters can be pretty long), Syracuse and Utica are less than an hour away, and a four-hour drive will get you to New York City. Most students choose to stay on campus or do outdoor activities in the Chenango Valley and nearby Adirondack Mountains.

Admissions

Average high school GPA:	3.6
Average freshman SAT verbal / math score:	669 / 677
Average freshman ACT score:	26
Application fee:	$55

Application deadlines:
1/15 (freshmen)
3/15 (transfer)
11/15 (early decision)

Total applicants:	7,873
Total accepted:	2,217 (28%)
Total accepted who enrolled:	744

Notification dates:
4/1 (freshmen)
5/1 (transfer)
12/15 (early decision)

Acceptance rate for early decision applicants:	60%

Students

Percentage of male / female students:	48% / 52%
Percentage of students from out of state:	69%
Percentage of students graduating in 4 years / 6 years:	88% / 91%

Money

Total endowment:	$557,100,000
Total tuition:	$34,795
Total cost with fees & expenses:	$45,400
Average financial aid package:	$31,355
Percentage of students who sought aid and received it:	100%
Percentage of students receiving financial aid:	37%

Also Check Out

Cornell University

Dartmouth College

Georgetown University

Middlebury College

Tufts University

College of Charleston

66 George Street
Charleston, SC 29424

(843) 953-5507
http://www.cofc.edu/

BIG PERSPECTIVE

Lots of learning and a touch of Southern charm

5 REASONS IT'S COOL

1. Talk about history! C of C is the **oldest college in South Carolina** and the thirteenth oldest in the United States.

2. Maymester, an annual three-week session, allows students to **study one subject intensively**.

3. The Tate Center of Entrepreneurship is just one of this college's **extra learning opportunities**.

4. No cookie-cutter dorms here: Live in one of the **twenty-one unique historic houses** surrounding campus.

5. If you can help it (and most can't), don't fall too hard for Charleston—students are **encouraged to study abroad**.

The Basics

Public / private: public state
Total enrollment / undergrads: 11,218 / 9,820
Campus setting: urban
Students call it: C of C
Students are called: Cougars
Notable alums: James Henry Carr (pro football player), James B. Edwards (governor, South Carolina), Orlando Jones (actor), Burnet R. Maybank (senator; governor, South Carolina), Arthur Ravenel Jr. (congressman)

From Maymester to Study Abroad, an Overflow of Learning

With the historic look of campus, it makes sense that C of C offers a major in historic preservation and community planning. There are a wide variety of majors here, from Hispanic studies to discovery informatics, an interdisciplinary combination of computer science and math. The Physics Department is a large one, and more than 35 percent of the physics students are female, which is greatly above the national average. The college focuses on a liberal arts base, requiring students to take classes in history, English, modern/classical languages, math, science, the arts, and social sciences. Students are encouraged to study abroad and can choose from programs in Chile, France, Argentina, Spain, and Cuba. In addition, bilateral programs allow students to study at a foreign university while paying C of C prices. African American studies majors can find internships and resources at the Avery Research Center for African-American History and Culture, which preserves the rich history

Graduation: A White or Black Tie Affair

In the spring, C of C graduates wear white—dresses for ladies, dinner jackets for men—and December grads wear tuxes or black dresses. Instead of caps and gowns, graduates accent their fancy attire with red roses—a bouquet for the women and a boutonniere for the men. Newly minted grads can't toss their caps in the air, but that's a small price to pay for elegance.

of the South's African Americans. Can't fit everything into a regular academic year? Consider taking a course during Maymester, a three-week intensive learning experience with classes on topics as varied as dinosaur biology, communications ethics, sailing, and accounting.

Historic Home Sweet Home

In addition to nine typical residence halls, C of C offers a unique housing alternative—old houses! The college's twenty-two historic houses were built between 1824 and 1907, so be prepared for creaky floors, leaky faucets, and charm. Students vie for space in these lovely homes, which are all within walking distance of campus. Most freshmen live in dorms, where they can take part in learning communities. Seventy percent of students are originally from South Carolina, and southern rules of decorum are still in effect here. Dorm members get to vote on the visitation rules for their residences at the start of each school year. The *Growl*, the student newsletter, has advice on what to do and where to go. One perennial recommendation: Cheer on Cougar basketball, one of the twenty Division I teams here. Cougar baseball, volleyball, golf, and sailing have also taken top titles.

The Stately South

The buildings are as appealing as you'd expect at an historic southern campus. Hang out on Cougar Plaza or in the Cistern Yard, admire the stately Wilson-Sottiel House, or venture off campus for a jog along the waterfront of Colonial Lake or Charleston Harbor. Water plays a big role in life here. Sailing is popular, and the Cistern, originally used to collect rainwater runoff, is a popular gathering spot. Incidentally, the Cistern is also where freshmen, in a rite of passage, used to get dunked. The small city of Charleston is, plain and simple, a great place to be a college student. From the beach to the bar scene, students don't have a hard time finding fun.

Admissions

Average high school GPA:	3.83
Average freshman SAT verbal / math score:	614 / 615
Average freshman ACT score:	24
Application fee:	$45

Application deadlines:
4/1 (freshmen)
4/1 (transfer)
11/1 (early action)

Total applicants:	8,673
Total accepted:	5,331 (61%)
Total accepted who enrolled:	1,968

Notification dates:
5/15 (freshmen)
continuous (transfer)
12/15 (early action)

Acceptance rate for early action applicants: —

Students

Percentage of male / female students:	35% / 65%
Percentage of students from out of state:	36%
Percentage of students graduating in 4 years / 6 years:	41% / 58%

Money

Total endowment:	$40,426,000
Total in-state tuition, fees & expenses:	$15,796
Total out-of-state tuition, fees & expenses:	$25,362
Average financial aid package:	$10,379
Percentage of students who sought aid and received it:	65%
Percentage of students receiving financial aid:	32%

Also Check Out

Clemson University

Tulane University

The University of Mississippi

Vanderbilt University

Wake Forest University

College of the Holy Cross

I College Street
Worcester, MA 01610

(508) 793-2011
http://www.holycross.edu/

BIG PERSPECTIVE

Cross my heart and hope to pass.

5 REASONS IT'S COOL

1. **All undergraduates, all the time.**

2. A Jesuit college, Holy Cross pledges to educate "men and women for others" through **a traditional liberal arts curriculum and service to the community.**

3. With its **small class sizes,** this college gives students lots of personal attention.

4. Campus traditions such as Purple Pride Day reinforce **the close-knit community.**

5. Grads are **admitted to medical school** at twice the national rate.

The Basics

Public / private: private religious
Total enrollment / undergrads: 2,821 / 2,821
Campus setting: suburban
Students call it: Holy Cross, HC
Students are called: Crusaders
Notable alums: James E. Burke (CEO, Johnson & Johnson), Ann Dowd (actress), Peter Jankowski (producer, *Law & Order*), Edward P. Jones (novelist) Chris Matthews (TV journalist), Joseph Murray (organ transplant pioneer), Clarence Thomas (U.S. Supreme Court justice)

No Grad Students Allowed

Among Holy Cross's strongest assets are its small class sizes, its 11:1 student-to-faculty ratio, and its focus on educating undergraduates in the liberal arts. A lot of attention means a lot of work, which students find both stressful and intensely rewarding. To help with the transition from high school to college, Holy Cross's new living and learning program, Montserrat, lets students choose from one of five interdisciplinary clusters, which form the curricular and residential communities for students' first year. Students can design their own majors or minors within the areas of faculty members' expertise. Fenwick Scholars are selected for this prestigious honors program during their junior year, and as seniors, they complete an independent project that comprises the curriculum. Students can study abroad in variety of countries, and there's considerable flexibility offered to students who also complete an extracurricular Independent Cultural Immersion Project. The premedical program

Countdown Dance

One hundred school days before graduation, you can find seniors boogying down at the 100 Days Dance. Hosted by the infamous Purple Key Society, this dinner and dance starts seniors' last huzzah before they leave the hilly campus for the working world.

at HC boasts twice as many med school admits as the national average. Economics, English, psychology and political science are the most popular majors at Holy Cross, whose strong Jesuit identity is strengthened by a well-deserved reputation as an excellent school.

The Color Purple

HC is a small school, but there's certainly enough space to study and socialize. This close-knit feeling is reinforced by the many traditions. On Purple Pride Day, the Purple Key Society—the campus's service and spirit group—hands out purple tchotchkes and munchies. Sports participation—whether it's varsity, IM, or club—is popular at Holy Cross, where the dorms form students' core communities. Basketball is the big ticket here: the men's and women's teams have had recent strong showings. Studying, however, takes up most of students' time. Ninety percent of students live on campus, so the library and classrooms are never far. Neither is the Pub in Hogan Campus Center (open only to students of legal age). The popular Tuesday Night 10 Spot takes place next to Hogan, and features Holy Cross music groups. Bigger musical acts come to campus for Spring Weekend, which is held as classes end. HC students' service to others is typified by the Giving Tree, from which students take an ornament listing a wished-for gift. The Purple Key society then hands these presents out to children in need just in time for Christmas.

Make New Buildings and Keep the Old

Students do have to climb up and down Mount St. James to get to class or the dorms, a route that can be especially tricky to navigate when it snows. But if they have a chance to look up, they will see beautiful views and gorgeous trees—HC has been designated an arboretum. The 174-acre campus is the oldest Catholic college in New England, and the third oldest in the United States. Not content with its historic buildings alone, Holy Cross is in the process of adding a new science complex, to the tune of $60 million. Shuttle buses transport students to local shopping areas and to Boston (forty-five miles away) and Providence (forty miles away), which is a real bonus since Worcester life is about as glamorous as it sounds. Seriously, though, there's plenty to do in Worcester, and there's even *more* to do in Boston.

Admissions

Average high school GPA:	—
Average freshman SAT verbal / math score:	640 / 644
Average freshman ACT score:	—
Application fee:	$50
Application deadlines: 1/15 (freshmen) 5/1 (transfer) 12/15 (early decision)	
Total applicants:	6,706
Total accepted:	2,313 (34%)
Total accepted who enrolled:	751
Notification dates: 4/1 (freshmen) 6/1 (transfer) 1/15 (early decision)	
Acceptance rate for early decision applicants:	69%

Students

Percentage of male / female students:	45% / 55%
Percentage of students from out of state:	62%
Percentage of students graduating in 4 years / 6 years:	89% / 91%

Money

Total endowment:	$544,347,000
Total tuition:	$32,820
Total cost with fees & expenses:	$43,593
Average financial aid package:	$25,264
Percentage of students who sought aid and received it:	100%
Percentage of students receiving financial aid:	55%

Also Check Out

Boston College

Fordham University

Georgetown University

Tufts University

University of Notre Dame

The College of New Jersey

PO Box 7718
Ewing, NJ 08628

(609) 771-1855
http://www.tcnj.edu/

BIG PERSPECTIVE

Stellar education? Sounds great. At a low price? Sounds even better.

5 REASONS IT'S COOL

1. TCNJ is a public liberal arts college. Roughly translated, that means **small classes at state school prices.**

2. Ready to take the lead? The Leadership in Public Affairs program will **jump-start your career in government.**

3. Founded as a teacher's college, the college's **strong Education Department produces leading educators** of tomorrow.

4. TCNJ is regularly ranked one of the **top public institutions of higher education.**

5. **Philly and New York** are easy to get to when the big city calls.

The Basics

Public / private: public state
Total enrollment / undergrads: 6,934 / 6,094
Campus setting: suburban
Students call it: TCNJ
Students are called: Lions
Notable alums: Holly Black (author), Sheila Callaghan (playwright), Jim Florio (governor, New Jersey), Tom McCarthy (sports broadcaster), Ty Treadway (actor)

Educators and Leaders

Academics at TCNJ are divided into seven schools: business, art, media and music, science, culture and society, nursing, engineering, and education, the most popular school. Students choose from a total of over fifty degree programs, with education, business, and English among the most popular choices. The college's Liberal Learning program requires students to take interdisciplinary classes, such as Exploring Concert Music and the History of New Jersey. TCNJ prides itself on providing small class sizes and professors who are accessible both in- and outside of the classroom. The student to faculty ratio is 13:1; and 88 percent of the faculty members have terminal degrees. Students can enroll in a unique certificate program in public leadership, where they take classes such as Citizen Democracy and learn how to tackle tough issues like urban sprawl. The Global Student Teaching program places students at schools in Croatia, Ireland, Costa Rica, and Venezuela, among other locations. Other study-abroad opportunities include programs in Thailand and England.

Which TCNJ Is Which?

Talk about a name game. Recently, Princeton University lost a legal battle with TCNJ over naming rights. In 1996, TCNJ changed its name from Trenton State College to the College of New Jersey in an attempt to reposition itself. The problem is that up until 1896, when it changed its name to Princeton, TCNJ's Ivy League neighbor was also known as—you guessed it—the College of New Jersey. Eventually, Princeton's legal case was dismissed, and today TCNJ is widely known (well, except by Princetonians!) as *The* College of New Jersey.

New Jersey's Brightest

An overwhelming percentage of TCNJ students are New Jersey residents, so if you're coming from out of state, expect students to know their way around the area already. While about half of upperclassmen live off campus, the college guarantees housing for all freshmen and sophomores in one of fourteen residence halls. Freshmen live with other members of their first-year seminars. As the New Jersey Lions, TCNJ has won more championships than any other Division III school in the country. In total, twenty-one teams, including lacrosse and field hockey, compete. Club and intramural offerings range from coed flag football to whitewater rafting. All told, about 65 percent of students play on a varsity or intramural team. Among the more than 150 student organizations are five student-run publications, the All College Theater, and the Lions Paintball Club. Recently, TCNJ has tried to recruit a more diverse study body, and participation in such groups as the African American Cultural Awareness Association and the Multicultural Lecture Series has increased as a result.

Capital City Attractions

TCNJ's 289-acre campus is located in the sleepy town of Ewing, a suburb of Trenton, the New Jersey state capital. Administrators are spending $250 million on campus facilities, and it's paying off. You'll find a mix of old Georgian façades and new, state-of-the-art buildings, such as Green Hall and the Science Complex, along with the bustling 97,000-square-foot Brower Student Center. Trenton is home to the New Jersey State Museum; the Contemporary Victorian Museum; the Old Barracks Museum, dedicated to the Revolutionary War; and the Cybis Porcelain Galleries. Nearby Princeton has quaint stores and restaurants, as well as delicious ice cream at Halo Pub and Ricky's Candy, Cones & Chaos. Philadelphia is about thirty minutes away by train, and New York City is about an hour away.

Admissions

Average high school GPA:	—
Average freshman SAT writing / math / critical reading score:	618 / 647 / 623
Average freshman ACT score:	—
Application fee:	$60
Application deadlines: 2/15 (freshmen) 2/15 (transfer) 11/15 (early decision)	
Total applicants:	8,185
Total accepted:	3,570 (44%)
Total accepted who enrolled:	1,270
Notification dates: 4/1 (freshmen) continuous (transfer) 12/15 (early decision)	
Acceptance rate for early decision applicants:	43%

Students

Percentage of male / female students:	42% / 58%
Percentage of students from out of state:	5%
Percentage of students graduating in 4 years / 6 years:	60% / 81%

Money

Total endowment:	$7,611,473
Total in-state tuition, fees & expenses:	$20,396
Total out-of-state tuition, fees & expenses:	$26,942
Average financial aid package:	$9,207
Percentage of students who sought aid and received it:	55%
Percentage of students receiving financial aid:	40%

Also Check Out

College of William & Mary

The Pennsylvania State University–University Park

University of North Carolina at Chapel Hill

University of Virginia

College of William & Mary

PO Box 8795	(757) 221-4000
Williamsburg, VA 23187	http://www.wm.edu/

 **BIG BRAIN**    **BIG PERSPECTIVE**    **BIG RESEARCH**

Heck, it was good enough for Thomas Jefferson . . .

5 REASONS IT'S COOL

1. There's **tradition and history in everything** from the architecture to the initials carved in your desk—W&M is America's second oldest college.

2. W&M offers both **high-quality teaching and high-level research opportunities** for students.

3. Succeed in business (while really trying) at the college's prestigious **undergraduate management program**.

4. The **money you'll save** at this prestigious public college will buy you a thousand or so day passes to nearby amusement park Busch Gardens.

5. **Frat life:** It's there if you want it, not *too* in your face if you don't.

The Basics

Public / private: public state
Total enrollment / undergrads: 7,709 / 5,734
Campus setting: small town
Students call it: William & Mary, W&M
Students are called: The Tribe
Notable alums: Henry Clay (statesman), Glenn Close (actress), Perry Ellis (designer), Thomas Jefferson (founding father), Jon Stewart (host, *The Daily Show*), Mike Tomlin (pro football coach)

Best of the Best

William & Mary's faculty have been recognized by national auditors for providing one of the nation's best undergraduate educations. The college's management major is among the most rigorous undergraduate business programs around; other difficult and well-respected departments include hard sciences like biochemistry, physics, and computer science. Across the board, there are opportunities to assist professors in their research. Even freshmen—the particularly high-achieving ones, that is—have the opportunity to contribute to and learn from the faculty's work during summer assistantships. In fact, the cream of the crop gets the red carpet from start to finish at W&M: In an effort to attract more of the nation's top high school graduates, the college operates the Monroe Program, which dangles the prospect of $1,000 and $4,000 research grants before the eyes of the most talented incoming freshmen. All W&M students face distribution requirements that mandate classes in the sciences, humanities, and, interestingly, creative or performing arts.

I Had to Throw Him In, Really.

If, on a visit to campus, you pass someone looking scorned in sopping wet clothes, assume they've just come from the bridge over Crim Dell Pond. One of William & Mary's many local legends has it that if a couple kisses there, they're bound to get married—unless one throws the other into the drink.

Cheers, Sort Of

At a school attended by Thomas Jefferson and chancellored by George Washington, it's not surprising that traditions are integral to the rhythm of life at W&M. Mention the Yule Log or the King and Queen Dance to any alum, and you'll get a big smile in return. Another time-less tradition, drinking, has also long been a part of the culture. Lately, though, this has begun to change. Due to alcohol violations, William & Mary's infamous booze-fueled fraternities and sororities have been losing their charters and houses, and so the Greek system, in general, is becoming a less visible part of campus life. True, 30 percent of students still belong to a fraternity or sorority, but the majority of these organizations are essentially social and community service groups. More and more, social life revolves around intramural teams and extracurricular organizations; a cappella groups, in particular, are popular.

Ye Olde Universitie

William & Mary's campus, located in Williamsburg, comes complete with shady trees and centuries-old buildings. Students agree that the place is drop-dead gorgeous, period. Historically, William & Mary has suffered from less than ideal town-gown relationships. Resident complaints about noise and vandalism have resulted in strict on-campus alcohol laws. These, in turn, have led to even more ill will toward the locals from students, who already blame the touristy part of town for high prices and cheesiness. That said, nearby amusement park Busch Gardens *can* be fun, and, if reliving history is your thing, Colonial Williamsburg is certainly the place to be. Especially if you don't mind wearing tri-corner hats.

Admissions

Average high school GPA:	4.0
Average freshman SAT verbal / math score:	672 / 665
Average freshman ACT score:	26
Application fee:	$60

Application deadlines:
1/1 (freshmen)
2/15 (transfer)
11/1 (early decision)

Total applicants:	10,772
Total accepted:	3,468 (32%)
Total accepted who enrolled:	1,344

Notification dates:
4/1 (freshmen)
4/15 (transfer)
12/1 (early decision)

Acceptance rate for early decision applicants:	50%

Students

Percentage of male / female students:	46% / 54%
Percentage of students from out of state:	32%
Percentage of students graduating in 4 years / 6 years:	81% / 91%

Money

Total endowment:	$491,652,269
Total in-state tuition, fees & expenses:	$16,272
Total out-of-state tuition, fees & expenses:	$32,692
Average financial aid package:	$12,252
Percentage of students who sought aid and received it:	84%
Percentage of students receiving financial aid:	27%

Also Check Out

Duke University

Georgetown University

University of North Carolina at Chapel Hill

University of Virginia

Vanderbilt University

College of Wooster

1189 Beall Avenue
Wooster, OH 44691

(330) 263-2000
http://www.wooster.edu/

 **BIG PERSPECTIVE**

College, *your* way

5 REASONS IT'S COOL

1. The highlight of a Wooster education is the unique, **three-semester Independent Study project.**

2. After handing in their I. S. projects, tradition dictates that students receive an **I DID IT button and a Tootsie Roll** to mark the sweet occasion.

3. **Small classes, personal attention from professors, and a flexible curriculum** are a small part of what comes with tuition.

4. **Merit- and need-based financial assistance** is provided to more than 90 percent of students.

5. The campus features a **white castle springing up from neatly manicured grounds.**

The Basics

Public / private: private religious
Total enrollment / undergrads: 1,819 / 1,819
Campus setting: small town
Students call it: Wooster
Students are called: Fighting Scots, Scots
Notable alums: Vince Cellini (sports broadcaster), Arthur Holly Compton (Nobel Laureate, Physics), Mary F. Crow (poet), Stephen R. Donaldson (novelist), John Dean (lawyer, political advisor), James V. Neel (geneticist), Timothy Smucker (CEO, The J. M. Smucker Co.), Susan Stranahan (journalist)

Where Students Reign

Wooster's take on the liberal arts is totally inimitable. The required Independent Study project has gained national acclaim. All seniors must complete this three-semester capstone program, where they conduct original research, write a thesis paper, or create a work of art or a performance with the support and guidance of a faculty advisor. This wholly original program not only gives students a high degree of academic flexibility and independence, but it also provides excellent training for grad school or other postcollege pursuits. Wooster's many majors and minors range from urban studies to communication sciences and disorders to Chinese; English, history, and psychology are popular choices. Students can also choose from eleven pre-professional programs, including pre-medicine and pre-veterinary. The student-to-faculty ratio is 12:1, and about 70 percent of classes have fewer than twenty students.

Can't They at Least Spring for Snickers?

When Wooster seniors submit their completed Independent Study project to the registrar on the first Monday after spring break (a day known on campus as I. S. Monday), they receive a yellow button that says I DID IT! and a Tootsie Roll. Why a Tootsie Roll? Registrar Lee Culp began this tradition about twenty years ago, choosing Tootsie Rolls because they were so cheap in bulk. Many Wooster students give their candy prizes more value—they get them bronzed for posterity.

Something to Cheer About

Wooster students share a love of athletics, academics, and traditions. Just about everybody lives on campus, in one of twelve residential halls, including some first-year-only dorms. About 30 percent of students play on one of the twenty-two Division III varsity teams, the Fighting Scots. Fans show up in droves to cheer on the baseball team, which has made three appearances in the NCAA Division III World Series, and the men's basketball team, which touts nine NCAC championships and tournament titles. Led into battle by the Scottish pipe band, the football team is also a big hit on campus. For less hard-core athletes, there are many intramural and club teams for such sports as badminton and billiards. Some of the hundred-plus activities include the Jenny Investment Club, the Juggling Club, the Personal Foul Dance Team, and a student-run coffee house known as Common Grounds. About 15 percent of students participate in one of the college's five sororities or four fraternities (referred to as "clubs" and "sections"), which are unaffiliated with national Greek organizations.

Idyll Times

Wooster's campus occupies about 240 idyllic acres of abundant trees and grass. While the small town of Wooster doesn't offer too much by way of student-friendly excitement, it does have a few restaurants and bars, as well as a farmer's market, an art and jazz festival, and frequent concerts. Nearby Cuyahoga Valley National Park and Mohican State Park offer trails and picnic spots, while Cedar Point, the self-styled Roller Coaster Capital of the World, boasts sixty-eight different rides. A thirty-minute drive gets students to Canton and the Pro Football Hall of Fame. Home to the Rock and Roll Hall of Fame, the Browns (NFL), and the Indians (MLB), Cleveland is just an hour away.

Admissions

Average high school GPA:	3.5
Average freshman SAT writing / math / critical reading score:	605 / 605 / 605
Average freshman ACT score:	24
Application fee:	$40

Application deadlines:
2/15 (freshmen)
6/1 (transfer)
12/1 (early decision)

Total applicants:	2,504
Total accepted:	2,011 (80%)
Total accepted who enrolled:	493

Notification dates:
4/1 (freshmen)
continuous (transfer)
12/15 (early decision)

Acceptance rate for early decision applicants:	87%

Students

Percentage of male / female students:	49% / 51%
Percentage of students from out of state:	54%
Percentage of students graduating in 4 years / 6 years:	68% / 75%

Money

Total endowment:	$228,462,000
Total tuition:	$30,060
Total cost with fees & expenses:	$38,390
Average financial aid package:	$24,981
Percentage of students who sought aid and received it:	94%
Percentage of students receiving financial aid:	56%

Also Check Out

Bennington College

Grinnell College

Kenyon College

Oberlin College

Wheaton College

Colorado College

14 East Cache La Poudre
Colorado Springs, CO 80903

(719) 389-6000
http://www.coloradocollege.edu/

 **BIG IDEA**

 **BIG WORLD**

A place for outdoor enthusiasts and focused studiers

5 REASONS IT'S COOL

1. The unique Block Plan allows **intensive investigation of one subject**.

2. **Friendly professors** are eager to continue discussions outside of class.

3. **The campus, located right at the base of Pike's Peak**, is the perfect jumping-off point for an adventure in the Rockies.

4. **The close-knit community** is open-minded, eco-friendly, and service-oriented.

5. Whether it's studying at CC's mountain cabin, their Baca campus, or overseas through popular study-abroad programs, students do **plenty of learning outside the classroom**.

The Basics

Public / private: private nonprofit
Total enrollment / undergrads: 1,998 / 1,970
Campus setting: urban
Students call it: CC
Students are called: Tigers
Notable alums: Lynne Cheney (wife of Vice President Dick Cheney), Alison Dunlap (cyclist), James Heckman (Nobel Laureate, Economics), Glenna Goodacre (sculptor), Ken Salazar (senator)

One Course at a Time

Under CC's unique Block Plan, students take eight three-and-a-half-week courses per year, one course at a time. Classes meet for three hours a day. The location is tailored to suit the material, so class meetings might alternate between a room and a lab, or they might take place entirely at the site of an archeology dig. Students build their own schedules through a bidding process, in which they use points to show preference for a particular course. With a 9:1 student-to-faculty ratio and an average class size of thirteen, CC offers an intimate learning environment to match its unusual academics. Knowledgeable and friendly faculty members are known to invite students over for end-of-block dinners. For those students who prefer to focus on one subject without the distraction of competing classes, the Block Plan is a rare opportunity. It's particularly well suited to study in the sciences, as students have plenty of time for fieldwork or laboratory analyses. Accordingly, biology is one of the most popular majors. Foreign languages and music aren't as fashionable. There

Luck of the Dog

Looking for a little luck? Inside Palmer Hall is a plaque of Colorado Springs founder General William Palmer—with his beloved dog. On their way to an exam, students in need of luck rub the mutt's nose, which has tuned shiny from all those years of finals.

are some core liberal arts requirements, but students find these relatively easy to fulfill. Many students take part in independent study projects or study abroad. The college also has a Baca campus in southwestern Colorado and a mountain cabin in the Rockies that is often used as a base for fieldwork.

The Happy Bubble

Founded in 1874, CC has grown from one building to a blend of historic and modern buildings on a ninety-acre campus at the base of Pike's Peak in the Rocky Mountains. What hasn't changed is the close-knit and famously open-minded nature of the college community. Freshmen live in Loomis, Slocum, or Bemis residence halls (Loomis is known as the party dorm). A three-year on-campus residence policy aims at sustaining community, and 80 percent of students live on campus. Upperclassmen have a variety of living options, including dorms, theme and language houses, and apartments in the recently completed Western Ridge Complex. CC is a liberal outpost in the conservative town of Colorado Springs, and relations with the town and the nearby Air Force Academy are somewhat strained. Most students are socially and environmentally conscious—over 80 percent are involved in some form of community service. About 30 percent hail from Colorado. During the four-day block break that separates courses, most students explore the skiing, hiking, rafting, and climbing available in the Rockies. Varsity athletics aren't a huge focal point, but men's ice hockey and women's soccer are Division I, and most students participate in intramural or club sports.

Rocky Mountain High

CC's campus is a five-minute walk from downtown Colorado Springs, a spread-out city of 500,000 without much nightlife. More exciting than the subpar bar scene are the opportunities for outdoor adventure afforded by the Rocky Mountains, especially during the winter months, when a drive to Breckenridge takes only two hours. If students are looking for a change of pace, the cities of Denver and Boulder are a little over an hour away.

Admissions

Average high school GPA:	—
Average freshman SAT writing / math / critical reading score:	653 / 663 / 663
Average freshman ACT score:	26
Application fee:	$50
Application deadlines:	
1/15 (freshmen)	
3/1 (transfer)	
11/15 (early action)	
Total applicants:	4,386
Total accepted:	1,487 (34%)
Total accepted who enrolled:	492
Notification dates:	
4/1 (freshmen)	
5/1 (transfer)	
1/15 (early action)	
Acceptance rate for early action applicants:	—

Students

Percentage of male / female students:	46% / 54%
Percentage of students from out of state:	73%
Percentage of students graduating in 4 years / 6 years:	77% / 83%

Money

Total endowment:	$438,711,000
Total tuition:	$32,124
Total cost with fees & expenses:	$41,080
Average financial aid package:	$29,982
Percentage of students who sought aid and received it:	91%
Percentage of students receiving financial aid:	40%

Also Check Out

Colby College

Dartmouth College

Lewis & Clark College

Middlebury College

University of Colorado at Boulder

Colorado State University– Fort Collins

1062 Campus Delivery
Fort Collins, CO 80523

(970) 491-1101
http://www.colostate.edu/

BIG CHOICE

BIG RESEARCH

Education doesn't get any higher than this.

5 REASONS IT'S COOL

1. Attention, science geeks! CSU's programs in **atmospheric, biomedical, and environmental science** are particularly strong.

2. Students here love to take it outside: **Hiking, biking and skiing in the nearby mountains** are all popular between-class pursuits.

3. Got your sights set on a professional degree? The university has top-notch **pre-vet, pre-law, and pre-med programs.**

4. Fort Collins is a **great college town** at the foot of the Rocky Mountains.

5. Research, thy name is CSU: Students have **countless hands-on research opportunities.**

The Basics

Public / private: public state
Total enrollment / undergrads: 26,723 / 21,283
Campus setting: urban
Students call it: CSU, Colorado State
Students are called: Rams
Notable alums: John Amos (actor), Keith Carradine (actor), Mary L. Cleave (astronaut), Amy Van Dyken (Olympic swimmer), Becky Hammon (pro basketball player), Bill Ritter (governor, Colorado)

Hands-On Sciences

CSU students delve deep into their own research. With twelve research centers across Colorado, a foothills campus for atmospheric research, and a mountain campus for natural resource studies, CSU offers plenty of hands-on research opportunities. Freshmen enroll directly into one of eight colleges or choose an "open option" where they explore different areas of study before choosing a focus. Programs in the sciences are popular here, and standout options include atmospheric, biomedical, and environmental science. Engineering, business, pre-med, and pre-law are also popular choices. Pre-vet students can take advantage of the many resources at CSU's top-notch Veterinary School and its affiliate Veterinary Teaching Hospital. Originally founded as an agricultural college, the university maintains strong programs in landscape architecture, agricultural economics, and animal science, among others. The Honors Program offers small classes with top professors and priority registration for about a thousand select students. While some

A Whole Lotta Love

There's a lot of love on the CSU campus on April 18, the annual "I Love CSU Day." Students wear green, one of the school colors, to show their love. Even Colorado's governor couldn't resist the love-fest—he signed a proclamation declaring "I Love CSU Day" across the state of Colorado!

students gripe about large class sizes and the difficulty of enrolling in choice courses, overall students find the coursework to be challenging and professors to be remarkably caring and accessible.

Happy and Healthy

It's safe to say the CSU students are probably healthier than the average college students. The great outdoors are easily accessible from campus, and typical between-class activities include biking, skiing, rock climbing, or lifting weights at CSU's recently revamped Recreation Center. Eighty percent of students play an intramural sport, and the Outdoor Program organizes classes and expeditions year-round. Freshmen are required to live on campus in one of ten residence halls. Most dorms have Living-Learning Floors that help students form communities based on similar interests, academic or otherwise. Upperclassmen generally move off campus, as Fort Collins offers a good deal of affordable housing options. Greek life is lively but not overwhelming: About 8 percent of students join. Far more popular among students is community service; in fact, CSU has one of the highest percentages of Peace Corps volunteers nationwide.

The Best College Town in the Rockies

CSU's expansive campus is centered on the Oval, a manicured lawn lined with elms almost as old as the university itself. While the campus's architecture leaves much to be desired aesthetically, facilities like the modern Lory Student Center are impressive. The campus is just a bike ride away from the many restaurants, coffee shops, bars, and clubs that make Fort Collins such a cool, friendly college town. The Rocky Mountains are nearby, and Denver is just a one-hour drive away. Students have the best of both worlds: They can raft the Cache LaPoudre River, go skiing at Breckenridge, or backpack in Rocky Mountain National Park and then hit up the bars and clubs of Denver or Fort Collins proper.

Admissions

Average high school GPA:	3.5
Average freshman SAT verbal / math score:	554 / 567
Average freshman ACT score:	23
Application fee:	$50
Application deadlines: 7/1 (freshmen) 7/1 (transfer)	
Total applicants:	11,310
Total accepted:	9,692 (86%)
Total accepted who enrolled:	4,010
Notification dates: continuous (freshmen) continuous (transfer)	

Students

Percentage of male / female students:	47% / 53%
Percentage of students from out of state:	18%
Percentage of students graduating in 4 years / 6 years:	34% / 63%

Money

Total endowment:	$152,225,082
Total in-state tuition, fees & expenses:	$12,219
Total out-of-state tuition, fees & expenses:	$23,747
Average financial aid package:	$8,455
Percentage of students who sought aid and received it:	82%
Percentage of students receiving financial aid:	34%

Also Check Out

Colorado College

University of California–Santa Cruz

University of Colorado at Boulder

The University of Montana–Missoula

Columbia University

116th Street and Broadway
New York, NY 10027

(212) 854-1754
http://www.college.columbia.edu/

 **BIG BRAIN**

 **BIG PERSPECTIVE**

 **BIG RESEARCH**

Big ideas begin here.

5 REASONS IT'S COOL

1. **Hello, diversity!** More than 40 percent of Columbia students identify themselves as students of color.

2. The **Manhattan location** means the greatest restaurants, theater, concerts, shops, bars, and clubs in the world.

3. **Columbia holds the nation's Nobel record:** Seventy-three alumni and current or former faculty are Nobel Prize winners.

4. The university **meets 100 percent of demonstrated financial need** for all admitted freshmen.

5. **Dual degrees** are available from Julliard and Columbia, as are bachelor's/graduate programs in law or international affairs.

The Basics

Public / private: private nonprofit
Total enrollment / undergrads: 4,184 / 4,184
Campus setting: urban
Students call it: Columbia
Students are called: Lions
Notable alums: Isaac Asimov (author), Michael Gould (CEO, Blooming-dale's), Maggie Gyllenhaal (actress), Alexander Hamilton (founding father), Ben Stein (actor, political commentator)

As Good as It Gets

Columbia expects a lot of its students and in return gives them the best education possible for their hard work. Most students enroll in either Columbia College (CC) or the Fu Foundation School of Engineering and Applied Science (SEAS). CC offers about ninety majors, the most popular of which are English and economics. All CC students must complete the Core Curriculum, a set of small, discussion-based classes that use important texts in literature, philosophy, science, art, music, and history. SEAS offers sixteen majors, including the popular biomedical/medical engineering, and has its own Core Curriculum. In addition to classes in literature or history, music or art, and university writing, SEAS Core classes include chemistry, physics, calculus, computer science, and a professional-level course that gives students hands-on experience. A renowned research university, Columbia offers all undergrads opportunities to work on groundbreaking research projects. And with an impressive 5:1 student-to-faculty ratio in CC and a 7:1 ratio in SEAS, students get lots of personal attention.

Strike Up a Tune

The night before the organic chemistry final exam—an evening known as **Orgo Night**—the Columbia University Marching Band stomps into Butler Library to distract studiers. It then travels around bothering—er, serenading—students studying in their rooms. Among the stops is the residential quad of Barnard, where women merrily throw trash at band members from their dorm windows.

Live and Learn

Whether on campus or off, you're likely to find Columbia students engaged in spirited debates about everything from hip-hop to the classics. But don't mistake Lions for nerds. While students here are devoted to their studies, they also know how to balance work with play and tend to wear their love for their school on their chests. During the week, students—almost all of whom live in campus housing—usually limit their socializing to the student union, the site of many meetings and events, or the dorms, where many students make their closest friends. But on the weekends (which sometimes begin on Thursday), students take advantage of the millions of different activities the city has to offer. About 10 percent to 15 percent of students go Greek, and just about everyone gets involved in at least one or two of the campus's more than four hundred student organizations and clubs.

Big City Campus, College Town Feel

Columbia is one of Manhattan's gems. Unlike most schools in the city, Columbia actually has a campus—and a beautiful one at that. Situated in the Upper West Side's Morningside Heights neighborhood, the main campus harks back to nineteenth-century Paris with its Beaux Arts architecture. Currently, the campus takes up more than thirty-two acres on six blocks, but there are plans to expand to Manhattanville, the neighborhood just to the north. With Columbia, Barnard, the Union Theological Seminary, and the Jewish Theological Seminary all within a few blocks, Morningside Heights feels like its own college town, packed with restaurants, bars, and bookstores. Lions can also be found checking out lectures, performances, and parties on campus or in the dorms. On the weekends, students often venture out farther, enjoying concerts, cultural events, bars, clubs, restaurants, or museum exhibits in other parts of the city, which are easily accessible by the subway (there's a 1/9 stop right in front of the main campus gates).

The data presented here refers to Columbia College. For more stats on SEAS and other colleges at Columbia University, check out http://college.sparknotes.com.

Admissions

Average high school GPA:	3.8
Average freshman SAT verbal / math score:	705 / 702
Average freshman ACT score:	—
Application fee:	$65

Application deadlines:
1/2 (freshmen)
3/15 (transfer)
11/1 (early decision)

Total applicants:	17,151
Total accepted:	1,662 (10%)
Total accepted who enrolled:	1,022

Notification dates:
4/4 (freshmen)
5/15 (transfer)
12/15 (early decision)

Acceptance rate for early decision applicants:	32%

Students

Percentage of male / female students:	48% / 52%
Percentage of students from out of state:	74%
Percentage of students graduating in 4 years / 6 years:	85% / 93%

Money

Total endowment:	$4,294,967,295
Total tuition:	$33,664
Total cost with fees & expenses:	$45,842
Average financial aid package:	$27,749
Percentage of students who sought aid and received it:	100%
Percentage of students receiving financial aid:	46%

Also Check Out

Brown University

Harvard University

Massachusetts Institute of Technology

University of Chicago

University of Pennsylvania

Connecticut College

270 Mohegan Avenue
New London, CT 06320

(860) 447-1911
http://www.connecticutcollege.edu/

 **BIG PERSPECTIVE**

 **BIG WORLD**

Small, smart, and proud of it

5 REASONS IT'S COOL

1. Conn's honor code **instills the campus with maturity, seriousness of purpose**, and cool perks like the ability to choose your own exam schedule.

2. Even without a Greek system, the **campus vibe is "work hard and play hard."**

3. Kids rule! Well, sort of. Student representatives here **serve (and wield actual influence) on the college president's advisory cabinets.**

4. Yanks or BoSox? The college is **close to New York City and Boston**.

5. The **hilltop campus is a designated arboretum** offering terrific views of the nearby Long Island Sound and Thames River.

The Basics

Public / private: private nonprofit
Total enrollment / undergrads: 1,886 / 1,872
Campus setting: suburban
Students call it: Conn, Conn College
Students are called: Camels
Notable alums: Allen Carroll (cartographer), Clap Your Hands Say Yeah (musicians), Judy Irving (filmmaker), Estelle Parsons (actress), Shelley Taylor (psychologist), Martha Witt (novelist)

On Campus, Around the World

If you're looking for that classic liberal arts college experience, look no further than Conn. Most classes here are discussion-based, and the student-faculty ratio is 10:1. Conn's most popular majors are English, political science, and psychology, while the campus's hard science facilities get strong reviews. Conn also boasts stellar programs in the arts. For instance, the Eugene O'Neill Theater Institute has a strong record of producing working actors, and dance majors frequently find themselves taking semesters off to tour with professional companies. Conn students also take advantage of a program that allows them to earn certificates in one of four interdisciplinary centers, including arts and technology, conservation biology, environmental science, community action and public policy, and international studies and the liberal arts. Conn is committed to getting students to experience the world beyond campus. Every student is guaranteed a $3,000 grant from the college to defray the costs of a summer internship. Conn also has renowned

Camel Competition

Connecticut students pride themselves on their myriad methods of relieving stress during study breaks. The annual Camelympics, a campuswide event held every fall, puts this pride on full display. For twenty-four straight hours, dorms compete against others in various events, athletic and otherwise. Better sharpen your Scrabble skills and stretch your Capture-the-Flag muscles, because we hear the competition gets pretty fierce.

study-abroad programs, including the Study Away/Teach Away initiative, which allows a small group of students and a pair of professors to travel to a foreign university and "reinvent" the Conn experience for a semester.

The Wild, Wild East

Whether you prefer massive keggers or more intimate gatherings, you'll find what you're looking for on this über-social campus. Conn's smorgasbord of clubs and intramural teams matches the wide variety of parties firing up the campus nights on Thursday through Saturday. While there's no Greek life here, students still report that there's plenty of drinking happening on campus. The entire student body lives on campus, and there is specialty housing available for all sorts of "isms"— whether you're an advocate of environmentalism, multiculturalism, or what have you. One downside of living on this lovely campus is that some facilities may need an update: Students complain in particular about the athletic center. Your opinion of Conn's demographics will probably have a lot to do with where you grew up. If you're from someplace metropolitan, you're unlikely to be impressed by the diversity. On the other hand, if you come from a small town, here's your chance to meet students from all over the world: Students here hail from forty-one countries.

New London Calling

Conn's campus sits on a hill and comes complete with natural wonders such as wetlands, ponds, forests, and hiking paths. The town of New London itself, however, is not the high point of most Conn students' experience. Aside from its seaside location, the town doesn't have a whole lot to recommend it. It's important to have a car if you have any plans of spending time off campus, and that's true whether you're taking I-95 to Boston or New York or staying closer to home; public transport in and around New London is, ahem, sparse.

Admissions

Average high school GPA:	—
Average freshman SAT verbal / math score:	666 / 658
Average freshman ACT score:	26
Application fee:	$60

Application deadlines:
1/1 (freshmen)
4/1 (transfer)
11/15 (early decision)

Total applicants:	4,278
Total accepted:	1,624 (38%)
Total accepted who enrolled:	490

Notification dates:
3/31 (freshmen)
5/15 (transfer)
12/15 (early decision)

Acceptance rate for early decision applicants:	66%

Students

Percentage of male / female students:	40% / 60%
Percentage of students from out of state:	84%
Percentage of students graduating in 4 years / 6 years:	84% / 87%

Money

Total endowment:	$192,481,000
Total tuition:	—
Total cost with fees & expenses:	$45,140
Average financial aid package:	$28,154
Percentage of students who sought aid and received it:	100%
Percentage of students receiving financial aid:	40%

Also Check Out

Colgate University

Hamilton College

Skidmore College

Trinity College

Wesleyan University

Cooper Union for the Advancement of Science and Art

30 Cooper Square
New York, NY 10003

(212) 353-4100
http://www.cooper.edu/

 **BIG BRAIN**

 **BIG PLAN**

 **BIG RESEARCH**

Full tuition scholarships for every single student!

5 REASONS IT'S COOL

1. At Cooper Union, all admitted students receive full scholarships.

2. Only 10 percent of applicants are accepted, making the school one of the most competitive in the nation.

3. If you want to study **art, architecture, or engineering**, you'll be hard-pressed to find a more respected place to do it.

4. Successful alums give back, big time, and the university's **endowment is over $450 million.**

5. Located in Astor Place on the border of the now-posh East Village, the school is in the **very heart of Manhattan.**

The Basics

Public / private: private nonprofit
Total enrollment / undergrads: 968 / 920
Campus setting: urban
Students call it: Cooper Union
Notable alums: Thomas Edison (inventor), Milton Glaser (creator of the I Love NY icon; founder, *New York* magazine), Russell Hulse (Nobel Laureate, Physics), Arnold Schmidt (painter), Jeffrey Epstein (investor)

Best Students, Best City

Cooper Union for was founded by Peter Cooper, first U.S. maker of the steam railroad engine, in the mid-nineteenth century. Originally offering adult education classes in such subjects as shorthand and architectural drawing, the school has become one of the most selective colleges in the nation, offering three challenging courses of study: architecture, art, and engineering. Its full scholarships for all students reflect the desire of its founder, who had less than a year of schooling, to provide free educations to talented youth. With an outstanding student-to-faculty ratio of 7:1, Cooper Union gives its students close contact with leading researchers, inventors, and artists. The focus is on both research and hands-on practice. Students are given the flexibility to concentrate on specific areas, such bioengineering, as well as access to great facilities. For instance, architectural students enjoy an 8,000-square-foot drafting studio and a computer design studio. No matter your area of study, you can count on access to important people, all of whom will be impressed by your credentials.

Great Hall History

Cooper Union's Great Hall has hosted many illustrious speakers, including philosopher Joseph Campbell, author Salman Rushdie, and politicians Ralph Nader and Rudolph Giuliani. Perhaps the most notable speech, however, was given in 1860 by Abraham Lincoln, who spoke out about the role of the federal government in slavery regulation. Some call that speech the turning point that led to Lincoln's nomination for the presidency.

Happy Birthday, Peter Cooper

Cooper Union students enjoy hitting the books, but they also know how to make the most of a stellar college campus and its insanely fun surroundings. The school has around sixty-five student organizations. Sports aren't particularly popular, but you'll find basketball, soccer, tennis, and volleyball teams. Cooper Union students are politically minded and mostly liberal. Student government plays an important role on campus, and each school has its own council. School-sponsored events are planned each year, including the Fall Festival, Pumpkin Carving, and winter ski trips. One annual tradition honors Peter Cooper's February birthday. Students, faculty, and anyone else affiliated with the school gather to sing the college song, raise a cupcake to Peter, and lay a wreath on his statue. If school-sponsored events don't appeal, there are countless other options on Cooper Union's doorstep.

All in a New York Minute

It may be difficult to tell where the Cooper Union campus leaves off and New York City begins, as it blends so well into the bustling neighborhood that surrounds it. The campus sits at the north end of Cooper Square, near Third Avenue, St. Mark's Place, Astor Place, and the East Village. The headquarters for the *Village Voice* are located up the street, as are buildings belonging to NYU. If you plan to hit the many clubs, theaters, restaurants, cafés, boutiques, and galleries that thrive in this area, you're bound to run into fellow students from NYU, Columbia, Baruch, and other local colleges.

Admissions

Average high school GPA:	3.5
Average freshman SAT verbal / math score:	649 / 686
Average freshman ACT score:	—
Application fee:	$65
Application deadlines:	
1/1 (freshmen)	
1/1 (transfer)	
12/1 (early decision)	
Total applicants:	2,600
Total accepted:	260 (10%)
Total accepted who enrolled:	203
Notification dates:	
4/1 (freshmen)	
5/1 (transfer)	
12/24 (early decision)	
Acceptance rate for early decision applicants:	21%

Students

Percentage of male / female students:	62% / 38%
Percentage of students from out of state:	41%
Percentage of students graduating in 4 years / 6 years:	69% / 85%

Money

Total endowment:	$454,621,612
Total tuition:	—
Total cost with fees & expenses:	$15,050
Average financial aid package:	$27,500
Percentage of students who sought aid and received it:	93%
Percentage of students receiving financial aid:	31%

Also Check Out

Auburn University

Case Western Reserve University

Columbia University

Massachusetts Institute of Technology

Rensselaer Polytechnic Institute

Cornell University

410 Thurston Avenue
Ithaca, NY 14850

(607) 255-2000
http://www.cornell.edu/

 **BIG BRAIN**

 **BIG CHOICE**

 **BIG RESEARCH**

Any person, any study

5 REASONS IT'S COOL

1. Enjoy the waterfalls, gorges, and gardens that grace **one of the loveliest campuses in the country.**

2. **A research institution of the highest caliber,** Cornell has world-class laboratories and one of the largest library systems in North America.

3. With seven schools, over four thousand courses, and at least five hundred clubs and organizations, **the university offers something for everyone.**

4. Its reputation as the **Ivy League party school** isn't far off the mark.

5. Study under Nobel laureates and Pulitzer Prize winners: Cornell **professors are the leading scholars and researchers in their fields.**

The Basics

Public / private: private nonprofit
Total enrollment / undergrads: 19,639 / 13,562
Campus setting: small town
Students call it: Cornell
Students are called: Cornellians, Big Red
Notable alums: Pearl S. Buck (writer), Ruth Bader Ginsberg (U.S. Supreme Court justice), Bill Maher (comedian, TV personality), Toni Morrison (writer), Christopher Reeve (actor), Janet Reno (U.S. attorney general)

Oh, the Possibilities!

Ezra Cornell wasn't kidding when, in 1865, he vowed to "found an institution where any person can find instruction in any study." With seven undergraduate colleges, seventy majors, and over four thousand courses, Cornell students certainly have options. Most enroll in the College of Arts and Sciences or the College of Engineering. Three of the colleges are funded by New York state, meaning that New Yorkers get a break on the hefty tuition. Class size can be large (the infamous Psychology 101 is a class of two thousand!), but higher-level classes usually stay between fifteen and fifty students. The sheer number of options can be daunting, and although the professors are accessible, you need to be motivated and take initiative. The core curriculum isn't too extensive, which gives students the chance to take electives from any of the seven schools (Wine Tasting at the Hotel School is popular). Cornell professors are at the top of their fields and expect their students to work hard.

The Mystery of Pumpkin Tower

One Halloween back in 1997, a pumpkin mysteriously appeared atop the pointed spire of McGraw clock tower. The resilient gourd kept its perch for five months, leading many to doubt the verity of the vegetable. One group even floated up a mini hot-air balloon to collect pumpkin samples, but the Great Pumpkin Mystery remained unsolved.

Working Hard and Letting Loose

Students accepted by Cornell tend to be motivated overachievers. The university abounds with opportunities for extracurricular activities, such as writing for the popular *Cornell Daily Sun* newspaper or volunteering through the Public Service Center. If you're into sports, there's a climbing wall, tons of intramural teams, and the much-anticipated hockey game against Harvard, in which students release pent-up tension by throwing dead fish at the Crimson players. Most students are heavily involved in one or two extracurriculars, balancing them with their academic load. And make no mistake, the academics are tough; Uris library is a popular hangout. Come the weekend, though, Cornellians let loose. The Greek system dominates the party scene, but there's also Collegetown, an area of off-campus housing with bars and restaurants. The largest party of the year is Slope Day, outdoor festivities on the last day of classes (when the snow has finally melted). As for housing, freshman from all seven schools live on the recently renovated North Campus. Upperclassmen have the option of living on West Campus, in one of the ten university-run "program" houses, or off campus in Collegetown. Big plus: The food service, run by the Hotel School, is known for cooking up some of the best campus grub in the country.

One Gorges Campus

The pun "Ithaca is Gorges," which you'll see emblazoning T-shirts across campus, sums up the Finger Lakes region: It's stunning and filled with, well, gorges. You're bound to pass over one, as well as an accompanying waterfall, on your way to class. The 745-acre hilltop campus also features the Cornell Plantations, three hundred acres of trails, gardens, and natural areas. From the 173-foot Jennie McGraw Tower, the focal point of campus, chime masters play daily tunes. Cornell overlooks the tip of Cayuga Lake and the small, artsy town of Ithaca. Although some students find Ithaca sleepy, they don't deny that it boasts great restaurants, like Maxie's, and occasional live music. Ithaca is also within ten miles of four natural parks. Students can rent gear from the outdoor education program for activities like climbing, skiing, biking, and hiking.

Admissions

Average high school GPA:	—
Average freshman SAT verbal / math score:	670 / 697
Average freshman ACT score:	26
Application fee:	$65

Application deadlines:
1/1 (freshmen)
3/15 (transfer)
11/1 (early decision)

Total applicants:	28,098
Total accepted:	6,935 (25%)
Total accepted who enrolled:	3,188

Notification dates:
4/3 (freshmen)
6/15 (transfer)
12/15 (early decision)

Acceptance rate for early decision applicants:	44%

Students

Percentage of male / female students:	51% / 49%
Percentage of students from out of state:	62%
Percentage of students graduating in 4 years / 6 years:	84% / 92%

Money

Total endowment:	$4,294,967,295
Total tuition:	$32,800
Total cost with fees & expenses:	$44,457
Average financial aid package:	$28,682
Percentage of students who sought aid and received it:	100%
Percentage of students receiving financial aid:	46%

Also Check Out

Brown University

Harvard University

Tufts University

University of Pennsylvania

Yale University

eighton University

2500 California Plaza
Omaha, NE 68178

(402) 280-2700
http://www.creighton.edu/

BIG JOB

A great school, plains and simple

5 REASONS IT'S COOL

I. Creighton's **well-regarded biomedical programs** give future doctors and nurses a head start.

2. The **exhaustive gen-ed curriculum** makes well-roundedness mandatory.

3. The cool, newly made-over **Old Market district of Omaha** gives students an excuse to wander off campus.

4. At this Catholic university, **religion is a presence,** but not an overwhelming one.

5. **Bluejay sports** get fans seeing red when it comes to the competition.

The Basics

Public / private: private religious
Total enrollment / undergrads: 6,981 / 4,075
Campus setting: urban
Students call it: Creighton
Students are called: Bluejays
Notable alums: Michael P. Anderson (astronaut killed in the Space Shuttle *Columbia*), Todd Fink (singer), Bob Gibson (pro baseball player), Ron Hansen (writer), J. Joseph Ricketts (founder, Ameritrade), Paul Silas (pro basketball player)

Is There a Doctor in the House?

Creighton's pre-med and nursing programs are the some of the strongest the school has to offer. For this reason, they are also quite popular. Also solid is the College of Business Administration. While the university's emphasis is on the practical vocations, Creighton still takes pains to make sure that its students are well rounded. This emphasis irritates some of the more pragmatic, secular minds, especially since the gen-ed requirements may involve a brush with (Roman Catholic) theology. Most students report, however, that doctrine and dogma seldom encroach on their intellectual lives and certainly don't detract from the quality of the learning experiences they've had. Faculty members are accessible and student oriented, so you're unlikely to hear them ask that familiar question: "And you are?" A cozy faculty-to-student ratio of 14:1 makes it hard for students to get lost in the shuffle.

Mass Romantic

After weeks of burning the midnight oil, Bluejays turn to candles. A hit among adherents and nonadherents alike, the candlelight mass held at St. John's, the campus chapel, is a "microwave" service meant to fit students' schedule. Stand, kneel, sit, and twenty minutes later, you're done!

"There's No Coast of Nebraska"

Life on the prairie offers multiple forms of entertainment. The Greek scene makes its largely keg-centric contributions to campus social life, but for those who quickly tire of ragers, there are the hip and edgy enticements of Omaha's Old Market district, or the closer-to-home offerings of the unfortunately named Skutt Student Center. Because Creighton is a Roman Catholic university, there are some pretty strict rules concerning coed commingling, but all but the most wild and crazy students should find these rules easy to live with. At this regional school, nearly half the student population hails from the Midwest. The administration has implemented an initiative to improve diversity, and people of color now make up 15 percent of the student body.

OMG! Omaha!

Most people think of two things when they hear the word *Omaha*: steak and insurance. That characterization couldn't be more inaccurate. Downtown Omaha's Old Market district is currently undergoing hipster-fication to such an extent that the city recently showed up on the *New York Times*'s radar. And Creighton is just a five-minute car ride away from this up-and-coming scene, meaning students have the best of neo-Bohemia right at their fingertips. Unfortunately, the area immediately adjacent to Creighton is a little sketchy, so caution and prudence are a must. Food service at the university is just so-so, and students rate the dorms as serviceable, if nothing special. Fitness freaks gravitate to the Kiewit Fitness Center (known by its rather humorous acronym, KFC), where they can cardio their cares away.

Admissions

Average high school GPA:	3.7
Average freshman SAT verbal / math score:	594 / 607
Average freshman ACT score:	25
Application fee:	$40

Application deadlines:
8/1 (freshmen)
8/1 (transfer)

Total applicants:	3,403
Total accepted:	3,030 (89%)
Total accepted who enrolled:	965

Notification dates:
continuous (freshmen)
continuous (transfer)

Students

Percentage of male / female students:	40% / 60%
Percentage of students from out of state:	55%
Percentage of students graduating in 4 years / 6 years:	63% / 75%

Money

Total endowment:	$267,766,000
Total tuition:	$24,166
Total cost with fees & expenses:	$33,968
Average financial aid package:	$21,260
Percentage of students who sought aid and received it:	91%
Percentage of students receiving financial aid:	50%

Also Check Out

Loyola University

Purdue University

Saint Louis University

University of Notre Dame

Valparaiso University

CUNY–Baruch College

I Bernard Baruch Way New York, NY I00I0	(646) 312-I000 http://www.baruch.cuny.edu/

BIG JOB

This way to vertical possibilities

5 REASONS IT'S COOL

I. Diversity university: Baruch students come from more than I20 countries, making it **one of the most diverse university's in the country.**

2. The tuition is **super-affordable, even for out-of-state students.**

3. The Zicklin School of Business is one of the nation's best places to study, with facilities that include a **state-of-the-art simulated trading floor.**

4. Plus, if you're interested in a career in business, there's **no better place to get started than in New York City.**

5. Get to know your profs: faculty members have a reputation for being **friendly and accessible.**

The Basics

Public/private: public state and local
Total enrollment/undergrads: 15,730 / 12,796
Campus setting: urban
Students call it: Baruch
Students are called: Bearcats
Notable alums: Fernando Ferrer (politician), Ralph Lauren (attended; fashion designer), Jennifer Lopez (attended; singer/actress), Bill McCreary (broadcaster)

Small World, Big City

Baruch students choose from among twenty-three majors and enroll in one of three colleges: the Zicklin School of Business, the School of Public Affairs, or the Mildred and George Weissman School of Arts and Sciences. With twelve thousand undergrads, Baruch can feel like a big place (a feeling that's probably amplified by the university's big-city Manhattan location). And while you'll be hard-pressed to avoid taking at least a few large lecture-style classes, most classes at Baruch have fewer than thirty students. The university's Freshman Seminar program helps kick things off for students with small, discussion-based classes and lots of personal attention from professors. Outside of the classroom, profs tend to be accessible and helpful. The unbeatable Manhattan location means that tons of internships and other opportunities for outside-of-the-classroom learning are at students' fingertips. Baruch's robust alumni network also helps hook students up with internships at nearby companies.

Showdown on Lexington Avenue

In recent years, Baruch has been working hard to rally enthusiasm for its athletic programs. The new Bearcat mascot clawed its way into the world in 2005. And in 2006, the Lexington Avenue Classic, a basketball doubleheader between Baruch and its CUNY rival, Hunter College, was introduced. Between unveiling an athletics website and lining the campus in banners, the university welcomed its first sellout crowd of 1,500 fans. The Lexington Avenue Classic is now an annual tradition.

A Community of Commuters

A stroll down the halls at Baruch can feel like a lesson in world geography and culture. The word *diverse* just begins to describe the colorful kaleidoscope that is the university's student body. Students come not only from all over New York City but from more than 120 countries. Baruch is a commuter school with no dorms, so getting to know fellow students can be challenging. Many students live far out on Long Island or in other parts of the city and leave campus as soon as they're finished with class. That said, students can—and many do—make friends at Baruch. The third-floor common area at the school's amazing seventeen-floor Newman Vertical Campus building is a great place to get started, and many students participate in clubs ranging from choral groups to the school radio station to pre-professional organizations. Students also join together to cheer on some of the school's Division III athletic teams or hang out at bars in the East Village or Baruch's Gramercy Park neighborhood.

Campus? What Campus?

Baruch's Newman Vertical Campus building covers nearly an entire square block between Third and Lexington avenues and 24th and 25th streets in Manhattan. This amazing, all-in-one facility is home to high-tech classrooms and research labs, a three-level athletics complex and recreation center, a student activities center, a performing arts complex, a TV studio, a food court, a bookstore, and a five-hundred-seat auditorium. When you finally run out of options inside, it's easy to find plenty of bars, restaurants, and shops right outside the door in Baruch's Gramercy Park neighborhood. Or you can hop on subway and make your way to theater performances, restaurants, bars, clubs, museums, an internship, or even home.

Admissions

Average high school GPA:	3.0
Average freshman SAT verbal / math score:	530 / 585
Average freshman ACT score:	—
Application fee:	$65

Application deadlines:
2/1 (freshmen)   12/13 (early decision)
3/1 (transfer)   12/15 (early action)

Total applicants:	15,066
Total accepted:	4,734 (31%)
Total accepted who enrolled:	1,493

Notification dates:
5/15 (freshmen)   1/7 (early decision)
5/1 (transfer)   1/7 (early action)

Acceptance rate for early action / early decision applicants:	— / 10%

Students

Percentage of male / female students:	49% / 51%
Percentage of students from out of state:	3%
Percentage of students graduating in 4 years / 6 years:	28% / 59%

Money

Total endowment:	$103,389,705
Total in-state tuition, fees & expenses:	$5,199
Total out-of-state tuition, fees & expenses:	$9,839
Average financial aid package:	$4,800
Percentage of students who sought aid and received it:	63%
Percentage of students receiving financial aid:	62%

Also Check Out

CUNY–Brooklyn College

CUNY–City College

CUNY–Hunter College

SUNY–Stony Brook University

CUNY–Brooklyn College

2900 Bedford Avenue
Brooklyn, NY 11210

(718) 951-5000
http://www.brooklyn.cuny.edu/

BIG CHOICE

An academic buffet with all the fixin's

5 REASONS IT'S COOL

1. BC richly deserves its reputation as **a great school and a great bargain**.

2. The beautiful campus, complete with wide-open lawns and lots of trees, is **a peaceful haven for city-weary students**.

3. Recent renovations have given BC the **most technologically advanced library** in the CUNY system.

4. Like to be challenged? The Honors Academy offers especially **rigorous coursework for aspiring doctors, engineers, and other ambitious students**.

5. The First College Year program eases the transition and helps **freshmen get to know their professors and peers**.

The Basics

Public / private: public state and local
Total enrollment / undergrads: 15,947 / 12,111
Campus setting: urban
Students call it: Brooklyn College, BC
Students are called: Bridges
Notable alums: Barbara Boxer (senator), Shirley Chisholm (senator, congresswoman), Bruce Chizen (president and CEO, Adobe Systems), Stanely Cohen (Nobel Laureate, Medicine), Alan Dershowitz (law professor, writer), Sam Levenson (humorist), Paul Moses (journalist), Gloria Naylor (novelist), Steve Riggio (CEO, Barnes & Noble), Jimmy Smits (actor)

Options, So Many Options

With twelve thousand undergrads, BC is big in terms of both size *and* academic options. Students choose from more than seventy majors, not including the eight different programs within the college's Honor Academy. BC's core curriculum requires all undergrads to take eleven interrelated classes and study a foreign language. As part of the First College Year program, freshmen are urged to enroll in Learning Communities, which allow them to take core classes together and receive mentoring and academic support. Professors are reportedly challenging and engaging, especially once students begin taking classes in their selected major. Many BC students are nontraditional and part-time, which lowers the percentage of students who graduate in four years to less than 20 percent. To help up this figure, the college recently began offering the On-Course Advantage program to help students graduate in four years.

Bells Are Ringing

You'd expect to hear the sounds of cars honking and traffic whirring in Brooklyn, but bells? The pretty sounds of bells are exactly what BC students hear emanating from the campus's LaGuardia Tower Carillon. The college's bell system can be programmed to play more than a hundred classical, patriotic, and holiday melodies. When President Clinton visited campus, for instance, the carillon played "Hail to the Chief" to announce his arrival. The carillon never plays while classes are meeting. It does, however, sound a two-bell strike to signal the beginning and end of classes.

A Little Bit of This, a Little Bit of That

It's tough to generalize about BC students, other than to say that—like the New York City borough they study in—they are an incredibly diverse bunch. BC is a commuter college with no on-campus housing and a mix of full-time and part-time and nontraditional students. After class ends, students usually leave campus for home or work. When they do stick around, students can usually be found hanging out in the student center or getting involved in one or more of the college's 140 student organizations. Clubs range from the unusual—cricket, the Desi Fashion Show Committee, the Francophone Committee—to more common groups like the Art Group and the TV & Radio Club. There are fraternities and sororities on campus, but fewer than 5 percent of students get involved.

A Tree (Well, Several—and a Nice Big Lawn) Grows in Brooklyn

BC's grassy campus is widely considered to be one of the most beautiful in the region. In recent years, the campus's peaceful vibe has been disturbed by the sounds of construction crews. The college recently completed a state-of-the-art library that is the most technologically advanced in the CUNY system. Other coming additions include a new West Quad; updated façades on the Roosevelt and James Hall buildings; a new building for classroom space, offices, the Department of Physical Education and Exercise Science, gymnasiums, and a swimming pool; and a center for the performing arts. BC is located in Midwood, a largely residential section of Brooklyn that offers little in the way of student-friendly bars and activities. Luckily, hipper parts of Brooklyn and Manhattan are easily accessibly by both subway and buses.

Admissions

Average high school GPA:	3.0
Average freshman SAT verbal / math score:	514 / 551
Average freshman ACT score:	—
Application fee:	$65
Application deadlines: continuous (freshmen) — (transfer)	
Total applicants:	13,615
Total accepted:	6,072 (45%)
Total accepted who enrolled:	1,379
Notification dates: continuous (freshmen) continuous (transfer)	

Students

Percentage of male / female students:	40% / 60%
Percentage of students from out of state:	1%
Percentage of students graduating in 4 years / 6 years:	17% / 39%

Money

Total endowment:	—
Total in-state tuition, fees & expenses:	$5,175
Total out-of-state tuition, fees & expenses:	$9,815
Average financial aid package:	$5,400
Percentage of students who sought aid and received it:	99%
Percentage of students receiving financial aid:	49%

Also Check Out

CUNY–Baruch College

CUNY–City College

CUNY–Hunter College

CUNY–Queens College

New York University

CUNY–City College

138th Street and Convent Avenue
New York, NY 10031

(212) 650-7000
http://www.ccny.cuny.edu/

BIG CHOICE

BIG RESEARCH

Movin' on up(town)!

5 REASONS IT'S COOL

1. Even out-of-state students get a great deal on tuition—and **about 70 percent of students receive need-based financial aid.**

2. **Colleges don't get more diverse than this:** Name a place, any place, and you'll find a City College student who hails from there.

3. No public college in the country can claim more **Nobel laureates among its alums.**

4. Students in the **Teacher Academy get tons of hands-on experience**—and free tuition.

5. Located **right next to Harlem,** the campus is within easy reach of cool restaurants, bars, and shops.

The Basics

Public / private: public state and local
Total enrollment / undergrads: 13,244 / 10,314
Campus setting: urban
Students call it: City College, City, CCNY
Students are called: Beavers
Notable alums: Kenneth Arrow (Nobel Laureate, Economics), Julius Axelrod (Nobel Laureate, Medicine), Ira Gershwin (songwriter), Ed Koch (mayor, New York City), Bernard Malamud (writer), General Colin Powell (U.S. Army), Mario Puzo (writer), Upton Sinclair (writer)

Heading Uptown?

Throughout its 150-plus-year history, City College has been one of the area's best deals in higher education. It offers dozens of majors, with architecture, psychology, and electrical engineering among the most popular. Freshmen participate in Freshman Year Programs, which ease the transition to college life; the required New Student Seminar teaches essential college survival skills. Ambitious students who enroll in the Honors College or special programs offered by CCNY Honors Center benefit from tiny, discussion-oriented classes taught by the campus's most renowned professors. The student-to-faculty ratio is 12:1, one of the lowest in the CUNY system. One of the state's best science and research programs, City College's Division of Science offers small seminars, academic and financial support for science majors, and four university-run research centers and institutes. Biomedical programs are particularly strong, and for future doctors, the seven-year BS/MD program knocks a year off of medical studies (and tuition).

A Tuition-Free State of Mind

What a deal! For most of its history, City College charged a grand total of nothing for tuition. Founded in 1847 as the Free Academy, the college's founders aimed to provide the children of the city's immigrants and the poor with a free college education. Admission to the college was based solely on merit. Only in 1976, when the Free Academy–turned–City College began to suffer economically, was tuition collected. To this day, however, City College remains committed to educating students from all walks of life at a modest price.

Something for Everyone

There's no such thing as a typical student at City College: The student body is simply too diverse to merit generalizations. Suffice to say, students come from every corner of the globe, representing more than a hundred countries and speaking more than eighty languages. If you're looking for that cozy, community-oriented college experience, you're probably best off looking elsewhere. City College provides minimal housing, and the vast majority of students leave campus after classes end for jobs, homes, or families. Despite the commuter nature of campus life, plenty of students can be found commingling at the Finley Student Center, which holds movie screenings, salsa lessons, belly-dancing performances, and special events and offers food. Finley is also the meeting site for most of City College's more than eighty-five student organizations, which range from Greek organizations to social service groups to fun stuff like clubs devoted to domino playing, rock climbing, and yoga.

The Top of the Town

City College's campus features a gorgeous cluster of historic Gothic-style buildings. Just a few years ago, the surrounding neighborhood of Manhattanville was considered the "middle of nowhere" by many. But thanks to a recent resurgence, the neighborhood has become more student friendly, offering nightlife options such the hip-hop producer Timbaland's nightclub, the Cherry Lounge. Other restaurants, bars, and clubs are beginning to crop up along the burgeoning West Harlem Pier as well. Most students head out of Manhattanville when they want to hang out, and they don't have to go far. Harlem is to just to the east, and student-friendly Morningside Heights—which is home to several institutions, including Columbia University and Barnard College—is just to the south. Of course, students can always venture farther down into Manhattan, which is an easy subway ride away.

Admissions

Average high school GPA:	2.81
Average freshman SAT verbal / math score:	489 / 524
Average freshman ACT score:	—
Application fee:	$65
Application deadlines: 3/1 (freshmen) continuous (transfer)	
Total applicants:	13,528
Total accepted:	6,295 (47%)
Total accepted who enrolled:	1,528
Notification dates: 8/1 (freshmen) 8/1 (transfer)	

Students

Percentage of male / female students:	51% / 49%
Percentage of students from out of state:	4%
Percentage of students graduating in 4 years / 6 years:	5% / 32%

Money

Total endowment:	—
Total in-state tuition, fees & expenses:	$5,237
Total out-of-state tuition, fees & expenses:	$9,797
Average financial aid package:	$8,400
Percentage of students who sought aid and received it:	77%
Percentage of students receiving financial aid:	51%

Also Check Out

CUNY–Baruch College

CUNY–Brooklyn College

CUNY–Hunter College

Fordham University

New York University

CUNY–Hunter College

695 Park Avenue
New York, NY 10021

(212) 772-4000
http://www.hunter.cuny.edu/

 **BIG CHOICE**

 **BIG RESEARCH**

The best deal in New York City

5 REASONS IT'S COOL

1. Want to be in the center of it all? Hunter's **Upper East Side Manhattan location is** just that.

2. Get hands-on experience through internships at Manhattan companies such as CNN, the Metropolitan Museum of Art, and more.

3. Get top-notch teacher training at Hunter's Teacher Academy, where tuition is free for accepted students.

4. See the world without leaving campus: Hunter students come from 150 different countries.

5. Students in the Macaulay Honors College enjoy more challenging classes, along with **free tuition, a free laptop, and a stipend to study abroad or intern.**

The Basics

Public / private: public state and local
Total enrollment / undergrads: 20,899 / 15,805
Campus setting: urban
Students call it: Hunter College, Hunter
Students are called: Hawks
Notable alums: Bella Abzug (congresswoman), Ellen Barkin (actress), Maurice Berger (art critic/historian), Vin Diesel (actor), Gertrude Elion (Nobel Laureate, Medicine), Ada Louise Huxtable (architecture critic), Terrance Lindall (artist), Audre Lorde (poet)

Have We Got a Deal for You

It would be tough to find a college that offers more academic bang for the buck than Hunter. Notable for its strong programs in nursing, education, health sciences, and social work, Hunter has one of the best academic reputations for the sciences and social sciences of any CUNY school. The university offers nearly seventy majors, including popular choices like accounting, English, and psychology. Students enrolled in the Honors College and the Teacher Academy enjoy small classes, plenty of mentoring, and, best of all, free tuition. Freshmen take a required First Year Seminar, and block scheduling means that students stick together in small groups throughout their first-year courses. Hunter students praise the quality of professors but lament the administrative bureaucracy. With hundreds of credit-bearing internships at their disposal, as well as opportunities to help top-notch faculty with their research, students leave Hunter well prepared for the real world.

A House with History

While many of Hunter's buildings are relatively new, there's one building on campus that boasts an older and more distinguished pedigree. The Roosevelt House, an English Georgian-style townhouse on 65th Street, was once the home of former president Franklin D. Roosevelt and First Lady Eleanor Roosevelt. It was at this residence that FDR recovered from polio in 1921, plotted his first campaign, and received congratulatory telegrams upon his victory in the 1932 presidential election. In 1943, the First Lady dedicated the building to Hunter, offering it as a center for students to use. Roosevelt House is currently undergoing a renovation and will, upon completion, serve as a public policy academic center.

Where Hard Work Rules

Hunter is home to large percentages of first-generation Americans and nontraditional students who juggle work, school, and families. This combination makes for students with reputations for being hardworking, open-minded, and diverse. Hunter is predominately a commuter campus, and as such students tend not to stick around on campus when classes are over. About 4 percent of students live in the dorms located at the college's secondary Gramercy Park campus. Hunter offers approximately 130 student organizations, with options ranging from the four Greek organizations to the College Senate to a wide range of intramural sports. And students often gather to cheer on the college's Division III sports teams, particularly if they're playing the school's biggest rival, nearby Baruch College.

Where the Action Is

Hunter is made up of a total of five campuses in Manhattan. The primary campus, consisting of a cluster of buildings joined by cool skywalks, is located in Manhattan's Upper East Side on East 68th Street at Lexington Avenue. While Hunter students by and large shuffle to other parts of the city as soon as classes are over, those who want to stick around enjoy the campus's proximity to Central Park (great for in-between classes picnics) and the restaurants, bars, and museums nearby. Hunter's dorms, as well as its health science classes, are located at the downtown campus near Gramercy Park. While public transportation is easily accessible from all campuses, the college runs a bus service that shuttles students from one campus to another.

Admissions

Average high school GPA:	3.0
Average freshman SAT verbal / math score:	534 / 553
Average freshman ACT score:	—
Application fee:	$65
Application deadlines: 3/15 (freshmen) 3/15 (transfer)	
Total applicants:	21,830
Total accepted:	7,350 (34%)
Total accepted who enrolled:	1,813
Notification dates: 1/3 (freshmen) continuous (transfer)	

Students

Percentage of male / female students:	32% / 68%
Percentage of students from out of state:	4%
Percentage of students graduating in 4 years / 6 years:	10% / 37%

Money

Total endowment:	—
Total in-state tuition, fees & expenses:	$4,349
Total out-of-state tuition, fees & expenses:	$11,149
Average financial aid package:	$4,809
Percentage of students who sought aid and received it:	—
Percentage of students receiving financial aid:	—

Also Check Out

CUNY–Baruch College

CUNY–Brooklyn College

CUNY–City College

Fordham University

CUNY–Queens College

65-30 Kissena Boulevard
Flushing, NY 11367

(718) 997-5000
http://www.qc.cuny.edu/

**BIG
CHOICE**

**BIG
HAND**

Check out one of New York City's best liberal arts values.

5 REASONS IT'S COOL

1. Boasting **strong academic programs and distinguished faculty**, it's not hard to see why they call Queens College the "jewel of the CUNY system."

2. Everybody's welcome! The **diverse student body** represents over 140 different countries.

3. When the college finishes construction of its new dorms, it will become **one of three colleges in the CUNY system that offers on-campus housing.**

4. Students pay **low tuition**, and more than half receive need- or merit-based financial aid.

5. Did we mention that **Jerry Seinfeld is a graduate?**

The Basics

Public / private: public state and local
Total enrollment / undergrads: 18,107 / 13,662
Campus setting: urban
Students call it: Queens College, Queens, QC
Students are called: Knights
Notable alums: Gary Ackerman (congressman), Fran Drescher (actress, comedienne), Marvin Hamlish (composer), Ron Jeremy (actor), Carole King (singer-songwriter), Robert Moog (inventor, Moog synthesizer), Mary Murphy (TV reporter), Jerry Seinfeld (actor, comedian), Paul Simon (singer-songwriter), Charles Wang (founder, Computer Associates)

Discover Your Academic Interests

Queens College offers a wide range of classes in both the liberal arts and pre-professional programs. Nearly a hundred majors are offered, including new programs in finance, international business, actuarial studies, graphic design, and neuropsychology. The college's Freshman Year Initiative is designed to help students make a smooth transition into college life as well as explore their academic interests. Freshmen are organized into groups of about forty. These groups, or "learning communities," take classes together during the first semester and are assigned professors, mentors, and TAs to teach them the college ropes. All freshmen must complete a writing class and at least two other classes toward core requirements. Students who prefer smaller classes and an extra challenge may apply for one of the university's honors programs or CUNY's Honors College, which awards free tuition,

Thank God It's Monday

Few people say, "Thank God it's Monday"—unless they happen to be students at Queens College, where Mondays and Wednesdays from noon to one are known as "free hour." During this time, no classes are held, and instead programs take place that are designed to bring the campus community together. Sometimes, student organizations meet. Other times, the campus hosts parties, speakers, or discussions and serves food. Students love free hour because it forces them to take a break and enjoy themselves.

a study-abroad or internship grant, and a computer to all participating students. The college often brings renowned artists and writers to campus: Past guests include Toni Morrison, Billy Joel, Frank McCourt, V. S. Naipaul, Doris Lessing, and the New York Philharmonic.

Commuter Campus with a Collegiate Community

Like other colleges in the CUNY system, Queens has a commuter campus. This means that making friends can be tough, due to the fact that most students flee campus for home or work come the end of classes. Despite the "come and go" feel of the campus, Queens still maintains a surprisingly collegial atmosphere. Students hail from every corner of the globe and are as diverse—culturally, politically, religiously, and more—as the city around them. Bonding opportunities are plentiful if students look hard enough for them: Try hanging out in the campus cafeteria between classes or joining the crowds cheering on the college's Division II athletic teams. Many Queens students participate in clubs or student organizations, which include everything from fashion and knitting clubs to Model UN and the fencing team.

A Bit of Green in NYC

With its seventy-seven-acre campus, Queens College offers plenty of grass, trees, and other natural amenities you might not expect from a city school. In addition to Spanish-style stucco and tile buildings, the campus is home to the newly renovated Powdermaker Hall, where most classes are held. Campus renovation projects include updates to the Student Union, new cafés and dining areas, and new landscaping. The college is located in a residential area of Flushing, Queens, just off the Long Island Expressway. Manhattan, the skyline of which can be seen from all over campus, is easily accessible by a subway ride of an hour or so.

Admissions

Average high school GPA:	3.3
Average freshman SAT verbal / math score:	525 / 554
Average freshman ACT score:	—
Application fee:	$65
Application deadlines: 1/1 (freshmen) 3/1 (transfer)	
Total applicants:	12,911
Total accepted:	5,502 (43%)
Total accepted who enrolled:	1,627
Notification dates: continuous (freshmen) continuous (transfer)	

Students

Percentage of male / female students:	39% / 61%
Percentage of students from out of state:	1%
Percentage of students graduating in 4 years / 6 years:	23% / 52%

Money

Total endowment:	$12,085,000
Total in-state tuition, fees & expenses:	$4,376
Total out-of-state tuition, fees & expenses:	$11,176
Average financial aid package:	$5,000
Percentage of students who sought aid and received it:	90%
Percentage of students receiving financial aid:	25%

Also Check Out

CUNY–Baruch College

CUNY–Hunter College

Fordham University

New York University

SUNY–Stony Brook University

Dartmouth College

6016 McNutt Hall
Hanover, NH 03755

(603) 646-1110
http://www.dartmouth.edu/

 **BIG BRAIN**

 **BIG IDEA**

 **BIG WORLD**

Great professors, great students, great outdoors

5 REASONS IT'S COOL

1. Dartmouth is the smallest of the eight Ivies. Make no mistake: This means that **undergraduate education is this college's heart and soul.**

2. The **unusual academic calendar** features four ten-week terms offered year-round.

3. Curious about life at other schools? Dartmouth offers **exchange programs with over fifty colleges and universities.**

4. Overachieve much? Students have myriad opportunities for **self-directed research, service projects abroad, and internships.**

5. Students go wild over the college's **27,000 acres of wilderness** up north.

The Basics

Public / private: private nonprofit
Total enrollment / undergrads: 5,753 / 4,085
Campus setting: small town
Students call it: Dartmouth
Notable alums: Michael Arad (architect), Owen Chamberlain (Nobel Laureate, Physics), Rachel Dratch (actress), Robert Frost (poet), Buck Henry (actor, filmmaker), Laura Ingraham (political analyst), Mindy Kaling (actress, writer), Nelson Rockefeller (businessman, politician), Daniel Webster (statesman)

Doing the D-Plan

Dartmouth's core curriculum requires a freshman seminar, foreign language proficiency, three world culture courses, and ten additional courses from a variety of disciplines. The Dartmouth Plan (or "D-Plan") divides the academic year into fall, winter, spring, and summer terms that are only ten weeks long. The condensed class schedule means that students face more intense workloads, but they also get more flexibility in planning their schedules. During their time off, students may opt to study anywhere from Brazil to Zimbabwe, take an internship or co-op, or take courses at any of the other member schools in the Twelve College Consortium. Dartmouth promotes collaborative, independent research projects with its Presidential Scholars Program and the Senior Fellowship Program for interdisciplinary studies. Aspiring actors can also spend a semester at the National Theater Institute either in Waterford (CT), Moscow, or London.

A College with a Crazy Streak

From bonfire-frenzied welcoming parties to inaugurate each school year, to barbeques and concerts over Green Key weekend, to snow sculpting and ski racing at the annual Winter Carnival, Dartmouth students relish their many campus traditions. One rite of passage, however, is not exactly school sanctioned: streaking. While it's true that many colleges have a streaking tradition, Dartmouth takes this oldie-but-goody prank to a whole new level. During the campus's Blue Light Challenge, students strip off their sweaters and winter coats and streak around while setting off the blue safety phones stationed around the campus. The challenge? Steering clear of the security guards who respond to the calls.

Greeks and Geeks

Like the great outdoors? Try joining Dartmouth's Outing Club, the oldest collegiate outdoors club in the nation. At Dartmouth, you'll find mountain, rivers, and even a stretch of the Appalachian Trail close by, so you can hike, ski, climb, and otherwise get close to nature to your heart's content. Dartmouth students tend to be a sporty bunch. Although the university doesn't offer athletic scholarships (in accordance with Ivy League rules), a large majority of students participate in intramural sports, and a quarter play for a varsity team. Greek life is a big deal here, and around half of all students participate. Students praise the dining food for its diversity and quality and for the healthy fare offered by Homeplate and Collis Café. A contributing factor to the diversity of the student body is the exclusively need-based scholarships offered by the college, attracting students from varied economic backgrounds. Indeed, many students work their way through school.

Ain't It Quaint?

Dartmouth students love their picture-perfect campus with its idyllic, small-town New England setting. Stately old buildings such as Baker Library and Dartmouth Hall share the campus with decidedly more modern buildings such as the Hopkins Center (affectionately known as the Hop), a glassy modern building with a colorful interior that is home to the college's Art and Drama departments. Dartmouth has recently finished constructing a new residence hall and new buildings to house its Engineering and Math departments. Although most students are perfectly content to hang out close to campus, both Boston (at 130 miles away) and Montreal (at 200 miles away) are within reach for weekend excursions. New Hampshire and Vermont also offer limitless opportunities for skiing, hiking, and other outdoors activities.

Admissions

Average high school GPA: —

Average freshman SAT writing / math / critical reading score: 709 / 714 / 708

Average freshman ACT score: —

Application fee: $70

Application deadlines:
1/1 (freshmen)
3/1 (transfer)
11/1 (early decision)

Total applicants: 13,938

Total accepted: 2,186 (16%)

Total accepted who enrolled: 1,086

Notification dates:
4/10 (freshmen)
4/25 (transfer)
12/15 (early decision)

Acceptance rate for early decision applicants: 30%

Students

Percentage of male / female students: 49% / 51%

Percentage of students from out of state: 96%

Percentage of students graduating in 4 years / 6 years: 84% / 93%

Money

Total endowment: $3,092,094,000

Total tuition: $33,297

Total cost with fees & expenses: $43,137

Average financial aid package: $31,840

Percentage of students who sought aid and received it: 100%

Percentage of students receiving financial aid: 51%

Also Check Out

Bucknell University

Cornell University

Middlebury College

Williams College

Yale University

Davidson College

Box 7156
Davidson, NC 28035

(704) 894-2000
http://www.davidson.edu/

 **BIG BRAIN**

 **BIG PERSPECTIVE**

Doin' the honors

5 REASONS IT'S COOL

1. At Davidson, **no class has more than fifty students,** and most are much smaller than that.

2. The honor code infuses the campus with **a powerful sense of communal trust.** Plus, you can schedule your finals on your own time. How cool is that?

3. When you finish learning here, you're really just getting started. A full **70 percent of grads eventually go on to earn graduate degrees.**

4. Did someone say money, honey? Forty percent of grads go immediately into high-paying business fields.

5. Campus traditions abound, and there's **plenty of southern charm, y'all.**

The Basics

Public / private: private religious
Total enrollment / undergrads: 1,667 / 1,667
Campus setting: small town
Students call it: Davidson
Students are called: Wildcats
Notable alums: Patricia Cornwell (writer), Dean Rusk (diplomat), Tony Snow (political strategist, columnist), Woodrow Wilson (U.S. president)

Serious about the Business at Hand

A lot of colleges pay lip service to the importance of quality classroom teaching. Davidson actually mandates that professors' passion for teaching and ability to teach be taken into account when considering promotions. The result? Time and again, Davidson students praise their professors for the kind of teaching that makes classroom topics come alive through real-world examples. The most popular majors are biology, English, and history; the science programs are also well respected. All departments, it should be said, hold in common the campus-wide honor code, which forbids dishonesty, cheating, and the tolerance thereof. Davidson students take their honor system seriously and report that it constitutes more than a simple injunction against copying answers on exams. More important is the feeling of purity the system adds to one's studies. The honor system lifts academics above the fussiness of grade point averages and into the serenity of something worth doing for its own sake. Both students and professors come to the classroom serious about the business at hand.

Honor All Around

A story meant to illustrate the effectiveness of Davidson's honor system takes as its premise a twenty-dollar bill, lying on the sidewalk. The first time you pass it, you leave it there, because it's not yours. The second time you pass it, you see someone's taped it down so it won't blow away. The third time you see it, it's in a photograph, on a poster with a phone number and message reading "Call me if you lost this."

A Spiritual Place

Speaking broadly, the students at Davidson are more spiritual than at the average American campus. While there's a lot to do besides going to church, students enthusiastically report the edifying benefits of living with and among people of differing degrees of religiosity. At any given moment, a Davidson student is most likely to be either studying or participating in athletics. Twenty sports are Division I here, and the administration encourages nonvarsity athletes to join intramural teams at whatever level of competitiveness suits them. Social life tends to revolve around Patterson Court, location of the fraternities (for men) and eating clubs (for women), neither of which are residential. Drinking is popular, but the large number of religious students on campus ensures that there's usually nonalcoholic entertainment available at the student union. The honor system is just as important to life outside the classroom as in; students report that thefts simply do not occur at Davidson.

Headin' South?

At least as far as size and appearance goes, Davidson has a lot in common with the classic New England college town. But make no mistake about it: This is North Carolina. Southern gentility and mores are more than a vague memory here. Students from other parts of the country are often startled by the "southernness" of the town, but almost everyone eventually falls in love with the romance and slow rhythm of life. The town is situated on the shore of Lake Norman, a popular spot for boating and jet-skiing. Cornelius, small-town home of Rusty Wallace and Will Ferrell, is a popular destination for day trips, and Charlotte (twenty miles away) is not so far as to be unreachable for a night out on the town. Further a field, the famous lighthouses of the Outer Banks are a half-day's drive away.

Admissions

Average high school GPA:	—
Average freshman SAT verbal / math score:	680 / 683
Average freshman ACT score:	26
Application fee:	$50

Application deadlines:
1/2 (freshmen)
3/15 (transfer)
11/15 (early decision)

Total applicants:	3,895
Total accepted:	1,185 (30%)
Total accepted who enrolled:	461

Notification dates:
4/1 (freshmen)
5/15 (transfer)
12/15 (early decision)

Acceptance rate for early decision applicants:	45%

Students

Percentage of male / female students:	50% / 50%
Percentage of students from out of state:	82%
Percentage of students graduating in 4 years / 6 years:	84% / 87%

Money

Total endowment:	$421,672,470
Total tuition:	$29,119
Total cost with fees & expenses:	$38,784
Average financial aid package:	$19,045
Percentage of students who sought aid and received it:	100%
Percentage of students receiving financial aid:	34%

Also Check Out

Dartmouth College

Duke University

University of Virginia

Washington & Lee University

Vanderbilt University

Denison University

P.O. Box 740
Granville, OH 43023

(740) 587-0810
http://www.denison.edu/

 BIG PERSPECTIVE

 BIG RESEARCH

Small-town life, big-time opportunities

5 REASONS IT'S COOL

1. **Surround yourself with smarties:** Over 50 percent of incoming students were in the top 10 percent of their high school classes.

2. The university offers **tons of research opportunities**, and every year 125 students get $3,300 to conduct their own research projects.

3. **Save a buck (or several thousand):** Ninety-four percent of students who ask get some type of financial aid, and 56% get merit awards.

4. **Welcome to small town America.** Granville and its residents (all 3,170) epitomize small-town life.

5. How do students blow off steam in such a small town? One word: parties!

The Basics

Public / private: private nonprofit
Total enrollment / undergrads: 2,263 / 2,263
Campus setting: small town
Students call it: Denison
Students are called: Big Red, Big R
Notable alums: Steve Carrell (actor), James Frey (writer), Michael Eisner (CEO, Walt Disney Company), Jennifer Garner (actress), Richard Lugar (senator), Bobby Rahal (pro race car driver)

Student-Centered and Flexible

Denison recently reduced its distribution requirements with the hopes of encouraging students to develop a greater sense of ownership over their academic programs. The reduced list of required classes still includes two seminars and coursework in fine arts, sciences, social sciences, humanities, and foreign languages, but students may double-count courses to fulfill the requirements more quickly. The most popular majors are communications, economics, and English, although the university's science programs are coming on strong with the help of a new laboratory complex and the university's 350-acre biological preserve. Denison encourages undergrads to take on research projects, whether independently or with faculty supervision, and the school's small size facilitates the process of finding professors who are willing to acts as advisors. Across the board, in fact, faculty members are very accessible, but they do expect their attentiveness to *you* to be reciprocated with attentiveness to *them*; attendance and homework policies

Green Acres Is the Place for Them

Sure, Denison is a moderate-to-conservative, fairly preppy school that requires students to live on campus, but to every rule there's an exception. Meet the Homesteaders: a small group of students who—with permission—live on a farm a mile from campus, grow their own food, and sleep in solar-powered cabins.

at Denison are strict. Support services, including a writing center, are readily available, and students of all GPAs use these programs to address the weak spots in their academic repertoires.

Denison's Denizens

Greek life at Denison used to be a nationally recognized phenomenon until the administration recently declared the school to be entirely residential. This means that all but a handful of students live on campus, and that Denison's fraternities and sororities no longer have any boarders. Some students gripe about the change, while others note with satisfaction that the campus is now, not surprisingly, much less cliquish than it used to be. Drinking remains a common pastime, and students note with grudging thankfulness that, although the administration went hard after the frats, the school's alcohol policies remain relatively lax. An undisputed upside to the dismantling of Denison's Greek life has been the construction of a half-dozen beautiful residences to house the students who otherwise would have lived in Greek housing. Housing options range from singles to standard double rooms to apartment-style arrangements holding ten people. Increasing diversity is one of the administration's biggest goals—and is likely to remain one for a while.

Home Sweet Granville

Without spending a dollar on travel, you can crystallize your thoughts on Denison's location by noting your instinctive reaction to this statement: Granville is a genuine, salt-of-the-earth small town, and unembarrassed to be so. There's not much to do, and most businesses close early—although two town bars host nightly, informal reenactments of the frat life now gone with the wind. The nearest big town, Columbus, is about thirty minutes away, and students with access to a car often head there on the weekends or simply tour the lovely rolling hills surrounding Granville. Denison itself is safe and pretty; the campus was designed by the architect/planner of New York's Central Park, and the common parentage shows.

Admissions

Average high school GPA:	3.6
Average freshman SAT verbal / math score:	639 / 641
Average freshman ACT score:	26
Application fee:	$40

Application deadlines:
1/15 (freshmen)
7/1 (transfer)
11/1 (early decision)

Total applicants:	5,010
Total accepted:	1,942 (39%)
Total accepted who enrolled:	573

Notification dates:
4/1 (freshmen)
continuous (transfer)
11/15 (early decision)

Acceptance rate for early decision applicants:	87%

Students

Percentage of male / female students:	43% / 57%
Percentage of students from out of state:	54%
Percentage of students graduating in 4 years / 6 years:	75% / 79%

Money

Total endowment:	$533,159,000
Total tuition:	$29,860
Total cost with fees & expenses:	$39,820
Average financial aid package:	$26,424
Percentage of students who sought aid and received it:	94%
Percentage of students receiving financial aid:	43%

Also Check Out

Davidson College

DePauw University

Kenyon College

Miami University

DePauw University

313 South Locust Street
Greencastle, IN 46135

(765) 658-4800
http://www.depauw.edu/

 BIG JOB

 **BIG PERSPECTIVE**

Goin' back to Indiana . . .

5 REASONS IT'S COOL

1. Like personal attention? Not a single class at DePauw has more than fifty students, and **the overall student-to-faculty ratio is 10:1.**

2. DePauw Fellows, a select group of media, management, and science students, get the chance to put their careers in overdrive through **internships, small classes, and senior capstone projects.**

3. Get your Greek on: the **fraternity and sorority scene is huge.**

4. The unique Winter Term offers students the chance to **spend a month doing a cool internship.**

5. This is the heartland. If you like **living slowly and smelling the roses,** you'll enjoy being in Greencastle, Indiana.

The Basics

Public / private: private religious
Total enrollment / undergrads: 2,326 / 2,326
Campus setting: small town
Students call it: DePauw
Students are called: Tigers
Notable alums: Joseph P. Allen (astronaut), Charles Beard (historian), Mary Ritter Beard (historian), Stephen F. Hayes (journalist), Vernon Jordan (businessman, political advisor), Barbara Kingsolver (novelist), Richard Peck (author), Dan Quayle (senator, U.S. vice president)

One Eye on Books, One Eye on the World

Top-quality professors and facilities form the twin pillars of academics at DePauw. Profs in the economics, music, and English departments are particularly well respected, and the equipment at the Center for Contemporary Media rivals what you'd find at a professional studio. Indeed, DePauw prides itself on providing its students with preparation for and access to the working world. A recent study ranked DePauw the eighth most successful liberal arts college in the country at producing corporate leaders. This is a tribute both to DePauw's Management Fellows Program and to its internship initiatives, which allow students to set aside up to eight months to gain experience in their prospective career fields. A January term also gives upperclassmen an opportunity to do brief internship stints or to travel abroad to participate in the Winter Term in Service program. Freshmen, meanwhile, spend the winter session with small peer groups in the "depauw.year1" program,

As White as Snow

A beloved DePauw tradition is the Boulder Run, in which students celebrate the first snowfall of the year by stripping down and running from their residences to the Columbia Boulder at the center of campus. The rite has withstood the test of time, although the police have gradually been getting less tolerant, and most participants now wear footwear for better traction. At this, of course, purists can only shake their heads.

which integrates seminars, advising, and social activities. All seniors are required to complete a culminating, comprehensive project in their majors.

All Greek to Us

Over 70 percent of DePauw students belong to fraternities and sororities. Greek life dominates the social scene and its calendar: Rushing, pledging, and various Greek events mark the rhythm of the school year from August all the way to June. As a result, life can sometimes be tough for independents. There are, of course, ways to get involved and make connections on campus that have nothing to do with Deltas or Thetas. DePauw offers over a hundred extracurricular clubs and organizations, including one of the country's best college radio stations and popular intramural sports and community service programs. About three-quarters of students perform volunteer work, and two-thirds participate in at least one intramural league. Politically speaking, the student body is right-of-center, but liberal students report that their opinions are by and large respected.

Hoosierland, USA

When you consider the fact that DePauw is located in Greencastle, it's not too difficult to imagine why and how the school's thumping Greek life got its start. Greencastle is a fairly small town, home to about nine thousand people, and it offers relatively little in the way of exciting goings-on after 8 P.M. Students seeking nightlife that doesn't involve Greek letters usually end up in Indianapolis or at Indiana University's Bloomington campus, both of which are a forty-five-minute drive away. For those without access to a car, getting out of Greencastle can be difficult. Fortunately, it's possible to make your own adventure right on DePauw's campus, which includes a 480-acre nature preserve with facilities for hiking, running, and canoeing.

Admissions

Average high school GPA:	3.6
Average freshman SAT verbal / math score:	614 / 621
Average freshman ACT score:	26
Application fee:	$40

Application deadlines:
2/1 (freshmen)	11/1 (early decision)
3/1 (transfer)	12/1 (early action)

Total applicants:	4,074
Total accepted:	2,751 (68%)
Total accepted who enrolled:	596

Notification dates:
4/1 (freshmen)	1/1 (early decision)
4/1 (transfer)	2/15 (early action)

Acceptance rate for early action/early decision applicants:	85% / 91%

Students

Percentage of male / female students:	44% / 56%
Percentage of students from out of state:	46%
Percentage of students graduating in 4 years / 6 years:	75% / 79%

Money

Total endowment:	$490,547,616
Total tuition:	$27,400
Total cost with fees & expenses:	$36,280
Average financial aid package:	$24,873
Percentage of students who sought aid and received it:	98%
Percentage of students receiving financial aid:	47%

Also Check Out

Boston University

Bucknell University

Clemson University

Denison University

Kenyon College

Dickinson College

PO Box 1773
Carlisle, PA 17013

(717) 243-5121
http://www.dickinson.edu/

 **BIG PERSPECTIVE**

 **BIG WORLD**

Want an education with an international twist?

5 REASONS IT'S COOL

1. At Dickinson, **small, seminar classes are the norm**—so be sure to read up before you show up.

2. There's **an international twist to almost everything** here. The best example? The university's acclaimed study-abroad program.

3. Humanities programs and the business school coexist symbiotically, **creating well-rounded students.**

4. Pack your hiking boots: The **Appalachian Trail passes ten minutes from campus** and opportunities for outdoors adventures abound.

5. **School spirit,** manifested in sports rivalries and campus traditions, is serious (and seriously fun) business.

The Basics

Public / private: private nonprofit
Total enrollment / undergrads: 2,400 / 2,400
Campus setting: suburban
Students call it: Dickinson
Students are called: Red Devils
Notable alums: James Buchanan (U.S. president), Jennifer Haigh (writer), Susan Stewart (poet), Rosie O'Donnell (attended; TV personality), Rich Smolan (photojournalist), Roger Taney (U.S. Supreme Court chief justice)

"Usefulness," Refined over Centuries

Just days after the Treaty of Paris officially ended the Revolutionary War, Dickinson was founded for the purpose of providing a "useful" education to the young citizens of the new nation. Dickinson's foreign language programs offer coverage not only of Romance language stand-bys but also languages such as Arabic, Hebrew, and Chinese. Dickinson's highly acclaimed study-abroad program sends students packing to twenty-four countries; more than 80 percent of students spend at least a semester abroad. Students who know where they're headed from day one can enroll in a partnership program with Penn State Law School that awards a bachelor's degree and a JD after six years. One of the strongest departments is biology, where the emphasis on "usefulness" also applies: Science courses, even introductory ones, are workshop-, rather than lecture-, based. This, and the fact that 80 percent of classes are capped at twenty-five students, enables professors to push their charges beyond familiar patterns of thinking.

Mermaidology

Benjamin Latrobe, the architect of Dickinson's original academic building, ordered the construction of a grand statue of Triton for his building's cupola, but local craftsmen forged a four-breasted, three-foot-tall bronze mermaid instead. For many years, it was traditional for first-year students to steal the statue from its perch and then return it to Dickinson's president at Homecoming. This ritual fell out of favor, however, after a student undertaking the theft hurt himself while leaping from a tree.

A Global Society

Sure, they look preppy on the surface, but there's actually a fair amount of economic and racial diversity among Dickinson's student body. The college has had more success with its diversity-promotion policies than many other small liberal arts schools have. African American, Asian American, Hispanic American, and international students each constitute about 5 percent of the student population. Nineteen percent of men and 24 percent of women join Greek houses, all of which are college owned and subject to strict alcohol regulations. Monitors check IDs at campus parties, four underage drinking violations trigger expulsion, and kegs are not permitted anywhere in any of the college residences. Only seniors may live off campus, although housing is guaranteed for four years; special interest housing for language buffs or community-service enthusiasts is available. The most powerful unifier of the student body, aside from irritation at the alcohol policies, is the series of rivalries Dickinson maintains with nearby schools. Every year, the Red Devils battle with Franklin and Marshall for the Conestoga Wagon Trophy and challenge Gettysburg for the Little Brown Bucket.

Cradled by Mountains and History

Situated in the Appalachian foothills of central Pennsylvania, Dickinson's campus is spotted with gray buildings built with limestone from the college-owned quarry. Carlisle, the college's hometown, is definitely not a cosmopolitan place, but there are some student-oriented bookshops and ethnic restaurants buried among the fast-food joints and big-box retail centers. There are also a number of historic sites and small museums in the area. Big Brother Big Sister and similar organizations have helped to increase contact between the campus and the town in recent years. Harrisburg, the state capital, is just twenty minutes away, although Philadelphia and Washington, D.C., two hours away, are the nearest big cities. The beaches of Maryland and Delaware are close enough for a weekend trip, and skiers can be on the slopes after just a forty-minute drive.

Admissions

Average high school GPA:	—
Average freshman SAT verbal / math score:	651 / 646
Average freshman ACT score:	—
Application fee:	$60

Application deadlines:
2/1 (freshmen)
4/1 (transfer)
11/15 (early decision)
12/1 (early action)

Total applicants:	5,298
Total accepted:	2,273 (43%)
Total accepted who enrolled:	618

Notification dates:
3/31 (freshmen)
continuous (transfer)
12/15 (early decision)
1/31 (early action)

Acceptance rate for early action/early decision applicants:	52% / 69%

Students

Percentage of male / female students:	44% / 56%
Percentage of students from out of state:	73%
Percentage of students graduating in 4 years / 6 years:	81% / 84%

Money

Total endowment:	$241,981,000
Total tuition:	$35,450
Total cost with fees & expenses:	$44,764
Average financial aid package:	$26,239
Percentage of students who sought aid and received it:	96%
Percentage of students receiving financial aid:	47%

Also Check Out

Gettysburg College

Hamilton College

Lafayette College

Muhlenberg College

Drew University

36 Madison Avenue
Madison, NJ 07940

(973) 408-3000
http://www.drew.edu/

BIG PERSPECTIVE

An up-to-date education in an old-fashioned setting

5 REASONS IT'S COOL

1. At this tech-friendly school, **every student has a laptop and network access**.

2. Drew's **proximity to New York City** means loads of internship opportunities in finance, art, and government.

3. **SAT-phobes, take note:** SAT scores are *not* required for admission.

4. Religious groups, particularly the **United Methodist Church**, have an important presence here.

5. Those with a travel bug will appreciate the International Seminars Program, which **exposes undergrads to other cultures, heritages, and religions**.

The Basics

Public / private: private religious
Total enrollment / undergrads: 2,647 / 1,656
Campus setting: suburban
Students call it: Drew
Students are called: Rangers
Notable alums: Young-Ho Chin (theologian), Fred Garrigus Holloway (bishop of the Methodist Church), Soon Yi Priven (wife of Woody Allen), Aileen Quinn (star of *Annie*)

Learning in the Global Classroom

Like other elite schools, Drew prizes independent research, student-designed majors, and group learning. Unlike its peer schools, though, Drew does not require applicants to submit their SAT scores. The university offers twenty-seven majors, and most students opt to study history, the social sciences, and visual and performing arts. Classes are taught by 122 full-time faculty members, nearly all of whom hold terminal degrees. Thomas Kean, former president of the university and governor of New Jersey, taught a class here. The 12:1 student-to-faculty ratio means that students won't get lost in the shuffle. Students can expect personal attention from their professors; Drew was recently recognized for excellent classroom interactions. The International Seminars Program allows students a unique opportunity to immerse themselves in other cultures while completing their majors. This means you can earn credit hours in Brazil, China, Eritrea, or Italy while the university foots most of the bill.

Admitted, Banned, Admitted Again

In 1920, women were permitted to enroll at Drew in seminary classes. But coeducation didn't fly for long, and eventually the university barred women altogether. Female undergrads were welcomed back during World War II to make up for the plummeting enrollment caused by the draft.

Play Well, Eat Well

Almost all Drew undergraduates live on campus, and they give themselves plenty to do. There are eighty student-run organizations; media groups such as radio and television stations; and the *Acorn*, Drew's student newspaper, which was recently voted Best College Newspaper by the New Jersey Collegiate Press Association. If political, social, or environmental issues get you fired up, you're sure to find a relevant group at Drew. There are even student houses devoted to particular religious affiliations, such as the Spirituality House and the Islamic Culture House. If being a spectator is more your style, check out the three hundred annual performances, lectures, conferences, and exhibits, or take in a game involving one of the university's fifteen sports teams. In addition to cross-country, basketball, soccer, swimming, and fencing, this university boasts an equestrian riding team. Students give Drew's eating options two thumbs up. Healthy food choices abound at three campus locations, and a variety of meal plans are offered.

At the Intersection of Old and New

Despite being just thirty miles from New York City, Drew is a quiet and peaceful place. Set on 186 acres in Madison, New Jersey, the campus is dotted with historic buildings. The newly renovated F. M. Kirby Shakespeare Theater houses the Shakespeare Theater of New Jersey. The university also enjoys the benefits of proximity to the research and development capital of the nation. Special seminars, speakers, and assistantships are de rigueur for many students.

Admissions

Average high school GPA:	3.39
Average freshman SAT writing / math / critical reading score:	588 / 581 / 595
Average freshman ACT score:	25
Application fee:	$50

Application deadlines:
2/15 (freshmen)
8/1 (transfer)
12/1 (early decision)

Total applicants:	4,532
Total accepted:	2,906 (64%)
Total accepted who enrolled:	479

Notification dates:
3/15 (freshmen)
4/1 (transfer)
12/24 (early decision)

Acceptance rate for early decision applicants:	89%

Students

Percentage of male / female students:	41% / 59%
Percentage of students from out of state:	41%
Percentage of students graduating in 4 years / 6 years:	67% / 73%

Money

Total endowment:	$241,450,000
Total tuition:	$32,508
Total cost with fees & expenses:	$45,158
Average financial aid package:	$23,242
Percentage of students who sought aid and received it:	82%
Percentage of students receiving financial aid:	45%

Also Check Out

College of William & Mary

Dartmouth College

Lafayette College

Muhlenberg College

University of Virginia

Drexel University

3141 Chestnut Street
Philadelphia, PA 19104

(215) 895-2000
http://www.drexel.edu/

 **BIG CHOICE**

 **BIG JOB**

Ready to get to work?

5 REASONS IT'S COOL

1. Drexel's mandatory co-op program allows students to **gain up to eighteen months of paid internship experience**—*before* graduation.

2. The **top-rated engineering and business programs** are among the best anywhere.

3. The university's **acclaimed career development center** helps place students with great companies.

4. You'll have no trouble staying connected: Drexel was **the first major university to go wireless,** and its campus features at least 6,500 computers.

5. Like cheesesteak sandwiches? The university is smack dab **in the heart of Philly.**

The Basics

Public / private: private nonprofit
Total enrollment / undergrads: 19,882 / 12,908
Campus setting: urban
Students call it: Drexel
Students are called: Dragons
Notable alums: Michael Anderson (pro basketball player), Chuck Barris (TV personality), Chris McKendry (ESPN anchor), Susan Seidelman (filmmaker)

I Get *Paid* for This?

Drexel is widely recognized for its mandatory co-op program, which sends students out of the classroom and into the workplace through a wide array of paid internships. Work opportunities are available at some 1,500 companies, including Boeing, UNYSIS, Comcast, Dupont, Lockheed Martin, and Sun Company. Students choose between one and three separate six-month internships, which they complete in alternating cycles with regular classroom studies. Those who complete three internships graduate in five years rather than the regular four. The university comprises thirteen colleges and schools, including colleges of engineering, business, arts and sciences, media arts and design, information science and technology, and the Pennoni Honors College. A total of seventy undergraduate programs are offered, and engineering and business are especially popular and well regarded. Most professors have terminal degrees, and the university boasts a student-to-faculty ratio of 10:1. A wide variety of study-abroad (and co-op

All in Good Time

J. Peterson Ryder, Drexel's first dean of men, had a major pet peeve: lateness. The punctual administrator used to note which students did (and didn't) make it to class on time. With his help, a large clock, known as the Ryder Clock, was installed in the campus's Great Court. Its inscription read, "Be On Time."

abroad) opportunities are available in places such as Japan, Turkey, China, and Jordan.

All Work and Some Play

Drexel may score high on surveys about its use of technology and academic programs, but it has received some low marks on the overall student experience, with complaints in particular about the small campus and need for more student housing. The Undergraduate Student Government Association has been instrumental in helping administrators address student issues. Housing is guaranteed for all first-year students, and about one-quarter of students live on campus. The university offers thirteen fraternities and six sororities. Popular student organizations include the Campus Activities Board, which sponsors a wide range of events; KWDU, the campus radio station; Mad Dragon Records, a recording studio; and the *Triangle*, the student newspaper. There are eighteen Division I varsity sports teams that compete in the Colonial Athletic Association Conference, along with a variety of intramural and club sports options.

Philly at Your Fingertips

Drexel is located in Philadelphia in the neighborhood called University City. The University of Pennsylvania is close by, as are many other universities and colleges. Philadelphia is the fourth largest metropolitan area in the country and is rich with cultural attractions, including museums, galleries, and historic buildings and neighborhoods. Public transportation is easily accessible, including buses, trolleys, and the SEPTA train. Students can also walk two blocks to the 30th Street Station, where Amtrak trains depart to destinations such as New York City, Boston, and Washington, D.C.

Admissions

Average high school GPA:	3.47
Average freshman SAT verbal / math score:	586 / 617
Average freshman ACT score:	—
Application fee:	$50
Application deadlines:	
3/1 (freshmen)	
continuous (transfer)	
Total applicants:	12,093
Total accepted:	9,946 (82%)
Total accepted who enrolled:	—
Notification dates:	
continuous (freshmen)	
continuous (transfer)	

Students

Percentage of male / female students:	57% / 43%
Percentage of students from out of state:	44%
Percentage of students graduating in 4 years / 6 years:	14% / 60%

Money

Total endowment:	$511,684,486
Total tuition:	$26,000
Total cost with fees & expenses:	$38,660
Average financial aid package:	$15,076
Percentage of students who sought aid and received it:	59%
Percentage of students receiving financial aid:	50%

Also Check Out

Babson College

Case Western Reserve University

Northeastern University

The Pennsylvania State University–University Park

Rutgers University

Duke University

2138 Campus Drive
Durham, NC 27708

(919) 684-8111
http://www.duke.edu/

 **BIG BRAIN**

 **BIG RESEARCH**

Brains and basketball

5 REASONS IT'S COOL

1. At Duke, rooting for **Blue Devils basketball is a way of life.**

2. With campus architecture this stunning, you'll never want to leave the **"Gothic Wonderland."**

3. The FOCUS Program creates an **interdisciplinary learning and living experience** for freshmen and sophomores.

4. Lemurs are cute! Students have an unusual opportunity to study and care for these precious primates at the **world-renowned Duke Lemur Center.**

5. Duke is **strong on scientific research:** Scientists here recently mapped the final human chromosome in the Human Genome Project.

The Basics

Public / private: private religious
Total enrollment / undergrads: 13,373 / 6,330
Campus setting: suburban
Students call it: Duke
Students are called: Dukies, Blue Devils
Notable alums: Elizabeth Dole (senator), Paul Farmer (physician), Grant Hill (pro basketball player), John J. Mack (CEO, Morgan Stanley), Charlie Rose (broadcast journalist), William Styron (novelist)

First-Rate and Flexible

Duke students enroll in either Trinity College of Arts & Sciences or the Pratt School of Engineering. Economics, psychology, public policy, political science, and biology are the most popular majors; Trinity students also have the option of designing their major. Pratt, one of the top undergrad engineering programs of its kind, boasts the new $97 million Fitzpatrick Center for Interdisciplinary Engineering, Medicine, and Applied Sciences. Research opportunities abound through the Duke University Medical Center, top-notch campus research centers, or the nearly 120 off-campus study programs. Most classes at Duke have twenty-five or fewer students, and the Small Group Learning Experiences program requires students to take at least three courses as tutorials, seminars, or independent studies. The Sanford Public Policy Institute gives future politicos the chance to study media, nonprofit organizations, and government agencies. The DukeEngage program offers full support to students in summer or semester-long service projects.

Doin' Time in K-Ville

Duke students camp out for weeks to secure tickets to the annual UNC basketball game, forgoing the comforts of dorm living for decidedly more rugged sleeping arrangements. Every year, a temporary tent city known as Krzyzewskiville, or *K-ville*, after men's basketball coach Mike Krzyzewski, becomes student central. Students devise schedules and alliances to enable themselves to attend class while friends—or perhaps the merest of acquaintances—hold their places in line.

Let's Go Cameron Crazy!

You don't have to be basketball fan to enjoy your time at Duke, but loving Blue Devils basketball certainly doesn't hurt your chances for having fun. Every year, archrival UNC comes to town for a match-up, and the game is as important a part of the calendar as finals or Thanksgiving break. Fans are known as "Cameron Crazies" after Cameron Indoor Stadium, home to Blue Devils basketball. Southern culture is an important influence on campus life—this is North Carolina, after all—and students tend to take above-average pride in the neatness of their dress. Greek life, too, is a large, although not dominating, part of the Duke experience: 29 percent of men belong to fraternities, and 42 percent of women belong to sororities. Frat parties are open to everyone, and alcohol is easy to come by—some would say too easy. In recent years the administration has tried to tweak Duke's housing assignment structure to limit out-of-control behavior. The success of these efforts is debatable, but students by and large seem happy with their living situations.

Cool Durham

Duke is set apart from the city of Durham by the Duke Forest and the Sarah P. Duke Gardens, leaving its students (happily) confined to their stunning campus. The Georgian-style East Campus, where all freshmen now reside, was the site of the original Trinity College, which moved to Durham in 1892. Colorful Duke stone, mined from a nearby quarry, forms the characteristic Gothic architecture of West Campus, including the picturesque Duke Chapel, which has a 210-foot tower and a fifty-bell carillon. Durham has a number of restaurants and bars that cater to students, but the city is a far cry from being an ideal place for a night on the town. Duke is part of the Research Triangle, made up of Durham, Raleigh, and Chapel Hill, which is home to the one of world's highest concentrations of PhDs and MDs. Durham is close to the Atlantic Ocean, the Appalachians, and the Great Smoky Mountains, making it an ideal starting point for outdoor adventures.

Admissions

Average high school GPA:	—
Average freshman SAT verbal / math score:	700 / 719
Average freshman ACT score:	26
Application fee:	$75

Application deadlines:
1/2 (freshmen)
3/15 (transfer)
11/1 (early decision)

Total applicants:	19,411
Total accepted:	4,123 (21%)
Total accepted who enrolled:	1,683

Notification dates:
4/1 (freshmen)
5/1 (transfer)
12/15 (early decision)

Acceptance rate for early decision applicants:	36%

Students

Percentage of male / female students:	51% / 49%
Percentage of students from out of state:	87%
Percentage of students graduating in 4 years / 6 years:	88% / 94%

Money

Total endowment:	$3,915,925,000
Total tuition:	$32,845
Total cost with fees & expenses:	$45,615
Average financial aid package:	$29,449
Percentage of students who sought aid and received it:	100%
Percentage of students receiving financial aid:	40%

Also Check Out

Georgetown University

Rice University

Stanford University

University of North Carolina at Chapel Hill

Washington University in St. Louis

Duquesne University

600 Forbes Avenue
Pittsburgh, PA 15282

(412) 396-6000
http://www.duq.edu/

BIG CHOICE

The prize of Pittsburgh

5 REASONS IT'S COOL

1. Duquesne is an internationally recognized, **top-notch Catholic university.**

2. Enjoy the main campus in **downtown Pittsburgh, or head to Italy**, where the university has a walled campus near downtown Rome.

3. **Programs in the health sciences are strong,** including majors such as nursing, pharmacy, physical therapy, and sports medicine

4. Feel the spirit watching **the NCAA Division I football team** and the Atlantic 10 men's basketball team.

5. The **living-learning centers** create close communities.

The Basics

Public / private: private religious
Total enrollment / undergrads: 10,110 / 5,678
Campus setting: urban
Students call it: Duquesne
Students are called: Dukes
Notable alums: John Clayton (sportscaster), Michael Hayden (director, CIA), Art and Dan Rooney (founder and owner, respectively, the Pittsburgh Steelers), Bobby Vinton (singer)

The Fast Track to Success

With a student-to-faculty ratio of 15:1, Duquesne offers plenty of personal attention. This Catholic school emphasizes morality and spirituality, aiming to create future leaders with a strong ethical sense to match their strong scholarly background. Students can choose from ten different schools within the university that focus on everything from business and education to medicine and law to music and liberal arts. The university also has a special school of leadership for those looking to take the world by storm. Ambitious students can also take advantage of a variety of programs that allow them to do more and do it faster, including accelerated degree programs, double majors, honors degrees, internships, off-campus study, and student-designed majors. In addition to the standard gamut of study-abroad programs, Duquesne also has its own campus in bustling Rome and another in picturesque Galway, Ireland, for those students who are itching to get out and see the world.

Humble Beginnings

Duquesne may be one of the top Catholic institutions in the country now, but it wasn't always so exalted. In the late nineteenth century, legend has it, classes were held over a bakery in Pittsburgh, and many of the students were struggling to get by. With its over ten thousand students and two campuses abroad, the school has come a long way.

A Town unto Itself

With more than 135 student organizations, you're sure to find your niche. Sign up for the one of many campus choral groups or for the American Chemical Society or the Dukettes Dance Troupe. The university also has an active Catholic ministry on campus. The Duquesne Union NiteSpot offers a late-night space where students can lounge around, update their Facebook profiles, or play pool, skee-ball, or Ping-Pong. Other recent campus additions include a state-of-the-art health science building, two recording studios, parking garages, a recreation center, and a Victorian throughway. Plus, there's always the great outdoors, which is easily accessible through university-sponsored weekend skiing, whitewater rafting, horseback riding, and spelunking trips. Athletics have always been big at Duquesne: The wresting squad, track team, rifle team, and ice hockey teams have all performed well, as have the school's men's basketball team and NCAA Division I football team.

They're Not Bluffing

Campus is small—it takes less than fifteen minutes to walk from one end to the other—but distinctive. Located on a forty-eight-acre plot of land, Duquesne looks down on downtown Pittsburgh from its hilltop perch, which is often referred to as "The Bluff." Students enjoy the hustle and bustle of urban life in Pittsburgh, which has lots to offer. Music buffs will enjoy the Pittsburgh Symphony Orchestra and the Pittsburgh Opera. The punk rock scene is respectable, and there are plenty of local clubs with live jazz, blues, and bluegrass. If the quiet of a museum is more your style, spend a day in the Andy Warhol Museum, the Carnegie Museum of Natural History, or the Carnegie Museum of Art. When it's time to party, students from Carnegie Mellon and the University of Pittsburgh are just down the street. And for those times when you're a little short on spending money, there are discounted tickets for Duquesne students at many venues, including the Pittsburgh Public Theater and the Pittsburgh Ballet.

Admissions

Average high school GPA:	3.65
Average freshman SAT writing / math / critical reading score:	558 / 576 / 564
Average freshman ACT score:	24
Application fee:	$50

Application deadlines:
7/1 (freshmen)
7/1 (transfer)
11/1 (early decision)
12/1 (early action)

Total applicants:	5,252
Total accepted:	3,807 (72%)
Total accepted who enrolled:	1,323

Notification dates:
continuous (freshmen)
continuous (transfer)
12/15 (early decision)
1/15 (early action)

Acceptance rate for early action/early decision applicants:	82% / 95%

Students

Percentage of male / female students:	42% / 58%
Percentage of students from out of state:	19%
Percentage of students graduating in 4 years / 6 years:	55% / 69%

Money

Total endowment:	$137,673,593
Total tuition:	$20,855
Total cost with fees & expenses:	$31,561
Average financial aid package:	$15,204
Percentage of students who sought aid and received it:	89%
Percentage of students receiving financial aid:	62%

Also Check Out

Seton Hall University

University of Delaware

The University of Pittsburgh

West Virginia University

Earlham College

801 National Road West
Richmond, IN 47374

(765) 983-1200
http://www.earlham.edu/

 **BIG PERSPECTIVE**

 **BIG WORLD**

Whole lotta Quakin' going on

5 REASONS IT'S COOL

1. **Quakers!** They founded the school, and their influence can still be felt today: Earlham grads care what their jobs mean to the community and the planet.

2. Around the world in four years: The academic program is designed to help **students engage with global issues.**

3. Alcohol is not the all-consuming obsession it is at many schools, and there's still **plenty to do on campus every weekend.**

4. More than half the students participate in **intramural leagues.**

5. Students do **over fifty thousand hours of volunteer work** every year.

The Basics

Public / private: private religious
Total enrollment / undergrads: 1,410 / 1,248
Campus setting: small town
Students call it: Earlham
Students are called: Quakers
Notable alums: Joseph M. Dixon (governor, Montana), Michael C. Hall (actor), Robert Quine (guitarist), Marc Reisner (writer), Andrea Seabrook (NPR correspondent)

Globally Aware and Intense

Inspired by the idea that there are different "ways of knowing," Earlham recently rejiggered its distribution requirements. Rather than taking a certain number of English courses, a certain number of math courses, and so on, students construct academic programs that include interpretive, analytical, abstract, quantitative, and scientific modes of inquiry. In practice, there's not a huge difference between the old system and the new, although the new setup makes it easier for students to avoid taking classes in which they have no interest. Earlham professors are highly accessible. Students play a formal role in the faculty-hiring practice, and some professors team up with small groups of students to travel to foreign countries during the May term. For example, the Biology Department frequently organizes expeditions to Costa Rica and the Galapagos islands. The study-abroad office helps students find semester- and year-long programs in such nontraditional places as India, Northern Ireland, and East Africa. On campus, over two hundred

Seeking Consensus

Because of its Quaker roots, Earlham is officially committed to governance by consensus, rather than by majority rule. The idea is that as opposed to majority rule, which reaches decisions through adversarial processes, consensus incorporates the wisdom and perspective of all interested parties. Sound like a pipe dream? Well, students and staff collaborate successfully more than you might imagine. And in any case, the positive vibes seep into the rhythms of daily life.

courses have an international bent, the Japanese Studies Department is a national standout, and team-taught programs in peace and global studies and human development and social relations take an interdisciplinary approach to current world affairs.

Somewhere Between Soaked and Dry

In a nod to the school's Quaker founders, Earlham tries to foster a spirit of community, peace, and justice on campus. Politics and volunteerism are important here, and there's a high degree of tolerance among the student body, which is 12 percent nonwhite and includes both preppy student government types and left-leaning hippy types. About nine out of ten students live on campus in single, double, and triple dorms. Earlham has no fraternities or sororities, but thirty small houses owned by the school provide special-interest housing (peace, service learning, Jewish culture, etc.). These houses sometimes take on Greek-esque roles, but they do not serve alcohol. Officially, the campus is dry, although students say it's more like "moist." Large-scale social events are usually organized by the student activities board. About a third of students are on intercollegiate teams, and half do intramurals.

Get Ready to Care About High School Basketball

Earlham's campus is dominated by Georgian buildings and striking landscaping. Japanese gardens symbolize the school's strong academic links with Japan. Beyond the two hundred acres that constitute the main part of campus lies what's called the "back campus": another six hundred acres of woods, fields, and farmland owned by the university. Earlham is located in Richmond, Indiana, a conservative city of forty thousand people that boasts low crime, proximity to Indianapolis and Cincinnati, and not a whole lot else. Some say the Richmond-haters are just whiners: Stores don't close nearly as early as they would in a truly small town, and there are a healthy number of cafés and boutiques. A car is almost essential for anyone with wanderlust, but keep in mind that freshman aren't allowed to keep wheels on campus.

Admissions

Average high school GPA:	3.5
Average freshman SAT writing / math / critical reading score:	597 / 594 / 621
Average freshman ACT score:	25
Application fee:	$30

Application deadlines:
2/15 (freshmen) 12/1 (early decision)
4/1 (transfer) 1/1 (early action)

Total applicants:	1,554
Total accepted:	1,092 (70%)
Total accepted who enrolled:	300

Notification dates:
3/15 (freshmen) 12/15 (early decision)
4/15 (transfer) 2/1 (early action)

Acceptance rate for early action / early decision applicants: — / 82%

Students

Percentage of male / female students:	43% / 57%
Percentage of students from out of state:	69%
Percentage of students graduating in 4 years / 6 years:	54% / 68%

Money

Total endowment:	$313,257,000
Total tuition:	$28,600
Total cost with fees & expenses:	$35,520
Average financial aid package:	$21,215
Percentage of students who sought aid and received it:	95%
Percentage of students receiving financial aid:	59%

Also Check Out

Grinnell College

Kalamazoo College

Kenyon College

Macalester College

Oberlin College

Eckerd College

4200 54th Avenue South
St. Petersburg, FL 33711

(727) 867-1166
http://www.eckerd.edu/

 **BIG HAND**

 **BIG PERSPECTIVE**

Fast learners by the open sea

5 REASONS IT'S COOL

1. Eckerd's **nationally recognized marine biology program** lets students spend time at the Woods Hole Oceanographic Institute.

2. Incoming freshmen build strong relationships with professors during the **month-long pre-semester autumn term.**

3. Unwind from a hard day's work with **a dip in the Gulf.**

4. The college has quickly ascended the academic ranks, recently becoming one of only 270 schools with a **Phi Beta Kappa charter.**

5. **A quarter of grads go straight to grad school** and two-thirds have jobs waiting for them.

The Basics

Public / private: private religious
Total enrollment / undergrads: 1,845 / 1,845
Campus setting: suburban
Students call it: Eckerd, EC
Students are called: Tritons
Notable alums: Dorothy Allison (writer), Brian Sabean (pro baseball general manager), Sterling Watson (writer), Steven Reuther (film producer)

Hitting the Ground Running

Eckerd's strongest programs are in marine biology, psychology, and international relations. The Chinese and Japanese departments are also gaining a reputation for demanding and rewarding courses. Incoming freshmen jump right in with a month-long autumn term, in which small student groups partner with professors in courses ranging from Coastal Oceanography to Religion and Public Policy. Freshmen then take a year-long survey course in canonical reading that alternates between lecture and small seminar formats. The focus on developing well-rounded students culminates in a senior course that combines a majors-based capstone project with a community service requirement. For all its convention bending, however, Eckerd has yet to achieve the consistency of an older institution. Fine arts are a bit neglected, and math professors are notoriously unable or unwilling to approach complicated material from an intro student's perspective. But the future is wide open for this relative newcomer, which provides an excellent bargain and an innovative student-centered experience.

The Senior Class

Eckerd has created a program that takes advantage of an often-overlooked natural resource of the Tampa Bay area: retirees. The Academy of Senior Professionals is a group of three hundred locals who take classes, work with professors, and lead workshops. They also mentor students and, in some cases, pick them up at the airport.

Life Is a Beach

Hard work may be the norm at Eckerd, but high stress is not. The calm atmosphere may be the result of the close proximity to the open ocean and its attendant water skiing, fishing, and sun bathing. Sandals pass for formal dress, and even professors occasionally wear shorts to class. For many, the easygoing vibe is second nature: A third of the students are native Floridians. The largest contingent of outsiders hail from the Northeast, and another 7 percent are international. These non-Floridians waste no time adopting the local custom. The vibe is generally liberal, although students of a conservative or religious bent find no lack of community. All students share a strong eco-friendly ethos, which the administration encourages. Fraternities and sororities are nonexistent, and alcohol policies are strict, both on campus and off. Over-21 wristbands are required at campus parties. Most underage students resign themselves to partying sober, but low-key boozing in the dorms, which house nearly three-quarters of the student body, is always an option.

Dalí, Disney, and Dolphins

Students have a tough time leaving Eckerd. To find out why, grab one of the school's free bikes and take a spin around the lush campus. The school owns a mile of shoreline along a peninsula jutting into the Boca Ciega Bay. Students gazing out their windows often spot a frolicking dolphin or two. Eckerd maintains a stock of canoes, kayaks, snorkeling equipment, and other water sport gear, free for use. Campus buildings are modern, especially the gigantic new library and the chapel-in-the-round located on a small island. As for hometown diversions, shops and restaurants in St. Petersburg tend to close early, in large part because of the significant senior population. Spring break central it ain't. On the bright side, students have free access to the Salvador Dalí Museum and other museums, and Orlando, Miami, and New Orleans are all a road-trip away.

Admissions

Average high school GPA:	3.3
Average freshman SAT verbal / math score:	562 / 562
Average freshman ACT score:	23
Application fee:	$35

Application deadlines:
continuous (freshmen)
continuous (transfer)

Total applicants:	2,774
Total accepted:	2,006 (72%)
Total accepted who enrolled:	540

Notification dates:
continuous (freshmen)
continuous (transfer)

Students

Percentage of male / female students:	44% / 56%
Percentage of students from out of state:	75%
Percentage of students graduating in 4 years / 6 years:	58% / 63%

Money

Total endowment:	$21,940,367
Total tuition:	$27,352
Total cost with fees & expenses:	$36,486
Average financial aid package:	$18,961
Percentage of students who sought aid and received it:	79%
Percentage of students receiving financial aid:	50%

Also Check Out

College of Charleston

Florida State University

Rollins College

Stetson University

Elon University

2700 Campus Box
Elon, NC 27244

(336) 278-2000
http://www.elon.edu/

 **BIG PERSPECTIVE**

 **BIG WORLD**

All aboard the leader-ship!

5 REASONS IT'S COOL

1. Elon's service learning, internship, and leadership programs give students plenty of opportunities to **learn outside of the classroom.**

2. Eighty percent of students study abroad—**one of the highest study-abroad rates in the country.**

3. Rising stars take to the stage in the **acclaimed performing arts programs.**

4. College Coffee, the **weekly coffee klatch attended by students and professors,** is one of the university's oldest traditions.

5. The **Elon Experiences transcript** lists students' extracurricular activities, to show prospective employers or grad schools.

The Basics

Public / private: private religious
Total enrollment / undergrads: 5,230 / 4,849
Campus setting: suburban
Students call it: Elon
Students are called: Phoenix
Notable alums: Rich Blomquist (writer, *The Daily Show*), Ward Burton (NASCAR racer), Jo Craven McGinty (journalist), Jack McKeon (pro baseball manager), Patrick Singleton (Olympic bobsledder), Kenneth Utt (film producer, actor)

Preparation for Life

Four undergraduate colleges make up Elon: the School of Education, the School of Communications, the Love School of Business, and the College of Arts and Sciences. The university offers 50 majors, the most popular of which include communications, business, educations, and biology. All freshmen must take the four First Year Core courses—College Writing, the Global Experience, Contemporary Wellness Issues, and General Statistics. Additionally, students must complete eight semester hours in subject areas such as expression, civilization, society, and science. Winter Term gives students an opportunity to do four weeks of concentrated study between semesters. On campus, students choose from an array courses, including the Business of NASCAR and Wealth and Poverty. But many students elect to study off campus, participating in such programs as Astronomy in Mexico and Ghana: West African History and Culture. Outside-of-the-classroom learning is encouraged.

Phoenix Rising

For many years, Elon's athletic teams went by the moniker "the Fighting Christians." As the university has grown, so too has its diversity, and in 1999 university president Leo Lambert led the effort to change the mascot to reflect the diverse faiths practiced on campus. The new mascot? A Phoenix—fitting for a university that in 1923 was ravaged by a devastating fire and managed to recover and thrive.

About 80 percent of students participate in internships and 70 percent study abroad, while others find service learning and leadership opportunities through the Kernodle Center for Service Learning and the Center for Leadership.

Leading the Way

The student vibe at Elon can be decidedly preppy, but that's changing as the student body continues to expand in size. Residential options include traditional dorms, such as the all-women West Hall; co-ed apartment-style suits at the Jordan Center; and theme housing, such as the Isabella Cannon International Studies Pavilion for students majoring in international studies or foreign languages. Among the myriad student organizations are ten fraternities, 11 sororities, 16 Division I athletic teams, and ESTV, the campus television station. Leadership opportunities abound, including serving as a student senator or officer with the Student Government Association. The university is affiliated with the United Church of Christ, and students may attend interfaith services held at Whitely Auditorium. Those without cars can sign up with Zipcar and take advantage of wheels as needed—a real must at this suburban campus.

In Good Company

Elon's 575-acre campus is located in the small town of Elon, in North Carolina's Piedmont Region. The entire campus has been designated a botanical garden, and the grounds feature not one but *two* lakes. In 2006, the university opened a new law school, and new dining and residence halls have also recently opened. The surrounding town has several restaurants and clubs, including Morazi's Pizza and the Lighthouse, while nearby Burlington has the Paramount Theatre, the Burlington Aquatics Center, the large City Park, and the Burlington Indians, a minor league baseball team. Other academic heavy hitters, such as Duke, UNC–Chapel Hill, and Wake Forest, are all about an hour away. The closest city, Raleigh, is about an hour away by car, and Washington, D.C. is about five hours away.

Admissions

Average high school GPA:	3.9
Average freshman SAT verbal / math score:	608 / 616
Average freshman ACT score:	25
Application fee:	$40
Application deadlines:	
1/10 (freshmen)	
continuous (transfer)	
11/1 (early decision)	11/10 (early action)
Total applicants:	9,204
Total accepted:	3,838 (42%)
Total accepted who enrolled:	1,283
Notification dates:	
3/15 (freshmen)	
continuous (transfer)	
12/1 (early decision)	12/20 (early action)
Acceptance rate early action / early decision applicants:	— / 68%

Students

Percentage of male / female students:	40% / 60%
Percentage of students from out of state:	71%
Percentage of students graduating in 4 years / 6 years:	69% / 76%

Money

Total endowment:	$66,951,000
Total tuition:	$20,171
Total cost with fees & expenses:	$28,191
Average financial aid package:	$12,794
Percentage of students who sought aid and received it:	70%
Percentage of students receiving financial aid:	31%

Also Check Out

Furman University

James Madison University

North Carolina State University

University of North Carolina at Chapel Hill

Wake Forest University

Emerson College

120 Boylston Street
Boston, MA 02116

(617) 824-8500
http://www.emerson.edu/

 **BIG PLAN**

The path to stardom starts here.

5 REASONS IT'S COOL

1. **Media production is among the best** and most popular majors; with state-of-the-art equipment and well-known professors.

2. Small, creative seminars allow students to **think outside the boundaries.**

3. **Exciting study-abroad opportunities** take students to the Netherlands and Prague. Emerson also offers a program in Los Angeles.

4. Between the nightly campus events and the **bustling tempo of the city,** it's hard to get bored.

5. **Diverse extracurriculars** include two radio stations, a handful of literary magazines, and ten performance troupes.

The Basics

Public / private: private nonprofit
Total enrollment / undergrads: 4,324 / 3,402
Campus setting: urban
Students call it: Emerson
Students are called: Lions
Notable alums: Bobbi Brown (makeup artist), Spalding Gray (performance artist), Laura Kightlinger (comedienne), Denis Leary (comedian), Jay Leno (TV personality), Henry Winkler (actor)

So Many Choices

Emerson is divided into two schools, one for arts and the other for communications. Although students pick their school and major after their first year (and many come to freshman orientation knowing exactly what they want to study), they are required to take an array of classes at both schools. Double majoring is popular, as is double minoring and designing one's own major. Communications, journalism, and media studies are favorite majors. Some notoriously difficult and less popular majors are writing, theater, and communication disorders. Class size is usually under twenty-five students, and TAs are virtually nonexistent. Emerson is part of the Boston ProArts Consortium, which allows students to take classes at six other area arts schools including the School of the Museum of Fine Arts and the Massachusetts College of Art. With its emphasis on hands-on learning and internships outside of class, Emerson is dedicated to educating the next generation of artists and communications professionals.

Stagecraft and Statecraft

Theater-minded Emerson students put their training to use in 2005 when their teachers were protesting the school administration's union-busting tactics. Two students enacted a dire allegory by dressing in skeleton costumes representing miscommunication and mismanagement and toting a black coffin that signified the death of academic freedom. The protests didn't immediately produce results, but they certainly made an impression.

Glitz, Glamour, Award Shows

Emerson students tend to be political, leftist, and accepting of difference. Although gay students are a big presence on campus, students of color and lower-income students are not. There is a grain of truth in the axiom that Emerson students are predominately white and wealthy. The Greek scene is almost nonexistent, and campus life revolves around events such as poetry slams, film shoots, comedy sketches, and cocktail parties. The Evvy Awards, Emerson's Emmy-style show, is a well-attended production that attracts big-name presenters. Students who want to contend for a prize must submit their work for review by superstar professionals in the relevant field. Aside from the occasional high-glamour event, day-to-day life at Emerson matches the pace of Boston. The campus blends with the city, as Emerson tends to purchase local buildings and incorporate them into its campus. The residence halls are primarily occupied by freshmen, but it's not uncommon for upperclassmen to return to campus for parties.

I Art Boston

Situated in the heart of Boston's theater district and overlooking the Commons (a huge park), Emerson looks to the city for nightlife and vitality. On-campus facilities and dorms are also a big draw. Emerson has completed the fifteen-year project of renovating the Cutler Majestic Theater, an exquisite building that combines classical style with ornate Art Nouveau. The theater—students call it "House of Gold" because of its huge amount of gilded plasterwork—is used for student shows and outside artist performances. Emerson recently built a sleek new gym—its first indoor athletic facility—and renovated its soccer field to cater to an increase in students. For a more relaxed atmosphere, students can take the T to nearby Cambridge. Newbury Street is another popular destination for students and tourists alike, with high-end retail stores and lots of restaurants.

Admissions

Average high school GPA:	3.59
Average freshman SAT writing / math / critical reading score:	623 / 597 / 632
Average freshman ACT score:	25
Application fee:	$60

Application deadlines:
1/5 (freshmen)
3/15 (transfer)
11/1 (early action)

Total applicants:	4,849
Total accepted:	2,289 (47%)
Total accepted who enrolled:	727

Notification dates:
4/1 (freshmen)
5/1 (transfer)
12/15 (early action)

Acceptance rate for early action applicants:	55%

Students

Percentage of male / female students:	45% / 55%
Percentage of students from out of state:	63%
Percentage of students graduating in 4 years / 6 years:	66% / 70%

Money

Total endowment:	$85,000,000
Total tuition:	$25,248
Total cost with fees & expenses:	$37,484
Average financial aid package:	$13,777
Percentage of students who sought aid and received it:	67%
Percentage of students receiving financial aid:	48%

Also Check Out

Boston University

Ithaca College

New York University

Syracuse University

University of Southern California

Emory University

1380 South Oxford Road Atlanta, GA 30322	(404) 727-6123 http://www.emory.edu/

 **BIG BRAIN**    **BIG RESEARCH**

Ivy-caliber education, minus the down coat

5 REASONS IT'S COOL

1. Emory's **endowment of $4.3 billion** is the country's seventh largest.

2. You don't have to be loaded to attend: **Emory Advantage reduces loans** for students from families with annual incomes of $100,000 or less.

3. With a **7:1 student-to-faculty ratio,** students really get to know their profs.

4. With one of the country's largest student populations, **Atlanta is a great college town.**

5. Get some real-world experience: Nearly **90 percent of students intern or conduct research** while in college.

The Basics

Public / private: private religious
Total enrollment / undergrads: 12,338 / 6,646
Campus setting: suburban
Students call it: Emory
Students are called: Eagles
Notable alums: Kenneth Cole (fashion designer), Glenda Hatchett (judge), Lucius Quintus Cincinnatus Lamar II (politician, U.S. Supreme Court justice), Sam Nunn (businessman, senator)

The Healing Sciences and More

Emory is home to some of the country's brightest students and most notable profs. Professors push students to the limit but are also accessible and open. Few of the predominantly discussion-oriented classes are taught by TAs, and students find ample opportunities to join faculty on research projects. Emory's Nursing and Business schools are two of the country's top institutes in their respective fields, but that's not to say the options are limited to those programs. Students choose from over seventy majors and fifty-five minors, including ten four-year combined bachelor's/master's programs and nine pre-professional programs. Emory encourages students to hold off on declaring a major until the end of their sophomore year. That extra time can be used to sample the school's fantastic offerings—and maybe even try out an internship or study-abroad program—before making a commitment.

Every Eagle Needs a Black Knight

Dooley is a black-clad skeleton with origins dating back to 1899. He is the unofficial mascot of Emory. During Dooley's Week, an annual spring event, the cavorting cadaver roams the campus accompanied by bodyguards, making unscheduled appearances in classrooms and asking profs to release their students. At week's end, all convene on McDonough Field for Dooley's Ball, a costume party with dancing and spirits of the liquid kind.

Debating and Volunteering

While the stereotypical Emory student is a wealthy northerner or local southerner, the campus actually has a surprising amount of diversity. Emory Advantage, the financial aid program that aims to make education accessible to a range of students, promotes economic diversity on campus. Students are known to engage in healthy debates about ethnic, racial, political, and religious issues outside of the classroom. Greek life is a big campus draw, but there are plenty of options for students who don't want to rush. When they're not studying in the library or under a tree on the tranquil campus, nearly 80 percent of Eagles volunteer on campus and off. Among the over three hundred campus organizations are several popular student publications and nationally recognized chess and debate teams. Intramural sports are also extremely popular, in part because the school's Division III athletics program doesn't include a football team.

Big City Sanctuary

Location is one of Emory's biggest selling points. Situated in Atlanta's Druid Hills neighborhood, the 635-acre campus feels hidden away from the rest of the world. The gorgeous buildings are made of Georgia marble and terracotta tile, and the red and orange leaves on the deciduous trees make for a postcard-ready scene come autumn. Students frequent the local shops and trendy restaurants and cafés. Those in need of debauchery can always find a Greek party or two. While campus may feel like a remote sanctuary, all the riches of downtown Atlanta are a fifteen-minute bus ride away. Some students go to concerts or Atlanta Braves games, but most head straight for the neighborhood of Buckhead, where hip clubs and great restaurants cement Atlanta's reputation as one of the country's best college towns.

Admissions

Average high school GPA:	3.7
Average freshman SAT writing / math / critical reading score:	664 / 689 / 661
Average freshman ACT score:	26
Application fee:	$50

Application deadlines:
1/15 (freshmen)
6/1 (transfer)
11/1 (early decision)

Total applicants:	14,222
Total accepted:	4,535 (32%)
Total accepted who enrolled:	1,665

Notification dates:
4/1 (freshmen)
continuous (transfer)
12/15 (early decision)

Acceptance rate for early decision applicants:	60%

Students

Percentage of male / female students:	43% / 57%
Percentage of students from out of state:	71%
Percentage of students graduating in 4 years / 6 years:	84% / 89%

Money

Total endowment:	$4,294,967,295
Total tuition:	$33,900
Total cost with fees & expenses:	$45,356
Average financial aid package:	$27,971
Percentage of students who sought aid and received it:	100%
Percentage of students receiving financial aid:	38%

Also Check Out

Duke University

Northwestern University

University of Pennsylvania

Vanderbilt University

Washington University in St. Louis

Eugene Lang College, The New School for Liberal Arts

65 West 11th Street
New York, NY 10011

(212) 229-5600
http://www.lang.edu/

**BIG
IDEA**

Out with the old, in with the New

5 REASONS IT'S COOL

1. **Independent thinkers** will love Lang's academic freedom, interdisciplinary studies, and nontraditional teaching methods.

2. You'll find top-notch programs in the **social sciences, writing, and the arts**.

3. Forget large lectures; **classes are capped at eighteen**.

4. This **most urban of all urban campuses** is set in the heart of Greenwich Village.

5. Students at this rapidly growing school have **unique access to internships**.

The Basics

Public / private: private nonprofit
Total enrollment / undergrads: 1,164 / 1,164
Campus setting: urban
Students call it: Lang
Notable alums: Ani DiFranco (singer-songwriter), Elisa Donovan (actress), Mike Doughty (singer-songwriter), Emily Gould (editor, Gawker)

The Lang Way

Lang is one of the eight colleges that make up the New School. Although Lang is small, its academic freedoms and Manhattan location confer huge benefits. Incoming freshmen are required to take courses to help them adjust to college/city life, including Writing the Essay, Reading NYC, and an Advising Seminar taught by their faculty mentor. After that, they are free to design their own course of study in one of twelve areas. In the seminar-style courses, lively discussion and debate are encouraged. Nontraditional learning is embraced, and students are encouraged to think critically and examine issues from the standpoint of political and social justice. Advising is taken seriously, and students get plenty of guidance. Instruction varies in quality. While Lang's location ensures that some profs are esteemed scholars, writers, or artists, the turnover rate is high. Students may take classes at any of the New School's eight schools, and Lang's shared libraries with Cooper Union and New York University provide access to over 3.3 million volumes. This college emphasizes putting knowledge into practice, allowing students to enroll in experiential courses that send them out into the world, as well as offering a host of

Bright, Shiny, and Growing

The New School really is new! The Eugene Lang College was found in 1985 with the help of a generous donation from the eponymous philanthropist.

coveted internships at places like Random House, Comedy Central, or the UN Relief Work Agency. Study-abroad options include short courses in South Africa, Sri Lanka, Scotland, and Germany, and semesters in places like Paris, Bermuda, Amsterdam, and Florence. Lang also has an exchange program with nearby Sarah Lawrence College.

To Do, or . . . to Do?

Lang's campus, which consists of several buildings scattered around Greenwich Village, is just a few blocks from Union Square and Washington Square Park. Three dorms are situated close to the academic buildings, and space is guaranteed for freshmen. Upperclassmen, however, may have to find housing in New York, which is no mean feat. There's a surfeit of stuff to do at this school. From live music to readings to political rallies to nightclubs, the list goes on and on. Lang In The City offers students discounted tickets to film, art, and dance events, and the Outdoor and Wellness program has courses in yoga, mural painting, and marathon running, among others. Beyond that, though, there aren't many organized extracurriculars, so independence is key. Most students are attracted to Lang precisely because it's a place for self-sufficient urbanites and liberal hipsters. When they're not hanging out on the steps of the Lang building on 11th Street, this diverse, progressive student body can be found in the clubs and cafés of the West Village taking in all that New York City has to offer.

Small School, Big City

Lang is located in downtown Manhattan. If you're envisioning skyscrapers, revise your mental image. The building that houses most of the classrooms sits on a lovely tree-lined street far from the hustle of Times Square and midtown. Much of the learning experience at Lang occurs outside the classroom, both because the administration encourages it and because it could hardly be otherwise in this zippy city. Students are bound to learn life lessons just by cruising around Greenwich Village, a vibrant hub of nightlife, music, gay pride, historic buildings, and restaurants. New York University and Cooper Union are close by, and students often mingle at the same bars or cafés. For students who want an urban college experience, Lang couldn't be better situated.

Admissions

Average high school GPA:	3.22
Average freshman SAT writing / math / critical reading score:	607 / 562 / 616
Average freshman ACT score:	24
Application fee:	$50

Application deadlines:
2/1 (freshmen)
5/15 (transfer)
11/15 (early decision)

Total applicants:	1,458
Total accepted:	960 (66%)
Total accepted who enrolled:	283

Notification dates:
4/1 (freshmen)
6/1 (transfer)
12/15 (early decision)

Acceptance rate for early decision applicants: 81%

Students

Percentage of male / female students:	32% / 68%
Percentage of students from out of state:	71%
Percentage of students graduating in 4 years / 6 years:	38% / 50%

Money

Total endowment:	—
Total tuition:	$28,600
Total cost with fees & expenses:	$43,010
Average financial aid package:	$19,478
Percentage of students who sought aid and received it:	80%
Percentage of students receiving financial aid:	59%

Also Check Out

Bard College

Hampshire College

New York University

Reed College

Sarah Lawrence College

The Evergreen State College

2700 Evergreen Parkway, NW
Olympia, WA 98505

(360) 867-6000
http://www.evergreen.edu/

 **BIG IDEA**

 **BIG PERSPECTIVE**

 **BIG WORLD**

Forget everything you know about what college is supposed to be like.

5 REASONS IT'S COOL

1. **No majors? No grades? No kidding!** Evergreen's wholly unique approach to academics allows students to create their own courses of study.

2. **Radicals R Us:** students tend to be **passionate, eco-friendly activists.**

3. Set among fir trees and bordering Puget Sound, the thousand-acre campus doubles as an **outdoor laboratory for environment students.**

4. Many students take their **learning outside of the classroom** through internships, community service, or study abroad.

5. Olympia, **a small, hip city with a cool music and arts scene,** is just six miles away.

The Basics

Public / private: public state
Total enrollment / undergrads: 4,416 / 4,124
Campus setting: rural
Students call it: Evergreen, TESC
Students are called: Greeners, Geoducks (a species of massive clam)
Notable alums: Lynda Barry (cartoonist), Carrie Brownstein (musician), Matt Groening (cartoonist), Benjamin Hoff (writer), Bruce Paritt (founder, Sub Pop Records), Christine Quinn-Brintnall (judge), Michael Richards (actor)

Unique Academics for Unique Students

Evergreen offers perhaps one of the most unusual academic programs of any public college or university in the country: Rather than individual classes, the college has coordinated studies programs, in which students examine one theme, event, or phenomenon through several disciplines. For example, students in Art's Sources spend one quarter reading literature about art and one quarter creating their own art in the fine metals studio. The two-quarter program Consuming Utopia: From Wilderness to Wal-Mart draws on readings from philosophy, film studies, and history to examine the idea of "utopia." Rather than offering majors, students customize their coursework through "learning contracts," drawn up with the assistance of faculty members and often involving internships and study abroad. At the end of each quarter, students get written feedback from professors (not letter grades). Faculty members offer lots of advising and stress the educational opportunities found beyond the confines of the classroom. Evergreen's campus,

Lettin' It All Hang Out

Evergreen's unofficial motto is *Omnia Extares*, which translates loosely to "Let It All Hang Out." Students live by the motto every June, when members of the graduating class take part in the Mud Bay Run—some clothed, some not.

located right on Puget Sound, is a veritable outdoor laboratory for the college's strong environmental studies program; media arts is also popular. For students ready to take on the responsibilities of academic freedom, Evergreen can provide an education like no other.

Keen to Be Green

Although students resist the label, Evergreen has a reputation for being a haven for "pot-smoking hippies." While it's true that many students do, in fact, inhale, Evergreen is by no means a party school, and there are plenty of other social options available. About 40 percent of students are over twenty-five, and about 70 percent are Washingtonians. Social activism abounds in this eco-friendly crowd, and students often pass protests or petition gatherers on their way to class. While liberal ideals prevail on campus, to feel at home the main requirement is having an open mind. Housing options include traditional dorms and apartment-style housing on the north end of campus. Freshman can elect to live in theme areas, such as Community Action House. Evergreen recognizes more than fifty student organizations—from the Electronic Music Collective to the Chemistry Club.

The Heart of the Pacific Northwest

Evergreen's secluded campus is set in a lovely fir forest about six miles outside of Olympia. Campus highlights include a student-run organic farm, 3,300 feet of undeveloped Puget Sound beach, and Seminar II, a "green" educational and arts complex and the newest building on campus by about thirty years. Olympia, a small city of about 45,000, is home to a lively alternative music, art, and theater scene. Old-growth forests, wildlife refuges, Mt. St. Helens, and Olympic National Park are all close by, and on a clear day, Mt. Rainer is visible in the distance. Hiking, biking, and skiing are all accessible, and Seattle is only a one-hour drive away.

Admissions

Average high school GPA:	3.07
Average freshman SAT verbal / math score:	592 / 537
Average freshman ACT score:	23
Application fee:	$50
Application deadlines: continuous (freshmen) continuous (transfer)	
Total applicants:	1,602
Total accepted:	1,525 (95%)
Total accepted who enrolled:	578
Notification dates: 12/1 (freshmen) 4/1 (transfer)	

Students

Percentage of male / female students:	45% / 55%
Percentage of students from out of state:	23%
Percentage of students graduating in 4 years / 6 years:	42% / 56%

Money

Total endowment:	$2,395,656
Total in-state tuition, fees & expenses:	$12,925
Total out-of-state tuition, fees & expenses:	$23,116
Average financial aid package:	$11,066
Percentage of students who sought aid and received it:	81%
Percentage of students receiving financial aid:	51%

Also Check Out

Hampshire College

Reed College

Sarah Lawrence College

University of Oregon

University of Puget Sound

Fairfield University

1073 North Benson Road
Fairfield, CT 06824

(203) 254-4000
http://www.fairfield.edu/

 **BIG PERSPECTIVE**

 **BIG WORLD**

An up-and-comer on the Sound

5 REASONS IT'S COOL

1. **Individualized instruction** is a priority at Fairfield, where **TAs do not exist.**

2. **Study abroad** is an increasingly integral part of the Fairfield experience.

3. The **Jesuit members of the faculty**, known for being wonderful teachers and advisors, enrich the academic and personal lives of students of all faiths.

4. **These kids know how to party.** From small apartment gatherings to enormous bashes on the beach, students enjoy their free time.

5. **Campus is gorgeous**, immaculately maintained, and located smack dab in the middle of the East Coast corridor.

The Basics

Public / private: private religious

Total enrollment / undergrads: 5,091 / 4,008

Campus setting: suburban

Students call it: Fairfield

Students are called: Stags

Notable alums: Larry Bossidy Jr. (pro baseball player), E. Gerald Corrigan (president, Federal Reserve Bank of New York), Jeff Campbell (CEO, Burger King), William Egan (founder, Alta Communications), Joe DeVito (comedian), Alexandra McHale (comedienne)

Low-Key Smarts

Fairfield students belong to one of three undergraduate schools: Arts & Sciences, Business, or Nursing. The core curriculum includes five components: science and math; history and social science; philosophy, religion, and ethics; literature and performance; and foreign language. Professors are known for being demanding but also friendly and helpful. As for the students, they're bright but not aggressively brainy or overly competitive. Impressive merit scholarships are available for top incoming freshman, and students who prove they've got the goods during their first year are invited to design their own majors and/or join the honors program as sophomores. All classes are capped at fifty students, and there are no teaching assistants. Study abroad, with a hundred programs in fifty countries, is a large and growing draw. Professors organize short academic trips during January term, spring break, and summer vacations, so travel can be a part of the Fairfield experience even for students

Fighting for Their Right

Long the most popular annual event at Fairfield, the Clam Jam was permanently cancelled in 2001 when neighbors of the school complained that the weekend-long April beach festival made their lives essentially unlivable. Fairfield students went down fighting: It took a temporary injunction to bring the Jam to a halt.

who don't want to leave campus for a full year or semester. Meanwhile, the administration has been working to cultivate international relationships for Fairfield's at-home departments. The Irish studies program has strong ties to the University of Galway, for example, while Italian studies is linked with the Florence University of the Arts.

Cups Up

Fairfield's unofficial nickname is J. Crew U, and as hard as it's tried, the administration can't get the minority population over 10 percent. In the near term, therefore, incoming freshmen should expect to find plenty of affluent white kids in country-club-ready attire. Students put up with hit-or-miss housing options for three years in the hope that, as seniors, they will be rewarded with a berth on the Beach, a four-mile strip of rental houses looking out on Long Island Sound. Boozing is big time at Fairfield, and the Beach is the epicenter of the debauchery. The Student Association has been working hard to provide nonalcoholic programming on the weekends—think movies, comedians, and bowling. Intramurals are popular, but the intercollegiate teams aren't a big deal. Football, formerly the marquee varsity sport, is now, for budgetary reasons, a club team. The transition has put a bit of a damper on school spirit. School pride remains intact, though: Fairfield's students believe they are among the best-looking undergrads in America.

Beautiful and in the Right Place

Fairfield spends enormous sums of money to make sure the buildings and grounds are as pretty as the students are. There's lots of landscaping, and the architecture is a mixture of college Gothic, English manor, and modern. Town-gown relations are rough around the edges, due mostly to the concrete-cracking noise emanating from the Beach three nights a week. Fairfield is a wealthy town, which can be intimidating for some Stags, but those on a budget will have plenty of options. The nearby city of Bridgeport is definitely less rarified. It's here that Fairfield students do most of their volunteering and community-service work. New York is ninety minutes down the road, Boston two hours in the other direction.

Admissions

Average high school GPA:	3.47
Average freshman SAT verbal / math score:	588 / 603
Average freshman ACT score:	—
Application fee:	$55
Application deadlines: 1/15 (freshmen) 5/1 (transfer) — (early decision)	
Total applicants:	8,035
Total accepted:	4,866 (61%)
Total accepted who enrolled:	899
Notification dates: 4/1 (freshmen) continuous (transfer) — (early decision)	
Acceptance rate for early decision applicants:	72%

Students

Percentage of male / female students:	43% / 57%
Percentage of students from out of state:	80%
Percentage of students graduating in 4 years / 6 years:	79% / 81%

Money

Total endowment:	$209,283,000
Total tuition:	$31,450
Total cost with fees & expenses:	$42,435
Average financial aid package:	$19,101
Percentage of students who sought aid and received it:	66%
Percentage of students receiving financial aid:	42%

Also Check Out

Boston College

Fordham University

Loyola College in Maryland

Providence College

Villanova University

Florida Agricultural and Mechanical University

400 Lee Hall Drive
Tallahassee, FL 32307

(850) 599-3000
http://www.famu.edu/

 **BIG CHOICE**

Is FAMU for you?

5 REASONS IT'S COOL

1. Students rave about the **warm, approachable admissions staff**, who truly put applicants' interests above the bottom line.

2. Test your standup routine or vocal stylings on **the Stoop, FAMU's version of the Apollo Theater.**

3. With state-of-the-art, campuswide wireless coverage, your **online research will be blazingly fast.**

4. The renowned marching band, **the Marching lOO,** really turns it out at football games.

5. The **student/teacher exchange with China** is the first of its kind among historically black colleges and universities.

The Basics

Public / private: public state
Total enrollment / undergrads: 13,064 / 10,576
Campus setting: urban
Students call it: Florida A&M, Florida A&M University, FAMU (rhymes with "Shamu")
Students are called: Rattlers
Notable alums: Cannonball Adderley (musician), Common (rapper), Kim Godwin (broadcast news director), Marquis Grissom (pro baseball player), T'Keyah Crystal Keymah (actress), Kwame Kilpatrick (mayor, Detroit), Pam Oliver (sports anchor)

Nationally Renowned, Yet Friendly

In 1997, *Time* magazine named FAMU College of the Year, an honor it richly deserves. The university attracts National Achievement scholars in numbers that rival Harvard's. It has also granted more diplomas to African American scholars than has any other college in the nation. Academic standards are high, but students are relieved to find their professors accommodating. While the 22:1 student-faculty ratio is less than intimate, FAMU's commitment to its students is a point of pride for administrators and alums. The university has particularly strong programs in architecture, the allied health sciences, education, engineering, and journalism. The most popular majors are in business and pharmacy (also strong programs). While campus facilities have been modernized for the twenty-first century, the administration is less tech friendly: Students complain about the impenetrable bureaucracy.

Band on the Run

FAMU's renowned Marching 100 band has often found itself in the national and international spotlight. The 100 performed with Kanye West and Jamie Foxx during the 2006 Grammy Awards show and with Prince during the Super Bowl XLI halftime show. In 1989, they represented the United States during the commemoration ceremony of France's Bastille Day bicentennial.

Not Easily Rattled

While cross-town rival FSU may have a monopoly on Tallahasseans' football loyalties, the Rattlers enjoy rabid popularity among FAMU faithful, especially since the recent upgrade to Division I-A status has brought stiffer competition and a higher profile. For socializing, students often frequent area clubs as an alternative to the typical Greek-dominated party scene. Although the university has experienced record-breaking growth in the past two decades, students describe the student body as a close-knit community of diverse personalities and diverse interests. That, however, is about as far as diversity goes at FAMU; originally founded as State Normal College for Colored Students, the student body is overwhelmingly African American and overwhelmingly native Floridian. Hispanics, whites, and Asians make up the 2 percent of the remaining student body. Students generally approve of campus culture and amenities, although some complain that student union food could use some improvement, despite the several fast-food options available.

FAMU Fab (and Drab)

The Tallahassee ZIP code forces FAMU to often play David to Florida State's Goliath, whose high-achieving men's football and basketball teams claim the lion's share of fan and media attention. In terms of real estate, however, FAMU has got it pretty good. Perched atop the highest hill in Tallahassee, the sprawling campus covers 419 acres. Prospective Rattlers, however, are advised to bring wheels. Despite being the state capital, FAMU's hometown elicits a lukewarm response from students, who take every occasion they can to get out of town. Residence halls are generally lackluster, particularly the notoriously bug-infested Palmetto North and Paddyfoote Hall, which students often describe as "straight ghetto." Gibbs and McGuinn halls fair better in the estimation of former residents, but many Famuans opt for off-campus housing.

Admissions

Average high school GPA:	3.18
Average freshman SAT verbal / math score:	486 / 485
Average freshman ACT score:	20
Application fee:	$20
Application deadlines:	
5/9 (freshmen)	
5/1 (transfer)	
Total applicants:	5,709
Total accepted:	4,029 (71%)
Total accepted who enrolled:	1,973
Notification dates:	
8/1 (freshmen)	
8/1 (transfer)	

Students

Percentage of male / female students:	43% / 57%
Percentage of students from out of state:	20%
Percentage of students graduating in 4 years / 6 years:	15% / 63%

Money

Total endowment:	—
Total in-state tuition, fees & expenses:	$10,630
Total out-of-state tuition, fees & expenses:	$21,984
Average financial aid package:	$8,353
Percentage of students who sought aid and received it:	69%
Percentage of students receiving financial aid:	79%

Also Check Out

Florida State University

Howard University

Morehouse College

Spelman College

Florida State University

282 Champions Way
Tallahassee, FL 32306

(850) 644-2525
http://www.fsu.edu/

BIG CHOICE

Books, beer, and bowl bids

5 REASONS IT'S COOL

1. Think you're the next Coppola or Kubrick? FSU's **School of Motion Picture, Television, and Recording Arts is consistently rated among the best** in the nation.

2. **Seminoles football sends students on the warpath—** especially when it comes time to battle the Gators!

3. **High-tech amenities saturate the campus:** Round-the-clock computer labs and eight campus libraries serve every research need.

4. Campus life is **decidedly laid-back.**

5. The student body generates **legendary amounts of school spirit.**

The Basics

Public / private: public state
Total enrollment / undergrads: 39,973 / 31,347
Campus setting: suburban
Students call it: Florida State, FSU
Students are called: Seminoles, 'Noles
Notable alums: Alan Ball (screenwriter), Sam Beam (musician), Lee Corso (sports broadcaster), Meg Crofton (president, Walt Disney World Resort), Neil Frank (meteorologist), Tony La Russa (pro baseball coach), Christine Lahti (actress), Burt Reynolds (actor), Richard Simmons (fitness guru)

From Silver Screen to Specimen Slide

FSU's standout School of Motion Picture, Television, and Recording Arts has won accolades for its excellent faculty and state-of-the-art amenities. As you might expect, gaining entrance to the program is highly competitive. But film isn't the only thing that FSU does well: Its programs in English, engineering, and fine arts put in strong showings year in and year out. The sciences have also been coming on of late, biology being especially well regarded. But as a large state school, FSU presents the typical large-state-school pitfalls. The student-to-faculty ratio is an impersonal 22:1, and many courses are of the big-lecture variety. Professors labor under the often-competing obligations of teaching and research, and the administration confronts students with a bureaucracy some describe as Byzantine. All of these factors may leave a lone 'Nole feeling lost in the shuffle. The onus is on the students to find their place and strike a balance between studying and partying.

Chopping Mad

The "war chant" and accompanying "tomahawk chop" may have been popularized by the Atlanta Braves and Kansas City Chiefs, but their origins are pure FSU. Meant to demoralize visitors and spur the home team on to victory, the chop and chant have been criticized by some Native American groups. Still, the Seminole Tribe of Florida supports the university, and FSU's Seminole tradition remains strong.

You Can't Fall off the Floor

At FSU, partying is a serious pursuit. The school is a perennial contender in *Playboy*'s party school rundown, and campus shindigs tend to be Greek dominated and football oriented. Seminoles consecrate home games with beer kegs in defiance of the campus's official dry status. Such conspicuous displays of consumption aside, the sun-kissed students are a self-professed laid-back and conservative bunch, which is perhaps a reflection of the fact that 93 percent are Florida-grown. Two-thirds of the student population is white, with blacks and Latinos comprising the two most represented minorities. A small miscellany of international students round out the figures. Campus amenities vary, and seasoned 'Noles advise incoming freshmen to stick to dorms on the campus's east side and avoid Dorman, Deviney, Smith, Kellum, and Salley Halls. The pricey meal plan is mandatory for students living in residence halls.

A Seminole Influence

Situated on the outskirts of Tallahassee, less than an hour from the Gulf Coast, FSU offers a small-town pace with big-city resources. Students find such living generally agreeable but are often eager to go off the reservation, enjoying spring break capitals such as Panama City or celebrating Mardi Gras in New Orleans. But Seminole fever infects students and townies alike, and relations between FSU and its host city are generally friendly. Although the student body is large, the campus is a compact 451 acres. There is a dearth of parking options, and the residence halls vary in quality. These hassles are offset by the palpable school spirit pervading the student body, largely a result of the shared passion for football and its attendant festivities.

Admissions

Average high school GPA:	3.62
Average freshman SAT writing / math / critical reading score:	560 / 593 / 586
Average freshman ACT score:	24
Application fee:	$30
Application deadlines:	
2/14 (freshmen)	
7/1 (transfer)	
Total applicants:	23,687
Total accepted:	14,027 (59%)
Total accepted who enrolled:	6,176
Notification dates:	
3/28 (freshmen)	
7/15 (transfer)	

Students

Percentage of male / female students:	43% / 57%
Percentage of students from out of state:	12%
Percentage of students graduating in 4 years / 6 years:	42% / 65%

Money

Total endowment:	$463,179,746
Total in-state tuition, fees & expenses:	$11,385
Total out-of-state tuition, fees & expenses:	$24,517
Average financial aid package:	$8,890
Percentage of students who sought aid and received it:	67%
Percentage of students receiving financial aid:	26%

Also Check Out

University of California–Los Angeles

University of Central Florida

University of Florida

University of Georgia

The University of Miami

Fordham University

441 East Fordham Road
New York, NY 10458

(718) 817-1000
http://www.fordham.edu/

 BIG JOB

 **BIG PERSPECTIVE**

Where education and character meet

5 REASONS IT'S COOL

1. Fordham's **five under-graduate colleges** give students plenty of academic options.

2. The university is spread across three campuses in **Manhattan, Little Italy in the Bronx, and suburban Tarrytown.**

3. **Internship opportunities abound** thanks to the university's connections to over 2,600 corporations and agencies.

4. The university's Jesuit roots mean students are encouraged to **develop mentally, physically, and spiritually.**

5. Fordham's **twenty-two Division I athletic teams** always draw huge crowds.

The Basics

Public / private: private religious
Total enrollment / undergrads: 14,732 / 7,701
Campus setting: urban
Students call it: Fordham
Students are called: Rams
Notable alums: Alan Alda (actor), Mary Higgins Clark (writer), Geraldine Ferraro (congresswoman), Denzel Washington (actor)

Four Colleges, One Serious Education

One of the country's leading Jesuit universities, Fordham offers students a great academic experience. The student-to-faculty ratio is just 11:1, and 95 percent of the 645-member faculty holds terminal degrees in their fields. Incoming freshmen enroll in one of four undergraduate colleges: Fordham College at Rose Hill, the College of Business Administration, Fordham College at Lincoln Center, and Fordham College of Liberal Studies. While these colleges vary widely in focus, all of them offer a solid liberal arts education centered on a common core curriculum of seventeen to twenty courses. Students have a wide range of majors to choose from, everything from business administration to theater to dance. The university provides a wide range of partnership programs with high-profile facilities in New York City. Dance majors work with professionals at the internationally recognized Alvin Ailey American Dance Theatre; engineering students take courses at Columbia University or Case Western Reserve University; and future business leaders enjoy university-sponsored breakfasts at the New

Fordham Stories

The Reverend John Hughes, founder of the college that became Fordham, was nicknamed "Dagger John," which is also the name of a campus pub named after him. Edgar Allen Poe spent a lot of time on campus, and it's said that his poem "The Bells" was inspired by the university church bell. On a more modern note, several film crews have filmed on campus. Look for Fordham buildings in *Love Story*, *A Beautiful Mind*, and *The Exorcist*.

York offices of current CEOs. Top-notch on-campus resources include the Center for Entrepreneurship, the National Principal's Leadership Institute, the Center for Ethics Education, the Center on European Union Law, and the Donald McGannon Communication Research Center.

A Clean, Well-Lighted Place

Fordham sponsors over 130 different student groups, including theater groups, media organizations, and musical troupes. The four campus libraries, with their combined 2.5 million books, are one of the university's most valuable assets. There is little to no Greek presence on campus. There is some rivalry between residential and commuter students, but many students say there is a feeling of cohesion despite the fact that not all undergrads live in the same place. One factor that unites these students: an impulse toward community service. Many undergrads get involved with on- and off-campus projects. Global Outreach, a group concerned with social justice, sponsors trips to places as close as New Orleans and as far away as India.

New York, New York

Gothic architecture and cobblestone streets offer a classic college atmosphere nestled in the heart of one of the world's most adventuresome and modern cities. Rose Hill in the Bronx is the oldest campus. Just outside of the gates is Belmont's Arthur Avenue, otherwise known as the Bronx's Little Italy. You'll also find the Bronx Zoo, the New York Botanical Garden, and the Enrico Fermi Cultural Center. For commuters, parking is a cinch. There are two safe, well-lit lots at the main university entrance. Lincoln Center is on the Upper West Side of Manhattan, where students can soak up all the culture they can without straying more than a few blocks from their dorms. The Marymount campus in Tarrytown, established in 2002, lies just twenty-five miles from New York City. While campus food isn't the greatest, that hardly matters when the best restaurants in the world are on your doorstep.

Admissions

Average high school GPA:	3.7
Average freshman SAT writing / math / critical reading score:	593 / 604 / 610
Average freshman ACT score:	25
Application fee:	$50
Application deadlines: 1/15 (freshmen) 7/1 (transfer) 11/1 (early action)	
Total applicants:	18,161
Total accepted:	8,449 (47%)
Total accepted who enrolled:	1,702
Notification dates: 4/1 (freshmen) continuous (transfer) 12/25 (early action)	
Acceptance rate for early action applicants:	51%

Students

Percentage of male / female students:	42% / 58%
Percentage of students from out of state:	45%
Percentage of students graduating in 4 years / 6 years:	72% / 78%

Money

Total endowment:	$357,342,000
Total tuition:	$30,000
Total cost with fees & expenses:	$43,085
Average financial aid package:	$19,953
Percentage of students who sought aid and received it:	77%
Percentage of students receiving financial aid:	56%

Also Check Out

Boston College

Fairfield University

Georgetown University

Loyola University

Franklin & Marshall College

PO Box 3003
Lancaster, PA 17604

(717) 291-3911
http://www.fandm.edu/

 **BIG HAND**

 **BIG PERSPECTIVE**

Science, studying, and some relaxing

5 REASONS IT'S COOL

1. Poetic physicists are welcome! **Many students double major**, often in widely disparate fields.

2. Unpoetic physicists are welcome too! The college has made its name from its **rigorous natural science programs.**

3. 115. That's how many **clubs and organizations** you, as a Fummer, will be able to choose from.

4. Beer or soda? It's your call. **Weekend life is vibrant for drinkers and nondrinkers alike.**

5. Lancaster, a surprisingly with-it town, is surrounded by **miles of rolling hills and countryside** perfect for short trips and hikes.

The Basics

Public / private: private nonprofit
Total enrollment / undergrads: 2,028 / 2,028
Campus setting: suburban
Students call it: Franklin & Marshall
Students are called: Dips, Fummers
Notable alums: James Lapine (playwright), Ken Mehlman (campaign manager for George W. Bush), Franklin Schaffner (film director), Spliff Star (rapper), Major Dick Winters (U.S. Army)

Down to a Science, and Then Some

Franklin & Marshall has long emphasized the strength of its science programs, and these remain its top departments. The pre-med track is very popular and very difficult. Those who do survive the pre-med gauntlet are accepted to med school at above-average rates. F&M isn't only about calculators and test tubes, however. Popular nonscience majors include psychology and politics, and research opportunities are available across the academic spectrum, from literature to chemistry. In every department, accessibility is the name of the game. The student-professor ratio is 10:1, lectures only very rarely have more than fifty students, and faculty are known for inviting small groups of students over for home-cooked meals. Ninety percent of students participate in the First Year Seminar program, in which clusters of sixteen students live and study together, examining a broad theme through a handful of interdisciplinary classes.

Clubbing on the Weekends

The list of Franklin & Marshall's student clubs proves that students do, eventually, stop studying and relax—in some charmingly unusual ways. In addition to the old standards, you'll find the African Drumming Club, the Anime Club, the Dance Dance Revolution Club, and the Toastmasters Club.

See You in the Library

Minorities constitute about 10 percent of the population at Franklin & Marshall, and a growing contingent of Fummers defies easy classification. Still, it's fair to say that many of the students are preppy, white, wealthy, northeastern, and scholarly. The campus is not overly competitive, but people take their classes seriously. As a result, there's relatively little time and passion left over for the kinds of activism and high-octane political awareness that characterize many campuses. School spirit is also muted—that is, on the 364 days of the year that Franklin & Marshall is not doing battle with Dickinson for the Conestoga Wagon Trophy. Students spend any extra energy on club activities or community service in Lancaster. The annual Spring Arts festival is a marquee event, bringing concerts, art exhibits, barbecues, and a carnival atmosphere to campus. The rest of the year, the frats try to pick up the slack. Greek houses claim 35 percent of men and 15 percent of women and hold their share of enormous parties. Meanwhile, amidst concerns about binge drinking, the administration is fine-tuning its regulation of the fraternities and sororities.

Pennsylvania Farm Country

Lancaster, located in the gentle hills of Pennsylvania's Amish country, has 60,000 inhabitants, but it sits in a larger metropolitan area of around 400,000. Many Franklin & Marshall students say it's a better place to live than they expected. The city has plenty of history, and it's done a fine job of changing with the times. There are a few nightclubs and a number of excellent restaurants. Amish farmer's markets are, at least occasionally, a good source of diversion, and when the simple life grows dull, Philly and Baltimore are each an hour and a half away. The campus itself is a 125-acre collection of Gothic and colonial buildings connected by shady pathways and surrounded by a quiet residential neighborhood.

Admissions

Average high school GPA:	—
Average freshman SAT verbal / math score:	630 / 651
Average freshman ACT score:	—
Application fee:	$50

Application deadlines:
2/1 (freshmen)
5/1 (transfer)
11/15 (early decision)

Total applicants:	4,059
Total accepted:	1,853 (46%)
Total accepted who enrolled:	524

Notification dates:
4/1 (freshmen)
— (transfer)
12/15 (early decision)

Acceptance rate for early decision applicants:	72%

Students

Percentage of male / female students:	51% / 49%
Percentage of students from out of state:	66%
Percentage of students graduating in 4 years / 6 years:	75% / 82%

Money

Total endowment:	$321,074,000
Total tuition:	$34,400
Total cost with fees & expenses:	$43,640
Average financial aid package:	$26,165
Percentage of students who sought aid and received it:	96%
Percentage of students receiving financial aid:	44%

Also Check Out

Allegheny College

Bucknell University

Denison University

Dickinson College

Muhlenberg College

Furman University

3300 Poinsett Highway
Greenville, SC 29613

(864) 294-2000
http://www.furman.edu/

BIG WORLD

Want to get engaged?

5 REASONS IT'S COOL

1. **Students live what they learn** through Furman's engaged learning mission.

2. The required Cultural Life Program **keeps tabs on students' enrichment.**

3. With its Baptist heritage, Furman aims to **deepen students' faith and knowledge** at the same time.

4. Greenville's downtown and Main Street provide **student-friendly shopping, dining, and entertainment sites.**

5. Students rave about the **big and beautiful campus.**

The Basics

Public / private: private nonprofit
Total enrollment / undergrads: 3,010 / 2,759
Campus setting: suburban
Students call it: Furman
Students are called: Paladins
Notable alums: Amy Grant (musician), Herman Lay (founder, Lay's Corporation), Mark Sanford (governor, South Carolina), Charles Townes (Nobel Laureate, Physics), John B. Watson (psychologist)

Change and Time

Furman's roots lie in the Baptist tradition, and the university's current mission marries learning and faith. The school is engaged in a vigorous campaign to increase its profile beyond the South. The university's signature "engaged learning" ethos means more projects and experience-based education for its students. Forty-two majors make up the undergraduate academic offerings at Furman, where students' educations rest upon Furman's Five Pillars: active learning, research, internships, service learning, and technology. In the past, the university has been on the trimester system, but it has recently switched to two semesters plus a two-week May Experience. This new system is still being fine-tuned, but once it's in place, it will give students the same number of academic options—if not more. A healthy 11:1 student-to-faculty ratio suggests how connected professors are to their students. Many students study at international universities in yearlong programs or hold internships throughout the nation and the world.

A Stroke of Luck

In an old tradition revived in 2004, football players greet fans on the Paladin Walk before home games. The purple power is in full effect as the players prepare to take to the field. In a final display of team building, they rub the base of the Paladin Statue and "polish the diamond F" (Furman's logo) before entering the stadium.

Add It Up

Perhaps because of the emphasis on engaged learning, there's a lot of book-hitting and project-finishing going on outside of the classroom. Furman students are also required to participate in nine Cultural Life Program (CLP) events each year. The university specifies what does and does not count as a CLP event, but the basic idea behind the requirement is to engender a deeper understanding of community and culture in students. Fewer than 10 percent of students come from minority groups. Thirty-five percent of men join fraternities, and 40 percent of women join sororities—all that adds up to raging Greek parties off campus. Furman's four-year on-campus residence requirement means that 90 percent of students live in university housing. Seventeen NCAA Division I athletic teams draw crowds. Football is popular, especially when Furman plays Georgia Southern. Cheerleaders and fans yell, "FU one time, FU two times, FU three times, FU all the time!"

Just a Patch of Green

Furman is located five miles north of bustling Greenville, which boasts a charming downtown and an award-winning Main Street. The university provides shuttle service to Greenville on the weekends, providing lots of dining and entertainment options. Students can catch top music acts at the BI-LO Center in town. Furman's current campus is relatively new, although the university's history goes back to the nineteenth century. The Bell Tower, with its fifty-nine-bell Burnside Carillon, is the iconic center of campus. The sprawling 800-acre campus includes an eighteen-hole golf course, the Stone Soccer Stadium, and a thirty-acre lake. The American Society of Landscape Architects has honored the university for its lush and lovely campus.

Admissions

Average high school GPA:	3.6
Average freshman SAT verbal / math score:	642 / 645
Average freshman ACT score:	26
Application fee:	$50

Application deadlines:
1/15 (freshmen)
6/1 (transfer)
11/15 (early decision)

Total applicants:	3,887
Total accepted:	2,158 (56%)
Total accepted who enrolled:	683

Notification dates:
3/15 (freshmen)
6/15 (transfer)
12/1 (early decision)

Acceptance rate for early decision applicants:	85%

Students

Percentage of male / female students:	44% / 56%
Percentage of students from out of state:	71%
Percentage of students graduating in 4 years / 6 years:	79% / 84%

Money

Total endowment:	$478,834,000
Total tuition:	$28,352
Total cost with fees & expenses:	$37,142
Average financial aid package:	$23,132
Percentage of students who sought aid and received it:	83%
Percentage of students receiving financial aid:	39%

Also Check Out

Clemson University

Davidson College

Emory University

Sewanee: The University of the South

Vanderbilt University

George Mason University

4400 University Drive
Fairfax, VA 22030

(703) 993-1000
http://www.gmu.edu/

BIG CHOICE

Making a name for itself

5 REASONS IT'S COOL

1. Mason offers a host of **accelerated BA/MA programs** for students who want to graduate with a dual degree.

2. It's just fifteen miles from the **politics, activism, and nightlife of Washington, D.C.**

3. Students from more than 120 countries call Mason home, and **the university is proud of its ethnic diversity.**

4. The programs in **public policy and economics are renowned.**

5. Students learn from **deeply respected professors** who are leaders in their fields.

The Basics

Public / private: public state
Total enrollment / undergrads: 29,889 / 18,221
Campus setting: suburban
Students call it: GMU, Mason
Students are called: Patriots
Notable alums: Hala Gorani (CNN anchor), Jai Lewis (pro basketball player), Ryan Mulkay (actor), Debora J. Wilson (president, the Weather Channel)

Top Professors! Dual Degrees! Unique Majors!

All Mason students are required to take a core curriculum that includes classes in literature, fine arts, natural science, oral communication, and Western civilization. They can then choose from a hundred majors, including unique degree programs in neuroscience and the administration of law. Integrative studies majors enroll in the New Century College, which incorporates experiential and service learning into the academic experience. Accelerated BA/MA programs in biology, chemistry, telecommunications, and civil and infrastructure engineering, among others, allow students to earn a dual degree in only five years. Academically, Mason has taken long strides in recent years, attracting top professors from the likes of Harvard and Yale. Economics students can study with Nobel Prize–winner Vernon Smith, while the school's proximity to Washington draws important political figures in for lectures or visiting professorships. If you're wondering how to turn your big ideas into reality, try the excellent classes and resources for budding entrepreneurs.

Decorating George

GMU's namesake is George Mason, author of the Virginia Declaration of Rights and contributor to the Bill of Rights. A towering, seven-foot-tall statue of Mason stands at the center of the Fairfax campus. Students decorate him to promote events and rub his toe when they need luck before exams.

A Commuter School with Patriot Pride

At this mostly commuter campus, the majority of students drive in from the suburbs of Northern Virginia. While only around four thousand students currently live on campus, housing options are growing and now include both apartment-style housing and traditional dorms. Students from 127 countries attend Mason, and the university is known for its diversity. Students are encouraged to study abroad. There are exchange agreements with universities in Korea, Chile, Sweden, and Japan; internships in China; and a semester at Oxford University for students with high GPAs. Plenty of opportunities exist right at home as well. The university's proximity to the nation's capital means endless internships and job possibilities. Despite the commuter status of many students, there is plenty of school pride, especially for the twenty-two Division I sports teams. The men's basketball team, in particular, enjoys a lot of support, especially after rocketing from underdog status to the Final Four in 2006.

To the Nation's Capital!

Mason is split up across three campuses in Northern Virginia, a large suburban area just outside of Washington, D.C. Of the three campuses (Arlington, Fairfax, and Prince William counties), Fairfax is the biggest and is just fifteen miles from downtown D.C. The modern campus is currently undergoing quite a bit of renovation. The new Aquatics Center has state-of-the-art equipment, and there are plans in the works for a new dining hall. The Patriot Center, a large arena on campus, hosts large concerts, basketball games, and other sporting events. Most students have cars, and although they may have to fight traffic, it takes only about thirty minutes to get to the museums, music, and nightlife of D.C. Equally handy is the Mason-to-Metro Shuttle, which runs late on Friday and Saturday nights.

Admissions

Average high school GPA:	3.41
Average freshman SAT writing / math / critical reading score:	546 / 564 / 553
Average freshman ACT score:	22
Application fee:	$70
Application deadlines: 1/15 (freshmen) 3/15 (transfer)	
Total applicants:	11,015
Total accepted:	6,724 (61%)
Total accepted who enrolled:	2,414
Notification dates: 4/1 (freshmen) 4/1 (transfer)	

Students

Percentage of male / female students:	46% / 54%
Percentage of students from out of state:	12%
Percentage of students graduating in 4 years / 6 years:	33% / 52%

Money

Total endowment:	$38,000,000
Total in-state tuition, fees & expenses:	$13,968
Total out-of-state tuition, fees & expenses:	$26,112
Average financial aid package:	$8,341
Percentage of students who sought aid and received it:	69%
Percentage of students receiving financial aid:	28%

Also Check Out

American University

College of William & Mary

Drexel University

Hofstra University

University of Maryland–College Park

The George Washington University

21211 Street, NW
Washington, DC 20052

(202) 994-1000
http://www.gwu.edu/

 BIG CHOICE

 BIG JOB

Capital city campus, founding father namesake

5 REASONS IT'S COOL

1. GW's co-op program and internship opportunities allow students to **work in their prospective fields while in school.**

2. **Top-ranked programs in international affairs and business** make this a smart choice for tomorrow's global business leaders.

3. Campus is just a short distance from the **White House, National Mall, and Library of Congress.**

4. D.C. is of course **home to all things political**, but it also offers a multitude of cultural attractions.

5. GW's **seven-year Integrated BA/MD program** allows students to build a strong foundation in the liberal arts en route to an MD.

The Basics

Public / private: private nonprofit
Total enrollment / undergrads: 24,531 / 10,813
Campus setting: urban
Students call it: George Washington, GW
Students are called: Colonials
Notable alums: Courtney Cox Arquette (actress), J. Edgar Hoover (director, FBI), L. Ron Hubbard (author; founder, Scientology), Jacqueline Kennedy Onassis (former first lady), General Colin Powell (secretary of state; chairman, the Joint Chiefs of Staff), Syngman Rhee (president, South Korea), Harry Reid (senator), Chet Simmons (founder, ESPN), Kenneth Starr (lawyer), Rachel Zoe (stylist)

Academics with a Real-World Twist

Freshmen at GW choose from one of six undergraduate schools, each with its own set of general requirements, and some with as many as fifteen mandatory classes. All schools require freshmen to take a writing composition class. Social sciences, international affairs, and business are the most popular programs, but strong suits include the sciences, including astronomy, biology, and computer science. The highly selective arts and sciences honors program gives students the opportunity to enroll in special seminars and study independently with professors. The Enosinian Scholars Program prepares the most promising research-oriented undergrads for advanced study in their fields by supporting senior thesis work. The honors program in engineering offers one-on-one collaboration with professors and student-faculty

So Much for Free Pancakes

GW is not necessarily a tradition-bound school. Take Midnight Breakfast, which used to offer students free food to ease the pain of studying for finals. In the spring of 2007, Midnight Breakfast got the boot when it was deemed too costly.

research opportunities. Although the majority of classes have twenty-five students or fewer, TA-led discussions are not uncommon in large lecture courses or labs. Across the disciplines, most profs hold PhDs, and all are committed, research-oriented scholars.

A Diverse Set of Open-Minded City Slickers

GW boasts an active and political student body. Most Colonials make friends through classes or popular outside organizations. Freshmen and sophomores must live on campus, typically in one of the former hotels now converted into spacious residence halls. Students also have the option of living in one of twenty-four Living and Learning Communities, which offer field trips to places like the United Nations headquarters in New York. Securing on-campus housing after the second year can be a competitive proposition, and D.C. apartments can be cost prohibitive, leading some students to move to surrounding suburbs in Maryland and Virginia (a fifteen- to thirty-minute subway ride away). Although students complain about the lack of healthy eating options, the debit card meal plan provides some flexibility. As for sports, basketball games are popular, but don't expect much in the way of athletics.

Capital City, Capital Times

As the extravagant, multimillion-dollar buildings and state-of-the-art facilities attest, GW spends on its students. Most of the architecture on the main undergraduate campus in DC's Foggy Bottom neighborhood is modern and blends into the surroundings. The capacious, glass-sided Marvin Center is a one-stop shop for students seeking food, work space, groceries, a bowling alley, or travel advice. The newly acquired Mount Vernon campus, three miles away across the Potomac River, boasts architecturally vibrant buildings, including the barn-shaped, redbrick main building, set against green athletic fields. For those looking to get away for the weekend, New York City and Philadelphia are a three- to four-hour's drive. The nearby beaches of Ocean City, Maryland, and Virginia Beach, Virginia, are other popular excursions.

Admissions

Average high school GPA:	—
Average freshman SAT writing / math / critical reading score:	636 / 645 / 643
Average freshman ACT score:	26
Application fee:	$70

Application deadlines:
1/15 (freshmen)
continuous (transfer)
12/1 (early decision)

Total applicants:	19,426
Total accepted:	7,342 (38%)
Total accepted who enrolled:	2,440

Notification dates:
3/15 (freshmen)
continuous (transfer)
12/15 (early decision)

Acceptance rate for early decision applicants:	63%

Students

Percentage of male / female students:	44% / 56%
Percentage of students from out of state:	98%
Percentage of students graduating in 4 years / 6 years:	72% / 78%

Money

Total endowment:	$621,110,000
Total tuition:	$39,210
Total cost with fees & expenses:	$50,760
Average financial aid package:	$33,196
Percentage of students who sought aid and received it:	91%
Percentage of students receiving financial aid:	38%

Also Check Out

American University

Boston College

Boston University

Georgetown University

New York University

Georgetown University

37th and O Streets, NW
Washington, DC 20057

(202) 687-5055
http://www.georgetown.edu/

 **BIG BRAIN**

 **BIG PERSPECTIVE**

Live in the capital, study the world.

5 REASONS IT'S COOL

1. Georgetown's programs in global politics and foreign languages are top notch.

2. Everyone loves a Jesuit. The university's Jesuit professors are well-loved and respected, and many are more liberal politically than secular professors.

3. Washington, D.C., offers unparalleled internship opportunities.

4. When you live on a campus within a city, you can head out for a night on the town or stick around for the classic party scene.

5. After a long drought, the basketball team made it to the Final Four in 2007.

The Basics

Public / private: private religious
Total enrollment / undergrads: 14,148 / 6,853
Campus setting: urban
Students call it: Georgetown
Students are called: Hoyas
Notable alums: King Abdullah II (King of Jordan), Bill Clinton (U.S. president), Patrick Ewing (pro basketball player), Linda Gradstein (NPR correspondent), Antonin Scalia (U.S. Supreme Court justice)

We Want to Be President

Students enroll in one of four schools: the College of Arts and Sciences, the School of Business, the School of Nursing, or the School of Foreign Service. Each school has a separate administration, but most academic departments are autonomous. With few exceptions, students complete a traditional liberal arts curriculum, including work in literature, social science, philosophy, theology, natural science, and mathematics. By far, the most prestigious and academically demanding of Georgetown's divisions is the School of Foreign Service, all of whose ultra-ambitious students are happy to remind you that Bill Clinton is an alum. The nursing and business schools have excellent reputations, though the business school is considered by the rest of the university as a refuge for slackers. Georgetown's faculty includes some real all-stars. But the less famous the professor, the greater the chance that she's actually a good teacher. The Jesuit professors, while not always leaders in their fields, take extraordinary interest in students' needs.

What's a Hoya?

The correct answer to the question "What's a Hoya?" is, simply, "Yes." To explain: The story goes that Georgetown's first football cheer was *Hoya Saxa*, ancient Greek for "What Rocks!" After the ancient language requirement had been eliminated, students, no longer knowing any better, dropped the *saxa* (rocks) and kept the *hoya* (what). So a *Hoya* is a *What*. What's a Hoya? Yes! Get it?

Living Among the Elite of Many Nations

Georgetown has a reputation of being a haven for students who were rejected from Ivy League schools. And while it's true that many students are preppy and Wall Street–bound, the student body is a fascinating constellation of ethnic, national, and religious backgrounds. The good news: Everyone finds his or her niche. The bad news: Groups are somewhat self-segregating. The most prominent of the religious identities is, not surprisingly, Catholicism, but aside from a highly public Mass held at the beginning of each year, there's not too much to make non-Catholics or non-Christians feel out of place. Multiculturalism is celebrated—not just nodded at—with regular campus events sponsored by student groups. Clubs and organizations of all kinds are enormously popular, especially considering all the attractions clamoring for students' attention off campus in the nation's capital. Thursday through Saturday, student apartments and townhouses, as well as the bars on M Street, fill with drunken Hoyas who often wind up arguing about multilateral agricultural trade policy.

The Capital at Your Doorstep

The campus is situated in the über-wealthy neighborhood of, yes, Georgetown, once a city in its own right and now an enclave of senators, lobbyists, and Supreme Court justices who *really* do not appreciate waking up on Sunday mornings to find "Hoyas Kick Ass" spray-painted on their front doors. Many blame the ill will between the students and the Georgetown residents on the fact that the latter have for decades refused to let the city build a subway station in Georgetown. As a result of this refusal, students have to take a shuttle or walk across a bridge to a *different state*—Virginia—to access the Metro. The warring sides find themselves reunited during the week, as Georgetown students intern at just about every federal office in existence. Hoyas interested in a more nitty-gritty approach to changing the world participate in one of the school's dozens of community service projects, many of which enable students to combine volunteering with academic work. For this reason, and because of the array of entertainment that DC offers, Georgetown's location is one of its major drawing cards.

Admissions

Average high school GPA:	—
Average freshman SAT verbal / math score:	691 / 694
Average freshman ACT score:	—
Application fee:	$65
Application deadlines:	
1/10 (freshmen)	
3/1 (transfer)	
11/1 (early action)	
Total applicants:	15,070
Total accepted:	3,367 (22%)
Total accepted who enrolled:	1,588
Notification dates:	
4/1 (freshmen)	
6/1 (transfer)	
12/15 (early action)	
Acceptance rate for early action applicants:	29%

Students

Percentage of male / female students:	46% / 54%
Percentage of students from out of state:	98%
Percentage of students graduating in 4 years / 6 years:	88% / 93%

Money

Total endowment:	$880,300,000
Total tuition:	$35,568
Total cost with fees & expenses:	$47,714
Average financial aid package:	$27,317
Percentage of students who sought aid and received it:	100%
Percentage of students receiving financial aid:	37%

Also Check Out

Brown University

Duke University

Rice University

United States Military Academy–West Point

University of Pennsylvania

Georgia Institute of Technology

225 North Avenue, NW
Atlanta, GA 30332

(404) 894-2000
http://www.gatech.edu/

Yellow jackets in white coats

5 REASONS IT'S COOL

1. A public university, Georgia Tech offers budget-minded students **terrific bang for their buck.**

2. **Co-ops put students to work,** allowing them to gain on-the-job experience for their post-graduate careers.

3. Stealing the T from the TECH sign gives students the chance to **connect with tradition while engineering the perfect crime.**

4. **Atlanta provides students with plenty to do**—if they can find the time.

5. **Super-fast Internet connections** means downloading notes or the day's lecture is a snap.

The Basics

Public / private: public state
Total enrollment / undergrads: 17,936 / 12,361
Campus setting: urban
Students call it: Georgia Tech, Tech, GT
Students are called: Yellow Jackets, Jackets, Ramblin' 'Recks
Notable alums: Michael Arad (architect), Charles Betty (CEO, Earthlink), Jimmy Carter (attended; U.S. president), Jeff Foxworthy (comedian), Nomar Garciaparra (pro baseball player), Bobby Jones (pro golfer), Vern Yip (interior designer), John Young (astronaut)

Stressing Excellence . . . and Students!

Google "nose to the grindstone" and you might find an image of Georgia Tech students. Immense workloads start from the first day of classes. Engineering is Georgia Tech's premier program, and the competition for a place at the table is fierce. Curve wreckers thrive in the Engineering and Computer Science departments. Many students find jobs before graduation, thanks to the popular co-op program. The electrical engineering and management programs are excellent, as are the liberal arts programs of Ivan Allen College. The notoriously remote faculty members tend to concern themselves more with research than with instruction, and students hoping to bend a professor's ear must first breach multiple firewalls in the form of TAs or course newsgroups. It's not uncommon to find sixth- or even seventh-year seniors roaming the grounds. Although their time at GT may be challenging, and often protracted, students leave with enviable qualifications and promising prospects.

Taking High T

Every year, Georgia Tech students steal the T from the TECH sign on the spire of the Tech Tower administration building. The administration has installed high-tech countermeasures to prevent the theft, but these have only sparked the ingenuity of the school's future engineers, who have kept the tradition alive and well despite official discouragement. T-taking techies will not be denied!

All Work and No Play?

Georgia Tech students are far too invested in making the grade to concern themselves with hedonistic hijinks. The Greeks put on respectably wild parties, but many students decompress with tamer activities, such as computer games. The student body is overwhelmingly male (although the Women in Engineering program hopes to change that) and native Georgian. After whites, Asians represent the largest ethnic bloc, with African Americans, Latinos, and Native Americans putting in a modest showing. Whatever their ethnicity, gender, or place of origin, however, students are united in their love of the Yellow Jackets sports teams. As a member of the Atlantic Coast Conference, Georgia Tech regularly battles with adversaries such as Duke, Florida State, North Carolina, and, of course, the University of Georgia, the school's fiercest rival.

Two's Company, Three's a Party

Georgia Tech is situated in Atlanta, a bustling southern metropolis that puts many diversions at students' fingertips. Unfortunately, the school's midtown locale also puts students' possessions at thieves' fingertips. Car break-ins are common in the neighborhoods around campus, but the yearly housing crunch means many students brave the baddies and seek off-campus digs. Among the least desirable housing options: the triples, 156 three-person occupancy rooms found in Towers, Folk, and Caldwell Halls. Atlanta's big-city setting gives students plenty of options for shopping, eating, drinking, and other amusements, and both beach and wilderness are a reasonable car ride away.

Admissions

Average high school GPA:	3.7
Average freshman SAT writing / math / critical reading score:	623 / 688 / 638
Average freshman ACT score:	26
Application fee:	$50
Application deadlines: 1/15 (freshmen) — (transfer)	
Total applicants:	9,389
Total accepted:	6,454 (69%)
Total accepted who enrolled:	2,837
Notification dates: 3/15 (freshmen) — (transfer)	

Students

Percentage of male / female students:	71% / 29%
Percentage of students from out of state:	29%
Percentage of students graduating in 4 years / 6 years:	29% / 76%

Money

Total endowment:	$1,312,679,309
Total in-state tuition, fees & expenses:	$14,243
Total out-of-state tuition, fees & expenses:	$29,589
Average financial aid package:	$9,033
Percentage of students who sought aid and received it:	51%
Percentage of students receiving financial aid:	29%

Also Check Out

Duke University

Massachusetts Institute of Technology

Stanford University

University of North Carolina at Chapel Hill

University of Virginia

Gettysburg College

300 North Washington Street
Gettysburg, PA 17325

(717) 337-6000
http://www.gettysburg.edu/

BIG PERSPECTIVE

The blue and the gray, every day

5 REASONS IT'S COOL

1. Classes rarely have more than twenty people, and **your professors will know you**—and not just by name.

2. **Study-abroad programs are popular and well run;** administrators make it easy to integrate foreign university classes into your transcript.

3. If you're looking to **go Greek**, this might be the place. Frats—and, to a lesser extent, sororities—are central to campus social life.

4. **Historic battlefields abut campus,** and even non–Civil War buffs enjoy exploring the grounds from time to time.

5. No wearing PJs to class, please. **Gettysburg is preppy**, and people pay a lot of attention to how they look.

The Basics

Public / private: private religious
Total enrollment / undergrads: 2,689 / 2,689
Campus setting: small town
Students call it: Gettysburg
Students are called: Bullets
Notable alums: Carol Bellamy (executive director, UNICEF), Bruce S. Gordon (head of the NAACP), Carson Kressley (style expert), Ron Paul (congressman), Jerry Spinelli (writer)

Teeny Tiny Classes

Gettysburg's biggest academic draw is its small, quality classes. The collegewide student-to-teacher ratio is 11:1, all classes are taught by professors, and almost all professors teach every semester. As a result, you won't have to wait until your senior year to get personal attention from members of the faculty. Students say introductory classes are often duller than they need to be, though the First-Year Seminars—sixteen-student classes intended to introduce freshman to college-level discussion and writing—get serious praise. Political science, psychology, history, and management are the most popular majors. Management, incidentally, is also reputed to be the easiest. Natural sciences, among the hardest majors, boast excellent lab facilities. Most everyone seems impressed by the library, particularly given Gettysburg's small size. Study abroad is popular and growing more so, particularly now that one of the administration's official goals is to squeeze as many international and interdisciplinary opportunities into the curriculum as possible.

Older Members of the Community

History lives, perhaps literally, in Gettysburg, said to be one of the most haunted towns in America. Several buildings on campus are reputed to house wandering ghosts and other specters of the Civil War era. Stevens Hall, for example, is the supposed home of the Blue Boy, a child who froze to death on a window ledge.

Popped Collars Unite

This is a preppy campus. Politically conservative, Gettysburg students tend to hail from upper-middle-class families of the Northeast. Racial and ethnic diversity are noticeably lacking—only 11 percent of students are nonwhite—but the administration is working hard to improve its numbers. Fraternities are a dominant, though not domineering, force in Gettysburg social life; Greek parties are major and frequent events. Fortunately, they're open to everyone—as long as you're a girl. If you're not, bring one, or you might be hanging out on the porch for the evening. The college has been spending generously to provide entertainment options that don't involve alcohol, but the free comedians and movies have yet to detract much from the frats' popularity. Freshmen and sophomores are required to live on campus (first-years are grouped in dorms with classmates from their Seminar classes), while juniors and seniors can move off. Few do, however. A full 90 percent of the student body lives in college-owned housing. Secondary social hubs include sports and volunteering. In fact, many students think of the Division III teams more as party throwers than as athletes.

Nice Costume

Gettysburg is an economically diverse small town with a historic movie theater, lots of outlet shopping, and, oh yeah, the most famous battlefield in the country. When the weather's nice, you can't swing your arms without hitting a tourist. For this reason, many students spend most of their time on campus—itself a gorgeous and immaculately maintained place. Others love strolling through the crowds of reenactors eating hardtack and arguing about what Abraham Lincoln plans to do in his second term. Setting aside the issue of the seasonal circus outside the campus gates, students say this is a pretty good place to go to college. Baltimore and Washington, D.C. are within a few hours' drive, the surrounding countryside is charming, and Gettysburg's facilities, from its computer labs to its athletic fields, are in great shape.

Admissions

Average high school GPA:	—
Average freshman SAT verbal / math score:	652 / 633
Average freshman ACT score:	—
Application fee:	$45

Application deadlines:
2/15 (freshmen)
continuous (transfer)
11/15 (early decision)

Total applicants:	5,310
Total accepted:	2,183 (41%)
Total accepted who enrolled:	730

Notification dates:
4/1 (freshmen)
continuous (transfer)
12/15 (early decision)

Acceptance rate for early decision applicants:	77%

Students

Percentage of male / female students:	46% / 54%
Percentage of students from out of state:	72%
Percentage of students graduating in 4 years / 6 years:	70% / 76%

Money

Total endowment:	$241,466,706
Total tuition:	$33,700
Total cost with fees & expenses:	$42,310
Average financial aid package:	$26,108
Percentage of students who sought aid and received it:	100%
Percentage of students receiving financial aid:	56%

Also Check Out

Bucknell University

College of William & Mary

Dickinson College

Franklin & Marshall College

Lehigh University

Gonzaga University

502 East Boone Avenue
Spokane, WA 99258

(509) 328-4220
http://www.gonzaga.edu/

BIG PERSPECTIVE

Intimate university, gorgeous location

5 REASONS IT'S COOL

1. Small classes, no TAs—Gonzaga offers a personalized education in an intimate environment.

2. The **Comprehensive Leadership Program** gets select students ready for the real world.

3. In keeping with **Jesuit tradition**, the university aims to educate the whole person through a broad liberal arts curriculum, including nine credits of religious studies classes.

4. There's **tons of Bulldog spirit**, especially when it comes to the NCAA Division I men's basketball team.

5. The **lovely Northwest campus** offers views of the Spokane River and Mt. Spokane.

The Basics

Public / private: private religious
Total enrollment / undergrads: 6,610 / 4,275
Campus setting: urban
Students call it: Gonzaga, Zag
Students are called: Bulldogs, Zags
Notable alums: Tony Canadeo (pro football player), Bing Crosby (singer), Thomas Foley (speaker, House of Representatives), Christine Gregoire (governor, Washington), Carl Pohlad (owner, Minnesota Twins)

Mind, Body, Spirit

One of the defining characteristics Gonzaga is the personal attention students receive from professors. The student-to-faculty ratio is 12:1, and classes are 100 percent professor taught. Classes average fewer than twenty-five students. As a school in the Jesuit tradition, Gonzaga shapes the entire person, mind, body, and spirit. Students praise the well-rounded education they receive. All Zag students take the University Core Curriculum, a thirty-one-credit lineup that covers philosophy, religious studies, math, English literature, and critical thinking. Popular majors include business, political science, and psychology. Freshman can apply to the Comprehensive Leadership Program, which involves years of leadership-focused classes and extracurricular activities such as serving as a scholarship judge, attending leadership retreats, and spending the summer volunteering in Zambia. The competitive Honors College offers students free rein of Hopkins House, which provides computer stations, study spaces, and a hangout spot.

Long Live the Bulldog(s)!

Spike, Gonzaga's official mascot, is a kid in a bulldog costume. Look a little closer at the court, though, and you might spot Q, Gonzaga's live bulldog mascot. Q has been around since 1999 and lives with an Athletic Department member. But he might need to watch his back—not all past bulldogs have enjoyed long, healthy lives. Corrigan, the bulldog of the 1940s, died after being fed poisoned meat, and another mascot died after just four days on the job.

Study abroad is encouraged, and many students spend their junior year at Gonzaga's campus in Florence, Italy, or at other programs in England, France, Spain, Japan, China, or Mexico.

Brother, Where Art Thou?

Faith and spirituality play a large role in academic and social life at Gonzaga. About half of the student body is Catholic, and there are forty-three Jesuits on campus who serve as residence hall chaplains and celebrate Mass. Still, quite a few other religions are represented, although in small numbers. Students must live on campus for at least two years and can do so in suites, apartments, or traditional residence halls, which have coed and single-gender options. About 45 percent of students are from Washington, while others tend to be from surrounding states. Students admit that there isn't much to do on campus, but the school is making an effort to provide more events and activities. The lack of on-campus activities doesn't seem to affect the Zags' fierce school pride in their men's basketball team. Home games draw huge crowds, and based on the Bulldogs' impressive home-court record, fans don't often leave disappointed.

Attention, Outdoors Lovers

The 108-acre Gonzaga campus is situated in a quiet residential area only half a mile from Spokane's downtown business district. The university features views of Mt. Spokane and is situated on the Spokane River. The midsized city of Spokane, located in the inland Northwest, is only thirty minutes from Idaho and four hours from Seattle. The campus has grown in the past few years to accommodate increased enrollment. The most notable new construction is the McCarthey Athletic Center, which students pack during home basketball games. For nature lovers, the surrounding region offers plenty of outdoor activities, such as skiing, rock climbing, hiking, and fishing.

Admissions

Average high school GPA:	3.63
Average freshman SAT verbal / math score:	600 / 608
Average freshman ACT score:	25
Application fee:	$45

Application deadlines:
2/1 (freshmen)
6/1 (transfer)
11/15 (early action)

Total applicants:	4,965
Total accepted:	3,331 (67%)
Total accepted who enrolled:	977

Notification dates:
3/15 (freshmen)
continuous (transfer)
1/15 (early action)

Acceptance rate for early action applicants:	78%

Students

Percentage of male / female students:	46% / 54%
Percentage of students from out of state:	49%
Percentage of students graduating in 4 years / 6 years:	55% / 74%

Money

Total endowment:	$132,676,479
Total tuition:	$24,590
Total cost with fees & expenses:	$33,032
Average financial aid package:	$18,004
Percentage of students who sought aid and received it:	88%
Percentage of students receiving financial aid:	56%

Also Check Out

Loyola Marymount University

Saint Mary's College of California

Santa Clara University

Seattle University

Goucher College

1021 Dulaney Valley Road
Baltimore, MD 21204

(410) 337-6000
http://www.goucher.edu/

 **BIG HAND**

 **BIG PERSPECTIVE**

 **BIG WORLD**

Calling all jetsetters and adventurers!

5 REASONS IT'S COOL

1. Goucher really wants you to see the world—in fact, it was the first college in the country to **require students to study abroad.**

2. Smile! In 2004, *Newsweek* named **Goucher students the happiest in the United States.**

3. Hope you like crabs. Baltimore is **a cool city with great bars and restaurants**—many of which specialize in Maryland's local delicacy.

4. **Small classes, a supportive community, caring professors**—Goucher students are more than just a number.

5. Guys will enjoy the **high female-to-male ratio**—66% of students are women.

The Basics

Public / private: private nonprofit
Total enrollment / undergrads: 2,310 / 1,446
Campus setting: suburban
Students call it: Goucher
Students are called: Gophers
Notable alums: Mildred Dunnock (actress), Jonah Goldberg (cultural commentator), Sarah T. Hughes (judge), Judith Lewent (CFO, Merck), Darcey Steinke (novelist)

Go Global . . . Just Don't Forget to Write Home

Goucher adds an international twist to its curriculum. A few years ago, the college became the first in the country to require students to study abroad for at least three weeks. Two popular options for fulfilling this requirement are the intensive courses abroad (ICAs) and the International Scholars Program (ISP). ICAs are three-week classes that usually take place during the winter, spring, or summer breaks. Recent offerings include courses such as "China: Past, Present, and Future" and "French in Avignon." ISP participants take several classes addressing global perspectives and then study abroad in the country of their choice, including such far-flung destinations as Ghana and India. Goucher offers a wide range of majors, including social sciences, history, psychology, and peace studies. All students must fulfill course requirements in areas such foreign languages and math, among other liberal arts fields. The college also offers several service learning courses, where students volunteer as part of the course requirements.

Stress Busters

Before fall semester finals begin, Goucher hosts Winter Meltdown, a day packed with creative ways of relieving stress. Students jump on trampolines, get massages, play games—and bash a car with sledgehammers.

Feminine Accents

Goucher was originally founded as a women's college, and women still significantly outnumber men—66 percent of the student body is female. The college offers five separate residence halls, and housing is guaranteed for all four years. On-campus housing options range from the nonsmoking, coed (by room) Tuttle House to Robinson House, which requires residents to communicate in a language other than English at all times. Students choose from over sixty organizations, including the African Dance Club, Club Francais, Ultimate Frisbee, the Hip-Hop Club, and Sacred Ground, which combines dancing and Christianity. Anyone can submit essays for publication in *Verge*, a prestigious on-campus journal that publishes research papers and nonfiction. Goucher's Community Auxiliary for Service connects service-minded students with opportunities such as tutoring local children, preparing meals in soup kitchens, and building houses through Habitat for Humanity.

No Need to Be Crabby Here

Goucher's 287-acre campus is located in Baltimore. To get to the restaurants and shops of downtown Towson, a nearby Baltimore suburb, students can walk or hop on the Collegetown shuttle, which also stops at nearby Johns Hopkins University and Loyola College. Each year, Towson hosts the Spring Festival, one of the largest street fairs on the East Coast, featuring games, food, and entertainment. Baltimore is home to the Orioles, a Major League baseball team, and to the Inner Harbor, a renovated neighborhood on Chesapeake Bay with attractions such as the Maryland Science Center and Harborplace, a huge mall. Washington, D.C. is about an hour away by car.

Admissions

Average high school GPA:	3.18
Average freshman SAT verbal / math score:	618 / 583
Average freshman ACT score:	—
Application fee:	$40
Application deadlines:	
2/1 (freshmen)	
5/1 (transfer)	
12/1 (early action)	
Total applicants:	3,171
Total accepted:	2,221 (70%)
Total accepted who enrolled:	451
Notification dates:	
4/1 (freshmen)	
6/1 (transfer)	
2/15 (early action)	
Acceptance rate for early action applicants:	83%

Students

Percentage of male / female students:	34% / 66%
Percentage of students from out of state:	71%
Percentage of students graduating in 4 years / 6 years:	57% / 64%

Money

Total endowment:	$174,296,847
Total tuition:	$28,900
Total cost with fees & expenses:	$39,050
Average financial aid package:	$19,917
Percentage of students who sought aid and received it:	82%
Percentage of students receiving financial aid:	49%

Also Check Out

Barnard College

Beloit College

Bryn Mawr College

The George Washington University

Vassar College

Grinnell College

1121 Park Street
Grinnell, IA 50112

(641) 269-4000
http://www.grinnell.edu/

 **BIG BRAIN**

 **BIG IDEA**

 **BIG PERSPECTIVE**

A pioneering approach to liberal arts

5 REASONS IT'S COOL

1. **Grinnell professors tend to work students hard** and give a lot in return.

2. There's **only one required course**, and even that one is offered in myriad different forms.

3. It's official policy to let **students, as far as is practicable, run their own lives.**

4. **Campus has an inclusive atmosphere**, and students tend to encourage, rather than sabotage, one another's academic pursuits.

5. The administration, apparently embracing the motto "you can't take it with you," has been spending fiendishly lately to **update tons of campus facilities.**

The Basics

Public / private: private nonprofit
Total enrollment / undergrads: 1,589 / 1,589
Campus setting: small town
Students call it: Grinnell
Students are called: Pioneers, Grinnellians
Notable alums: Herbie Hancock (musician), Harry Hopkins (advisor to FDR), Robert Noyce (cofounder, Intel)

It's on You

Most Grinnell professors are both respected scholars and talented educators, and the school's atmosphere encourages deep intellectual journeys. The only required course is the Freshman Seminar, which, through a survey of subjects from extraterrestrials to veganism, acclimates first-year students to the standards and customs of academia. Coursework is intense, and professors expect you to put just as much effort into your classes as they do. The school's small size makes it impossible to offer the vast course catalog available at many other places, and popular courses fill up quickly. Fortunately, if you can't get into—or if Grinnell doesn't offer—the class you're looking for, the Mentored Advanced Project program will give you the opportunity to build it from scratch. MAP students work with a professor to plan and execute an independent, supervised work of scholarship or art. Meanwhile, the Experimental College (ExCo) allows townies, students, and staff to design and teach their own non-credit courses in whatever subject they choose. The sciences are reputed to be the most difficult departments.

Officially Time to Party

Grinnellians who grew up in cities might feel as though they're going to school on Mars, but one benefit of the campus's isolation is the we're-in-this-together spirit that animates the students. Official school-sponsored events that might get eyes rolling elsewhere are quite popular here. Annual theme parties include the Mary B. Jane cross-dressing dance; the Waltz; the Disco; the Alice in Wonderland music festival; and the 10/10 party—celebrating, on October 10, the cutting of the first student-employment paychecks of the academic year.

It's on You, Vol. II

There's a big, not to mention codified, emphasis on privacy and personal responsibility at Grinnell. The Self-Governance policy entrusts students with their own well-being and encourages them to resolve conflicts without involving the administration. This means the campus security team will sooner make sure drunk students get home safely than they will bust them for underage consumption. Despite its small size, Grinnell has several dozen extracurricular activities and clubs, which range from the standard (foreign language clubs, community service groups) to the more unusual (e.g., an association for the appreciation of beards and mustaches). Athletics aren't too important. Grinnell competes in Division III, and students aren't wowed by the varsity teams. Those who do want to participate in intercollegiate sports find it easy to do so, thanks to Grinnell's no-cut policy. Intramurals are, depending on whom you ask, either nonexistent or nothing less than the school's lifeblood.

A Well-Endowed Oasis in the Middle of Nowhere

Transfers aren't any more common at Grinnell than they are at other schools, but when students *do* leave, they often blame their desertion on the size and isolation of Grinnell's hometown. This is Iowa, and it's not even the busy part of Iowa. Some embrace that; others abhor it. The two streets in town with any commerce to speak of are ten minutes by foot from campus. The college, no doubt aware of the downsides of its environs, has spent big bucks on making the campus inviting and well appointed. Even moderately out-of-date buildings have been replaced or completely refurbished. Recent years have seen the construction of new dorms, a new gym, a new dining hall, a new student center, and a new *wing* of campus. Not surprisingly, life on campus and in town is extremely safe.

Admissions

Average high school GPA:	—
Average freshman SAT verbal / math score:	673 / 665
Average freshman ACT score:	26
Application fee:	$30

Application deadlines:
1/20 (freshmen)
5/1 (transfer)
11/20 (early decision)

Total applicants:	3,104
Total accepted:	1,401 (45%)
Total accepted who enrolled:	405

Notification dates:
4/1 (freshmen)
5/20 (transfer)
12/20 (early decision)

Acceptance rate for early decision applicants:	78%

Students

Percentage of male / female students:	46% / 54%
Percentage of students from out of state:	78%
Percentage of students graduating in 4 years / 6 years:	83% / 87%

Money

Total endowment:	$1,471,804,000
Total tuition:	$28,566
Total cost with fees & expenses:	$37,330
Average financial aid package:	$25,972
Percentage of students who sought aid and received it:	100%
Percentage of students receiving financial aid:	54%

Also Check Out

Carleton College

Kalamazoo College

Kenyon College

Macalester College

Swarthmore College

Guilford College

5800 West Friendly Avenue
Greensboro, NC 27410

(336) 316-2000
http://www.guilford.edu/

 **BIG HAND**

 **BIG PERSPECTIVE**

Here's where things get personal. Very personal.

5 REASONS IT'S COOL

1. At this easygoing school, even the **professors go by their first names.**

2. If you want real-world experience, check out the **variety of internship and study-abroad options** offered here.

3. Every student is **assigned a faculty advisor** who helps with course selection and the fulfillment of academic and career goals.

4. Guilford puts its money where its mouth is: Around 80 percent of students receive some form of **merit- or need-based financial aid.**

5. Students at this Quaker school pride themselves on their **commitment to social justice.**

The Basics

Public / private: private religious
Total enrollment / undergrads: 2,687 / 2,687
Campus setting: suburban
Students call it: Guilford
Students are called: Quakers
Notable alums: Rick Ferrell (pro baseball player), World B. Free (pro basketball player), Marilyn McIntyre (actress), Tony Womack (pro baseball player)

Liberal Arts with a Quaker Twist

With fewer than 2,600 students, this college offers many of the perks of a small liberal arts school—and much more. A Quaker school, Guilford stresses simplicity, equality, justice, integrity, and diversity in addition to academics. Not only do students have an extraordinary amount of influence on the college's governance, but professors treat students as equals from the moment they first arrive on campus. All freshmen must take a First Year Experience (FYE) course, which is a discussion-oriented interdisciplinary seminar that helps students understand their roles as members of the college community. Faculty members recognize that students learn in many different ways, which is why the school offers many hands-on courses and independent study opportunities. Guilford also helps students design internships and encourages them to volunteer in the community and study abroad. Biology, business, psychology, and theater are among the college's most popular areas of study. Whatever your major, expect to challenge your preconceptions.

Meet the Big Man on Campus

With his tall hat and buckled shoes, Guilford's Fighting Quaker resembles the Quaker Oats cereal guy, who adorns oatmeal canisters across America. But don't be fooled: The hot breakfast cereal mascot and Guilford have nothing in common.

A Society of Friends

"Close knit" is perhaps the most accurate term to describe Guilford. The college's vibrant community spirit stems from the centrality of dorm life, the lack of frats and sororities, and the school's egalitarian philosophy, which eschews elitism, preferential treatment, and discrimination. Students typically see their peers as fellow social activists who will help them change the world. While most students are politically liberal, even the most conservative students manage to find a place on this campus, where everyone is a little quirky and, many students say, a bit impractical. Quakers find it easy to make friends by volunteering or participating in one of the forty-plus student organizations on campus, which cover everything from politics to social clubs to student media. The student-run radio station, WQFS (90.9 FM), is particularly esteemed. Artsy students also enjoy the many exhibits that come to campus, as well as theater performances and a touring choir. Sorry, sports fans: Athletics are not a big deal here. While the college does have a Division III athletics program, some students say that athletes have a tough time fitting in with their nonjock peers.

Little Campus in the Big Woods

If you like the idea of spending four years on 348 wooded acres, removed from the bustle of the big city, then this school might be just the place for you. Located on the western edge of Greensboro, Guilford puts students within a few hours' drive of several recreational parks and ski areas, in addition to the Atlantic coast. Students sometimes make day trips to these areas or even weekend trips to Atlanta or Washington, D.C., both of which are a five-hour drive away. This isn't a school that empties out on weekends, though. By and large, students spend their free time on campus, where outdoor activities abound. Some of the more popular entertainment options include drum circles, late night firelight jam sessions, and hiking, climbing, and rafting trips with the Great Outdoor Club. When they opt to stay indoors, students usually take advantage of school-sponsored film screenings, guest speakers, art exhibits, concerts, open-mic nights, dance parties, and theater performances.

Admissions

Average high school GPA:	3.14
Average freshman SAT verbal / math score:	581 / 559
Average freshman ACT score:	23
Application fee:	$25

Application deadlines:
2/15 (freshmen)
4/1 (transfer)
1/15 (early action)

Total applicants:	2,603
Total accepted:	1,900 (73%)
Total accepted who enrolled:	430

Notification dates:
4/1 (freshmen)
5/1 (transfer)
2/15 (early action)

Acceptance rate for early action applicants:	75%

Students

Percentage of male / female students:	41% / 59%
Percentage of students from out of state:	64%
Percentage of students graduating in 4 years / 6 years:	44% / 55%

Money

Total endowment:	$55,155,409
Total tuition:	$22,690
Total cost with fees & expenses:	$30,510
Average financial aid package:	$11,661
Percentage of students who sought aid and received it:	67%
Percentage of students receiving financial aid:	38%

Also Check Out

College of Charleston

Earlham College

Elon University

Grinnell College

Oberlin College

Hamilton College

198 College Hill Road
Clinton, NY 13323

(315) 859-4011
http://www.hamilton.edu/

BIG PERSPECTIVE

Liberated liberal arts

5 REASONS IT'S COOL

1. Hamilton has **no distribution requirements.** Students take a broad and enriching range of whatever classes interest them most.

2. Students have **almost-unlimited access to their professors,** who consider teaching their first and most important job.

3. Sports are popular, whether you're playing or watching, and there's **more school spirit** than you'll find at many colleges.

4. Is this England? Research is inconclusive, but it's been suggested that Hamilton **students drink more beer than water.**

5. Clinton, New York, is the **ideal place** for four years of quiet, unhurried study.

The Basics

Public / private: private nonprofit
Total enrollment / undergrads: 1,821 / 1,821
Campus setting: small town
Students call it: Hamilton
Students are called: Continentals, Hamiltonians
Notable alums: Henry Allen (critic), Ezra Pound (poet), Paul Greengard (neuroscientist), B. F. Skinner (behavioral psychologist)

It's Your Call

Liberal arts are the name of the game at Hamilton. Rather than setting distribution requirements, the administration expects students to expose themselves voluntarily to a broad range of disciplines. First-years do take a proseminar—a sixteen-student class with lots of writing and discussion—and sophomores work through an interdisciplinary program culminating in a presentation. The introductory classes in most departments are sometimes overcrowded, but classes at higher levels get rave reviews. Professors are enthusiastic and approachable whether you're a star student or a struggling schlub. There are no TAs. The hard sciences have sometimes lagged behind humanities and social sciences, but the construction of a large science center has already given the naturals a shot in the arm. Government and economics are two of the most popular majors; both are strengthened by the presence of the Arthur Levitt Public Affairs Center on campus. A 3-2 program in engineering and a 3-3 program in law are both offered in conjunction with Columbia University.

Oranges on Ice, Please

The Citrus Bowl, a long-standing Hamilton tradition, calls for students to smuggle oranges and other citrus contraband into the first hockey game of the season and toss the fruit onto the ice after the Continentals score their first goal. To cut down on delay-of-game penalties, the college administration has tried to discourage the practice in recent years, thus disappointing local citrus vendors.

Rah-Rah in the Woods

For a lot of Hamiltonians, life outside the classroom is built on the twin pillars of alcohol and sports. Intramural leagues are popular; this is the kind of campus where people aren't going to look at you funny if you say you're going to the gym. There are twenty-eight intercollegiate varsity teams, and Continentals take All-American honors frequently. Some teams, especially hockey, draw large, enthusiastic, and drunk crowds. Many Hamilton students report that alcohol is appealing because there's not always much else to do on campus or in Clinton. The campus pub is a cornerstone of social life, and there are fraternities, although they're no longer permitted to have campus houses. Almost all students live in university-owned housing. These residences run the gamut from typical dorms to refurbished former frat houses that are described, unanimously, as gorgeous. The main dining facilities get decent marks, but most Hamiltonians prefer the smaller "boutique" eateries. A great coffeehouse concert series has recently brought Ben Folds and the Shins for acoustic performances.

Getting Along with the Neighbors

Hamilton's campus is dominated by handsome architecture and surrounded by more than a thousand acres of college-owned forest, fields, and woodlands. Down a hill is the village of Clinton, a small, rural town. Prospective students shouldn't overestimate Clinton's size. There are shops and restaurants, but not too many. Fortunately, relations between the college and the village are good. Every year, Clinton holds a fall festival on the village green; students are encouraged to attend, and the event reinforces the friendly bonds between town and gown. All the goodwill in the world, however, can't change the fact that when the wind and snow of an Upstate winter arrive, there's relatively little to do on campus or in Clinton aside from watch hockey and drink. An important part of many Hamilton students' experiences is an annual or semiannual freak-out, culminating in a road trip to New York City, Boston, or Montreal.

Admissions

Average high school GPA:	—
Average freshman SAT verbal / math score:	672 / 674
Average freshman ACT score:	—
Application fee:	$50
Application deadlines:	
1/1 (freshmen)	
4/15 (transfer)	
11/15 (early decision)	
Total applicants:	4,266
Total accepted:	1,425 (33%)
Total accepted who enrolled:	501
Notification dates:	
4/1 (freshmen)	
6/1 (transfer)	
12/15 (early decision)	
Acceptance rate for early decision applicants:	47%

Students

Percentage of male / female students:	50% / 50%
Percentage of students from out of state:	65%
Percentage of students graduating in 4 years / 6 years:	82% / 88%

Money

Total endowment:	$660,808,000
Total tuition:	$34,780
Total cost with fees & expenses:	$44,390
Average financial aid package:	$29,148
Percentage of students who sought aid and received it:	100%
Percentage of students receiving financial aid:	49%

Also Check Out

Bowdoin College

Colby College

Colgate University

Middlebury College

Williams College

Hampshire College

893 West Street
Amherst, MA 01002

(413) 549-4600
http://www.hampshire.edu/

 **BIG IDEA**

 **BIG PERSPECTIVE**

Nothing ordinary about it

5 REASONS IT'S COOL

1. **No grades.** Hampshire encourages students to **think independently** and **creatively** and evaluates them in a similarly unusual fashion.

2. **Strong programs in film, television, and cognitive science** attract students who want to step outside their comfort zones.

3. **Students are proud of their academic work and see it as an integral part of life,** not just something they're required to do.

4. The Amherst location means that students **enjoy plenty of New England charm.**

5. The Pioneer Valley is a great place for anyone who likes to **hike, ski, camp, or see the stars** now and then.

The Basics

Public / private: private nonprofit
Total enrollment / undergrads: 1,448 / 1,448
Campus setting: small town
Students call it: Hampshire
Students are called: Frogs
Notable alums: Ken Burns (documentary filmmaker), Edward Humes (journalist), Jon Krakauer (mountaineer, writer), Daniel Horowitz (criminal defense attorney), Liev Schreiber (actor), Elliot Smith (musician), Barry Sonnenfeld (film director), Naomi Wallace (playwright)

Choose Your Own Adventure

Hampshire is sometimes referred to as the "undergraduate graduate school," because it gives students freedom to pursue their interests. In return, it expects them to produce high-caliber, self-directed research and writing. Students move through three divisions. Division I loosely follows the pattern of a general education program; classes in cognitive science, social science, natural science, humanities, and disciplinary arts are required. Division II, analogous to departmental major requirements at other schools, is a self-designed phase that takes place over the course of several semesters. Division III consists of a single large project on the scale of a master's thesis. The heterodoxy doesn't end there: Hampshire issues no grades. Instead, faculty members complete written evaluations. Profs are generally considered accessible and supportive, and get good reviews for their teaching skills. The number of courses available to students is vastly increased by Hampshire's

Economics 101

All the independence and innovative spirit in the world can't change the fact that Hampshire's endowment is small—$39.5 million. And that's not just a number. One of the most common complaints from Hampshire students is that their gym, library, dorms, and laboratory facilities—not to mention the student center, which doesn't exist—fail to meet expectations. The facilities at the other nearby colleges are better, and available for use.

membership in the Five College Consortium. Students take over 1,200 classes every year at other schools, which include Amherst, Mount Holyoke, the University of Massachusetts, and Smith.

Straight Talk

Ninety-three percent of students live on campus in one of two types of college housing: basic dorms and "mods." In the mods, which are mostly for upperclassmen, four to ten students live together and share housework responsibilities. Singles are available for most who want them. The student body is not especially diverse, and many students tend to be left-leaning and politically vocal. Discussing "issues" is definitely one of the most popular pastimes on campus. There are a lot of outdoorsy-types at Hampshire (free mountain biking, cross-country skiing, and kayaking equipment is available), but organized sports, even at the intramural level, are extremely low-key. Spirit for varsity sports is almost completely nonexistent, and casual games of soccer or basketball are often at risk of disintegrating into political debates.

Focus on the Trees

Hampshire's campus is dominated by less-than-beautiful buildings dating from the 1960s. Fortunately, the surrounding Pioneer Valley is gorgeous, and western Massachusetts is an excellent staging ground for urban or rural expeditions, with Boston and the East Coast just as accessible as the deeper wilderness of New England. Amherst itself is a charming town. Shops and restaurants stay open pretty late, and, with the University of Massachusetts and Amherst College in the neighborhood, there are always lectures and cultural events taking place. Students report feeling safe in their home away from home, although some complain that the size and poor outdoor lighting of Hampshire's campus makes late-night wandering a riskier enterprise than it needs to be.

Admissions

Average high school GPA:	3.42
Average freshman SAT writing / math / critical reading score:	646 / 605 / 661
Average freshman ACT score:	26
Application fee:	$55

Application deadlines:
1/15 (freshmen)
3/1 (transfer)
11/15 (early decision)
12/1 (early action)

Total applicants:	2,454
Total accepted:	1,386 (56%)
Total accepted who enrolled:	392

Notification dates:
4/1 (freshmen)
4/15 (transfer)
12/15 (early decision)
2/1 (early action)

Acceptance rate for early action/early decision applicants:	89% / 62%

Students

Percentage of male / female students:	41% / 59%
Percentage of students from out of state:	83%
Percentage of students graduating in 4 years / 6 years:	51% / 71%

Money

Total endowment:	$39,695,448
Total tuition:	$33,855
Total cost with fees & expenses:	$44,135
Average financial aid package:	$27,990
Percentage of students who sought aid and received it:	97%
Percentage of students receiving financial aid:	56%

Also Check Out

Bard College

Bennington College

Brown University

Smith College

Hampton University

Tyler Street
Hampton, VA 23668

(757) 727-5000
http://www.hamptonu.edu/

BIG
PERSPECTIVE

The real HU

5 REASONS IT'S COOL

1. Students at this historically black college have a **strong sense of community and purpose.**

2. Business, nursing, and education are just some of the **strong pre-professional programs.**

3. **Throw out your sneakers!** HU students turn the university-imposed dress code into an opportunity to show off their fashion sense.

4. The **lovely waterfront campus** boasts a number of historic buildings.

5. Small classes, dedicated professors, and an emphasis on discipline ensure that students are on the ball.

The Basics

Public / private: private nonprofit
Total enrollment / undergrads: 6,152 / 5,135
Campus setting: urban
Students call it: Hampton, HU
Students are called: Pirates
Notable alums: Ruth Carter (costume designer), Spencer Christian (weatherman), Alberta Williams King (mother of Martin Luther King Jr.), Angela Burt-Murray (editor in chief, *Essence*), Charles Phillips (president, Oracle), Wanda Sykes (actress), Booker T. Washington (educator, leader)

Education for Life

Since Mary Peake conducted the first classes in 1863 under the Emancipation Oak, HU has remained committed to the principle of "education for life." While less well known than some other historically black colleges, Hampton still offers its students a quality education, especially in the pre-professional domain. The school is made up of six undergraduate colleges, with a third of the student body enrolling in the College of Business. The School of Nursing offers a strong undergrad degree program, as does the School of Pharmacy. Quite a few students gravitate toward the recently expanded journalism and communications program, which holds classes in a state-of-the-art facility completed in 2002. Those with an interest in oceanography can take advantage of the interdisciplinary marine and environmental science program, as well as the many research opportunities that result from the university's proximity to Chesapeake Bay. HU also has a number of

Living History

Located on HU's campus is the Emancipation Oak, the site of the first southern reading of the Emancipation Proclamation. This large oak tree has been designated one of the Ten Great Trees of the World.

academic enrichment programs, including the W. E. B. Dubois Honor Society, which gives its members priority registration and individualized advising. All these opportunities come at a price: strict rules. Although students consistently praise their professors, some wish for more academic independence and personal freedom.

Discipline and Direction

As you might guess from the university's motto ("My home by the sea"), the 254-acre campus sits directly on the Hampton waterfront. The Student Center, with its movie theater, bowling alley, game room, and comfy reading rooms, is a hot spot for socializing. Discipline at HU is of utmost importance, and the administration imposes strict rules on its students. There is a dress code and limited male-female dorm visitation. Some students balk at these restrictions, while others accept and appreciate them. As might be expected, there are severe penalties for alcohol or drug abuse. Students do party, but they go off-campus to do so—or try to. The dearth of nightlife in the surrounding area draws a universal thumbs down. However, the lack of outside stimuli strengthens the sense of community on campus, where students are heavily involved in clubs, and events are well-attended. Fraternities, sororities, student government, dance companies, and religious organizations are just some of the activities students pursue. The dorms are historic, but slightly run down, and many upperclassmen jump at the opportunity to move to Hampton Harbor, a small shopping and apartment area nearby. Women outnumber men significantly.

Hampton History

The university is located in the city of Hampton, on the southeast end of the Virginia Peninsula. The campus boasts a number of historic buildings including the University Museum, the oldest African American museum in the United States. Hampton, along with Norfolk, Virginia Beach, Newport News, Portsmouth, Suffolk, and Chesapeake, make up the larger Hampton Roads area. Between Fort Monroe and the large naval base in Norfolk, there's a strong military presence in the area. This does nothing to improve the nightlife in Hampton proper. Most students find that a car is essential. Virginia Beach, a thirty-minute drive away, has a bit more going on.

Admissions

Average high school GPA:	3.2
Average freshman SAT verbal / math score:	536 / 511
Average freshman ACT score:	19
Application fee:	$25

Application deadlines:
3/1 (freshmen)
— (transfer)

Total applicants:	5,401
Total accepted:	2,433 (45%)
Total accepted who enrolled:	1,100

Notification dates:
7/31 (freshmen)
— (transfer)

Students

Percentage of male / female students:	35% / 65%
Percentage of students from out of state:	85%
Percentage of students graduating in 4 years / 6 years:	40% / 54%

Money

Total endowment:	$185,833,752
Total tuition:	$13,358
Total cost with fees & expenses:	$22,334
Average financial aid package:	$3,220
Percentage of students who sought aid and received it:	46%
Percentage of students receiving financial aid:	65%

Also Check Out

Florida Agricultural and Mechanical University

Howard University

Morehouse College

Spelman College

University of Maryland–College Park

Harvard University

86 Brattle Street
Cambridge, MA 02138

(617) 495-1000
http://www.harvard.edu/

 **BIG BRAIN**    **BIG PERSPECTIVE**    **BIG RESEARCH**

Believe the hype.

5 REASONS IT'S COOL

1. Harvard's at the **top of the college heap,** and everyone knows it.

2. Individually, Harvard students include some of the **nation's brightest.** Gather them all up on one college campus, and you'd better wear shades.

3. The residential system of houses offer unique, small communities where **students live, learn, and dine together.**

4. The **obscenely large endowment** means that the buildings and facilities are as good as money can buy.

5. **Cambridge is a cool college town** with lots of student-friendly attractions—and neighboring Boston's just a short T-ride away.

The Basics

Public / private: private nonprofit
Total enrollment / undergrads: 19,538 / 6,715
Campus setting: urban
Students call it: Harvard
Students are called: Crimson, Cantabs (an abbreviation of Cantabrigian, meaning "a person who lives in Cambridge")
Notable alums: William S. Burroughs (writer), T. S. Eliot (Nobel Laureate, Literature), Susan Faludi (journalist), Al Gore (U.S. vice president; Nobel Laureate, Peace), Brian Greene (physicist), Tommy Lee Jones (actor), John F. Kennedy (U.S. president), Natalie Portman (actress)

It's the Harvard of . . .

Harvard's reputation precedes it. Fortunately, the university's strong academics make good on all the hype. Students select from over forty concentrations, and they have the option of creating their own blend of studies from the areas available. The most popular and largest majors include biology, economics, English, political science, and psychology. Harvard's core program requires all students to complete courses in areas such as foreign cultures, literature, science, and history. Faculty members excel as teachers and scholars and include luminaries such as scientists James D. Watson and E. O. Wilson. Students who want an even greater challenge than what Harvard already doles out can join the honors program, where they complete a thesis or research project during their senior year. Class sizes tend be small, especially in the upper levels, where seminars can feel like graduate-level courses.

Open Ye the Gates

Anyone entering Harvard Yard must pass through one of several wrought-iron gates, most of which were donated by various graduating classes over the past two centuries. The main entrance to the Yard is Johnston Gate, located on the west side of campus and featured on dozens of postcards. Superstition has it that Harvard undergrads may walk through Johnston Gate only on their first and last days at Harvard and will fail or drop out if they pass through it any other time.

Yard Work

Yes, Harvard students work hard. And while it's true that they spend tons of time studying, they also find time to take advantage of Harvard's many student organizations. These include the *Harvard Crimson*, the daily student newspaper; the Harvard Lampoon, the legendary campus humor organization; Hasty Pudding Theatricals, the study theater society; the Harvard Glee Club; and many more. The university offers forty-one intercollegiate sports teams, and the campus's athletic facilities include basketball courts, two swimming pools, and forty-eight tennis courts. Freshmen live in their own dorms in centrally located Harvard Yard. From sophomore year on up, students cohabitate in the university's twelve residential "houses." Each house has its own dining hall, library, and resident faculty member. On-campus housing is guaranteed for all four years, and most students choose to stay on in the luxe accommodations provided.

Building on History

Harvard's buildings reflect the styles that have come and gone since its inception in 1636, from the iconic Memorial Hall to the modern Gund Hall. The largest college library in the world, with a collection numbering over 15 million, is conveniently located right on campus. The stately Annenberg Hall, featuring vaulted ceilings and stained-glass windows, is reserved for freshman dining. New construction in adjacent Allston is in the works, and the new science facilities will focus on sustainability in their design. Cambridge is considered by many to be a quintessential college town. Harvard Square lies right next to the campus, and the larger metropolis of Boston is easy to get to on the T. The rest of the New England region offers plenty of other diversions—namely skiing, hiking, and urban exploring.

Admissions

Average high school GPA:	—
Average freshman SAT verbal / math score:	— / —
Average freshman ACT score:	—
Application fee:	$65

Application deadlines:
1/1 (freshmen)
2/1 (transfer)
11/1 (early action)

Total applicants:	22,754
Total accepted:	2,125 (9%)
Total accepted who enrolled:	1,686

Notification dates:
4/1 (freshmen)
5/31 (transfer)
12/15 (early action)

Acceptance rate for early action applicants:	14%

Students

Percentage of male / female students:	51% / 49%
Percentage of students from out of state:	84%
Percentage of students graduating in 4 years / 6 years:	87% / 98%

Money

Total endowment:	$4,294,967,295
Total tuition:	$30,275
Total cost with fees & expenses:	$44,655
Average financial aid package:	$33,625
Percentage of students who sought aid and received it:	100%
Percentage of students receiving financial aid:	49%

Also Check Out

Massachusetts Institute of Technology

Princeton University

Stanford University

University of Pennsylvania

Yale University

Harvey Mudd College

301 East 12th Street
Claremont, CA 91711

(909) 621-8000
http://www.hmc.edu/

 **BIG BRAIN**

 **BIG JOB**

 **BIG RESEARCH**

Do you have what it takes to be a "Mudder"?

5 REASONS IT'S COOL

1. **Surround yourself with smarties:** One out of every four Mudd students was valedictorian of his or her high school class.

2. **Like science?** Mudd has some of the country's **strongest programs in technical science and engineering.**

3. **Ride unicycles to class!** Read the next page for further details.

4. Grads go on to **earn PhDs at a rate of 40 percent**—the highest of any school.

5. The college boasts a **100 percent job placement rate for grads** by November 1 after their graduation.

The Basics

Public / private: private nonprofit
Total enrollment / undergrads: 729 / 729
Campus setting: suburban
Students call it: Harvey Mudd, Mudd, HMC
Students are called: Mudders
Notable alums: Donald D. Chamberlin (coinventor, SQL), Karl Mahlburg (mathematician), George Nelson (astronaut), Michael G. Wilson (filmmaker)

Dive into the Mudd

No bones about it: Harvey Mudd students work hard, and the academic environment can be intense. But that hard work comes with rewards: Mudd grads post phenomenal job placement and PhD acceptance rates. The college emphasizes peer collaboration, and students often work together on challenging projects. Mudd offers a unique blend of training in both technical subjects and the liberal arts: Students select from the nine math, science, and engineering majors that are offered, and they all must complete a liberal arts core curriculum constituting about a third of their coursework. Mudd students take advantage of the college's association with the Claremont Colleges system and all the course offerings and facilities the association brings with it. Students can also design their own major or select from several rigorous dual degree programs. The college's honor code means that students have 24-hour access to buildings and labs, as well as take-home, closed-book exams. The Mudd experience is rounded out by a required research project or senior thesis.

Calling All Pranksters

Maybe it's because all of the academic pressure requires letting off steam, but pranks (however elaborate) are commonplace at Mudd. In December 2006, after a semester on the job, President Maria Klawe entered her office to find in it a detailed reconstruction of the Mudd campus's Zen garden, complete with a fountain and benches. And if imitation is the sincerest form of flattery, MIT must have a big crush on Harvey Mudd: MIT students recently repeated the theft of a cannon from the Caltech campus that Harvey Mudd students first pulled back in 1986.

Unicycles and Uniqueness

For a small school of fewer than one thousand students, Mudd offers quite a bit of variety when it comes to the campus scene. Students choose from eight residence halls, divided between the Quad and the newer Outer Dorms. The newer dorms are known by the names North, South, East, and West, but they don't exactly correspond to the normal cardinal directions. While course loads are über-demanding and hitting the books is a common pastime, Mudders still have time for fun. Students from Claremont McKenna, Scripps, and Harvey Mudd compete in NCAA Division III athletics together; the men's teams are known as the Stags, and the women's teams are known as the Athenas. Students from all schools in the Claremont Colleges system socialize together, and leadership opportunities are plentiful, as are campus clubs. The college even has a unicycle club, although membership has been waning since the club's 1970s heyday.

Home, Warty Home

While Mudd's campus architecture is rather utilitarian, many buildings are adorned with cinder block "warts" added as decorative trim. Altogether, Mudd's buildings contain more than 25,000 warts. In fact, warts are so plentiful on campus that the college's unofficial mascot, Wally the Wart, is even one of them. The Sontag Residence Hall is the first building in the Claremont Colleges system to be officially certified for its greenness and sustainability. Off campus, students can easily walk over to quaint Claremont Village for shopping and treats; Los Angeles and its beaches are a bit farther afield—thirty-five miles to be exact.

Admissions

Average high school GPA:	—
Average freshman SAT writing / math / critical reading score:	705 / 741 / 714
Average freshman ACT score:	—
Application fee:	$50
Application deadlines: 1/15 (freshmen) 4/1 (transfer) 11/15 (early decision)	
Total applicants:	2,119
Total accepted:	645 (30%)
Total accepted who enrolled:	180
Notification dates: 4/1 (freshmen) 5/1 (transfer) 12/15 (early decision)	
Acceptance rate for early decision applicants:	49%

Students

Percentage of male / female students:	71% / 29%
Percentage of students from out of state:	51%
Percentage of students graduating in 4 years / 6 years:	78% / 85%

Money

Total endowment:	$229,721,079
Total tuition:	$34,670
Total cost with fees & expenses:	$46,082
Average financial aid package:	$27,752
Percentage of students who sought aid and received it:	100%
Percentage of students receiving financial aid:	54%

Also Check Out

California Institute of Technology

Cooper Union for the Advancement of Science and Art

Massachusetts Institute of Technology

Stanford University

University of California–Berkeley

Haverford College

370 Lancaster Avenue
Haverford, PA 19041

(610) 896-1000
http://www.haverford.edu/

 **BIG BRAIN**

 **BIG PERSPECTIVE**

A genuine community of scholars

5 REASONS IT'S COOL

1. Haverford enjoys a well-deserved reputation as an elite college that offers **stellar academics in a cozy small-school atmosphere.**

2. **Access to faculty is unparalleled**, and many students consider their professors friends.

3. The **student-designed and -enforced honor code** cultivates a deep sense of trust and common purpose.

4. Get more bang for your buck: **Nearby colleges Bryn Mawr and Swarthmore allow cross-registration** at no extra charge.

5. **Social life is laid-back and inclusive,** and it's easy to start a conversation with just about anyone.

The Basics

Public / private: private nonprofit
Total enrollment / undergrads: 1,168 / 1,168
Campus setting: suburban
Students call it: Haverford
Students are called: Fords
Notable alums: Nicholson Baker (writer), Dave Barry (humorist), Henry J. Cadbury (Nobel Laureate, Peace), Charles Mathias (senator), Maxfield Parrish (painter)

Out of the Rat Race

Haverford requires students to fulfill distribution requirements in humanities, sciences, social sciences, a foreign language, and writing. Students are also expected to complete coursework in social justice, a requirement that demonstrates the ongoing influence of the school's Quaker founders (although the college has severed its official ties with the Society of Friends). The workload at Haverford is heavy, and students take their academics seriously, but the environment is anything but cutthroat. An unwritten rule discourages people from talking about their grades, which means that the struggle for success doesn't usually feel like a zero-sum game pitting friend against friend. The welcoming and approachable professors do a lot to keep the tone positive. The student-faculty ratio is 8:1, and the average class size is sixteen, meaning that it's easy for professors to treat students as academic partners. Most professors live on campus, which deepens students' sense that they're part of a special community.

The Honor Code

Many colleges have honor codes, but Haverford's is unique because it is completely run by students. Fords review the Code, consider the need for changes, and reratify it before the start of every semester. Students take the Code very seriously, including its mandate to report the actions of anyone they observe violating it.

Dorky and Proud of It

There's one trait that most Haverford students have in common: students cheerfully acknowledge that they are, as a group, a little on the nerdy side. Quaker ideals of inclusiveness prohibit Greek houses, and 96 percent of students live on the quiet and relaxed campus. Freshman dorms are reputed to be better than upperclassmen apartments, although students who wish to are usually able to live in private rooms for all four years. There are some theme houses, including Drinker House, which is the closest the college comes to having a fraternity. Weekend parties are populated not only by Haverford students but also by Bryn Mawr students, who ride the shuttle bus to Haverford from their campus two miles down the road. A sizeable contingent of students don't party much at all, preferring to spend their free time making new friends or meeting up with old ones at low-key get-togethers.

Surrounded by Choices

Haverford is a wealthy suburb ten miles from downtown Philadelphia, and whether students are out for a night on the town or a museum visit, they benefit from their close proximity to the City of Brotherly Love. East Coasters have an easy trip home up or down I-95, and when warm whether hits, the Jersey shore beckons. The nearby and enormous King of Prussia Mall is popular with shopaholics, although Haverford itself has all the stores, restaurants, and cafés you could want, provided you don't mind paying slightly inflated prices. Campus is famously safe—not surprising, considering its location—and pretty, with a nature walk and duck pond accenting its eclectic collection of architecture.

Admissions

Average high school GPA: —

Average freshman SAT writing / math / critical reading score: 691 / 689 / 691

Average freshman ACT score: —

Application fee: $60

Application deadlines:
1/15 (freshmen)
3/31 (transfer)
11/15 (early decision)

Total applicants: 3,351

Total accepted: 869 (26%)

Total accepted who enrolled: 314

Notification dates:
4/15 (freshmen)
6/1 (transfer)
12/15 (early decision)

Acceptance rate for early decision applicants: 44%

Students

Percentage of male / female students: 47% / 53%

Percentage of students from out of state: 86%

Percentage of students graduating in 4 years / 6 years: 81% / 88%

Money

Total endowment: $452,933,000

Total tuition: $33,394

Total cost with fees & expenses: $45,294

Average financial aid package: $28,881

Percentage of students who sought aid and received it: 100%

Percentage of students receiving financial aid: 43%

Also Check Out

Amherst College

Brown University

Bryn Mawr College

Swarthmore College

Williams College

Hendrix College

1600 Washington Avenue
Conway, AR 72032

(501) 329-6811
http://www.hendrix.edu/

 **BIG PERSPECTIVE**

 **BIG WORLD**

Where learning is living

5 REASONS IT'S COOL

1. Located **just outside Little Rock, Arkansas**, Hendrix is a small-town school with a major metropolis in its backyard.

2. **Professors go out of their way to help students**, often forming close bonds with them that last well beyond graduation.

3. The interdisciplinary studies program gives students the **option of designing their own majors.**

4. Ninety-nine percent of students receive **some form of financial aid.**

5. The new Hendrix Odyssey program ensures that **all** students get hands-on experience in their fields of study.

The Basics

Public / private: private religious
Total enrollment / undergrads: 1,095 / 1,088
Campus setting: suburban
Students call it: Hendrix
Students are called: Warriors
Notable alums: Natalie Canerday (actress), May Ann Gwinn (journalist), Mary Steenburgen (actress), Joan Wagnon (mayor, Topeka, KS)

A World of Opportunities

If you think small schools mean small opportunities, think again. Even Hendrix students themselves gape at the quality of the academic opportunities available to them. Whether you major in English or psychology, both highly popular, or buck convention and design your own course of study, you'll learn from faculty members who push their students to do their absolute best. Students in all departments must complete the Hendrix Odyssey, which requires the completion of three projects in the arts, global awareness, internships, community service, research, or other areas. Students leave this college with a well-rounded education and a reputation for preparedness among grad schools and employers. An impressive 60 percent of students pursue postgraduate degrees in law, medicine, business, and the arts and sciences after leaving Hendrix.

Out with the Greeks

Hendrix is perhaps the only school where students rush to join frats and sororities that don't exist. Every September, the college holds what it calls Faux Rush Week, during which each residence hall hosts a different event, ranging from mud wrestling to a pie-eating contest to water balloon dodge ball. Students compete to earn points for their dorms, and the week culminates with a foam dance party and the Hendrix Olympix, where the winning dorm receives cash and prizes.

Do unto Others

Hendrix students by and large come from upper-middle-class backgrounds, and espouse liberal political beliefs. They are deeply interested in addressing social injustices, and many complain that their school doesn't actively recruit more minorities. Students are likely to spend their downtime talking politics, debating systems of government, or campaigning to right one of the world's wrongs. When students aren't hanging out in the dorms, where 80 percent of them live, they tend to congregate in the Brick Pit, an open pavilion in the middle of campus, and in the student center, affectionately called the Burrow. The college-sponsored Friday Afternoon Discussions are also popular. They feature panel discussions on topics ranging from the meaning of dreams to social policy issues.

My Campus, My Life

Going to school thirty minutes outside of Little Rock gives Hendrix students the best of both worlds: a close campus community with big-city opportunities. While the proximity to Little Rock is much appreciated, most students spend their evenings and weekends on campus, where there is always something to do. The Office of Student Activities coordinates student social events ranging from concerts and movies to dances and open-mic nights. When the weather's nice, students walk along the nature trail or hang out in the gazebo or pecan court.

Admissions

Average high school GPA:	3.7
Average freshman SAT verbal / math score:	622 / 612
Average freshman ACT score:	25
Application fee:	$40

Application deadlines:
8/1 (freshmen)
8/1 (transfer)

Total applicants:	1,263
Total accepted:	1,077 (85%)
Total accepted who enrolled:	396

Notification dates:
continuous (freshmen)
continuous (transfer)

Students

Percentage of male / female students:	45% / 55%
Percentage of students from out of state:	46%
Percentage of students graduating in 4 years / 6 years:	55% / 61%

Money

Total endowment:	$159,678,000
Total tuition:	$22,616
Total cost with fees & expenses:	$30,554
Average financial aid package:	$16,968
Percentage of students who sought aid and received it:	80%
Percentage of students receiving financial aid:	58%

Also Check Out

Austin College

Baylor University

Rhodes College

Trinity University

Hobart and William Smith Colleges

629 S. Main Street
Geneva, NY 14456

(315) 781-3000
http://www.hws.edu/

 **BIG IDEA**

 **BIG PERSPECTIVE**

When one is better than two

5 REASONS IT'S COOL

1. Hobart and William Smith pulls off the neat trick of being **two schools in one:** a men's college and a women's college.

2. There are no **formal distribution requirements,** and students design their educations across academic disciplines.

3. **Classes are small,** and professors take a genuine interest in their students.

4. The campus sits beside Seneca Lake, which makes for pleasant **afternoons out on the water.**

5. **Sports and service are big** deals here. The lacrosse team always draws a crowd, and students form lasting, meaningful bonds with residents of Geneva.

The Basics

Public / private: private nonprofit
Total enrollment / undergrads: 1,883 / 1,868
Campus setting: small town
Students call it: Hobart William Smith, H&WS
Notable alums: Elizabeth Blackwell (first woman MD in the United States), Eveyln Tooley Hunt (writer; creator, American-style haikus), Alan Kalter (announcer, *Late Show with David Letterman*), Bill Whitaker (TV journalist)

Encouraging Breadth

Hobart and William Smith emphasizes its marriage of liberal and interdisciplinary learning. Students are required to declare not only a major but also a minor or second major, one of which must be interdisciplinary. There are no distribution requirements, aside from a small interdisciplinary first-year seminar. One of the strongest selling points of an education here is the diminutive size of classes. Fewer than 10 percent of courses enroll more than fifty students, and around two-thirds of courses have fewer than twenty-five students. As a result, professors get to know their students quite well and keep in touch with them as the years go by. Psychology and economics are two of the most popular majors, and the hard sciences are coming on strong now that the lab facilities have undergone a major refurbishing. The Finger Lakes Institute gives students a chance to get work experience in their fields of concentration, and study-abroad programs are popular and far-flung—twenty-eight foreign and domestic cities host students every semester.

A Happy Marriage

Hobart and William Smith Colleges are, technically, independent institutions that share many of the same facilities. William Smith was founded in 1908, when a philanthropist by that name offered the college of Hobart (founded in 1822) a large donation—on the condition that a college for women be established alongside the men's school. Eventually, it seemed unnecessarily expensive to maintain two largely identical academic programs next door to each other, and by the early forties, almost all classes were coed.

More Together than Separate

Hobart (the men's college) and William Smith (the women's) maintain separate administrations, but for the most part, students at the two schools exist in a single community. Over 90 percent of the student body lives on campus; same-sex living arrangements are available, but coed dorms are just as common. Greek life is underwhelming. About 15 percent of men join fraternities, while there are no sororities. Students eager for alternative, non-Greek community living can apply for berths in small residential houses owned by the university. These houses, as well as most dorms, activity spaces, and athletic facilities, get high marks. There's a student-run dance club, lots of equipment available for water sports on Seneca Lake, and –an outdoor activities program that organizes day- and weekend-long adventures in the surrounding wilderness. Diversity is probably the area with the most room for improvement: 47 percent of students are New Yorkers, and only 12 percent are nonwhite.

Beauty, on Campus and Off

Combined, the Hobart and William Smith campuses stretch across two hundred lakeside acres. Buildings range from colonial to modern, with more than enough ivy to make you remember you're at college. Geneva, a resuscitating industrial community, is more of a "town with a college" than a true "college town," but there are nonetheless a few spots popular with students. The Smith Opera House, for example, brings in surprisingly big-time musical acts and gives students discounts on tickets. Meanwhile, state parks in the Finger Lakes region keep hikers, bikers, and campers happy. It's good to have a car, but first-years with wheels are often disappointed to realize that Syracuse and Rochester, the nearest cities, are relative duds.

Admissions

Average high school GPA:	3.22
Average freshman SAT verbal / math score:	593 / 599
Average freshman ACT score:	—
Application fee:	$45

Application deadlines:
2/1 (freshmen)
7/1 (transfer)
11/15 (early decision)

Total applicants:	3,410
Total accepted:	2,209 (65%)
Total accepted who enrolled:	545

Notification dates:
4/1 (freshmen)
continuous (transfer)
12/15 (early decision)

Acceptance rate for early decision applicants:	79%

Students

Percentage of male / female students:	46% / 54%
Percentage of students from out of state:	55%
Percentage of students graduating in 4 years / 6 years:	71% / 78%

Money

Total endowment:	$141,965,240
Total tuition:	$33,730
Total cost with fees & expenses:	$44,476
Average financial aid package:	$25,059
Percentage of students who sought aid and received it:	80%
Percentage of students receiving financial aid:	63%

Also Check Out

Colby College

Hamilton College

Skidmore College

St. Lawrence University

Union College

Hofstra University

100 Hofstra University
Hempstead, NY 11549

(516) 463-6600
http://www.hofstra.edu/

BIG CHOICE

An arboretum, a unique curriculum, and a train to NYC

5 REASONS IT'S COOL

1. Small classes and a great student-to-faculty ratio characterize academics at this **up-and-coming university**.

2. Students who take classes in the innovative New College **enjoy field trips, hands-on experience, and creative pairings of concentrations.**

3. The Odyssey Program **takes studying abroad to a new level:** Instead of staying in one place, students move from city to city.

4. Through the LEAP program, students can **earn a bachelor's and a law degree in just six years.**

5. **New York, New York!** The excitement of the Big Apple is twenty-five miles away.

The Basics

Public/private: private nonprofit
Total enrollment/undergrads: 12,550 / 8,498
Campus setting: suburban
Students call it: Hofstra
Students are called: Lions, the Pride
Notable alums: Alan Colmes (broadcaster), Francis Ford Coppola (filmmaker), Nelson DeMille (author), Philip Rosenthal (creator, *Everybody Loves Raymond*), Howard Safir (police commissioner, New York City)

Hey, Is That a New College?

Students praise the small classes and interdisciplinary options at this midsize university. With an average class size of twenty-three and a 14:1 student-to-faculty ratio, students can have plenty of personalized attention if they ask for it. Students taking classes at the New College follow a block schedule in which they take one class for three and a half weeks. These courses are open to all freshmen and sophomores and include a field trip component that takes advantage of the school's proximity to New York City. After a year of New College block courses, upperclassmen can choose from 130 majors or stick with the interdisciplinary environment of the New College. The latter option includes such unique concentrations as creative writing paired with psychology or molecular biology with business administration. Those following a more traditional route can enroll in the popular Frank G. Zarb School of Business or the School of Communication, among other undergraduate programs. To ease the transition to college, consider the First

Let's Go Dutch

William Hofstra, the university's namesake, had relatives from the Netherlands, and a Dutch connection lives on today. There's a dorm complex called the Netherlands, the design of the university's flag and seal were borrowed from the Dutch, and there is a Dutch festival on campus each year. The Dutch government even named a flower after the university: the Hofstra University Tulip.

Year Connections (FYC) program, which gives students instant study-buddies.

Love It, Leave It, or Both

One of the defining characteristics of Hofstra is its proximity to New York City, which provides a wealth of job and internship possibilities, as well as myriad entertainment options. There's a fairly sizeable commuter population, as the majority of students are originally from Long Island. Between students heading home or taking the Long Island Railroad into the city, the campus tends to empty out on the weekends. While some wish for more on-campus events, others seem pleased with the barhopping scene nearby, and everyone loves the Freak Formal that occurs every Halloween. There are over thirty-seven residence halls to house those who do live on the tree-lined campus. A strong Greek scene pervades most aspects of social life, and students aren't shy about their love of a good party. Whether at a party or at a desk, this is a well-dressed crowd—don't be surprised to find ladies donning heels for morning class.

What Beautiful Trees You Have

The 240-acre campus is located in Hempsted, just twenty-five miles from New York City. The campus, a registered arboretum (one of only 430 in the country), includes gardens, tree-lined walkways, and a two-acre bird sanctuary. Hempstead doesn't have much to offer the college student, but the beaches of Long Island are just a short drive away. Most students have wheels, and those who don't use public transport. The Long Island Railroad is just two miles from campus and will take you straight into Manhattan.

Admissions

Average high school GPA:	3.26
Average freshman SAT verbal / math score:	582 / 596
Average freshman ACT score:	23
Application fee:	$50
Application deadlines: continuous (freshmen) — (transfer) 11/15 (early action)	
Total applicants:	13,493
Total accepted:	8,366 (62%)
Total accepted who enrolled:	1,710
Notification dates: 2/1 (freshmen) continuous (transfer) 12/15 (early action)	
Acceptance rate for early action applicants:	74%

Students

Percentage of male / female students:	47% / 53%
Percentage of students from out of state:	32%
Percentage of students graduating in 4 years / 6 years:	36% / 55%

Money

Total endowment:	$204,639,084
Total tuition:	$23,800
Total cost with fees & expenses:	$35,630
Average financial aid package:	$17,353
Percentage of students who sought aid and received it:	51%
Percentage of students receiving financial aid:	53%

Also Check Out

Hobart and William Smith Colleges

Siena College

Skidmore College

Hope College

141 East 12th Street, PO Box 9000
Holland, MI 49422

(616) 395-7000
http://www.hope.edu/

BIG PERSPECTIVE

Wishin' and hopin' and dreamin' and studyin' . . .

5 REASONS IT'S COOL

1. **Traditions are bountiful** at Hope, and students benefit from the bonding this brings.

2. This **Christian-affiliated** school is in **the historically Dutch town of Holland.**

3. This school **celebrates student projects**, creative and research-based alike.

4. Major **campus improvements** have made life sweeter for students.

5. Students can **lounge lakeside** in minutes—Lake Michigan is just five miles away.

The Basics

Public / private: private religious
Total enrollment / undergrads: 3,203 / 3,203
Campus setting: suburban
Students call it: Hope
Students are called: Flying Dutch
Notable alums: Meredith Arwady (contralto), Rob "CmdrTaco" Malda (founder, Slashdot), Max De Pree (writer, business leader), Milton J. Nieuwsma (filmmaker, writer), Rachel Reenstra (TV host), Sufjan Stevens (singer-songwriter)

Hope Springs Eternal

Hope College is a liberal arts college affiliated with the Reformed Church in America. Although students from that particular denomination form less than twenty percent of the student body, Christianity still runs strong through this school. So do the arts: Hope is the only private liberal arts college to be nationally accredited in art, dance, music, and theater. Strong programs in the sciences, supported with tons of funding from the National Science Foundation Research Experiences for Undergraduates Program, complement the focus on creativity at Hope. Each spring, students show off the fruits of their labors in a performance. Many students collaborate with faculty on their research. The most popular majors at Hope fall into the areas of business, education, and psychology. All students start with a common general education curriculum and can take introductory First-Year Seminars. Later on, students can study abroad in over sixty countries; the summer semester in Vienna is a very popular choice.

Pull My Rope

"The Pull," an annual tradition at Hope for over a hundred years, pits thirty-six sophomores against the same number of freshmen in a grand tug-of-war from opposite banks of the Black River. Eighteen moralers from each team give directions to the pullers. Juniors and seniors pitch in as coaches to the young ones, who practice their tugging technique leading up to the main event. Parents, alumni, fellow students, and friends come out in droves to watch the exciting battle, which lasts about three hours.

Double Dutch

Hope College's emblem is an anchor, and with such a flurry of activity going on on this campus, it's important to focus on stability. There are eighteen men's (Flying Dutchmen) and women's (Flying Dutch) varsity sports, and the winning women's basketball team is ranked number one in NCAA Division III. In a fit of competition, freshmen and sophomore women compete for the Nykerk Cup each fall. The underclasswomen try to outdo each other through singing, acting, and orating—with only three weeks to prepare. The frenzy doesn't stop there: during the annual Dance Marathon, students dance for twenty-four hours to raise money for the DeVos Children's Hospital. The annual Christmas Vespers concert draws listeners from around the country to hear the melodious voices of Hope. The great majority of students here hail from states surrounding the Great Lakes. Although Hope has many strengths, diversity is not one of them.

Tiptoe Through the Tulips

Hope College is a mere five miles from the eastern shores of Lake Michigan. Long known as a summertime destination, Holland is full of lakeside charms and tulips—thousands and thousands of tulips. Each May, Tulip Time celebrates the blooms of the ubiquitous bulbs with Dutch folk dances, parades, and delicious dishes. Students can drive around the lake to Chicago or Milwaukee, and Grand Rapids is just a half an hour away. Hope's not resting on Holland's historic past, however. The college recently renovated the Schaap Science Center to the tune of $36 million. The DeVos Fieldhouse opened in 2005, and it can hold up to 3,400 Flying Dutch and Dutchmen fans. The Western Theological Seminary shares Hope's ninety-one acre campus, which has a lovely grove of pine trees at its center.

Admissions

Average high school GPA:	—
Average freshman SAT verbal / math score:	—/—
Average freshman ACT score:	—
Application fee:	$35
Application deadlines: continuous (freshmen) continuous (transfer)	
Total applicants:	2,666
Total accepted:	2,172 (81%)
Total accepted who enrolled:	778
Notification dates: continuous (freshmen) continuous (transfer)	
Acceptance rate for early action applicants:	—

Students

Percentage of male / female students:	40% / 60%
Percentage of students from out of state:	26%
Percentage of students graduating in 4 years / 6 years:	64% / 76%

Money

Total endowment:	$118,096,854
Total tuition:	$22,430
Total cost with fees & expenses:	$30,212
Average financial aid package:	$18,771
Percentage of students who sought aid and received it:	85%
Percentage of students receiving financial aid:	50%

Also Check Out

Kalamazoo College

Michigan State University

Valparaiso University

Howard University

2400 Sixth Street, NW
Washington, DC 20059

(202) 806-6100
http://www.howard.edu/

BIG HAND

A prestigious university in the nation's capital

5 REASONS IT'S COOL

1. This **historically black college/university (HBCU)** produces more African American PhDs than any other university in the nation.

2. The Moorland-Spingarn Research Center houses **one of the largest collections of black literature in the country.**

3. **Small classes** are the norm here; more than 60 percent of classes have twenty students or fewer.

4. **Washington, D.C.** offers culture, entertainment, and plenty of internship opportunities.

5. Students from **more than a hundred countries** make this university an enlightened place to be.

The Basics

Public / private: private nonprofit
Total enrollment / undergrads: 10,623 / 7,112
Campus setting: urban
Students call it: Howard
Students are called: Bison
Notable alums: Percival Broderick (deputy prime minister, Jamaica), Shauntay Hinton (Miss USA, 2002), Hon. Thurgood Marshall (first African American U.S. Supreme Court justice), Toni Morrison (author), Phylicia Rashad (actress)

Need a Change of Pace? Try a Different College!

Howard students are focused, motivated, and serious about academic success. The climate is far from competitive, however, and students are supported by both professors and peers. There are fifty-eight majors, from 3-D reality to comparative politics. Being in the nation's capitol is a plus for those students in the market for hands-on experience. Business, communications, engineering, and architecture students all have co-op programs available to them. If Howard doesn't offer a class or a location that suits your fancy, try the National Student Exchange (NSE). This domestic exchange program allows sophomores and juniors to study at any of 171 other colleges, including Columbia, Duke, and Rutgers. Howard students must complete a rather hefty core curriculum to graduate, including courses in composition, foreign language, African American history, and physical education. The student-to-faculty ratio is 7:1, and classes are small.

Howard's Happening Homecoming

Come October, make sure you stay close to campus for the annual weeklong homecoming extravaganza. Undergrads, alumni, and friends gather for fashion shows, poetry slams, gospel choirs, step shows—and, of course, the football game. For two days during homecoming week, everyone takes to the campus quad for Yardfest, which features food and live music. Howard's homecoming is so big that it's mentioned in songs by Ludacris and the Notorious B.I.G.

Out-of-Staters, Unite!

Don't feel anxious about going to college out of state—at Howard, you'll feel right at home no matter where you come from. Only 9 percent of students are from the capital area, while 75 percent come from other states. There's a strong international presence on campus as well, especially from Africa and the Americas. Students cite a strong sense of community as a defining feature of the university. Greek life also plays a major role. Many black fraternities were founded at Howard, and they promote not just partying but also service and unity among African Americans. There are more than 140 clubs and organizations on campus, and most students are highly involved in several. Popular options include dance teams, professional associations, and gospel choirs. First-year students should plan to live on campus. They can choose from among nine residences, including single-sex and coed halls. There are some pretty stringent visitation rules in the dorms, and the amenities vary from building to building. Major hangouts on campus are Punch-Out, a dining area with a food court feel, and the Blackburn Center, located at the center of campus. Looking for something to do? Hop on the nearby Metro to explore the nation's capital.

East, West, and Main

Howard's campus is divided into East Campus (where you'll find the Divinity School), West Campus (home of the Law School), and Main Campus. Stately brick buildings dot the campus, include a number of historic landmarks, including both Frederick Douglass Memorial Hall and Founders Library. Students tend to congregate on the "yard" in one of the many campus eateries. Getting around the city is easy on the Metro, which is accessible from the Main Campus. There's a wealth of things to do in D.C., from free museum visits at the Smithsonian to late-night clubbing. The bars and restaurants of Adams Morgan tend to draw students as well.

Admissions

Average high school GPA:	3.2
Average freshman SAT verbal / math score:	548 / 539
Average freshman ACT score:	22
Application fee:	$45
Application deadlines: 2/15 (freshmen) 4/1 (transfer) 11/1 (early action)	
Total applicants:	8,860
Total accepted:	4,156 (47%)
Total accepted who enrolled:	1,444
Notification dates: continuous (freshmen) continuous (transfer) 12/24 (early action)	
Acceptance rate for early action applicants:	—

Students

Percentage of male / female students:	33% / 67%
Percentage of students from out of state:	90%
Percentage of students graduating in 4 years / 6 years:	35% / 59%

Money

Total endowment:	$371,160,000
Total tuition:	$11,490
Total cost with fees & expenses:	$19,501
Average financial aid package:	$17,077
Percentage of students who sought aid and received it:	75%
Percentage of students receiving financial aid:	60%

Also Check Out

Florida Agricultural and Mechanical University

Hampton University

Morehouse College

Spelman College

Indiana University– Bloomington

107 S. Indiana Avenue
Bloomington, IN 47405

(812) 855-4848
http://www.iub.edu/

 **BIG CHOICE**

 **BIG RESEARCH**

Hoosier favorite team?

5 REASONS IT'S COOL

1. **A wide selection of academic program, majors, and research options** allows students to choose from a number of paths.

2. IU's **beautiful campus** sports historic limestone buildings along with impressive museums and recreation facilities.

3. **Research opportunities abound** at this major research university, even for freshmen.

4. **Hoosier spirit** dominates the student body, infusing all campus parties and festivities.

5. **On-campus residential neighborhoods make for a cozy community,** even at this large school.

The Basics

Public / private: public state
Total enrollment / undergrads: 38,247 / 29,828
Campus setting: small town
Students call it: IU, IUB
Students are called: Hoosiers
Notable alums: Joe Buck (sportscaster), Meg Cabot (author), Hoagy Carmichael (songwriter), Mark Cuban (technology entrepreneur; owner, Dallas Mavericks), Robert Gates (U.S. secretary of defense), Booker T. Jones (musician), Will Shortz (puzzle maker), Leonard Slatkin (conductor), Tavis Smiley (radio and TV host), Gary Snyder (poet), Mark Spitz (Olympic swimmer), Isaiah Thomas (pro basketball player), James Watson (Nobel Laureate, Medicine)

A Smorgasbord of Studies

With more than 130 majors across thirteen undergraduate schools and the College of Arts and Sciences, IU gives its students plenty of options. The University Division provides academic advising and support for freshmen, helping them navigate the big academic ocean and complete all requirements. The UD's Health Professionals and Pre-Law centers provide further specialized advising for advancement in those fields. The student-to-faculty ratio is 18:1. Optional Freshman Interest Groups (FIGs), which bring together small groups of students to live and study around a common theme, make the large school feel like a small one. For the science minded, the competitive IU STARS program provides four years of research opportunities beginning freshman year, which gives

The (Big) Little 500

The Little 500, modeled after the Indy 500 and immortalized in the movie *Breaking Away*, is an annual bicycle race that has been part of IU life since 1951. The "World's Greatest College Weekend," as the race and surrounding events have come to be known, draws more than twenty thousand people to Bloomington. Student teams compete in men's and women's relay-style races solely for the glory of winning; all proceeds go to a scholarship fund for working IU students.

participants an edge when they apply to grad school. But no matter what your field, the IU academic experience provides lots of options, from the renowned library, bursting with over 7 million volumes, to study-abroad programs, self-designed majors, and honors programs.

Pick Your Party

IU is home to over five hundred organizations and clubs, including over one hundred interests-based learning programs, but Greeks command the most attention, with about 17 percent of students participating in frats or sororities. As a result, IU is also home to lots of parties—big parties. There are big festivities, too, most prominently spring's IU Sing, during which musical and dance performances are on display. Big Ten Hoosier athletics drive school spirit, especially when teams play rival Purdue. Men's basketball is the hottest sport, and the one for which IU is most famous, but soccer, football, and swimming and diving are not far behind. The Indiana Memorial Union (IMU), the second largest student union in the United States, brings students (and guests) together with shops, salons, eateries, and even a hotel. IMU recreational options include bowling, movies, and art classes.

Love That Limestone

The Sample Gates open to over 1,800 acres of IU campus, where limestone mined from Indiana quarries forms the heart and soul of the older buildings. The collegiate Gothic architecture gives the grounds a stately, romantic feeling, most apparent at the Rose Well House. (The story goes that a female student isn't truly a Hoosier until she has been kissed there at midnight.) The Student Building, completed in 1905, is on the National Register of Historic Places, and the IU Auditorium houses the *Century of Progress* mural by Thomas Hart Benton and a 4,500-pipe Roosevelt Organ. Bloomington is the quintessential college town. Sprawling Indianapolis is only an hour's drive away, but Chicago (which is at least three hours away) it ain't.

Admissions

Average high school GPA:	3.5
Average freshman SAT verbal / math score:	556 / 576
Average freshman ACT score:	24
Application fee:	$50
Application deadlines: continuous (freshmen) continuous (transfer)	
Total applicants:	24,169
Total accepted:	19,252 (80%)
Total accepted who enrolled:	7,218
Notification dates: continuous (freshmen) continuous (transfer)	

Students

Percentage of male / female students:	48% / 52%
Percentage of students from out of state:	34%
Percentage of students graduating in 4 years / 6 years:	48% / 71%

Money

Total endowment:	$755,038,506
Total in-state tuition, fees & expenses:	$14,552
Total out-of-state tuition, fees & expenses:	$27,564
Average financial aid package:	$7,463
Percentage of students who sought aid and received it:	67%
Percentage of students receiving financial aid:	35%

Also Check Out

Michigan State University

Northwestern University

Purdue University

University of Illinois at Urbana-Champaign

University of Wisconsin–Madison

Ithaca College

100 Job Hall
Ithaca, NY 14850

(607) 274-3011
http://www.ithaca.edu/

 **BIG PERSPECTIVE**

Gorge yourself on learning!

5 REASONS IT'S COOL

1. Students take to the stage, screen, and airwaves with **top programs in the performing arts and communications.**

2. Faculty members really **pay attention** to students at Ithaca, where the focus is on educating undergrads.

3. **Well over 90** of graduates from the School of Health Sciences and Human Performance pass their licensure exams.

4. The campus's location in the Finger Lakes region mean **lots of recreation opportunities.**

5. Never has Division III football caused such a stir! The **rivalry for the Corata Jug** brings out the best in the Ithaca Bombers.

The Basics

Public / private: private nonprofit
Total enrollment / undergrads: 6,409 / 6,028
Campus setting: small town
Students call it: Ithaca
Students are called: Bombers
Notable alums: Kate Aldrich (mezzo-soprano), Giulio Capua (vice president and publisher, *Architectural Digest*), Robert Iger (president and CEO, The Walt Disney Co.), Ricki Lake (actress, TV host), Jessica Savitch (news anchor), Rod Serling (creator, *The Twilight Zone*)

Intrepid Explorers

Ithaca's film, music, and theater programs lure many students to this lovely campus. The School of Music's conservatory-style programs emphasize performance but also allow students to branch out into traditional liberal arts studies. The Park School of Communications provides an array of pre-professional preparation to budding filmmakers, journalists, and media moguls. Ithaca's complete undergraduate experience supports all kinds of scholars in the over one hundred majors here—including those who haven't made up their minds yet. Rather than stamping students "undeclared," Ithaca calls the undecided "exploratory students" and allows them to enroll in classes across the five schools and the Division of Interdisciplinary and International Studies. These explorers have two semesters to declare a major. Those still interested in going their own way can major in Planned Studies, which entails submitting a proposal in the area of inquiry.

Nice Jug!

The Division III football game between the SUNY Cortland Red Dragons and the Ithaca Bombers sounds like it deserves a fiercer trophy than what the winner actually receives. Each year since 1959, these two schools duke it out for the Cortaca Jug, whose name comes from the mash-up of *Cort*land and Ith*aca*. The colorful jug sports the four colors of these two schools—blue and gold for Ithaca and red and white for SUNY Cortland—along with each year's score.

Cold Fingers

About 45 percent of Ithaca students come from the state of New York, so they might already be used to the chilly winters of this region. Weather aside, there are lots of extracurricular activities on and off campus. Cornell University is nearby, and Ithaca students can enroll in courses there. There are no social fraternities, so social units form around activities like student government, the award-winning *Ithacan* newspaper, and students' schools. The School of Music has over three hundred concerts every year, and film screenings are plentiful. The Division III athletic champs include the women's crew team. Students praise the town of Ithaca for its street-side shopping, and the surrounding Finger Lakes region provides hiking and scenery aplenty. The numerous internships and professional preparation that is intrinsic to students' studies at Ithaca result in grads who are well-prepared for grad school and the job market. Well over 90 percent of graduates from the School of Health Sciences and Human Performance pass their licensure exams, and just as many find jobs after graduation.

Ithaca Is Gorges

Ithaca, a college town at heart, sits at the southern end of Cayuga Lake. Ithaca is also the home of Cornell University, and the two schools enjoy a warm relationship in this cool area. The Finger Lakes region has lakes, glacier-formed gorges, and award-winning wineries. The campus is sixty miles south of Syracuse, and is at roughly the halfway point between New York City and Toronto. On campus, the Dillinger Center for the Performing Arts looks onto Cayuga Lake and hosts numerous performances from Ithaca's talented students. The distinctive Muller Chapel welcomes students of all faiths for worship and meditation. The campus currently benefits from a slate of new construction, and the new School of Business building is the nation's first undergraduate business school to receive LEED Platinum certification.

Admissions

Average high school GPA:	—
Average freshman SAT writing / math / critical reading score:	588 / 598 / 592
Average freshman ACT score:	—
Application fee:	$60

Application deadlines:
2/1 (freshmen)
3/1 (transfer)
11/1 (early decision)

Total applicants:	11,312
Total accepted:	7,773 (69%)
Total accepted who enrolled:	1,521

Notification dates:
4/15 (freshmen)
4/15 (transfer)
12/15 (early decision)

Acceptance rate for early decision applicants:	50%

Students

Percentage of male / female students:	45% / 55%
Percentage of students from out of state:	53%
Percentage of students graduating in 4 years / 6 years:	64% / 73%

Money

Total endowment:	$140,789,568
Total tuition:	$26,832
Total cost with fees & expenses:	$38,151
Average financial aid package:	$22,694
Percentage of students who sought aid and received it:	86%
Percentage of students receiving financial aid:	67%

Also Check Out

Boston University

Cornell University

New York University

The Pennsylvania State University–University Park

Syracuse University

James Madison University

800 South Main Street
Harrisonburg, VA 22807

(540) 568-6211
http://www.jmu.edu/

 **BIG RESEARCH**

 **BIG WORLD**

Virginia is for lovers of learning.

5 REASONS IT'S COOL

1. Toss a Frisbee or just lounge on the quad with the rest of the **friendly, relaxed student body.**

2. Take an **innovative approach to science** at the College of Integrated Science and Technology.

3. Get **hands-on experience in filmography, video editing, or feature magazine production** at the School for Media and Arts Design.

4. Be part of a student body nationally recognized for its **focus on social responsibility and civic service.**

5. Oh Shenandoah! Go for a hike or bike ride in the **lovely Blue Ridge Mountains** surrounding quaint, historic Harrisonburg.

The Basics

Public / private: public state
Total enrollment / undergrads: 17,393 / 16,013
Campus setting: small town
Students call it: James Madison, JMU
Students are called: Duke Dogs, Dukes
Notable alums: Jim Acosta (news correspondent), Marcia Angell (physician, author), Charles Haley (pro football player), Phoef Sutton (TV producer, writer)

Hands-on and Happy

JMU is a rapidly growing research institution, but one that remains dedicated to teaching. Large lecture classes may be common in the first year, but professors are consistently described as accessible and eager to help. Freshmen admitted to the JMU Honors Program have access to smaller, high-level courses. JMU's six undergraduate colleges offer sixty-seven possible majors, including traditional liberal arts concentrations and specialized occupational tracks. The acclaimed College of Business draws a large number of students. The College of Education has a five-year dual BA/MA program in teaching, and the School of Media and Art Design (SMAD) provides hands-on training in cinema studies, interactive media, and print journalism, among other subjects. The College of Integrated Science and Technology (CISAT) offers innovative programs that focus on real-world application. Excellent lab facilities and ample research opportunities allow students to work on socially and environmentally relevant projects at home or abroad.

Growing Up

Founded in 1909, JMU was initially a school for women with an enrollment of just over two hundred students. My, how times have changed! Not only is JMU coed, but the institution has also nearly doubled in size in the past twenty years and now boasts an undergrad population of over sixteen thousand.

Life on the Quad

Dukes are a laid-back bunch content with all JMU has to offer (and some are more than content with the 3:2 girl-to-guy ratio). The large quad on central campus is always filled with students studying or just hanging out. The informal gathering spot known as Taylor Down Under, located under Taylor Hall, is perfect for a quick nap between classes. And the robust recreation facility, UREC, boasts a climbing wall, yoga sessions, and dozens of fitness classes. About 15 percent of students go Greek. Other diversions include over three hundred clubs and organizations, intramural and club sports, weekly movie screenings, theater productions, and live music. Although Dukes aren't wild about their varsity athletics, everyone goes to the huge homecoming bash. Nearly 70 percent of the student body is native Virginian, and many students give back through some form of community service. Thirty-five residence halls are spread over the large campus's six divided areas, but many upperclassmen move to apartments or houses off-campus, where most of the partying takes place.

The Burg

Interstate 81 runs right through the middle of campus and through the heart of Harrisonburg, a lovely town located in the Shenandoah Valley of central Virginia. "The Burg" doesn't offer much in the way of nightlife, but students appreciate its welcoming atmosphere and the great hiking and mountain biking close by. Eastern Mennonite University and Bridgewater College are in or near town, and the frats and bars of UVA are an hour away. For students hankering for a bit of city life, Richmond and Washington, D.C. are just a two-hour drive away.

Admissions

Average high school GPA:	3.69
Average freshman SAT writing / math / critical reading score:	560 / 570 / 560
Average freshman ACT score:	23
Application fee:	$40

Application deadlines:
1/15 (freshmen)   11/1 (early action)
3/1 (transfer)

Total applicants:	17,765
Total accepted:	11,137 (63%)
Total accepted who enrolled:	3,745

Notification dates:
4/1 (freshmen)   1/15 (early action)
4/15 (transfer)

Acceptance rate for early action applicants:	52%

Students

Percentage of male / female students:	39% / 61%
Percentage of students from out of state:	30%
Percentage of students graduating in 4 years / 6 years:	62% / 80%

Money

Total endowment:	$28,777,717
Total in-state tuition, fees & expenses:	$13,866
Total out-of-state tuition, fees & expenses:	$23,812
Average financial aid package:	$7,683
Percentage of students who sought aid and received it:	50%
Percentage of students receiving financial aid:	28%

Also Check Out

George Mason University

The Pennsylvania State University–University Park

University of Delaware

University of Virginia

Virginia Polytechnic Institute and State University

Johns Hopkins University

3400 North Charles Street
Baltimore, MD 21218

(410) 516-8000
http://www.jhu.edu/

 **BIG BRAIN**

 **BIG RESEARCH**

More than just pre-med!

5 REASONS IT'S COOL

1. Do a **dual degree in music performance** with the prestigious Peabody Conservatory.

2. Johns Hopkins was the nation's first research university, and it offers **sixty grants for undergraduate research.**

3. The **beautiful college campus** is only a short train ride from Annapolis and Washington, D.C.

4. Required courses for biomedical engineering majors include Physiological Foundations— **one of the hardest in the nation.**

5. **Academics are rigorous,** but all grades in first-year courses are pass/fail.

The Basics

Public / private: private nonprofit
Total enrollment / undergrads: 6,124 / 4,478
Campus setting: urban
Students call it: Hopkins
Students are called: Blue Jays
Notable alums: Madeleine Albright (U.S. secretary of state), John Barth (writer), Michael Bloomberg (mayor, New York City), Rachel Carson (environmentalist), Wes Craven (film writer/director), John Dewey (philosopher, reformer), John McLaughlin (director, CIA), Frank Oppenheimer (physicist who worked on the Manhattan Project), Woodrow Wilson (U.S. president)

Flexibility and Rigor

Johns Hopkins's well-known science programs attract a large number of biomedical/medical engineering and other science-oriented students. But while Hopkins is most famous for its pre-med programs, the Krieger School of Arts and Sciences offers equally outstanding courses. Around 70 percent of students conduct research projects during their tenure. Aside from a mandatory writing course, there are no required classes. With a student-to-faculty ratio of 9:1, students get lots of attention, particularly during their junior and senior years. While traditionally Hopkins has been known for its focus on grad students, in recent years it has increased its emphasis on undergrad education. The Writing Department boasts such luminaries as Stephen Dixon and National Book Award winner Alice McDermott.

Johns or John?

Since the university was founded in 1876, many have joked about the name "Johns." No less a humorist than Mark Twain jested that people might be wary of enrolling in a school "that didn't know how to spell the name 'John.'" There is a rather unexciting explanation for the peculiarity, however: "Johns" was the founder's great-grandmother's maiden name.

Here, There, and Spring Fair

Hopkins students are known for their work ethic and dedication. Most shoulder the heavy workload willingly. Students also know how to use their leisure time to good advantage. A fifth of the campus join frats and sororities, and many undergrads get involved with the more than two hundred student organizations. A cappella groups and student plays are popular, and the Diverse Gender and Sexuality Alliance is active on campus. The biggest social event is the student-run Spring Fair, a three-day festival during which thousands of local residents and students enjoy food, music, and games. As for campus dining, students appreciate the diverse selection at the dining halls. If the vegan and kosher options start to pale, "J-Cash" can be put toward meals at off-campus restaurants. Partying is not an overwhelming aspect of life at Hopkins. Caffeine pills to power through a long study session are about as wild as it gets. Some students channel their energy into cheering on their nationally recognized lacrosse team, even road-tripping with them to away games.

Home Sweet Homewood

Homewood, the main undergrad campus, lies three miles north of Baltimore's Inner Harbor. Students love to sunbathe, read, or just hang out on the Beach, a green area surrounded by the library and red-brick Georgian class buildings. The campus is beautiful and incredibly green, with well-trimmed lawns and buildings arranged into quads. Washington, D.C. is an hour-long commuter-rail ride away, and its wealth of internship opportunities particularly appeals to students on the popular international studies or politics track. Maryland's capital, Annapolis, is also less than an hour's drive away. Baltimore offers an aquarium and zoo, and its art museum is just next door to Homewood. The university continues to update its facilities. The newly renovated sports center is an athlete's dream, with squash courts, a rock-climbing wall, a pool, and a weight room. The newly built Mattin Center offers soundproof music rooms, darkrooms, and a black-box theater.

Admissions

Average high school GPA:	3.69
Average freshman SAT writing / math / critical reading score:	678 / 704 / 678
Average freshman ACT score:	26
Application fee:	$60
Application deadlines:	
1/1 (freshmen)	
3/15 (transfer)	
11/15 (early decision)	
Total applicants:	13,900
Total accepted:	3,726 (27%)
Total accepted who enrolled:	1,207
Notification dates:	
4/1 (freshmen)	
5/3 (transfer)	
12/15 (early decision)	
Acceptance rate for early decision applicants:	59%

Students

Percentage of male / female students:	53% / 47%
Percentage of students from out of state:	86%
Percentage of students graduating in 4 years / 6 years:	81% / 90%

Money

Total endowment:	$2,350,000,000
Total tuition:	$33,900
Total cost with fees & expenses:	$45,522
Average financial aid package:	$31,176
Percentage of students who sought aid and received it:	100%
Percentage of students receiving financial aid:	45%

Also Check Out

Cornell University

Duke University

Harvard University

University of Pennsylvania

Yale University

The Julliard School

60 Lincoln Center Plaza
New York, NY 10023

(212) 799-5000
http://www.juilliard.edu/

 **BIG PLAN**

The big apple of art's eye

The Basics

Public / private: private nonprofit
Total enrollment / undergrads: 808 / 481
Campus setting: urban
Students call it: Juilliard
Notable alums: Jamie Foxx (actor), William Hurt (actor), Val Kilmer (actor), Philip Glass (composer), Laura Linney (actress), Patti Lupone (singer, actress), Yo-Yo Ma (cellist), Wynton Marsalis (trumpeter), Itzak Perlman (violinist), Tito Puente (musician), Nina Simone (singer), Kevin Spacey (actor), Ving Rhames (actor), John Williams (composer)

Major Music Scene, Minor Academics

Julliard students must pick one of three majors: dance, drama, or music. The majority chooses music, with around 11 percent of students opting for drama and dance. Students receive training from eminent faculty members who have achieved great things in their fields. In addition to the required performance classes, students must fulfill a fair number of liberal arts requirements in literature, philosophy, social sciences, and languages. Third- and fourth-year students can choose from elective courses on topics such as the black arts movement, existentialism, and film. Academically ambitious students can complement their rigorous music or drama lessons with classes at Barnard or Columbia. The school also offers an accelerated BM/MM program that allows students to begin completing the requirements for a master's degree in music during their senior year.

The Centennial Dodge

Juilliard has no sports teams, but in celebration of the school's 100th anniversary, two drama students devised a homecoming and dodge ball competition. The Juilliard Penguins faced off against the Guilliard Minnows in a heated contest, as the Julliard Marching Band and cheerleaders performed on the sidelines. A Spirit Week was launched for the occasion, and students tailgated before the game. Unsurprisingly, the homecoming tradition didn't stick.

Cause: Practice; Effect: Brilliance

Because music, dance, and theater rehearsals are so arduous and all consuming, students have little time for non-performance-related activities. Although there are no sports teams or Greek chapters, some alternative activities include writing for the *Julliard Journal*, the school's monthly paper, and participating in a service club called ArtReach. Started as a response to the 9/11 terrorist attacks, ArtReach serves the community by promoting art through volunteer projects. The school encourages its students to take soak in the city's cultural offerings by giving them free or discount tickets to performances at the Metropolitan Opera, New York Philharmonic, and other venues. There are countless world-class arts events going on every night all around the city. On-campus social life revolves around Meredith Willson Residence Hall, which houses about 50 percent of the student body, and where there are social gatherings, film screenings, and talks given by alumni. Juilliard freshman are required to live in five-person suites in the residence hall, but upperclassmen have access to single rooms.

The Core of the Big Apple

Julliard is located on a sixteen-acre lot of modern buildings known as the Lincoln Center for the Performing Arts, adjacent to Broadway between 62nd and 66th streets in the heart of Manhattan. These grand yet conservative travertine edifices surround a gray cement plaza dotted with potted plants. The Metropolitan Opera is housed in the Lincoln Center complex, as is the New York City Ballet. Julliard's five-story building is an 8-million-cubic-foot space with fifteen huge rehearsal rooms, dozens of soundproof practice rooms, and a massive theater. The Lila Acheson Wallace Library houses one of the world's most impressive collections of music manuscripts and composer first editions, including scores by Bach, Stravinsky, and Mozart. Julliard students rarely venture outside of New York City, preferring to enjoy the urban social scene and multitude of shows and concerts. More traditional colleges, including Fordham University's Lincoln Center campus, are minutes away.

Admissions

Average high school GPA:	—
Average freshman SAT verbal / math score:	—/—
Average freshman ACT score:	—
Application fee:	$100
Application deadlines: 12/1 (freshmen) 12/1 (transfer)	
Total applicants:	2,523
Total accepted:	136 (5%)
Total accepted who enrolled:	96
Notification dates: 4/1 (freshmen) 4/1 (transfer)	

Students

Percentage of male / female students:	52% / 48%
Percentage of students from out of state:	85%
Percentage of students graduating in 4 years / 6 years:	73% / 81%

Money

Total endowment:	$478,100,000
Total tuition:	$25,610
Total cost with fees & expenses:	$38,705
Average financial aid package:	$21,298
Percentage of students who sought aid and received it:	83%
Percentage of students receiving financial aid:	79%

Also Check Out

Eugene Lang College, The New School for Liberal Arts

New York University

Oberlin College

Juniata College

1700 Moore Street
Huntingdon, PA 16652

(814) 641-3000
http://www.juniata.edu/

BIG PERSPECTIVE

Education has a new name: POE.

5 REASONS IT'S COOL

1. The Program of Emphasis (POE) allows students to **personalize their own curricula**.

2. Seventy-five percent of students gain real job experience via the school's **extensive internships program**.

3. Located in Huntingdon, Pennsylvania, Juniata offers **a wide variety of outdoor sports and recreation**.

4. **Forty percent of students study abroad** in programs in nearly twenty different countries.

5. Get in shape and have fun at the same time on the **popular varsity and intramural sports** teams.

The Basics

Public / private: private religious
Total enrollment / undergrads: 1,460 / 1,460
Campus setting: small town
Students call it: Juniata, JC
Students are called: Eagles
Notable alums: Bruce Davis (director, Academy of Motion Picture Arts and Sciences), Kristen C. Holloway (grassroots activist), Chuck Knox (pro football coach), William Phillips (Nobel Laureate, Physics)

Go Ahead, Be Self-Centered

With fewer than 1,500 students, JC guarantees that your education will be about *you* instead of your professors' pet projects. Students choose from nearly eighty majors, which gives them more options than they would have at the larger universities. The English, history, education, and philosophy programs are stellar, as are some of the more quirky offerings, such as museum studies and peace studies and conflict resolution. About half of all students also pick a Program of Emphasis (POE), which allows them to pursue academic interests in another, often unrelated department outside of their own program. So if you're a burgeoning biologist and also an aspiring journalist, you can enroll in a POE in the school's top-notch communication program. Whatever you study, you'll have the satisfaction that comes from demanding challenges and hard work under the guidance of excellent professors.

Go Yell It on the Mountain

Once a year, Juniata cancels all classes, and everyone—students, faculty, and staff alike—adjourns to a nearby park for lunch, nature hikes, crafts, music, tug-of-war, and a faculty/staff coed flag football game against the seniors. Mountain Day, as it's called, always comes in the fall, but the exact date remains a mystery until the last second.

For the Love of Learning

Students here tend to be smart, driven, and consumed with their studies. The result isn't a dour or spiritless campus but rather a unique kind of witty fun that's found at only a handful of colleges. It's not unusual to find JC students talking politics over breakfast and literature over lunch. When the conversation dries out, look for them in the gym and on the field, where many play varsity and intramural sports. Or they might be participating in one of the more than ninety student organizations on campus. And while 92 percent of Juniata's students are white, upper-middle-class Christians, the newly opened Office of Diversity is working to bring in students of different ethnic, racial, and religious backgrounds.

So Many Options, So Little Time

At Juniata, your biggest problem will be deciding what you'll have to skip in favor of some other fun activity. There are always tons of events going on, ranging from extracurricular offerings and intramural sports to concerts, guest lectures, plays, and movies. When it comes to volleyball and field hockey, the Division III Eagles draw big crowds. Students thirsting for something different often explore the wilderness surrounding the quiet town of Huntingdon. Outdoorsy types find that the area is great for hiking, camping, biking, picnicking, and jogging. Weekend road trips to Philadelphia and Pittsburgh are easily doable, and Altoona, home of one of Penn State's campuses, is an even closer thirty-minute ride away.

Admissions

Average high school GPA:	3.82
Average freshman SAT verbal / math score:	585 / 592
Average freshman ACT score:	—
Application fee:	$30

Application deadlines:
3/1 (freshmen)
6/15 (transfer)
11/1 (early decision)

Total applicants:	1,785
Total accepted:	1,168 (65%)
Total accepted who enrolled:	380

Notification dates:
continuous (freshmen)
continuous (transfer)
12/30 (early decision)

Acceptance rate for early decision applicants:	85%

Students

Percentage of male / female students:	47% / 53%
Percentage of students from out of state:	31%
Percentage of students graduating in 4 years / 6 years:	67% / 74%

Money

Total endowment:	$57,814,000
Total tuition:	$28,250
Total cost with fees & expenses:	$36,960
Average financial aid package:	$21,974
Percentage of students who sought aid and received it:	86%
Percentage of students receiving financial aid:	72%

Also Check Out

Bucknell University

Dickinson College

Muhlenberg College

The University of Pittsburgh

Ursinus College

Kalamazoo College

1200 Academy Street
Kalamazoo, MI 49006

(269) 337-7000
http://www.kzoo.edu/

 **BIG IDEA**

 **BIG PERSPECTIVE**

 **BIG WORLD**

Get on the K-Plan.

5 REASONS IT'S COOL

1. Kalamazoo is a **hotbed for political, economic, and religious debates** among students and professors.

2. Students get lots of **help finding internship opportunities.**

3. The Liberal Arts Colloquium sponsors about **a hundred concerts and lectures** each year.

4. **Eighty percent of K-Zoo students study abroad,** with programs located in countries all over the globe.

5. Students get **course credit for their volunteer projects** in the local community.

The Basics

Public / private: private religious
Total enrollment / undergrads: 1,345 / 1,345
Campus setting: suburban
Students call it: Kalamazoo, K-Zoo, K College, K
Students are called: Hornets
Notable alums: Selma Blair (actress), Holly Hughes (political activist, member of the Republican National Committee), Lisa Kron (actress, playwright), Nagai Kafu (novelist, playwright)

Your Plan, My Plan

Students at this school enjoy small classes, personal attention, and courses taught by distinguished professors. Unlike other colleges, Kalamazoo is on the quarter system, which means students attend school for three ten-week terms each year rather than two eighteen-week semesters. What really sets this college apart from other liberal arts schools, though, is the required K-Plan curriculum, a mix of liberal arts courses that culminate in a Senior Individualized Project (SIP) involving field research, student teaching, or artistic production. The K-Plan fosters a collaborative learning environment in which students get to know their professors while they take the first steps toward becoming well-rounded and engaged thinkers. The K-Plan also gives students the option of interning or studying abroad. It's so popular, in fact, that almost all students study abroad for three to ten months, and most find internships too.

Be Gracious. Very Gracious.

Students study hard, but they get at least one guilt-free day of goofing off every year. On the Day of Gracious Living, the college cancels all classes, and the entire student body takes a day trip to Lake Michigan. The Day of Gracious Living always has an air of mystery and excitement surrounding it, since the school doesn't announce its date until the night before.

Learning from the Best

Kalamazoo students represent all points along the political spectrum, from diehard conservative to tree-hugging liberal. Since all Hornets tend to be rather outspoken, there is plenty of heated debate and on-campus political activism. The college channels these debates into its Liberal Arts Colloquium (LAC), which sponsors lectures and concerts given by notable politicians, scholars, writers, and artists. In fact, so important are these lectures and performances to the mission of the college that students on the K-Plan are required to attend at least twenty-five of these events to graduate. Students are intense and driven, but more cooperative than cutthroat. When students do take time off to relax, they often participate in dorm mixers, cheer on the Kalamazoo athletic teams, attend concerts, or catch a movie. Kalamazoo has no frats or sororities, but party-loving students are invited to rush at nearby Western Michigan University.

The Quad at the Center of the World

With its expansive green space and neo-colonial architecture, Kalamazoo's campus feels like a special retreat tucked away from the rest of the world. The campus centers around a grassy hill called the Quad, where students sled on cafeteria trays in the winter. Students usually spend their spare time at Hicks Student Center or on the Quad, which is also the site of many university-wide events such as homecoming, Spring Fling, convocation, and commencement. Most students spend the weekend on campus, but when it's time to get away, they check out parties at nearby Western Michigan University or hit the bars in town. And when students itch to reacquaint themselves with the big city, they head to Chicago and Detroit, which are only about two and a half hours away.

Admissions

Average high school GPA:	3.58
Average freshman SAT verbal / math score:	653 / 637
Average freshman ACT score:	26
Application fee:	$35

Application deadlines:
2/15 (freshmen)   11/15 (early decision)
2/15 (transfer)   12/1 (early action)

Total applicants:	1,800
Total accepted:	1,241 (69%)
Total accepted who enrolled:	390

Notification dates:
4/1 (freshmen)   12/1 (early decision)
4/1 (transfer)   12/20 (early action)

Acceptance rate for early action/early decision applicants:	87% / 86%

Students

Percentage of male / female students:	43% / 57%
Percentage of students from out of state:	29%
Percentage of students graduating in 4 years / 6 years:	73% / 80%

Money

Total endowment:	$152,000,000
Total tuition:	$27,054
Total cost with fees & expenses:	$34,969
Average financial aid package:	$22,820
Percentage of students who sought aid and received it:	—
Percentage of students receiving financial aid:	50%

Also Check Out

Grinnell College

Hope College

Lawrence University

Michigan State University

University of Chicago

University of Michigan–Ann Arbor

Kenyon College

Ransom Hall
Gambier, OH 43022

(740) 427-5000
http://www.kenyon.edu/

Where small classes meet small town

5 REASONS IT'S COOL

1. **Classes are small**, and you'll never have to deal with a TA.

2. Even if you have no idea what you want to study, you can go here with confidence—**every academic program is excellent**.

3. Greek life is available, if you're interested, but **you won't feel like an extraterrestrial if you don't pledge**.

4. **Live the small-town life**: Gambier has fewer than seven hundred full-time residents.

5. At this **accepting, inclusive college**, it's perfectly normal to strike up conversations with strangers.

The Basics

Public / private: private nonprofit
Total enrollment / undergrads: 1,661 / 1,661
Campus setting: rural
Students call it: Kenyon
Students are called: Lords and Ladies
Notable alums: Rutherford B. Hayes (U.S. president), Allison Janney (actress), E. L. Doctorow (writer), Robert Lowell (poet), Paul Newman (actor), Kevin O'Donnell (director, U.S. Peace Corps), William Renquist (U.S. Supreme Court chief justice), Bill Watterson (cartoonist; creator, *Calvin and Hobbes*)

Slackers Beware

Kenyon's academics are very strong, and graduates are known among employers for their critical thinking abilities and intellectual dexterity. In the past, humanities and social sciences got all the attention, but the construction of a new science quad has begun to even the playing field. Fine arts classes are also well-respected and widely available. All faculty members teach undergraduates, most classes have fewer than twenty students, and there are only ten students for every professor, most of whom live on or very near campus. To graduate, students must complete coursework in fine arts, a foreign language, humanities, natural science, and social science, as well as their major requirements. English, political science, and psychology are the most popular majors; about half of all graduates take degrees in humanities, arts, or social sciences. Seniors complete a "comp" project intended as a capstone

All Together Now

At the start of every school year, freshmen take the Founder's Oath, which requires them to follow the rules of the college and to promote its health as an institution. They also gather on the steps of Rosse Hall to sing Kenyon songs while the senior class makes fun of them. Three years later, of course, the singers—at least, the ones who have kept the oath—become the teasers.

to their four undergraduate years, and there's heavy emphasis on one-on-one interaction with professors in every field. All classrooms have wireless Internet connections, and professors increasingly integrate technology into their lessons.

The Good Old College Smorgasbord

All students live in college-owned housing, the quality of which occupies a spectrum from *just fine* to *deeply uninspiring*. The food gets even worse reviews. Frats play an important, but not dominating, role in the social scene. Twenty-seven percent of men join one of eight fraternities, and 19 percent of women join one of four sororities. Drinking is widespread but not pressure based; there's a lot to do on campus whether you're sober or not. Over 120 clubs—including student publications, performance troupes, and political activist organizations—are available to interested Lords and Ladies on campus. Sporting events do not normally draw large crowds, but one in five students does participate in intramurals. Dating was last popular during the Reagan Administration, some students report; these days, almost everyone at Kenyon is either practically engaged or enjoying a streak of random hookups.

Isolated Entertainment

The campus and the town of Gambier are woven together to create a very small, rural community situated in the rolling hills of central Ohio. Students and townies get along well enough, and the two blocks that make up downtown are pretty and quaint. Mt. Vernon, about five miles down the road, presents the closest thing to a shopping center, and free shuttles are available for travel to nearby small towns. The weather is also more extreme than a lot of non-Ohioans expect it to be. Fortunately, Kenyon compensates for some of these downers with a campus chock full of art galleries, theaters, music halls, and other student facilities, including a nature preserve. And, of course, it's very safe. Someone's book was stolen in 1983, but that's about it.

Admissions

Average high school GPA:	3.78
Average freshman SAT verbal / math score:	681 / 662
Average freshman ACT score:	26
Application fee:	$50
Application deadlines:	
1/15 (freshmen)	
4/1 (transfer)	
12/1 (early decision)	
Total applicants:	3,929
Total accepted:	1,420 (36%)
Total accepted who enrolled:	440
Notification dates:	
4/1 (freshmen)	
5/1 (transfer)	
12/15 (early decision)	
Acceptance rate for early decision applicants:	72%

Students

Percentage of male / female students:	47% / 53%
Percentage of students from out of state:	77%
Percentage of students graduating in 4 years / 6 years:	80% / 83%

Money

Total endowment:	$158,053,000
Total tuition:	$34,990
Total cost with fees & expenses:	$41,950
Average financial aid package:	$27,275
Percentage of students who sought aid and received it:	98%
Percentage of students receiving financial aid:	44%

Also Check Out

Amherst College

Bowdoin College

Denison University

Oberlin College

Swarthmore College

Knox College

2 East South Street
Galesburg, IL 61401

(309) 341-7000
http://www.knox.edu/

 **BIG IDEA**

 **BIG WORLD**

Ready to get focused?

5 REASONS IT'S COOL

1. During the Green Oaks Term, students can live and study near a **remote biological field station.**

2. Applicants **aren't required to report SAT or ACT scores.**

3. Most of the residence halls are suite style, and more than **95 percent of students live on campus.**

4. Students take only **three classes at a time** during each of the three trimesters.

5. About **60 percent of graduates go on to grad school** within five years—and the latest medical school acceptance rate was a world-beating 100 percent.

The Basics

Public / private: private nonprofit
Total enrollment / undergrads: 1,351 / 1,351
Campus setting: small town
Students call it: Knox
Notable alums: Barry Bearak (Pulitzer Prize winner, International Reporting), Eugene Field (writer), Ismat Kittani (president, United Nations), Robert Hanssen (spy), Hiram Revels (first African American senator), Ellen Browning Scripps (founder, Scripps-Howard News Syndicate)

Take Charge of Your Education

Students at Knox are self-directed. The administration and professors trust students in turn, as evidenced by the unproctored exams and the freedom students have to develop a personalized education plan with their advisers. Sixty-seven percent of students come from the top quarter of their high school classes, and most of them enjoy creating their own academic adventure. Knox prepares its undergrads for successful engagement with the world. The Peace Corp Preparatory Program (the first of its kind in the country) includes courses in a foreign language, education, and international studies. Peace Corp Prep students are also required to do an internship, get work experience, or study off campus. About half of Knox's roughly 1,350 students study abroad. Programs are offered in seventeen countries, including China, Costa Rica, Argentina, and Tanzania. But you don't have to go far to get a unique experience. Twenty miles from campus is Green Oaks, seven hundred acres of college-owned prairie land. Every few years, the school offers Green Oaks

Unite as One People Throughout This Land

Knox's founders were antislavery activists, and the National Underground Railroad Freedom Center named the college a Freedom Station for its efforts in research and education about the Underground Railroad. At Old Main, now a National Historic Landmark, Abraham Lincoln debated Stephen A. Douglas and asserted that slavery was immoral.

Term, during which interested students can live and take classes on the prairie.

Creative and Involved

With three literary journals on campus, plus a student newspaper and twelve music/dance ensembles, Knox students might seem strictly creative. But they're also athletic, with more than half taking part in some manner of sport, whether it's one of twenty-one Division III teams or a club or intramural sport. Students have a tradition of getting involved, which they can do by joining one of the college's one hundred clubs or an outside organization. The diversity of the student body is a point of pride: 15 percent of students are minorities, and 7 percent are international students. The vast majority of students live on campus, where their housing options include townhouses, apartments, and special-interest houses. Although deciding where to live might be a challenge, deciding on the meal plan shouldn't be. All five of Knox's meal plans are allocated differently but priced the same. Menus are put online and updated daily.

A Town That's Oh So Nice

Galesburg, Illinois, is a quintessential Midwestern college town, complete with brick streets and a downtown shopping and eating district called Seminary Street. The town is within walking distance of the college and about three and a half hours from both Chicago and St. Louis. Campus itself has an interesting mix of different brick buildings, including Old Main, at the center of campus, and the lovely Seymour Library. The Old Jail, which used to be the county lockup, is now home to the Center for Global Studies. When a snowstorm hits, fun-loving students take cafeteria trays over to the Knox Bowl, home to Prairie Fire football and the best sledding on campus.

Admissions

Average high school GPA:	—
Average freshman SAT writing / math / critical reading score:	630 / 611 / 633
Average freshman ACT score:	26
Application fee:	$40

Application deadlines:
2/1 (freshmen)
4/1 (transfer)
12/1 (early action)

Total applicants:	2,085
Total accepted:	1,535 (74%)
Total accepted who enrolled:	407

Notification dates:
3/31 (freshmen)
4/30 (transfer)
12/31 (early action)

Acceptance rate for early action applicants:	94%

Students

Percentage of male / female students:	44% / 56%
Percentage of students from out of state:	49%
Percentage of students graduating in 4 years / 6 years:	67% / 75%

Money

Total endowment:	$66,218,594
Total tuition:	$27,606
Total cost with fees & expenses:	$34,725
Average financial aid package:	$22,477
Percentage of students who sought aid and received it:	94%
Percentage of students receiving financial aid:	64%

Also Check Out

Beloit College

DePauw University

Grinnell College

Lawrence University

Lafayette College

Quad Drive
Easton, PA 18042

(610) 330-5000
http://www.lafayette.edu/

**BIG
PERSPECTIVE**

Ya want liberal arts? Come and get 'em.

5 REASONS IT'S COOL

1. **Classes are small, professors are friendly,** and just about every course is perspective-altering.

2. They're in the money. Lafayette's endowment ranks among the top 100 in the United States, and **students enjoy top-of-the-line facilities and other perks.**

3. Lafayette's got a **lovely hilltop campus** that's within striking distance of New York and Philadelphia.

4. The **football rivalry with nearby Lehigh** is the stuff of sporty dreams.

5. Life on **campus is fun and full of options,** from the popular Greek scene to the many clubs and organizations.

The Basics

Public / private: private religious
Total enrollment / undergrads: 2,381 / 2,381
Campus setting: suburban
Students call it: Lafayette
Students are called: Leopards
Notable alums: Stephen Crane (writer), General George Decker (chief of staff, U.S. Army), Haldan Keffer Hartline (Nobel Laureate, Medicine), Phillip S. Hench (Nobel Laureate, Medicine), Joel Silver (filmmaker)

Well-Rounded by Design

In recent years, Lafayette has worked hard to get students in the habit of considering their roles as global citizens. As freshmen, students engage in a year-long exploration of post-9/11 American values, and the college's study-abroad program continues to see high rates of participation. Engineering, Economics, English, and Government are the most popular departments. Core requirements ensure that science and engineering students are, just like everyone else, required to take a first-year seminar in writing—while scholars of Romantic poetry are, just like everyone else, required to take a second-year seminar in technology and science. Students report that professors are friendly, engaging, and accessible once class is over. The student-to-faculty ratio is 11:1, and class sizes are manageable.

Lafayette vs. Lehigh

Lafayette and Lehigh University hold two fierce competitions every year. The first takes place when hundreds of high school seniors admitted to both Pennsylvania schools decide which to attend. The second comes when the Lafayette Leopards take on the Lehigh Mountain Hawks in what is the longest continually played college football rivalry in the country.

Yeah, We've Got That

Whether you're a jock, a nerd, or a nerdy jock, Lafayette provides excellent facilities for your enrichment, including a new $35 million sports center and $25 million residential complex. A member of the Patriot League, Lafayette offers more than twenty varsity sports. It also has fifty intramural sports and more than two hundred other nonathletic organizations. Fraternities and sororities are important social hubs, although not necessarily key party sites. Twenty-five percent of men join one of the nine frats, while 45 percent of women join one of six sororities. All Greek houses are officially dry, meaning that low-key, under-control late night gatherings are vastly more common than raging bacchanals. The campus, perched on a hill as it is, can feel like an island at times, and students tend to stick close by: more than 90 percent live on campus. Volunteering is popular, and alternative spring break programs send students abroad to perform community service and learn about international socioeconomic challenges.

Fun in the Poconos

The Lafayette campus sits on a hill overlooking the town of Easton and the nearby Delaware River. The campus grounds are well kept with plenty of green spaces. Many buildings are new or have been recently refurbished. Easton, a small town of about thirty thousand people, isn't quite as picturesque as the college it plays host to. Best known for its Crayola factory, it doesn't appeal hugely to the college crowd. In recent years, however, more and more businesses catering to students have opened. The larger region, known as the Lehigh Valley, is a bit short on entertainment options that don't require hiking gear, although students enjoy great skiing in the Poconos and, in warmer weather, an enormous waterslide park at Dorney Kingdom. Musikfest, a popular ten-day festival, is held in the nearby town of Bethlehem just before the start of the academic year. Students can easily drive to Philadelphia (about sixty miles away) and New York City (about seventy miles away).

Admissions

Average high school GPA:	3.78
Average freshman SAT verbal / math score:	625 / 653
Average freshman ACT score:	26
Application fee:	$60

Application deadlines:
1/1 (freshmen)
6/1 (transfer)
12/1 (early decision)

Total applicants:	5,875
Total accepted:	2,169 (37%)
Total accepted who enrolled:	630

Notification dates:
4/1 (freshmen)
continuous (transfer)
3/15 (early decision)

Acceptance rate for early decision applicants:	68%

Students

Percentage of male / female students:	52% / 48%
Percentage of students from out of state:	70%
Percentage of students graduating in 4 years / 6 years:	87% / 90%

Money

Total endowment:	$633,413,800
Total tuition:	$33,634
Total cost with fees & expenses:	$44,188
Average financial aid package:	$22,888
Percentage of students who sought aid and received it:	99%
Percentage of students receiving financial aid:	52%

Also Check Out

Bucknell University

Colgate University

Lehigh University

Muhlenberg College

University of Pennsylvania

Lake Forest College

555 North Sheridan Road Lake Forest, IL 60045	(847) 234-3100 http://www.lakeforest.edu/

 **BIG HAND**

 **BIG PERSPECTIVE**

Liberal arts, Chicago-style

5 REASONS IT'S COOL

1. The First-Year Studies Program will **ease your transition to college** with small classes and strong academic advising.

2. The **12:1 student-to-faculty ratio** and small classes ensure that you'll get plenty of personal attention.

3. The Center for Chicago Program provides **elite internship opportunities** with top-notch employers.

4. With **Chicago in your backyard,** you'll be able to take advantage of some of the best restaurants and cultural attractions.

5. No TAs here: **Professors teach every class.**

The Basics

Public / private: private nonprofit
Total enrollment / undergrads: 1,448 / 1,422
Campus setting: suburban
Students call it: Lake Forest
Students are called: Bears, Foresters
Notable alums: Blair Butler (comedienne), Jacqueline Carey (writer), Ed Janus (journalist)

A Face to the Name

Lake Forest is not a place for slackers. With just over 1,400 students, it's almost impossible to vanish into the woodwork. Classes are small, with between ten and twenty students each. They are also often discussion oriented, which means that professors know their students by name and are familiar with their work. If you're the type of student who tends to catch a few Z's in the back of a lecture hall, or blend in with the crowd on those days you haven't done your homework, you'll need to step up your game considerably if you want to make it here. Professors aren't trying to catch their students slacking, though; they're eager to see undergrads succeed, and they make themselves accessible outside of class. You'll get up close and personal attention no matter which of the twenty-six majors you choose. Settling on a major is less difficult here than it is at other schools, since profs encourage students to sample lots of different disciplines before settling down in one field. One of the college's few required courses is the First-Year Studies class, which begins with a trip to Chicago during orientation week, where you'll learn about the city firsthand.

Get Out and Enjoy the Greenery

Lake Forest, which is surrounded by woodlands, has always been devoted to studying and protecting the natural environment. In addition to the standard green initiatives found on nearly every twenty-first-century college campus, Lake Forest also offers prime wildlife viewing. Birders from all over the state trek out to Lake Forest College Bird Observatory each year to spot raptors, warblers, vultures, nighthawks, shoebirds, and cranes. Students, professors, and community members also work together in the Shaw Woods Avian Monitoring Program (SWAMP) in the college's own savanna and ravine woodlands.

Your Clique, My Clique, Our Community

While many Lake Forest students are white, upper-middle-class kids from the Chicago area, the monotony is broken up by the large body of international students. Some students complain that campus social life is a little cliquish, with the athletes hanging out in one corner and the artists in another. Still, a good number of students branch out by participating in student organizations, which include student government, frats and sororities, honor societies, community service and political interest groups, media, music, theater, religious groups, intramurals, and more. Students are given a voice in the management of the college, and some of the campus's most concerned members participate in governance committees such as the College Council. More than anything else, though, it's the school's seventeen intercollegiate athletic teams that unite the student body and give it something to cheer about.

On Chicago's Back Doorstep

The 107-acre campus is wooded and surrounded by ravines, natural prairies, Lake Michigan's beaches, and biking and jogging trails. Campus parties are popular on weekends, as are treks out to parties at Northwestern University, just thirty minutes away. Downtown Chicago is just thirty miles away, which means that students here enjoy the perks of both the great outdoors and the big city. Chicago offers outstanding shopping, culture, and eating, and students enjoy day-tripping to see a show or catch a ballgame. A train station just minutes away from campus makes Chicago even more accessible, although even the short walk from campus can be grueling during the blustery winter months.

Admissions

Average high school GPA:	3.5
Average freshman SAT writing / math / critical reading score:	574 / 582 / 582
Average freshman ACT score:	25
Application fee:	$40

Application deadlines:
2/15 (freshmen)
continuous (transfer)
12/1 (early decision)
12/1 (early action)

Total applicants:	2,197
Total accepted:	1,390 (63%)
Total accepted who enrolled:	386

Notification dates:
3/20 (freshmen)   12/20 (early decision)
continuous (transfer)   1/20 (early action)

Acceptance rate for early action/early decision applicants:	79% / 67%

Students

Percentage of male / female students:	42% / 58%
Percentage of students from out of state:	64%
Percentage of students graduating in 4 years / 6 years:	63% / 70%

Money

Total endowment:	$61,208,507
Total tuition:	$28,700
Total cost with fees & expenses:	$36,824
Average financial aid package:	$23,024
Percentage of students who sought aid and received it:	100%
Percentage of students receiving financial aid:	74%

Also Check Out

Beloit College

Boston University

Loyola University

Northwestern University

Skidmore College

Lawrence University

PO Box 599
Appleton, WI 54912

(920) 832-7000
http://www.lawrence.edu/

 **BIG HAND**

 **BIG PERSPECTIVE**

Where nerds rule the school

5 REASONS IT'S COOL

1. Nearly 90 percent of students take **one-on-one courses with their professors**.

2. Administrators strive to create an **atmosphere of tolerance** for all students.

3. Nearly **half of students study abroad**, perhaps because Lawrence offers several need-based scholarships for participating students.

4. Eleven percent of students are international, which makes this college **one of the country's most internationally diverse**.

5. Appleton, Wisconsin, too hectic for you? **Get away from it all at Björklunden,** the school's 425-acre haven for retreats and seminars.

The Basics

Public/private: private nonprofit
Total enrollment/undergrads: 1,480 / 1,480
Campus setting: small town
Students call it: Lawrence, LU
Students are called: Vikings
Notable alums: Jennifer Baumgardner (author), Walter Samuel Goodland (governor, Wisconsin), Lorena Hickok (journalist), Terry Moran (news anchor)

Rising to the Occasion

No matter your major, you'll be challenged at Lawrence. The quarter system ensures that students stay on top of their work, especially since exams and papers come on a fairly regular three-week schedule. Professors are notorious for pushing their students to think critically from the moment they set foot in the classroom. A two-term seminar known as Freshman Studies teaches students to argue persuasively, both aloud and on paper. There are also Individualized Studies, one-on-one classes that promote intellectual maturity, self-direction, and the synthesis and application of knowledge. While they might grumble about the rigorous academics, students know that the tough love will help them become better thinkers and better communicators, not to mention more appealing job applicants. And while such a demanding environment might tempt other students to cheat, Lawrence students abide by a strict honor code that promotes academic integrity and stresses cooperation and collaboration over competition.

No Trivial Pursuit

Lawrence is home to the Annual Great Midwest Trivia Contest, a fifty-hour trivia marathon. Originally broadcast on the radio, in 2006 the contest moved to a webcast-only format to allow trivia buffs both on and off campus to participate. And despite the absurd prizes—ranging from plastic pink flamingos to stainless-steel bedpans— Lawrence students take the competition very seriously.

Home of Band Camp Alumni

At this school, everyone is a little bit of a nerd—and that's a compliment! Lawrence students study hard and log more than their fair share of hours in the library. And even when it's time to kick back and unwind with friends in the Union or the Coffee House, conversations usually drift to more academic topics, such as politics, economics, and the latest literary movements. Students are also an active lot, and many belong to a handful of the eighty-plus student clubs on campus. Popular student events include winter camping on Lake Michigan, campus concerts, an international film festival, IM sports, plays, and parties. And for those of you who want to pledge, there are five frats and three sororities.

A Tight-Knit Campus

Lawrence's campus, which overlooks the Fox River, offers spectacular views. While some students complain that the eighty-four-acre campus is too small, most enjoy the close sense of community it inspires. There's always an event going on somewhere, particularly on weekends, when there are concerts, plays, and maybe even a Greek-sponsored Jell-O wrestling match or two. The nearby town of Appleton has a number of popular bars and coffee shops, all of which are within walking distance of Lawrence. Those who are willing to venture even farther into the city will discover more distractions, such as shopping, museums, good restaurants, and theater performances.

Admissions

Average high school GPA:	3.45
Average freshman SAT writing / math / critical reading score:	650 / 652 / 657
Average freshman ACT score:	26
Application fee:	$40

Application deadlines:
1/15 (freshmen)
5/1 (transfer)
11/15 (early decision)
12/1 (early action)

Total applicants:	2,315
Total accepted:	1,304 (56%)
Total accepted who enrolled:	361

Notification dates:
4/1 (freshmen)
— (transfer)
12/1 (early decision)
1/15 (early action)

Acceptance rate for early action/early decision applicants:	86% / 82%

Students

Percentage of male / female students:	45% / 55%
Percentage of students from out of state:	57%
Percentage of students graduating in 4 years / 6 years:	59% / 76%

Money

Total endowment:	$200,436,073
Total tuition:	$29,376
Total cost with fees & expenses:	$37,155
Average financial aid package:	$23,900
Percentage of students who sought aid and received it:	96%
Percentage of students receiving financial aid:	63%

Also Check Out

Carleton College

Grinnell College

Juniata College

Northwestern University

University of Wisconsin–Madison

Lehigh University

27 Memorial Drive West
Bethlehem, PA 18015

(610) 758-3000
http://www.lehigh.edu/

BIG PERSPECTIVE

Engineering, business, and liberal arts, oh my!

5 REASONS IT'S COOL

1. Civil, environmental, mechanical, electrical, chemical . . . name a type of engineering, and Lehigh's **top-notch engineering program covers it.**

2. Got your sights set on conquering the world of business? The **College of Business and Economics is a great place** to start.

3. Lehigh offers **combined seven-year BA/MD, DMD, and OD programs** with Pennsylvania professional medical schools.

4. The **fun, lively Greek scene** means fun, lively parties. Lots of 'em.

5. Country living has its charms, but Lehigh is also within a short drive from **Philadelphia and New York City.**

The Basics

Public / private: private nonprofit
Total enrollment / undergrads: 6,858 / 4,743
Campus setting: suburban
Students call it: Lehigh
Students are called: Engineers
Notable alums: William P. Gottlieb (photographer, journalist), Terry Hart (astronaut), Lee Iacocca (CEO, the Chrysler Corporation), Joe Morgenstern (film critic), Roger Penske (owner, Penske Racing)

Making Money and Building Stuff

Lehigh is divided into four colleges: Arts and Sciences, Business and Economics, Engineering and Applied Sciences, and Education (which is largely populated by graduate students). The most popular departments are Finance and Engineering; in fact, two-thirds of Lehigh students major in some form of business, economics, or engineering. Fields such as biotechnology and nanotechnology are also strong here. All Lehigh students, regardless of their major, are required to complete coursework in computers, English, writing, humanities, math, natural science, and social science. Workloads are tough across the board, as is the grading policy, but students are rewarded with committed professors and small-ish classes, especially after freshman year. The student-to-faculty ratio is 9:1, and all professors, 99 percent of whom hold PhDs, teach at least one class of undergrads. Lehigh's unique Global Citizenship program puts an international spin on learning, and students may choose from fifty study-abroad programs in thirty countries.

Clubbing, Lehigh style

Partying is the most popular way to unwind at **Lehigh**, but the administration, keen to promote social opportunities that don't involve alcohol, has been very supportive of campus organizations and of the students who want to start new ones. For evidence of this, look no further than, say, the Real Estate, Bhangra, Robotics, Equestrian, Mariachi, Hellenic, Paint Ball, and Cricket clubs.

We Like to Party

Lehigh students are hard workers. They want to make the dean's list, and they want to ace their exams. They're not all work and no play, however. If studying *and* partying (sometimes at the same time) are your passions, then you'll fit right in. The college's fraternities and sororities play a major role in the campus social scene. Thirty-five percent of men and 38 percent of women join Greek houses, and the rush/pledge process shapes, to a large degree, the social calendar. Even volunteer work—one of the *least* raucous thing students do—is often coordinated through the Greek houses. Still, the majority of upperclassmen don't go Greek, and independent students still have fun. Students choose from housing options like university-owned theme houses. School spirit gets especially rabid during the annual football game against rival Lafayette. You can leave your books on the shelf that weekend. They may very well be ripped from your hands by overzealous football fans if you don't.

Life on a Mountain Side

Lehigh's 1,600-acre campus is carved into the side of a mountain. A sharp economic disparity exists between campus-dwellers and residents of the surrounding town of Bethlehem, and students tend to stay on campus and have limited interaction with the locals. A fair (and growing) number of businesses in town cater to students, and students report feeling safe when they do venture off campus. Surrounding Lehigh Valley is a lovely and tempting wilderness for outdoor adventurers, while the proximity of New York City and Philadelphia (at seventy-five miles and fifty miles away, respectively) pleases those who'd rather hike up Fifth Avenue than a mountain trail.

Admissions

Average high school GPA: —

Average freshman SAT verbal / math score: 632 / 678

Average freshman ACT score: —

Application fee: $65

Application deadlines:
1/1 (freshmen)
4/1 (transfer)
11/15 (early decision)

Total applicants: 10,689

Total accepted: 4,182 (39%)

Total accepted who enrolled: 1,216

Notification dates:
4/1 (freshmen)
5/1 (transfer)
12/15 (early decision)

Acceptance rate for early decision applicants: 56%

Students

Percentage of male / female students: 58% / 42%

Percentage of students from out of state: 73%

Percentage of students graduating in 4 years / 6 years: 75% / 86%

Money

Total endowment: $939,473,000

Total tuition: $33,470

Total cost with fees & expenses: $43,690

Average financial aid package: $26,584

Percentage of students who sought aid and received it: 96%

Percentage of students receiving financial aid: 47%

Also Check Out

Bucknell University

Carnegie Mellon University

Cornell University

The Pennsylvania State University–University Park

University of Pennsylvania

Lewis & Clark College

0615 SW Palatine Hill Road
Portland, OR 97219

(503) 768-7000
http://www.lclark.edu/

BIG PERSPECTIVE

BIG WORLD

Westward ho!

5 REASONS IT'S COOL

1. Find your inner (or outer) hippie on this **laid-back, environmentally conscious campus.**

2. Blaze some trails! Lewis & Clark's **study-abroad program is one of the best in the region,** with opportunities to live and learn on every continent.

3. The pioneering spirit of the college's namesakes lives on: Students are required to **complete coursework in international studies.**

4. Small classes and a 13:1 student-faculty ratio ensure that **students receive plenty of personal attention.**

5. **The eclectic neighborhoods of downtown Portland** are a five-minute drive from campus.

The Basics

Public / private: private nonprofit
Total enrollment / undergrads: 3,641 / 1,985
Campus setting: suburban
Students call it: Lewis & Clark, L&C
Students are called: Pioneers
Notable alums: Earl Blumenauer (congressman), Markie Post (actress), Monica Lewinsky (White House intern)

Explore and Discover

Exploration & Discovery, a required interdisciplinary course for freshmen, captures the pioneering essence of academics at Lewis & Clark. Students are encouraged to pursue a wide set of interests, develop civic responsibility, and become global citizens. There's even an international studies requirement, which over half the students fulfill through studying abroad. In another effort to expand horizons, the 3-2 engineering program allows students to divide their study time with participating schools in New York, St. Louis, Los Angeles, and Beaverton, OR. Lewis & Clark offers twenty-six majors, including the option of designing your own. English, international relations, and foreign languages are especially strong programs. Classes are 100 percent professor taught and are usually capped at twenty students. The workload is as challenging as you make it. The academic freedom encourages some to grow and allows others to slack. There are a number of new facilities on campus. The Watzek library, with its large windows and cozy reading rooms, is a hot spot to study and socialize.

Clothing: Optional

Speaking of the spirit of exploration, Lewis & Clark's most revealing tradition by far is the Naked Mile, a springtime jog around campus to celebrate, well, nakedness. Students have also been known to show up to class naked. This cheeky tradition began as a fundraiser to raise money for students arrested at a protest.

Feeling Green?

Lewis & Clark students are concerned with the state of the world and their place in it, so much so that their college has earned the nickname the "school with a conscious." There are four green buildings on campus, including the recently completed J. R. Howard Hall, and college policies reflect a commitment to sustainability. Students are generally laid-back and friendly. Residency on campus is required for the first two years, and 80 percent of students stay on campus for all four years. Housing consists of eight residence halls with theme-based options; Copeland is the most social of the bunch. The newer four-bedroom suites called Apartments are reserved for upperclassmen. Students gravitate toward outdoors activities more than they do team sports. Indeed, the football team was disbanded altogether a few years ago (the program has since been reinstated). When they're not conquering the great outdoors, students can choose from over sixty clubs, as well as annual celebrations on campus, like the much-loved luau. While Lewis & Clark's small size can lead to feelings of claustrophobia at times, it also engenders a great sense of community. Plus, a trip to downtown Portland on the Pioneer Express (the free shuttle service) takes only fifteen minutes.

Studying Up a Storm

The Lewis & Clark campus rests on a hill in a wealthy suburban community a mere six miles from Portland. Students can easily drive or bus downtown to the progressive, eclectic, and, yes, rainy city. Despite the frequent storm clouds, students find plenty of activities to brighten their days, like the cafés on Pearl St., the bars in Hawthorne, or readings at Powell's, the largest independent bookstore in America. On campus, the spectacular view of Mt. Hood serves as a reminder that the college is located in the heart of the Pacific Northwest. Skiing and beaches are less than an hour and a half away, Seattle is a three-hour drive, and there's plenty of hiking, biking, and climbing to keep students active.

Admissions

Average high school GPA:	3.68
Average freshman SAT writing / math / critical reading score:	640 / 636 / 664
Average freshman ACT score:	26
Application fee:	$50

Application deadlines:
2/1 (freshmen)
7/1 (transfer)
11/15 (early action)

Total applicants:	4,698
Total accepted:	2,744 (58%)
Total accepted who enrolled:	509

Notification dates:
4/1 (freshmen)
continuous (transfer)
1/15 (early action)

Acceptance rate for early action applicants:	—

Students

Percentage of male / female students:	39% / 61%
Percentage of students from out of state:	77%
Percentage of students graduating in 4 years / 6 years:	62% / 71%

Money

Total endowment:	$180,549,197
Total tuition:	$29,556
Total cost with fees & expenses:	$38,820
Average financial aid package:	$25,018
Percentage of students who sought aid and received it:	91%
Percentage of students receiving financial aid:	54%

Also Check Out

Reed College

University of California–Santa Cruz

University of Oregon

University of Puget Sound

Louisiana State University– Baton Rouge

101 Thomas Boyd Hall
Baton Rouge, LA 70803

(225) 578-3202
http://www.lsu.edu/

BIG CHOICE

A smart Louisiana Purchase

5 REASONS IT'S COOL

1. In an effort to reverse its reputation as a football-'n'-beer school, the university has **invested in infrastructure like blazingly fast Internet connectivity and a massive library.**

2. But not to worry: **LSU still cancels classes for Mardi Gras!**

3. Campus, formerly a plantation, is **the very picture of southern charm.**

4. **STRIPES: a freshman camp** where you can learn all of the LSU traditions, songs, and superstitions.

5. A surprisingly **diverse liberal arts curriculum** means a course for just about every interest.

The Basics

Public / private: public state
Total enrollment / undergrads: 29,925 / 24,583
Campus setting: urban
Students call it: LSU
Students are called: Tigers
Notable alums: James Carville (political commentator), Joanne Woodward (actress), "Pistol" Pete Maravich (pro basketball player), Rex Reed (film critic), Shaquille O'Neal (pro basketball player)

Pigskin or Sheepskin?

By reputation, classes at LSU are little more than a way to kill time between football games. But recently, administrators have taken measures to win credibility as a flagship institution by shifting research into overdrive. Results have been mixed. On the one hand, the research push has generated much-needed revenue for the school, which has seen its share of the state tax kitty grow smaller and smaller. On the other hand, some say the emphasis on research has taken away from the emphasis on teaching. In addition, many students are more concerned with the Big Game than with the Great Tradition. Biology, chemistry, and physics are some of LSU's strongest and most popular majors, especially for those on the med-school track, but enough bookworms arrive at LSU to make English and French curricular powerhouses. Those who are not so easily discouraged by large classes and taciturn profs can enjoy a rich gumbo of learning, enrichment, and fun.

Driving Old Dixie Down

In its earlier inception as a military academy known as "The Ole War Skule," LSU's superintendent was none other than William Tecumseh Sherman. A man reviled by southerners to this day, General Sherman held his position at LSU until 1861, when the outbreak of war forced the school's closure. The Union general informally known as Cump went on to launch Sherman's March, which turned the tide of the Civil War. The school reopened after Confederate Louisiana rejoined the Union in 1865, but, needless to say, General Sherman never sought to resume his superintendent's duties.

Get 'Em, Tiger

Football is king at LSU, and the raucous stadium, known infamously as Death Valley, is the king's throne (one particularly thunderous game actually registered on the campus Richter scale). Students' passion for *le grande fête* is inflamed by LSU's proximity to New Orleans, just eighty miles down Interstate 10. Every year, Tigers can be found in full force among the ranks of Mardi Gras revelers. Student life does have a serious side, which tends to be channeled into religious, as opposed to political, expressions. Not many campus political organizations exist, and tension often simmers between the largely conservative and native-Louisianan student body and the left-leaning faculty and students hailing from lands north of the Mason-Dixon. African Americans represent about 10 percent of the population, with Asians and Latinos each claiming roughly 3 percent.

High Times in the Deep South

Formerly a plantation overlooking the Mississippi River, LSU boasts one of the loveliest campuses in the nation. Azaleas, magnolias, and oaks line the grounds between the lakes and Italian Renaissance–style buildings dotting the campus. The campus borders an economically depressed area of Baton Rouge, but the campus is generally safe. The neighborhood adjacent to LSU is home to some fantastic restaurants: Mike Anderson's Seafood and The Chimes are particular favorites of Tigers fans, along with popular haunts such as Canes and Louie's. Devotion to the football team infects all of Baton Rouge, so on game day, expect to find few businesses open. The campus itself has residence halls that are populated by only around 20 percent of undergrads; the rest seek digs off campus. Sorority members enjoy the stately graces of the antebellum mansions that serve as their chapter houses. Baton Rouge's central location is within easy distance of party mecca New Orleans and the beaches of the Gulf Coast.

Admissions

Average high school GPA:	3.53
Average freshman SAT writing / math / critical reading score:	565 / 606 / 589
Average freshman ACT score:	24
Application fee:	$40

Application deadlines:
4/15 (freshmen)
4/15 (transfer)

Total applicants:	10,135
Total accepted:	7,455 (74%)
Total accepted who enrolled:	4,503

Notification dates:
continuous (freshmen)
continuous (transfer)

Students

Percentage of male / female students:	48% / 52%
Percentage of students from out of state:	13%
Percentage of students graduating in 4 years / 6 years:	27% / 59%

Money

Total endowment:	$285,227,135
Total in-state tuition, fees & expenses:	$12,447
Total out-of-state tuition, fees & expenses:	$20,747
Average financial aid package:	$8,011
Percentage of students who sought aid and received it:	58%
Percentage of students receiving financial aid:	35%

Also Check Out

Florida State University

Tulane University

University of Georgia

The University of Mississippi

The University of Texas at Austin

Loyola College in Maryland

4501 North Charles Street
Baltimore, MD 21210

(410) 617-2000
http://www.loyola.edu/

BIG PERSPECTIVE

Go greyhound!

5 REASONS IT'S COOL

1. The College of Arts and Sciences immerses students in **great traditions of learning**—whether they like it or not.

2. The urban Baltimore campus means **great bars are only a cab ride away**.

3. The School of Business and Management incubates **tomorrow's corporate movers and shakers.**

4. A 13:1 student-to-faculty ratio means **you'll never be just a face in the crowd.**

5. **Greyhound sports** gets fans' hearts racing.

The Basics

Public / private: private religious
Total enrollment / undergrads: 6,035 / 3,502
Campus setting: urban
Students call it: LC, Loyola
Students are called: Greyhounds
Notable alums: Mark Bowden (writer), Frank Cashen (Major League Baseball executive), Tom Clancy (writer), Edwin A. Fleishman (psychologist), Jim McKay (sports journalist), Steven B. Smith (poet), Jimmy McNulty (attended; detective in *The Wire*)

Get Your Learn On

Academic rigor is the order of the day at LC. Before they can dream of earning a degree in one of the school's many fine programs, underclassmen must complete a demanding gen-ed curriculum. Once they pass through this crucible, students have an array of options. The School of Business and Management, a perennially popular choice, allows students to nurture their inner hedge fund manager. The College of Arts and Sciences offers many degree options from among the hard and human sciences (and is also responsible for the gen-ed requirements). Loyola is affiliated with the Roman Catholic Church, and while it's possible to major in Catholic studies, religion isn't an overbearing part of the academic experience. Although demanding, classes feature a dynamic, elegant blend of approaches. You won't find dull lectures or touchy-feely group therapy sessions here. And the strictures of undergrad academics are lessened by the intimate student-to-faculty ratio of

This Old House

For the first three years of its existence, LC's campus consisted of a single house in downtown Baltimore. In 1855, the school relocated to more spacious digs in the Mount Vernon neighborhood, before finally settling into it's current home in the 1920s. Situated on the property formerly known as the Evergreen Estate—hence the campus nickname of Evergreen—LC provides current students with a blend of modern facilities and picturesque early nineteenth century architecture, exemplified by the Reverend Francis X. Knott, S. J., Humanities Center.

13:1. Going Greyhound will get you where you want to go educationally, and you'll likely learn more than you bargained for along the way.

If You Pour It, They Will Come

LC students tend to be clean cut and friendly. Because the Greek scene is nonexistent, Greyhounds must turn to the many welcoming bars of Falls Point, Federal Hill, and York Road to satisfy their tippling urges. If barhopping funds are running short, students sometimes crash parties at nearby Towson and Johns Hopkins. Although LC's rich and varied social atmosphere generally wins high praise, some students claim that their peers are bland Abercrombie androids. Administrators have recently taken measures to court minorities. If you love to learn and like the sound of a social life featuring cocktails, cab rides, and cover charges, then LC is definitely the place for you.

Baltimore and More

Baltimore is the city Greyhounds call home. It's also the city of Edgar Allen Poe and John Waters, two fascinating iconoclasts. While Baltimore's bars are popular destinations, students also appreciate the aquarium, the art museum, and the restaurants. When in need of a different urban environment or a political internship, Greyhounds can take the train to D.C. The campus offers its own delights. Students rave about the dorms, especially Butler, Campion, and Newman Halls, which are notably spacious and comfortable. One campus demerit is the library, which features really creepy stairwells. It is, however, currently undergoing a renovation and expansion. Already up-to-date is the ever-popular Fitness and Aquatic Center, where students can work off the previous night's mojitos.

Admissions

Average high school GPA:	3.46
Average freshman SAT verbal / math score:	598 / 614
Average freshman ACT score:	24
Application fee:	$50
Application deadlines: 1/15 (freshmen) 7/15 (transfer)	
Total applicants:	7,909
Total accepted:	5,024 (64%)
Total accepted who enrolled:	946
Notification dates: 4/1 (freshmen) continuous (transfer)	

Students

Percentage of male / female students:	41% / 59%
Percentage of students from out of state:	82%
Percentage of students graduating in 4 years / 6 years:	78% / 83%

Money

Total endowment:	$156,800,000
Total tuition:	$30,615
Total cost with fees & expenses:	$42,073
Average financial aid package:	$20,830
Percentage of students who sought aid and received it:	98%
Percentage of students receiving financial aid:	42%

Also Check Out

Boston College

College of the Holy Cross

Fairfield University

Georgetown University

University of Notre Dame

Villanova University

ola Marymount University

One LMU Drive
Los Angeles, CA 90045

(310) 338-2700
http://www.lmu.edu/

City smarts meet shoreline cool.

5 REASONS IT'S COOL

1. **Roman Catholic values** are at the center of education and student life.

2. In the **laid-back atmosphere of Los Angeles**, sunshine and studying go hand in hand.

3. Students can get a **head start in business, communications, and film** while completing a traditional liberal arts education.

4. **Community service is at the heart** of life here, and the Center for Service and Action coordinates the university's service work.

5. Students are smitten with campus thanks to its **breathtaking location** and ongoing renovation.

The Basics

Public / private: private religious
Total enrollment / undergrads: 8,903 / 5,746
Campus setting: suburban
Students call it: Loyola Marymount, LMU
Students are called: Lions
Notable alums: Johnnie Cochran (lawyer), Carson Daly (TV personality), Bob Denver (actor), Colin Hanks (actor)

The Complete Package

In 1973, Marymount College and Loyola University merged and became Loyola Marymount University. The school is governed by the Jesuit and Marymount principles of educating the whole person and focusing on ethics, faith, and social justice. An upper-division ethics course is required of all students. Students choose to enroll in one of six undergraduate colleges: the Bellarmine College of Liberal Arts, the College of Communication and Fine Arts, the College of Business Administration, the Frank R. Seaver College of Science and Engineering, the School of Education, or the School of Film and Television. Popular majors include communications, psychology, biology, and business, while the film program gives cinephiles a shot at greatness in Hollywood. All undergrads have a similar core curriculum and can choose from over eighty majors, all of which focus on the traditional liberal arts. Small class sizes of about nineteen students plus lots of local internship opportunities later on make LMU a solid choice.

Very Shifty

In the early part of the twentieth century, the Loyola College and the Religious of Sacred Heart of Mary educated local Los Angeles young men and women, respectively. After relocating several times throughout the Los Angeles area, Loyola College eventually became Loyola University in 1930. In 1933, the Religious of Sacred Heart of Mary started the Marymount Junior College in Westwood (home of UCLA), which moved to Palos Verdes and then finally to the Westchester campus of Loyola University in 1968. Finally in 1973, the two schools settled down, merged, and became the Loyola Marymount University we know today.

Warm Weather, Cool Students

The LMU lifestyle consists of serving others, studying, and soaking up the sun. Over three-quarters of students are from California, and 60 percent are Catholic. These generally conservative students also tend to be social and athletic. Roughly half live in one of the sixteen comfortable residence halls. With so many students commuting to school every day, parking can be problematic. On weekends, the campus clears out a bit, and remaining students usually head into the city, the suburbs, or the beach. The Center for Service and Action (CSA) organizes community service programs, including the popular Alternative Breaks program. Campus clubs create a stir with frequent activities, and most organizations, including the Greeks, participate in projects that lend a helping hand. LMU competes in NCAA Division I, mostly in the West Coast Conference. The men's basketball games aren't as big as they once were, but they still draw large crowds.

California, Californiaaaaaaaaa

LMU's campus is situated on the Westchester bluffs overlooking the Pacific Ocean, with spectacular views of the Playa Del Rey community. On the Fourth of July, you can see all of L.A.'s fireworks displays right from the comfort of campus. At this truly lovely locale, palm trees sway in the ocean breeze, and lush lawns provide perfect spots for reading a book or having a chat. The centerpiece of the Upper Campus is Sacred Heart Chapel, with the Sunken Gardens and Alumni Mall below. Current campus facilities include the former Raytheon/Hughes Corporate headquarters, which means lots of extra classroom space, and a bookstore, dining hall, fitness center, and office space. The complex is now called University Hall, and it's located on the lower Leavey Campus. Downtown L.A. is not far away by car, and the beach, with its many oceanfront restaurants and recreations, is just down the road.

Admissions

Average high school GPA:	3.62
Average freshman SAT writing / math / critical reading score:	584 / 592 / 583
Average freshman ACT score:	24
Application fee:	$50
Application deadlines: 1/15 (freshmen) 6/1 (transfer)	
Total applicants:	8,168
Total accepted:	4,370 (54%)
Total accepted who enrolled:	1,262
Notification dates: continuous (freshmen) continuous (transfer)	

Students

Percentage of male / female students:	41% / 59%
Percentage of students from out of state:	26%
Percentage of students graduating in 4 years / 6 years:	62% / 73%

Money

Total endowment:	$325,000,000
Total tuition:	$29,198
Total cost with fees & expenses:	$41,124
Average financial aid package:	$17,254
Percentage of students who sought aid and received it:	76%
Percentage of students receiving financial aid:	57%

Also Check Out

Pepperdine University

University of California–Los Angeles

University of California–San Diego

University of California–Santa Barbara

University of San Diego

University of Southern California

Loyola University

820 North Michigan Avenue
Chicago, IL 60611

(773) 274-3000
http://www.luc.edu/

 **BIG CHOICE**

Get ready to ramble!

5 REASONS IT'S COOL

1. The **School of Business Administration** throws students right into the mix, sending them to downtown Chicago to gain work experience.

2. The school's **Chi-town address** means there's always something going on.

3. **Jesuit ideals rule** at this Catholic university.

4. Get in touch with your feminine side! **Women outnumber men by around two to one.**

5. **Ramblers sports** get the crowd howling along with mascot Lou Wolf.

The Basics

Public / private: private religious
Total enrollment / undergrads: 15,194 / 9,725
Campus setting: urban
Students call it: LUC, Loyola
Students are called: Ramblers
Notable alums: Susan Candiotti (journalist), Sandra Cisneros (writer), James Iha (musician), James McManus (writer), Jennifer Morrison (actress), Bob Newhart (comedian)

Loyola to a Fault

LUC's pursuit of academic excellence has shifted into overdrive recently. Enrollment is at record highs, which has proven beneficial overall. Still, not all Ramblers are happy campers. Though the student-to-faculty ratio remains a decent 13:1, class sizes have been swelling. With the high price tag accompanying an undergraduate career at LUC, some feel that real value has declined with recent growth. However, many students applaud the surging applications and focus on academics. LUC boasts a number of strong programs, most notably biology, nursing, and psychology. Many students come to LUC to get on the healthcare track. Another perennial draw is the School of Business Administration, which gives students real-life experience in the bustling milieu of downtown Chicago. No matter which major you choose, you can expect to find professors who are friendly, accessible, and always willing to work with students.

The Sixth Man

During the 1963 NCAA Men's Basketball Tournament, LUC made a small contribution to eliminating racial segregation in the United States. Coaches had an implicit agreement to limit the number of black players who played in each game. Ramblers coach George Ireland violated this compact when he played as many as five black players. The Ramblers went on to win the championship.

Chi-Town Stomping Grounds

Greeks maintain only a token presence here; the alpha and omega of student social life is Chicago, Loyola's hometown. Strict rules governing on-campus residents mean that Ramblers are all too happy to repair to local bars. As soon as they're able, students move out of campus housing and into Chicago apartments, which gives LUC a commuter school vibe. Word also has it that students divide into three camps: preppie, hipster, and the sartorially undecided. Students are united by their largely upper-middle-class standing. LUC is known for attracting well-heeled Catholics, but its ethnic and regional diversity are nothing to sneeze at. Whites represent 62 percent of the student population, and some 34 percent hail from states other than Chicago. And if you happen to be a current or aspiring player, you'll be happy to know that at LUC, girls outnumber guys by more than two to one.

That Town of Towns

The "Second City" is certainly first in Ramblers' hearts. They love the many opportunities to see a show, visit a museum, or just have a few beers. The campus offers ready access to these delights courtesy of the CTA El train, which stops practically at the school's front door. LUC's campus overlooks Lake Michigan, a view everyone loves. When the weather's fair, there are good times to be had. But students warn that in general, the climate is not for the faint of heart. The origins of the nickname "The Windy City" may be controversial, but no one is arguing that the winter wind is pleasant. Campus is currently straining under greatly increased enrollment, and facilities sometimes fall short of demand. Students say the dorms are livable, if slightly cramped, but they complain about the tough rules governing on-campus housing. The Halas Sports Center draws approving reviews.

Admissions

Average high school GPA:	3.53
Average freshman SAT writing / math / critical reading score:	575 / 582 / 586
Average freshman ACT score:	24
Application fee:	$25
Application deadlines: 4/1 (freshmen) 7/1 (transfer)	
Total applicants:	15,178
Total accepted:	11,754 (77%)
Total accepted who enrolled:	2,130
Notification dates: continuous (freshmen) continuous (transfer)	

Students

Percentage of male / female students:	35% / 65%
Percentage of students from out of state:	33%
Percentage of students graduating in 4 years / 6 years:	41% / 66%

Money

Total endowment:	$305,664,000
Total tuition:	$27,200
Total cost with fees & expenses:	$37,896
Average financial aid package:	$21,689
Percentage of students who sought aid and received it:	77%
Percentage of students receiving financial aid:	64%

Also Check Out

Creighton University

DePauw University

Saint Louis University

University of Notre Dame

Macalester College

1600 Grand Avenue
St. Paul, MN 55105

(651) 696-6000
http://www.macalester.edu/

 **BIG BRAIN**

 **BIG PERSPECTIVE**

An elite college in Minnesota? Snow kidding.

5 REASONS IT'S COOL

1. You won't be left out in the cold: Macalester **students are easygoing, accepting, and super-smart**.

2. Go global without even stepping foot off campus: the study body has a **decidedly international flavor**, with one in ten students hailing from a foreign country.

3. If you're pining for **small classes, caring professors, and a nurturing community**, pine no further.

4. Hungry brains find food for thought in the **satisfying academic environment**.

5. The **urban location in St. Paul** is a rarity among Midwestern liberal arts colleges.

The Basics

Public / private: private religious
Total enrollment / undergrads: 1,918 / 1,918
Campus setting: urban
Students call it: Mac, Macalester
Students are called: Fighting Scots
Notable alums: Kofi Annan (Nobel Laureate, Peace), Duane Hanson (artist), Bob Mould (musician), Tim O'Brien (novelist), DeWitt Wallace (businessman, philanthropist)

Rhodes to Glory

Macalester grads have racked up impressive numbers of Fulbright, Rhodes, and other prestigious scholarships. One of the college's biggest selling points is the small size of its classes. The student-to-faculty ratio is 11:1, and it's common for students to develop friendly working relations with professors—some even play together on intramural sports teams. Macalester's general education requirements include two courses in social science, two in natural science and mathematics, and two in fine arts and humanities. Students must also take courses that include a multicultural component and complete a comprehensive capstone project during their senior year. Depending on a student's major, this capstone project can take the form of a major research paper, original work of art, or self-designed scientific experiment. Macalester's most popular programs are in economics, chemistry, biology, and psychology. The college's science facilities are excellent and feature an astronomical observatory and electron spectroscopy facility. About

Ready, Aim . . .

Minnesota's weather is often cited as a downside of life at Macalester. But students certainly know how to find the silver lining in their snow clouds. Every year on the night of the first snowfall, the Grand Avenue Snowball Fight gives students an excuse to take a break from studying. Students line up on the north and south sides of the avenue, teaming with neighbors to pelt the enemy army across the street with snow.

5 percent of students participate in stipend-supported research with professors over the summer. More than half of students take advantage of the robust study-abroad program, which offers travel opportunities in more than sixty countries.

Hippy and International

Life is laid-back at Macalester. The campus is known as a haven for hippies, smart kids, and international students. Students by and large consider themselves liberal and politically aware, and over 10 percent are international, with more than ninety nations represented. There are no fraternities or sororities. Seventy percent of students live on campus, but those who live off campus are reportedly happy to do so: The surrounding neighborhoods are welcoming to students, and much of Macalester's social life happens off campus, anyway. Intramural sports are popular with a passionate minority, but athletics aren't a big deal here. Most students are barely conscious of the fact that their school fields varsity athletic teams. Over $90 million has been spent in fifteen years to improve Macalester's physical amenities. Students are happy with the culinary options but report that the recreational facilities are ripe for renovation.

Twin City Living

Macalester's campus is a picture of red brick prettiness, and the row of Victorian homes on nearby Summit Avenue provides a pleasant destination for mind-clearing walks. The campus's small size—it's just fifty-three acres—can feel a little cramped. The residential neighborhoods of St. Paul that surround the campus are pleasant and safe. And the city itself comes with the theaters, ethnic enclaves, and cool nightlife that you'd expect from one of the Midwest's major metropolitan areas. There are more than a dozen other colleges and universities nearby, and cultural attractions like the Guthrie Theatre and the Minneapolis Institute of Art are accessible by public transportation.

Admissions

Average high school GPA:	—
Average freshman SAT verbal / math score:	677 / 664
Average freshman ACT score:	26
Application fee:	$40
Application deadlines:	
1/15 (freshmen)	
4/15 (transfer)	
11/15 (early decision)	
Total applicants:	4,826
Total accepted:	1,881 (39%)
Total accepted who enrolled:	501
Notification dates:	
4/1 (freshmen)	
5/15 (transfer)	
12/15 (early decision)	
Acceptance rate for early decision applicants:	48%

Students

Percentage of male / female students:	42% / 58%
Percentage of students from out of state:	79%
Percentage of students graduating in 4 years / 6 years:	79% / 85%

Money

Total endowment:	$525,000,000
Total tuition:	$33,494
Total cost with fees & expenses:	$41,914
Average financial aid package:	$25,238
Percentage of students who sought aid and received it:	100%
Percentage of students receiving financial aid:	66%

Also Check Out

Carleton College

Denison University

Grinnell College

Oberlin College

University of Chicago

Vassar College

Manhattan College

Manhattan College Parkway
Riverdale, NY 10471

(718) 862-8000
http://www.manhattan.edu/

BIG PERSPECTIVE

Bright students, big city

5 REASONS IT'S COOL

1. **There are no TAs.** Every class is taught by a professor.

2. Looking for an extra challenge? The **Honors Enrichment Program** will prepare you to be an intellectual leader.

3. With **Manhattan just a short ride away,** you'll never get bored.

4. Run, baby, run: the Draddy Gymnasium is home to **the largest indoor track in New York City.**

5. **There are no outsiders here.** Students at this Catholic school have a reputation for getting along with one another.

The Basics

Public / private: private religious
Total enrollment / undergrads: 3,357 / 3,021
Campus setting: urban
Students call it: Manhattan, MC
Students are called: Jaspers
Notable alums: Alexandra Chando (actress), James W. Cooley (mathematician), Rudy Guiliani (mayor, New York City), Barnard Hughes (actor), Ray Kelly (police commissioner, New York City), James Patterson (novelist)

A Broad Focus and Personal Attention

MC is a Lasallian Catholic school, but its academic focus is not just religious. All MC students must take classes in math, writing, religion, and a foreign language. The individual colleges—Education, Business, Arts and Sciences, and Engineering—have additional requirements. No matter what school you enroll in or which of the dozens of majors you choose, you'll enjoy small, discussion-oriented classes and lots of personal attention. You'll also have the option of enrolling in the Honors Enrichment Program, which offers interdisciplinary classes and encourages students to apply what they learn in the classroom. Profs and administrators know students by name and go out of their way to make sure everyone is engaged. Jaspers particularly appreciate this kind of personal attention when it comes time to seek out internships or jobs. A strong alumni network and a great career service department also go a long way toward ensuring that MC grads are able to take advantage of New York City's amazing opportunities.

Take Me Out to the Ballgame

In the late 1800s, the **MC** baseball team was playing the Metropolitans, a semipro team. As Manhattan came to bat during the seventh inning of a close game, the coach, Brother Jasper (for whom the school mascot is named), noticed that the Manhattan students in the crowd were getting fidgety. He called a timeout and directed fans to get up and stretch for a few minutes. At least, that's how the legend goes.

Two Groups, One Unifying Basketball Team

MC has just over three thousand undergrads, about 70 percent of whom live on campus. While the student body is reasonably diverse, many Jaspers are middle to upper class, preppy, Catholic, and white. While the commuting students miss out on some of the bonding experiences the dorm dwellers enjoy, there's little friction between the two groups. Many students get involved with Greek life or one of MC's sixty-plus registered organizations, which include everything from the school radio station to an electronics club to a club for commuters. And during basketball season, everyone comes together to rally around the men's Division I basketball team, which often plays in the NCAA Tournament.

World-Class Fun Is Just a Subway Ride Away

Don't be fooled by the name: Manhattan College isn't actually in Manhattan. Not anymore, anyway. The school was originally founded on Canal Street in lower Manhattan, but today, the campus is located in the Bronx's Riverdale neighborhood, a relatively posh area with a suburban flavor about ten miles north of midtown Manhattan. To make room for all the students who want to live on campus, the college is building a new dorm, called East Hill Tower II. There are also plans to turn one of the current dorms, Chrysostom Hall, into offices. While the green MC campus is visually appealing, many students don't find it or the Riverdale neighborhood nearly as enticing as Manhattan. Luckily, New York City's excellent subway and bus system make it easy for students to zip downtown, where they can get their fill of the Guggenheim, the Met, or any of the city's zillions of other attractions.

Admissions

Average high school GPA:	3.37
Average freshman SAT writing / math / critical reading score:	554 / 528 / 548
Average freshman ACT score:	23
Application fee:	$50

Application deadlines:
4/15 (freshmen)
7/1 (transfer)
11/15 (early decision)

Total applicants:	5,078
Total accepted:	2,616 (52%)
Total accepted who enrolled:	707

Notification dates:
4/15 (freshmen)
8/15 (transfer)
12/1 (early decision)

Acceptance rate for early decision applicants:	61%

Students

Percentage of male / female students:	50% / 50%
Percentage of students from out of state:	30%
Percentage of students graduating in 4 years / 6 years:	60% / 67%

Money

Total endowment:	$43,764,852
Total tuition:	$20,350
Total cost with fees & expenses:	$31,875
Average financial aid package:	$16,440
Percentage of students who sought aid and received it:	78%
Percentage of students receiving financial aid:	58%

Also Check Out

Boston University

Fordham University

New York University

Northeastern University

Massachusetts Institute of Technology

77 Massachusetts Avenue
Cambridge, MA 02139

(617) 253-1000
http://web.mit.edu/]

 **BIG BRAIN**

 **BIG JOB**

 **BIG RESEARCH**

Brilliant techies, innovative profs, stellar school

5 REASONS IT'S COOL

1. **Professors' research and work** inspires and motivates students.

2. Although the undergrad population is thickly studded with academic stars, **collaboration between peers is the norm.**

3. **Pranks, hacks, practical jokes**—whatever you call them, they add some levity to the atmosphere of academic brilliance.

4. MIT's location on the Charles River provides **beautiful views and plentiful extracurricular options.**

5. **Serious research opportunities** are available from day one.

The Basics

Public / private: private nonprofit
Total enrollment / undergrads: 10,253 / 4,127
Campus setting: urban
Students call it: MIT
Students are called: Beavers
Notable alums: Buzz Aldrin (astronaut), Ben Bernanke (chairman, Federal Reserve), William R. Hewlett (cofounder, Hewlett-Packard), Charles Koch (CEO, Koch Industries), I. M. Pei (architect)

UROP at the Top

Perhaps the best science and technology school in the world, MIT is a haven for brilliant young minds. The most popular majors are electrical engineering and computer science, mechanical engineering, manage- ment, and biology. Wait, management? Yup. The institute's offerings extend beyond the realm of computers and labs to a slate of profes- sional and liberal arts majors. Freshmen are graded "pass/no record" during their first term and "A/B/C/no record" during the second, mean- ing no D or F grades will show up on students' transcripts during their first year. Professors, leaders in their fields, are passionate about their work. Twenty-five MIT profs have won Nobel Prizes. With a remarkable 7.5:1 student-to-faculty ratio and an emphasis on professors, rather than TAs, teaching classes, it's easy for students to benefit from their teach- ers' enthusiasm and expertise. Opportunities for collaborative work are supported through such endeavors as the Undergraduate Research and Opportunities Program (UROP) and partnerships such as the

Nightwork

MIT students are known for *hacks*, as their witty and benign pranks are called. Hacks sometimes take friendly aim at local rival Harvard University and far-flung competitor Caltech. In 2006, for example, MIT students stole a three-ton cannon from Caltech (whose students stole it back a few days later). Other famous hacks have involved placing various objects on the Great Dome, including a fire truck and a replica of the Wright brothers' airplane. Want more hacks? Check out *Nightwork: A History of Hacks and Pranks at MIT*, by T. F. Petersonn.

Summer Undergraduate Research Fellowship (SURF), which operates through the National Institute of Standards and Technology.

Busy Beavers

While the academic pressure can be intense at MIT, students are able to temper the pressure-filled atmosphere. In addition to being doers, makers, and innovators, many undergrads are also pranksters and collaborators. The institute respects its young scholars, as its website demonstrates: The MIT Admissions website, an early adopter of web 2.0 technology, is built around student and staff blogs. Five sororities and twenty-seven fraternities draw students into Greek life. There's a good showing of cultural groups, support programs, and activities on campus. MIT competes in a staggering forty-two varsity sports, and many teams have had historically strong showings. Housing is guaranteed for four years, and students can select their dorm and floor, which leads to interesting enclaves.

Boston Bonanza

MIT is located in Cambridge, right along the Charles River and just down the road from Harvard. MIT and Harvard might be the marquee names in town, but there are over fifty other colleges and universities in the Boston area, making it a paradise for the eighteen-to-twenty-one set. Art and culture abound, and there are more affordable bars and restaurants than you can shake a calculator at. MIT isn't particularly renowned for its beauty; busy Mass Ave. runs through the center of campus, which is a blend of original buildings with traditional columns and domes, and new, more contemporary buildings. Still, many dorms have stunning views of the Charles River and Boston beyond. The on-campus buildings are interconnected and easy to navigate (except when students are trying to race down the Infinite Corridor, which runs through buildings 7, 3, 10, 4, and 8).

Admissions

Average high school GPA:	—
Average freshman SAT verbal / math score:	703 / 737
Average freshman ACT score:	27
Application fee:	$65

Application deadlines:
1/1 (freshmen)
3/15 (transfer)
11/1 (early action)

Total applicants:	11,374
Total accepted:	1,514 (13%)
Total accepted who enrolled:	1,002

Notification dates:
3/25 (freshmen)
5/15 (transfer)
12/15 (early action)

Acceptance rate for early action applicants:	15%

Students

Percentage of male / female students:	56% / 44%
Percentage of students from out of state:	91%
Percentage of students graduating in 4 years / 6 years:	82% / 94%

Money

Total endowment:	$4,294,967,295
Total tuition:	$33,400
Total cost with fees & expenses:	$44,650
Average financial aid package:	$29,831
Percentage of students who sought aid and received it:	100%
Percentage of students receiving financial aid:	60%

Also Check Out

California Institute of Technology

Duke University

Harvard University

Harvey Mudd College

Stanford University

Merrimack College

315 Turnpike Street
North Andover, MA 01845

(978) 837-5000
http://www.merrimack.edu/

 **BIG PERSPECTIVE**

 **BIG WORLD**

Where doing unto others is a way of life

5 REASONS IT'S COOL

1. The **blend of liberal arts and professional education** provides intellectual breadth and hands-on experience.

2. The **strong emphasis on community service** at this Roman Catholic school will appeal to charitable students.

3. **Professors make themselves available** to their students.

4. With **Boston twenty-five miles away,** there are plenty of internship opportunities, cultural hot spots—and bars.

5. The college has invested in a **new campus center,** a **new center for the arts,** and two **new residence halls.**

The Basics

Public / private: private religious
Total enrollment / undergrads: 2,251 / 2,213
Campus setting: suburban
Students call it: Merrimack, MC, Mack
Students are called: Warriors
Notable alums: Greg Classen (pro hockey player), Steve McKenna (pro hockey player), Adam Shephard (author), Carl Yastrzemski (pro baseball player)

Liberal Arts with an Augustinian Twist

The Augustinian tradition is strong at this Roman Catholic school. Not only is the campus community close-knit, but students and professors also consistently demonstrate a commitment to helping others. And it's not just that Merrimack encourages students to participate in community service; professors are also committed to helping students think critically and act morally. Students are urged to undertake independent studies, participate in internships, and study abroad so they can gain a broader understanding of the world and acquire the tools they'll need to excel after graduation. The Cooperative Education Program, meanwhile, allows students to work in career-related jobs while completing their bachelor's degrees. Students have their choice of thirty majors in the liberal arts, business, engineering, and the sciences, including more specialized majors in digital media arts, international business, and sports medicine.

Home Sweet Home

During the weekend-long homecoming extravaganza, known officially as Family Weekend, there's tailgating, a football game, a men's ice hockey game, a comedy show, a concert, a meet-the-deans event, and coed flag football. And for those more civic-minded families, there are even opportunities to do some community service.

One Big, Happy Family

For most of its history, Merrimack was predominately known as a commuter school, but it has become a residential college of late, with 80 percent of students living on campus. Most students hail from white, upper-middle-class New England families, but the campus is slowly becoming more diverse. Students tend to be outgoing and friendly, and many participate in intramurals or one of the school's Division II sports teams. And while only a small number of students participate in Greek life, many find their niche in one of the student organizations, which range from the Poker Club to Model UN to the Merrimack Program Board, which organizes concerts and comedy events on campus.

Next Stop: Wonderland

Merrimack's 220-acre campus epitomizes the small New England liberal arts college. Colored by green grass in the spring and summer, multihued leaves in the fall, and snow in the winter, the campus makes each of the four seasons a cause for celebration. While many students study or socialize outside during the warmer months, there's plenty to do indoors when the mercury drops. The recently renovated Sakowich Campus Center brings students together for athletic and social functions ranging from dances to movies and games. And the Rogers Center for the Arts offers concerts, theater performances, and comedy acts. When students begin to hanker for some big-city action, they can make the half-hour drive or train ride to Boston, where bars, restaurants, museums, sporting events, and other college students abound.

Admissions

Average high school GPA:	3.34
Average freshman SAT writing / math / critical reading score:	563 / 573 / 562
Average freshman ACT score:	22
Application fee:	$50

Application deadlines:
2/1 (freshmen)
12/30 (transfer)
11/30 (early action)

Total applicants:	3,424
Total accepted:	2,452 (72%)
Total accepted who enrolled:	532

Notification dates:
4/1 (freshmen)
1/10 (transfer)
12/20 (early action)

Acceptance rate for early action applicants:	68%

Students

Percentage of male / female students:	47% / 53%
Percentage of students from out of state:	27%
Percentage of students graduating in 4 years / 6 years:	54% / 71%

Money

Total endowment:	$33,555,506
Total tuition:	$26,620
Total cost with fees & expenses:	$38,625
Average financial aid package:	$18,000
Percentage of students who sought aid and received it:	65%
Percentage of students receiving financial aid:	54%

Also Check Out

Boston College

Boston University

Northeastern University

University of Connecticut

University of Massachusetts Amherst

Miami University

501 East High Street
Oxford, OH 45056

(513) 529-1809
http://www.muohio.edu/

BIG CHOICE

Brains, good looks—what's not to love?

5 REASONS IT'S COOL

1. Miami's **prestigious Farmer School of Business** has produced numerous CEOs and other bigwigs.

2. Students are treated to **hefty career resources and lots of visits from recruiters**.

3. Ohio residents receive more scholarship dollars than out-of-staters, though **everyone gets their money's worth** at this challenging school.

4. The school's **dining services have won more first-place awards** than those of any other North American university.

5. Poet Robert Frost once proclaimed Miami University **"the most beautiful campus there is."**

The Basics

Public / private: public state-related
Total enrollment / undergrads: 16,329 / 14,551
Campus setting: small town
Students call it: Miami of Ohio, Miami
Students are called: RedHawks
Notable alums: Brad Alford (CEO and chairman, Nestlé), Art Clokey (creator, Gumby and Pokey), Rita Dove (poet), Wayne Embry (first African American NBA general manager), Benjamin Harrison (U.S. president), Nick Lachey (singer), Chris Rose (sportscaster)

Miami and Me

Though Miami University offers masters and doctoral degrees, under-graduates are the real stars here. The academic atmosphere can be intense, but student are aided by energetic professors and modest class sizes that average around twenty five students. The liberal arts tradition remains alive and well through the mandatory Miami Plan for Liberal Education, which includes a broad range of interdisciplinary Foundation courses, a Thematic Sequence outside of the major, and a Senior Capstone Experience. More than a hundred majors are offered across the College of Arts and Science and five schools. The most popular options include business, marketing, zoology, psychology, and finance. Economics, music, and botany are also strong. Miami also boasts unique offerings such as pulp and paper science technology. Three Honors and Scholars Programs provide participating students with scholarships and special housing. Around 40 percent of students study abroad, including

Rock the Cradle

There's something about the RedHawks nest that inspires coaching greatness. Miami University is so well known for nurturing future coaches, managers, and owners that it has been dubbed the Cradle of Coaches. The best of this group are even formally inducted into the athletic department's official Cradle of Coaches at a yearly ceremony.

at the satellite campus in Luxembourg. Miami has a high graduation rate compared to similar public schools, and supports graduating students with a huge career fair.

Count Me In

Though the mascot is the RedHawk, students here could easily be called the Eager Beavers. Students choose from tons of extracurriculars, including over 300 campus groups. The on- and off-campus social scene is lively, and the Greek scene draws around 25 percent of men and women. Sports are popular, and the school hosts competitive teams in football, basketball, swimming, tennis, and volleyball. Diversity isn't a particularly strong point. The student body is just under 75 percent Ohioan and 90 percent white, and preppiness abounds. The university, however, is attempting to branch out with efforts like the Minority Professional Leadership Program and forums to address minority issues. A free wireless network blankets the campus, allowing students to connect while lounging on any of the school's plentiful lawns. Freshmen are required to live on campus, but that's not a drawback. Campus safety is a nonissue, and new living-learning communities based on themes like "Celebrate the Arts" and "RedHawk Traditions" provide students with interesting housing options.

Small Is Beautiful

Miami University is named for the Miami River Valley and the Native American tribe that lived there. Located thirty miles from Cincinnati in the town of Oxford, the campus is a gorgeous collection of Georgian architecture, lovely lawns, and copious trees. Such splendor is complimented by a slate of construction projects, including a new business school and performing arts complex. Oxford is a true college town: It's a manageable six miles square, and over 40 percent of the residents are between twenty and twenty-four, with students dominating the population. If the bucolic charm gets to be too much, besides Cincinnati, the urban delights of Indianapolis are about two hours away.

Admissions

Average high school GPA:	3.7
Average freshman SAT verbal / math score:	596 / 620
Average freshman ACT score:	25
Application fee:	$45

Application deadlines:

1/31 (freshmen)	11/1 (early decision)
5/1 (transfer)	12/1 (early action)

Total applicants:	15,468
Total accepted:	12,060 (78%)
Total accepted who enrolled:	3,557

Notification dates:

3/15 (freshmen)	12/15 (early decision)
continuous (transfer)	2/1 (early action)

Acceptance rate for early decision applicants:	78%

Students

Percentage of male / female students:	46% / 54%
Percentage of students from out of state:	29%
Percentage of students graduating in 4 years / 6 years:	66% / 80%

Money

Total endowment:	$320,188,000
Total in-state tuition, fees & expenses:	$19,782
Total out-of-state tuition, fees & expenses:	$32,297
Average financial aid package:	$17,573
Percentage of students who sought aid and received it:	74%
Percentage of students receiving financial aid:	40%

Also Check Out

Case Western Reserve University

Indiana University–Bloomington

The Ohio State University

University of Connecticut

University of Michigan–Ann Arbor

Michigan State University

250 Hannah Administration Building
East Lansing, MI 48824

(517) 355-1855
http://www.msu.edu/

 **BIG CHOICE**

 **BIG RESEARCH**

 **BIG WORLD**

The only thing that's *not* big is the price.

5 REASONS IT'S COOL

1. MSU has more **study-abroad opportunities** than any other public university in the country, with more than 250 programs in 60 countries.

2. The **renowned School of Journalism** is a proving ground for would-be Woodwards and Bernsteins.

3. **Live like a king** in one of the largest and best dormitory systems in the country.

4. The **agricultural sciences and biotechnology programs** are first rate.

5. Recently named one of the **top 100 Global Universities**, MSU itself has connections in nearly 50 different countries.

The Basics

Public / private: public state
Total enrollment / undergrads: 45,520 / 35,821
Campus setting: suburban
Students call it: Michigan State, MSU
Students are called: Spartans
Notable alums: Kirk Gibson (pro baseball player), Magic Johnson (pro basketball player), Sam Raimi (film director), Don Gronyeal (journalist), Jim Harrison (author)

Not Just Another State School

With more than 200 different majors in seventeen colleges to choose from, you're sure to find your academic calling at MSU. Michigan State's agricultural programs in the sciences, agribusiness, and horticulture have ranked among the best in the nation for more than one hundred years. The university's programs in elementary and secondary school education are also top notch, as are its programs in journalism, communications, psychology, and physics. MSU students have more opportunities to study abroad than students at any other public university in the country. Pick from scores of interesting programs in different disciplines in dozens of different countries on every continent—even Antarctica. The MSU library system, meanwhile, packs a head-spinning five million books, which doesn't even include the millions of microfilm. And for those gunning for even greater challenges, the MSU Honors College allows students to plan their own curricula, take graduate-level courses, and even engage in original research.

A Towering Presence

If you've seen a photo of the MSU campus, odds are you've seen Beaumont Tower, the iconic red brick edifice that is the face of Michigan State. The 105-foot clock tower houses a carillon of nearly fifty bells, which star in free summer concerts. According to legend, an MSU alum who died fighting in World War II haunts the tower looking for his long lost love and calls to her by making the bells ring. In a less ghostly but equally romantic tradition, people kiss in the shadow of the tower.

Spartan, not *Spartan*

Despite its mascot, Michigan State is anything but austere. With more than 35,000 undergrads, MSU ranks in the top ten largest universities in the country. Most students agree, though, that the university's size is one of its greatest strengths. People of every interest and background flourish here. Join one or more of the 500 different campus organizations, rally with one of the many active political organizations on campus, or report for the *State News*, one of the largest campus newspapers in the country. If you need a break, hang out in the Brody Complex, a cluster of dorms that's also home to the enormous student cafeteria, and a great place to meet someone new. With more than fifty nationally affiliated frats and sororities, MSU's vibrant Greek life ensures that a good time is always just around the corner. Culturally minded students can get lost in the Wharton Center for Performing Arts, the Breslin Student Events Center, the Abrams Planetarium, horticultural and botanical gardens, and the several art and natural history museums on campus. And, of course, there are always Spartan sports, which include twenty NCAA Division I teams.

A Beacon of Light

Michigan State sits on nearly 5,000 acres of land in the small town of East Lansing. MSU dominates the community, and more than two-thirds of East Lansing's 50,000 residents are students. With its many museums, gardens, and sporting events, the university campus serves in many ways as the cultural hub of the community. While East Lansing itself is nothing to write home about, many students feel a special attachment to the local shops, bars, cafés, and restaurants along Grand River Avenue. East Lansing is also only a few miles away from Lansing, the state capital, and part of a much larger metropolitan area of over half a million people. MSU's proximity to Lansing offers great internship opportunities, especially for students interested in government and politics. Detroit and Chicago are also just a few hours down the road and offer big-city culture, dining, shopping, and entertainment.

Admissions

Average high school GPA:	3.61
Average freshman SAT writing / math / critical reading score:	553 / 598 / 566
Average freshman ACT score:	24
Application fee:	$35
Application deadlines: continuous (freshmen)* continuous (transfer)	
Total applicants:	23,247
Total accepted:	17,046 (73%)
Total accepted who enrolled:	7,308
Notification dates: 9/1 (freshmen) 9/1 (transfer)	

Students

Percentage of male / female students:	46% / 54%
Percentage of students from out of state:	8%
Percentage of students graduating in 4 years / 6 years:	36% / 71%

Money

Total endowment:	$1,050,854,297
Total in-state tuition, fees & expenses:	$14,887
Total out-of-state tuition, fees & expenses:	$27,532
Average financial aid package:	$9,307
Percentage of students who sought aid and received it:	75%
Percentage of students receiving financial aid:	37%

Also Check Out

Cornell University

The Pennsylvania State University–University Park

Purdue University

University of Illinois at Urbana–Champaign

University of Wisconsin–Madison

Middlebury College

5405 Middlebury College
Middlebury, VT 05753

(802) 443-5000
http://www.middlebury.edu/

 **BIG BRAIN**

 **BIG PERSPECTIVE**

 **BIG WORLD**

First-rate academics, picture-perfect setting

5 REASONS IT'S COOL

1. At this **top school for languages**, intensive summer language programs prepare students for studying abroad.

2. It's easy to fall in love with the campus's rural Vermont setting, which includes **110 acres of ski trails, glades, and a terrain park.**

3. The honor code, which allows self-scheduled, unproctored exams, fosters **a sense of trust and community.**

4. **Professors are known for their expert knowledge** and willingness to work with students.

5. While the nightlife may be lacking, **dozens of campus clubs make up the difference.**

The Basics

Public / private: private nonprofit
Total enrollment / undergrads: 2,406 / 2,406
Campus setting: small town
Students call it: Middlebury
Students are called: Panthers
Notable alums: Eve Ensler (author, *The Vagina Monologues*), Ari Fleischer (White House press secretary), Andrea Koppel (TV news correspondent), Dana Reeve (philanthropist), Frank Sesno (CNN Washington bureau chief)

Rigor, Excellence, and Honor

Middlebury students are required to take at least one class in seven of the following fields: deductive reasoning and analytical processes, social analysis, languages, historical studies, philosophical and religious studies, physical and life sciences, the arts, and literature. On top of these, students have physical education, civilization, and writing classes to take. When it comes time to choose a major, students will find top programs in foreign languages and English, among others. In 1965 Middlebury became the first school to establish an undergraduate major in environmental science, a program that is still strong today. The student-to-faculty ratio is 9:1, and class sizes are normally around ten to twenty students, often fewer. Languages taught via immersion give students a jump-start on the numerous study-abroad opportunities offered by the college. The school also offers a wide array of international studies majors in cultures such as the Middle East, East Asian, and Russian and East European Studies.

Going Polar

Members of Middlebury's Polar Bear Club brave the subfreezing temperatures and snow banks for a late-night skinny-dip in Lake Dunmore just after the ice has thawed. If nothing else, the activity establishes a bond between fellow warm-blooded adventurers.

Commons Life

Middlebury's small size makes for close bonds between students, who participate in tons of activities outside of class, including sailing, competing in triathlons, and bird-watching. The Sunday Night Group attracts a politically active crowd dedicated to ending global warming. Social houses, Middlebury's version of the Greek system, draw around a sixth of the student body. The annual student-run Winter Carnival includes ice shows, ski competitions, parties, and performances by the Middlebury Figure Skating Club. Students tend to be an outdoorsy, athletic bunch. Watching sports, particularly varsity hockey matches, is a popular pastime, as is participating in intramurals. Although the school was the first college or university in the United States to graduate an African American student, the majority of students are white and from wealthy New England families, notwithstanding an international student population of around 10 percent. Students live in one of five resident communities known as Commons, which are self-governing, living-learning communities. Each commons has its own dining hall, games, and intramural sports, which leads to rivalries. Because housing is included with the cost of tuition, almost all students stay on campus throughout their time at Middlebury.

Club Midd

The picturesque campus is so luxurious that students refer to it as "Club Midd." Nestled between Vermont's Green Mountains and the Adirondacks, the campus lays claim to the oldest standing college building in Vermont, Painter Hall, a large granite structure built in 1816. Middlebury is always updating both its athletic and academic facilities. It recently retrofitted Hillcrest Hall, a wood-framed farmhouse built in the late nineteenth century, to conform to environmental green standards. The town and school enjoy a historically close and positive relationship, and local residents often cheer on the school's hockey team. Despite the wealth of activities and history, students can sometimes feel isolated by the ultra-rural environs. Popular weekend road-trip destinations include Burlington, about thirty-five miles north, Montreal, 130 miles up, and Boston, 200 miles southeast.

Admissions

Average high school GPA:	—
Average freshman SAT verbal / math score:	—/—
Average freshman ACT score:	—
Application fee:	$65

Application deadlines:
1/1 (freshmen)
3/1 (transfer)
11/1 (early decision)

Total applicants:	6,205
Total accepted:	1,339 (22%)
Total accepted who enrolled:	563

Notification dates:
4/1 (freshmen)
4/10 (transfer)
12/15 (early decision)

Acceptance rate for early decision applicants:	38%

Students

Percentage of male / female students:	48% / 52%
Percentage of students from out of state:	94%
Percentage of students graduating in 4 years / 6 years:	84% / 93%

Money

Total endowment:	$721,839,000
Total tuition:	—
Total cost with fees & expenses:	$44,330
Average financial aid package:	$28,413
Percentage of students who sought aid and received it:	100%
Percentage of students receiving financial aid:	44%

Also Check Out

Amherst College

Bowdoin College

Dartmouth College

Hamilton College

Williams College

Mills College

5000 MacArthur Boulevard
Oakland, CA 94613

(510) 430-2255
http://www.mills.edu/

 **BIG HAND**

 **BIG PERSPECTIVE**

Nothing run-of-the-mill about it

5 REASONS IT'S COOL

1. Looking for that classic women's college experience? At Mills, it's **ladies first and ladies only.**

2. Live in luxury at Mills's **super-cushy dorms**, some of which have sleeping porches.

3. Small classes + personal attention from professors + supportive advisors = **a nurturing community.**

4. Already know your career or academic goals? Mills offers six **dual-degree programs,** including a 4+1 BA/MBA program.

5. Mills's **Bay Area location** is a prime home base for checking out San Francisco, the mountains, the ocean, and more.

The Basics

Public / private: private nonprofit
Total enrollment / undergrads: 1,410 / 927
Campus setting: urban
Students call it: Mills
Students are called: Cyclones
Notable alums: Renel Brooks-Moon (first female pro baseball announcer), Trisha Brown (choreographer), Ariel Gore (writer), Joanna Newsome (musician), Susan Perrine (physician)

A Top Academic Choice in the Bay Area

A small, liberal arts college, Mills offers bachelor's degrees to women and grad degrees and certificates to both sexes. The most popular undergraduate majors are English; psychology; political, legal, and economic analysis; biology; and anthropology and sociology. Students can also design their own majors with the input of three faculty members. Multiple-degree programs, including a 4+1 MBA degree, and pre-professional programs give focused students excellent outlets. Mills's music program is particularly strong and has produced some innovative graduates. First-year students begin their college careers with a series of general-education courses, which introduce them to the liberal arts by examining various women's issues. General education requirements encompass three main areas—skills, perspectives, and disciplinary experiences—and include studies of culture and gender as well as major prep. After developing a firm foundation of skills, students take a series of sophomore seminars that meld certain disciplines into

No Boys Allowed

In 1990, Mills College trustees voted to admit men in an effort to bolster the school's finances. The students would not have it, and intense protests were mounted. Ultimately, the women were victorious, and Mills continues to admit only women at the undergraduate level.

a single, cohesive course. In keeping with the school's commitment to lots of interaction with faculty, the average class size is a mere fifteen students, and the student/faculty ratio clocks in at 11:1.

A Supportive Community of Women

As "freshwomen," students at Mills join Living Learning Communities, located within the college's posh on-campus housing. The vibe on campus is peaceful, and arts and culture offerings are plentiful. Students tend to be hardworking, philanthropic, and humanist. Thirty-five percent of Mills students identify themselves as students of color, and nontraditional or older students add to the abundant student diversity. Six NCAA Division III sport teams draw athletic undergrads, and for-credit P.E. courses round out schedules while helping students stay in shape. A career services center offers support with individual counseling, assessment, and comprehensive job prep resources, including mock interviews. Socializing may best be pursued off campus. Students can cross-register at nearby UC Berkeley, and many others head over to the city of Berkeley to meet new people, including guys—a scarce commodity on campus. What's not scarce are on-campus dining options, which include organic and vegetarian fare for discerning palates.

Plenty of Room to Mill Around

Beautiful Richards Road serves as the entrance to the Mills campus, which occupies 135 acres in the city of Oakland. Mill's Mediterranean-style buildings are very California, complete with red tile roofs, and new construction preserves that same architectural flair, with a nod to the environmentally green. The Vera M. Long Building for the Social Sciences opened in 2004 and features new technology housed in airy and comfortable spaces. An exception to this style is the Victorian Mills Hall, which once served as the campus's only building. The school's plum location in the Bay Area makes it a frequent stop for visitors and an ideal launching pad for students to explore San Francisco, go wine tasting in Napa, or groove out in Berkeley. While the neighborhoods surrounding the schools are improving steadily, there are still sketchy areas, and students should exercise caution.

Admissions

Average high school GPA:	3.57
Average freshman SAT verbal / math score:	577 / 537
Average freshman ACT score:	23
Application fee:	$40
Application deadlines:	
5/1 (freshmen)	
3/1 (transfer)	
11/15 (early action)	
Total applicants:	1,122
Total accepted:	727 (65%)
Total accepted who enrolled:	200
Notification dates:	
3/30 (freshmen)	
4/1 (transfer)	
12/15 (early action)	
Acceptance rate for early action applicants:	77%

Students

Percentage of male / female students:	— / 100%
Percentage of students from out of state:	29%
Percentage of students graduating in 4 years / 6 years:	59% / 69%

Money

Total endowment:	$177,800,000
Total tuition:	$30,300
Total cost with fees & expenses:	$44,364
Average financial aid package:	$24,002
Percentage of students who sought aid and received it:	83%
Percentage of students receiving financial aid:	73%

Also Check Out

Mount Holyoke College

Scripps College

Smith College

University of California–Berkeley

University of California–Santa Cruz

Morehouse College

830 Westview Drive, SW
Atlanta, GA 30314

(404) 681-2800
http://www.morehouse.edu/

BIG PERSPECTIVE

Morehouse for the money

5 REASONS IT'S COOL

1. The "Morehouse Man" has long been a **symbol of collegiate pride and excellence.**

2. The prestige factor is undeniable: Morehouse enjoys its reputation as the **best of the nation's historically black college and universities.**

3. The college's Atlanta location puts **culture and fun within easy reach.**

4. Morehouse's participation in the Atlanta University Center, a consortium of six area colleges, means you'll have **six times the resources at your disposal.**

5. Life at all-male Morehouse isn't monastic due to the college's **close ties with nearby Spelman.**

The Basics

Public / private: private nonprofit
Total enrollment / undergrads: 2,933 / 2,933
Campus setting: urban
Students call it: Morehouse, House
Students are called: Morehouse Men, Maroon Tigers
Notable alums: Julian Bond (civil rights leader), Samuel L. Jackson (actor), Martin Luther King Jr. (Nobel Laureate, Peace), Spike Lee (filmmaker), Edwin Moses (Olympic track and field athlete, diplomat), David Satcher (U.S. surgeon general), Saul Williams (poet, musician)

House Rules

Since its inception in 1867 as a college for former slaves, Morehouse, the only all-male representative of the HBCUs (historically black colleges and universities), has maintained a level of academic excellence that has made it the gold standard of that group. Morehouse participates in the Atlanta University Center, a consortium of local historically black colleges that pool resources and maximize educational options for their students. At its core, Morehouse features a liberal arts curriculum that not even science majors can escape. For a college with a reputation for academic rigor, the college has fairly relaxed admission policies. But don't be fooled: Academics at Morehouse are competitive, and the learning environment can be intense (faculty and administrators are committed to transforming raw youth into "Morehouse men"). Many students major in biology and business, two of the school's strongest programs, and the theology and history programs are also strong.

Ready for Its Close-up

Morehouse has exerted quite a bit of influence on popular culture. Alum Spike Lee channeled his college experience in to his 1988 film *School Daze*, even filming some scenes on the campus. Writers for the Bill Cosby–produced 1980s sitcom *A Different World* translated their visits to Morehouse into episode storylines. And Morehouse's marching band had a featured role in the 2002 film *Drumline*.

Loosen Up That Tie!

At times, campus life here can seem like a throwback. Not only is Morehouse one of the few remaining all-male colleges, but the donnish air of faculty members also inspires a respect among students not often seen on campuses these days. Formality pervades interactions and attire among the students, who might be as inclined to wear a jacket and tie as a T-shirt and jeans. The Greek system dominates the college's vibrant, highly communal social life, although it has recently suffered a spate of hazing scandals. Athletic teams enjoy strong support among the student body, and the school's House of Funk Marching Band is nationally renowned. Morehouse's close relation with nearby Spelman, a women's college, dispels the potentially monastic implications of an all-male campus. Each Morehouse student has an assigned Spelman "sister," and opportunities for mixing abound both on and off campus.

Georgia on My Mind

Atlanta, also known as "Hot-lanta," is dense with colleges: Georgia Tech, Emory, and the historically black colleges that make up the Atlanta University Center are all nearby, providing plenty of opportunities for cross-college socializing. Morehouse's Atlanta location also puts students within easy reach of both sand and surf and mountains. Although an urban school, Morehouse experiences little crime, and at 61 acres, the campus is a study in diminutive collegiate stateliness. Residence halls offer varying degrees of comfort and cleanliness. Students recommend the housing provided by historic Graves Hall and warn against DuBois Hall. The administration requires students living on campus to participate in a meal plan, which draws both praise and complaints.

Admissions

Average high school GPA:	3.2
Average freshman SAT verbal / math score:	526 / 534
Average freshman ACT score:	21
Application fee:	$45

Application deadlines:
2/15 (freshmen)
2/15 (transfer)
10/15 (early decision)

Total applicants:	2,368
Total accepted:	1,297 (55%)
Total accepted who enrolled:	676

Notification dates:
4/1 (freshmen)
4/1 (transfer)
12/15 (early decision)

Acceptance rate for early action applicants:	—

Students

Percentage of male / female students:	100% / 0%
Percentage of students from out of state:	68%
Percentage of students graduating in 4 years / 6 years:	33% / 54%

Money

Total endowment:	$117,863,600
Total tuition:	$16,276
Total cost with fees & expenses:	$27,910
Average financial aid package:	$11,079
Percentage of students who sought aid and received it:	25%
Percentage of students receiving financial aid:	83%

Also Check Out

Florida Agricultural and Mechanical University

Georgia Institute of Technology

Hampton University

Howard University

Washington University in St. Louis

Mount Holyoke College

50 College Street
South Hadley, MA 01075

(413) 538-2000
http://www.mtholyoke.edu/

BIG PERSPECTIVE

Where women leaders are primed for greatness

5 REASONS IT'S COOL

1. The college is known for its **open-mindedness.**

2. Because Mount Holyoke is a member of the Five College Consortium, students may **choose from more than five thousand courses** a year.

3. As the first of an elite group of women's colleges, Mount Holyoke **fosters the female leaders of tomorrow.**

4. Almost a third of students major in the sciences or math, and **many graduates go on to earn PhDs.**

5. The college has **study-abroad programs in France and Senegal** and offers one-to-one exchanges with students in Hong Kong, Paris, and Germany.

The Basics

Public / private: private nonprofit
Total enrollment / undergrads: 2,153 / 2,149
Campus setting: small town
Students call it: Mount Holyoke
Students are called: Lyons
Notable alums: Virginia Apgar (developer, Apgar test), Elaine Chao (U.S. secretary of labor), Suzan-Lori Parks (playwright, screenwriter), Frances Perkins (U.S. secretary of labor), Wendy Wasserstein (playwright)

More than Your Average Core

Students at Mount Holyoke must take a heavy load of core requirements, but they have flexibility among specific courses. The brightest students can join the First-Year Honors Tutorial Program, which pairs a few students with a professor to examine particular topics in depth. There are many other opportunities for independent study and honors thesis writing under faculty supervision. The school offers a total of forty-nine majors, a third of which are interdisciplinary. While the most popular majors are English, psychology, and biology, the school also offers nontraditional majors in film studies, ancient studies, and critical social thought, among others. Additionally, thirty to forty students each year graduate with majors they've created themselves. Students may take classes at any of the other schools in the Five College Consortium: Amherst, Hampshire, Smith, and the University of Massachusetts–Amherst, all of which are within twelve miles of Mount Holyoke. The college also offers five-year, dual-degree programs in engineering.

Traditions Evergreen

Laurels feature prominently in school lore. According to Mount Holyoke superstition, a laurel leaf tucked under the pillow can inspire graduating seniors. As a mark of achievement and honor, a chain of laurels unites each graduating class as they march shoulder to shoulder during commencement, festooned in green and white. The tradition dates back to 1902 and symbolizes Mount Holyoke solidarity.

For Whom the Bell Tolls

Half of the notably diverse student body represents minorities, and seventy different countries are represented. There are a variety of economic and religious backgrounds as well. The school has a vocal lesbian contingent, but the four coeducational schools nearby supply plenty of testosterone for students of all orientations. More than 90 percent of Lyons live in the campus dorms, which tend to be plush, with high ceilings, baby grand pianos, wide windows, and TV lounges. Meal plans are required for those living on campus, but this is no hardship, as the dining halls offer a great variety of food including vegan, halal, and kosher options. Sports aren't big on campus, aside from the occasional rugby game against rival Smith, but school spirit runs high. The many traditions include Big Sister/Little Sister mentoring, which matches juniors with "firsties," and Mountain Day, when classes are cancelled and leaf peeping takes over. Despite Las Vegas Night, a huge yearly party, students do more low-key hanging than wild raging.

Natural Wonders and Space to Ride Horses

A mix of architectural styles, from Gothic to modern, characterizes this 800-acre campus. One of the most recent additions to the green, hilly campus is the Blanchard Campus Center, featuring a 5,000-foot, glass-walled room. The labs and facilities are state-of-the-art and include a solar greenhouse, thermal cyclers, and DNA sequencing equipment. For outdoorsy fun, students can go canoeing on one of the school's two lakes, skating on the outdoor ice rink, or climbing on the school's namesake mountain (now called Mount Skinner), where a 390-acre state park offers hiking trails and a stunning view of the valley below. An art museum, eighteen-hole golf course, Japanese meditation garden and teahouse, and spacious equestrian center with two indoor arenas and a cross-country course add to the splendor. The surrounding town of South Hadley is underwhelming, but it offers some low-key entertainment options such as unique bookstores, coffee shops, and a movie theater. For those with urban longings, train and bus service puts Boston and New York City within three hours' distance.

Admissions

Average high school GPA:	3.66
Average freshman SAT writing / math / critical reading score:	665 / 644 / 671
Average freshman ACT score:	26
Application fee:	$60

Application deadlines:
1/15 (freshmen)
5/15 (transfer)
11/15 (early decision)

Total applicants:	3,065
Total accepted:	1,632 (53%)
Total accepted who enrolled:	556

Notification dates:
4/1 (freshmen)
6/15 (transfer)
1/1 (early decision)

Acceptance rate for early decision applicants:	61%

Students

Percentage of male / female students:	— / 100%
Percentage of students from out of state:	75%
Percentage of students graduating in 4 years / 6 years:	74% / 80%

Money

Total endowment:	$516,147,751
Total tuition:	$34,090
Total cost with fees & expenses:	$45,056
Average financial aid package:	$28,464
Percentage of students who sought aid and received it:	100%
Percentage of students receiving financial aid:	62%

Also Check Out

Barnard College

Bryn Mawr College

Smith College

Tufts University

Wellesley College

Muhlenberg College

2400 Chew Street
Allentown, PA 18104

(484) 664-3100
http://www.muhlenberg.edu/

BIG PERSPECTIVE

Welcome to the 'Berg!

5 REASONS IT'S COOL

1. Bombed the SAT or the ACT? No worries: At Muhlenberg, **standardized test scores are not required** for admission.

2. Muhlenberg's **innovative curriculum** wants to educate the *whole* you.

3. The **first-rate theater program** gives every student a chance to shine in the spotlight.

4. While Muhlenberg is proud of its Lutheran affiliation, **religious diversity is a major emphasis.**

5. A cooperative program lets students **take classes at other local colleges,** including Lafayette and Lehigh, at no extra cost.

The Basics

Public / private: private religious
Total enrollment / undergrads: 2,500 / 2,500
Campus setting: suburban
Students call it: Muhlenberg, 'Berg
Students are called: Mules
Notable alums: Anthony Azizi (actor), Richard Ben-Veniste (member, 911 Commission), David Fricke (editor), Jack McCallum (sportswriter)

Friends and Mentors

Muhlenberg faculty members are not only enthusiastic about the courses they teach, but many also continue to be involved in their students' lives well after the term has ended. All students are required to take classes in four big areas: academic skills, perspectives, exploration and integration, and physical education. Perspectives help students expand their worldviews through classes in such areas as history and the fine arts, while an interdisciplinary, writing-intensive first-year seminar fulfills exploration and integration. The more than forty majors include everything from African American studies to the natural sciences. Students speak highly of the college's pre-med, business, political science, theater, dance, and visual arts programs. Those who can't find a major that's right for them can design their own. Students are encouraged to expand their minds outside of the classroom as well, through over forty study-abroad programs or the unique semester-in-Washington program. Academic resources range from the Baker Biological Field Station and Wildlife Sanctuary to the Holocaust Resource Center.

A Hazy Controversy

Although Muhlenberg's Greek scene is pretty tame today, it wasn't always so. In 1998 the university was the subject of the documentary film *Frat House*, which explores the dark underbelly of Greek life. The film primarily featured the spring hazing rituals of the now-banned Alpha Tau Omega frat. HBO shelved the documentary when it discovered that many of the scenes had been staged. The university, meanwhile, came down hard on ATO after proof surfaced that ATO had conducted hazing rituals at all, albeit off-camera.

Where Tolerance Reigns

Muhlenberg students balance academic ambition with a deep sense of compassion for others. Despite the homogeneity of the student body, students have earned a reputation for being accepting of people from other faiths, races, ethnicities, and sexual orientations. Most students participate in at least one of the university's hundred-plus student organizations, which cover everything from politics to foreign languages to student media and intramurals. Community service is also extremely popular. About 20 percent of students join one of the school's four frats or four sororities, although the Greek scene tends to be less rambunctious than at other schools, possibly because of the administration's crackdown on alcohol and drug use in recent years. Those looking for nightlife are best off heading to local student bars just off campus. Freshmen generally live in West Quad, Walz, Prosser, and Brown Halls, while upper-class students might live in the apartments of MacGregor Village, the suites of BenFer Hall, and the Muhlenberg Independent Living Experience. The recently renovated Life Sports Center offers practice space for the twenty Division III teams and amateurs, including the air hockey club.

Living Here in Allentown

Many students lament that Allentown—made famous by Billy Joel's song of the same name—leaves much to be desired for the fun-loving college student. There are a handful of bars, restaurants, and movie theaters within walking distance of campus, but not much else in a town that is in many ways still reeling from recession. There is always something going on around campus, though, from concerts and movies to theater performances and stand-up. Those looking for a little more action or big-city culture usually head to nearby Philadelphia on the weekends, just about an hour away by bus. New York is only ninety minutes away.

Admissions

Average high school GPA:	3.41
Average freshman SAT verbal / math score:	617 / 617
Average freshman ACT score:	26
Application fee:	$45

Application deadlines:
2/15 (freshmen)
6/15 (transfer)
2/1 (early decision)

Total applicants:	4,347
Total accepted:	1,903 (44%)
Total accepted who enrolled:	615

Notification dates:
3/15 (freshmen)
7/1 (transfer)
specific (early decision)

Acceptance rate for early decision applicants:	71%

Students

Percentage of male / female students:	41% / 59%
Percentage of students from out of state:	72%
Percentage of students graduating in 4 years / 6 years:	81% / 85%

Money

Total endowment:	$114,242,721
Total tuition:	$30,490
Total cost with fees & expenses:	$38,990
Average financial aid package:	$16,847
Percentage of students who sought aid and received it:	95%
Percentage of students receiving financial aid:	39%

Also Check Out

Bucknell University

Lafayette College

Lehigh University

Ursinus College

New Mexico State University

PO Box 30001
Las Cruces, NM 88003

(505) 646-0111
http://www.nmsu.edu/

BIG CHOICE

BIG RESEARCH

Attention starry-eyed students!

5 REASONS IT'S COOL

1. Whether you're a space cadet or a farmer Joe, NMSU has got you covered: It has been **designated as both a space grant and a land grant school.**

2. *¡Que bueno!* NMSU consistently rates highly as **a top school for Latino students.**

3. NMSU has taken steps toward becoming **a zero-greenhouse-emissions campus.**

4. Hate winter? The university's **southwestern location** means you'll never have to worry about being snowed under.

5. NMSU hosts an **annual student rodeo.**

The Basics

Public / private: public state
Total enrollment / undergrads: 16,415 / 13,210
Campus setting: suburban
Students call it: NMSU, New Mexico State
Students are called: Aggies
Notable alums: Lou Henson (college basketball coach), Charley Johnson (pro football player), Kenton Keith (pro football player)

Academic Careers That Are Ready for Liftoff

NMSU students' nickname, the Aggies, hearkens back to the university's previous inception as New Mexico College of Agriculture and Mechanic Arts. While agriculture remains a strong and popular program, NMSU has since set its sights on the heavens as well as the earth. The university enjoys a special (and lucrative) relationship with NASA as one of fifty-two space grant programs in the nation. This NASA program, intended to encourage competitive engineering research among participating institutions, means that students will find a slew of well-funded engineering programs. NMSU's astronomy program in particular is quite strong (the clear desert skies here surely encourage a lot of stargazing). NMSU also offers students of the arts and humanities solid value for their tuition dollars, especially with its notable literature of the Southwest program.

Cosmically Collegiate

NMSU went cosmic in 2004 when alum Wendee Wallach-Levy, wife of comet hunter David Levy, won approval to name an asteroid for her alma mater. The asteroid was named "Nemsu," a variation of NMSU, to skirt the International Astronomical Unions ban on acronyms. Nemsu has a girthy five-mile waistline and pursues an orbit around the sun—which means NMSU boasts a satellite campus that's actually a satellite!

Saddlin' Up for a Great Time

Aggies are overwhelmingly a homegrown bunch: More than 80 percent of students hail from New Mexico. Latino students represent more than 40 percent of the student population, with blacks, Asians, Native Americans, and various nationalities among the other minority students. Nonnatives to the area generally express contentment with the university's location, but the fact that Las Cruces isn't exactly a party town is a common complaint. Whatever Las Cruces's deficiencies in this department, they are more than compensated for by the campus Greek scene, which manages to kick up the jams despite NMSU's official "dry campus" status. Other festivities include KRUXfest, a spring music festival put on by the university's student-run radio station, and Aggie Rodeo, the university's annual rodeo.

Hot in the Shade

NMSU is located in Las Cruces, some forty miles north of El Paso, the next nearest city and home to regional rival University of Texas–El Paso. The climate is typical American Southwest: Winters are almost nonexistent, and summers are long and blazing, although nights in every season can be surprisingly chilly. NMSU's campus sprawls across six thousand acres. Students report that residence halls are generally decent. In recent years, NMSU administrators have "themed" certain residence halls, earmarking Garcia Hall for freshman and a portion of the WRC Center for honors students. The spanking new Chamisa Village campus apartments are another desirable spot.

Admissions

Average high school GPA:	3.37
Average freshman SAT verbal / math score:	— / 501
Average freshman ACT score:	20
Application fee:	$15

Application deadlines:
8/19 (freshmen)
8/14 (transfer)

Total applicants:	5,434
Total accepted:	4,735 (87%)
Total accepted who enrolled:	1,913

Notification dates:
continuous (freshmen)
continuous (transfer)

Students

Percentage of male / female students:	45% / 55%
Percentage of students from out of state:	16%
Percentage of students graduating in 4 years / 6 years:	12% / 42%

Money

Total endowment:	$57,809,523
Total in-state tuition, fees & expenses:	$10,623
Total out-of-state tuition, fees & expenses:	$20,197
Average financial aid package:	$7,438
Percentage of students who sought aid and received it:	58%
Percentage of students receiving financial aid:	43%

Also Check Out

Arizona State University

The University of Arizona

University of New Mexico

University of Utah

New York University

70 Washington Square South
New York, NY 10012

(212) 998-1212
http://www.nyu.edu/

BIG CHOICE

It's up to you, NYU.

5 REASONS IT'S COOL

1. Located in the heart of **Greenwich Village and Union Square**, NYU has one of the most exciting college campuses in the country.

2. Tisch School of the Arts produces some of **the world's most renowned actors and filmmakers.**

3. With students hailing from more than 120 countries, this school is **genuinely and thoroughly diverse.**

4. Past and present **high-achieving faculty** include literally hundreds of winners of top prizes

5. The **$1.6 billion endowment** allows NYU to invest in top faculty and state-of-the-art facilities.

The Basics

Public / private: private nonprofit
Total enrollment / undergrads: 40,870 / 20,965
Campus setting: urban
Students call it: NYU
Notable alums: Woody Allen (film director), Candace Bushnell (writer), Clive Davis (founder, Arista Records), Philip Seymour Hoffman (actor), Alan Greenspan (chairman, Federal Reserve), Frank McCourt (writer), Martin Scorsese (film director)

So Many Possibilities, So Little Time

Location is NYU's biggest asset. Students are surrounded by galleries, theaters, independent movie theaters, and performance venues. The university often nabs Ivy-caliber profs who jump at the chance to teach in the country's most vibrant neighborhood. Students in the renowned Tisch School of the Arts don't just get to create art in the city; their professors often take them to study the works of renowned artists and actors as it is being debuted or shown. Whatever you study at NYU, you'll discover that the university offers seemingly infinite possibilities, including eight undergrad schools and colleges, 2,500 courses, and 160 majors. While they are dedicated and accomplished, NYU profs don't baby their students. Some faculty make themselves available, but others wait for students to seek them out. If students are willing to be assertive, they can reap rewards ranging from research opportunities to internships to connections that can help in the postcollege job search.

Got Strawberries?

Each spring, NYU hosts Strawberry Fest, a street festival that spans several blocks of West Fourth in Manhattan's Greenwich Village. In addition to the bouncy castles, carnival games, and free stuff, the carnival features New York City's longest strawberry shortcake.

Do It Yourself

Like the city they call home, NYU students are diverse and tolerant. Hard workers, they also take advantage of their surroundings. Some students find that the urban nature of the campus makes it difficult to forge friendships, but others say the trick is to get involved in campus and dorm life. And that isn't difficult, given the sheer number of student organizations and clubs. NYU offers 275 intramural sports, twenty-one UAA varsity teams, and hundreds of student organizations ranging from the campus ratio station to community service to wilderness adventures to religious organizations. There are also seventeen frats and thirteen sororities on campus, although a measly 2 percent of NYU students rush. While the university doesn't put a ton of emphasis on campus activities, it does host a number of free events, including concerts, plays, lectures, and film screenings.

In the Heart of It All

Like many urban schools, NYU doesn't have much in the way of a traditional campus. Instead, its buildings are scattered around Greenwich Village and Union Square, blending in with the neighborhood. Undergrads are guaranteed housing, and many of the dorms are built in converted apartments, hotels, or, in the case of Palladium, a once-famous nightclub of the same name. Dorms range from standard to luxurious. The recently built Kimmel Center for University Life houses most of NYU's student services offices, a performing arts center, student center, and an auditorium. Kimmel sits across the street from Washington Square Park, whose arch has become synonymous with NYU. University buildings are also clustered in Greenwich Village and Union Square, located just a few blocks away from each other in lower Manhattan. A free trolley system ferries students from building to building, and New York's countless other attractions—ranging from the hipsters in Williamsburg to the mummies at the Metropolitan Museum of Art to the plays on Broadway and off—are just a few minutes from campus by subway.

Admissions

Average high school GPA:	3.6
Average freshman SAT writing / math / critical reading score:	664 / 670 / 663
Average freshman ACT score:	27
Application fee:	$65

Application deadlines:
1/15 (freshmen)
4/1 (transfer)
11/1 (early decision)

Total applicants:	35,448
Total accepted:	12,842 (36%)
Total accepted who enrolled:	4,707

Notification dates:
4/1 (freshmen)
5/1 (transfer)
12/15 (early decision)

Acceptance rate for early decision applicants:	53%

Students

Percentage of male / female students:	39% / 61%
Percentage of students from out of state:	66%
Percentage of students graduating in 4 years / 6 years:	73% / 82%

Money

Total endowment:	$1,591,687,498
Total tuition:	$31,534
Total cost with fees & expenses:	$45,900
Average financial aid package:	$20,707
Percentage of students who sought aid and received it:	66%
Percentage of students receiving financial aid:	48%

Also Check Out

Boston College

Columbia University

Emory University

Fordham University

Tufts University

North Carolina State University

203 Peele Hall
Raleigh, NC 27695

(919) 515-2011
http://www.ncsu.edu/

 **BIG CHOICE**

 BIG JOB

From Raleigh to the real world

5 REASONS IT'S COOL

1. In the Cooperative Education Program, students **alternate semesters of classes and full-time, paid work.**

2. The **top-rated textile program** places 95 percent of its students in jobs within three months of graduation.

3. **Friendliness and school spirit** bring together this diverse student body.

4. A unique **Professional Golf Management Program** sets up students with an internship and interdisciplinary coursework.

5. **Located in Raleigh** and near Duke and UNC in the hub of the Research Triangle, NC State offers access to world-renowned tech companies and state government organizations.

The Basics

Public / private: public state
Total enrollment / undergrads: 31,130 / 23,730
Campus setting: urban
Students call it: NC State, NCSU, State
Students are called: The Wolfpack
Notable alums: John Edwards (senator), Torry Holt (pro football player), General Henry H. Shelton (chairman, Joint Chiefs of Staff)

Lots of Opportunity, Lots of Variety

Entering students choose between several colleges including schools of agriculture, design, education, and engineering. Those undecided on a major enter the First Year College, which helps them assess their interests. NC State is known for its strong science, technology, and textile programs, and the most popular majors are engineering, business management, and communications. General requirements in all majors are hefty and include many math, sciences, humanities, and social science credits, along with writing and communication, physical education, and computer literacy courses. As at any state school, classes can be large, with sizes ranging from twenty to one hundred. An exceptional cohort of honors students takes smaller seminars taught by the most talented faculty in each department. These students also have access to extra independent study and study-abroad options. For textile students, the prestigious Centennial Scholarship Program provides additional opportunities to develop leadership skills or travel abroad to enrich classroom knowledge.

Race for the Kreme

In 2004, an NC State sophomore decided to dash from the school's bell tower to the nearest Krispy Kreme doughnut shop two miles away, eat twelve donuts (144 grams of fat, for those counting), and run back to the tower—in under an hour. The challenge has become a tradition that raises money for North Carolina Children's Hospital. The record time? Twenty-four minutes.

Play Hard, Cheer Loud

NC Staters are serious about school spirit, and extracurricular activities revolve around the Division IA varsity football and basketball teams. Decked out in red-and-white T-shirts, and the occasional red clown wig for good measure, thousands of students cheer on the Wolfpack. But it's not just about spectatorship—intramural and club sports are competitive and popular too. The campus also hosts many religious groups, such as the popular Campus Crusade for Christ and an active gay pride group. The College of Design and the College of Textiles sponsor yearly fashion shows in which majors in those schools present their work. Runways, models, and makeup are provided in part by a Chapel Hill beauty school. Although more than 90 percent of students come from North Carolina, the student body is diverse partly due to the sheer size of the school (23,000 undergrads). Most freshmen live on campus, but upperclassmen tend to move off. Same-sex, all-freshman, and international student housing is available. Sororities and fraternities have an increasingly diminished presence on campus, with less than 10 percent of students joining.

Life in Jolly Raleigh

The vast NC State campus is divided into six regions. Notable landmarks include Lake Raleigh, a small arboretum, and the Court of North Carolina, a green expanse with zigzagging brick walkways set among the school's oldest buildings. Brick is the material of choice for all but two buildings on campus, and brick-paved walkways and sculptures can be found in almost every corner. Building designs range from the flat-roofed, simplistically styled Pullen Hall, to the gargantuan, diagonally shaped 1911 building (built in 1909), to the columned and stately Alumni Memorial Building. Hillsborough Street, a busy, four-lane thoroughfare with coffee shops, restaurants, and bars, runs along the northern part of campus. A somewhat unreliable bus system connects students with Duke and UNC campuses, and beaches near Wilmington are around two hours away.

Admissions

Average high school GPA:	4.0
Average freshman SAT writing / math / critical reading score:	561 / 613 / 573
Average freshman ACT score:	23
Application fee:	$60

Application deadlines:
2/1 (freshmen)
4/1 (transfer)
11/1 (early action)

Total applicants:	15,500
Total accepted:	9,470 (61%)
Total accepted who enrolled:	4,668

Notification dates:
continuous (freshmen)
continuous (transfer)
1/15 (early action)

Acceptance rate for early action applicants:	53%

Students

Percentage of male / female students:	57% / 43%
Percentage of students from out of state:	7%
Percentage of students graduating in 4 years / 6 years:	36% / 71%

Money

Total endowment:	$412,298,000
Total in-state tuition, fees & expenses:	$12,490
Total out-of-state tuition, fees & expenses:	$24,688
Average financial aid package:	$8,925
Percentage of students who sought aid and received it:	79%
Percentage of students receiving financial aid:	32%

Also Check Out

Clemson University

University of North Carolina at Chapel Hill

Virginia Polytechnic Institute and State University

Wake Forest University

Northeastern University

360 Huntington Avenue
Boston, MA 02115

(617) 373-2000
http://www.northeastern.edu

BIG CHOICE

BIG JOB

Get your career in gear!

5 REASONS IT'S COOL

1. Northeastern's **highly-rated co-op program** is the largest at any university.

2. You'll get a leg up on the competition: Students graduate with **up to eighteen months of work experience** under their belts.

3. Like choice? The university offers **eighty majors in six different colleges.**

4. College towns don't get more collegiate than Boston. We're talking more than a **hundred colleges and universities in the immediate area.**

5. The pretty campus is located in **the heart of the Back Bay** and just a stone's throw from the city's top art museums.

The Basics

Public / private: private nonprofit
Total enrollment / undergrads: 20,605 / 15,195
Campus setting: urban
Students call it: Northeastern, NU
Students are called: Huskies
Notable alums: Michelle Bonner (sports broadcaster), Richard Egan (business leader), Shawn Fanning (founder, Napster), Reggie Lewis (pro basketball player)

Workin' It

The Northeastern experience is defined largely by the university's co-op program, the largest and most acclaimed in the country. Students participate in a broad range of internships starting during their sophomore year and then alternate between six months of paid, full-time work and a semester of classes. Past placements have included the Boston Red Sox broadcast booth, BBC Thailand, MTV Europe, and Atari. The university offers eighty majors in six undergraduate colleges of health sciences, arts and sciences, business, computer and information science, engineering, and criminal justice. The most popular majors include business, engineering, and health fields. The Faculty Undergraduate Research Initiative (FURI) connects students with research opportunities, and the Office of the University Provost awards fellowships of up to $1,000 to fund faculty-student research projects. The university has recently hired 130 new full-time faculty members. Professors here get good reviews, and the student-to-faculty ratio is 16:1.

What Lies Beneath

Underneath Northeastern's campus are tunnels running between thirteen buildings. The city of Boston has forbidden Northeastern to expand the tunnels to newer buildings, but when campus is buried under snow, students are grateful for any tunnels they get.

In Heavy Rotation

Student life at Northeastern has a somewhat disjointed feel because students participating in the university's co-op program constantly rotate on and off campus. The prime location in Boston, along with the proximity to other area colleges, mean that there's always something to do, and the university has earned a reputation as a party school. Seventeen athletic teams are offered, with teams partipating in the NCAA Colonial Athletic League Association (the men's hockey team competes in the prestigious Hockey East league). The university also has a signficant club sports program, with its men's and women's rugby teams—the MadDogs and Lady MadDogs—leading the way.

Beautiful Boston

Northeastern is located in the Back Bay area of Boston. The leafy, sixty-seven-acre campus faces Huntington Avenue, home to the city's top cultural institutions, including the Museum of Fine Arts (free to many Boston-area students, including Huskies) and the Boston Symphony Orchestra. Other nearby attractions include the Boston Ballet, Fenway Park, the Museum of Science, the Isabella Stewart Gardner Museum, and the New England Aquarium. Students also take advantage of the Esplanade, the jogging and biking path that runs along the Charles River, and the Quincy Market, home to food vendors galore.

Admissions

Average high school GPA:	—
Average freshman SAT verbal / math score:	605 / 634
Average freshman ACT score:	25
Application fee:	$75
Application deadlines: 1/15 (freshmen) 5/1 (transfer)	
Total applicants:	27,168
Total accepted:	12,173 (45%)
Total accepted who enrolled:	2,955
Notification dates: 4/1 (freshmen) continuous (transfer)	

Students

Percentage of male / female students:	50% / 50%
Percentage of students from out of state:	65%
Percentage of students graduating in 4 years / 6 years:	— / 60%

Money

Total endowment:	$611,562,000
Total tuition:	$29,910
Total cost with fees & expenses:	$42,179
Average financial aid package:	$16,433
Percentage of students who sought aid and received it:	60%
Percentage of students receiving financial aid:	60%

Also Check Out

Boston University

Brandeis University

Columbia University

New York University

Tufts University

Northern Arizona University

South San Francisco Street
Flagstaff, AZ 86011

(928) 523-9011
http://www.nau.edu/

BIG CHOICE

A mountain "do"

5 REASONS IT'S COOL

1. With enrollment under fifteen thousand, the university offers **an intimate college experience without the huge price tag.**

2. Can't wait to get your career in gear? NAU offers a fast-track, **three-year bachelor's degree program.**

3. Students can get into the wild while they earn college credit with **the Grand Canyon Semester.**

4. Hooray for diversity: NAU was recently rated **one of the top schools for Latinos.**

5. **Miles of mountain wilderness** provide a refuge from the typical college stresses—and from the blazing heat that afflicts the rest of Arizona.

The Basics

Public / private: public state
Total enrollment / undergrads: 20,562 / 14,526
Campus setting: small town
Students call it: NAU
Students are called: Lumberjacks
Notable alums: Andy Devine (actor), Diana Gabaldon (writer), R. Carlos Nakai (artist, composer), Jennifer Roberson (writer), Claudio Sanchez (NPR correspondent)

From Concierges to Campfires

For a long time, NAU faculty members weren't expected to do research. Instead, they were encouraged to concentrate on teaching. While there is more emphasis on research today, the quality of teaching remains high. In contrast to Arizona State and the University of Arizona, its massive neighbors to the south, NAU boasts a fairly cozy student-to-faculty ratio of 17:1. NAU used to be a teacher's college, and the education program remains one of the university's strongest. Another excellent program—one of the top 10 in the nation, in fact—is hotel and restaurant management, which is endowed by the heirs of the founder of Ramada Inns. This program, along with a host of others, participates in the three-year bachelor's curriculum offered by NAU. The university also makes the most of its proximity to the Grand Canyon by offering students a Grand Canyon Semester, in which research and rugged living combine for fifteen units of credit.

That's How We Roll

For decades, in a cherished **NAU** tradition, the homecoming king and queen were rolled across campus in a huge lumber wagon to honor Flagstaff's logging heritage. Students had to discontinue the custom temporarily when the wheels deteriorated. Luckily, the **NAU** Alumni Association came to the rescue with a $25,000 pledge drive for the wheels' restoration. This wagon's wood is truly worth its weight in gold!

Tree Huggin' and Beer Chuggin'

With its close proximity to natural wonders, NAU has traditionally attracted hippies, hikers, and other crunchy sorts, although a 2005 image makeover has drawn a greater variety of students. When not skiing or hiking, students engage in typical college shenanigans. Like many other universities, NAU has implemented a First-Year Experience (FYE) aimed to boost freshman retention. There are freshmen-only dorms, while sophomores and upperclassmen can choose among dorms, suites, and apartments. NAU is respectably diverse. The student body is 12 percent Latino, 6 percent Native American, 2 percent African American, and 2 percent Asian American. In the tasty treats department, NAU gets poor reviews. Students complain about the bland and predictable food on offer. Freshmen are especially disgruntled, because NAU requires they purchase meal plans.

In the Pines

Flagstaff isn't exactly a bustling metropolis. With only around sixty thousand residents, "Flag," as it's affectionately called by native Arizonans, is slow paced. It does offer easy access to natural delights such as Sunset Crater, Oak Creek Canyon, the Grand Canyon, and the San Francisco Mountains, where students can camp, hike, or hit the slopes. NAU's mountain high may not be for everyone, but for the granola set, it inspires an undying devotion. The large campus comprises some 738 alpine acres of aspen and ponderosa pine. The lack of affordable off-campus apartments keeps around 40 percent of students in university housing for the four years they're there. Students in search of hustle and bustle can get to Phoenix by car in three hours, or to Tucson or Albuquerque in five. For those without wheels of their own, Flagstaff does have a local bus system.

Admissions

Average high school GPA:	3.4
Average freshman SAT writing / math / critical reading score:	518 / 539 / 535
Average freshman ACT score:	22
Application fee:	$25
Application deadlines: continuous (freshmen) continuous (transfer)	
Total applicants:	9,072
Total accepted:	2,930 (32%)
Total accepted who enrolled:	2,607
Notification dates: continuous (freshmen) continuous (transfer)	

Students

Percentage of male / female students:	41% / 59%
Percentage of students from out of state:	17%
Percentage of students graduating in 4 years / 6 years:	26% / 48%

Money

Total endowment:	$13,561,389
Total in-state tuition, fees & expenses:	$11,634
Total out-of-state tuition, fees & expenses:	$20,574
Average financial aid package:	$7,885
Percentage of students who sought aid and received it:	64%
Percentage of students receiving financial aid:	41%

Also Check Out

Arizona State University

Colorado State University–Fort Collins

Pepperdine University

San Diego State University

Northwestern University

633 Clark Street
Evanston, IL 60208

(847) 491-3741
http://www.northwestern.edu/

 **BIG BRAIN**

 **BIG CHOICE**

Where first-rate doesn't mean cutthroat

5 REASONS IT'S COOL

I. Northwestern students are **nerds who like to smile**. They're super-serious about academics, but they also love to have fun.

2. The Medill School of Journalism is one of the **most prominent journalism programs** in the country.

3. **Chicago is just a short train ride away**, and internships and entertainment abounds.

4. With a **7:1 student-to-faculty ratio**, Northwestern can give more personal attention to students than almost any college in the country.

5. Northwestern **encourages student-directed projects**, including research, independent study, and off-campus field studies.

The Basics

Public / private: private nonprofit
Total enrollment / undergrads: 17,460 / 8,153
Campus setting: suburban
Students call it: Northwestern, NU, NWU
Students are called: Northwesterners
Notable alums: Zach Braff (actor), Stephen Colbert (comedian), Dick Gephardt (congressman), Charlton Heston (actor), Nicole Lapin (TV news anchor), Michael Wilbon (sports writer)

Prestige Without Pretension

Despite the extremely high caliber of students and professors, Northwestern's classrooms are surprisingly unpretentious. Perhaps that's because undergrads get so much personal attention, particularly in upper-level courses. The university has a 7:1 student-to-faculty ratio, and nearly three-quarters of undergrad classes have fewer than twenty students, which means that Wildcats don't have to compete with one another for attention. Since Northwestern is on the quarter syste m, things move quickly: Whereas students at other schools have eighteen weeks per term, Northwestern students have only ten, which leaves no time for slacking. The university's 8,000 undergrads choose from eighty majors in six undergraduate schools focusing on the arts and sciences, communication, education and social policy, engineering, journalism, and music. Northwestern's world-renowned Kellogg School of Management now offers certificate programs for undergrads preparing for future careers in finance, law, or academia.

Mark Your Territory

You can't spend much time at Northwestern without hearing someone mention the Rock. A six-foot-high quartzite boulder, the Rock was brought to campus all the way from Wisconsin by the class of 1902. Although the Rock was originally intended to be a drinking fountain to quench the thirst of parched students walking between Harris and University Halls, Northwestern's fraternities and sororities have transformed it into the heaviest billboard on earth. Unfortunately for vandals and would-be pranksters, painting the Rock is so popular that it's often done and redone over several times each night, which means your midnight artwork might be buried beneath someone else's by the time morning rolls around.

Books, Greeks, and Wildcats

Schoolwork is serious business at Northwestern, where it's not uncommon for students to hit the library on a Saturday night. Then again, during football season, it's not uncommon for even the most studious students to set aside their books and cheer on the Wildcats. Greek life has a healthy presence, and about a third of students join fraternities and sororities. Students who opt to live on campus live in one of the college's eleven residential colleges, where they can room with fellow Northwesterners who share their own interests. Each residential college is organized around a theme—such as business, engineering, community service, and the arts—and residents plan activities and special programs that suit these interests. Most students also participate in at least one of the 250 student organizations, which include everything from intramural sports and political and religious groups to community service clubs, theater, and the twelve-time national champion Northwestern Debate Society.

My Kind of Town

Located in a wooded area right on Lake Michigan, Northwestern's campus has more than a few fantastic scenic viewpoints and plenty of places to play Ultimate Frisbee when the weather is nice. Temperatures dip below freezing during the winter, which can extend all the way into April, but when the temperature finally climbs back up into the fifties, students celebrate in their shorts, T-shirts, and flip-flops. Northwestern's hometown of Evanston has a number of great restaurants, shops, coffee shops, bars, and even an independent movie theater. The biggest draw for students, though, is the bustling city of Chicago, which is just a stone's throw away. Once in the city, students have options galore, ranging from sporting events to museums and restaurants, from bars and clubs to concerts and literary events.

Admissions

Average high school GPA:	—
Average freshman SAT verbal / math score:	690 / 708
Average freshman ACT score:	26
Application fee:	$65

Application deadlines:
1/1 (freshmen)
5/1 (transfer)
11/1 (early decision)

Total applicants:	18,385
Total accepted:	5,434 (30%)
Total accepted who enrolled:	2,062

Notification dates:
4/15 (freshmen)
7/1 (transfer)
12/15 (early decision)

Acceptance rate for early decision applicants:	50%

Students

Percentage of male / female students:	47% / 53%
Percentage of students from out of state:	75%
Percentage of students graduating in 4 years / 6 years:	84% / 92%

Money

Total endowment:	$4,294,967,295
Total tuition:	$33,408
Total cost with fees & expenses:	$45,313
Average financial aid package:	$26,573
Percentage of students who sought aid and received it:	100%
Percentage of students receiving financial aid:	41%

Also Check Out

University of Chicago

University of Michigan–Ann Arbor

University of Pennsylvania

University of Wisconsin—Madison

Washington University in St. Louis

Oberlin College

173 West Lorain Street
Oberlin, OH 44074

(440) 775-8121
http://www.oberlin.edu/

 **BIG BRAIN**

 **BIG PERSPECTIVE**

Making their own kind of music

5 REASONS IT'S COOL

1. Three words: **first name basis.** Classes are small, and professors work hard to know their students.

2. You'll put your sign-making markers to good use. Campus is a **hotbed for progressive political activism.**

3. Catch a world-class music performance any day of the week. The Oberlin **Conservatory of Music is among the country's best.**

4. Lots of schools talk about their **commitment to diversity,** but Oberlin really means it. After all, it was the first college in the country to admit women.

5. The innovative Winter Term gives students a chance to **pursue cool self-directed projects** on or off campus.

The Basics

Public / private: private nonprofit
Total enrollment / undergrads: 2,841 / 2,829
Campus setting: small town
Students call it: Oberlin
Students are called: Yeomen/Yeowomen
Notable alums: Jim Burrows (TV producer), Tracy Chevalier (novelist), Carl Dennis (poet), Adam Moss (editor), Liz Phair (singer-songwriter), Jane Pratt (magazine publisher), William Grant Still (composer), Julie Taymor (film/theater director), George Walker (composer)

Lots of Options, All of 'Em Good

Oberlin is made up of two distinct divisions: the College of Arts and Sciences, with approximately 2,300 students, and the Conservatory of Music, with approximately 550 students. Many students take classes in both divisions, and some enroll in Oberlin's dual-degree program, which, after five years, awards a bachelor of arts and a bachelor of music. Another five-year option, for students of somewhat different skill sets, is the 3-2 engineering program, run in conjunction with Washington University in St. Louis, Case Western, and the California Institute of Technology. Oberlin's academic calendar is a 4-1-4 system, which includes a fall semester, a spring semester, and a short Winter Term, during which students pursue internships or intensive academic projects. Oberlin's facilities are mostly top notch; the science center is state-of-the-art, and the Conservatory offers 153 practice rooms and 168 Steinway grand pianos. The library, too, gets high marks for ease of use

Me First!

Oberlin has a long-standing tradition of firsts. Way back in the 1830s, the school made it a goal to pioneer higher education for African Americans and women, and by the turn of the twentieth century, about half of all African Americans with college degrees were graduates of Oberlin. Seventy years later, the school took another crucial step toward the future by becoming one of the first colleges in the country with coed dorms.

and depth of resources. Nonmajor graduation requirements follow the rule of threes: three classes in humanities, three in natural science, and three in social science, as well as three Winter Term projects and three classes dealing with cultural diversity.

Living and Studying in Harmony

Students at the College of Arts & Sciences and the Conservatory of Music share dorms and dining halls, forming one harmonious academic community (pun intended). Student/faculty concerts and recitals are popular campus activities with music and nonmusic students alike, and more than four hundred are given every year. Club sports and IM leagues are another popular way of unwinding, although varsity athletics don't make much of an impact on those students who are not athletes. Oberlin students tend to be committed to social justice and sharply attuned to politics, both of the national and local variety. Almost every faculty governance committee has an undergraduate member or liaison. About eight in ten students live on campus, and program and theme residential houses are beloved by upperclassmen for bringing together peers with similar interests and for drastically increasing the campus's stock of single bedrooms.

The Oberlin Bubble

Oberlin students report that they like their school's location, and this affinity gives rise to the Oberlin Bubble, a mystical force that saps many students' desire to stray far from campus. Oberlin, Ohio, is a community of eight thousand, located thirty-five miles southwest of Cleveland. It's the sort of charming throwback town you'd expect to have an old-style movie theater, complete with a marquee. And indeed it does. It also offers a vibrant music and arts scene. The college is at the center of town within easy walking distance of many student-oriented shops and hangouts. Every year, a certain percentage of the freshman class comes to campus thinking it doesn't snow all that much in Ohio, and every year they are unpleasantly surprised.

Admissions

Average high school GPA:	3.58
Average freshman SAT verbal / math score:	693 / 667
Average freshman ACT score:	25
Application fee:	$35
Application deadlines:	
1/15 (freshmen)	
3/15 (transfer)	
11/15 (early decision)	
Total applicants:	6,686
Total accepted:	2,266 (34%)
Total accepted who enrolled:	701
Notification dates:	
4/1 (freshmen)	
5/1 (transfer)	
12/10 (early decision)	
Acceptance rate for early decision applicants:	63%

Students

Percentage of male / female students:	44% / 56%
Percentage of students from out of state:	91%
Percentage of students graduating in 4 years / 6 years:	67% / 81%

Money

Total endowment:	$550,000,000
Total tuition:	$34,216
Total cost with fees & expenses:	$43,976
Average financial aid package:	$24,255
Percentage of students who sought aid and received it:	100%
Percentage of students receiving financial aid:	55%

Also Check Out

Amherst College

Brown University

Swarthmore College

Wesleyan University

Yale University

Occidental College

1600 Campus Road
Los Angeles, CA 90041

(323) 259-2500
http://www.oxy.edu/

 BIG PERSPECTIVE

 BIG WORLD

Where "L.A." stands for "liberal arts"

5 REASONS IT'S COOL

1. Oxy is where **a small liberal arts campus meets the big city**—and that's an exciting (and unusual) place to be.

2. Like to think globally? Look no further than the **strong world affairs program**.

3. Students live in a variety of **cool theme-based residential options**—just one of the many ways Oxy builds friendships and communities.

4. Goshdarnit, **this is one pretty campus**. No wonder so many films, from *Real Genius* to *Clueless*, have shot scenes here.

5. **Attention aspiring filmmakers!** You can learn your craft and then snag industry job without having to move.

The Basics

Public / private: private nonprofit
Total enrollment / undergrads: 1,825 / 1,804
Campus setting: urban
Students call it: Occidental, Oxy
Students are called: Tigers
Notable alums: Alphonze Bell (congressman), Steve Coll (journalist), Ramesh Flinders (filmmaker), Terry Gilliam (filmmaker), Pete McCloskey (congressman), Jim Mora Sr. (pro football coach), Patt Morrison (radio personality, columnist), Luke Wilson (actor)

A Real Learning Community

Occidental's academic centerpiece is its Learning Communities Program for freshmen, which places students in intimate seminars on any number of topics such as "stupidity" (religious studies), the "pursuit of happiness" (philosophy), or "food politics" (urban and environmental policy). Students even share the dorms with their seminar mates. Occidental offers thirty majors, the most popular of which include economics, English, and psychology; students can also design their own courses of study. Internationally minded students can take advantage of the world affairs program as well as the Occidental-at-the-United Nations Program, where they can intern with the United Nations Secretariat or a related institution. There are also standing exchange agreements with schools like Cambridge University and the Chinese University of Hong Kong. To graduate, seniors must produce original work or conduct original research for a project known as senior comp.

Splashy Birthday to You!

Occidental's fountain played a starring role in *Star Trek III: The Search for Spock*, and now it's playfully called the "Star Trek fountain." One, uh, wet campus tradition involves tossing your pals in the fountain on their birthdays. You may want to keep your big day a secret—or risk spending it searching for dry socks.

Everybody Get Together

Occidental's residential options include eleven coed dormitories, along with themed living areas such as Multicultural Hall and the Women's Center. Weekly residence hall gatherings, called "hall spreads," bring residents together for games, movies, or discussions. Students gather for meals at the Marketplace in Johnson Student Center or at the Tiger Cooler, which serves quick bites. Half of Occidental's students come from California, and the campus's economic and ethnic diversity is encouraged by generous merit scholarships and financial aid packages. Students tend to be worldly and broad-minded. While three-quarters of them live on campus, only a small number elect to join one of the three fraternities and three sororities, whose membership and parties are open to all. There are about a hundred school clubs, and they recruit new members each fall on Club Day. Campus events keep students entertained on the weekends, as do the distractions that abound in Los Angeles.

This Place Deserves an Oscar

Occidental has appeared in many movies—not always playing itself. *Beverly Hills 90210* called Oxy "California University," and in *Clueless*, Oxy played the part of a Beverly Hills high school. The school's frequent big screen appearances testify to its beauty. Popular campus haunts include the Mary Norton Clapp Library and the Student Quad, which sits in between the Tiger Cooler and the Johnson Student Center. The new Hameetman Science Center matches the Mediterranean style of the other campus buildings and features twenty-three teaching and research labs. Occidental is located at the hub of the hipster area of Eagle Rock, which is gentrifying quickly. International flavors and cheap eats abound on Colorado Boulevard. The campus is a short drive to Glendale and Pasadena.

Admissions

Average high school GPA:	3.55
Average freshman SAT verbal / math score:	640 / 648
Average freshman ACT score:	26
Application fee:	$50

Application deadlines:
1/10 (freshmen)
3/15 (transfer)
11/15 (early decision)

Total applicants:	5,309
Total accepted:	2,229 (42%)
Total accepted who enrolled:	458

Notification dates:
4/1 (freshmen)
5/1 (transfer)
12/15 (early decision)

Acceptance rate for early decision applicants:	64%

Students

Percentage of male / female students:	44% / 56%
Percentage of students from out of state:	51%
Percentage of students graduating in 4 years / 6 years:	78% / 84%

Money

Total endowment:	$313,700,000
Total tuition:	$34,400
Total cost with fees & expenses:	$44,833
Average financial aid package:	$29,089
Percentage of students who sought aid and received it:	100%
Percentage of students receiving financial aid:	50%

Also Check Out

Claremont McKenna College

Pitzer College

Pomona College

University of California–Los Angeles

University of Southern California

The Ohio State University

Enarson Hall, 154 W. 12th Avenue
Columbus, OH 43210

(614) 292-6446
http://www.osu.edu/

 **BIG CHOICE**

 **BIG RESEARCH**

Welcome to Planet Buckeye!

5 REASONS IT'S COOL

1. Ohio State's high academic standards and commitment to research make it **a "public Ivy" if ever there was one**.

2. Fancy yourself a people person? The **huge student body** will afford you plenty of opportunities to put your social skills to the test.

3. Be prepared to join the local cult—**Buckeyes football**.

4. Corporate types will find the **Fisher School of Business** the perfect place to gear up for the rat race.

5. Like **big-city life**? Ohio State is located in Columbus, the biggest city in the state.

The Basics

Public / private: public state
Total enrollment / undergrads: 51,818 / 38,479
Campus setting: urban
Students call it: The Ohio State University, Ohio State, OSU
Students are called: Buckeyes
Notable alums: William A. Fowler (Nobel Laureate, Physics), Patricia Heaton (actress), Paul F. Iams (founder, the Iams Company), Bobby Knight (college basketball coach), Roy Lichtenstein (artist), Jesse Owens (Olympic track and field athlete), Cynthia Ozick (author), Dwight Yoakam (singer-songwriter)

Where High Enrollment Meets High Standards

When it comes to academic quality, Ohio State proves that sometimes bigger really is better. The university's curriculum favors practical and pre-professional programs and is distributed across eighteen different colleges and schools. The Fisher School of Business attracts a large number of undergrads, as does the engineering program. Other popular majors include biology, psychology, and English. No matter their intended major, underclassmen must complete a typical liberal arts sampler platter. Getting the right classes can lead to unsavory encounters with the administrative bureaucracy, and many classes will likely be huge, but self-starters can flourish because of Ohio State's all-around commitment to academic excellence. Research funding is well over $420 million with fellowships and grants from places such as the American Association for the Advancement of Science and the

One from the Grooveyard

"Hang on Sloopy," a familiar sixties pop hit by **The McCoys**, is a staple of oldies radio stations. In 1965, it also became the unofficial Buckeyes song when a marching band member begged the conductor to let the band take a stab at it. It's been played at Buckeye football games ever since and is now even played at Cincinnati Bengals and Cleveland Indians games. "Sloopy," incidentally, was the nickname of a real life Ohioan.

Guggenheim Foundation. A fully operational hospital, one of the nation's leading cancer studies centers, the world's first Mathematical Biosciences Institute (funded by the National Science Foundation . . . OSU has it all.

It's a Riot

With some fifty thousand students and an urban location, Ohio State is anything but restful. Buckeyes party hard, especially during football season—a bit too hard at times, perhaps, as the school experienced a postgame riot in 2002. Such events are not the norm, however, and the student body is a rather conservative, homegrown one. The university draws its students overwhelmingly from the state of Ohio, but a diversity initiative has achieved results: African Americans constitute 11 percent of the student population, Asians 6 percent, and Latinos 3 percent. Opportunities for fun and socializing abound, although at a school as huge as this one is, students may have to leave their shells a bit to make the necessary associations. The Greek system is a big draw, but it doesn't dominate—the study body is just too huge for any one faction to take over.

Hello, Columbus

Unlike many big state universities, which tend to have rural locations, Ohio State is located smack dab in Columbus, the largest city in Ohio. Shopping, restaurants, and nightclubs are all within easy reach of campus. Buckeyes rely on the Easton Mall for the latest fashions and on nightclubs such as 4 Kegs, Ledo's, and Miani's for showing them off. Artsy types might prefer coffee houses such as Kafé Kerouac, which hosts a Poetry Potluck every Thursday, or Shi-Sha, which offers hookah pipes. The Ohio State campus has many amenities of its own. Neighborhoods adjacent to South Campus skew toward shabbiness, so crime can sometimes be an issue.

Admissions

Average high school GPA:	—
Average freshman SAT writing / math / critical reading score:	583 / 623 / 591
Average freshman ACT score:	25
Application fee:	$40
Application deadlines:	
2/1 (freshmen)	
6/25 (transfer)	
Total applicants:	18,286
Total accepted:	12,417 (68%)
Total accepted who enrolled:	6,266
Notification dates:	
continuous (freshmen)	
continuous (transfer)	

Students

Percentage of male / female students:	53% / 47%
Percentage of students from out of state:	10%
Percentage of students graduating in 4 years / 6 years:	35% / 68%

Money

Total endowment:	$1,996,839,412
Total in-state tuition, fees & expenses:	$16,359
Total out-of-state tuition, fees & expenses:	$28,254
Average financial aid package:	$10,149
Percentage of students who sought aid and received it:	67%
Percentage of students receiving financial aid:	47%

Also Check Out

Miami University

The Pennsylvania State University–University Park

University of Cincinnati

Purdue University

University of Illinois at Urbana-Champaign

Ohio Wesleyan University

6l South Sandusky Street Delaware, OH 43015	(740) 368-2000 http://www.owu.edu/

BIG PERSPECTIVE

Get ready for prime time.

5 REASONS IT'S COOL

1. The academic program blends traditional **liberal arts with nuts-and-bolts pre-professional training**.

2. **Study-abroad programs in twenty countries**, plus a semester in Washington, let you indulge your wanderlust.

3. **Students have a say in their own lives.** The university president meets frequently with the student-composed Archway Committee.

4. **You'll have a good time.** It's no longer a big party school, but there's a pub on campus.

5. Delaware is a charming town, and **Columbus comes in handy** when you're ready for a big night out or a great internship.

The Basics

Public / private: private religious
Total enrollment / undergrads: 1,935 / 1,935
Campus setting: small town
Students call it: Ohio Wesleyan
Students are called: Battling Bishops
Notable alums: Charles Fairbanks (U.S. vice president), Wendie Malick (actress), Frank Sherwood Rowland (Nobel Laureate, Chemistry), Mildred Elizabeth Sisk (convicted traitor)

Not All Pie-in-the-Sky

The Ohio Wesleyan educational experience is founded on the twin pillars of liberal arts and professional preparation. The idea is that after four years, a student should not only be acquainted with the broad themes of thought and knowledge but also have a fighting chance at getting a job. This approach seems to be working. Ohio Wesleyan is one of only five schools in the country that makes the top 20 both for undergraduates who go on to receive PhDs *and* for undergraduates who go on to become corporate leaders. Graduates' rate of acceptance to medical school is around 90 percent, a number that is expected to rise now that the $35 million renovation of the campus science center is complete. The strongest departments are Biology, Psychology, Political Science, and Pre-Law; economics and business are the most popular majors. All students must complete three courses in humanities, social sciences, and natural sciences, as well as two courses in foreign language and one in performing or fine arts. A four-year honors program allows top

No Boys Allowed

The Monnett Weekend began as a women's athletic festival on Mother's Day, 1896. Barred from attending, many male students hid in nearby trees and spied on the girls running around the maypole. These days, the maypole is still a part of the celebration, but men are welcome.

incoming freshmen to conduct research and enjoy one-on-one faculty partnerships. Professors are accessible and friendly. Most introductory classes have about thirty-five students, and the overall average is sixteen.

Calming Down

Ohio Wesleyan has long had a reputation as a hard-drinking, out-of-control place. That's changing, due almost entirely to a serious administration crackdown. $150 fines are routinely issued for underage drunkenness, Greek rush is dry, and armband systems are required at parties. In practice, this means things have simmered down to a level of average debauchery. Thirty-nine percent of men join one of ten fraternities, and 26 percent of women join one of six (nonresidential) sororities; 85 percent of the student body lives in university-owned residences, and housing is guaranteed for four years. The student body is relatively diverse: About 15 percent of students are racial minorities, and forty-one foreign countries are represented. Almost 60 percent of students are from Ohio. The two top draws, in terms of extracurricular activities, are community service and intramural sports. Theater troupes, choral groups, and special- and ethnic-interest groups are also popular.

Can You Name the Fifteenth Largest City in America?

Several buildings on the Ohio Wesleyan campus are on the National Register of Historic Places, but aside from these lookers, the place is rather bland. A highway cuts right through the middle, dividing the academic buildings from the residences. The town of Delaware boasts pretty, tree-lined streets; 26,500 people; and the Little Brown Jug, the annual harness-racing championship that constitutes the middle leg of that sport's Triple Crown. Twenty miles to the south of Delaware lies Columbus and all of the accoutrements of big-city life. Hiking, camping, golf, and skiing are all within a few hours' drive.

Admissions

Average high school GPA:	3.36
Average freshman SAT verbal / math score:	608 / 608
Average freshman ACT score:	25
Application fee:	$35

Application deadlines:
3/1 (freshmen)   12/1 (early decision)
5/15 (transfer)   12/15 (early action)

Total applicants:	3,579
Total accepted:	2,257 (63%)
Total accepted who enrolled:	565

Notification dates:
10/1 (freshmen)
continuous (transfer)
12/30 (early decision)
1/15 (early action)

Acceptance rate for early action/early decision applicants:	93% / 86%

Students

Percentage of male / female students:	48% / 52%
Percentage of students from out of state:	46%
Percentage of students graduating in 4 years / 6 years:	62% / 68%

Money

Total endowment:	$158,400,000
Total tuition:	$29,870
Total cost with fees & expenses:	$40,130
Average financial aid package:	$20,854
Percentage of students who sought aid and received it:	82%
Percentage of students receiving financial aid:	56%

Also Check Out

College of Wooster

Denison University

DePauw University

Kenyon College

Miami University

Oregon State University

104 Kerr Administration Building
Corvallis, OR 97331

(541) 737-1000
http://oregonstate.edu/

BIG CHOICE

BIG RESEARCH

Oh, to be a Beaver!

5 REASONS IT'S COOL

1. As one of **Oregon's largest public research institutions,** OSU offers endless resources, including fourteen thousand acres of research forest.

2. Beavers vs. Ducks! Join in the madness that surrounds the **OSU-UO football rivalry.**

3. There's a reason Lewis & Clark passed through the Willamette Valley. The area features **lush surroundings and proximity to both beaches and mountains.**

4. OSU students love the **cozy, small-town vibe of Corvallis.**

5. OSU has a branch campus in Bend, the Hatfield Marine Science center in Newport, and **research facilities all over the state.**

The Basics

Public / private: public state
Total enrollment / undergrads: 19,362 / 15,829
Campus setting: small town
Students call it: OSU, Oregon State
Students are called: Beavers
Notable alums: Christopher Howell (poet), Chad Johnson (pro football player), Bernard A. Newcomb (cofounder, E*Trade), Linus Pauling (Nobel Laureate, Chemistry, Peace), Gary Payton (pro basketball player)

Land, Sea, Sun, Space—OSU Has It All

A leading recipient of funding for research, OSU is one of just two schools in the country to receive designation as a land grant, sea grant, space grant, *and* sun grant institution. That's a lot of federal dollars, and the excellent research facilities, faculty, and resources at OSU show this money at work. Students can take courses in ten different colleges, with colleges of liberal arts, business, and engineering drawing the most enrollees. Programs such as business administration, pre-pharmacy, and biotechnology are popular. OSU's history as an agricultural university (students sometimes call the university "Moo-U") is evident in the strong forestry and agricultural sciences programs. The school's pre-veterinary medicine program is one of just a few of its kind in the Northwest. The university offers a fairly extensive core curriculum that elicits mixed feelings from students. Freshmen will have a hard time escaping large lecture-style classes, but upperclassmen are usually rewarded with small higher-level classes. A select number of OSU

Do Beavers Eat Ducks?

The OSU Beavers do, each and every night of the week leading up to the big game against rival University of Oregon, whose mascot is the duck. Talk about eating up the competition—hope you like the taste of water fowl!

students may gain admittance to the University Honors College, where classes are smaller and honors degrees are awarded. Study-abroad programs and internships send students to the far reaches of the globe.

A Civil War—In Oregon?

OSU students are an active group, and nothing gets them more revved up than cheering on their Division I varsity sports teams. OSU's baseball team recently won the College World Series for the second year in a row, and the consistently strong wrestling team won the 2007 Pac-10 Championship. School spirit is fierce. In the week before the Civil War Game against rival University of Oregon, OSU students wear only the school colors of orange and black and get their vocal chords primed for some intense cheering. Greek organizations play a large role in the social scene, and about 20 percent of students participate. Thirsty Thursdays draw crowds week after week, and house parties, local bars, and an impressive lineup of on-campus events hosted by the Memorial Union keep students plenty busy. Students rave about the newly renovated Dixon Recreation Center, which houses a gym, indoor climbing wall, tennis pavilion, pool, and basketball, volleyball, and racquetball courts. OSU has fourteen residence halls and four student-run co-op houses, but most upperclassmen opt for off-campus housing.

Small Town, Big Heart

OSU's 400-acre campus is located in Corvallis, a friendly college town in the heart of the Willamette Valley. Theaters, coffee shops, bars, and restaurants are all an easy walk or bike ride from campus. Students appreciate the cozy atmosphere, with its farmers markets and rodeos, as well as the perpetually green surroundings. The price paid for the lush setting is persistent rain, but the primarily Oregonian student body is used to the weather. If students get an itch for the big city, Portland is a ninety-minute drive away. Outdoor enthusiasts have plenty of options, from biking on backcountry roads to rafting down the Rogue River. The lovely Oregon coast is an hour away, as are the Cascade Mountains with skiing, hiking, and camping.

Admissions

Average high school GPA:	3.49
Average freshman SAT verbal / math score:	532 / 553
Average freshman ACT score:	23
Application fee:	$50

Application deadlines:
9/1 (freshmen)
5/1 (transfer)
11/1 (early action)

Total applicants:	9,077
Total accepted:	8,387 (92%)
Total accepted who enrolled:	2,856

Notification dates:
continuous (freshmen)
continuous (transfer)
— (early action)

Acceptance rate for early action applicants:	—

Students

Percentage of male / female students:	54% / 46%
Percentage of students from out of state:	14%
Percentage of students graduating in 4 years / 6 years:	31% / 61%

Money

Total endowment:	$440,042,746
Total in-state tuition, fees & expenses:	$14,430
Total out-of-state tuition, fees & expenses:	$26,346
Average financial aid package:	$9,022
Percentage of students who sought aid and received it:	68%
Percentage of students receiving financial aid:	42%

Also Check Out

The University of Montana–Missoula

University of Oregon

University of Puget Sound

University of Washington

Parsons, The New School for Design

66 Fifth Avenue New York, NY 10011	(212) 229-8900 http://www.parsons.newschool.edu/

BIG PLAN

Fashion your career in the heart of the city.

5 REASONS IT'S COOL

1. Parsons' **renowned Fashion Department** offers classes with designers such as Tim Gunn and visiting critics such as Donna Karan.

2. The first art and design school in the United States to start a campus overseas, **Parsons supports affiliate schools in France, South Korea, the Dominican Republic, and Japan.**

3. Students take advantage of the **incredible culture, art, and internships** available in New York City.

4. The **unique course offerings** include Royal Furnishings of Versailles and New York Trend Spotting.

5. Enroll in the **five-year dual degree program** and get both a BA and a BFA.

The Basics

Public / private: private nonprofit
Total enrollment / undergrads: 3,598 / 3,180
Campus setting: urban
Students call it: Parsons
Notable alums: Tom Ford (designer), Donna Karan (designer), Norman Rockwell (artist), Steven Meisel (photographer), Joel Schumacher (filmmaker)

Success by Design

Students work hard at Parsons. The Foundation Program, the first-year core course load most students shoulder, is designed to weed out the less serious aspiring artists and designers. The program includes twelve courses in studio design, drawing, critical reading and writing, and world art, along with field trips to professional design studios in the city. The majority of professors at Parsons are leaders in their fields. This means they're great resources for establishing connections in the art and design worlds but not very available for one-on-one learning. Only 10 percent of the faculty teaches full-time. To supplement classroom work, each department sponsors lectures from visiting artists, who meet with students individually and critique their work. The Office of Career Services helps students secure required internships at marquee companies, including the *New York Times*, Marc Jacobs, and the Museum of Modern Art. The most popular majors include design and visual communications, fashion design, and illustration.

A Jury of Their High-Fashion Peers

At the end of senior year, each student submits her or his work to be judged by a jury of over 350 designers, journalists, and retailers. The best work is presented at the Benefit Fashion Show, which draws such notable attendees as Oscar de la Renta, Marc Jacobs, and department store mogul Susan Kronick. Top students win a Designer-of-the-Year award, which has helped many graduates launch their careers.

Globalization Starts Here

What Parsons lacks in gender equality (the female-to-male ratio is 80:20), it makes up for in diversity. Almost a third of the students come from foreign countries, mostly in Asia and Europe. As freshmen, most students live in one of six undergraduate residence halls. After freshmen year, though, many move off campus. Parsons students tend to be career focused and hardworking. Most have their eye on the prize of gainful employment following graduation. Fashion design majors, in particular, have a reputation for extreme competitiveness. But students know how to have fun too. The plethora of clubbing and drinking opportunities in the city more than makes up for the absence of Greek life. New York's galleries, music, and museums make it hard for students to justify holing up in their rooms during downtime. The Latino/Latina Student Group, Chinese Student Association, and a large gay pride community stand out among student groups.

It's All About the City

Located in the hub of the fashion, art, and design world, Parsons has two main campuses: one in Greenwich Village and one in Midtown Manhattan. The majority of buildings, including the schools' three libraries and five of the residence halls, are situated around Washington Square and Union Square. The Angelo Donghia Materials Library and Study Center includes a library, a gallery (with its own full-time curator), computers, and a lecture hall. Parsons invests a lot in updating its resources, and a new Design Center is in the works. This new center will include additional classroom space, a design store, and expanded gallery room for innovative exhibitions. Architecture students also have access to a spacious studio loft with wireless technology. The school invests heavily in keeping its design and media equipment up-to-date. Fashion design majors will appreciate the Fashion Computer Center on Seventh Avenue (where *Project Runway* is filmed), with its top-of-the-line workstations outfitted with graphic and modeling design programs, scanners, and color printers.

Admissions

Average high school GPA:	3.2
Average freshman SAT writing / math / critical reading score:	536 / 553 / 551
Average freshman ACT score:	—
Application fee:	$50
Application deadlines:	
3/1 (freshmen)	
3/1 (transfer)	
Total applicants:	2,394
Total accepted:	1,094 (46%)
Total accepted who enrolled:	487
Notification dates:	
continuous (freshmen)	
continuous (transfer)	

Students

Percentage of male / female students:	22% / 78%
Percentage of students from out of state:	47%
Percentage of students graduating in 4 years / 6 years:	48% / 66%

Money

Total endowment:	—
Total tuition:	$30,270
Total cost with fees & expenses:	$42,680
Average financial aid package:	$9,940
Percentage of students who sought aid and received it:	53%
Percentage of students receiving financial aid:	44%

Also Check Out

Cooper Union for the Advancement of Science and Art

Eugene Lang College, The New School for Liberal Arts

Rhode Island School of Design

SUNY–Fashion Institute of Technology

The Pennsylvania State University–University Park

201 Old Main
University Park, PA 16802

(814) 865-4700
http://www.psu.edu/

 **BIG CHOICE**

 **BIG RESEARCH**

Happy times in Happy Valley

5 REASONS IT'S COOL

1. With its roughly 35,000 fulltime undergrads, Penn State has a **legendary social scene**.

2. Good news for those who dream of a career in front of the green screen: this school produces **tons of meteorologists**.

3. The Nittany Lions, who compete in the Big Ten, **are one of the winningest teams in college football history**.

4. **It's not called Happy Valley for nothing:** When you're not hitting the books, you can hit the slopes.

5. Those with CEO dreams could do worse than the **Smeal College of Business**, which has a solid national reputation.

The Basics

Public / private: public state-related
Total enrollment / undergrads: 42,914 / 36,613
Campus setting: small town
Students call it: Penn State, PSU
Students are called: Lions, Nittanies
Notable alums: Benjy Bronk (writer, *The Howard Stern Show*), Julius Epstein (screenwriter, *Casablanca*), Jonathan Frakes (actor), Alan Furst (writer), Jenny Gardiner (writer), Franco Harris (pro football player), Chip Kidd (designer), Rick Santorum (senator), Lara Spencer (TV host)

The View from the Cheap Seats

Penn State is the school to which just about every college-bound Pennsylvanian applies. Many are disappointed: The university's acceptance rate of 62 percent is one of the lowest in the nation among state institutions. Those who do make it in find a wide array of majors to choose from, once a forty-five-unit general education requirement has been satisfied. Incoming students should brace themselves for the lecture-hall hoards. Weathering these difficulties pays off, especially if you're into weather; Penn State has a renowned meteorology program. Other strong programs include engineering and those offered by the Smeal School of Business, but virtually every major here is nationally renowned. Especially driven students will want to check out the reputable Schreyer Honors College. Students in all programs report generally positive experiences with their professors.

Where's the Love?

Beginning in the 1960s, Penn State observed Gentle Thursday, a self-created holiday held every April. The tradition was originally a celebration of peace, love, fellowship, and just plain grooviness. As the sixties gave way to the seventies, Gentle Thursday disintegrated into a drug-fueled free-for-all. It was eventually abandoned in 1980.

Lions of Winter

There are 35,000 eighteen-to-twenty-one-year-olds tucked away among mountains in the middle of Pennsylvania, where winters are long and cold. As you might expect, there's quite a bit of drinking at Penn State. Despite the ever-more-restrictive underage-drinking countermeasures implemented by administrators over the years, students bravely carry on the boozing tradition. Much of the revelry revolves around the football season, when Penn State's vaunted Nittany Lions take the field. The other big game on campus is the Greek scene. Partying isn't the only thing to do, though. Activities abound, and the school's entertainment venues draw top bands. Out-of-state students will find that being smack dab in the middle of Pennsylvania also means being smack dab in the middle of Pennsylvanians: Some 75 percent of the student body hails from PA.

C'mon, Get Happy!

Residence halls are generally well regarded, with Pollock Hall and West Halls as standouts. Penn State requires its freshmen to live on campus—and purchase pricey meal plans, of course! To university powers and the postal service, Penn State is located in University Park; to everyone else, it's in Happy Valley. This unlikely, sitcom-esque moniker reflects the small-town pace of life. For both students and locals, the university is quite literally the biggest game in town. Beaver Stadium, where the Nittany Lions play, seats over 100,000 fans, and getting tickets is a cutthroat competition. To celebrate victories or numb the agony of defeat after games, students hit the Lion's Den, Players, the Cell Block, or the Saloon. Other students prefer The Brewery's lack of pretension. Students not in search of keggers can repair to The Hub, the main student union. This university's mountain environs mean skiing and snowboarding are popular winter pastimes. There are plenty of urban amenities in town, but students are very happy with life on campus.

Admissions

Average high school GPA:	3.53
Average freshman SAT verbal / math score:	577 / 613
Average freshman ACT score:	—
Application fee:	$50
Application deadlines:	
continuous (freshmen)	
continuous (transfer)	
Total applicants:	29,904
Total accepted:	18,423 (62%)
Total accepted who enrolled:	8,027
Notification dates:	
continuous (freshmen)	
continuous (transfer)	

Students

Percentage of male / female students:	55% / 45%
Percentage of students from out of state:	23%
Percentage of students graduating in 4 years / 6 years:	48% / 84%

Money

Total endowment:	$1,390,000,000
Total in-state tuition, fees & expenses:	$20,374
Total out-of-state tuition, fees & expenses:	$30,922
Average financial aid package:	$15,295
Percentage of students who sought aid and received it:	70%
Percentage of students receiving financial aid:	44%

Also Check Out

Temple University

University of Connecticut

University of Delaware

University of Maryland–College Park

The University of Pittsburgh

Pepperdine University

24255 Pacific Coast Highway
Malibu, CA 90263

(310) 506-4000
http://www.pepperdine.edu/

**BIG
PERSPECTIVE**

There's no trouble in *this* paradise.

5 REASONS IT'S COOL

1. Check out that view! Pepperdine's **gorgeous campus** rests on the Santa Monica Mountains, overlooking the Malibu coastline.

2. The university's Christian tradition makes it a great place for **intellectual** *and* **spiritual growth.**

3. Craving personal attention from your profs? Pepperdine offers **small classes and a midsized student body.**

4. The winning **Waves athletics program** is making waves in the NCAA (even without a football team).

5. Live the *suite* life in the cool communal living spaces.

The Basics

Public / private: private religious
Total enrollment / undergrads: 7,593 / 3,297
Campus setting: small town
Students call it: Pepperdine, Pepp
Students are called: Waves
Notable alums: Adam Firestone (wine entrepreneur), James Hanh (mayor, Los Angeles), Brandy Norwood (actress, singer), Kenneth Starr (lawyer, independent council), Neil Clark Warren (founder, eHarmony)

An Education with a View

At Seaver College, Pepperdine's undergraduate liberal arts college, students find a mix of research-oriented and professional programs. The most popular majors are business administration, advertising, psychology, political science, and international studies. Pepperdine prides itself on providing close contact with profs—the student-to-faculty ratio is 12:1, and class sizes tend to be low. Professors share the university's core Christian values. Students have their choice of three ways to complete their general-education requirements: the Great Books program, the Social Action and Justice track, or a selection of courses handpicked by the students. Great Books students gain a thorough introduction to Western culture through four seminars that examine history, culture, philosophy, and literature in their original texts. Students on the four-course Social Action and Justice track examine human rights and social movements within historical, political, and economic contexts. While the Malibu campus keeps students safe and

The Hills Are Alive . . .

. . . with the sounds of Songfest. This annual singing competition, a tradition at Pepperdine since 1973, goes beyond typical singing competitions at other colleges and universities. Student groups stage elaborate twelve-minute extravaganzas at six sold-out performances, all for the chance to win the Songfest Sweepstakes Award. Pepperdine alumni come back to campus in droves to witness the exuberant students put on wacky costumes and sing their hearts out.

happy, the university's international programs are very popular, with over half of undergrads choosing to go abroad. Pepperdine can be challenging, and students really do have to work hard despite the easygoing campus feeling.

Togetherness, 24/7

There's an intense feeling of community on the Pepperdine campus. All that togetherness is certainly facilitated by the university's requirement that all students attend one convocation (or convo) program per week, designed to affirm Christian values in student life. Left-leaning or not-so-religious students may find that the campus—one of the more conservative in Southern California—is not their cup of tea. Pepp students get to know each other better through living in comfortable suites, where they may gripe together over less-than-savory food from the caf. Another campus bonding experience is cheering on the Waves, who have sweet facilities and a sweet rep as a winning athletics program. Students here have a long tradition of community service, especially within a Christian context, and the university's Volunteer Center hooks students up with a wide range of service activities.

Your Own Personal Pacific

One of Pepperdine's strongest suits is its location in Malibu. The area's canyons, hills, and ocean make for a beautiful backdrop to this tidy campus. The neutral-colored Mediterranean-style buildings populate the terraced landscape, which rises up the Santa Monica Mountains. Be ready to hike up flights and flights of stairs! Nearer to shore, there's shopping and opportunities for celeb-sightings, but not too many eateries catering to students. A quick drive down Highway 1 puts you in Santa Monica, which is host to more student-friendly dining and shopping, as well as additional beachy recreation. The rest of Los Angeles completes the Pepperdine experience.

Admissions

Average high school GPA:	3.67
Average freshman SAT verbal / math score:	610 / 621
Average freshman ACT score:	25
Application fee:	$65
Application deadlines: 1/15 (freshmen) 1/15 (transfer)	
Total applicants:	7,483
Total accepted:	2,098 (28%)
Total accepted who enrolled:	705
Notification dates: 4/1 (freshmen) 4/1 (transfer)	

Students

Percentage of male / female students:	42% / 58%
Percentage of students from out of state:	50%
Percentage of students graduating in 4 years / 6 years:	71% / 79%

Money

Total endowment:	$538,233,000
Total tuition:	$32,620
Total cost with fees & expenses:	$43,040
Average financial aid package:	$30,991
Percentage of students who sought aid and received it:	89%
Percentage of students receiving financial aid:	40%

Also Check Out

Boston College

Loyola Marymount University

Pomona College

University of California–Los Angeles

University of Southern California

Pitzer College

1050 North Mills Avenue
Claremont, CA 91711

(909) 621-8000
http://www.pitzer.edu/

 BIG IDEA

 **BIG PERSPECTIVE**

 **BIG WORLD**

Know thyself, know thy neighbor.

5 REASONS IT'S COOL

1. Pitzer's unique curriculum encourages students to engage in **multicultural and multidisciplinary thinking.**

2. Students **perform community service for credit.** It's part of Pitzer's Social Responsibility Objective.

3. New additions to campus include **three new residence halls.**

4. Pitzer is a small, nurturing community. But students enjoy big university resources, thanks to the college's association with the **Claremont Consortium of schools.**

5. **City lights, sunny beaches, gorgeous mountains . . .** whatever your pleasure, it's all within an easy drive.

The Basics

Public / private: private nonprofit
Total enrollment / undergrads: 958 / 958
Campus setting: suburban
Students call it: Pitzer
Students are called: Sagehens
Notable alums: Anne Archer (actress), Max Brooks (actor, author), Mablean Ephriam (judge, *Divorce Court*), Amy Gerstler (author), Jennipher Goodman (filmmaker), Jana Sue Memel (documentarian)

All in the Family

Pitzer offers one of the most unusual academic programs in the country. The college doesn't prescribe general education courses, just a set of six Educational Objectives, and instead of departments, there are cohorts. Required work starts with the First-Year Seminar, topics for which have included popular culture, propaganda, and environmental toxicology. The curriculum encourages interdisciplinary thought, and all students must select an issue to examine from the perspectives of at least two different cultures and two different disciplines. Disciplines can be pretty wild; after all, Pitzer was the first college in the country to offer a course on YouTube. Community-service learning activities are also encouraged. The most popular majors are psychology, sociology, political studies, media studies, environmental studies, and art. Pitzer's unconventional approach yields great results: In the 2006 and 2007, students and alums won a combined 18 Fulbrights, a school record. Because Pitzer is a member of the prestigious Claremont Consortium,

One Anti-Climactic Comet

In 1973, Lubous Kohoutek predicted that a comet he discovered would be so bright that it would light up the night sky. This was supposed to be *the* comet to watch. Instead, when stargazers gathered on the Pitzer Mounds to see this stellar event, they saw, well, nothing. The would-be comet now lends its name to a two-day art and music party held at the very same Pitzer Mounds. Even though the comet was a bust, the Kohoutek Music and Arts Festival has hot bands and student booths that provide entertainment.

students are given the opportunity to take courses at nearby Harvey Mudd, Pomona, Claremont McKenna, and Scripps Colleges.

Free to Be

Social life at Pitzer is not intensely structured, and there are no fraternities or sororities. Academics here are focused on individual growth and community service, and students continue to develop both ideals when they're not in the classroom. Almost all students are politically liberal, and an appreciation for diverse people and ideas is one of the college's hallmarks. About half of the students come from California, and 73 percent of students live on campus. Pitzer has five residence halls, now that three new dormitories opened in the summer of 2007. On the weekends, students can catch some sun while playing Ultimate Frisbee, hanging out on the Pitzer Mounds, or checking out some of the events happening on the other Claremont campuses, since it takes just about ten or fifteen minutes to walk anywhere within the Consortium's campus. In sports, Pitzer students join up with Pomona College to form the Sagehens and compete on NCAA Division III teams.

On the Mounds

Known as the "city of trees and PhDs," Claremont sits below the San Gabriel Mountains in the Pomona Valley, about thirty miles east of Los Angeles. Students can ride the rails on the Metrolink to go downtown. Pasadena lies between the two cities and has a smattering of shops, restaurants, and activities that students enjoy. The Claremont Village offers its own charming diversions too. On campus, Grove House serves as a meeting place and dining commons for students, while the Gold Student Center boasts fitness facilities, a gallery, student organization resources, and a new café. The unusual Pitzer Mounds at the center of campus provide visual interest as well as perfect spots for relaxation.

Admissions

Average high school GPA:	3.65
Average freshman SAT verbal / math score:	—/—
Average freshman ACT score:	—
Application fee:	$50
Application deadlines: 1/1 (freshmen) 4/15 (transfer) specific (early action)	
Total applicants:	3,437
Total accepted:	1,263 (37%)
Total accepted who enrolled:	229
Notification dates: 4/1 (freshmen) 5/15 (transfer) specific (early action)	
Acceptance rate for early action applicants:	—

Students

Percentage of male / female students:	41% / 59%
Percentage of students from out of state:	42%
Percentage of students graduating in 4 years / 6 years:	61% / 70%

Money

Total endowment:	$86,336,000
Total tuition:	$31,000
Total cost with fees & expenses:	$44,608
Average financial aid package:	$30,802
Percentage of students who sought aid and received it:	100%
Percentage of students receiving financial aid:	36%

Also Check Out

Bard College

Hampshire College

Occidental College

Sarah Lawrence College

Scripps College

Skidmore College

Pomona College

333 North College Way
Claremont, CA 91711

(909) 621-8000
http://www.pomona.edu/

 **BIG BRAIN**

 **BIG PERSPECTIVE**

A liberal arts gem in a lovely setting

5 REASONS IT'S COOL

1. Pomona's faculty is **outstanding and committed.**

2. The **science and art facilities** can't be beat.

3. Get **five colleges for the price of one!** Pomona is a member of the Claremont Consortium, giving students the resources of all five member colleges.

4. This college has **one of the most beautiful campuses in the state**—and since that state is California, that's saying a lot.

5. Pomona is considered **the West Coast's premier liberal arts college.**

The Basics

Public / private: private nonprofit
Total enrollment / undergrads: 1,545 / 1,545
Campus setting: suburban
Students call it: Pomona
Students are called: Sagehens
Notable alums: Richard Chamberlain (actor), Kris Kristofferson (singer-songwriter, actor), Roy E. Disney (senior executive, Walt Disney Company), Lynda Obst (filmmaker), George C. Wolfe (playwright)

Four Pillars

Academics at Pomona center around four pillars: critical inquiry, the general education requirements, the student's major, and the Senior Exercise. With the exception of the initial critical inquiry seminar, there are no required courses (just areas). Right from the start, students link up with a faculty advisor who helps them plan out their courses. Pomona offers a wide selection of classes (600 offered on campus; 2,500 offered across the Claremont Colleges consortium each year) and a great deal of freedom when it comes to its programs of study. Independent study opportunities exist in all forty-four of the school's academic majors. Students are free to plan and direct their own research and creative projects under the guidance of faculty mentors or design an entire major with the help of staffed advisors. Study, work, and intern-abroad experiences may be incorporated into every major. Students can either choose from one of Pomona's thirty-four international programs or plan their own global excursion for credit.

What's in a Number?

At Pomona, the number 47 isn't just any old number. Back in the sixties, students concluded that the number turned up more often in nature than other random numbers. Ever since, the number 47 and Pomona have been mystically and inexorably linked. Students point out that Pomona's exit off of the San Bernardino Freeway is Exit 47. The number of organ pipes in Lyman Hall is 47. In 2000, there were 47 high school valedictorians in Pomona's freshman class. And the list goes on . . .

Share and Share Alike

Students here are smart, driven, and multifaceted. Sharing the resources of five colleges enriches student life. The college (in partnership with nearby Pitzer College) competes on nineteen varsity sports teams as part of the NCAA Division III Southern California Intercollegiate Athletic Conference. The oldest cross-town sports rivalry in California is between Pomona's Sagehens and the Occidental College Tigers. When they're feeling hungry, students fill up at any of the Claremont Consortium's twelve dining halls. The five-college system's three hundred student organizations are also open to students. Pomona, however, is unique among the five colleges in being the only one with a fraternity system. Students here are known to be friendly and supportive of each other both inside and outside of the classroom. Room Draw in April causes a frenzy for students searching for their ideal abode, but there's space for almost all students to live on campus. Another Pomona fave is the Ski-Beach Day in February or March, when students hit the slopes in the morning and the beach that same afternoon.

Natural or Big-City Splendors, Take Your Pick

The Pomona campus lies within an hour of the desert, the ocean, mountains, and Los Angeles. Environmentally minded students recently convinced the campus administration to provide a shared Flexcar, so now students can easily tour around Claremont, which *Money* magazine ranked in 2007 as the no. 5 best place to live in the country. On campus, the new Seaver Biology Building boasts energy-efficient labs and classrooms. Several campus buildings and residences have been recently renovated, including the outdoor Sontag Greek Theater. The Bridges Hall of Music also got an update a few years back and now has a new pipe organ. The Smith Campus Center centers campus life with eateries, rec facilities, and a store. The Claremont Wilderness Park, just a few minutes away, is a great place to squeeze in some between-class hiking.

Admissions

Average high school GPA:	—
Average freshman SAT writing / math / critical reading score:	711 / 715 / 717
Average freshman ACT score:	26
Application fee:	$60

Application deadlines:
1/2 (freshmen)
3/15 (transfer)
11/15 (early decision)

Total applicants:	5,440
Total accepted:	963 (18%)
Total accepted who enrolled:	379

Notification dates:
4/10 (freshmen)
5/15 (transfer)
12/15 (early decision)

Acceptance rate for early decision applicants:	31%

Students

Percentage of male / female students:	50% / 50%
Percentage of students from out of state:	68%
Percentage of students graduating in 4 years / 6 years:	81% / 90%

Money

Total endowment:	$1,457,213,000
Total tuition:	$31,580
Total cost with fees & expenses:	$44,006
Average financial aid package:	$32,100
Percentage of students who sought aid and received it:	100%
Percentage of students receiving financial aid:	52%

Also Check Out

Claremont McKenna College

Dartmouth College

Princeton University

Stanford University

University of Southern California

Princeton University

PO Box 430
Princeton, NJ 08544

(609) 258-3000
http://www.princeton.edu/

**BIG
BRAIN**

**BIG
PERSPECTIVE**

Calling all future leaders!

5 REASONS IT'S COOL

1. It's pretty darn cool to be a part of Princeton's **amazing community of smarties and overachievers**.

2. The **star-studded faculty roster** includes household names like Toni Morrison and Cornell West.

3. Princeton, a beautiful town itself, is just an easy train ride away from the bright lights of **Philadelphia and New York City**.

4. Hungry for more than just knowledge? Join one of the **famous eating clubs** (social clubs that are part fraternity, part dining hall).

5. The **Woodrow Wilson School of Public and International Affairs** accepts a select number of policy-loving undergrads.

The Basics

Public / private: private nonprofit
Total enrollment / undergrads: 7,242 / 4,923
Campus setting: suburban
Students call it: Princeton
Students are called: Princetonians
Notable alums: David Duchovny (actor), F. Scott Fitzgerald (writer), Steve Forbes (publisher), James Madison (U.S. president), Ralph Nader (consumer advocate), Brooke Shields (actress), Jimmy Stewart (actor)

Reach with the Stars

Academics at Princeton are serious business. Students must complete both a junior essay and a senior thesis, and the substantial core requirements include classes in writing, a foreign language, epistemology, ethics, history, English, math, and science (including two labs). Engineering students, meanwhile, choose majors from six academic departments and interdepartmental programs such as architecture and engineering, geological engineering, and robotics. Class sizes at Princeton range from small and cozy to huge and impersonal, depending on one's major. The most popular majors, like politics, economics, and history, tend to attract larger enrollments. That said, even the biggest classes do not impede professor-student interaction, as all professors hold office hours and tend to be available outside of class. The relative scarcity of grad programs—unlike Harvard and Yale, Princeton lacks business, law, and medical schools—ensures that the lion's share of faculty attention is aimed squarely at undergrads.

Faster, Higher, Stronger, Nakeder

All hail the naked athletes! The Nude Olympics was a Princeton tradition that proved to be rather short-lived. In 1970, at the first sign of snow, hundreds of Princeton sophomores frolicked about Holder Courtyard clad in nothing but thick boots, winter hats, and a modest amount of body paint. The tradition quickly caught on and became an annual event—until the university's trustees put the kibosh on it in 1999, citing safety concerns. It's all fun and games until someone slips on the ice and hurts his bum.

Food for Thought

Instead of a Greek system—which officially ended (or unofficially went underground) in 1855 when the university banned fraternities—Princeton has eating clubs. A uniquely culinary social tradition, eating clubs range from exclusive groups, which students must "bicker" to get into (bickering is equivalent to rushing), to more inclusive clubs that just require signing up. Students choose from one of six residential colleges (Butler, Forbes, Mathey, Rockefeller, Whitman, and Wilson), where they live either for their first two years only or for all four years. Ninety-eight percent of undergrads live in campus housing. Extracurriculars at Princeton are just as varied as you'd expect from an Ivy. One standout is the Princeton Triangle Club, the national's oldest touring undergraduate musical comedy group, whose members write and perform original musicals and even take their show on the road. Sports have a healthy presence on campus: There are thirty-eight varsity teams and an equal number of club sports, not to mention plenty of Frisbee action on the quads.

Glorious Gothic

Predominantly Gothic-styled architecture set amid green quads and towering oak trees gives Princeton's pristine campus a decidedly Old World feel. A manmade lake borders the northern edge of campus and serves the Princeton crew team. The university has put lots of money into updating its fitness and campus centers, which are outfitted with all of the latest equipment. The city of Princeton is wealthy, cute, and a terrific place to do some upscale shopping, but it offers little by way of nightlife. Events such as Communiversity, a yearly street fair with games, food, music performers, and vendors, attempt to bridge the divide between town residents and students. When students have a hankering for city life, New York City and Philadelphia are just a short train ride away.

Admissions

Average high school GPA:	3.85
Average freshman SAT verbal / math score:	715 / 722
Average freshman ACT score:	27
Application fee:	$65

Application deadlines:
1/1 (freshmen)
— (transfer)
specific (early decision)

Total applicants:	17,564
Total accepted:	1,790 (10%)
Total accepted who enrolled:	1,228

Notification dates:
4/10 (freshmen)
— (transfer)
specific (early decision)

Acceptance rate for early decision applicants:	32%

Students

Percentage of male / female students:	54% / 46%
Percentage of students from out of state:	86%
Percentage of students graduating in 4 years / 6 years:	90% / 97%

Money

Total endowment:	$4,294,967,295
Total tuition:	$33,000
Total cost with fees & expenses:	$43,980
Average financial aid package:	$28,792
Percentage of students who sought aid and received it:	100%
Percentage of students receiving financial aid:	49%

Also Check Out

Dartmouth College

Harvard University

Massachusetts Institute of Technology

Stanford University

Yale University

Providence College

549 River Avenue
Providence, RI 02918

(401) 865-1000
http://www.providence.edu/

BIG PERSPECTIVE

Your well-rounded education starts here.

The Basics

Public / private: private religious
Total enrollment / undergrads: 4,835 / 3,998
Campus setting: suburban
Students call it: Providence, PC
Students are called: Friars
Notable alums: Doris Burke (sports reporter), Billy Donovan (college basketball coach), Peter Farrelly (filmmaker), Janeane Garofalo (comedienne, actress), Mike Leonard (broadcast journalist), Lenny Wilkens (pro basketball coach)

A Civilized Curriculum

The rigorous academic environment at Providence College is rooted in the liberal arts tradition. Courses in natural science, social science, philosophy, theology, math, and fine arts are mandatory, but the curricular cornerstone is the Development of Western Civilization program. This twenty-credit, four-semester experience is designed to give students an interdisciplinary overview of just about everything that's happened in or said about the West over the past several thousand years. For those that hunger for more, an invitation-only, intensive liberal arts honors program follows the basic outline of the Western Civ curricula. Forty-two percent of all classes have fewer than twenty enrollees. The student-to-faculty ratio is a cozy 12:1. Of the fifty majors offered, marketing, business administration, and English are the most popular. A pre-med studies program is also available and offers early admission to Brown University's medical school.

A Tradition of Secrecy

An air of mystery surrounds the annual Junior Ring Weekend. On Friday night, juniors board buses that whisk them away to a party at an unnamed location. Class rings are presented on Saturday morning, and that evening a formal dinner is held at another undisclosed locale.

Go Friars!

Annual events at PC include Junior Ring Weekend and the Midnight Madness rally for the Friars basketball team. The nearly 100 student organizations on campus include choral groups, drama troupes, and media outlets, but no Greeks. The Cavanaugh Art Gallery, Blackfriar Theater, and Smith Center for the Arts contribute to the potent artistic atmosphere. Only five intramural sports leagues exist, but the school's recreational athletic facilities include an ice rink and a ballet studio. Among the intercollegiate athletic teams, the biggest sports draw is men's basketball, for which tickets are often hard to secure. Indeed, Friars are more likely to shout about three-pointers than about politics. While activism is relatively low-key on campus, many students participate in community service through the Campus Ministry. Eighty-three percent of students live on campus, though housing is not guaranteed for all four years. Eighty-eight percent of students are white; seventeen foreign countries are represented, and 12 percent of students are Rhode Island natives.

PC: Party College

PC's 105-acre campus has tons of open space and architecture that shifts between historic and modern. The surrounding neighborhood can be a little dangerous, though many incidents would be prevented if students didn't walk back to campus drunk and alone. Relations with the neighbors are tense, especially when the weekend parties get cranked up. By most reports, the city of Providence is a great place for college students. Free buses ferry students between the campus and the downtown area two miles away, where Friars can mix with students from Brown University and the Rhode Island School of Design. For those looking to get away, beaches and Boston are both about an hour away, and NYC is a three-hour ride.

Admissions

Average high school GPA:	3.46
Average freshman SAT writing / math / critical reading score:	616 / 611 / 597
Average freshman ACT score:	25
Application fee:	$55

Application deadlines:
1/15 (freshmen)
4/1 (transfer)
11/1 (early action)

Total applicants:	8,799
Total accepted:	4,188 (48%)
Total accepted who enrolled:	1,024

Notification dates:
4/1 (freshmen)
5/30 (transfer)
1/1 (early action)

Acceptance rate for early action applicants:	63%

Students

Percentage of male / female students:	44% / 56%
Percentage of students from out of state:	88%
Percentage of students graduating in 4 years / 6 years:	86% / 87%

Money

Total endowment:	$134,519,321
Total tuition:	$26,780
Total cost with fees & expenses:	$37,810
Average financial aid package:	$17,906
Percentage of students who sought aid and received it:	86%
Percentage of students receiving financial aid:	58%

Also Check Out

Boston College

Boston University

College of the Holy Cross

Fairfield University

Villanova University

Purdue University

475 Stadium Mall Drive
West Lafayette, IN 47907

(765) 494-4600
http://www.purdue.edu/

 **BIG CHOICE**

 **BIG RESEARCH**

Where learning takes flight

5 REASONS IT'S COOL

1. Purdue is among the few American universities with undergraduate flight training programs *and* **its own airport.**

2. The School of Aeronautics and Astronautics is **the perfect training ground for future astronauts.**

3. Purdue is **one of the nation's strongest science schools,** with first-rate programs across the board.

4. **One of the largest international student populations in the country** call the university home.

5. Ready to cheer yourself hoarse? The eighteen NCAA Division I teams make this Big Ten school **a dream for sports fans.**

The Basics

Public / private: public state
Total enrollment / undergrads: 39,228 / 31,290
Campus setting: suburban
Students call it: Purdue
Students are called: Boilermakers, Boilers
Notable alums: Neil Armstrong (astronaut), Ted Allen (actor), George Peppard (actor), Booth Tarkington (novelist), Jong Woo Park (president, Samsung), Kyle Orton (pro football player)

Excellence in the Sciences

For nearly 150 years, Purdue has offered some of the world's best academic training in technology, agriculture, and the sciences. Students can pursue degrees in approximately 200 different majors through eight different colleges, including the colleges of engineering, liberal arts, health sciences, and education, among others. Purdue is particularly renowned for its unique undergraduate aviation and aeronautics programs, which prepare future Neil Armstrongs for space travel. NASA has sent more than twenty Purdue alums into space, which is a testament to the strength of the university's program. Purdue also has a strong track record in physics, engineering, and the biological sciences. Boilermakers have the opportunity to study abroad with nearly 150 different programs in roughly fifty different countries, usually at no extra cost. Small classes and a student-to-faculty ratio of 15:1 ensure that students get lots of one-on-one attention from their instructors.

And a Nickname was Forged . . .

Who wants to be associated with some boring, common mascot like a wildcat, a bruin, or a pirate? Students at Purdue have the unusual fortune of being known as Boilermakers. The nickname harkens back to Purdue's roots as a school of industry and technology. Reporters first coined the nickname "boilermakers" back in the 1890s, when Purdue's football players were also experienced metallurgists who spent just as much time fueling the fires of their forges as they did perfecting the forward pass. The name quickly stuck and a new, albeit odd, legend was born.

Something for Everyone

Eighty percent of Purdue students choose to live on campus for all four years in the university's extensive system of residence halls, which consists of fifteen dorms and twelve cooperative living homes. This high percentage of student residency is unusual for large state schools, and bolsters the sense of community here. Five thousand students live in the fifty-plus fraternities and sororities, which make up a significant component of social life for most Purdue students. As a result, finding a good party on campus is never a problem, though neither is finding other things to do. There are nearly 800 student-run organizations operating on campus. Find your niche with the outdoor clubs, the environmentalists, the campus humanists, faith-based organizations, or the campus daily, the *Purdue Exponent*. Intramural sports are also extremely popular, as is cheering on Purdue's eighteen Division I sports teams. Football fans sing the praises of Joe Tiller, who has led the Boilers to several straight bowl appearances.

The Talk of the Town

Spread out across 2,500 acres of land, Purdue is the heart and soul of West Lafayette, a small town in Indiana. Purdue's Slayter Center for the Performing Arts is a massive, 20,000-seat outdoor amphitheater that serves as a venue for summer concerts and plays. During the colder months, similar productions are performed in the Elliott Music Hall, one of the largest theaters of its kind in the world. The horticultural gardens, meanwhile, contain over 200 different species and are open to the public. Tens of thousands of people also flock to the Mackay Arena every year to watch the Purdue Boilermakers basketball team. And for those students looking for big-city excitement, Indianapolis and Chicago, Columbus, and Louisville are nearby.

Admissions

Average high school GPA:	3.5
Average freshman SAT verbal / math score:	557 / 588
Average freshman ACT score:	24
Application fee:	$30
Application deadlines: 3/1 (freshmen) continuous (transfer)	
Total applicants:	24,883
Total accepted:	21,042 (85%)
Total accepted who enrolled:	7,363
Notification dates: continuous (freshmen) — (transfer)	

Students

Percentage of male / female students:	59% / 41%
Percentage of students from out of state:	27%
Percentage of students graduating in 4 years / 6 years:	31% / 64%

Money

Total endowment:	$1,341,000,000
Total in-state tuition, fees & expenses:	$14,642
Total out-of-state tuition, fees & expenses:	$28,812
Average financial aid package:	$12,131
Percentage of students who sought aid and received it:	92%
Percentage of students receiving financial aid:	40%

Also Check Out

Cornell University

University of Chicago

University of Illinois at Urbana-Champaign

University of Michigan–Ann Arbor

University of Notre Dame

Quinnipiac University

275 Mount Carmel Avenue Hamden, CT 06518	(203) 582-8200 http://www.quinnipiac.edu/

BIG JOB

Ready for the real world?

5 REASONS IT'S COOL

1. Quinnipiac is a great place for **top-notch career training** in fields such as health, physical therapy, communications, and nursing.

2. Education students can earn both their bachelor's and master's degrees thanks to a **five-year accelerated program**.

3. **Future media moguls** can run the campus television station, two radio stations, and a newspaper.

4. The **Fred Friendly First Amendment Award** honors those who have shown courage in preserving First Amendment rights.

5. Nature lovers will appreciate the proximity to a **cool state park**.

The Basics

Public / private: private nonprofit
Total enrollment / undergrads: 7,341 / 5,821
Campus setting: suburban**Students call it:** Quinnipiac
Students are called: Bobcats
Notable alums: Murray Lender (founder, Lender's Bagels), William Weldon (CEO, Johnson & Johnson), Turk Wendell (pro baseball player)

A World of Opportunities

Quinnipiac has traditionally catered to students looking for pre-professional training. The university offers fifty-one majors through six undergraduate colleges and schools of liberal arts, communications, health sciences, business, physical therapy, and nursing. Students may also choose the Division of Education, a special five-year accelerated program that leads to both a bachelor's degree in a chosen major and a master's degree in education. Each year, up to sixty incoming freshmen are invited to join the University Honors Program, which features special seminar courses, lectures, and other activities. No matter their major, though, all Quinnipiac students must enroll in a three-course series that allows them to explore how people interact with each other in larger communities and in global contexts. Students wishing to study abroad can go away for a semester or a full year or can take shorter two- to six-week study trips with their own professors. Internships are also encouraged, and in many majors, real-world experiences are integrated into the curriculum. The university has 280 full-time faculty members, and the student-to-faculty ratio is 16:1.

Sportscasting 101

In June 2007, Quinnipiac invited nine former and current National Hockey League (NHL) players to practice their sportscasting skills under the tutelage of ESPN's John Buccigross. The idea was to give hockey players experience they could possibly parlay into journalism gigs. The players got to interview pro baseball players, analyze clips, and take classes.

Service, Growth, and Learning

Quinnipiac students are a lively bunch who mix fun with learning and activism. The university sponsors more than seventy student organizations and sponsors a host of events throughout the year, ranging from comedians to student trips to a campus film series. Students interested in careers in media can get practical experience from the two campus radio stations, a student-run television station, and the *Chronicle*, the student newspaper that has been in continuous publication for nearly eighty years. The university is also home to one of the world's largest collections of art commemorating the Great Irish Famine. The new York Hill area of the campus is under development; it features a sports complex that opened in January 2007, a student center, dormitories, and a parking garage. And when the snow finally melts in the spring, many students participate in Quinnipiac's Alternative Spring Break, during which they serve on humanitarian missions in Barbados, Nicaragua, and throughout the United States.

Ah, New England

Quinnipiac's 500-acre campus is located at the foot of Sleeping Giant State Park in the community of Hamden, Connecticut. Students are deeply integrated into Hamden life, and many pursue community service projects in the community. Art and history lovers will enjoy the many museums and galleries in the area, including those that commemorate the region's indigenous Quinnipiac peoples and the Puritan settlers who arrived in Connecticut in the mid-seventeenth century. Hamden lies just outside the city of New Haven, ninety minutes from New York and two hours from Boston, which gives students plenty of opportunities for both internships and weekend excursions. The colorful New England foliage also draws large crowds of students in the fall.

Admissions

Average high school GPA:	3.4
Average freshman SAT verbal / math score:	556 / 579
Average freshman ACT score:	25
Application fee:	$45

Application deadlines:
2/1 (freshmen)
4/1 (transfer)

Total applicants:	10,313
Total accepted:	5,973 (58%)
Total accepted who enrolled:	1,425

Notification dates:
3/1 (freshmen)
continuous (transfer)

Students

Percentage of male / female students:	39% / 61%
Percentage of students from out of state:	70%
Percentage of students graduating in 4 years / 6 years:	60% / 68%

Money

Total endowment:	$155,156,000
Total tuition:	$27,600
Total cost with fees & expenses:	$39,920
Average financial aid package:	$15,338
Percentage of students who sought aid and received it:	65%
Percentage of students receiving financial aid:	54%

Also Check Out

Colby College

New York University

Northeastern University

University of Connecticut

Randolph College

2500 Rivermont Avenue
Lynchburg, VA 24503

(434) 947-8000
http://www.randolphcollege.edu/

BIG PERSPECTIVE

New name, new gender, same excellence

5 REASONS IT'S COOL

1. Be part of a new chapter in Randolph's history—as of 2007, **this former women's college has opened its doors to men.**

2. Students bond with their professors at this small school, where the **average class size is just twelve.**

3. Ring Week, Daisy Chain, Pumpkin Parade—**traditions are of the utmost importance** for this tight-knit group.

4. Go global! **Over 40 percent of students study abroad.**

5. The **quiet Virginia campus** is filled with gardens and gazebos, and the pastoral Blue Ridge Mountains are a short drive away.

The Basics

Public / private: private religious
Total enrollment / undergrads: 715 / 706
Campus setting: suburban
Students call it: Randolph
Students are called: Wildcats
Notable alums: Pearl S. Buck (Nobel Laureate, Literature), Candy Crowley (TV news correspondent), Blanche Lincoln (senator), Suzanne Patrick (deputy undersecretary of defense for industrial policy)

Welcome, Fellas!

As of July 2007, the institution formerly known as Randolph-Macon Women's College has a new name and a new addition to the student body: men! This is quite a change from the old rules, which prohibited men from walking around campus alone. Apart from the coed transformation, not much will change here. Academics are at the forefront, and the seminar-style courses are challenging across the board. Students are motivated and serious and treat the honor code with the utmost reverence. Professors teach all courses, demand hard work, and mentor their students. The student-to-faculty ratio is 8:1. There are twenty-five majors, and students may create their own courses of study. Biology, English, math, psychology, and history are most popular. Pre-professional programs are offered in law, medicine, education, and business, as well as a 3-2 programs in engineering and nursing. The Randolph curriculum emphasizes teaching from a global perspective and broadening horizons. Students are encouraged to study abroad, and over 40 percent do.

Ode to a Tree

In the 1960s, students began decorating a weeping cherry tree on campus with poems. In homage to their flower-power sisters, students still poem-ify the tree each spring.

Sisterhood—and Brotherhood

Aside from weekend jaunts to other universities, life at this former women's college is centered on campus. Students are required to live in one of the six palatial dorms that are, except for Webb, all mixed-year. Due to its central location, Main Hall (nicknamed "The Hilton") is one of the most popular choices, but there is no bad option. All the dorms have TV lounges and old fashioned "date parlors." Students are highly involved in the campus community and its many beloved traditions. In the Even/Odd Rivalry, for example, students play practical jokes on their rival class. And everyone looks forward to MacDoodle Day, when classes are cancelled and community-building activities take place. This tight-knit group has tons of school pride. Some find the campus a bit too insular, and those students who crave anonymity should probably look elsewhere. Lynchburg doesn't offer much excitement, but the college brings bands, comedians, and lecturers to campus on the weekends for events that are heavily attended. Almost 20 percent of the student body participates in varsity sports. Male teams include soccer, tennis, basketball, riding, and cross-country. Randolph also has a nationally recognized riding program that has won three ODAC championships since 2002.

Ah, Serenity!

Randolph's lovely campus is in a suburban neighborhood of Lynchburg, VA, near the James River and the Blue Ridge Mountains. Many of the buildings on campus have been around since the early days. From red-brick structures covered in wisteria to the open-air amphitheater of the Dell, students have plenty of places to study, reflect, or hang out with friends. The quaint city of Lynchburg doesn't have more than a few bars and coffeehouses, and some students tire of the rural isolation. The livelier college town of Charlottesville is only one hour north, and Washington, D.C, Richmond, and Virginia Beach are all within three or four hours.

Admissions

Average high school GPA:	3.4
Average freshman SAT verbal / math score:	596 / 564
Average freshman ACT score:	—
Application fee:	$35

Application deadlines:
3/1 (freshmen)
6/1 (transfer)
11/15 (early decision)

Total applicants:	745
Total accepted:	664 (89%)
Total accepted who enrolled:	187

Notification dates:
10/1 (freshmen)
continuous (transfer)
12/15 (early decision)

Acceptance rate for early decision applicants:	91%

Students

Percentage of male / female students:	— / —
Percentage of students from out of state:	60%
Percentage of students graduating in 4 years / 6 years:	— / 63%

Money

Total endowment:	$142,854,000
Total tuition:	$23,900
Total cost with fees & expenses:	$34,210
Average financial aid package:	$23,411
Percentage of students who sought aid and received it:	89%
Percentage of students receiving financial aid:	60%

Also Check Out

College of William & Mary

Randolph-Macon College

Smith College

University of Virginia

Randolph-Macon College

PO Box 5005
Ashland, VA 23005

(804) 752-7200
http://www.rmc.edu/

BIG PERSPECTIVE

Score a great education—or a touchdown.

5 REASONS IT'S COOL

1. Learn from **dedicated professors** who truly care about teaching.

2. No one's just a number here. In this **tight-knit community**, everybody knows your name.

3. **Sports, beer, and studying** take center stage for the well-balanced student body.

4. If you're into the Greek scene, you'll be right at home: **There's always a frat party going on.**

5. With the bars and restaurants of **downtown Richmond** only ten minutes away from the secluded campus, students get the best of both worlds.

The Basics

Public / private: private religious
Total enrollment / undergrads: 1,146 / 1,146
Campus setting: suburban
Students call it: RMC, Randolph-Macon
Students are called: Yellow Jackets
Notable alums: Macon Brock (founder, Dollar Tree), J. Rives Childs (diplomat), Beth Dunkenberger (women's college basketball coach), Randy Forbes (congressman), Gregory R. Smith (human rights activist)

Working Hard, Working Together

Founded by Methodists in 1830, Randolph-Macon College is an oft-overlooked liberal college in central Virginia. Not to be confused with the college formerly known as Randolph-Macon Women's College (now Randolph College), RMC is a small school with a focus on developing the minds and character of its students. It's a solid choice for those who want a broad, well-rounded education, but not for those who want specialized, pre-professional programs. Professors get high marks from students for their friendliness and dedication to teaching. Students work closely with their profs and their peers, and everyone takes academics seriously. During the First-Year Experience Program, freshmen work with two professors from different disciplines to explore the same topic. The college offers a number of enrichment programs, such as the Summer Undergraduate Research Fellowship (SURF), a program that allows students to explore wide-ranging topics, from child development to acid rain, and also requires them to write

Moving Through History

Although campus is dotted with historical buildings, it wasn't actually the first site of the college. Originally located in Boydton, near the North Carolina border, RMC moved to Ashland after the railroad link to Boydton was destroyed in the Civil War.

their own proposals and apply for their own grant money. J-term is a month in January set aside for internships or courses abroad.

The Busy Bees

Yellow Jackets may take academics seriously, but they don't neglect their social lives. Over 40 percent of the student body goes Greek, and frat parties dominate the weekends. Hailing mostly from Virginia, Pennsylvania, or other states along the Eastern Seaboard, students are generally smart, friendly, athletic, somewhat conservative, and largely upper class. Diversity is most present in the school's small international population, but students are quick to note the strong sense of inclusion everyone feels here. Most students are heavily involved in campus activities, which run the gamut from BBQs on the lawn to a Battle of the Bands at the Blackwell Center for the Performing Arts. Community service is popular, as is working for the school newspaper, the *Yellow Jacket*. No matter what the season, sports are the biggest deal on campus. Though the teams aren't powerhouses, they garner powerful support. Over half the students are involved in intramurals. The Brock Sports and Recreation Center, with its new weight rooms, indoor track, swimming pool, and climbing wall, attracts a lot of visitors. A small-town atmosphere prevails on campus, and while this means everyone knows you, it also means everyone feels supported.

Centrally Located in Central Virginia

RMC's small 117-acre campus sits in a wooded, suburban neighborhood in the historic town of Ashland, VA. Campus buzzes with events, including the annual Springfest, an outdoor concert at the Fountain Plaza. When students want a change of pace, the bars and cultural activities of downtown Richmond are just a ten-minute drive away. For those lacking wheels or looking to travel longer distances, the Amtrak station is conveniently located just yards away from campus. Less than two hours will get you to Virginia Beach and Washington, D.C., while Ashland's location in the heart of central Virginia allows for unfettered access to the natural beauty of the Blue Ridge Mountains.

Admissions

Average high school GPA:	3.3
Average freshman SAT writing / math / critical reading score:	542 / 549 / 553
Average freshman ACT score:	—
Application fee:	$30

Application deadlines:
3/1 (freshmen)
4/1 (transfer)
11/15 (early decision)

Total applicants:	2,878
Total accepted:	1,670 (58%)
Total accepted who enrolled:	398

Notification dates:
4/1 (freshmen)
5/1 (transfer)
12/1 (early decision)

Acceptance rate for early decision applicants:	81%

Students

Percentage of male / female students:	45% / 55%
Percentage of students from out of state:	31%
Percentage of students graduating in 4 years / 6 years:	62% / 74%

Money

Total endowment:	$116,545,594
Total tuition:	$24,710
Total cost with fees & expenses:	$33,040
Average financial aid package:	$17,459
Percentage of students who sought aid and received it:	82%
Percentage of students receiving financial aid:	57%

Also Check Out

College of William & Mary

James Madison University

Randolph College

University of Virginia

Reed College

3203 Southeast Woodstock Boulevard Portland, OR 97202	(503) 771-1112 http://www.reed.edu/

 **BIG BRAIN**    **BIG IDEA**    **BIG PERSPECTIVE**

And now for something *completely* different

5 REASONS IT'S COOL

1. If you like **your politics liberal and your academics demanding**, Reed might just be the school for you.

2. Fully 25 percent of grads eventually pursue PhDs, making Reed the largest per capita **producer of doctoral candidates** of any liberal arts college.

3. Reed students are a breed apart: They study hard, play hard, and have **tons of unique organizations and cool traditions.**

4. Portland is a **big city with a relaxed attitude** that offers music, arts, culture, and decent nightlife galore.

5. The wilderness of **the Pacific Northwest is at your doorstep**, whether for study or recreation.

The Basics

Public / private: private nonprofit
Total enrollment / undergrads: 1,436 / 1,407
Campus setting: urban
Students call it: Reed
Students are called: Reedies
Notable alums: James Beard (chef, food writer), Miles Davis (attended; musician), Barbara Ehrenreich (writer), Janet Fitch (novelist)

No Grades! Well, Sort Of . . .

The freshman academic experience at Reed is built around Humanities 110, a yearlong interdisciplinary program that focuses on important works from Western civilization. Other requirements include courses in math, physical education, and social sciences. Grades are deemphasized at Reed; students put much more stock in the long evaluations professors write for each student after a course has concluded. Unless a student receives a C, D, or F, she will only see the feedback (not the letter grade). Among the strongest departments are biology, chemistry, psychology, and English. Unusually for a liberal arts college, Reed also has an excellent physics program. Reed maintains a number of impressive academic partnerships with other institutions: There's a forestry program available at the Nicholas School of the Environment at Duke; a studio art program at the Pacific Northwest College of Art; a 3-2 engineering program with Columbia and the California Institute of Technology; and an oceanography program at Woods Hole. There are excellent facilities on campus; a $2 million improvement to the studio

Happy Endings

Every year, Reed's three-day Renn Fayre festival marks the end of spring classes. The event used to be a renaissance fair, but now the theme changes every year. The celebration, which includes insect-eating contests and a nude Slip 'N Slide, kicks off when the senior class marches together to hand in their theses to the registrar's office.

art facility was recently completed, and Reed has the only nuclear reactor in the country staffed predominantly by undergraduates. Classes in all departments are small, with the average course having fourteen students, and professors are engaging and friendly.

Atheism, Communism, and Free Love

Unofficially, Reed's motto is "atheism, communism, free love." Most Reed students are politically liberal; many are proudly nonconformist. The Honor Principle—an unwritten guide to behavior that basically suggests controlling oneself—is taken seriously by most students. In return, many exams are take-home, and a spirit of harmony pervades campus. Freshmen must live on campus, but after that, about a third of students move into the surrounding neighborhoods, where cheap housing is possible to find. There are no Greek houses or varsity sports. Club sports are popular, although students don't take them too seriously. Theme dorms let students bond over similar interests, such as watching cartoons in Running with Scissors or being outdoors in Outhouse. Most students are pleased with the facilities, which include a free pool hall, student darkrooms, band practice spaces, and a comic book library.

Cool Campus, Cool City, Cool Weather

Reed's 110-acre campus, located five miles from downtown Portland, features big lawns, small creeks, a protected wetlands area, and a visible commitment to environmental sustainability. Beaches, mountains, and high desert are all within a two-hour drive (Mount Hood, on which Reed maintains a ski cabin, is less than two hours away). Getting around Portland is relatively painless, and there's plenty of reason to get around. Artistic and cultural events abound, and there are tons of young people in the area. There's also a lot of rain. For this and other reasons, Portland is often compared to Seattle. Powell's, the largest independent bookstore in the world, is a popular spot for Reed students, as are the many music venues incubating up-and-coming acts.

Admissions

Average high school GPA:	3.9
Average freshman SAT writing / math / critical reading score:	690 / 670 / 705
Average freshman ACT score:	26
Application fee:	$40

Application deadlines:
1/15 (freshmen)
3/1 (transfer)
11/15 (early decision)

Total applicants:	3,049
Total accepted:	1,223 (40%)
Total accepted who enrolled:	376

Notification dates:
4/1 (freshmen)
5/15 (transfer)
12/15 (early decision)

Acceptance rate for early decision applicants:	60%

Students

Percentage of male / female students:	45% / 55%
Percentage of students from out of state:	87%
Percentage of students graduating in 4 years / 6 years:	52% / 73%

Money

Total endowment:	$390,227,000
Total tuition:	$34,300
Total cost with fees & expenses:	$44,480
Average financial aid package:	$27,257
Percentage of students who sought aid and received it:	100%
Percentage of students receiving financial aid:	47%

Also Check Out

Amherst College

Georgetown University

Oberlin College

University of California–Berkeley

University of Chicago

Rensselaer Polytechnic Institute

110 8th Street
Troy, NY 12180

(518) 276-6000
http://www.rpi.edu/

 **BIG BRAIN**

 **BIG PLAN**

 **BIG RESEARCH**

Changing the world, one gadget at a time

5 REASONS IT'S COOL

1. Rensselaer has one of the **most respected engineering programs** in the country.

2. Academics here are tough, but students are rewarded with **top professors and incredible research opportunities.**

3. The **inventor of email?** A Rensselaer grad. The inventor of the microprocessor? Yep, he went here too. So did the engineer for the Brooklyn Bridge, and so on.

4. The campus has been dubbed one of the **most well-connected campuses** in the United States.

5. It's an **easy drive to New York City**, Montreal, Boston, the Adirondacks, and the tons of colleges nearby.

The Basics

Public / private: private nonprofit
Total enrollment / undergrads: 7,433 / 5,193
Campus setting: suburban
Students call it: Rensselaer
Students are called: Redhawks
Notable alums: Myles Brand (president, NCAA), Marshall Brain (founder, HowStuffWorks.com), Bobby Farrelly (filmmaker), Ivar Giaever (Nobel Laureate, Physics), Theodore Judah (designer, transcontinental railroad), Raymond Tomlinson (inventor, email), Edward Zander (CEO, Motorola)

Get Ready to Work

Most students come to Rensselaer to study engineering. The engineering program here is one of the nation's oldest and most respected, and it's also known for being one of the toughest. The institute offers a total of 140 degree programs through its five schools of architecture, engineering, humanities and social sciences, management and technology, and science. Students may also pursue multidisciplinary studies in the area of information technology. There are many opportunities for students to pursue research and to gain real-world experience through the co-op program. Upperclassmen work one semester and one summer in their chosen fields. Rensselaer boasts 450 tenured faculty members, all of whom have strong reputations as researchers, and the student-to-faculty ratio is 15:1. The institute recently scored a $3.2 million grant from the National Science Foundation for its interdisciplinary fuel cell

Crackpot Ideas

Each year, twenty creative students at Rensselaer enroll in Inventor's Studio, a class in which they are challenged to come up with brilliant, patentable inventions. Past ideas include the Automatic Double Dutch Turner, a device that turns two jump ropes, and the Microinfuser, a machine you can use to administer drugs to yourself. Rensselaer alums dream up methods and technologies that change the world.

science, engineering, and entrepreneurship program and opened a $20 million research facility specifically for the study of renewable fuel systems and energy conservation.

The Ratio of Fun to More Fun

Students here are nerdy and proud of it. They're less psyched about the dearth of girls. Like most tech schools, Rensselaer has far more men (75 percent) than women (25 percent). The imbalance is so notorious that most students simply refer to it as "the ratio." Luckily, the institute offers plenty of on-campus activities to keep the gender-disparity blues at bay. The thirty-five fraternities and sororities play a big role in the social scene, although parties tend to be pretty low-key. More than 160 student clubs and organizations are offered, including ballroom dancing, drama, a student-run newspaper called the *Polytechnic*, an astrophysical society, a game development club, and a model railroad society. All organizations are run out of the Rensselaer Union, a unique student-run center. Students take advantage of on-campus resources such as the Mueller Fitness Center, with its weight rooms, tennis courts, and swimming pools, and RPI Playhouse, which is home to a wide array of theater performances.

Capital Region

Rensselaer sits on 275 beautiful acres on a hill overlooking both the city of Troy and the Hudson River. New York's capital city, Albany, is only nine miles away, while the resort of Saratoga Springs is a little more than thirty miles away. The area is home to many other colleges, including Union College, SUNY–University at Albany, Siena College, the College of Saint Rose, Russell Sage College, and Skidmore College, which means that there's always a good time to be had *somewhere* nearby. The Capital District also sports a large mega-mall and plenty of parks with hiking and biking trails, and the Adirondacks offer more hardcore outdoor recreation opportunities. New York City is about two hours away by train or car.

Admissions

Average high school GPA:	4.0
Average freshman SAT writing / math / critical reading score:	619 / 690 / 635
Average freshman ACT score:	25
Application fee:	$70

Application deadlines:
1/15 (freshmen)
— (transfer)
11/1 (early decision)

Total applicants:	6,875
Total accepted:	4,574 (67%)
Total accepted who enrolled:	1,270

Notification dates:
3/15 (freshmen)
continuous (transfer)
12/31 (early decision)

Acceptance rate for early decision applicants:	84%

Students

Percentage of male / female students:	75% / 25%
Percentage of students from out of state:	55%
Percentage of students graduating in 4 years / 6 years:	61% / 81%

Money

Total endowment:	$702,712,000
Total tuition:	$32,600
Total cost with fees & expenses:	$45,181
Average financial aid package:	$26,650
Percentage of students who sought aid and received it:	86%
Percentage of students receiving financial aid:	67%

Also Check Out

Case Western Reserve University

Massachusetts Institute of Technology

New York University

Purdue University

Rhode Island School of Design

2 College Street
Providence, RI 02903

(401) 454-6100
http://www.risd.edu/

Get your creative juices flowing.

5 REASONS IT'S COOL

1. Want to use your art skills to better the world? RISD emphasizes **environmental sustainability and the practical side of art.**

2. The **college art library** displays work by students and faculty, as well as by Monet, Picasso, and many Roman and Egyptian artists.

3. Around **90 percent of RISD alumni work** in fields related to what they studied in school.

4. Students have access to **Brown University**'s classes and other resources.

5. The European Honors Program allows juniors and seniors to **study in Rome,** learn Italian, and soak up the art and architecture.

The Basics

Public / private: private nonprofit
Total enrollment / undergrads: 2,259 / 1,863
Campus setting: urban
Students call it: RISD (pronounced RIZ-Dee)
Notable alums: Martha Coolidge (film director), Martin Mull (comedian, painter), Seth MacFarlane (creator, *Family Guy*), Nicole Miller (fashion designer), Gus van Sant (film director)

All Day in the Atelier

RISD students are extremely dedicated to their art, which helps them handle the significant workload. Freshmen must take the year-long Foundation Studies Program, which includes both artistic and critical analysis and features classes in drawing, design, art history, and writing. Fourteen liberal arts courses are required, and they are larger and more lecture-oriented than the close-knit studio classes. Once the foundational coursework is finished, students choose from sixteen undergraduate majors. The most popular are illustration, architecture, and graphic design. The school also offers majors in ceramics, film/animation/video, jewelry, and glass. With a student-to-faculty ratio of 10:1, students can expect lots of face time with their professors, and average class size falls at about thirteen students. Another plus: There is a six-week winter term during which small groups of students can travel with faculty to countries such as New Zealand, Egypt, and India. RISD invests heavily in career services, sponsoring professional development programs, seminars, and individual counseling sessions.

Thinking Outside the Microwave

Imagine a kitchen with pop-up dishwashers, retractable burners, and countertop waste disposal. That's just what a team of RISD students and faculty did in the early 1990s. Dissatisfied with the typical residential kitchen, which requires bending, reaching, and kneeling, they designed a Universal Kitchen in which heights and depths can be adjusted for each chef. Their idea was so well received, Maytag bought exclusive rights. Who says *starving* and *artist* have to go together?

State-of-the-Art School

Although studio work tends to consume students, those who find time to socialize outside class have options ranging from the popular gay pride alliance to the many lectures and gallery talks sponsored by the school. One of the most eagerly anticipated events is the Artists' Ball, where students compete for best costume prizes. There is no Greek system, but that's the way students like it. Those longing for frat-esque events can head to parties at Brown or to area dance clubs. RISD has a diverse student body, with international students making up 11 percent of the student population and Asian Americans 14 percent. Men aren't as well-represented, constituting only about 34 percent of the student body, and most undergrads come from the upper end of the class scale. All students live on campus their first year, but most move off afterward. While on campus, they're required to buy meal plans. Students applaud Carr Haus, a student-run café, and the Met, the main dining hall, which features a vegan bar, a stir-fry station, and a bakery.

The Crossroads of Art and History

Set on top of a hill in Providence—the second-largest city in New England after Boston—RISD lies in the more upscale section of the city, a short walk away from downtown Providence. Most buildings are tall colonial and Victorian structures. Originally constructed in the eighteenth and nineteenth centuries, they reflect the school's proximity to the town's historic district, where picturesque, brick-lined walkways flanked with lampposts are lined with a gorgeous mix of Greek revival, colonial, and Italianate buildings. Freshman dorms and the main dining hall are located in the redbrick Quad building, where students have access to the campus computer network and communal studios. Students seeking a breather from city life can travel eleven miles to the RISD Farm, known as Tillinghast, which has a beach, woods, and a field. Boston is nearby on the train, and New York City is not too far in the opposite direction. Martha's Vineyard, Nantucket, and lots of ski resorts are also within a few hours.

Admissions

Average high school GPA:	3.3
Average freshman SAT verbal / math score:	592 / 625
Average freshman ACT score:	—
Application fee:	$50

Application deadlines:
2/15 (freshmen)
3/15 (transfer)
12/15 (early action)

Total applicants:	2,557
Total accepted:	854 (33%)
Total accepted who enrolled:	422

Notification dates:
4/1 (freshmen)
5/1 (transfer)
1/25 (early action)

Acceptance rate for early action applicants:	49%

Students

Percentage of male / female students:	34% / 66%
Percentage of students from out of state:	94%
Percentage of students graduating in 4 years / 6 years:	78% / 90%

Money

Total endowment:	$293,293,069
Total tuition:	$32,858
Total cost with fees & expenses:	$42,978
Average financial aid package:	$17,000
Percentage of students who sought aid and received it:	69%
Percentage of students receiving financial aid:	49%

Also Check Out

Cooper Union for the Advancement of Science and Art

Parsons, The New School for Design

SUNY–Fashion Institute of Technology

Rhodes College

2000 North Parkway
Memphis, TN 38112

(901) 843-3000
http://www.rhodes.edu/

BIG PERSPECTIVE

Where every student is a Rhodes scholar

5 REASONS IT'S COOL

1. Looking for the **classic small college experience** with big-city amenities and a dash of down-home Tennessee flavor?

2. Rhodes **professors really care** about teaching.

3. **The Honor System is a source of school pride:** All students pledge to act honorably and treat others with respect.

4. **Students love Memphis**, home not only to the blues but also to great nightlife and Graceland, Elvis Presley's grand estate.

5. **Over 95 percent of grads applying to business schools are accepted**, and the med school acceptance rates are similarly impressive.

The Basics

Public / private: private religious
Total enrollment / undergrads: 1,696 / 1,687
Campus setting: suburban
Students call it: Rhodes
Students are called: Lynxes
Notable alums: Dixie Carter (actress), Abe Fortas (U.S. Supreme Court justice), Charlaine Harris (writer)

Book Smarts

Rhodes emphasizes a "cover all the bases" liberal arts curriculum. All Rhodes students take one of two four-semester courses: Search for Values explores important texts in Western history, while Life: Then and Now draws on religious and philosophical texts. Rhodes has more than twenty departmental majors, seven interdisciplinary majors, and close to thirty minors, including computer science. Foundation requirements develop communication skills; students fulfill the requirements by taking courses in such liberal arts subjects as literature and a foreign language. There's also a senior seminar in every major, and students must execute a for-credit project that connects their academic work to the real world. Biology, business, and English are the most popular majors; the campus's science facilities are excellent, and the international relations program is also very strong. Half of Rhodes students study abroad, and 60 percent do an internship. Professors, 96 percent of whom have PhDs, take the time to get to know their students. The majority of classes have around twenty students.

The Name Game

You name it, Rhodes has probably been called it. Rhodes was named the Masonic University of Tennessee when it was founded in 1848. Two years later, the name was changed to Montgomery Masonic College. After a stint as Stewart College, the name was changed again to Southwestern Presbyterian University and eventually to just Southwestern. This name lasted until 1945, when it was changed to Southwestern at Memphis. At last, in 1984, the school was renamed Rhodes College in honor of Nalle Rhodes, a former university president.

Get up and Go

Rhodes students maintain busy schedules, to say the least. Volunteering is popular among this engaged, worldly, and friendly bunch: More than 80 percent of Rhodes students do some type of community service. The Rhodes Center for Academic Research and Education through Service (CARES) offers students and faculty the opportunity to connect intellectual endeavor with service. One in four students plays in intercollegiate varsity sport, and nearly 70 percent participate in intramural sports. All told, there are ninety student organizations on campus, which sponsor upward of 250 events per year, from theater productions to mock trials to weekly outings with the film society. Freshmen and sophomores are required to live on campus, in traditional dorms, town houses, and theme housing, and about half of juniors and seniors do so too. The Greek system claims about half the student body as members. And a final caveat: The odds of finding love at Rhodes are better for guys than girls, as the Joe-to-Jane ratio is 2:3.

No Singin' the Blues Here

Rhodes's hundred-acre campus is located in Memphis's historic district. Many of the campus's Gothic-style buildings are on the National Register of Historic Places. Students sweat off any academic stress at the Bryan Campus Life Center, home to a gymnasium, indoor track, the Lynx Lair food court, and the McCallum Ballroom, which is used for dances and other special events. Within walking distance of campus are the Memphis Brooks Museum of Art and the Memphis Zoo. As the birthplace of rock and roll and the unofficial home of the blues, Memphis has several attractions devoted to music, including Beale Street, Graceland, and the Rock 'n' Soul Museum. Nashville and its music scene is just a three-hour car ride away.

Admissions

Average high school GPA:	3.85
Average freshman SAT verbal / math score:	639 / 630
Average freshman ACT score:	26
Application fee:	$45

Application deadlines:
continuous (freshmen)
2/1 (transfer)
11/1 (early decision)

Total applicants:	3,786
Total accepted:	1,873 (49%)
Total accepted who enrolled:	452

Notification dates:
4/1 (freshmen)
4/1 (transfer)
12/1 (early decision)

Acceptance rate for early decision applicants:	73%

Students

Percentage of male / female students:	41% / 59%
Percentage of students from out of state:	73%
Percentage of students graduating in 4 years / 6 years:	77% / 81%

Money

Total endowment:	$222,890,000
Total tuition:	$28,802
Total cost with fees & expenses:	$37,196
Average financial aid package:	$25,184
Percentage of students who sought aid and received it:	84%
Percentage of students receiving financial aid:	39%

Also Check Out

Duke University

Emory University

Northwestern University

Sewanee: The University of the South

Vanderbilt University

Rice University

6100 Main Street, PO Box 1892
Houston, TX 77251

(713) 348-0000
http://www.rice.edu/

 **BIG BRAIN**

 **BIG RESEARCH**

Deep in the academic heart of Texas

5 REASONS IT'S COOL

1. Rice students get an **Ivy League–caliber education without the Ivy League price.**

2. The university prides itself on the **diversity of its student body:** students rub elbows daily with people of all races, classes, ethnicities, religions, and sexual orientations.

3. At 5:1, Rice has **one of the lowest student-to-faculty ratios** around.

4. With nearly $4 billion in the bank, Rice has the **fifth-largest per-student endowment** in the country.

5. The **elite architecture program** offers undergrads one of the most rigorous and prestigious educations in architecture anywhere.

The Basics

Public / private: private nonprofit
Total enrollment / undergrads: 5,119 / 3,049
Campus setting: urban
Students call it: Rice
Students are called: Owls
Notable alums: Lance Berkman (pro baseball player), Robert Curl (Nobel Laureate, Chemistry), Alberto Gonzales (U.S. attorney general), Howard Hughes (attended; industrialist), Ricky Pierce (pro basketball player), Shannon Walker (astronaut)

Trailblazing Through Academia

Academics are serious business at Rice, which boasts more National Merit Scholars than any other university and the highest percentage of National Science Fellowships per capita. Most classes have fifteen students or fewer, while labs generally have fewer than ten. And with 91 percent of faculty holding PhDs, students can rest easy knowing they're learning from the best of the best, especially since so few courses have graduate student teaching assistants. Rice is a trailblazer in many areas of research, including artificial hearts, nanotechnology, space science, and structural chemical analysis. In addition to the sciences, Rice also has a stellar music program and one of the most prestigious undergraduate architectural programs in the country. There are so many options at Rice that students often complain they have a tough time settling on just one major, which is why roughly two-thirds of students end up double majoring.

Make a Run for It

At 10 P.M. on the 13th, 26th, and 31st of each month, a group of students known as the Baker 13 streaks through campus clad in nothing but shaving cream. The streakers run across campus to visit every residential college, chanting the Baker 13 cheer: "Join us! Join us!" For those students who forget what day or time it is, the streakers leave a reminder by pressing their shaving cream-covered bodies onto each college's windows and doors.

Building Communities

About 65 percent of Rice students live in one of the nine campus dorms, called residential colleges. Students eat, sleep, study, and hang out primarily in their college. These colleges are the cornerstone of students' Rice experience, especially since there are no campus fraternities or sororities. Not surprisingly, friendly rivalries develop between colleges, which play out during events such as student orientation and the annual Beer Bike contest—part bike race, part drink-a-thon. And since students are randomly assigned to their colleges, everyone gets to mix and mingle with people from different racial, ethnic, religious, and socioeconomic backgrounds. All Rice students come together to cheer on the Division I football and baseball teams, though, and to participate in the more than two hundred campus clubs and organizations.

An Urban Oasis

Despite its location just blocks from Houston's Museum District and the world-renowned Texas Medical Center, Rice has the tucked-away feel of a suburban campus. Interspersed between the university's quadrangles of Mediterranean-style buildings are acres of greens, which are usually covered with students sprawled out in the Texas sun. When students want to head off campus, they don't have to go far. The trendy Rice Village neighborhood is stocked with shops, bars, and restaurants. Many students also enjoy running, biking, and picnicking in nearby Hermann Park, which also features a zoo, a museum, and outdoor theatrical productions. Those looking for pro sports, theaters, and nightlife can hop on the Houston METRO light rail, which stops just outside the campus gates.

Admissions

Average high school GPA:	—
Average freshman SAT writing / math / critical reading score:	685 / 710 / 691
Average freshman ACT score:	26
Application fee:	$50

Application deadlines:
1/10 (freshmen)
3/15 (transfer)
11/1 (early decision)
12/1 (early action)

Total applicants:	8,776
Total accepted:	2,080 (24%)
Total accepted who enrolled:	712

Notification dates:
4/1 (freshmen)
6/1 (transfer)
12/15 (early decision)
2/10 (early action)

Acceptance rate for early action/early decision applicants:	28% / 30%

Students

Percentage of male / female students:	51% / 49%
Percentage of students from out of state:	47%
Percentage of students graduating in 4 years / 6 years:	76% / 90%

Money

Total endowment:	$3,990,000,000
Total tuition:	$28,400
Total cost with fees & expenses:	$39,150
Average financial aid package:	$22,048
Percentage of students who sought aid and received it:	99%
Percentage of students receiving financial aid:	35%

Also Check Out

Duke University

Georgetown University

Northwestern University

The University of Texas at Austin

University of Pennsylvania

Rochester Institute of Technology

One Lomb Memorial Drive
Rochester, NY 14623

(585) 475-2411
http://www.rit.edu/

 **BIG CHOICE**

 BIG JOB

 **BIG RESEARCH**

RIT wants to hook you up . . . with a great job.

5 REASONS IT'S COOL

1. **Degrees are available in a number of unique areas,** such as biotechnology, film and animation, and microelectronic engineering.

2. RIT is internationally recognized for its **co-op program,** one of the largest and oldest in the country.

3. Students study abroad in countries **such as Japan, Scotland, Russia, Japan, China, and South Africa.**

4. RIT is unique for its **high percentage of deaf and hearing-impaired students.**

5. Park Point, the **brand new apartment complex and bookstore,** is one of many improvements administrators are making on campus.

The Basics

Public / private: private nonprofit
Total enrollment / undergrads: 15,557 / 13,140
Campus setting: suburban
Students call it: Rochester Institute, RIT
Students are called: Tigers
Notable alums: Bernie Boston (photojournalist), Daniel Carp (chairman, Eastman Kodak), Tom Curley (president and CEO, Associated Press), N. Katherine Hayles (literary critic)

Twenty-first-Century Science

Over two hundred degree programs are available through RIT's eight colleges, but the emphasis is on applied sciences. Computer science, art and design, and engineering are among the strongest programs. Business and photography are also popular, and excellent programs in American crafts provide training in ceramics, woodworking, glass, metals, and jewelry making. The school has also instituted a degree in new media, which combines studies in printing, graphic design, and information technology. Some of the more unusual degrees include film and animation, imaging science, microelectronic engineering, software engineering, and biotechnology, which benefits from a recently completed education and training facility. The core curriculum gives students a foundation in liberal arts with coursework in the humanities, social sciences, writing, and literature. Students are allowed to jump right in by taking courses in their major early on. Undergrad research is a priority, and juniors and seniors in many

Maybe Fractions Weren't Their Thing

The RIT campus is divided into two sections. One has the academic buildings, and the other has the residence halls and apartments. Connecting these two sections is a wide walkway affectionately known as the Quarter Mile, although it actually measures only a third of a mile.

programs participate in co-ops, through which they get paychecks and hands-on experience.

Now *This* Is College Life

RIT students represent all fifty states and almost one hundred countries, although nearly half are from New York. The skewed male-to-female ratio of 7:3 is typical of engineering schools in the United States, but the administration is taking steps to recruit more female students. Given the mix of art, engineering, business, and science students, the campus atmosphere is fairly diverse. Students have plenty of distractions to choose from with numerous student clubs and organizations, including an ambulance corps, a magazine, TV and radio stations, an interfaith center, and a small Greek system. Sports are also popular, and among the twenty-three varsity teams, hockey is the biggest draw. The gigantic new recreational complex and fitness center features concerts and other performances. RIT offers a generous number of housing options, and over 60 percent of students take advantage. The many comfortable living options include houses for the small Greek population, special-interest residence halls, lifestyle floors, and on-campus apartments.

Brick City

"Brick City," as campus is otherwise known, is a collection of brick buildings sitting on 1,300 acres of wooded wetlands in Rochester, New York, a city that also hosts six other colleges. The city is packed with shopping options and cultural fare, including the local philharmonic orchestra, George Eastman House, several art museums and galleries, and a leading professional theater center. Students who prefer the great outdoors can choose from several nearby parks, including the Highland Botanical Park, Durand-Eastman Park, and Ontario Beach Park. A number of annual festivals are held in the city, including an international jazz festival, arts and crafts festivals, and two film festivals.

Admissions

Average high school GPA:	3.7
Average freshman SAT verbal / math score:	587 / 624
Average freshman ACT score:	25
Application fee:	$50

Application deadlines:
2/1 (freshmen)
— (transfer)
12/1 (early decision)

Total applicants:	10,219
Total accepted:	6,593 (65%)
Total accepted who enrolled:	2,370

Notification dates:
continuous (freshmen)
continuous (transfer)
1/15 (early decision)

Acceptance rate for early decision applicants:	76%

Students

Percentage of male / female students:	69% / 31%
Percentage of students from out of state:	47%
Percentage of students graduating in 4 years / 6 years:	— / 64%

Money

Total endowment:	$572,990,473
Total tuition:	$24,627
Total cost with fees & expenses:	$34,659
Average financial aid package:	$17,100
Percentage of students who sought aid and received it:	88%
Percentage of students receiving financial aid:	53%

Also Check Out

Case Western Reserve University

Cooper Union for the Advancement of Science and Art

Massachusetts Institute of Technology

Purdue University

Rensselaer Polytechnic Institute

Rollins College

1000 Holt Avenue
Winter Park, FL 32789

(407) 646-2000
http://www.rollins.edu/

BIG PERSPECTIVE

Small school, sunny days

5 REASONS IT'S COOL

1. **Small classes, caring professors, and no TAs** make for a personalized and challenging educational experience.

2. **Sun, surf, sand, and Disney World** are only a short drive away.

3. Between the lovely **architecture and the stunning views of Lake Virginia**, campus feels more like a villa than a college.

4. Take advantage of the **many international study opportunities** including study abroad, internship, and fieldwork programs.

5. The five-year Accelerated Management Program offers a **dual BA/MBA**.

The Basics

Public / private: private nonprofit
Total enrollment / undergrads: 2,454 / 1,720
Campus setting: suburban
Students call it: Rollins, Rolly
Students are called: Tars
Notable alums: Donald Cram (Nobel Laureate, Chemistry), Meg Crofton (president, Walt Disney World Resort), Olcott Deming (U.S. ambassador), Buddy Ebsen (actor), Jack Kramer (pro tennis player)

Everything (Academic) Under the Sun

One of the South's stronger liberal arts schools, Rollins offers an interdisciplinary education in a sunny Florida setting. The Rolly experience begins with the College Conference Program—small freshmen seminars that span the disciplines. The extensive, sometimes groan-inducing general education requirements include three terms of physical education. But minor complaints about the curriculum disappear when the conversation turns to the dedicated faculty. According to students, professors don't just know your name, they know your life story—hardly a surprise, considering the 11:1 student-to-faculty ratio. The high-tech Bush Science Center has thirty-eight laboratories open to undergrads, and the modern Cornell Campus Center is a hub for student activity. Rollins boasts strong programs in psychology, English, and the arts. Pre-professional options include pre-law, pre-med, and a well-respected five-year BA/MBA business program. All students are encouraged to pursue independent research projects and participate in the

Crazy like a Fox

One of Rolly's most beloved traditions is Fox Day, when the president signals the cancellation of classes by placing a statue of a fox on Mills Lawn. No one knows when the fateful day will arrive, but when the chapel bell rings, students know it's time to put away their books and head for the beach.

faculty-mentored Rollins Summer Research Program. High-achievers may be selected for the Honors Degree Program, which provides access to special seminars and a living/learning community.

College Campus or Tropical Paradise?

Often drawing comparisons to a country club, the Rollins campus has stucco buildings, manicured lawns, an outdoor pool, and picturesque views of Lake Virginia. All-Campus Events (ACEs) bring in live music, lectures, and comedians. Theater productions, "dive-in" movies at the campus pool, and waterskiing rank among the most popular pastimes. Tars enjoy a good party, and the Greek scene attracts about 40 percent of the student body. Alcohol and drugs are prevalent, although the administration has been cracking down of late. There's a palpable sense of community at Rolly, but critics are quick to point out the homogenous nature of the student body, which skews white, wealthy, and well-coiffed. You won't see students wearing sweatpants to class. Polo shirts and designer handbags are the norm. Finding affordable housing nearby is difficult, but 40 percent of juniors and seniors move off-campus anyway.

From Disney to Daytona

Rolly is situated in the quaint town of Winter Park, five minutes from the bright lights of Orlando. The city has some cultural offerings, a decent nightlife, and, of course, a bevy of theme parks, most notably Universal Studios, Disney World, Sea World, and Discovery Cove. The University of Central Florida and Stetson are nearby, and so are a selection of beaches. Daytona and Cocoa Beaches are an hour away, and Tampa and Miami are two- and three-hour-drives away, respectively.

Admissions

Average high school GPA:	3.4
Average freshman SAT verbal / math score:	583 / 595
Average freshman ACT score:	24
Application fee:	$40

Application deadlines:
2/15 (freshmen)
4/15 (transfer)
11/15 (early decision)

Total applicants:	2,998
Total accepted:	1,658 (55%)
Total accepted who enrolled:	501

Notification dates:
4/1 (freshmen)
continuous (transfer)
12/15 (early decision)

Acceptance rate for early decision applicants:	70%

Students

Percentage of male / female students:	40% / 60%
Percentage of students from out of state:	47%
Percentage of students graduating in 4 years / 6 years:	49% / 63%

Money

Total endowment:	$310,300,000
Total tuition:	$30,420
Total cost with fees & expenses:	$41,162
Average financial aid package:	$29,865
Percentage of students who sought aid and received it:	93%
Percentage of students receiving financial aid:	42%

Also Check Out

Emory University

Florida State University

Stetson University

Tulane University

University of Florida

The University of Miami

Rose-Hulman Institute of Technology

5500 Wabash Avenue
Terre Haute, IN 47803

(812) 877-1511
http://www.rose-hulman.edu/

BIG PLAN

BIG RESEARCH

Engineering success, one student at a time

5 REASONS IT'S COOL

1. Rose-Hulman has one of the **top-ranked undergraduate engineering schools** in the country.

2. **Ready to get focused?** Degree options here are limited to math, science, and engineering.

3. The **unique biomedical engineering program** prepares students for careers in one of the most rapidly growing fields in science.

4. The Rose-Hulman Ventures program hooks students up with **top-notch internships.**

5. The **low student-to-faculty ratio** ensures that students get lots of personal attention from their professors.

The Basics

Public / private: private nonprofit
Total enrollment / undergrads: 1,963 / 1,862
Campus setting: suburban
Students call it: Rose-Hulman
Students are called: Fightin' Engineers
Notable alums: Frederick Garry (jet designer), John Hostettler (congressman), Abe Silverstein (center director, NASA), Leroy Wilson (president, AT&T)

Adventures in Engineering

Who says you have to go to a big school to get top-notch training in the sciences and technology? At Rose-Hulman, students can immerse themselves in a small-college community while taking advantage of state-of-the-art programs in engineering, science, and math. A 12:1 student-to-faculty ratio keeps classes small, and students get a lot of face time with their professors. Not surprisingly, most students major in engineering, although Rose-Hulman offers several different tracks within the department: chemical, computer, electrical, mechanical, and software engineering. The biomedical engineering track has become especially popular in recent years. When not in the classroom, students intern through Rose-Hulman Ventures, a well-funded internship program that gives students valuable working experience in the real world. Ninety-nine percent of all faculty members hold terminal degrees, and 100 percent of them play multiple roles, acting as professor, researcher, author, inventor, outside consultant, or all of the above.

CANDLES in the Wind

Terre Haute is a small but thriving town housing several universities and a variety of cultural museums. One of those is the CANDLES museum for the Children of Auschwitz Nazi Deadly Lab Experiment Survivors. In 2003 the CANDLES museum was destroyed by a fire set by a neo-Nazi, and many priceless works of art and artifacts were forever lost. The museum has since been rebuilt through fundraising drives and donations.

Science In, Science Out

The vast majority of Rose-Hulman students hail from the Midwest, and roughly 80 percent are male. The administration is currently working hard to increase the number of women on campus as well as the number of students from other regions of the country and the globe. Many students participate in the popular Army and Air Force ROTC programs. The institute assigns students to the nine residence halls based on grade and gender; some residence halls feature amenities such as convenience stores, laundry facilities, and even barber shops. There are eighty student organizations, including the gun club, French club, an outdoors club, media clubs, and, of course, multiple engineering clubs—there's even a robotic club. The campus radio station is WMHD 90.7 FM, "The Monkey," and the school's weekly newspaper, the *Rose Thorn*, is run entirely by students. Students choose from eight fraternities and three sororities and participate in a number of outreach programs geared to high school students, such as the Homework Hotline and Operation Catapult, a summer science camp.

A Pocket of Culture

Terre Haute may be a small, Midwestern town, but don't equate "small and Midwestern" with "nothing to do." Students enjoy taking in live theater performances and attending film series at the Community Theatre of Terre Haute, one of the oldest theaters in Indiana. Local museums include the Clabber Girl Museum and Country Store, where visitors learn all about baking powder, and the Sheldon Swope Art Museum, which features late nineteenth- and early twentieth-century works by Thomas Hart Benton, Andy Warhol, and Edward Hopper. The National Road Heritage Trail and the Fairbanks Park River Walk offer plenty of fresh air and greenery. Terre Haute is also home to other colleges and universities, including Indiana State University and its eleven thousand students. The nearest big cities, Indianapolis and Chicago, are 60 miles away and 165 miles away, respectively.

Admissions

Average high school GPA:	—
Average freshman SAT writing / math / critical reading score:	598 / 677 / 621
Average freshman ACT score:	26
Application fee:	$40
Application deadlines: 3/1 (freshmen) — (transfer)	
Total applicants:	3,059
Total accepted:	2,205 (72%)
Total accepted who enrolled:	525
Notification dates: continuous (freshmen) continuous (transfer)	

Students

Percentage of male / female students:	81% / 19%
Percentage of students from out of state:	57%
Percentage of students graduating in 4 years / 6 years:	73% / 82%

Money

Total endowment:	$190,686,519
Total tuition:	$28,530
Total cost with fees & expenses:	$38,364
Average financial aid package:	$22,011
Percentage of students who sought aid and received it:	79%
Percentage of students receiving financial aid:	66%

Also Check Out

Case Western Reserve University

Harvey Mudd College

Purdue University

Rensselaer Polytechnic Institute

Rochester Institute of Technology

University of Illinois at Urbana-Champaign

Rutgers University

605 Davidson Road, Room 202
Piscataway, NJ 08854

(732) 932-4636
http://www.rutgers.edu/

BIG CHOICE

A world of choices

5 REASONS IT'S COOL

1. Rutgers offers **four thousand courses** between its three campuses.

2. The administration **celebrates the diversity of its student body** by bringing top speakers to campus and holding conferences on race relations.

3. **Two honors programs** offer students personalized advising, funding for research, and special honors seminars.

4. The **Ecological Preserve and Natural Teaching Area** features 370 acres of old-growth forests.

5. This university boasts a **prestigious training program for pharmacists.**

The Basics

Public / private: public state
Total enrollment / undergrads: 34,392 / 26,691
Campus setting: urban
Students call it: Rutgers
Students are called: Knights
Notable alums: Just Blaze (hip-hop producer), Stanley Norman Cohen (geneticist), Calista Flockhart (actress), Milton Friedman (Nobel Laureate, Economics), James Gandolfini (actor), Natalie Morales (*Today Show* correspondent), Robert Pinsky (U.S. poet laureate)

Around the World in 80 Ways

At New Brunswick-Piscataway, Rutgers's largest campus, there are twelve colleges focused on fields such as environmental sciences, nursing, theater and visual arts, and social work. The schools offer almost a hundred majors, including many interdisciplinary ones. The pharmacy program is a particularly well-respected and popular choice. Rutgers' size makes TA-taught classes a fact of life for most, with professors leading roughly 70 percent of undergraduate courses. All freshman are required to take an Expository Writing course in which they learn to write lengthy academic essays. Other distribution requirements tend to be flexible given the vast list of courses, which span topics such as obesity, sustainable agriculture, Cleopatra, and immigrant workers' rights. For those seeking to broaden their academic horizons, Rutgers offers more than forty study-abroad programs in twenty countries, including Brazil, Namibia, and South Korea.

No More Chicken

A giant felt rooster named Chanticleer (a fighting rooster featured in medieval fables and later appropriated by Geoffrey Chaucer for his *Canterbury Tales*) was Rutgers' mascot for thirty years, but after as many years of mockery, he was superseded by the Scarlet Knight in 1955.

Making a Difference

Although over 90 percent of students hail from New Jersey, Rutgers students are extremely ethnically and economically diverse. Asian Americans make up 23 percent, Latino students 8 percent, African Americans 9 percent, and international students 2 percent of the student body. The New Jersey Folk Festival, a student event that highlights a particular music and cultural tradition each year, features a cappella concerts, food, and dancing lessons. Community service programs are also popular, including a neighborhood relations program that matches students up with seniors and disabled residents, and a project that bring seniors and students together to watch classic films. The over four hundred other extracurriculars include a cryptography club and a Minority Investors Network. While there are many commuters, roughly half the student body lives on campus. There are a variety of dorm options.

By the Banks

Set in suburban New Brunswick, Piscataway, Rutgers' main campus, is divided into five smaller campuses at the edge of the Raritan River. Students praise the Cook College Campus in particular for its vast green spaces and trees. This campus also has an outdoor roller rink, greenhouses, a sheep barn and piggery, and horse stables. Rutgers's main sister campus in Newark offers a more urban feel, while its Camden campus lies ten minutes across the river from Philadelphia. A somewhat unreliable bus system links each of the campuses. Just as Rutgers locations run the rural-to-urban gamut, the buildings on Rutgers's sprawling campuses represent a wide range of architectural styles. The oldest building, Old Queens, with its ornate white cupola, wrought-iron entrance gate, and stained-glass windows, is in the Federal style, while the college's first dorm, Winants Hall, is a stately neoclassical design. Newer architectural additions tend to embrace modern redbrick. Rutgers is currently in the planning stages of revamping its campus. For those seeking to escape campus life altogether, New York City and Philadelphia are within an hour's train ride of New Brunswick.

Admissions

Average high school GPA:	—
Average freshman SAT verbal / math score:	586 / 622
Average freshman ACT score:	—
Application fee:	$60
Application deadlines: continuous (freshmen) — (transfer)	
Total applicants:	27,560
Total accepted:	16,049 (58%)
Total accepted who enrolled:	5,259
Notification dates: 3/1 (freshmen) 5/15 (transfer)	

Students

Percentage of male / female students:	50% / 50%
Percentage of students from out of state:	7%
Percentage of students graduating in 4 years / 6 years:	46% / 71%

Money

Total endowment:	$497,914,000
Total in-state tuition, fees & expenses:	$20,170
Total out-of-state tuition, fees & expenses:	$28,675
Average financial aid package:	$12,536
Percentage of students who sought aid and received it:	70%
Percentage of students receiving financial aid:	46%

Also Check Out

Boston College

The College of New Jersey

The George Washington University

The Pennsylvania State University–University Park

University of Delaware

Saint Louis University

221 North Grand Boulevard
St. Louis, MO 63103

(314) 977-2222
http://www.slu.edu

BIG CHOICE

The spirited students of Saint Louis

5 REASONS IT'S COOL

1. It looks good for its age! SLU is the **oldest university west of the Mississippi.**

2. The **Jesuit-inspired curriculum** aims to educate the *whole* you, not just your brain, through service and spiritual development.

3. Want a **career-focused education?** SLU offers training in fields such as business, nursing, physical therapy, and much more.

4. Students soar to new heights in **unique aviation programs.**

5. St. Louis and students go well together—there's a lot to do for **arts buffs, sports aficionados, and science geeks** alike.

The Basics

Public / private: private religious
Total enrollment / undergrads: 12,034 / 7,479
Campus setting: urban
Students call it: SLU (pronounced "slew")
Students are called: Billikens
Notable alums: Enrique Bolaños (president, Nicaragua), James Gunn (filmmaker), Andreas Katsulas (actor), Gene Kranz (flight director, NASA), Ed Macauley (pro basketball player), Brian McBride (pro soccer player), Joseph Teasdale (governor, Missouri), Jerry Trupiano (sportscaster)

A SLU of Choices

SLU offers strong programs in career prep, including popular programs in business, nursing, health sciences, pre-law, and engineering. With roots in the Jesuit tradition, the university also emphasizes social justice and spiritual development in its broad-based curriculum. More than eighty-five majors are offered through nine different undergraduate schools. The student-faculty ratio of 12:1 ensures that students get face time with professors, 99 percent of whom hold terminal degrees in their fields. SLU offers a number of unique courses. At the Doisy College of Health Sciences, for example, students can enroll in culinary arts classes that emphasize agriculturally sustainable cuisine. And the unique Parks College of Engineering, Aviation, and Technology hosts the nation's first federally certified flight school. SLU has a second campus in Madrid, Spain, which hosts six hundred international students in four-year programs.

Bender's Billikens

The Billiken: one of the most unique, if unattractive, of college mascots. The impish, babylike character was created in 1908 by Missouri art teacher and entrepreneur Florence Pretz. Pretz sold her design to a manufacturing company, and soon the market was flooded with bestselling Billiken dolls and collectibles. So how did the nutty little guy end up as SLU's mascot? The story goes that a local sportswriter thought athletic coach John Bender looked like a Billiken and dubbed the football team "Bender's Billikens." Although the Billiken-collecting craze didn't last long, the mascot name stuck for good.

Flex Your Faith and Your Muscles

Sports are a major component of campus life at SLU. The men's soccer team has won ten national titles, more than any other NCAA team, and the Billikens compete in sixteen NCAA Division sports as part of the Atlantic 10 Conference. Things get particularly spirited during basketball games, when students wear blue and cheer with the Blue Crew, the student cheering section. About 90 percent of freshmen live on campus in one of four freshmen dorms. After their first year, students can choose whether to stay in one of the four additional dorms, three apartment complexes, or three language houses. Faith is important to many students, and resident priests assigned to every residence hall hold Mass at least once per week. Students also volunteer frequently in the community, serving meals, working with the campus ministry, and participating in various service projects. The university offers twelve fraternities and sororities (about 20 percent of students participate) and 170 student organizations.

Artfully Growing

SLU has over 250 acres of prime real estate in the St. Louis arts district, the most culturally rich region of the city. The green Doisy Research Center was completed in 2007, while the renovated Busch Student Center (BSC) has a large ballroom, eateries, and stores catering to student needs. The massive Chaifetz Arena will serve as the brand new home court for SLU basketball teams. The nearby St. Louis Museum of Art shows modern and contemporary works, and the Samuel Cupples house displays fine and decorative arts. St. Louis also offers pro sports teams, an active nightlife, and, of course, the famous Arch, which is conveniently located just five minutes away from campus.

Admissions

Average high school GPA:	3.68
Average freshman SAT verbal / math score:	592 / 606
Average freshman ACT score:	25
Application fee:	$25
Application deadlines:	
8/1 (freshmen)	
continuous (transfer)	
Total applicants:	12,120
Total accepted:	8,160 (67%)
Total accepted who enrolled:	1,709
Notification dates:	
10/1 (freshmen)	
10/1 (transfer)	

Students

Percentage of male / female students:	42% / 58%
Percentage of students from out of state:	53%
Percentage of students graduating in 4 years / 6 years:	61% / 75%

Money

Total endowment:	$824,850,844
Total tuition:	$26,250
Total cost with fees & expenses:	$35,918
Average financial aid package:	$19,034
Percentage of students who sought aid and received it:	60%
Percentage of students receiving financial aid:	53%

Also Check Out

Boston College

Georgetown University

University of Notre Dame

Washington University in St. Louis

Saint Mary's College of California

1928 Saint Mary's Road
Moraga, CA 94575

(925) 631-4000
http://www.stmarys-ca.edu/

BIG PERSPECTIVE

A Catholic choice in the Bay Area

5 REASONS IT'S COOL

1. A Saint Mary's education emphasizes the Lasallian traditions of **respect, social justice, and learning**.

2. January is *really* cool here. During **the January Term**, students do internships, take a nontraditional class, or study abroad in faraway places like India and Morocco.

3. All students are required to take **Great Books seminars**, in which they read Plato, Dante, Shakespeare, and other great writers.

4. Students can easily **study abroad** at other Lasallian colleges and universities around the world.

5. A **pretty campus and Bay Area proximity** make Saint Mary's a great home base.

The Basics

Public / private: private religious
Total enrollment / undergrads: 3,962 / 2,835
Campus setting: suburban
Students call it: Saint Mary's, SMC
Students are called: Gaels
Notable alums: Joseph Alioto (mayor, San Francisco), Alfred Brousseau (mathematician), Robert Haas (poet), Tony Martin (singer, actor), Tom Meschery (pro basketball player, poet)

Great Books for Great Students

The Lasallian tradition is strong at this Catholic college run by the Christian Brothers, who emphasize faith, social justice, education, and respect for all people. Students can enroll in one of four schools: the School of Liberal Arts, the School of Economics & Business Administration, the School of Education, or the School of Science. The most popular majors include communications, liberal studies (teacher prep), and business. Saint Mary's requires all students to complete a series of four Great Books seminars, in which they explore Greek, Roman, Christian, Renaissance, and modern thinkers. The month-long January Term is popular because of its laid-back vibe and interesting selection of classes. During this term, students concentrate on one course, internship, research project, or study-abroad trip to destinations including South Africa, Nicaragua, and Morocco. Many students also study abroad during the full fall and spring terms at other Lasallian colleges and universities around the world.

De La Salle Forth

Held each spring, De La Salle Week commemorates the life of Saint John Baptist de La Salle and the traditions on which Saint Mary's is founded. Activities include the Carnival for Kids, which brings East Bay youth to the campus. The entire student body caps the celebration with a barbeque on the campus quad and an all-school convocation.

From Breezy to Gail Force

Saint Mary's students are a diverse bunch. More than half are Catholic, and most are happy to live and study on their cool campus. They tend to be a friendly, laid back, and traditional. The largest student group is the Gael Force, the student spirit club that cheers on Gael athletics. The college offers several strong NCAA Division I teams, including women's soccer and volleyball and men's basketball and baseball. The college offers a wide range of student organizations, ranging from political groups such as the Black Student Union and College Republicans to the *Collegian*, the campus newspaper, and KSMC, the campus radio station. About 60 percent of students live on campus. The collections of the Hearst Art Gallery, located on campus, provide inspiration for students and members of the community alike.

Easy Going

Located in the hills of the Moraga Valley, Saint Mary's 400-acre campus is about twenty miles east of San Francisco. Although the Moraga itself is decidedly suburban, the area's rolling hills, plentiful trees, and moderate climate make peace easy to come by. The campus's original Spanish villa-style buildings, including the picturesque chapel, date back to the 1920s. Saint Mary's is currently undergoing comprehensive renovations to redo and increase the number of classrooms, dining areas, and student dorms. The new Brousseau Hall focuses on science education and inquiry. Nature-loving students can head to the mountains, forests, ski slopes, several national parks, and ocean, all of which are easy to reach by car. Nearby San Francisco, Oakland, and San Jose offer museums, shopping, restaurants, and plenty of pro sports options.

Admissions

Average high school GPA:	3.33
Average freshman SAT verbal / math score:	545 / 549
Average freshman ACT score:	—
Application fee:	$55

Application deadlines:
1/15 (freshmen)
7/1 (transfer)
11/15 (early action)

Total applicants:	4,991
Total accepted:	3,508 (70%)
Total accepted who enrolled:	610

Notification dates:
3/15 (freshmen)
continuous (transfer)
12/24 (early action)

Acceptance rate for early action applicants:	51%

Students

Percentage of male / female students:	37% / 63%
Percentage of students from out of state:	11%
Percentage of students graduating in 4 years / 6 years:	58% / 66%

Money

Total endowment:	$143,387,480
Total tuition:	$28,900
Total cost with fees & expenses:	$40,768
Average financial aid package:	$21,717
Percentage of students who sought aid and received it:	69%
Percentage of students receiving financial aid:	50%

Also Check Out

Loyola Marymount University

Santa Clara University

University of San Diego

University of Notre Dame

San Diego State University

5500 Campanile Drive
San Diego, CA 92182

(619) 594-5200
http://www.sdsu.edu/

BIG CHOICE

A sunny state (school) of mind

5 REASONS IT'S COOL

1. The next generation of global business leaders learns the ropes at San Diego State's **outstanding College of Business Administration**.

2. **Par-tay!** You'll have no excuse for staying home Thursday through Sunday. Or Monday through Wednesday.

3. **One out of every seven San Diegans** who hold a college degree claims San Diego State as his or her alma mater.

4. **Service-learning programs, internships, and volunteer opportunities** are plentiful.

5. Two words: **beach and sun.** San Diego State delivers both in spades.

The Basics

Public / private: public state
Total enrollment / undergrads: 34,305 / 28,527
Campus setting: urban
Students call it: San Diego State, SDSU
Students are called: Aztecs
Notable alums: Marshall Faulk (pro football player), Tony Gwynn (pro baseball player), Julie Kavner (actress), Kathleen Kennedy (filmmaker), Art Linkletter (TV personality), Kathy Najimy (actress), Ellen Ochoa (astronaut), Gregory Peck (actor), Jerry Sanders (mayor, San Diego), Carl Weathers (actor)

From Global Business to Global Travel

Big on options, San Diego State offers more than eighty majors. The university is divided into seven undergraduate colleges, including the colleges of business administration, education, engineering, health and human services, sciences, professional studies, and fine arts. Popular majors include business administration, psychology, liberal studies (for elementary school teachers), and journalism. The program in international business wins especially high praise from students. The optional Freshman Success Program helps freshmen adjust to big-school life through small seminars, "packages" of classes that groups of the same students take together, and residential learning communities. Interdisciplinary options abound, and the university also offers a prestigious honors program. Many students study abroad, choosing from approximately 190 programs in forty-four different countries. Students

Towering Toilet Tank

The Hardy Memorial Tower rises high above the San Diego State campus. Built in 1931 in the mission style, the eleven-story tower is the campus's most prominent landmark. To many students, the tower's height represents the higher ideals of the university. The original campus architects, however, had a more utilitarian purpose in mind: The tower originally disguised a 5,000-gallon water tank that created pressure for the plumbing system on campus. Today, the tower houses a fifty-bell carillon that rings out daily across campus.

make the most of the urban location through more than a hundred local paid and unpaid internships and cooperative learning programs. The student-to-faculty ratio is 19:1, which is typical of larger schools where graduate students take on some teaching responsibilities.

Catching Rays or Catching Up on Studies?

Simply put: San Diego State students like to party. The healthy Greek presence of about forty fraternities and sororities certainly adds to the jovial atmosphere. While about 90 percent of students live off campus or commute, the campus vicinity still tends to be party central. Other popular activities include swimming and surfing at nearby Pacific Beach and heading south of the border, literally—Tijuana, Mexico, is just a thirty-mile drive to the south and is a popular weekend destination. The university offers more than three hundred student clubs, including the KPBS student television and radio stations, the *Daily Aztec* student newspaper, twenty-eight honor societies, and the Marching Aztecs marching band. While ethnic and cultural diversity runs high, over 90 percent of students hail from California.

Montezuma's Abode

San Diego State is located in a peaceful, suburban section of San Diego. The campus itself is situated high on a mesa known as Montezuma Mesa (the campus is sometimes referred to by this name). Mission-style buildings hearken to the area's Spanish heritage, and a statue of Montezuma greets drivers at the entrance to the university on Campanile Drive. The university recently completed a flurry of new construction, opening three new buildings: the BioScience Center, the Calpulli Center, and the College of Arts and Letters. San Diego's Gaslamp Quarter, an entertainment district with restaurants and shops, is a popular with students, as is Balboa Park, an urban park with cultural attractions like museums and gardens.

Admissions

Average high school GPA:	3.45
Average freshman SAT verbal / math score:	520 / 541
Average freshman ACT score:	22
Application fee:	$55

Application deadlines:
11/30 (freshmen)
11/30 (transfer)

Total applicants:	40,959
Total accepted:	19,708 (48%)
Total accepted who enrolled:	4,109

Notification dates:
3/1 (freshmen)
3/1 (transfer)

Students

Percentage of male / female students:	42% / 58%
Percentage of students from out of state:	5%
Percentage of students graduating in 4 years / 6 years:	17% / 57%

Money

Total endowment:	$99,628,917
Total in-state tuition, fees & expenses:	$14,536
Total out-of-state tuition, fees & expenses:	$24,706
Average financial aid package:	$7,300
Percentage of students who sought aid and received it:	70%
Percentage of students receiving financial aid:	38%

Also Check Out

California Polytechnic University–San Luis Obispo

University of California–San Diego

University of California–Santa Barbara

University of California–Santa Cruz

University of San Diego

Santa Clara University

500 El Camino Real
Santa Clara, CA 95053

(408) 554-4000
http://www.scu.edu/

 **BIG HAND**

 **BIG JOB**

 **BIG PERSPECTIVE**

Where old (school) meets new (technology)

5 REASONS IT'S COOL

1. **Educate your mind, body and spirit:** Jesuit ideals shape the Santa Clara experience in every way.

2. Students get to know each other inside and out (of the classroom) through the university's unique **Residential Learning Communities.**

3. Be a part of history: Santa Clara is **the oldest university in California.**

4. The **engineering and business programs** are among the best in the state.

5. Attention, tech heads! The Silicon Valley location means there are lots of opportunities to get **real-world experience at top tech firms.**

The Basics

Public / private: private religious
Total enrollment / undergrads: 7,952 / 4,613
Campus setting: suburban
Students call it: Santa Clara, SCU
Students are called: Broncos
Notable alums: Reza Aslan (author), Brandi Chastain (pro soccer player), Khaled Hosseini (novelist), Janet Napolitano (governor, Arizona), Steve Nash (pro basketball player), Gavin Newsom (mayor, San Francisco), Leon Panetta (White House chief of staff)

Jesuit-Flavored Academics

A Jesuit university, Santa Clara adds a dash of Catholic ideals to its three academic programs: arts and science, business, and engineering. Students must complete a set of core requirements, which include writing, religious studies, and traditional liberal arts courses. The Leavey School of Business is one of the top three business schools in the state and trains students by using experiential activities and the latest technology. The school's Accelerated Cooperative Education program gives students the chance to get their feet in the door with top Silicon Valley companies. Each year, juniors and seniors score paid, part-time work with companies such as Lockheed Martin, Bank of America, Logitech, SAP Labs, and Agile Software. The School of Engineering is also one of the best in the state, offering five undergraduate degree programs. Santa Clara's University Honors Program admits a select number of students every year. About a third of students venture abroad.

Just Kickin' It

The women's soccer program at Santa Clara was recently immortalized on the silver screen. In the 2003 movie *Bend It like Beckham*, the film's soccer-playing main character, Jess, received a scholarship to attend Santa Clara.

The Buddy System

Community spirit is alive and well at Santa Clara, where students are friendly, preppy, and athletic. The university offers a unique system of themed Residential Learning Communities (RLCs), where students live and study side by side. Certain courses are reserved for students from the same RLCs, and community building is emphasized. Santa Clara is home to eleven coed residence halls, which are split up into nine RLCs. Most freshmen live on campus, but overall about half of students eventually move to off-campus accommodations. Many students aren't shy about their religious leanings, but religious participation is not required in any way. Santa Clara offers a huge a variety of student organizations, many of which are service oriented. The Ruff Riders, the official student booster club, is the largest campus organization. Women's soccer is hugely popular: Olympic champion Brandi Chastain cut her teeth here, and the team continues to be one of the hottest in the nation.

A Study in Contrasts

Santa Clara's campus is where old and new come together. As the oldest university in California, Santa Clara is home to traditional mission architecture, including the Mission Santa de Asis, the campus's historical centerpiece, which dates back to 1777, and the surrounding Mission Gardens, whose olive trees also date back to late-mission times. On the other end of the spectrum, a new building for the Leavey School of Business will be wired to the gills, and the new Learning Commons & Library will open soon. The spiffy Leavey Center hosts the women's volleyball and men's and women's basketball games. The Sunday night service in the Mission Church is well-attended, and students also gather in the Benson Memorial center to shop, eat, and socialize. The Silicon Valley lies just beyond campus, and San Francisco is forty miles to the north.

Admissions

Average high school GPA:	3.52
Average freshman SAT verbal / math score:	603 / 619
Average freshman ACT score:	25
Application fee:	$55
Application deadlines:	
1/15 (freshmen)	
5/1 (transfer)	
11/1 (early action)	
Total applicants:	8,670
Total accepted:	5,762 (66%)
Total accepted who enrolled:	1,339
Notification dates:	
4/1 (freshmen)	
6/1 (transfer)	
12/31 (early action)	
Acceptance rate for early action applicants:	81%

Students

Percentage of male / female students:	45% / 55%
Percentage of students from out of state:	45%
Percentage of students graduating in 4 years / 6 years:	77% / 84%

Money

Total endowment:	$598,657,000
Total tuition:	$30,900
Total cost with fees & expenses:	$42,594
Average financial aid package:	$19,689
Percentage of students who sought aid and received it:	68%
Percentage of students receiving financial aid:	40%

Also Check Out

Boston College

Gonzaga University

Loyola Marymount University

University of San Diego

Sarah Lawrence College

I Mead Way
Bronxville, NY 10708

(914) 337-0700
http://www.sarahlawrence.edu/

 **BIG IDEA**  **BIG PERSPECTIVE**

Academic freedom for the creative and quirky

5 REASONS IT'S COOL

1. Do you go against the grain? Sarah Lawrence encourages **independent thinking** and celebrates difference.

2. With **no majors, tests, or grades**, the college offers anything but a traditional academic experience.

3. **Pop into Manhattan**—the cozy suburban campus is only thirty minutes away from NYC.

4. Enjoy a **personalized academic experience** with your own course of study, small classes, and dedicated professors.

5. Into all things creative? Sarah Lawrence boasts **great writing, theater, film, and visual arts programs**.

The Basics

Public / private: private nonprofit
Total enrollment / undergrads: 1,709 / 1,391
Campus setting: suburban
Students call it: Sarah Lawrence, SLC
Notable alums: J. J. Abrams (TV and film producer), Brian DePalma (film director), Cary Elwes (actor), Tea Leoni (actress), Yoko Ono (artist, musician), Barbara Walters (TV journalist), Vera Wang (fashion designer)

Freedom Is at Hand

Unique is the word that best describes academics here. Students get extensive evaluations from their professors, rather than grades. This system creates a supportive, noncompetitive atmosphere. Students enjoy a 6:1 student-to-faculty ratio and work with a don (a faculty advisor) throughout their four years to design a personalized course of study. Music, theater, and dance majors work on what's called the component system, taking complementary courses that balance theory with practice. All other disciplines operate on the conference system: eleven-person seminars accompanied by one-on-one meetings with professors every other week (every week for first years). Sarah Lawrence is particularly strong in writing and the arts. Faculty members include esteemed members of the New York literary, theater, and art scenes, who are not only talented pros but also dedicated teachers. The recently opened Heimbold Visual Arts Center provides beautiful work spaces, including printmaking studios and postproduction editing suites. Sarah Lawrence offers six study-abroad programs and

The Times They Are a-Changin'

Seventy-five years ago, Sarah Lawrence was an all-women's school that aimed to teach refined manners to the young ladies of high society. Now, the school encourages students to question authority, speak their minds, and dye their hair green if the mood strikes them—young ladies and young gentlemen alike.

semester exchange programs with Reed College, in Portland, Oregon, and Eugene Lang College, The New School for Liberal Arts, in New York City.

Everyone Is Different

The Sarah Lawrence motto, "You are different. So are we," captures the school's celebration of individuality. There's a fairly large gay, lesbian, bisexual, and transgender population, and a general willingness to accept people as they are. Some students describe Sarah Lawrence as the perfect place for those who didn't fit in during high school. It's also the perfect place for all artsy, independent thinkers who thrive in an intimate environment. Sarah Lawrence students tend to be creative, left-leaning activists. Poetry readings, film viewings, and theater productions are popular on campus. Other highlights include the annual Coming Out Dance and Bacchanalia, a springtime festival of beer and bands on the North Lawn. Team sports aren't too popular, but there is a great gym on campus. Sarah Lawrence used to be a women's college, and it shows in the disproportionate ratio of women to men. Ninety percent of the student body lives in the unique dorms on the small, Tudor-styled campus.

Suburban to Urban

The lovely forty-one-acre Sarah Lawrence campus, filled with ivy-covered buildings, boulders, and gardens, is a safe and quiet enclave flanked by the ritzy suburb of Bronxville and the city of Yonkers. Town-gown relations are somewhat strained, and neither Bronxville nor Yonkers provides much excitement. When they tire of campus activities, most students take a half-hour train ride to New York City, often availing themselves of the free nighttime shuttle to the train station and other locations in Bronxville. The bustling excitement of the Big Apple, filled with museums, shows, and live music, offsets any ennui students may feel on the suburban campus.

Admissions

Average high school GPA:	3.7
Average freshman SAT verbal / math score:	—/—
Average freshman ACT score:	—
Application fee:	$60

Application deadlines:
1/1 (freshmen)
3/1 (transfer)
11/15 (early decision)

Total applicants:	2,727
Total accepted:	1,261 (46%)
Total accepted who enrolled:	381

Notification dates:
4/1 (freshmen)
4/1 (transfer)
12/15 (early decision)

Acceptance rate for early decision applicants:	44%

Students

Percentage of male / female students:	26% / 74%
Percentage of students from out of state:	77%
Percentage of students graduating in 4 years / 6 years:	65% / 74%

Money

Total endowment:	$66,752,000
Total tuition:	$35,280
Total cost with fees & expenses:	$48,840
Average financial aid package:	$26,435
Percentage of students who sought aid and received it:	91%
Percentage of students receiving financial aid:	51%

Also Check Out

Bard College

New York University

Oberlin College

Smith College

Vassar College

Scripps College

1030 Columbia Avenue
Claremont, CA 91711

(909) 621-8000
http://www.scrippscollege.edu

 **BIG HAND**

 **BIG PERSPECTIVE**

Ladies, lead the way!

5 REASONS IT'S COOL

1. Scripps encourages the development of **strong, intellectual women.**

2. Students can **pursue interdisciplinary work** if a single major doesn't fit their needs.

3. **Cookies every Wednesday!** Every week, students gather for the traditional Wednesday Tea.

4. The **gorgeous campus** is full of gardens, fountains, and quiet spots for pursuing knowledge.

5. The **shared resources of the Claremont Consortium** enhance the already impressive offerings.

The Basics

Public / private: private nonprofit
Total enrollment / undergrads: 890 / 869
Campus setting: suburban
Students call it: Scripps
Students are called: Scrippsies
Notable alums: Serena Altschul (TV journalist), China Chow (actress, model), Gabrielle Giffords (congresswoman), Judith Keep (federal judge), Beth Nolan (White House chief counsel), Edith Pattou (author)

Study on, Sisters

Scripps gives bright young women the necessary knowledge, intellectual skills, and liberal arts foundation to become leaders in their chosen fields. The most popular majors are visual and performing arts, area and ethnic studies, women's studies, and the social sciences. First-year students launch their academic careers with the three-semester Core Program of interdisciplinary seminars, and all students are required to present a senior thesis, project, or performance during their senior year. The student-to-faculty ratio is roughly 11:1, and intimate academic communities encourage students to be creative and find their own intellectual modes of expression. The reciprocal agreement with the other four colleges in the Claremont Consortium—Claremont McKenna, Harvey Mudd, Pitzer, and Pomona—means that students can take up to two-thirds of their classes at the neighboring colleges.

Do Not Enter

Even though the doors to wisdom are always open at Scripps, students are permitted to pass through Dennison Library's wooden front doors only twice. Matriculation marks the first time, when students sign a book as a symbolic rite of passage into the college. They walk through the doors again just before commencement ceremonies, when they say goodbye to their college years and step into the new world that awaits them.

Female Focused

Scripps prides itself on providing a close-knit community for its supportive, opinionated, and creative students. And when they say close-knit, they mean it: total enrollment is limited to a cozy one thousand students. The university's nine residential halls are reportedly quite comfortable. Students gather every week for Wednesday Teas held at Seal Court at the Malott Commons, where they sip tea, eat cookies, and otherwise bond with their fellow students. The four other Claremont colleges are all within walking distance, putting the resources and social options—not to mention the *men*—of the participating schools at students' disposals. More than 200 student organizations and 150 monthly events are offered through the five colleges. Scripps's Career Planning & Resources (CP&R) program offers an innovative slate of services to help grads plan for their lives and careers.

Serenity and Sun

Situated in suburban Claremont, Scripps is just over thirty miles east of Los Angeles. The campus offers picture-perfect beauty with its many historic buildings (many of which are listed on the California Register of Historic Places) and Mediterranean flare. Recent updates to the campus include an expansion of the athletic facilities. The student-run Motley Coffeehouse serves up fair-trade coffee and provides a social center for student life. Scripps shares buildings, including libraries and medical facilities, with the four other colleges in the Claremont Consortium, all of which are within walking distance. Mountains, beaches, and deserts can be reached by car, and Los Angeles is connected to Claremont by the Metrolink train.

Admissions

Average high school GPA:	4.0
Average freshman SAT verbal / math score:	676 / 662
Average freshman ACT score:	26
Application fee:	$50

Application deadlines:
1/1 (freshmen)
4/1 (transfer)
11/1 (early decision)

Total applicants:	1,873
Total accepted:	846 (45%)
Total accepted who enrolled:	223

Notification dates:
4/1 (freshmen)
5/1 (transfer)
12/15 (early decision)

Acceptance rate for early decision applicants:	40%

Students

Percentage of male / female students:	— / 100%
Percentage of students from out of state:	58%
Percentage of students graduating in 4 years / 6 years:	81% / 84%

Money

Total endowment:	$228,329,821
Total tuition:	$33,506
Total cost with fees & expenses:	$44,600
Average financial aid package:	$29,642
Percentage of students who sought aid and received it:	100%
Percentage of students receiving financial aid:	40%

Also Check Out

Barnard College

Occidental College

Pomona College

University of California–San Diego

Wellesley College

Seattle University

902 12th Avenue, PO Box 222000
Seattle, WA 98122

(206) 296-6000
http://www.seattleu.edu/

BIG WORLD

A school with a conscience

5 REASONS IT'S COOL

1. SU's 13:1 student-to-faculty ratio allows you to work closely with **dedicated and passionate professors**.

2. The student body is **one of the most diverse** in the Pacific Northwest.

3. Take advantage of **many international opportunities**, from study abroad to internships with NGOs.

4. In keeping with its **Jesuit traditions**, SU emphasizes service and social justice.

5. As far as location goes, you can't beat **Seattle's lively Capitol Hill neighborhood.**

The Basics

Public / private: private religious
Total enrollment / undergrads: 7,226 / 4,160
Campus setting: urban
Students call it: SU
Students are called: Redhawks
Notable alums: General Patrick Brady (recipient of the Congressional Medal of Honor), John Hopcroft (theoretical computer scientist), Carolyn S. Kelly (president, *Seattle Times*), Duff McKagan (musician), Jim Whittaker (first American to climb Mount Everest)

Breathe In, Breathe Out

The SU motto, "Inhale tradition, exhale innovation" aptly describes the approach to academics at this midsized Jesuit university. Academics are taken seriously and are informed by a commitment to service learning and social justice. Students enroll in the Albers School of Business and Economics, the College of Arts and Sciences, the College of Nursing, the College of Science and Engineering, or the Matteo Ricci College, which offers pre-education and humanities degrees. Business, nursing, and engineering are quite strong, as are English, criminal justice, and psychology. The small classes are 100 percent professor taught. Community service is required in many courses, and students in the business school learn how to be leaders "for a just and humane world." There are study-abroad programs in a variety of countries, and the International Development Internship programs place students with NGOs (nongovernmental organizations) in Africa, Asia, or Latin America.

Ladies: Welcome

SU has long been committed to innovative thinking. In 1931, twenty years before the Jesuits officially sanctioned coeducation, SU became the first Jesuit school to admit women, a move that incited controversy as far away as Rome.

Well Balanced, Service Oriented

There is no typical way SU students dress, vote, or think. What they do have in common is a desire to be balanced, civic-minded individuals. The Center for Service and Community Engagement provides opportunities to get involved in the local community, including one-week service immersions and the Student Leaders for the Common Good program. SU has recently become NCAA Division I, which means more athletic scholarships and more excitement surrounding sports. Currently, the varsity soccer team is great, and many students get involved in intramural teams. Although Jesuit traditions are important and about half the students are Catholic, all faiths are welcome. SU has more diversity that its northwestern counterparts, which students cite as a great aspect of the school. Women far outnumber men, and the straight ones bemoan their lack of romantic options. However, there are plenty of social outlets in the city. Students are required to live on campus for their first two years. The dorms get good marks, and each has its own personality. The Archbishop Murphy Apartments are designated for juniors and seniors, but many upperclassmen move into the surrounding neighborhoods rather than stay on campus.

Peaceful Urbanity

SU's campus provides students a quiet escape from Seattle. The campus ministry is there for those who wish to explore their faith, and the architecturally revered Chapel of St. Ignatius is a special place for all. The Quad is the heart of campus and the site of Quadstock, an annual party at which student bands play alongside big-name acts. Although some of the campus facilities are a bit run-down, plans are underway to renovate the Pigott Auditorium and to build a new arts center. The surrounding neighborhood of Capitol Hill, a historically gay district, is one of the most diverse in all of Seattle. Bars, restaurants, shops, and coffeehouses line the streets and provide students a lively atmosphere in which to have fun. Students should avoid walking alone on Broadway Ave. after dark, but the area is otherwise very safe. Despite the rain, students love all that Seattle has to offer.

Admissions

Average high school GPA:	3.56
Average freshman SAT verbal / math score:	591 / 583
Average freshman ACT score:	24
Application fee:	$45
Application deadlines: continuous (freshmen) 8/15 (transfer)	
Total applicants:	4,532
Total accepted:	2,933 (65%)
Total accepted who enrolled:	783
Notification dates: continuous (freshmen) continuous (transfer)	

Students

Percentage of male / female students:	38% / 62%
Percentage of students from out of state:	40%
Percentage of students graduating in 4 years / 6 years:	43% / 63%

Money

Total endowment:	$184,657,000
Total tuition:	$24,615
Total cost with fees & expenses:	$33,378
Average financial aid package:	$23,740
Percentage of students who sought aid and received it:	74%
Percentage of students receiving financial aid:	60%

Also Check Out

College of the Holy Cross

Gonzaga University

University of Notre Dame

University of Puget Sound

Seton Hall University

400 South Orange Avenue	(973) 761-9000
South Orange, NJ 07079	http://www.shu.edu/

BIG WORLD

Excellence in everything from business to basketball

5 REASONS IT'S COOL

1. SH is the oldest and one of the largest **Roman Catholic diocesan universities** in the United States.

2. The campus is totally wireless, from dorms to lawns, and **all incoming freshmen receive a laptop** with an upgrade after two years.

3. Every Fall, SHU 500 brings together students, faculty, and alumni for **a day of community service**.

4. Students **go global through** studying abroad or interning with an international company.

5. South Orange is just **fourteen miles from New York City**.

The Basics

Public / private: private religious
Total enrollment / undergrads: 9,637 / 5,335
Campus setting: suburban
Students call it: Seton Hall, SH
Students are called: Pirates
Notable alums: Samuel Alito (U.S. Supreme Court justice), Craig Biggio (pro baseball player), Chuck Connors (journalist), Samuel Dalembert (pro basketball player), Donald DiFrancesco (state senator, governor, New Jersey), Andy Stanfield (Olympic sprinter), Max Weinberg (musician)

It's a Big World out There

Seton Hall's sixty majors offer everything from business to education to international relations to theology. And though the student body is sizeable, the school prides itself on the close interaction between students and professors. Fewer than 4 percent of classes are taught by TAs, and the student-to-faculty ratio is 15:1. Technology plays a major part in classroom instruction: Streaming video is frequently used, and students participate in online activities. Global affairs are also important to Seton Hall academics. The Whitehead School, founded in conjunction with the United Nations Association, offers a diplomacy program, which presents a forum in which ambassadors and international affairs experts work directly with students. Internships are available at global companies such as CNN, Johnson & Johnson, and Pfizer, and at the United Nations. Pirates regularly study abroad in countries such as Russia, China, Spain, France, and Italy, or spend a semester interning in D.C.

A Fiery Past

Seton Hall has been plagued by fire. An 1867 fire destroyed the school's original building. Almost twenty years later, a second fire gutted the university's main building. A fire in 1909 destroyed the dormitories and a classroom. And sadly, a fire in 2000 killed three students.

Media Matters

Pirates choose from over a hundred student-run clubs and organizations and twenty-five Greek chapters. This isn't the most politically active campus in the world, but future journalists can write for the *Setonian*, the school's newspaper, while future satirists can write for the *Rampage*, the school's underground spoof paper. SH also boasts one of the best student-run college radio stations in the country. For sports fans, the Division I men's basketball program incites the most passion. Golf, soccer, softball, swimming, tennis, track and field, and volleyball also draw cheers. The facilities are state-of-the-art: All classrooms in Jubilee Hall are Internet connected, the new Science and Technology Center opened in 2007, and the $20 million Walsh Library is an excellent resource for research. Although the student body represents a multitude of ethnicities and cultures, some complain that the amount of diversity divides students rather than unites them.

Apples and Oranges

Seton Hall's campus occupies fifty-eight acres in South Orange, a quaint town that holds tight to history, as the gas lamps on streets might suggest. The small village is perfect for students with low-key social ambitions, but the sleepy vibe bothers more hearty partiers. Crackdowns from the local police and the administration have driven many revelers to confine their debauchery to the frat houses. Others head into Manhattan, where every manner of shopping, food, arts, and nightlife can be found. The vast majority of students are New Jersey or New York natives, and many head home for the weekends, often leaving town and campus deserted.

Admissions

Average high school GPA:	3.26
Average freshman SAT verbal / math score:	561 / 568
Average freshman ACT score:	—
Application fee:	$55

Application deadlines:
3/1 (freshmen)
6/1 (transfer)

Total applicants:	4,982
Total accepted:	4,160 (84%)
Total accepted who enrolled:	1,115

Notification dates:
12/1 (freshmen)
1/1 (transfer)

Students

Percentage of male / female students:	47% / 53%
Percentage of students from out of state:	26%
Percentage of students graduating in 4 years / 6 years:	41% / 56%

Money

Total endowment:	$197,725,000
Total tuition:	$22,770
Total cost with fees & expenses:	$36,386
Average financial aid package:	$14,664
Percentage of students who sought aid and received it:	68%
Percentage of students receiving financial aid:	57%

Also Check Out

College of the Holy Cross

Duquesne University

Rutgers University

Saint Louis University

Sewanee: The University of the South

735 University Avenue
Sewanee, TN 37383

(931) 598-1000
http://www.sewanee.edu/

BIG PERSPECTIVE

The school so nice they named it twice

5 REASONS IT'S COOL

1. The **venerable** *Sewanee Review* is the longest-running lit journal in the country.

2. Sewanee's **scenic 10,000-acre campus** has all the hiking, biking, and spelunking an outdoorsy type could want.

3. The **strong affiliation with the Episcopal Church** is evident: Semesters are even referred to as Advent and Easter terms.

4. **Curve wreckers and other overachievers** can join the Order of Gownsmen.

5. The **world-class creative writing program** receives funding from the estate of Tennessee Williams.

The Basics

Public / private: private religious
Total enrollment / undergrads: 1,611 / 1,518
Campus setting: small town
Students call it: Sewanee
Students are called: Tigers
Notable alums: Paul Harris Boardman (filmmaker), Radney Foster (singer-songwriter), H. T. Kirby-Smith (author, poet), Jon Meacham (editor), Anson Mount (actor), Raegan Payne (actress), Gene Robinson (Episcopalian bishop), John Shoop (pro football coach)

All Rhodes Lead to Sewanee

Sewanee's liberal arts curriculum includes nineteen core courses covering literature, history, foreign languages, math, science, religion and philosophy, social science, and the arts, as well as physical education requirements. The school's approach to academics is decidedly traditional, and standards of excellence follow the old English model. The Gothic architecture seen across campus is modeled after that of Oxford and Cambridge, and those schools even donated the first volumes to Sewanee's library. Seniors labor through a comprehensive series of exams before graduation, and the accessible profs have a tendency to teach classes clad in academic robes. Respect for great traditions pays off in high achievement. Percentage-wise, Sewanee has graduated more Rhodes Scholars than any other U.S. school. English is the strongest and most popular program and serves up hefty doses of Shakespeare and Chaucer. History and theology are also well regarded.

I've Always Depended on the Kindness of Tennessee Williams

Playwright Tennessee Williams bequeathed future royalties to Sewanee in honor of his grandfather, an alumnus. With each publication or performance of a Williams play, a little more money drops into the university's coffers.

Prestigious and Preppy

Sewanee style nods toward the button-down fashion of yesteryear. It's not unusual to see male students sporting blazers and bowties and women wearing skirts or dresses, and members of the elite Order of the Gownsmen (an association of students with high GPAs) don signature dark robes. But the throwback digs aren't the result of school rules: Students and faculty have adopted this unofficial dress code as a mark of pride. If you haven't guessed already, let us spell it out for you: students here tend to be on the preppy, conservative side. Devotion to community is not just limited to fashion. Sports are popular, if not competitive, and Tigers are always up for a party. A popular Greek scene serves up fun for all, and drinking is prevalent. Episcopalians represent a sizeable contingent, and most students are Christians of some stripe. Administrators are taking measures to recruit more minorities into the fold.

Lord of Its Domain

Sewanee's campus and surroundings are known as the Domain or the Mountain, which are fitting nicknames, given the school's perch atop Lookout Mountain. The tiny town of Sewanee offers minimal excitement, but most students don't mind. The demanding studies and insular vibe combine to make campus a place that students are loath to leave. Standards of residential life vary for the more than 90 percent of students living on the campus. The new Humpheys Hall offers the best creature comforts. Nature lovers will find much to do on the campus's undeveloped acreage. Veterans warn, however, that the school's remote location means shopping and cell phone reception are both scarce. Atlanta, Nashville, and Chattanooga are close by, but wheels are needed to break the rural confines.

Admissions

Average high school GPA:	3.63
Average freshman SAT writing / math / critical reading score:	622 / 616 / 628
Average freshman ACT score:	26
Application fee:	$45

Application deadlines:
2/1 (freshmen)
4/1 (transfer)
11/15 (early decision)

Total applicants:	1,932
Total accepted:	1,368 (71%)
Total accepted who enrolled:	412

Notification dates:
4/1 (freshmen)
continuous (transfer)
12/15 (early decision)

Acceptance rate for early decision applicants:	77%

Students

Percentage of male / female students:	48% / 52%
Percentage of students from out of state:	79%
Percentage of students graduating in 4 years / 6 years:	79% / 82%

Money

Total endowment:	$270,928,000
Total tuition:	$30,438
Total cost with fees & expenses:	$39,440
Average financial aid package:	$21,439
Percentage of students who sought aid and received it:	97%
Percentage of students receiving financial aid:	45%

Also Check Out

Davidson College

University of North Carolina at Chapel Hill

Vanderbilt University

Wake Forest University

Washington & Lee University

Siena College

515 Loudon Road
Loudonville, NY 12211

(518) 783-2300
http://www.siena.edu/

 **BIG HAND**

 **BIG PERSPECTIVE**

Go ahead, be challenged!

5 REASONS IT'S COOL

1. Siena's **small, discussion-oriented classes** hone students' oral communication and critical thinking skills.

2. Students enjoy all the benefits of living and studying in a **close-knit community**.

3. Pack your scrubs: A **special BS/MD program** with Albany Medical College allows qualified students to shave time from medical school.

4. The **honors program** offers even smaller classes and the chance to register early.

5. Siena's proximity to Albany means students have access to **excellent internship opportunities**.

The Basics

Public / private: private religious
Total enrollment / undergrads: 3,220 / 3,220
Campus setting: suburban
Students call it: Siena
Students are called: Saints
Notable alums: George Deukmejian Jr. (governor, California), Harry Flynn (Roman Catholic archbishop), Ed Henry (news anchor), William J. Kennedy (author), John Lannan (pro baseball player), Ron Vawter (actor)

Foundations for Excellence

Siena's strong Franciscan tradition helps create a close-knit atmosphere on campus. This becomes apparent to students from their first semester when they participate in the First-Year Experience, which mixes social events with formal academic advising. The First-Year Experience puts newbies together in two small classes known as Foundations 100 and 105, which introduce the nature of academic enquiry and the meaning of responsibility. The experience also challenges students to critically examine society, humanity, nationalism, and the difference between religious and secular worldviews. By teaching students how to think critically and articulate their arguments, the Foundations sequence provides them with key skills they'll use repeatedly throughout college and their professional lives. Many students become attached to their First-Year Experience professors, who are helpful and encouraging. Siena offers twenty-eight majors, which are distributed throughout its three schools of liberal arts, business, and science.

One Happy Family

Each fall, Siena hosts Family Weekend, a three-day event during which students show off the college to their families. Siena makes certain the weekend is chock-full of activities, such as a family reception, a golf tournament, brunch with the deans, an arts and crafts fair, late-night events in the union, Sunday Mass, and the President's Pancake Sunday Brunch on Sunday. With so much to do, many students groan that Family Weekend is just about as fun as running a marathon—except that they have to hit the gym afterward to work off all that food.

Life Is What You Make of It

Siena is not particularly diverse. While there are some minorities and international students, the lion's share of students are wealthy, Catholic, and from New York. Intramural sports are popular, as is playing or rooting for one of the school's eighteen Division I athletic teams. Siena also boasts more than sixty student organizations. Political activism groups are especially popular, as are theater groups and student government. Many students write for the *Promethean*, Siena's student-run newspaper, and the *Pendragon*, a campus literary magazine. The Franciscan Center for Service and Advocacy provides a wide range of community service opportunities, including serving meals in local soup kitchens and building houses for the needy through Habitat for Humanity. Students say that most of their closest friendships develop out of the bonds they forge in their extracurricular activities. The Student Events Board sponsors a number of theater and musical performances, movie screenings, and open-mic nights.

Dude, Where's My Beer?

Siena's Loudonville setting is exactly what you might expect from Upstate New York: sprawling, colorful, and nestled among mountains that offer some of the country's best skiing and hiking. For some, though, the idyllic campus leaves something to be desired—mainly, alcohol. In the last few years, Siena's administration has begun cracking down on underage drinking. To monitor the amount of alcohol that enters the rooms of students who are twenty-one or older, security guards patrol the dorms and the townhouses in which the juniors and seniors live. Although many students complain about this, they seem to have found a solution: making the ten-minute drive to Albany, where bars, nightclubs, restaurants, and shops are plentiful. Or, if they yearn for even bigger city life, they take the two-hour train ride into Manhattan.

Admissions

Average high school GPA:	3.5
Average freshman SAT verbal / math score:	556 / 583
Average freshman ACT score:	24
Application fee:	$50

Application deadlines:
3/1 (freshmen)
8/15 (transfer)
12/1 (early decision)
12/1 (early action)

Total applicants:	5,094
Total accepted:	2,804 (55%)
Total accepted who enrolled:	690

Notification dates:
3/15 (freshmen)
continuous (transfer)
12/15 (early decision)
1/1 (early action)

Acceptance rate for early action/early decision applicants:	77% / 57%

Students

Percentage of male / female students:	44% / 56%
Percentage of students from out of state:	12%
Percentage of students graduating in 4 years / 6 years:	72% / 79%

Money

Total endowment:	$122,032,700
Total tuition:	$21,285
Total cost with fees & expenses:	$30,835
Average financial aid package:	$12,655
Percentage of students who sought aid and received it:	80%
Percentage of students receiving financial aid:	61%

Also Check Out

Boston College

New York University

SUNY–Binghamton University

SUNY–Geneseo

SUNY–University at Albany

Skidmore College

815 North Broadway
Saratoga Springs, NY 12866

(518) 580-5000
http://www.skidmore.edu/

BIG PERSPECTIVE

A cozy liberal arts haven through and through

5 REASONS IT'S COOL

1. Classes rarely have more than twenty students, and you'll have ample opportunities to **get to know your professors.**

2. Skidmore's First-Year Experience is **designed to help freshmen acclimate to college** academics.

3. Skidmore puts a big **emphasis on inter-disciplinary learning.**

4. Saratoga Springs is a **fun, laid-back town** that serves as a base camp for all manner of mountain adventures.

5. Fun, creative students and **campus parties that are open to everyone:** What's not to like about the social scene?

The Basics

Public / private: private nonprofit
Total enrollment / undergrads: 2,816 / 2,759
Campus setting: small town
Students call it: Skidmore
Students are called: Thoroughbreds
Notable alums: Barbara Bloom (TV executive, writer), Ben Cohen (attended; cofounder, Ben & Jerry's Ice Cream), Molly McGrann (novelist), Grace Mirabella (editor), Wilma Stein Tisch (philanthropist)

My Professor Knows My Name!

Skidmore students hit the books before they even hit campus. The college's First-Year Experience (FYE) program includes a summer reading assignment, workshops, and other academic programming. Freshmen take the Scribner Seminars, small-group, discussion-based classes populated by students who live near one another in the residence halls. About fifty seminars are offered, covering a wide range of topics, and Scribner professors double as academic advisors. Skidmore's faculty is well liked; students gush over the amount of personal attention they get. Business, English, and fine arts are the most popular fields of study, while economics and the natural sciences are generally considered to be the toughest. Skidmore students vary widely in the amount of effort they put into their academics: They range from study addicts to complete slackers, while most fall somewhere in between these two extremes. The college offers popular summer programs, including a month of readings, discussions, and social events with esteemed authors, a five-week Summer

But Is It Art?

Skidmore's emphasis on interdisciplinary study is most dramatically manifested—architecturally, at least—in the Frances Young Tang Teaching Museum and Art Gallery. Located on campus in a stunning facility, the museum works to expand the concept of what a gallery exhibition can be. The museum includes dedicated teaching space, and many professors hold classes there to help students consider subject matter in unusual ways.

Six session for art students, and the annual Summer Archaeological Field School in Colorado, to name just a few.

A Tight-Knit Community

The Skidmore community is close-knit and inclusive, with three-quarters of students living on campus. Traditionally, Skidmore's social life has revolved around campus parties, particularly those thrown by athletic teams. In recent years, however, more bars have been opening up in Saratoga Springs. Nights on the town have also become more popular as the college has begun to enforce its alcohol regulations more seriously. School spirit doesn't run especially high; most students seem to think their time is better spent on things other than bullhorns and pom-poms. Skidmore has eighty-three student organizations, including the popular outdoor activities club, which sponsors excursions in the nearby Adirondacks. Students tend to be politically aware, liberal, and from the Northeast, with a solid 30 percent hailing from New York State.

By George, a Great College Town

The Skidmore campus offers terrific views of the surrounding mountains and forests of the Adirondack region. If you're a hiker, biker, or skier, you'll find plenty of options to keep you more than busy on weekends. Lake George, a popular (if past its prime) resort destination, is about thirty minutes away. New York, Boston, and Montreal, all within driving distance, constitute the troika of long-weekend getaway destinations. The town Saratoga Springs itself strikes most students as an unexpectedly vibrant place. Skidmore's campus is about a mile from the center of town, where you'll find plenty of restaurants and shops, many catering to the outdoors-seeking tourists who pass through the area year-round. Students can catch a folk music show at Caffe Lena, purportedly the country's oldest coffeehouse.

Admissions

Average high school GPA:	3.31
Average freshman SAT writing / math / critical reading score:	627 / 630 / 630
Average freshman ACT score:	26
Application fee:	$60

Application deadlines:
1/15 (freshmen)
4/1 (transfer)
11/15 (early decision)

Total applicants:	6,652
Total accepted:	2,578 (39%)
Total accepted who enrolled:	672

Notification dates:
4/1 (freshmen)
— (transfer)
12/15 (early decision)

Acceptance rate for early decision applicants:	58%

Students

Percentage of male / female students:	41% / 59%
Percentage of students from out of state:	65%
Percentage of students graduating in 4 years / 6 years:	73% / 78%

Money

Total endowment:	$255,000,000
Total tuition:	$34,224
Total cost with fees & expenses:	$45,250
Average financial aid package:	$27,280
Percentage of students who sought aid and received it:	94%
Percentage of students receiving financial aid:	38%

Also Check Out

Amherst College

Connecticut College

Tufts University

Vassar College

Wesleyan University

Smith College

7 College Lane
Northampton, MA 01063

(413) 584-2700
http://www.smith.edu/

 **BIG BRAIN**

 **BIG HAND**

 **BIG PERSPECTIVE**

Women pioneers of academic excellence

5 REASONS IT'S COOL

1. Smith boasts the **nation's first and only engineering program at a women's college.**

2. The students are a **diverse, friendly, and outspoken bunch.**

3. Majors run the gamut from **interdisciplinary fields** such as landscape, urban, and Latino/a studies to more traditional fields.

4. Smith is unique in that it **guarantees funding for internships** related to students' studies.

5. The **popular study-abroad program** sends about half the junior class packing to locales around the world.

The Basics

Public / private: private nonprofit
Total enrollment / undergrads: 3,092 / 2,634
Campus setting: small town
Students call it: Smith
Students are called: Pioneers, Smithies
Notable alums: Barbara Bush (First Lady), Julia Child (chef, TV personality), Madeleine L'Engle (writer), Sylvia Plath (poet), Nancy Reagan (First Lady), Gloria Steinem (feminist)

Work and Passion

The Smith workload is hefty. While students have no core requirements save a first-year writing course, those gunning for honors must take courses in seven subjects including math, philosophy, and foreign languages. Classes are taught solely by professors, and the maximum class size is fifty. Smith has more than a thousand course offerings, and its membership in the Five College Consortium means students can take classes at Amherst, UMass–Amherst, Hampshire, and Mount Holyoke. Smith also offers many special independent and off-campus study opportunities, such as the Smith Scholars Program, in which students spend up to two years working on independent projects (such as a play or a thesis). The Semester-in-Washington Program allows government majors to study with a Smith professor while learning about the policymaking process firsthand through internships. Government, psychology, art, and English are the most popular majors, but around 25 percent of Smithies follow science and engineering tracks.

Celebrate Good Times

At convocation, Smithies celebrate the start of the school year. Each house has a different theme, such as restricting one's attire to a certain material (this is where duct tape comes in) or wearing as little as possible, but everyone is united in riotous clapping, yelling, and sometimes foghorn blowing.

Full Service

Students put lots of time into their demanding classes, but they're also likely to invest energy in extracurriculars. Service organizations involve students in various projects on campus and in local communities. Also popular are a cappella groups and club sports teams (rugby, in particular). There is a vocal gay community. Those rare Smithies who lament the lack of a Greek scene may pledge sororities at UMass–Amherst. The residence halls resemble sororities in their governmental structure: Two seniors run each house, and four first-years organize Friday afternoon tea parties. The name *residence hall* does not do justice to the housing situation at Smith. Students live in refurbished mansions accommodating anywhere from thirteen to one hundred students. All undergraduates except nontraditional students live on campus, and students mostly eat in their house's dining room, which is sometimes themed with Mediterranean, vegan, or Asian cuisines. A top hangout is the recently opened Campus Center, a massive white glass building, which has meeting spaces for faculty and students, a café with salads and sandwiches, and lounges.

Through the Gates

Smith is situated in historic Northampton, Massachusetts, a town the college's founder, Sophia Smith, hoped students would embrace. At the foot of the Berkshire Mountains, downtown Northampton is a ten-minute walk from campus and is home to several sushi restaurants, two movie theaters with independent and international films, bars, and boutiques. Inside the cast iron Grecourt Gates that mark the college entrance, a tall clock tower stands atop the campus's first building, College Hall. The 125-acre campus includes equestrian facilities with a forty-stall barn, four riding rings, and miles of trails; a croquet court; and Paradise Pond. Architectural styles, while predominately historic, range from Georgian and Greek revival to modern. Boston, Providence, and New Haven are all within two hours, New York City is a little farther south, and ski slops are only ten minutes away.

Admissions

Average high school GPA:	4.0
Average freshman SAT verbal / math score:	641 / 618
Average freshman ACT score:	25
Application fee:	$60
Application deadlines:	
1/15 (freshmen)	
5/15 (transfer)	
11/15 (early decision)	
Total applicants:	3,427
Total accepted:	1,819 (53%)
Total accepted who enrolled:	674
Notification dates:	
4/1 (freshmen)	
6/1 (transfer)	
12/15 (early decision)	
Acceptance rate for early decision applicants:	72%

Students

Percentage of male / female students:	— / 100%
Percentage of students from out of state:	78%
Percentage of students graduating in 4 years / 6 years:	82% / 86%

Money

Total endowment:	$1,156,349,000
Total tuition:	$32,320
Total cost with fees & expenses:	$44,038
Average financial aid package:	$32,659
Percentage of students who sought aid and received it:	100%
Percentage of students receiving financial aid:	61%

Also Check Out

Brown University

Bryn Mawr College

Mount Holyoke College

Vassar College

Wellesley College

Southern Methodist University

6425 Boaz
Dallas, TX 75275

(214) 768-2000
http://www.smu.edu/

BIG JOB

Attention future captains of industry!

5 REASONS IT'S COOL

1. Students take advantage of SMU's **unrivaled business networking opportunities.**

2. Read the greats, old and new, in the *Southwest Review*, the English program's **award-winning literary journal.**

3. **Like to swim and watch movies?** You can do both when films are shown at the Dedman Center's indoor pool.

4. **Cheer and drink beer** when the Mustangs tackle their Division I football opponents.

5. The **best shopping and dining in Dallas** lie minutes away from campus.

The Basics

Public / private: private religious
Total enrollment / undergrads: 10,941 / 6,296
Campus setting: suburban
Students call it: SMU, The Hilltop
Students are called: Mustangs
Notable alums: James A. Baker (Texas Supreme Court judge, secretary of the treasury, secretary of state), Kathy Bates (actress), Laura Bush (First Lady), Hacksaw Jim Duggan (pro wrestler), Jeffrey Skilling (chairman and CEO, Enron), Aaron Spelling (TV and film producer)

Taking Care of Business

To many people, the business of SMU is business. The school has long been popular among aspiring movers and shakers eager to ascend to the ranks of the Texas elite. Programs in finance, business, advertising, and political science are consistently among the most popular. Psychology is a popular major, and the engineering co-op program allows students to work directly with some of the many high-tech companies in the surrounding areas. Humanities-minded students are drawn to strong programs in history and English, and creative types can take advantage of the top-notch performing arts program, which recently upgraded with cutting-edge special-effects technology. The student-to-faculty ratio is a respectable 12:1, and opportunities for personal attention abound. The administration has made recent efforts to ratchet up academic standards and play down the school's rep as a giant networking opportunity.

My Little Pony

Everything's bigger in Texas, with the exception of SMU's mascot, Peruna. The diminutive Shetland pony gets its name from a potent nineteenth-century cure-all famous throughout Texas. For over seventy years, Peruna has appeared at every home football game accompanied by a select entourage of trained student handlers. Undoubtedly, the sight of the tiny black pony and its posse strikes fear into the heart of every visiting foe.

Preppie Does Dallas

Popped collars and designer handbags represent the dominant fashion sensibility on campus. Conservative mores are prevalent, and campus radicals are far and few between. Two Texas college mainstays, football and the Greeks, drive the social life, usually pulling a keg behind them despite the campus's official dry status. Students love their Mustangs as much as their drink, especially when rival Texas Christian steps onto the field. Empty calories can be burned off at the lavish student recreation facility, Dedman Center, which offers indoor and outdoor pools, weight-training equipment, and a rock-climbing wall. Students speak well of the food service and residence halls, the most desirable of which is the honors dorm, Virginia-Snider. All housing is coed, and themed floors cater to a variety of interests. Most of the student population hails from the Lone Star State, and ethnic diversity is laudable, with minorities representing roughly 20 percent of the student body.

Deep in the Heart of Dallas

SMU makes its home at the center of Dallas, right next to the affluent neighborhoods of University Park and Highland Park. Shopping, nightlife, and fine dining are in easy reach. The campus itself is lush and well groomed. The signature building, Dallas Hall, is a neoclassical postcard complete with columns and a rotunda. Among other campus highlights is the Meadows Museum of Art, whose 2001 grand opening was presided over by the king and queen of Spain.

Admissions

Average high school GPA:	3.5
Average freshman SAT writing / math / critical reading score:	604 / 626 / 610
Average freshman ACT score:	25
Application fee:	$60

Application deadlines:
1/15 (freshmen)
7/1 (transfer)
11/1 (early action)

Total applicants:	7,648
Total accepted:	4,106 (54%)
Total accepted who enrolled:	1,369

Notification dates:
continuous (freshmen)
continuous (transfer)
12/31 (early action)

Acceptance rate for early action applicants:	80%

Students

Percentage of male / female students:	46% / 54%
Percentage of students from out of state:	38%
Percentage of students graduating in 4 years / 6 years:	55% / 71%

Money

Total endowment:	$1,013,703,336
Total tuition:	$27,400
Total cost with fees & expenses:	$41,705
Average financial aid package:	$24,824
Percentage of students who sought aid and received it:	90%
Percentage of students receiving financial aid:	33%

Also Check Out

Rice University

Texas Christian University

Tulane University

The University of Texas at Austin

Vanderbilt University

Southwestern University

1001 East University Avenue
Georgetown, TX 78626

(512) 863-6511
http://www.southwestern.edu/

BIG PERSPECTIVE

Feel at home among your fellow geeks.

5 REASONS IT'S COOL

1. Fifty percent of Southwestern students graduated in the top 10 percent of their high school classes.

2. The university puts its money where its mouth is: **85 percent of students receive some form of financial aid.**

3. Want to make the world a better place? **Activism and community service are huge.**

4. **See the world while earning your degree:** 50 percent of students study abroad.

5. Because there are no graduate programs, **undergrads receive star treatment.**

The Basics

Public/private: private religious
Total enrollment/undergrads: 1,277 / 1,277
Campus setting: suburban
Students call it: Southwestern
Students are called: Pirates
Notable alums: J. Frank Dobie (writer), Bill Engvall (comedian), Pete Sessions (congressman), Mike Timlin (pro baseball player)

Get Involved

With an endowment of over a quarter billion and an undergrad population under 1,500, Southwestern invests more in each student than almost any other U.S. school. Such investment translates into an average class size of fourteen, a total lack of TAs, and a 10:1 student-to-faculty ratio. Professors often invite students to participate in their research, and they expect regular class attendance in return. This tradeoff isn't a problem for Southwestern's ambitious students, many of whom major in business administration, communication studies, or psych. Designing one's own degree is also an option. All freshmen participate in the university's First Year Seminar Program, and every student has numerous opportunities for hands-on experience. The Paideia Program, for example, seeks to engage students in and beyond their community and enables undergrad research and creative independent projects. Along with study-abroad programs in destinations as unique as Turkey and Jamaica, Southwestern offers internships in Manhattan for aspiring artists and a semester in D.C. for the politically inclined.

Bikes for the Taking

After alum Wally Meyer died in a cycling accident in 2004, his sister donated thirty yellow bikes to his alma mater in honor of her brother's beloved activity. Known as "Pirate bikes," the two-wheeled beauties scattered across campus are free for the taking. Students, faculty, and staff members can ride anywhere on campus, so long as they leave the bikes at their destination for the next person wishing to take a spin.

The Geek Life

One of the biggest perks of Southwestern's small size is the supportive community it engenders. All students are required to live on campus during their first year. Even when moving off campus becomes an option, though, most upperclassmen choose to remain at school. Each dorm has a unique personality, and students are fanatically loyal to their residence hall communities, teaming up to participate in intramural sports, the Homecoming Parade, and other campuswide events. Although the university is affiliated with the United Methodist Church, not all students are Christian, or even particularly religious. About 59 percent are female, and 79 percent are white. One unifying factor: dorkiness. Pirates are nerdy and proud of it. For extracurricular entertainment, there are 107 organizations to choose from, including frats and sororities, which claim about 59 percent of students. Southwestern also participates in a number of Division III sports, although it is one of the few Texas schools without a football team.

Find Your Own Adventure

Pirates have a love-hate relationship with Georgetown. They bemoan the town's almost total lack of nightlife and complain that the school does little to compensate. Weekend frat and sorority parties and Wednesday evening study break events help to break the monotony. Popular on-campus diversions, other than studying at the library, include playing Ultimate Frisbee and hanging out at the student center, which offers pool tables, foosball, shuffle puck, food, and (sometimes) BYOB events. The university screens a movie on the last Saturday of each month, and free pizza and sodas are served at the athletic center over the weekends. For those in need of escape, the most popular travel destination is Austin, a forty-five-minute drive away, where there's good food, great bars, tons of music, film, and art events, and a lively, young populace.

Admissions

Average high school GPA:	—
Average freshman SAT verbal / math score:	616 / 616
Average freshman ACT score:	25
Application fee:	$40
Application deadlines: 2/15 (freshmen) 4/1 (transfer) 11/1 (early decision)	
Total applicants:	1,955
Total accepted:	1,271 (65%)
Total accepted who enrolled:	345
Notification dates: 4/1 (freshmen) continuous (transfer) 12/1 (early decision)	
Acceptance rate for early decision applicants:	75%

Students

Percentage of male / female students:	41% / 59%
Percentage of students from out of state:	7%
Percentage of students graduating in 4 years / 6 years:	67% / 78%

Money

Total endowment:	$279,939,773
Total tuition:	$25,740
Total cost with fees & expenses:	$34,450
Average financial aid package:	$20,432
Percentage of students who sought aid and received it:	90%
Percentage of students receiving financial aid:	49%

Also Check Out

Austin College

Hendrix College

Rhodes College

Trinity University

The University of Texas at Austin

Spelman College

350 Spelman Lane, SW
Atlanta, GA 30314

(404) 681-3643
http://www.spelman.edu/

BIG PERSPECTIVE

A historically black college for smart women

5 REASONS IT'S COOL

1. Leadership and sisterhood play a part in every aspect of life at this **all-women's college.**

2. **Forty percent of freshmen are legacy students** following in the footsteps of another family member.

3. Students can **cross-register for classes** at Morehouse College and Clark Atlanta University.

4. Spelman is located just **five minutes from downtown Atlanta.**

5. Students are active in all sorts of organizations, from **sororities to jazz ensembles to varsity sports.**

The Basics

Public / private: private nonprofit
Total enrollment / undergrads: 2,290 / 2,290
Campus setting: urban
Students call it: Spelman
Students are called: Jaguars
Notable alums: Marian Wright Edelman (founder, Children's Defense Fund), Bernice King (author), Keisha Knight-Pulliam (actress), Dr. Deborah Prothrow-Stith (public health leader), Alice Walker (author), Nikki Lee Weldon (educator)

Ambitious African American Woman

As one of the top all-women's historically black colleges in the country, Spelman has a reputation for providing strong academics in an intimate setting. Popular majors include biology, psychology, political science, and English. The Women's Research and Resource Center, the first of its kind at a historically black college, offers a comparative women's studies major and classes in feminist theory. Undergrads can cross-register with Morehouse College, a historically black men's college, and Clark Atlanta University, a coed school right across the street. Through the Atlanta University Center, a consortium of the city's historically black schools, Spelman women can take part in the Dual Degree Engineering Program. This 3-2 program gives students a liberal arts background and then helps them transfer to engineering schools. Grads of this program receive bachelor's degrees from both universities. Study abroad is encouraged, and programs are available in Chile, Senegal, Argentina, and Japan, among others.

Little White Dress

Books, check. Dorm supplies, check. Conservative white dress . . . check? Spelman women don white dresses for formal events such as Founders Day, graduation, freshman orientation, and so on. These dresses must be proper (no thigh-skimming minis, please) and pure white (nope, ecru won't cut it).

Spelman Sisterhood

Sisterhood is a defining feature of the social life. Sororities are taken seriously and are quite active in campus life. Community service is popular, as are religious organizations and musical ensembles. Division III varsity sports include softball, tennis, golf, cross-country, soccer, volleyball, and basketball. While there is no typical Spelman student, most undergrads can be described as enterprising, motivated, and involved in their community. Most are from Georgia, although there are sizeable populations from California, New York, Maryland, and Illinois as well. Ninety-two percent of the student body is African American. There are ten residence halls on campus, each with its own character—and strict rules of decorum. Alcohol is strictly prohibited on campus, so most partying takes places at Spelman's brother school, Morehouse, which is just a short walk away.

Half a Mile to Downtown Hotlanta

Spelman's thirty-two acre campus is charming, dotted with historic buildings and exuding collegiate appeal. The Sisters Chapel, dedicated in the 1920s, hosts events throughout the school year, and the Robert W. Woodruff Library is shared by the Atlanta University Center (AUC) consortium. Despite their age, the majority of buildings on campus have stood the test of time. Still, this college is hardly living in the past. A new green suite-style residence hall shows that. Applicants wary of women's colleges shouldn't fret too much; with Clark Atlanta University and Morehouse in such close proximity, there are plenty of men around. If it's too hot to walk, count on AUC shuttles for transport to and from member campuses. And downtown Atlanta is just five minutes away. Spelman students receive discounts on MARTA, Atlanta's public transportation system, which means more dough for the restaurants, museums, and shopping of "Hotlanta."

Admissions

Average high school GPA:	3.58
Average freshman SAT verbal / math score:	548 / 529
Average freshman ACT score:	22
Application fee:	$35
Application deadlines:	
2/1 (freshmen)	
2/1 (transfer)	
— (early action)	
Total applicants:	5,248
Total accepted:	1,946 (37%)
Total accepted who enrolled:	569
Notification dates:	
4/1 (freshmen)	
4/1 (transfer)	
— (early action)	
Acceptance rate for early action applicants:	—

Students

Percentage of male / female students:	— / 100%
Percentage of students from out of state:	70%
Percentage of students graduating in 4 years / 6 years:	67% / 77%

Money

Total endowment:	$258,054,391
Total tuition:	$14,470
Total cost with fees & expenses:	$25,755
Average financial aid package:	$10,500
Percentage of students who sought aid and received it:	67%
Percentage of students receiving financial aid:	69%

Also Check Out

Birmingham-Southern University

Emory University

Georgia Institute of Technology

Howard University

University of Georgia

St. John's University

8000 Utopia Parkway
Queens, NY 11439

(888) 9ST-JOHNS
http://www.stjohns.edu

 **BIG CHOICE**

 **BIG WORLD**

Where big diversity meets the Big East

5 REASONS IT'S COOL

1. It's a helluva town! St. John's has **three New York City campuses**, the largest of which is in Queens.

2. All **incoming students are given a laptop**—which they can keep after graduation!

3. At this **Roman Catholic–affiliated school**, students volunteer and get involved with the local community.

4. The Discover the World program combines **community service with a study-abroad experience**.

5. This **diverse student body** hails from more than one hundred countries.

The Basics

Public / private: private religious
Total enrollment / undergrads: 20,069 / 14,983
Campus setting: urban
Students call it: St. John's, STJ
Notable alums: Susan M. Kropf (COO, Avon Products), Gary P. Muto (president, Gap Adult and Gapbody), Kate W. O'Beirne (editor, *National Review*), Patrick J. Purcell, (president, Herald Media and the *Boston Herald*)

Discover New York—and the World

St. John's offers over a hundred majors, including programs as varied as cytotechnology, theology, microcomputer technology, and public relations. The university integrates its geographic location into academics from the start. In their Discover New York class, which they must take as part of the core curriculum, freshmen learn about the history and cultural landscape of the Big Apple, complementing their studies with outings to museums and Broadway shows. Because of the university's religious affiliations, a Catholic theology course is also a requirement. Students in the Peter J. Tobin College of Business have an opportunity to earn course credit while interning at top companies such as Smith Barney and Donna Karan, among others. More interested in traveling than in buffing your resume to a high shine? The new Discover the World study-abroad program allows students to travel to several countries throughout the semester. Community service is stressed abroad and at home, and a list of agencies needing your help awaits.

Seeing Red

The Red Storm used to go by "Redmen," but in 1994, concerned because that term is a pejorative for Native Americans, the university adopted the new moniker. The new name has gone over well, but it has left the university mascot-less for the time being.

Beware the Red Storm

With more than twenty thousand students among its five campuses, St. John's is a big school—and its students have big school spirit. The men's basketball team, the Red Storm, are Division I players in the Big East Conference and play half their home games in Manhattan's famed Madison Square Garden. Half the student body is Roman Catholic. Theology courses are required, and STJ honors its Vincentian roots through an emphasis on serving the poor. In fact, community service is stressed in most aspects of student life, both in class and in groups such as fraternities and sororities. Like its metropolitan location, the university is wonderfully diverse. Its student body comprises 39 percent minorities and students from more than a hundred countries. Students regularly make the trip into Manhattan, whether for course require-ments or just for fun. They must get hooked; after graduation, 83 per-cent of alumni make their homes in the greater New York area.

Learn to Love the MTA

St. John's has campuses in Manhattan, Long Island, and Staten Island, but it's the Queens campus that draws the most undergrads. Students enjoy the traditional collegiate look of the Queens location and love the fact that Manhattan is just a subway ride away. From internships to entertainment, New York City offers college students plenty of activi-ties. Broadway shows, film festivals, comedy clubs—the list is endless. Access to other parts of the country is easy, as the Queens campus is a fifteen-minute drive from both Kennedy and La Guardia airports. Leave your car at home; New Yorkers are all about public transportation, and St. John's students are no exception.

Admissions

Average high school GPA:	3.2
Average freshman SAT verbal / math score:	531 / 551
Average freshman ACT score:	—
Application fee:	$30
Application deadlines:	continuous (freshman) continuous (transfer)
Total applicants:	25,594
Total accepted:	15,159 (59%)
Total accepted who enrolled:	3,260
Notification dates:	continuous (freshman) continuous (transfer)

Students

Percentage of male / female students:	44% / 56%
Percentage of students from out of state:	11%
Percentage of students graduating in 4 years / 6 years:	40% / 64%

Money

Total endowment:	$305,000,000
Total tuition:	$24,400
Total cost with fees & expenses:	$37,440
Average financial aid package:	$15,807
Percentage of students who sought aid and received it:	65%
Percentage of students receiving financial aid:	64%

Also Check Out

Fairfield University

Georgetown University

Syracuse University

Villanova University

St. Lawrence University

23 Romoda Drive
Canton, NY 13617

(315) 229-5011
http://www.stlawu.edu/

 **BIG HAND**

 **BIG PERSPECTIVE**

The operative world here is *nurturing*.

5 REASONS IT'S COOL

1. St. Lawrence's First-Year Program lets freshmen **live and learn with a small group of fellow newcomers.**

2. **Bachelor's-to-master's programs in business administration and engineering** allow students to take advantage of neighboring schools.

3. Nearly half the students participate in **study-abroad programs or off-campus study options.**

4. The university has launched a **$130 million campaign to improve facilities and student resources.**

5. Attention nature lovers! St. Lawrence is home to **a seventy-six-acre forest preserve.**

The Basics

Public / private: private nonprofit
Total enrollment / undergrads: 2,303 / 2,182
Campus setting: small town
Students call it: St. Lawrence, SLU
Students are called: Laurentians, Saints
Notable alums: Jeffrey H. Boyd (president and CEO, Priceline.com), Susan Collins (senator), Kirk Douglas (actor), Dave Jennings (pro football player), Martha MacCallum (news anchor), Jacques Martin (pro hockey coach), Lorrie Moore (author), Owen D. Young (founder, RCA)

Small School with Big Options

St. Lawrence promises small classes and lots of personal attention. The small-school touch is apparent from students' first day on campus, when they enroll in the First-Year Program and are assigned to an interdisciplinary, team-taught course. Not only do these classes give newcomers the chance to get to know their professors, but they also allow them to study with the same group that will make up their living community. Dozens of majors and minors include offerings such as conservation biology, environmental studies, neuroscience, and several ethnic and cultural studies. The most popular majors in recent years have been psychology, government, economics, English, and history. In addition to a student-exchange program, SLU's international programs send students to fourteen countries for study and independent or team research. Laurentians are known for their rigorous approach to academics, and the faculty is happy to challenge them.

The High Life

Upstate New York's autumn leaves inspire students in a unique way. During Peak Weekend, the school's Outing Club hits the Adirondacks. It's an annual tradition that at least one student reaches the summit of each of the Adirondack's forty-six highest peaks.

A student-to-faculty ratio of 11:1 and TA-free classes topping out in the mid-twenties also encourage strong academic engagement.

Where Work Meets Play

Laurentians may enjoy their studies, but they don't spend their lives buried in books. Just about everyone joins at least one of the university's one hundred student organizations, which range from the groups focused on arts to politics to community service to ski racing. Roughly 60 percent of students participate in intramural or intercollegiate athletics, and the men's ice hockey team is a fan favorite. Nearly a quarter of students participate in Greek life, although the influence of frats and sororities has declined in recent years. Ninety-five percent of students live on campus, and the school provides a number of theme-based residence options for students interesting in LGBT issues, environmental matters, and community service. Although the First-Year Program helps most students find a social and extracurricular niche, racial, ethnic, and class diversity is low, but the university is working to change this. SLU's diversity is mainly geographic, with students hailing from more than forty-one states and twenty-four countries.

Nature's Little Miracle

Canton, New York, may not be a bustling college town, but SLU students love it just the same. The breathtakingly green campus is mostly vehicle free, creating a sanctuary-like atmosphere and a sense of detachment from the rest of the world. Students take advantage of concerts, hockey games, themed parties, midnight breakfasts, and Greek festivities. Residents of the Java House coordinate music performances by contemporary bands, and a first-run theater brings in the latest movies. The school provides accessories for hiking and camping in the nearby Adirondacks, which are less than an hour's drive away. Syracuse and Albany are close by, and those looking for more cosmopolitan options can try out the abundant nightlife options in Montreal or Ottawa, both of which are a two-and-a-half hour drive away.

Admissions

Average high school GPA:	3.49
Average freshman SAT verbal / math score:	601 / 608
Average freshman ACT score:	25
Application fee:	$50

Application deadlines:
2/1 (freshmen)
4/1 (transfer)
11/15 (early decision)

Total applicants:	3,192
Total accepted:	1,878 (59%)
Total accepted who enrolled:	611

Notification dates:
3/31 (freshmen)
5/1 (transfer)
12/15 (early decision)

Acceptance rate for early decision applicants:	75%

Students

Percentage of male / female students:	47% / 53%
Percentage of students from out of state:	50%
Percentage of students graduating in 4 years / 6 years:	71% / 75%

Money

Total endowment:	$229,830,177
Total tuition:	$33,690
Total cost with fees & expenses:	$43,190
Average financial aid package:	$32,471
Percentage of students who sought aid and received it:	94%
Percentage of students receiving financial aid:	63%

Also Check Out

Bennington College

Colgate University

College of the Holy Cross

Macalester College

Skidmore College

St. Mary's College of Maryland

18952 East Fisher Road St. Mary's City, MD 20686	(240) 895-2000 http://www.smcm.edu/

BIG PERSPECTIVE

Little, public, different, *better*

5 REASONS IT'S COOL

1. **Saint Mary's is Maryland's official public honors college**, and that means students get a top-notch liberal arts education with a public school price tag.

2. **Rosaries not required:** in spite of its Catholic-sounding name, St. Mary's is not a religious school.

3. Classes are small and professor-student relations are tight, which might be part of the reason **half of students pursue graduate and professional degrees**.

4. Opportunities for **study abroad, internships, research, and self-directed study** abound.

5. Ply the **nearby Chesapeake Bay** with the sailing team . . . or with a cardboard boat.

The Basics

Public / private: public state
Total enrollment / undergrads: 1,957 / 1,948
Campus setting: rural
Students call it: St. Mary's, SMCM
Students are called: Seahawks
Notable alums: William Craft (poet), Julie Croteau (first female NCAA men's baseball player), John F. Slade III (judge, state assemblyman), Paul Reed Smith (guitar maker)

Serious Students Wanted

Saint Mary's is serious about academics. With a student-to-faculty ratio of 13:1, students know that they'll get a lot of personal attention from their professors, 98 percent of whom hold terminal degrees in their fields. Students choose from twenty-three different majors or create their own course of study. Those who enroll in the Honors College benefit from small seminar-style classes, prestigious internships, study-abroad opportunities, and a unique interdisciplinary course of study. Honors students are also required to complete a senior project, which represents the culmination of their studies. The projects can include elements of creative expression, internships, an informative international experience, or original research. With all these amazing academic opportunities available, it's no wonder that 50 percent of Saint Mary's students go on to earn graduate or professional degrees at top universities such as MIT, Stanford, Yale, and Cambridge.

Not Ready for the Sailing Team

St. Mary's annual Cardboard Boat Race takes place during homecoming/parents' weekend. Teams must construct boats entirely out of materials provided for them, which usually include cardboard, plastic, and balsa wood. Then they race their craft in a small loop on the St. Mary's River near the college boathouse and docks. There are cash prizes for the winners, although there's no word on how many boats actually finish the race.

Go Jump in a Lake . . .

Saint Mary's students participate in over seventy different student-run clubs and organizations, including music groups, improvisational troupes, poetry groups, and academic, religious, and political clubs. It's also a campus tradition to get tossed into St. John's pond once a year, usually on your birthday. The college offers thirteen varsity sports teams, including the nationally ranked sailing team. A full 70 percent of students join one or more of the twenty club and intramural sports teams. Saint Mary's is serious about helping students adjust to life after graduation too: Upperclassmen and women often live in townhouses and pay their own electric bills and can opt out of the university's meal plans to cook for themselves.

Oysters on the Half Shell

Southern Maryland is the oyster capital of the United States, and the annual Oyster Festival reflects this honor. Each year, in the third week of October, congregants consume more than 150,000 oysters and seventy kegs of beer while watching the oyster-shucking contest. If you aren't into shellfish, catch the Point Lookout Ghost Tour on Halloween, where you can tour the remains of a Civil War–era prison in nearby Point Lookout State Park. The Calvert Marine Museum in Calvert County is a regular venue for big-name performers, and the Saint Mary's county fair features livestock judging, fatty fair foods, and even a carnival with a Tilt-a-Whirl. If you tire of all the excitement, relax on campus, which is notably picturesque.

Admissions

Average high school GPA:	3.5
Average freshman SAT verbal / math score:	626 / 609
Average freshman ACT score:	—
Application fee:	$40
Application deadlines:	
1/15 (freshmen)	
2/15 (transfer)	
12/1 (early decision)	
Total applicants:	2,255
Total accepted:	1,271 (56%)
Total accepted who enrolled:	428
Notification dates:	
4/1 (freshmen)	
6/1 (transfer)	
12/31 (early decision)	
Acceptance rate for early decision applicants:	65%

Students

Percentage of male / female students:	43% / 57%
Percentage of students from out of state:	17%
Percentage of students graduating in 4 years / 6 years:	63% / 72%

Money

Total endowment:	$30,957,844
Total in-state tuition, fees & expenses:	$20,844
Total out-of-state tuition, fees & expenses:	$31,178
Average financial aid package:	$6,500
Percentage of students who sought aid and received it:	62%
Percentage of students receiving financial aid:	42%

Also Check Out

American University

College of William & Mary

Towson University

University of Delaware

University of Maryland–College Park

Stanford University

Montag Hall
Stanford, CA 94305

(650) 723-2300
http://www.stanford.edu/

 **BIG BRAIN**

 **BIG PERSPECTIVE**

 **BIG RESEARCH**

This Cardinal rules.

5 REASONS IT'S COOL

1. **Elite academics and year-round sunshine:** What more could you want?

2. Stanford enjoys a reputation as **a top national school with boundless research opportunities**.

3. The sprawling **campus is so beautiful** you'll never want to leave. And most students don't, preferring to live on-campus during their time here.

4. Stanford's **athletic teams kick butt** in NCAA Division I, and the rivalry with Berkeley is the one of the most legendary in college football.

5. Students enjoy **the relaxed Stanford lifestyle**.

The Basics

Public / private: private nonprofit
Total enrollment / undergrads: 17,747 / 6,422
Campus setting: suburban
Students call it: Stanford
Students are called: Cardinals
Notable alums: Chelsea Clinton (First Daughter), Michael Cunningham (novelist), Sandra Day O'Connor (U.S. Supreme Court justice), Daniel Pearl (journalist), Sally Ride (astronaut), Sigourney Weaver (actress), Tiger Woods (attended; pro golfer)

At the Tops of Their Games

Stanford enjoys a well-deserved reputation as one of the best universities in the country and a shining star of the West Coast academic world. Students choose from about sixty majors, including a slew of interdisciplinary options, or design their own course of study. The most popular majors are biology (or HumBio, for human biology), computer science, economics, English, and psychology. The university's core program is extensive. All students must take the Introduction to Humanities class (not a universally loved experience) and complete courses in the following areas: science technology and math; humanities and social sciences; and world culture, American culture, and gender studies. Nearly all classes are taught by faculty members, many of whom have Nobels, MacArthurs, and a variety of other top prizes in their trophy cases. All students are encouraged to study abroad, and nearly a third of students take advantage of the rich opportunities offered. Academic advisors,

Moonlight Makeout

You might expect people to howl at the full moon, but kiss? That's exactly what Stanford students do every year during the annual Full Moon on the Quad. On the evening of the academic year's first full moon, seniors and freshmen gather on the campus's Main Quad for one activity: smooching. The idea behind all of this lip action is for seniors to anoint freshmen as full-fledged Stanford men and women. Incidentally, sophomores and juniors have been known to steal a smooch or two too.

who are either staff or faculty, assist in guiding students through the university's extensive academic choices.

Sunny Dispositions

Nearly all students choose to live on campus, and for good reasons: Surrounding Palo Alto, while quite pretty, is also quite pricey, and life on campus rocks. The university guarantees housing for all four years and requires freshman to live on campus. Between marathon study sessions, students zip around campus on bikes, meet up for a study break at the CoHo (or coffee house), and take windsurfing lessons on nearby Lake Lagunita. Stanford students are generally preppy, smart, and driven. Fraternities and sororities draw about 12 percent of students. Sports figure largely on campus, and Stanford's NCAA Division I athletic teams inspire plenty of passion in fans. These passions peak every November during the "Big Game," the annual football game with longtime rival Berkeley. Be sure to enjoy the, uh, *interesting* song stylings of the Leland Stanford Junior Marching Band, which is one of the wackier pep bands in college athletics.

A California Classic

Stanford's campus, clocking in at more than eight thousand acres, is one of the largest in the world. Frederick Law Olmsted, who also designed Central Park, drew up the campus's original plans. Lovely mission-style architecture persists through most buildings, but there's still quite a bit of design diversity, especially in student housing. The campus is located Palo Alto, a safe, if stodgy, area full of historic homes and plenty of shopping and culinary diversions. Cross-pollination between the university and Silicon Valley is abundant; headquarters for firms such as Google, Adobe, and Intel are all nearby. San Francisco, the closest big city, is just under an hour away and can be reached by car or train.

Admissions

Average high school GPA:	4.0
Average freshman SAT writing / math / critical reading score:	701 / 713 / 701
Average freshman ACT score:	26
Application fee:	$75

Application deadlines:
12/15 (freshmen)
3/15 (transfer)
11/1 (early action)

Total applicants:	22,333
Total accepted:	2,444 (11%)
Total accepted who enrolled:	1,646

Notification dates:
4/1 (freshmen)
5/25 (transfer)
12/15 (early action)

Acceptance rate for early action applicants:	20%

Students

Percentage of male / female students:	52% / 48%
Percentage of students from out of state:	34%
Percentage of students graduating in 4 years / 6 years:	76% / 94%

Money

Total endowment:	$4,294,967,295
Total tuition:	$32,994
Total cost with fees & expenses:	$44,621
Average financial aid package:	$29,234
Percentage of students who sought aid and received it:	100%
Percentage of students receiving financial aid:	46%

Also Check Out

Duke University

Harvard University

Massachusetts Institute of Technology

Princeton University

University of California–Berkeley

Stetson University

421 North Woodland Boulevard
DeLand, FL 32723

(386) 822-7000
http://www.stetson.edu/

 **BIG HAND**

 **BIG PERSPECTIVE**

Hats off to Stetson!

5 REASONS IT'S COOL

1. Stetson is **Florida's first private university** and pioneered its first colleges of music and law.

2. Students enjoy **year-round sunshine and warm weather**.

3. The **outstanding music program** is housed in a building created to look like a piano.

4. Stetson touts **great creative writing programs** in fiction, poetry, drama, and literary nonfiction.

5. Students go wild for the Division I athletics, and the **men's basketball team** was the first in Florida to win one thousand games.

The Basics

Public / private: private nonprofit
Total enrollment / undergrads: 3,762 / 2,273
Campus setting: small town
Students call it: Stetson
Students are called: Hatters
Notable alums: Ted Cassidy (actor), Max Cleland (senator), Craig Crawford (political commentator), James Merritt (Baptist pastor; CEO, Touching Lives), Kevin Nicholson (pro baseball player), E. Clay Shaw Jr. (congressman)

Smaller Doesn't Always Mean Lesser

Stetson is all about community. The personal touch is apparent from day one, when freshmen are given the opportunity to enroll in small, frosh-only seminars taught by some of the university's best professors. They may also opt for living-learning communities, where students live with the same students from their classes. The university offers sixty different majors in three undergraduate colleges of arts and sciences, business, and music. Business, elementary education, and psych are some of the most popular areas of study, but there are more specialized opportunities, too, including family business and sports management. Business students have the unique opportunity of investing real money in the stock market and measuring their performance against those of other student investors (in the past, they've beaten Harvard Business School students). Regardless of their major, all students need to fulfill several basic requirements before graduating,

How About a NightCap?

Every Friday evening from 10 P.M. to midnight, Stetson hosts what's known as NightCap, a series of events that give students the chance to hang out and socialize. Each week brings a different activity, ranging from movies to concerts to parties to games. Whatever the venue, NightCap always offers free snacks, which is a big draw for many students.

which cover everything from writing and math to religious heritage and ethical decision making.

Where Greeks Rule

At Stetson, there's always something going on. Between the college's seven fraternities and six sororities, there's usually a party (or six) to be found. For those interested in something other than rushing or attending Greek bashes, the university offers about 120 student organizations, ranging from student publications to intramurals to religious organizations. Cheering on the Division I athletics teams is also a popular pastime, although football fans often lament the absence of a football team. The campus's Hollis Center houses first-rate fitness facilities, including a pool and fitness room.

A Sunshine State of Mind

Filled with palm trees and turn-of-the-twentieth-century buildings, Stetson's campus befits its coastal Florida setting. In fact, the school is even listed on the National Register of Historic Places. And while most of the buildings have since been renovated—including the Lyman Center, Stetson's first green building—the campus retains its Old World charm. Stetson students are known for their wild campus parties, but those looking for a little less alcohol and a little more culture can find what they're looking for in nearby Orlando, which has great restaurants, pro sports, art venues, and, of course, amusement parks.

Admissions

Average high school GPA:	3.76
Average freshman SAT verbal / math score:	571 / 560
Average freshman ACT score:	24
Application fee:	$40
Application deadlines:	
3/1 (freshmen)	
continuous (transfer)	
11/1 (early decision)	
Total applicants:	2,919
Total accepted:	1,896 (65%)
Total accepted who enrolled:	567
Notification dates:	
12/1 (freshmen)	
continuous (transfer)	
11/25 (early decision)	
Acceptance rate for early decision applicants:	84%

Students

Percentage of male / female students:	42% / 58%
Percentage of students from out of state:	20%
Percentage of students graduating in 4 years / 6 years:	57% / 65%

Money

Total endowment:	$124,428,000
Total tuition:	$27,100
Total cost with fees & expenses:	$36,748
Average financial aid package:	$22,727
Percentage of students who sought aid and received it:	83%
Percentage of students receiving financial aid:	50%

Also Check Out

Eckerd College

Florida State University

Rollins College

University of Florida

The University of Miami

Stevens Institute of Technology

Castle Point on Hudson
Hoboken, NJ 07030

(201) 216-5000
http://www.stevens.edu/

 BIG JOB

 **BIG PLAN**

 **BIG RESEARCH**

Where the future is now

5 REASONS IT'S COOL

1. Stevens is **the fourth-oldest technological university** in the United States.

2. Like a good challenge? Students here work hard, but they're rewarded with **one of the best science educations in the country.**

3. Research: You'll do tons of it here, as you collaborate with faculty members to **develop tomorrow's technologies.**

4. The Davidson Laboratory is home to **unique research in hydrodynamics, naval architecture, and ocean engineering.**

5. **Hoboken has great bars and restaurants,** plus it's directly across the river from a wee little hamlet they call New York City.

The Basics

Public/private: private nonprofit
Total enrollment/undergrads: 4,829 / 1,853
Campus setting: urban
Students call it: Stevens, S.I.T.
Students are called: Ducks
Notable alums: Evelyn E. Bailey (economist), James Corcoran (president and CEO, Lockheed Martin), Leon F. Cordero (president, Ecuador), Eugene McDermott (founder, Texas Instruments)

A Place for Techno-Geniuses

Stevens consists of five separate but equally challenging schools. The Charles Schaefer School of Engineering and Science gives students a mix of classroom, research, and internship opportunities in an effort to close the gap between engineering and the sciences. The Wesley Howe School of Technology Management, on the other hand, combines technology and science with business studies. The School of Systems and Enterprises offers a study of industry and government within a global framework, while the College of Arts and Letters provides coursework in history, literature, philosophy, and the social sciences. In addition to its five schools, Stevens also offers a nationally recognized co-op program, as well as plenty of research opportunities for undergraduates. Stevens's groundbreaking technogenesis program allows students, faculty, and companies to work together to develop new technologies. Students compete for $2,000 and $3,000 cash prizes, which are awarded to teams of graduating seniors whose technogenesis projects show the highest potential.

A Bloody Beginning

Castle Point, near Stevens, is not only the highest point in Hoboken, but it's also said to be the haunting grounds of a well-known ghost. On March nights when the wind howls, listen for Jan of Rotterdam, who was killed here during an Indian raid. It is said that he roams Castle Point in search of his missing scalp.

Calling All High Achievers

Stevens is for high achievers both in and out of the classroom. In fact, many students find that their academic interests *are* their personal interests (which may be why there are so many engineering and science clubs). The institute offers more than seventy student organizations, which range from multicultural groups to honor societies to the student-run radio station. About a third of students join one of the seventeen fraternities and sororities, and Greek life steers much of the social action on campus. There's also student government and the student honor board, which investigates instances of plagiarism and student misconduct, along with a variety of jazz bands, concert bands, and weekend film festivals. The NCAA Division III sports program is popular and offers twenty-four varsity teams, including men's and women's basketball and women's equestrian and field hockey.

The Best of Both Worlds

Stevens is located on a fifty-five-acre plot of land in Hoboken, just across the Hudson River from New York City. The city has a small-town, Main Street feel, belying its proximity to the concrete jungle of downtown Manhattan, which is no more than a couple miles away. Hoboken is becoming one of New Jersey's and greater New York's hotspots, as more and more young professionals move out of the city proper in search of cheaper rent and a quieter atmosphere. The influx has led to new bars, restaurants, pubs, shops, and cafés to explore in the evenings. Check out Weehawken Cove, take in the view at Castle Point, catch a play at the DeBaun Auditorium, or take a leisurely stroll along the Waterfront Walkway.

Admissions

Average high school GPA:	3.7
Average freshman SAT verbal / math score:	605 / 668
Average freshman ACT score:	25
Application fee:	$55

Application deadlines:
2/15 (freshmen)
7/1 (transfer)
11/15 (early decision)

Total applicants:	2,278
Total accepted:	1,224 (54%)
Total accepted who enrolled:	483

Notification dates:
3/15 (freshmen)
continuous (transfer)
12/15 (early decision)

Acceptance rate for early decision applicants:	83%

Students

Percentage of male / female students:	76% / 24%
Percentage of students from out of state:	38%
Percentage of students graduating in 4 years / 6 years:	31% / 72%

Money

Total endowment:	$130,237,000
Total tuition:	$31,750
Total cost with fees & expenses:	$44,015
Average financial aid package:	$21,139
Percentage of students who sought aid and received it:	85%
Percentage of students receiving financial aid:	66%

Also Check Out

Clark University

Cooper Union for the Advancement of Science and Art

Drexel University

Rensselaer Polytechnic Institute

Rochester Institute of Technology

SUNY–Binghamton University

PO Box 6000
Binghamton, NY 13902

(607) 777-2000
http://www.binghamton.edu/

 **BIG CHOICE**

 **BIG RESEARCH**

Great teachers and great classes are just the basics.

5 REASONS IT'S COOL

1. Binghamton **rivals many private northeastern colleges academically.** In terms of tuition, it blows them out of the water.

2. The university recently moved up to **NCAA Division I**, and its up-and-coming basketball team inspires Bearcat pride.

3. Make yourself at home at this **ethnically diverse** university.

4. The **Individualized Major Program** lets students design their own majors.

5. Sick of everyone knowing your business? As one of **more than ten thousand undergrads**, you won't have that problem here.

The Basics

Public / private: public state
Total enrollment / undergrads: 14,373 / 11,523
Campus setting: suburban
Students call it: SUNY-Binghamton, Binghamton, BU
Students are called: Bearcats
Notable alums: William Baldwin (actor), Steve Koren (screenwriter), Tony Kornheiser (sports journalist), Camille Paglia (feminist critic), Paul Reiser (actor), Madeleine Smithberg (cocreator, *The Daily Show*), Art Spiegelman (graphic novelist), Bob Swan (CFO, eBay)

Get Off on the Right Foot

Don't be fooled by the public school name and price tag. Binghamton is an academic powerhouse with many of the perks—and a few of the pitfalls—of a big research university. BU has strong programs in the sciences, business, political science, engineering, and nursing. Students have hefty workloads, but their labors pay off when they get into topnotch graduate programs or land jobs at notable companies. Consider enrolling in one of three programs that allow freshmen to live and take classes with a small community of fellow students. Area-Based Courses (ABCs) enable enrollees to take two classes, each of which has a different approach to the same subject—genetics, for example, or terrorism. First Year Experience Courses (FYEs) introduce students to profs and staff from across the campus and show them how they can get involved in the community. And Learning Communities gives students the chance to get to know their professors both inside and outside the classroom.

These Flip-Flops Were Made for Stomping

Each year during Spring Fling, Binghamton students celebrate their escape from the snowy winter of Upstate New York. The event features a palm reader, a magician, bumper cars, a mechanical bull, and music acts ranging from student bands to 50 Cent. The carnival's most beloved tradition is the "Stepping on the Coat" ceremony, during which students step—or stomp—on their coats in a symbolic farewell to winter.

Something for Everyone

Binghamton can seem overwhelming, particularly to students from Upstate New York who don't arrive with ready-made social groups, as many Bearcats from the city do. Going Greek can be one good way to carve out a niche; Binghamton has twenty-two frats and seventeen sororities to choose from. If that's not your thing, though, you'll find your place in one of the two hundred student organizations, which cover everything from sculpting to a student radio station to politics. Each residence hall develops its own identity and traditions. The dorms are also assigned faculty members who create learning opportunities outside the classroom in the form of film screenings, parties, and off-campus excursions. And if you want to hang out with friends from other dorms but don't want to go to a frat or sorority party, Late Nite Binghamton offers live music, parties, movies, games, and other activities on the weekends. Bearcats football and basketball games give sports fans reason to cheer.

Small Town, Big Options

Because many students don't venture off campus, undergrads sometimes think of Binghamton as boring. In reality, while Binghamton may not be big, it has a surprising number of attractions. Its art galleries are open late on the first Friday of every month, and there are plenty of good restaurants and bars, not to mention traveling opera and theater performances. Sports fans will enjoy the minor league hockey and baseball teams, and students who prefer to be outdoors will like the parks for hiking, biking, walking, and running and the rivers for fishing, boating, and kayaking when the weather's warm. It's easy to get in downhill skiing, snowboarding, and tubing during the snowy months. Binghamton's Getaway Bus Trips give students the chance to get off campus for a day and check out nearby attractions, including Mets games, the National Baseball Hall of Fame, Six Flags' Fright Fest, Howe Caverns, and Philadelphia. Or students can make a three-hour drive to Philly or New York City themselves.

Admissions

Average high school GPA:	3.7
Average freshman SAT verbal / math score:	614 / 655
Average freshman ACT score:	26
Application fee:	$40

Application deadlines:
continuous (freshmen)
continuous (transfer)
11/15 (early action)

Total applicants:	22,853
Total accepted:	9,861 (43%)
Total accepted who enrolled:	2,319

Notification dates:
continuous (freshmen)
continuous (transfer)
1/1 (early action)

Acceptance rate for early action applicants:	—

Students

Percentage of male / female students:	52% / 48%
Percentage of students from out of state:	7%
Percentage of students graduating in 4 years / 6 years:	67% / 79%

Money

Total endowment:	$56,280,000
Total in-state tuition, fees & expenses:	$15,298
Total out-of-state tuition, fees & expenses:	$21,558
Average financial aid package:	$11,878
Percentage of students who sought aid and received it:	78%
Percentage of students receiving financial aid:	44%

Also Check Out

New York University

SUNY–Geneseo

SUNY–Stony Brook University

SUNY–University at Buffalo

University of Delaware

SUNY–Fashion Institute of Technology

Seventh Avenue at 27th Street
New York, NY 10001

(212) 217-7999
http://www.fitnyc.edu/

 BIG JOB

 **BIG PLAN**

Got a passion for fashion?

5 REASONS IT'S COOL

1. FIT grads have **an astounding 90 percent job-placement rate.**

2. Students can **expand their sartorial horizons** in Florence, Melbourne, Hong Kong, India, and other locales worldwide.

3. FIT offers **the only accessories design degree program in the United States.**

4. Welcome to New York City, baby. The Seventh Avenue location puts students **right in the heart of the fashion world.**

5. How's this for a track record? **Calvin Klein, Caroline Herrera, Michael Kors**, and a slew of other superstars are FIT grads.

The Basics

Public / private: public state and local
Total enrollment / undergrads: 10,010 / 9,825
Campus setting: urban
Students call it: FIT
Students are called: Tigers
Notable alums: Caroline Herrera (fashion designer), Norma Kamali (fashion designer), Calvin Klein (fashion designer), Michael Kors (fashion designer), Daniel Vosovic (fashion designer)

The Fabric of a Great Career

FIT has two undergraduate schools: the School of Art and Design, which offers seventeen majors, and the Business and Technology school, with ten offerings. This top U.S. arts school seeks to give students a solid grounding in the liberal arts even as they hone the skills necessary in their chosen professions. FIT's core curriculum includes a physical education course and ten courses in fields such as math, natural science, foreign languages, and American history. Most majors require a degree-related internship. Because 40 percent of these internships lead to jobs, this part of the college experience is especially important. The college hosts guest lectures from top professionals to promote networking opportunities. FIT's New York location also gives it a rich pool from which to draw its faculty, who tend to be leaders in the fields of fashion and design. The school's Presidential Scholars program gives exceptional students access to special colloquia, field trips, priority course registration, monetary awards, and on-campus housing.

Like President, Like Students

Students at FIT are driven to succeed—and so is their president. Raised in Harlem, Dr. Joyce Brown, who as an African American woman reflects the diversity of her school, climbed the college administration ranks after working full-time as a financial aid counselor during graduate school. She now fosters confidence and a go-getting attitude among her students.

Fashionably Diverse

On-campus housing at FIT is a hot commodity, and even freshmen aren't guaranteed a spot. Some rooms require one of the meal plans, which are flexible but also restrictive, given the variety of eating options in New York City and the early closing time of dining halls (8:00 P.M. at the latest). Student activities center around the behemoth David Dubinsky Student Center, an eight-story modern structure that houses many student-run clubs, a student exhibition space, and food court. It's also home to the college's Internship Center, where full-time counselors help students choose sponsor companies. The sundry mix of student extracurricular activities includes the newspaper, *West 27*, the Black Student Union, Holistic Healing and Lifestyle, and a gospel choir. The student body at FIT is notably rich in diversity, consisting of 7 percent African American, 10 percent Asian American, 10 percent Latino American, and 11 percent international students. It lacks diversity, however, in its gender ratio: Only 14 percent of students are male.

Talk About a Perfect Location

FIT's campus is strategically located in Manhattan, the epicenter of those fields its students pursue—fashion and design. New York's fashion district and art galleries are right next door, providing students easy access to networking opportunities and internships. The campus features buildings with state-of-the-art facilities and rich research materials, and FIT is currently in the process of adding new buildings, one of which will include a rooftop garden and flexible venue for fashion shows, conferences, and events. Students are encouraged to soak up the countless cultural offerings available in the big city, including opera, dance, theater, and the art world.

Admissions

Average high school GPA:	3.1
Average freshman SAT verbal / math score:	—/—
Average freshman ACT score:	—
Application fee:	$40

Application deadlines:
2/1 (freshmen)
2/1 (transfer)
11/15 (early action)

Total applicants:	3,602
Total accepted:	1,539 (43%)
Total accepted who enrolled:	928

Notification dates:
continuous (freshmen)
continuous (transfer)
1/31 (early action)

Acceptance rate for early action applicants:	61%

Students

Percentage of male / female students:	14% / 86%
Percentage of students from out of state:	30%
Percentage of students graduating in 4 years / 6 years:	63% / 66%

Money

Total endowment:	$25,808,323
Total in-state tuition, fees & expenses:	$15,983
Total out-of-state tuition, fees & expenses:	$22,243
Average financial aid package:	$8,365
Percentage of students who sought aid and received it:	65%
Percentage of students receiving financial aid:	31%

Also Check Out

Eugene Lang College, The New School for Liberal Arts

Parsons, The New School for Design

Rhode Island School for Design

Syracuse University

SUNY–Geneseo

I College Circle
Geneseo, NY 14454

(585) 245-5211
http://www.geneseo.edu/

BIG PERSPECTIVE

They call it "SUNY's Honor College."

5 REASONS IT'S COOL

1. No lone wolves here—students are an active, involved bunch.

2. The **excellent profs** go out of their way to help students learn, and TAs don't teach undergrads.

3. **No one breaks the bank:** New York State residents pay just over $14,000 a year, while out-of-staters pay just over $20,000.

4. Geneseo boasts **the highest four-year graduation rate of any public university or college in the United States**.

5. With Ivy-clad buildings, tree-lined streets, and quaint shops, restaurants, and bars, this town has **charm to spare**.

The Basics

Public / private: public state
Total enrollment / undergrads: 5,530 / 5,358
Campus setting: small town
Students call it: SUNY-Geneseo, Geneseo State University, Geneseo
Students are called: Knights
Notable alums: Norma Holland (journalist), Chelsea Noble (actress), Curt Smith (sports broadcaster), Chet Walker (radio host)

What a Small Liberal Arts College Looks Like

Geneseo looks and feels more like a small liberal arts college than like an arm of the massive SUNY system. For one thing, the idyllic campus looks like it belongs in the catalog of a New England college. For another, the university focuses on teaching rather than research, which is great news for undergrads, who don't have to fight for profs' attention as they would at other state schools. Professors are accessible and teach discussion-based courses. Even big lecture classes are surprisingly enjoyable, perhaps because they're never taught by TAs. Since Geneseo is a liberal arts college in spirit, business administration and nursing are not among its thirty-seven major offerings. But there are plenty of other choices spanning the liberal arts, sciences, fine arts, and communication. Whatever you major in, you'll complete the Common Core, which includes requirements in humanities, foreign languages, non-Western tradition, U.S. history, critical writing and reading, and numeric and symbolic reasoning.

Grizzly Business

Just outside campus in the center of Main Street in the middle of a fountain stands a big bronze bear. Students often decorate him with leis and other objects or use him in pranks. And according to school legend, the bear will jump down and run away forever if a virgin graduates from Geneseo. At the time of publication, he was still firmly planted in the fountain.

Caffeine, Please

Visit Geneseo's library on any given night, and you're sure to find tons of students. But while Knights are a studious bunch (and tend to think of their school as the brainiest SUNY), they are also very involved in campus life. And although only about 56 percent of Geneseo students live on campus, most spend a lot of time there. Guest lectures and scholarly events grab students' attention, as does the Division III men's ice hockey team. And just about everyone is involved in at least one of the school's 169 student organizations, which range from the Accounting Society to the Club for Animal Rights Education to student media to a yoga club to a ski team. Greeks also have a decent presence on campus, with 9 percent of students in frats and 13 percent in sororities. These percentages might be a little misleading, though. Three-fifths of Geneseo's student are female, which makes for lots of jokes about the gender gap around campus.

The Hills Are Alive with the Swish of Sleds

Western New York is a beautiful, if somewhat remote, place to attend college. Situated on the western edge of the Finger Lakes, the hilly campus offers heavenly sunsets and fantastic views of the Genesee Valley. Students sled during the winter and mud slide once spring arrives. Outdoorsy types also enjoy hiking or jogging around campus or taking a twenty-minute drive to Letchworth State Park to go camping, picnicking, or hiking. Aside from outdoor activities, there's little to do in town. Luckily, there's always plenty happening on campus, including theater and music events, intramural sports, and parties. As an added bonus, the campus is full of beautiful buildings. One of the oldest is the 1932 James B. Welles building, which features arches, gables, and ivy overlaying a stone and brick façade. Frank Lloyd Wright's apprentice Edgar Tafel designed the Brodie Building (home to the School of the Arts), as well as the five dorms and dining hall that make up the campus's South Side complex. When students want to get off campus and out of the area, they can make the forty-minute drive up to Rochester.

Admissions

Average high school GPA:	3.8
Average freshman SAT verbal / math score:	644 / 656
Average freshman ACT score:	26
Application fee:	$40

Application deadlines:
1/15 (freshmen)
1/15 (transfer)
11/15 (early decision)

Total applicants:	9,043
Total accepted:	3,681 (41%)
Total accepted who enrolled:	1,080

Notification dates:
3/15 (freshmen)
3/15 (transfer)
12/15 (early decision)

Acceptance rate for early decision applicants:	58%

Students

Percentage of male / female students:	41% / 59%
Percentage of students from out of state:	1%
Percentage of students graduating in 4 years / 6 years:	64% / 79%

Money

Total endowment:	$7,672,105
Total in-state tuition, fees & expenses:	$14,148
Total out-of-state tuition, fees & expenses:	$20,408
Average financial aid package:	$9,526
Percentage of students who sought aid and received it:	86%
Percentage of students receiving financial aid:	44%

Also Check Out

Boston College

Colgate University

Cornell University

Ithaca College

SUNY–Binghamton University

SUNY–Stony Brook University

Nicolls Road
Stony Brook, NY 11794

(631) 632-6000
http://www.sunysb.edu/

 **BIG CHOICE**

 **BIG RESEARCH**

For math and science types on a budget

5 REASONS IT'S COOL

1. Students represent a dazzling array of ethnicities, religions, and countries.

2. The university pours money into its **science and engineering programs**.

3. Stony Brook faculty take credit for **628 inventions and 353 patents**.

4. **If research is your thing**, the Undergraduate Research & Creative Activities (URECA) will thrill you.

5. The Learning Communities Program (LCP) **creates the impression that you're attending a small college.**

The Basics

Public / private: public state
Total enrollment / undergrads: 22,522 / 14,847
Campus setting: small town
Students call it: SUNY-Stony Brook, SUNY-SB, Stony Brook University, Stony Brook, SB, SBU
Students are called: Seawolves
Notable alums: Diane Farr (actress), Christine Goerke (opera singer), Jef Raskin (cocreator, Macintosh computer)

Low Tuition, Bright Future

Stony Brook students use state-of-the-art facilities, professors conduct cutting-edge research, and there are tons of opportunities to participate in major research projects and take classes with first-rate scholars. Some of the most popular majors here are biology, business, computer science, and economics. In addition to the majors you'd expect at a large research university, Stony Brook offers natural resources/conservation and cytotechnology. Those who are more interested in the humanities won't suffer; with sixty-one majors and sixty-five minors, Stony Brook has lots of options to choose from. Whatever your major, you'll enjoy a 17:1 student-to-faculty ratio and challenging courses—although students in math, science, and engineering often complain that they have to work harder than their peers majoring in the liberal or fine arts.

Get It All Out

To ease pre-exam anxiety, Seawolves hold a **Midnight Scream**. At the stroke of twelve, they open their windows or walk outside to holler for a few minutes. Some find that screaming provides a welcome adrenaline rush; others argue that it stops them from losing their minds after countless hours hunched over books in the library.

Do It Your Way

Stony Brook's almost fifteen thousand undergrads are a diverse bunch. Commuters, who make up about half of the undergrad population, often spend little time on campus and don't always try to make friends. The university is trying to change that, though, and their efforts seem to be working, if the fact that about 75 percent of freshmen now opt to live in the dorms is any indication. Whether they live on campus or not, Seawolves have tons of ways to become active in campus life. There are more than three hundred student clubs and organizations, including fifteen frats and eighteen sororities. Between Student Activities–sponsored barbeques, DJs, and parties on Wednesday afternoons, theater, music, and Division I athletic events, campus is a pretty happening place. Not all students take advantage of these offerings, though. There is a large contingent of students who spend almost all of their time studying (math, science, and engineering students might argue they have no other choice, given their workload). There are also a good number of students who party all the time. But most Seawolves fall somewhere in between, balancing work and play.

An Island unto Itself

Occupying 1,100 wooded acres of Long Island's north shore, Stony Brook is ideally located. There are tons of shops, bars, and restaurants near campus, and students who want to hang out in (or go home to) New York City can easily make the 1.5-hour trek on the Long Island Railroad, which has a station right on campus. The excellent location could even be considered a detriment, since the school's proximity to NYC means it often clears out on weekends.

Admissions

Average high school GPA:	3.6
Average freshman SAT writing / math / critical reading score:	557 / 625 / 566
Average freshman ACT score:	—
Application fee:	$40

Application deadlines:
3/1 (freshmen)
4/15 (transfer)
11/15 (early action)

Total applicants:	21,292
Total accepted:	10,066 (47%)
Total accepted who enrolled:	2,709

Notification dates:
continuous (freshmen)
continuous (transfer)
1/1 (early action)

Acceptance rate for early action applicants: —

Students

Percentage of male / female students:	50% / 50%
Percentage of students from out of state:	4%
Percentage of students graduating in 4 years / 6 years:	— / —

Money

Total endowment:	$76,543,331
Total in-state tuition, fees & expenses:	$14,925
Total out-of-state tuition, fees & expenses:	$21,185
Average financial aid package:	$8,200
Percentage of students who sought aid and received it:	65%
Percentage of students receiving financial aid:	48%

Also Check Out

New York University

SUNY–Binghamton University

SUNY–Geneseo

SUNY–University at Albany

SUNY–University at Buffalo

SUNY–University at Albany

1400 Washington Avenue
Albany, NY 12222

(518) 442-3300
http://www.albany.edu/

BIG CHOICE

Capital school, capital opportunities

5 REASONS IT'S COOL

1. With **fifty-four possible majors and fifty-nine minors**, your biggest problem will be squeezing everything in.

2. Students have access to **tons of internship and job opportunities** in and beyond New York's capital.

3. UAlbany offers a **great education for a very low price**—and over $1 million in merit scholarships to incoming frosh.

4. The **College of Nanoscale Science and Engineering** is ranked the best in the nation by *U.S. News & World Report.*

5. The **diverse student body** represents many races, ethnicities, and countries.

The Basics

Public / private: public state
Total enrollment / undergrads: 17,434 / 12,457
Campus setting: suburban
Students call it: SUNY Albany, UAlbany, Albany, University at Albany
Students are called: Danes
Notable alums: Randy Cohen (columnist), Brian Lehrer (radio host), Phil Lewis (sportscaster), Harvey Milk (gay rights activist), Kate Stoneman (first woman admitted to the New York State Bar)

It Pays to Be Proactive

Craving freedom after attending a restrictive high school? UAlbany might be perfect for you. For starters, you'll be one of about twelve thousand students. You can choose from fifty-four majors and fifty-nine minors. Not everyone loves the large scale of UAlbany. Students complain that the administration is bureaucratic, that TAs teach too many courses, and that profs aren't very accessible. But while there's no handholding at UAlbany, most professors and even administrators are responsive and helpful if you seek them out. And it's possible to create a personalized academic experience at UAlbany. Freshmen may opt to participate in Project Renaissance, a series of interdisciplinary courses that allow students to live and study together while fulfilling some general requirements. Ambitious students in search of a challenge may also want to consider the Honors College, which offers classes taught by some of the university's best profs and provides post-college mentoring. There are also thirty departmental honors programs.

Shine Some Light on Me

UAlbany students may not be known for their school spirit, but graduation has a way of making people sentimental. Each May, on the Saturday of Commencement Weekend, UAlbany holds its annual Torch Night. Representatives of the graduating class pass a torch to their junior counterparts as a way of saying, "You're next."

Carve Out Your Place

Like most SUNY schools, UAlbany's student body consists primarily of state residents, many of whom self-segregate with people from their own region. That's not to say the school isn't diverse. The students represent an array of ethnicities, political beliefs, and, more prosaically, study creeds, which range from extremely studious to quite lazy. Whatever their interests, students usually have no trouble finding their own niche in one of the university's 200-plus student organizations, which run the gamut from sororities and frats, to the Albany Nanoscience Interest Group, to student media and religious organizations, to intramural sports. Despite moving into Division I of the NCAA in 1999–2000, UAlbany hasn't been able to draw big student crowds to football games or other sporting events. Instead, students typically flock toward the Campus Center, where lounge areas and chain restaurants abound. The Campus Center is also home to the Danes After Dark lounge, which features games including pool, air hockey, foosball, and Madden '07, music, tournaments, and free snacks.

Party—or Else

If you're looking for ivy and columns, look elsewhere. UAlbany's main campus, designed by Edward Durell Stone, is a modernist creation that some consider art and others consider an eyesore. While the city of Albany offers plentiful internship and job opportunities, as a center for recreation, it leaves much to be desired. It isn't particularly attractive and can be rather gray and depressing during the winter. For those willing to drive forty minutes east into Vermont, the winter offers great skiing possibilities. And during the rest of the year, the easternmost part of New York and western Vermont offer breathtaking views and some beautiful hiking and camping spots. Most often, students stay closer to home and hit Albany's restaurants and bars. Those who don't drink tend to feel limited in their social options, so they often study on campus or check out Danes After Dark.

Admissions

Average high school GPA:	3.3
Average freshman SAT verbal / math score:	565 / 590
Average freshman ACT score:	—
Application fee:	$40

Application deadlines:
3/1 (freshmen)
8/1 (transfer)
11/15 (early action)

Total applicants:	18,689
Total accepted:	10,436 (56%)
Total accepted who enrolled:	2,414

Notification dates:
continuous (freshmen)
continuous (transfer)
1/1 (early action)

Acceptance rate for early action applicants: —

Students

Percentage of male / female students:	51% / 49%
Percentage of students from out of state:	6%
Percentage of students graduating in 4 years / 6 years:	50% / 62%

Money

Total endowment:	$20,093,262
Total in-state tuition, fees & expenses:	$15,544
Total out-of-state tuition, fees & expenses:	$21,804
Average financial aid package:	$8,399
Percentage of students who sought aid and received it:	79%
Percentage of students receiving financial aid:	50%

Also Check Out

Fordham University

Ithaca College

SUNY–Binghamton University

SUNY–Stony Brook University

SUNY–University at Buffalo

SUNY–University at Buffalo

Capen Hall Buffalo, NY 14260	(716) 645-2000 http://www.buffalo.edu/

 **BIG CHOICE**

Choices, choices, choices—84, to be precise

5 REASONS IT'S COOL

1. Expand your horizons: UB has **one of the largest international student populations in the country**.

2. The **top-notch academics come at bargain-basement prices**. Even out-of-staters pay only $21,000.

3. With its $2.2 million budget, the Student Association can book **guests such as Dave Chapelle and Kanye West**, and the school's lecture series has brought in big names like Al Gore, Conan O'Brien, and the Dalai Lama.

4. No public university in New York or New England offers as **many academic programs**.

5. Thanks to Learning Communities, you'll **make friends easily**.

The Basics

Public / private: public state
Total enrollment / undergrads: 27,220 / 18,165
Campus setting: suburban
Students call it: UB, SUNY-Buffalo, Buffalo
Students are called: Bulls
Notable alums: Ellen Shulman Baker (astronaut), Wolf Blitzer (journalist), Ron Silver (actor), Tom Toles (editorial cartoonist), Harvey Weinstein (cofounder, Miramax)

Where Bigger Means Better

With more than eighteen thousand undergrads, UB is one of the largest schools in the SUNY system, but its 15:1 student-to-faculty ratio is one of the lowest. Students boast about how accessible their profs are, particularly those who teach upper-division classes and required first-year composition courses. It's also possible to achieve a small-community feel within the massive undergrad population thanks to UB's undergrad academies, groups of students and faculty that have classes and extracurriculars together. Outstanding students can also opt to join an honors community. While students work hard in just about every department, future scientists, engineers, pharmacists, architects, and businesspeople often complain that they have more work than their peers. With eighty-four majors to choose from, and the option of designing one's own major, UB allows even the pickiest students to find a program that fits.

Coed Clothed Mud Volleyball

Ooz-fest, the world's biggest mud-volleyball game, takes place each April at UB. Fire trucks drench dirt courts with water, creating the mud pits where teams compete. Awards are given out to the winners, as well as to the most creative dressers.

Friendship 101

The majority of UB students hail from Western New York, although there's a large international student population as well. Students who come from big cities can find it hard to adjust to life in a town with only a sliver of Manhattan's population and wealth. But typically, by mid-September, even students who commute—as a great number of UB students do—have struck up friendships with at least one or two of their peers. Students also find that joining one of the three hundred student organizations is a good way to make friends. The Student Union is a focal point for fast food, makeshift study groups, and gossip circles. Bulls basketball is growing increasingly popular.

North Campus, South Campus

UB has two campuses, and many undergrads spend time on both. North Campus (or "North," as it's commonly called) in Amherst, a suburb just north of Buffalo, is where most undergraduate courses are held. It's an unattractive compound of 1960s-era brown brick buildings and has little in the way of entertainment beyond the Student Union. South Campus (or "South") is in the middle of Buffalo and is home to the med school, public health school, nursing school, and architecture programs. It features attractive old architecture and plenty of bars, restaurants, and coffee shops right across the street. Both campuses have dorms, and first-year students are assigned to one without being able to express a preference. (No prizes for guessing whether ugly, dull North or pretty, entertaining South is the more desirable location.) When students want to escape, they often hang out on Elmwood or in Allentown, hip areas of town with a number of bars. Bulls longing for the big city may make the seven-hour trek to New York City or the more reasonable ninety-minute drive to Toronto.

Admissions

Average high school GPA:	3.1
Average freshman SAT verbal / math score:	560 / 595
Average freshman ACT score:	24
Application fee:	$40
Application deadlines:	
— (freshmen)	
— (transfer)	
11/1 (early decision)	
Total applicants:	18,391
Total accepted:	10,466 (57%)
Total accepted who enrolled:	3,216
Notification dates:	
continuous (freshmen)	
continuous (transfer)	
12/15 (early decision)	
Acceptance rate for early decision applicants:	74%

Students

Percentage of male / female students:	54% / 46%
Percentage of students from out of state:	3%
Percentage of students graduating in 4 years / 6 years:	33% / 58%

Money

Total endowment:	$463,214,506
Total in-state tuition, fees & expenses:	$15,129
Total out-of-state tuition, fees & expenses:	$21,389
Average financial aid package:	$6,079
Percentage of students who sought aid and received it:	69%
Percentage of students receiving financial aid:	52%

Also Check Out

Ithaca College

SUNY–Binghamton University

SUNY–Stony Brook University

SUNY–University at Albany

Syracuse University

Swarthmore College

500 College Avenue
Swarthmore, PA 19081

(610) 328-8000
http://www.swarthmore.edu/

 **BIG BRAIN**

 **BIG PERSPECTIVE**

I'm smart, you're smart, we're all smart.

5 REASONS IT'S COOL

1. **Academic intensity is the name of the game**, and students are some of the brainiest you'll find anywhere.

2. Unlike many other liberal arts colleges, Swarthmore offers a top-of-the-line **undergraduate engineering program.**

3. The **extra-tough honors program** puts academics in a league of their own.

4. Swarthmore is a shining example of that **nurturing, small college experience** you dream of.

5. The lovely campus, a designated arboretum, is just a **short train ride away from downtown Philadelphia.**

The Basics

Public / private: private nonprofit
Total enrollment / undergrads: 1,484 / 1,484
Campus setting: suburban
Students call it: Swarthmore
Students are called: Swatties
Notable alums: Michael Dukakis (governor, Massachusetts), Jonathan Franzen (novelist), Carl Levin (senator), James Michener (novelist), Alice Paul (suffragist leader), Valerie Worth (poet)

Where's It's Okay to Be Brainy

Swarthmore's "learning for learning's sake" ethos means that coursework can be pretty intense for students. Requirements include twenty non-major courses, at least nine of which must be distributed equally between three broad fields: humanities, natural science and engineering, and social science. Academic programs are strong on all fronts, from the engineering program to more unusual offerings such as peace and conflict studies. During the first semester of freshman year, students take classes on a pass-fail bases, which gives them some time to acclimate themselves to the demands of college-level academics. Most freshmen enroll in freshman seminars, which are small classes that cover a freewheeling range of topics. Upperclassmen may choose to join Swarthmore's highly regarded honors program, which is modeled on the Oxford tutorial system and culminates with students taking an oral examination reviewed by outside scholars. Nearly half of students go abroad at some point, and many exchange programs are available.

Running Amok

Swarthmore students run circles around competing institutions, both in the academic arena and in other, more creative ways. The campus was downright depressed when the men's and women's rugby teams, under pressure from their leagues, had to cancel the Dash for Cash fundraiser, in which naked athletes ran through a gauntlet of cheering, cash-throwing spectators. Fortunately, the McCabe Mile is still going strong. During this annual tradition, students race eighteen laps (the equivalent of one mile) around the basement of McCabe Library. The winning prize? A roll of Scott toilet paper, in honor of the library's namesake, who served on the board of the Scott paper company.

Full Speed Ahead

Students here tend to be intense, passionate, and eclectic. Balance is the name of their game. They take pride in their ability to reconcile daunting academic loads with ambitious extracurricular commitments and generous helpings of late-night unwinding. Greek life has a muted presence; 6 percent of men join one of two frats, and there are no sororities. This means that social life revolves around campus parties, which flower under the loosely enforced alcohol restrictions. Political activism attracts many students, as does volunteer work. The Eugene Lang Center for Civic and Social Responsibility has a national reputation for breaking new ground in the developing field of service learning. Student publications, culture groups, performance troupes, and quasi-intellectual salons are all popular. Most campus clubs and organizations have a heterogeneous membership profile, owing to the fact that Swarthmore's student body is a refreshingly diverse one: Only about 10 percent of students are Pennsylvanians, and a full third are nonwhite.

All Kinds of Green

Swarthmore has the twelfth-largest endowment per student of any college in the country, and this wealth is reflected in gorgeous facilities like the campus's new $77 million science center. The college's 357 acres are full of natural beauty and loveliness; they're so green and leafy, in fact, that they constitute an official arboretum. The village of Swarthmore lies just beyond campus. While quiet and safe, the surrounding town provides only moderately varied entertainment options for students. Fortunately, there's a train station on campus where students can catch a commuter train to downtown Philadelphia (a fifteen-minute ride), and other options like hiking trails and the enormous King of Prussia mall are all close by.

Admissions

Average high school GPA:	—
Average freshman SAT writing / math / critical reading score:	702 / 698 / 702
Average freshman ACT score:	26
Application fee:	$60

Application deadlines:
1/2 (freshmen)
4/1 (transfer)
11/15 (early decision)

Total applicants:	4,852
Total accepted:	923 (19%)
Total accepted who enrolled:	370

Notification dates:
4/1 (freshmen)
5/15 (transfer)
12/15 (early decision)

Acceptance rate for early decision applicants:	45%

Students

Percentage of male / female students:	48% / 52%
Percentage of students from out of state:	83%
Percentage of students graduating in 4 years / 6 years:	86% / 92%

Money

Total endowment:	$1,245,281,000
Total tuition:	$32,912
Total cost with fees & expenses:	$44,580
Average financial aid package:	$30,369
Percentage of students who sought aid and received it:	100%
Percentage of students receiving financial aid:	48%

Also Check Out

Amherst College

Brown University

Harvard University

Haverford College

Williams College

Yale University

Sweet Briar College

P.O. Box B
Sweet Briar, VA 24595

(434) 381-6100
http://www.sbc.edu/

 **BIG HAND**

 **BIG PERSPECTIVE**

Where women become sisters and leaders

5 REASONS IT'S COOL

1. This women's college is dedicated to giving its students a **personalized, challenging, and empowering education**.

2. From faculty mentors to big sisters, **students have a huge network of advisors** to guide them.

3. Junior Year in France and Junior Year in Spain are just two of the school's **renowned study-abroad programs**.

4. Located at the foothills of the Blue Ridge Mountains, the **campus is beautiful and expansive**.

5. The **tight-knit community** nurtures sisters for life.

The Basics

Public / private: private nonprofit
Total enrollment / undergrads: 751 / 739
Campus setting: rural
Students call it: SBC, Sweet Briar
Students are called: Vixens
Notable alums: Elaine Dundy (actress, journalist, author), Lendon Grey (Olympic dressage competitor), Diane Holloway (TV critic), Diana Muldaur (actress), Fleming Parker Rutledge (Episcopal priest, theologian)

Studying Vixens

Once a sort of glorified finishing school, Sweet Briar is now a liberal arts powerhouse whose graduates become doctors, lawyers, and CFOs. With over forty academic programs, including pre-med, pre-law, and pre-vet, motivated students have plenty to choose from—and many double- or even triple-major rather than settle on one program. Government, history, chemistry, and creative writing are all strong, and faculty across the board gets high marks. Coursework is challenging and somewhat competitive, although most Vixens thrive in the demanding academic environment. Most profs, often described as mentors, live on campus. The 9:1 student-to-faculty ratio and small class sizes speak to SBC's commitment to the individual. In addition to faculty advisors, students are assigned upper-class mentors their first year. Internship sponsors, work-study supervisors, and a dedicated alumni network all provide connections and guidance further down the road.

And to Honor Our Junior Women . . .

Sweet Briar is immersed in traditions, many of which involve seniors and first-years. Juniors shouldn't feel left out though: At the Junior Banquet, they are presented with their class rings, which they wear on their pinky fingers.

Suzy Sweet Briar

With the motto "Think Pink" and the nickname "Suzy Sweet Briar," SBC women might sound like preppy, traditional pearl wearers. But upper-classwomen maintain that Suzies are more Virginia Woolf than Emily Post. Academics, leadership, and tradition are important to Vixens, and many get involved in tap clubs, selective societies that focus on dancing, a cappella, volunteerism, or simply rivalry with other tap clubs. Founders Day and Lantern Bearing, during which sophomores accompany their senior sisters on a torchlight march, are among the most cherished traditions, but there are plenty of others to choose from. Vixens show their athletic prowess in eight varsity and club sports. The equestrian program, with its stellar Rogers Riding Center, is top-notch. On-campus living is required for all four years, but the rural locale doesn't provide many alternatives anyway. While weekdays are typically spent hanging out on the beautiful campus, the weekend sends Vixens to neighboring colleges like VMI, Washington & Lee, or all-male Hampden-Sydney. Despite the occasional bout of cabin fever, Sweet Briar ladies value their close-knit community. This isn't your typical beer-swilling college experience.

Perfectly Rural

Situated on 3,250 acres of central Virginia hill country, the Sweet Briar campus is a lovely expanse of nature sanctuaries and historic buildings. Designed in part by Ralph Adams Cram, who also worked on Princeton and West Point, SBC features decidedly stately architecture. Rolling meadows, lakes, and hiking trails around the grounds are perfect for endless hours of contemplative wandering, but don't lend themselves easily to partying. Most students say a car is an absolute necessity, and although Lynchburg is just a twenty-minute drive away, most students would rather drive an hour to Hampden-Sydney or Charlottesville, or three to Washington, D.C.

Admissions

Average high school GPA:	3.4
Average freshman SAT writing / math / critical reading score:	559 / 538 / 574
Average freshman ACT score:	24
Application fee:	$40

Application deadlines:
2/1 (freshmen)
5/1 (transfer)
12/1 (early decision)

Total applicants:	585
Total accepted:	470 (80%)
Total accepted who enrolled:	190

Notification dates:
3/1 (freshmen)
5/15 (transfer)
12/15 (early decision)

Acceptance rate for early decision applicants:	97%

Students

Percentage of male / female students:	2% / 98%
Percentage of students from out of state:	52%
Percentage of students graduating in 4 years / 6 years:	65% / 67%

Money

Total endowment:	$93,080,412
Total tuition:	$24,740
Total cost with fees & expenses:	$35,055
Average financial aid package:	$15,150
Percentage of students who sought aid and received it:	83%
Percentage of students receiving financial aid:	—

Also Check Out

College of William & Mary

Mount Holyoke College

Randolph College

University of Richmond

Syracuse University

P.O. Box 37324
Syracuse, NY 13244

(315) 443-1870
http://www.syracuse.edu/

 **BIG CHOICE**

You name it, this school has it.

5 REASONS IT'S COOL

1. Want to be the next Ted Koppel or Bob Costas? A slew of famous journalists graduated from Syracuse's **top-ranked Newhouse School of Communications.**

2. Students love the **Orange, their mascot,** and their winning NCAA Division I sports teams.

3. Syracuse is a **veritable superstore of majors,** with over two hundred to choose from.

4. **See the world:** SU operates centers in London, Florence, Beijing, and other cities.

5. Love snow? Syracuse is one of the **snowiest regions in the country.**

The Basics

Public / private: private nonprofit
Total enrollment / undergrads: 17,492 / 11,546
Campus setting: urban
Students call it: Syracuse, SU
Students are called: Orangemen
Notable alums: Jim Brown (pro football player), Dick Clark (TV personality), Eileen Collins (astronaut), Bob Costas (sportscaster), Taye Diggs (actor), Dwight Freeney (pro football player), Ted Koppel (journalist), Sol LeWitt (artist), Story Musgrave (astronaut), Lou Reed (attended; musician), William Safire (attended; social commentator, author), Alice Sebold (novelist), Bill Viola (artist)

Swing into Action

A Syracuse education is governed by the ideal of "scholarship in action." The university's academic and professional programs encourage student innovation, which may explain why so many alums go on to be leaders in their fields. With over two hundred majors in nine undergraduate colleges, it's easy for even the choosiest students to find their niches. Most students enroll in the College of Arts & Sciences, the Whitman School of Management, and the College of Visual and Performing Arts. The Newhouse School of Public Communications has also long been an academic powerhouse, producing a number of now-famous alums in journalism and media. Syracuse's most popular majors include marketing management, architecture, political science, and psychology.

What Rhymes with Orange?

Unlike many schools, who choose weapon-wielding or saber-toothed mascots for their sports teams, the Syracuse mascot is simply orange—*an* orange to be exact. Syracuses's mascot, however, wasn't always so pleasantly round and sweet. For most of the twentieth century, the mascot was the Saltine Warrior, an Indian chieftain who was finally deposed in 1978 amid protests from students who deemed it racist. After a brief flirtation with a Roman gladiator, Syracuse eventually settled on the uncontroversial orange in 1980.

Burr! It's Cold out Here!

Syracuse is on record as being the snowiest metropolitan area in the country. There are many campus activities and events on campus, though, to give the students warm fuzzies. Fraternities and sororities are tremendously popular; in fact, there are forty-four Greek groups to choose from. Division I men's lacrosse, football, and basketball games draw the university community together. So do the more than three hundred student clubs and organizations. Not surprisingly, journalism and media are popular extracurricular activities, including campus radio, TV, and newspapers—all helpful for the budding media moguls and newsies. Campus-wide parties also help break the ice, including the annual April Block Party, which includes concerts and carnival rides. The city of Syracuse has a lot to offer students too, such as movie theaters, shops, and a variety of bars and clubs located just off campus.

That's My Name Too

Smack in the middle of the state and 250 fifty miles away from New York City, Syracuse sits atop University Hill surrounded by the city that shares its name. The university's Quad is located at the center of campus and serves as the main pedestrian throughway. The campus itself is imbued with a deep sense of history, and several of its eclectic buildings are listed on the National Register of Historic Places. Hendricks Chapel, for example, harkens to the school's religious roots, despite the fact that Syracuse is no longer affiliated with any single denomination or faith. Other, less visually appealing buildings, such as the Carrier Dome, make up for their drab appearance with sheer functionality. In the case of the Dome, that function is hosting some of the country's best collegiate sporting events. There's also lots of construction and renovation going on, which gives students the impression that Syracuse isn't just about revering the past—it's also about building the future.

Admissions

Average high school GPA:	3.6
Average freshman SAT verbal / math score:	606 / 629
Average freshman ACT score:	—
Application fee:	$70

Application deadlines:
1/1 (freshmen)
1/1 (transfer)
11/15 (early decision)

Total applicants:	19,744
Total accepted:	10,157 (51%)
Total accepted who enrolled:	3,054

Notification dates:
3/15 (freshmen)
continuous (transfer)
12/31 (early decision)

Acceptance rate for early decision applicants:	63%

Students

Percentage of male / female students:	45% / 55%
Percentage of students from out of state:	58%
Percentage of students graduating in 4 years / 6 years:	66% / 79%

Money

Total endowment:	$835,900,000
Total tuition:	$28,820
Total cost with fees & expenses:	$41,620
Average financial aid package:	$23,600
Percentage of students who sought aid and received it:	82%
Percentage of students receiving financial aid:	—

Also Check Out

Boston College

Boston University

Cornell University

The Pennsylvania State University–University Park

Temple University

1801 North Broad Street Philadelphia, PA 19122	(215) 204-7000 http://www.temple.edu/

BIG CHOICE

Something's ticking in the heart of Philly.

5 REASONS IT'S COOL

1. Temple consistently ranks among the **most diverse campuses in the nation.**

2. Investments in technology and distance learning options make this **one of America's most connected campuses.**

3. In addition to several study-abroad programs, there are **campuses in London, Rome, and Tokyo.**

4. Two words: **Temple basketball.**

5. The university is located in the heart of Philadelphia, **a city rich in history, culture, and entertainment.**

The Basics

Public / private: public state-related
Total enrollment / undergrads: 33,865 / 24,674
Campus setting: urban
Students call it: Temple
Students are called: Owls
Notable alums: Ben Bova (author), Richard Brooks (filmmaker), Steve Capus (president, NBC News), Bill Cosby (comedian), Eddie Jones (pro basketball player), Joe Klecko (pro football player), Tom Sizemore (actor), John F. Street (mayor, Philadephia), Diana Vincent (jewelry designer)

For the Decided and Undecided

Temple undergrads choose from 125 different degree programs in virtually every field. The most popular degrees are in business and management, visual and performing arts, education, communication technology, and the social sciences. The university is also noted for its pre-professional programs in medicine, dentistry, podiatry, pharmacy, and law. Students unsure of where to jump in can enroll as undeclared in the Division of University Studies. The DUS provides academic advising, including specific services for those interested in the healthcare industry, and hosts several workshops specifically for freshmen. Recent and continued investments, to the tune of a half billion dollars, have led to construction and renovation of facilities across several Temple campuses. One highlight is the new TECH Center, one of the largest on-campus computer facilities of its kind in the United States. Typical of many schools its size, Temple has a student-to-faculty ratio of 17:1.

A Presidential Dressing-Down

Temple awarded its 1965 World Peace Prize to Canadian prime minister and Nobel Peace Prize recipient Lester Pearson. In a bold move, Pearson used his acceptance speech to criticize the U.S.'s bombing of Vietnam. The speech did not go over well with then-president LBJ, who reportedly laid into the contrary Canuck the next day. Pearson later apologized.

With average class sizes of twenty-six, this isn't the most intimate academic atmosphere. Nevertheless, professors tend to be supportive, and for students enrolled in the honors programs, classes are more intimate.

The Owls Take on Many Disguises

Temple has one of the most diverse student bodies in the country. There are more than two hundred student clubs and groups, including a reputable debate team, and many community service opportunities. Of the school's two dozen varsity teams, basketball draws the most passionate sports enthusiasts. Club sports also offter plenty of options, including men's and women's rugby. Twenty-four Greek organizations have Temple charters, but only 2 percent of students pledge. The recently renovated student complex offers amenities including a full-scale movie theater, game room, and computer lounge. The school also sponsors concerts, guest lectures, art exhibits, festivals, and workshops, but many students seek their fun off campus.

The Streets of Philadelphia

Temple has six campuses in Philadelphia's greater metropolitan area, but it's the main campus, about a mile and a half north of Center City, where most of the action takes place. The school hosts a variety of social and cultural events, and recent construction projects have yielded some top-notch educational and recreational sites, including loads of fitness and sports facilities. Still, most students head off campus to enjoy the finest of the city's museums, shopping districts, theater and music, professional sports, and food, as well as a wealth of historic sites. Although the neighborhoods immediately surrounding the main campus are often described as sketchy, the university employs a large police force, and the school is fairly safe. And when Philly gets a little old, NYC and D.C. are just a short trip away.

Admissions

Average high school GPA: 3.26

Average freshman SAT writing / math / critical reading score: 537 / 551 / 547

Average freshman ACT score: 22

Application fee: $50

Application deadlines:
4/1 (freshmen)
6/15 (transfer)

Total applicants: 18,140

Total accepted: 10,952 (60%)

Total accepted who enrolled: 3,851

Notification dates:
continuous (freshmen)
continuous (transfer)

Students

Percentage of male / female students: 45% / 55%

Percentage of students from out of state: 22%

Percentage of students graduating in 4 years / 6 years: 27% / 56%

Money

Total endowment: $196,165,000

Total in-state tuition, fees & expenses: $19,210

Total out-of-state tuition, fees & expenses: $27,254

Average financial aid package: $13,308

Percentage of students who sought aid and received it: 89%

Percentage of students receiving financial aid: 54%

Also Check Out

Gonzaga University

The Pennsylvania State University–University Park

Rutgers University

Syracuse University

The University of Pittsburgh

Texas A&M University– College Station

1265 TAMU
College Station, TX 77843

(979) 845-3211
http://www.tamu.edu/

BIG CHOICE

BIG RESEARCH

Not just a school, a way of life

5 REASONS IT'S COOL

1. A&M is triple designated as **a land-, sea-, and space-grant institution**.

2. Whether you're a Texan or not, **tuition is dirt cheap.**

3. Go abroad through the International Studies program or **at one of A&M's centers in Italy, Mexico, and Qatar.**

4. Only the U.S. military academies have more service members than **A&M's Corps of Cadets,** who play an important role in preserving the many Aggie traditions.

5. From bonfires to school yells to road trips following the team, **Aggies are hardcore football fanatics.**

The Basics

Public / private: public state
Total enrollment / undergrads: 45,380 / 36,580
Campus setting: suburban
Students call it: A&M, TAMU
Students are called: Aggies
Notable alums: Ray Childress (pro football player), Michael E. Fossum (astronaut), Patricia Gras (news broadcaster), Dante Hall (pro football player), Chuck Knoblauch (pro baseball player), Acie Law IV (pro basketball player), Lyle Lovett (singer-songwriter, actor), Kathleen McElroy (editor), George P. Mitchell (businessman), Rick Perry (governor, Texas)

The Ups and Downs of Research

Aggies choose from over 150 majors, with engineering and agriculture being the strongest, followed by veterinary medicine and business. Biological and physical sciences, interdisciplinary studies, and operations management and supervision are among the most popular majors. Research opportunities abound, particularly in the fields of nuclear science, space research, biotechnology, and oceanography. Undergrads can also participate in ongoing projects with NASA that include working at the Center for Space Power or building modularized satellites for the Air Force Research Lab. Heavy core requirements mandate courses across the sciences and humanities, including the arts, foreign language, and computer literacy. Class sizes average in the thirties, with more than 10 percent of classes reaching over one hundred students. Some students complain that faculty members are too focused

Join the Team

Aggie football fans, many of whom spend entire games on their feet, are collectively referred to as the 12th Man. The tradition dates back to a 1922 bowl game, during which an injury-depleted Aggies team looked to the stands for help. The coach called on student E. King Gill, an ex-football player who had left to play basketball. Gill rejoined the team, wearing an injured player's uniform. Although he didn't play, the Aggies won 22-14, and Gill's gesture of loyalty has been an inspiration ever since.

on their research, but others contend that most profs are eager to help their students.

Howdys All Around

A&M is one of the country's largest universities in terms of land area. Nearly forty dorms house 20 percent of the student population. Many freshmen live in Learning Living Communities where resident clusters share common interests. College Station is almost an extension of campus, so even off-campus dwellers enjoy A&M's close-knit community. It's not unusual for strangers to greet each other in the streets with "howdy," the university's official salutation. Students have no lack of options with over eight hundred extracurricular offerings, including a Greek system and numerous religious and cultural groups. Sports, both participatory and spectator, are also huge. Varsity teams excel in a number of areas including baseball, golf, soccer, and tennis, but students are most faithful to Aggies football, particularly when rival UT–Austin is in town. The student body is predominately Texas-born, white, and conservative. But the school also boasts a robust international community, and plans are underway to increase diversity.

Aggieland

Taken together, College Station and the neighboring town of Bryan are called Aggieland, a name that underscores their close relationship with A&M. With a population of just over 100,000, this metro area ranks as the most educated in Texas, due in no small part to the dominating presence of the university. Almost all restaurants have Aggie specials, and community service hits a high note during the Big Event, which is the nation's largest one-day service project. Weekends start on Thursday nights when students flock to the Dixie Chicken, one of the few local bars. Concerts are occasionally held on campus, but most students head to Houston, Austin, or Dallas—each of which is within two hundred miles of campus—to catch big music acts or enjoy any kind of club scene.

Admissions

Average high school GPA:	—
Average freshman SAT writing / math / critical reading score:	557 / 608 / 581
Average freshman ACT score:	24
Application fee:	$60

Application deadlines:
2/1 (freshmen)
3/15 (transfer)

Total applicants:	17,410
Total accepted:	13,334 (77%)
Total accepted who enrolled:	7,476

Notification dates:
continuous (freshmen)
continuous (transfer)

Students

Percentage of male / female students:	51% / 49%
Percentage of students from out of state:	3%
Percentage of students graduating in 4 years / 6 years:	35% / 77%

Money

Total endowment:	$4,294,967,295
Total in-state tuition, fees & expenses:	$15,806
Total out-of-state tuition, fees & expenses:	$24,056
Average financial aid package:	$10,747
Percentage of students who sought aid and received it:	87%
Percentage of students receiving financial aid:	33%

Also Check Out

College of William & Mary

Cornell University

Rice University

University of North Carolina at Chapel Hill

Vanderbilt University

Texas Christian University

2800 South University Drive
Fort Worth, TX 76129

(817) 257-7000
http://www.tcu.edu/

 **BIG CHOICE**

 **BIG JOB**

Where academic options are Texas-sized

5 REASONS IT'S COOL

1. Nearly every major **requires internships** or other hands-on experience.

2. The Honors Program pairs **great students with great professors** in some of the school's smallest and most rigorous classes.

3. The **top-ranked advertising program** prepares students for excellence in this competitive industry.

4. **Professors know their students' names** and are accessible in and out of the classroom.

5. Small first-year seminars let **newcomers get their feet wet** in courses such as Genius Minds, Broken Brains, and The Truth About Lies.

The Basics

Public / private: private religious
Total enrollment / undergrads: 8,865 / 7,267
Campus setting: suburban
Students call it: Texas Christian, TCU
Students are called: Frogs
Notable alums: Betty Buckley (actress), John Davis (entrepreneur), Kristin Holt (TV personality), Rod Roddy (announcer, *The Price Is Right*), Bob Schieffer (broadcast journalist), Kurt Thomas (pro basketball player), LaDainian Tomlinson (pro football player)

Small Campus Feel, Big Campus Opportunities

Of the nearly one hundred majors offered among TCU's seven schools, the most popular are in the communications and advertising program. Some of the more offbeat include e-commerce, criminal justice/safety studies, farm and ranch management, fashion merchandising, and voice and opera. Regardless of their major, students take classes in three core areas: heritage, mission, vision & values, which includes courses on culture and religion; human experiences and endeavors, which covers classes in the humanities, social sciences, natural sciences, and fine arts; and essential competencies, such as math and writing. TCU maintains an average class size of twenty-seven. Professors tend to be approachable and personable, sometimes even inviting overachievers to participate in research projects. But the kindness of professors isn't the only way students get hands-on experience. Most departments require two semesters of internships, and campus facilities include a

Out of This World

TCU is home to the Oscar E. Monnig Meteorite Gallery and all of its one thousand meteorites. The collection was donated to TCU beginning in 1978. Upon his death in 1999, Mr. Monnig left an astronomical sum of money for the Geology Department to maintain the collection, which opened to the public in 2003.

fully operational TV studio and radio station, GIS and remote sensing center, nuclear magnetic resonance facility, observatory, art gallery, and exceptional electrical engineering labs.

Greeks Rule

The Greek system has a strong presence at TCU. Close to 40 percent of students are in frats or sororities, and students who aren't in one may feel left out. More than two hundred registered organizations are available on campus, including many religious and service clubs. Student government and campus media, ranging from TV to radio to print, are popular among students, and the school hosts several music interest groups. As for athletics, the reinvigorated football program has given students something to cheer about in recent years. Basketball and tennis are also popular spectator sports. The school is affiliated with (though not governed by) the Disciples of Christ, and although students say it's not overly religious, few religious minorities are present. The stereotypical TCU student is wealthy, white, and conservative. Some students lament the lack of interaction between those of different races and social classes, although civility is the norm and the administration stresses that there's something for everyone.

Bigger and Better

TCU's campus is one of its big selling points. The university is currently undergoing a $255 million construction project that will bring four new residence halls; indoor football, baseball, and golf facilities, renovations to the football stadium; a new university union; and a full renovation and expansion of the School of Education. Popular campus events range from sports to music to theater to Greek parties. But students often head to off-campus hot spots in Fort Worth or Dallas. Both feature bars, restaurants, concerts, theater, museums, and professional sporting events, in addition to a healthy population of students from neighboring colleges.

Admissions

Average high school GPA:	—
Average freshman SAT verbal / math score:	—/—
Average freshman ACT score:	—
Application fee:	$40
Application deadlines:	
2/15 (freshmen)	
4/15 (transfer)	
11/15 (early action)	
Total applicants:	8,677
Total accepted:	5,442 (63%)
Total accepted who enrolled:	1,649
Notification dates:	
4/1 (freshmen)	
continuous (transfer)	
1/1 (early action)	

Students

Percentage of male / female students:	41% / 59%
Percentage of students from out of state:	21%
Percentage of students graduating in 4 years / 6 years:	—/ 69%

Money

Total endowment:	$1,117,209,000
Total tuition:	$22,980
Total cost with fees & expenses:	$31,350
Average financial aid package:	$14,771
Percentage of students who sought aid and received it:	73%
Percentage of students receiving financial aid:	40%

Also Check Out

Auburn University

Austin College

Clemson University

Pepperdine University

Texas Tech University

Texas Tech University

Box 45005	(806) 742-2011
Lubbock, TX 79409	http://www.ttu.edu/

 **BIG CHOICE**

 **BIG RESEARCH**

Sports, Southern hospitality, and academic options

5 REASONS IT'S COOL

1. Students in **the Honors College** take graduate courses, conduct research alongside profs, and live in a separate learning community.

2. The **Graduate-on-Time contract** cuts through the bureaucratic red tape and keeps students on track to ensure that they're out in four.

3. The **ROTC program** gives inductees the discipline necessary to tackle life's challenges—and sometimes even pays for their educations!

4. Students from Texas and bordering states **save on room, board, and tuition.**

5. **Red Raiders** are Texan through and through.

The Basics

Public / private: public state
Total enrollment / undergrads: 27,996 / 22,851
Campus setting: urban
Students call it: Texas Tech, Tech, TTU
Students are called: Red Raiders, Techsans
Notable alums: Charles Bassett (astronaut), Bob Bullock (lieutenant governor, Texas), Marcus Coleman (pro football player), George Eads III (actor), Robert Lewis (CEO, U.S. Bank), Scott Pelley (broadcast journalist), Sheryl Swoopes (pro basketball player), Steve Tanner (DJ), Dirk West (cartoonist)

Techin' Care of Business

At this large research university, students choose from over 150 majors, including some unusual offerings such as electronic media and communication, environmental toxicology, natural resource management, and plant and soil science. The most popular majors are health and physical education, mechanical engineering, and psychology. Among the ten schools and colleges, Agricultural Sciences and Natural Resources takes the lions share of research dollars. The university maintains an active archeological site, Lubbock Lake Landmark, which is nationally recognized for its historic significance. The world's largest collection of material on the Vietnam War is housed among the school's massive library resources. While most courses have fewer than forty students, many are taught by TAs. And with an 18:1 student-to-faculty ratio, undergrads have to take some initiative, though professors are usually

Who's That Guy?

The Red Raider might look like Zorro, but he's got a history all his own. Also known as the Masked Rider, the mysterious horseman made his first appearance at several football games in 1936, wearing a scarlet cape and circling the field on a palomino stallion. The mascot tradition was made official after the 1954 Gator Bowl when the masked rider led the team onto the field, stunning the crowd and spurring the team to victory.

approachable. With Tech looking to rise in the ranks of global education and research institutions, the administration is investing more in quality professors, groundbreaking research, and renovations for many academic buildings, including a new English/Philosophy/Education complex and university center.

Where's the Party?

Students are friendly and welcoming here, but those of a more liberal political stripe may have a tough time fitting in. All freshmen are required to live on campus, and students can choose from a number of themed learning communities, in addition to a number of halls and residential complexes. After first year, most students head off campus to escape the housing crunch. As a result, most of the weekend partying takes place away from the dry campus. For those interested in Greek life, the twenty-eight frats and twenty-one sororities have a big social presence. But although Tech has a reputation as a party school, alternative diversions are easy to find. There's a real community atmosphere on campus, and students are active in the nearly four hundred organizations and clubs, which range from publications to the Fashion Board to volunteer service to intramural sports. And just about everyone comes together to cheer on Red Raiders football and basketball.

Lubbock Is Texas

To those who haven't visited the state before, Lubbock may represent the quintessential Texas city. The region is vast and dry, and despite the size, it's a bit removed from big-city life. Unlike many parts of the state, Lubbock does enjoy distinct seasons. It also provides a friendly atmosphere for Tech students, who enjoy easy access to the Depot District's numerous bars and dance clubs. Meals at many of the restaurants here can also be charged to the Tech Express debit card. Students also take advantage of skiing opportunities in nearby New Mexico.

Admissions

Average high school GPA:	—
Average freshman SAT writing / math / critical reading score:	528 / 580 / 552
Average freshman ACT score:	23
Application fee:	$50

Application deadlines:
5/1 (freshmen)
continuous (transfer)

Total applicants:	13,809
Total accepted:	9,691 (70%)
Total accepted who enrolled:	3,862

Notification dates:
continuous (freshmen)
continuous (transfer)

Students

Percentage of male / female students:	55% / 45%
Percentage of students from out of state:	5%
Percentage of students graduating in 4 years / 6 years:	23% / 55%

Money

Total endowment:	$337,454,368
Total in-state tuition, fees & expenses:	$14,647
Total out-of-state tuition, fees & expenses:	$22,897
Average financial aid package:	$7,424
Percentage of students who sought aid and received it:	61%
Percentage of students receiving financial aid:	37%

Also Check Out

Baylor University

Texas A&M University–College Station

Texas Christian University

University of Oklahoma

The University of Texas at Austin

Towson University

8000 York Road
Towson, MD 21252

(410) 704-2000
http://www.towson.edu/

BIG CHOICE

Really good education, *really* good deal

5 REASONS IT'S COOL

1. Towson is the only university in Maryland to offer **undergraduate degrees in business.**

2. The **college of education** produces teachers ready to take on classrooms everywhere.

3. The number of academic choices is exceeded only by the number of **dollars students save on tuition.**

4. The Honors College offers small classes and the chance to **bunk with your fellow smarties in a living-learning community.**

5. Craving big-city excitement (or perhaps a **cool internship opportunity**)? Baltimore is close, and Washington, D.C. is only an hour farther.

The Basics

Public / private: public state
Total enrollment / undergrads: 18,921 / 15,374
Campus setting: suburban
Students call it: Towson, TU
Students are called: Tigers
Notable alums: Jermon Bushrod (pro football player), Jack L. Chalker (author), Charles S. Dutton (actor), D. J. Gallo (satirist), John Glover (actor), Mike Rowe (TV personality)

Big, but Not Too Big

With twelve thousand undergrads, Towson is big, but not so big that students are reduced to numbers or have to contend with stadium-sized lecture halls. Students choose from sixty-four majors, which are distributed across the university's six undergraduate colleges of liberal arts, business, education, fine arts, health professions, and science and mathematics. The most popular majors tend to be in pre-professional areas, and include business administration, psychology, elementary education, mass communication and nursing. The student-to-faculty ratio is 18:1, and more than 75 percent of professors hold terminal degrees in their fields. The Towson Honors College is open to a select group of about seven hundred students who live with other honors students in a "Living and Learning Community" and reap the benefits of tougher classes. Honors College professors are known for pushing students to think across disciplines.

Building a Better Tiger

When the Towson student government first installed the tiger that sat outside Cook Library in 1996, their hopes of boosting school spirit were quickly dashed. Ten years later, after repeated acts of vandalism, the statue was finally removed in early 2006. The following year, a new bronze tiger, designed to be resistant to vandalism, was unveiled outside the university's Stephens Hall.

Towson's Got You Connected

More than 3,500 of Towson's students live on campus, including roughly 75 percent of first-year students. Students can take in a game with one of Towson's twenty Division I varsity teams or lend their talents to one of more than 150 other organizations. In their off hours, Towson students tend to gather at the University Union, which houses the bookstore, dining facilities, a post office, and a student center with games, food, music, and a cyber café.

Charm City at Your Fingertips

The city of Towson is located just outside Baltimore. Extensive shopping is available within walking distance of campus, as are a number of coffee shops, restaurants, and a public library. Baltimore itself is the home of the National Aquarium, two professional sports teams (the Ravens and Orioles), and the Inner Harbor, a destination known for its shopping, seafood, art galleries, professional theater, and nightlife. The area is full of history too, stretching all the way back to the days before the Revolutionary War. Check out nearby Colonial Williamsburg, any one of the many nearby Civil War battlefields, or Fort McHenry National Monument, the birthplace of the Star-Spangled Banner. Go a little farther and you'll be in Washington, D.C., home to some of the nation's best museums, archives, and monuments, not to mention professional opportunities.

Admissions

Average high school GPA:	3.45
Average freshman SAT writing / math / critical reading score:	540 / 549 / 535
Average freshman ACT score:	22
Application fee:	$45
Application deadlines:	
2/15 (freshmen)	
2/15 (transfer)	
Total applicants:	13,470
Total accepted:	9,304 (69%)
Total accepted who enrolled:	2,690
Notification dates:	
continuous (freshmen)	
continuous (transfer)	

Students

Percentage of male / female students:	39% / 61%
Percentage of students from out of state:	20%
Percentage of students graduating in 4 years / 6 years:	31% / 58%

Money

Total endowment:	$4,864,870
Total in-state tuition, fees & expenses:	$14,670
Total out-of-state tuition, fees & expenses:	$24,028
Average financial aid package:	$7,887
Percentage of students who sought aid and received it:	66%
Percentage of students receiving financial aid:	34%

Also Check Out

George Mason University

University of Connecticut

University of Delaware

University of Maryland–College Park

University of New Hampshire

Trinity College

300 Summit Street
Hartford, CT 06106

(860) 297-2000
http://www.trincoll.edu/

 **BIG PERSPECTIVE**

 **BIG WORLD**

Engaged around the world and across the street

5 REASONS IT'S COOL

1. Academics at Trinity **are great across all disciplines,** from English to engineering.

2. Looking for that nurturing, small college experience? At Trinity, you'll find **small classes and caring professors.**

3. **Community spirit is strong, and membership rates for extracurriculars and public service organizations run high.**

4. **Study abroad is popular,** with half of students packing their bags at some point during their four years.

5. True, Hartford ain't the most happening city, but **revitalizing programs are underway.**

The Basics

Public / private: private nonprofit
Total enrollment / undergrads: 2,528 / 2,353
Campus setting: urban
Students call it: Trinity
Students are called: Bantams
Notable alums: Edward Albee (expelled; playwright), Charles McLean Andrews (historian), Stephen Gyllenhaal (filmmaker), Mary McCormack (actress), D. Holmes Morton (physician), Jane Swift (governor, Massachusetts), George Will (author)

Strong Across the Board

Trinity's academic programs are strong across the board. The top departments are Economics, Political Science, and Biology, and the college also operates an Engineering Department—one of just a handful of small colleges to do so. All Trinity students must complete required coursework in fine arts, humanities, natural science, social science, and math. The First Year Program for freshmen includes a writing-intensive seminar taught by professors who double as academic advisors. While Trinity professors produce leading research and writing, they are known primarily for teaching. The student-to-faculty ratio is 10:1, and a third of students take advantage of opportunities to collaborate with professors on research. Half of students study abroad, choosing from forty countries on five continents. Trinity maintains its own campus in Rome. Engineers show their stuff in the annual Firefighting Home Robot Contest, the biggest public robotics competition in the country.

Leading by Learning

Trinity has demonstrated its commitment to improving life for its neighbors by playing an indispensable role in the Learning Corridor project. This neighborhood initiative, led in part by a former Trinity president, has aimed to revitalize the downtrodden neighborhood surrounding the Trinity campus through the construction of an ambitious sixteen-acre "learning corridor" consisting of several newly built public schools. The project has proved to be a success so far, and other cities throughout the country have followed Trinity's lead.

Parties and Preppies

Trinity plays host to a vibrant party scene. About a fifth of students join fraternities or sororities, and Greek houses act as the center of weekend socializing. Trinity has long been known as a haven for preppy types, and while this is still somewhat the case, the student body has grown more diverse in recent years. You won't find a lot of school spirit in the traditional sense, although students get plenty fired up about varsity sports if it means a good party is in order. A full three-quarters of students participate in intramural sports; softball alone attracts over seven hundred students. The campus features nineteen acres of playing fields, and the Ferris Athletic Center has a pool, a fitness center, crew tanks, and squash courts. Another campus bright spot is the Underground Coffee House, home to java-drinking students and musicians and poets during the weekly open-mic sessions.

In the Heart of Hartford

Trinity's hundred-acre campus is located in the middle of Hartford. The pretty campus features Gothic-style buildings and is dominated by a picturesque chapel and a large quad. Step off campus, however, and the picture changes dramatically, as the surrounding neighborhoods have long struggled with various inner-city hardships. A community revitalization initiative is expected to lead eventually to $130 million in new construction in the area. Two-thirds of Trinity students complete at least one internship in Hartford, and classes in urban development and history often send students into what is essentially a living laboratory right on the campus's doorstep. Hartford is full of attractions waiting to be discovered, including the Mark Twain House and the Wadsworth Atheneum, the nation's oldest public art museum.

Admissions

Average high school GPA:	—
Average freshman SAT writing / math / critical reading score:	649 / 658 / 647
Average freshman ACT score:	26
Application fee:	$60

Application deadlines:
1/1 (freshmen)
4/1 (transfer)
11/15 (early decision)

Total applicants:	5,343
Total accepted:	2,289 (43%)
Total accepted who enrolled:	609

Notification dates:
4/1 (freshmen)
6/1 (transfer)
12/15 (early decision)

Acceptance rate for early decision applicants:	60%

Students

Percentage of male / female students:	51% / 49%
Percentage of students from out of state:	82%
Percentage of students graduating in 4 years / 6 years:	78% / 85%

Money

Total endowment:	$382,404,710
Total tuition:	$33,440
Total cost with fees & expenses:	$44,100
Average financial aid package:	$25,590
Percentage of students who sought aid and received it:	100%
Percentage of students receiving financial aid:	39%

Also Check Out

Boston College

Brown University

Georgetown University

Middlebury College

Tufts University

Trinity University

One Trinity Place
San Antonio, TX 78212

(210) 999-7011
http://www.trinity.edu/

**BIG
PERSPECTIVE**

Where students climb to success . . . and to class

5 REASONS IT'S COOL

1. **This is Texas, y'all!** Texan culture, history, and pride pervade all aspects of the Trinity experience.

2. Challenging classes and attention from profs add up to **a first-rate classroom experience**.

3. Get ready to reach and lunge for the top at this **pretty, hilly campus.**

4. There's always time to study (or surf) on the university's **campuswide wireless network.**

5. Lots of campus activities make for **happy, outgoing students, and friends are easily made.**

The Basics

Public / private: private religious
Total enrollment / undergrads: 2,693 / 2,467
Campus setting: urban
Students call it: Trinity
Students are called: Tigers
Notable alums: Naomi Shihab Nye (writer), Uma Pemmaraju (news anchor), Jaclyn Smith (actress), Jerheme Urban (pro football player), Alice Walton (Wal-Mart heiress)

Common Denominator

Trinity's 10:1 student-to-faculty ratio means it's hard to go unnoticed or unchallenged here. Both inside and out of the classroom, students are constantly offered ways to enhance their educations. Everyone must complete the Common Curriculum, which includes a first-year seminar, a writing workshop, and a slate of courses designed to hone students' critical and creative thinking skills. There's also a Fitness Education requirement—strong bodies as well as strong minds are important at this hilly campus. In addition to the Common Curriculum, students choose from thirty-seven majors, which span the liberal arts and sciences, and professional programs. Trinity offers two five-year programs, which culminate in a master's degree in teaching or in accounting. When all is (almost) said and done, seniors complete a required Senior Experience, which can include a thesis, a capstone course, or a project that hearkens back to the good old Common Curriculum.

Take It to the Top

New students would be wise to get their legs in shape before arriving at Trinity. A university tradition requires all incoming freshmen to climb the campus's 166-foot Murchison Memorial Tower to shake hands with the university president, who is waiting at the top. After graduation, students climb and shake again, as a farewell to their undergraduate years.

Nacho Average School

Every Wednesday at 3:33 P.M., the Trinity community gathers for the university's much-loved Nacho Hour. And while Tex-Mex food is plentiful in these parts, students burn off extra calories by huffing and puffing their way to the top of Cardiac Hill, where many classes are held. Trinity students tend to be quite friendly, and campus activities like the Trinity University Volunteer Action Community (TUVAC) and ever-popular fraternities and sororities keep students active and involved. Nearly eight percent of students live on campus. Students are a smart bunch, and about half of entering freshmen come from the top 10 percent of their high school graduating class. Diversions in San Antonio abound, and artsy Austin is under an hour and a half by car. Students can also get to Mexico in just over two hours.

Oh, Give Me a Home

Trinity moved to its present campus in San Antonio in 1952. Before that the university was located in Tehuacana, and then in Waxahachie (try saying the names of those Texas towns ten times fast). The posh campus sits on a hilltop overlooking San Antonio. Trinity students roam among 117 acres of native live oaks and red brick buildings. The campus's Laurie Auditorium seats up to 2,700 people and provides cultural edification for students and San Antonians alike. The city's skyline wouldn't be complete without Trinity's Murchison Memorial Tower. Down in the city below, the River Walk (or Paseo Del Rio) draws crowds. And remember the Alamo! The historic fort is just one of the historic delights in this decidedly Texan city.

Admissions

Average high school GPA:	3.52
Average freshman SAT verbal / math score:	641 / 651
Average freshman ACT score:	26
Application fee:	$50

Application deadlines:
2/1 (freshmen)
3/1 (transfer)
11/1 (early decision)
11/1 (early action)

Total applicants:	3,899
Total accepted:	2,360 (61%)
Total accepted who enrolled:	660

Notification dates:
4/1 (freshmen)   12/15 (early decision)
4/1 (transfer)   12/15 (early action)

Acceptance rate for early action/early decision applicants:	71% / 68%

Students

Percentage of male / female students:	46% / 54%
Percentage of students from out of state:	30%
Percentage of students graduating in 4 years / 6 years:	63% / 74%

Money

Total endowment:	$814,672,000
Total tuition:	$24,864
Total cost with fees & expenses:	$33,292
Average financial aid package:	$14,343
Percentage of students who sought aid and received it:	82%
Percentage of students receiving financial aid:	39%

Also Check Out

Baylor University

Rice University

Texas Christian University

The University of Texas at Austin

Vanderbilt University

Tufts University

Bendetson Hall
Medford, MA 02155

(617) 628-5000
http://www.tufts.edu/

 **BIG BRAIN**

 **BIG WORLD**

Elite academics? Check. Beautiful campus? Check.

5 REASONS IT'S COOL

1. Go global through Tufts's **acclaimed study-abroad program**, which is widely considered to be one of the best in the country.

2. Delve into top-rated programs in **international relations and engineering**.

3. Like to think outside the box? The **Experimental College** offers more than a hundred courses on everything from Rastafarianism to YouTube.

4. The **cozy, suburban campus** is just a hop, skip, and a T ride away from the excitement of Boston.

5. When it comes to size, many students find Tufts to be a happy medium: **neither too big, nor too small.**

The Basics

Public / private: private nonprofit
Total enrollment / undergrads: 9,638 / 4,995
Campus setting: suburban
Students call it: Tufts
Students are called: Jumbos
Notable alums: Tracey Chapman (singer-songwriter), Jamie Dimon (CEO, JP Morgan Chase), David Faber (news anchor), Leslie Gelb (journalist, scholar), Gregory Macguire (novelist), Daniel Patrick Moynihan (senator), Oliver Platt (actor), Meredith Vieira (journalist)

A Little Bit Traditional, a Little Bit Innovative

With its strong academics, Tufts isn't just a safety for students who don't get into Harvard or Princeton. It's an excellent school in its own right. The student-to-faculty ratio is 8:1. Professors are high achievers in their fields, but that doesn't mean they don't have plenty of time for their students. Tufts undergrads praise the personal attention and care they get from their profs. They also like the fact that full professors teach most classes, leaving TAs to handle smaller discussion groups and labs. In some ways, the Tufts curriculum is traditional, with distribution requirements for both engineering and liberal arts students. At the same time, though, Tufts encourages innovative learning. Students can design their own majors, get credit for internships, and do independent studies. The Experimental College gives students a chance to design and teach their own courses, as well as take classes from visiting lecturers and full-time faculty members. Popular majors include international relations, bio,

Grin and Bare It

In the 1960s, West Hall was the last all-male dorm on the Tufts campus. When the guys living there heard that women would be moving in the following year, they decided to protest by running naked across the academic quad. Their nude sprint didn't succeed in keeping women out, but it did become an annual tradition.

econ, English, and psychology. Study abroad is a big deal at Tufts, with 35 to 40 percent of juniors heading out of the country annually.

Uphill, Downhill

Tufts students take academics seriously. They're just as likely to hit the stacks as the bars. A fairly diverse bunch, Tufts students are also pretty liberal. Freshmen and sophomores must live in dorms, but many upper-classmen choose to stay on campus too. Students rave about their beautiful—and hilly—campus, which features great views of Boston. The campus is informally split into two areas, Uphill and Downhill. Although the campus is small, some students spend most of their time either Uphill or Downhill and scoff at denizens of the other area. Numerous activities are on offer at Tufts. Lots 'of students volunteer with the Leonard Carmichael Society, an umbrella organization for volunteers. There are also fun yearly events such as Halloween on the Hill. Greek life isn't a particularly powerful force—around 15 percent of men are in fraternities, and less than 5 percent of women are in sororities. Still, frat parties are plentiful and popular. A Division III school, Tufts isn't known for its sports.

Boston Area, You're My Home

Tufts is in the Boston area—emphasis on *area*. Medford and Somerville, where the campus is located, are most definitely suburbs. The 150-acre campus sits on a hill overlooking the city. Still, while you won't be able to step out of your dorm and into a teeming metropolis, Boston is just a fifteen-minute ride away on the T. And the Boston area is home to over fifty-five colleges and universities, which means there are over half a million students clogging the streets, hanging out at the bars, and generally taking advantage of this charming city. Tufts students like the proximity of Boston and Cambridge, and some enjoy retreating to a suburban campus after a wild night on the town or a pleasant afternoon in a café.

Admissions

Average high school GPA: —

Average freshman SAT writing / math / critical reading score: 700 / 705 / 701

Average freshman ACT score: 26

Application fee: $70

Application deadlines:
1/1 (freshmen)
3/1 (transfer)
11/1 (early decision)

Total applicants: 15,295

Total accepted: 4,096 (27%)

Total accepted who enrolled: 1,280

Notification dates:
4/1 (freshmen)
5/1 (transfer)
12/15 (early decision)

Acceptance rate for early decision applicants: 39%

Students

Percentage of male / female students: 50% / 50%

Percentage of students from out of state: 75%

Percentage of students graduating in 4 years / 6 years: 84% / 90%

Money

Total endowment: $1,181,972,000

Total tuition: $33,906

Total cost with fees & expenses: $44,500

Average financial aid package: $27,064

Percentage of students who sought aid and received it: 100%

Percentage of students receiving financial aid: 38%

Also Check Out

Brown University

Columbia University

Dartmouth College

Harvard University

The University of Pennsylvania–University Park

Tulane University

6823 St Charles Avenue
New Orleans, LA 70118

(504) 865-5000
http://www.tulane.edu/

 **BIG PERSPECTIVE**

 **BIG RESEARCH**

Big time academics in the Big Easy

5 REASONS IT'S COOL

1. **A member of the Southern Ivies**, Tulane rubs shoulders with Duke, Emory, Rice, and Vanderbilt.

2. The Renewal Plan has given the school **a twenty-first-century makeover** in the aftermath of Hurricane Katrina.

3. **Green Wave football** inspires eddies of joy and oceans of alcohol.

4. Students hail from all over the globe, creating **a cosmopolitan campus culture**.

5. It's smack-dab **in the middle of New Orleans**.

The Basics

Public / private: private nonprofit
Total enrollment / undergrads: 10,606 / 6,533
Campus setting: urban
Students call it: Tulane, The Green Wave
Students are called: Tulaners
Notable alums: Lauren Hutton (model, actress), Jerry Springer (talk show host), Newt Gingrich (speaker, House of Representatives), Paul Michael Glaser (actor, director), John Kennedy Toole (novelist), Ruth Kirschstein (director, National Institutes of Health), John "Hot Rod" Williams (pro basketball player)

Up for Renewal

Just when Tulane was attempting to rally from the financial difficulties it had struggled with for decades, Hurricane Katrina dealt it a serious blow. In the aftermath, there have been faculty layoffs, a pared-down set of offerings, and a continued brain drain as professors frustrated with comparatively low salaries go elsewhere. But the school's aggressive Renewal Plan, implemented in December 2005 to ensure financial stability and strengthen Tulane's role as a world-class education and research institution, has largely met with success. Engineering and philosophy are up to their pre-Katrina excellence. Tulane began it existence as a medical college, and pre-med, which has always been popular, is back on track. The humanities, especially English, continue to thrive. Students who manage to resist the siren song of the French Quarter will find attentive professors eager to help them thrive.

Catch a Tiger by Its Rag?

Tulane's annual football game against rival **LSU** is a big deal—a really big deal. After rioting ensued following a Tulane victory in 1938, the Victory Flag ("Tiger Rag" to LSU), which is decorated with both schools' logos, was created as a symbol of good sportsmanship. Although the original artifact was allegedly destroyed in a 1982 fire, the schools worked together from archival photos to create a reconstruction in 2001. Now the two teams vie for bragging rights as well as ownership of the Victory Flag/Tiger Rag.

Riding the Wave

As you might expect from a school situated in the Big Easy, drinking is the number-one recreational activity at Tulane. In fact, rather than attempt the impossible, Tulane simply cancels classes for Mardi Gras. While there is a lively Greek system, it faces stiff competition in a city where even underage students find no shortage of quaffing opportunities. A high number of Tulaners hail from outside Louisiana, with a large contingent coming from northeastern prep schools. The outsider mix gives Tulane a cosmopolitan vibe that can sometimes be at odds with the laissez-faire ambiance of New Orleans. The campus itself, which the storm didn't damage much, is a lovely amalgam of architectural styles set against ample green space and stately oaks. In terms of residence halls, social butterflies should consider Sharp and Monroe, while those seeking superior creature comforts should look into Paterson or Wall. Plenty of off-campus options are also available in the surrounding residential neighborhood.

Crescent City Connection

Tulane is situation at the uptown end of New Orleans, which, despite student claims of a near-total recovery, bears the scars Hurricane Katrina left. The city still thrives on its Mardi Gras celebration and Jazz Fest, among other celebrations. Students can also take advantage of numerous historic sites, walkable neighborhoods, parks, a zoo and aquarium, sports, shopping, and, of course, incredibly rich and delicious food. Although the public bus service has struggled since the storm, travel from campus to the downtown French Quarter area is eased by the streetcar line that runs along nearby St. Charles Avenue. The city, which has always had a high homicide rate, has seen violent crime spike in recent years. While the uptown area, a few miles from the worst-hit neighborhoods, is relatively safe, students should exercise caution and take advantage of available student safety programs.

Admissions

Average high school GPA:	3.45
Average freshman SAT writing / math / critical reading score:	641 / 639 / 662
Average freshman ACT score:	—
Application fee:	$55

Application deadlines:
1/15 (freshmen) 11/1 (early decision)
6/1 (transfer) 11/1 (early action)

Total applicants:	20,756
Total accepted:	7,824 (38%)
Total accepted who enrolled:	1,110

Notification dates:
4/1 (freshmen)
continuous (transfer)
12/15 (early decision)
12/15 (early action)

Acceptance rate for early action/early decision applicants: — / 39%

Students

Percentage of male / female students:	49% / 51%
Percentage of students from out of state:	66%
Percentage of students graduating in 4 years / 6 years:	— / —

Money

Total endowment:	$858,323,000
Total tuition:	$34,896
Total cost with fees & expenses:	$44,093
Average financial aid package:	$25,945
Percentage of students who sought aid and received it:	88%
Percentage of students receiving financial aid:	35%

Also Check Out

Boston University

Duke University

Emory University

Rice University

Vanderbilt University

Union College

807 Union Street
Schenectady, NY 12308

(518) 388-6000
http://www.union.edu/

BIG PERSPECTIVE

If you can spell the town it's located in, you're halfway there.

5 REASONS IT'S COOL

1. Union is a rare thing: an esteemed liberal arts college that's also **big in the sciences and engineering**.

2. You'll **know your professors** (and they'll know you too).

3. The **Greek scene rocks**, but you don't have to go Greek to have a good time.

4. Schenectady ain't the most happening city, but it does put students within range of **tons of other local colleges**.

5. Current and aspiring ski bums can enjoy **weekend getaways to the many nearby ski resorts**.

The Basics

Public / private: private nonprofit
Total enrollment / undergrads: 2,212 / 2,212
Campus setting: urban
Students call it: Union
Students are called: Dutchmen/Dutchwomen
Notable alums: Chester A. Arthur (U.S. president), Daniel Butterfield (U.S. general), Tom Riis Farrell (actor), Gordon Gould (physicist), Phil Alden Robinson (filmmaker), Kate White (author, editor)

Give a Lot, Get a Lot

Union operates on a trimester system, and most students take three classes per shortened term. The result: Students dig deeper into their courses and also have more opportunities for internships, independent studies, and studies abroad. Popular majors include biology, French, philosophy, political science, psychology, and economics. The programs in chemistry and engineering, not surprisingly, are among the most difficult. Union's curriculum mandates courses in history, literature, and civilization; social and behavioral science; math and natural science; and a foreign language and non-Western studies. Students also must complete an interdisciplinary cluster of classes that teaches them about a chosen topic from multiple academic perspectives. All freshmen take writing-intensive courses designed to introduce them to college-level scholarship. The Union Scholars program offers a range of enhanced opportunities to a select group of students; these include special study-abroad options, one-on-one collaborations with

Idol Worship

In 1875, a Union alumnus donated a giant Chinese stone lion to his alma mater. Thought to date back to the fifteenth century, the two-ton idol traveled all the way from Shanghai, where it was unearthed, to the Union campus, where it sits outside next to Bailey Field. The tradition of painting the idol began almost immediately after its arrival. Random acts of decoration have been perpetrated for every imaginable purpose: initiation ritual, class or frat rivalry, sports celebration, or simply because it's there.

professors, and extra mentoring. Ninety-four percent of Union's professors have PhDs, and the student-to-faculty ratio is 11:1.

Greek and Old

Preppy, wealthy, and agnostic is the typical profile of a Union student. About half of the college's two thousand students hail from New York, while the remaining come from elsewhere in the Northeast. The campus vibe is friendly and community oriented—nearly 90 percent of students live on campus, and over a hundred student groups help to strengthen the sense of togetherness. Greek roots run very deep at Union. In fact, the first three college fraternities in America were started here, beginning with the Kappa Alpha Society way back in 1825. Greek life anchors the social scene—about a third of students participate—and Union has developed something of a party-school rep. In response, the administration implemented the Minerva Housing program, in which faculty and students contribute to a shared intellectual, residential, and social atmosphere. Annual campus events include a lobster bake, Party in the Garden, and Spring Fest. Sports, both participatory and spectator, are popular.

Spring Will Come, We Think

Union's lovely hundred-acre campus includes well-manicured gardens and beautiful woodlands. The architectural centerpiece is Nott Memorial, a sixteen-sided lecture and exhibit space. Beyond campus lies Schenectady, a small city that's situated fifteen miles west of Albany, the state capital. Though not exactly an urban mecca, the region does have a sizeable population and tons of students. Schenectady itself is somewhat economically depressed and suffers from a dearth of student-friendly bars, restaurants, and shops. The livelier town of Saratoga Springs, however, is nearby for students with cars. Winters in Upstate New York are long and snowy, and the surrounding Catskill, Adirondack, Green, and Berkshire mountains provide plenty of hiking and skiing.

Admissions

Average high school GPA:	3.5
Average freshman SAT verbal / math score:	611 / 629
Average freshman ACT score:	25
Application fee:	$50

Application deadlines:
1/15 (freshmen)
5/1 (transfer)
11/15 (early decision)

Total applicants:	4,373
Total accepted:	1,862 (43%)
Total accepted who enrolled:	560

Notification dates:
4/1 (freshmen)
continuous (transfer)
12/15 (early decision)

Acceptance rate for early decision applicants:	68%

Students

Percentage of male / female students:	53% / 47%
Percentage of students from out of state:	60%
Percentage of students graduating in 4 years / 6 years:	80% / 84%

Money

Total endowment:	$298,300,000
Total tuition:	—
Total cost with fees & expenses:	$44,043
Average financial aid package:	$26,330
Percentage of students who sought aid and received it:	100%
Percentage of students receiving financial aid:	46%

Also Check Out

Brown University

Colgate University

Dickinson College

Hamilton College

Skidmore College

United States Air Force Academy

HQ USAFA/XPR, 2304 Cadet Drive, Suite 200
USAF Academy, CO 80840

(719) 333-1818
http://www.usafa.edu/

 **BIG BRAIN**

 **BIG JOB**

 **BIG PLAN**

Aim high into the wild blue yonder!

5 REASONS IT'S COOL

1. Where else will you learn to fly jets, skydive, and design rocket launchers?

2. **Cadets are commissioned as Air Force officers**, most as second lieutenants, for at least five years following graduation.

3. **All four years are free.** The Air Force pays for room, board, and medical and dental care.

4. Fellowship runs high as **cadets bond over shared ambitions** and a desire to serve their country.

5. The campus's **lush lawns, majestic architecture, historical ambiance, and sweeping landscape** attract tourists from across the country.

The Basics

Public / private: public federal
Total enrollment / undergrads: 4,524 / 4,524
Campus setting: suburban
Students call it: Air Force, the Academy, The Hill, The Zoo, The Wild Blue U
Students are called: Cadets, Zoomies
Notable alums: General Ron Fogleman (U.S. Air Force chief of staff), Fred Gregory (astronaut, NASA administrator), Susan Jane Helms (astronaut), Richard T. Schlosberg (businessman, publisher), Heather Wilson (congresswoman)

Aim (Really) High

The Air Force Academy produces a uniquely high number of astronauts. This isn't too surprising since the faculty, the majority of whom are Air Force officers, include the country's top people in the fields of aeronautics and astrophysics. The Academy's core curriculum includes extensive coursework in engineering and basic science. All cadets graduate with a BS no matter which of the school's twenty-five majors they select. Recent efforts have sought to broaden offerings in the humanities and social sciences, but 60 percent of students take degrees in science and engineering, with astronautical engineering and management topping the list of most popular programs. Morning classes, most of which start at 7:30 A.M., are followed by a steady regimen of studying, eating, more classes, training, more eating, and more studying. Curved scales turn up the heat on the grade-conscious, and the average student spends

I'm Ready for My Clothes, Mr. DeMille

Any good military corps needs a good uniform. Underwhelmed by the proposals from military tailors, the secretary of the Air Force approached director Cecil B. DeMille for help. The iconic Hollywood director was eager to comply, pulling staff from his production of *The Ten Commandments* to assist him. To this day, cadets sport his creation.

twenty hours a week on homework. But small class sizes guarantee personal attention.

Reveille, Day in and Day Out

Physical fitness is high on the list of priorities for cadets. Freshmen undergo a required five-week basic training session before the start of classes. During the academic year, there are a host of intercollegiate and intramural sports along with regular physical fitness and aerobics tests. The Academy's boxing, football, and rugby teams rank among the nation's best. Off-campus living is not an option and free time is a hot commodity, especially for freshmen. Students who fail a class or athletic requirement, or are found guilty of some infraction in conduct or honor, are denied leave. Daring cadets confined to campus take unsanctioned expeditions through the school's underground tunnels. While a no-alcohol policy is strictly enforced on campus, the surrounding town offers plenty of bars to choose from. Neighboring University of Colorado at Boulder and Colorado State University provide additional distractions. The overwhelmingly male (over 80 percent) student body tends to be conservative, white, and religious, although exchange programs with foreign academies enhance diversity.

The Rocky Mountain Sighs

Nestled in the foothills of the Rocky Mountains roughly forty miles from Denver, the Academy's 18,000-acre campus consists of numerous halls and memorials, a stadium, an airfield, and a cemetery. Valleys and ridges interrupt the level terrain, and it's not unusual to see deer or wild turkey wandering the park-like grounds. The famous Cadet Area, located at the peak of the ridges more than seven thousand feet above sea level, is home to an array of dazzlingly modern structures, most notably the ethereal Cadet Chapel with its thin, aluminum spires. Other notable landmarks include the War Memorial, which lists graduates killed in combat, the landscaped Air Gardens, and the Honor Wall, which bears the academy's honor code. Cadets tired of absorbing the surrounding majesty hit up the ski slopes or the nearby town of Colorado Springs.

Admissions

Average high school GPA:	3.86
Average freshman SAT verbal / math score:	—/—
Average freshman ACT score:	—
Application fee:	—
Application deadlines: 1/31 (freshmen) 1/31 (transfer)	
Total applicants:	9,255
Total accepted:	1,321 (14%)
Total accepted who enrolled:	1,266
Notification dates: 5/15 (freshmen) 5/15 (transfer)	

Students

Percentage of male / female students:	82% / 18%
Percentage of students from out of state:	94%
Percentage of students graduating in 4 years / 6 years:	78% / 79%

Money

Total endowment:	—
Total tuition:	—
Total cost with fees & expenses:	—
Average financial aid package:	—
Percentage of students who sought aid and received it:	—
Percentage of students receiving financial aid:	—

Also Check Out

California Institute of Technology

Carnegie Mellon University

Massachusetts Institute of Technology

United States Coast Guard Academy

United States Military Academy–West Point

United States Naval Academy–Annapolis

United States Coast Guard Academy

I5 Mohegan Avenue
New London, CT 06320

(860) 444-8444
http://www.cga.edu/

 **BIG BRAIN**

 **BIG JOB**

 **BIG PLAN**

In the service, out at sea

5 REASONS IT'S COOL

1. Summer training includes (paid!) work on ships traveling to exotic locations such as Hawaii and Bermuda.

2. The **free education and stipend** allow cadets to lead self-sufficient lives.

3. Positions as **deck watch officers or engineers in training** await cadets upon graduation.

4. As the smallest of the military service academies, CGA prides itself on the **close relationship between faculty and students**.

5. Cadets have the option of taking **elective classes at neighboring Connecticut College.**

The Basics

Public / private: public federal
Total enrollment / undergrads: 996 / 996
Campus setting: suburban
Students call it: Coast Guard Academy, USCGA, CGA
Students are called: Cadets, Bears
Notable alums: Ellsworth Price Bertholf (first commandant, Coast Guard), Daniel Burbank (astronaut), Bruce Melnick (astronaut), G. William Miller (chairman, Federal Reserve; secretary of treasury), Elmer Stone (commander, Coast Guard; naval aviator)

To Love, Honor, and Obey

Because admission to the Coast Guard Academy is purely merit based (not the case at other military academies, which allow congressional recommendations), CGA is often considered the most difficult college-level military institution to get into. Mandatory classes in calculus, chemistry, physics, ethics, government, criminal justice, health, economics, naval architecture, literature, and engineering take the first two years to complete. Cadets are limited to eight majors for their mandatory bachelor of science, and all programs, with the exception of government and management, are science intensive. The rigorous workload is made bearable by professors who are generous with attention and encouragement. Classes tend to be small, topping out at forty students, and the student-to-teacher ratio is a cozy 9:1. Coursework occasionally involves trips to nearby laboratories or high-tech companies and may take students to cities like New York City or Boston. Guest lecturers frequently

Objee Trouvé

In 1926, a cadet returning from leave brought back a live bear cub. Surprisingly, the academy permitted the cub to stay and eventually gave him the nickname **Objee**, short for "objectionable presence." Objee took to showering and eating with the cadets. The live bear remained a staple at CGA until changes in animal quarantine laws in 1984. Today, the bear lives on in the academy's mascot.

include alums returning to discuss their successes in science, business, or law. The academy also offers the bonus of free graduate school following the first obligatory tour of duty.

Shaping Up to Ship Out

The academy plans every hour of cadets' lives. In addition to a demanding academic schedule, there is military training, which requires exercise, ship time, and frequent room and uniform inspections. Cadets are considered active duty military personnel and train each summer aboard one of the academy's state-of-the-art ships or aircraft. The first summer includes a stay on the main training ship, the USCGC *Eagle*, a 295-foot barque and the only tall sailing ship in active service. Students are allotted time each afternoon to participate in one of twenty-three varsity teams or additional intramural sports. Military protocol and social etiquette require cadets to attend dances, concerts, and rallies. Those with time for outside activities can choose from eighteen student clubs, many of which are based around music, theater, or religion. Diversity isn't one of the academy's strong suits. The student body is less than 15 percent minority and 30 percent female.

The Quintessential Cadet Town

New London, situated where the Thames River empties into Long Island Sound, has a long maritime history, making it the perfect college town for CGA. The campus's architecture varies from stately redbrick colonial to sleek and modern. Monuments to heroic officers are sprinkled about the vast, well-manicured lawns. Foremost among campus landmarks is scenic Robert Crown Park, with a fieldstone-lined pond, a wartime memorial obelisk, and a gazebo. The starkly white Jacob's Rock, another unique structure, houses the sailing team and seamanship center. Athletic facilities are kept up-to-date, and the academy recently installed a synthetic field turf to replace the traditional grass surface on the Cadet Memorial Field. Students with the inclination, and the leave time, can break free of their insular surroundings with a trip to nearby New York City or Boston.

Admissions

Average high school GPA:	3.76
Average freshman SAT verbal / math score:	618 / 652
Average freshman ACT score:	26
Application fee:	—

Application deadlines:
3/1 (freshmen)
— (transfer)
11/1 (early action)

Total applicants:	1,633
Total accepted:	394 (24%)
Total accepted who enrolled:	250

Notification dates:
5/1 (freshmen)
— (transfer)
12/15 (early action)

Acceptance rate for early action applicants:	30%

Students

Percentage of male / female students:	72% / 28%
Percentage of students from out of state:	94%
Percentage of students graduating in 4 years / 6 years:	68% / 73%

Money

Total endowment:	—
Total tuition:	—
Total cost with fees & expenses:	—
Average financial aid package:	—
Percentage of students who sought aid and received it:	—
Percentage of students receiving financial aid:	—

Also Check Out

United States Air Force Academy

United States Military Academy–West Point

United States Naval Academy–Annapolis

Yale University

United States Military Academy–West Point

600 Thayer Road
West Point, NY 10996

(845) 938-4011
http://www.usma.edu/

 **BIG BRAIN**

 BIG JOB

 **BIG PLAN**

Become a lean, mean leadership machine.

5 REASONS IT'S COOL

1. Originally founded as an engineering school, West Point has top-ranked **civil and mechanical engineering** programs.

2. In addition to **free tuition, room, and board,** cadets are given around $7,000 a year for uniforms, books, and laptops.

3. As the motto attests, every cadet learns the value of **Duty, Honor, and Country.**

4. West Point's vast campus (one of the largest in the world at 16,000 acres) is **as beautiful as it is immense.**

5. From plebes to firsties, **each class gets its own weekend to celebrate every year,** culminating in a weeklong string of events at graduation.

The Basics

Public / private: public federal
Total enrollment / undergrads: 4,231 / 4,231
Campus setting: small town
Students call it: USMA, West Point, Army
Students are called: Cadets, Plebes (for the first-years), Yearlings/Yuks (sophomores), Cows (juniors), Firsties (seniors)
Notable alums: Buzz Aldrin (astronaut), Jefferson Davis (Confederate president), Abner Doubleday (alleged inventor of baseball), Dwight D. Eisenhower (U.S. president), Ulysses S. Grant (U.S. president), General Robert E. Lee (U.S. Army), General Douglas MacArthur (U.S. Army), General David Petraeus (U.S. Army), Fidel V. Ramos (president, Philippines), General Norman Schwarzkopf (U.S. Army)

Where Rules Rule

Teachers at this elite institution are known for their dedication. Class sizes average around sixteen students, and cadets get lots of individual attention (for better and worse). An extensive core curriculum consists of thirty-one courses in a broad array of arts and sciences courses. Only during junior and senior years do students start taking classes for their majors. Senior theses and final projects are common, and an impressive number of students win postgraduate scholarships to continue their research. West Point was the first school in the United States to offer a formal engineering program, and its engineering major remains most popular despite being one of the most challenging. Engineering majors frequently attend conferences and participate in outreach programs

Spirited Away

Cadets are known to carry out "spirit missions," which are spirit-building exercises executed under cover of darkness. Cadets, led by a team captain, sneak out of their barracks to conduct nightly raids and other missions. Missions can include anything from stealing mess hall dinner plates to adorning every statue on campus in battle rags before a football game.

such as the West Point Bridge Design Contest for middle- and high-school students. In recent years, course offerings have expanded to include an increasing number of foreign languages. And West Point is making it easier for cadets to study abroad and participate in exchange programs with foreign military academies.

Follow the Leader

West Point cadets are ambitious and driven to succeed, but they're also a close-knit bunch bonded by their shared experience. Physical and intellectual fitness is stressed upon entrance and continued throughout. Mandatory marching drills, duties, coursework, and sports activities leave little time for anything else. Twenty-four intercollegiate sports are available for men and women (who make up just 15 percent of the student body), including rugby, crew, and sailing. With such restriction on time, cadets are happy to join student organizations such as the fine arts forum, glee club, and radio station, or to go to dances with nearby colleges. The mess hall is majestic, with tall ceilings and historic artifacts lining the walls, but the food is oft maligned for its blandness and mediocrity. Strictly enforced rules prohibit underage drinking and ensure the fastidious tidiness of living quarters.

Living the Hudson High Life

Nicknamed Hudson High because of its location on the scenic banks of the Hudson River, West Point was originally a stronghold in the American Revolution (and under the command of the notorious traitor Benedict Arnold). Today, the school is surrounded by ski slopes rather than redcoats, and includes three major ski runs of its own, in addition to an artillery range and a nuclear reactor. The campus is sprinkled with Gothic-styled gray buildings, stately castles, monuments to illustrious graduates, and underpasses separating the lush green lawns and sports fields. Cadets with a spare moment can explore the surrounding town of Highland Falls, known as the "Historic Gateway to West Point." West Point is only 50 miles from New York City, though students don't have much free time to enjoy it—especially during their first year when they only have one weekend of leave per semester.

Admissions

Average high school GPA:	—
Average freshman SAT verbal / math score:	633 / 652
Average freshman ACT score:	26
Application fee:	—
Application deadlines:	
2/28 (freshmen)	
2/28 (transfer)	
Total applicants:	10,958
Total accepted:	1,555 (14%)
Total accepted who enrolled:	1,194
Notification dates:	
6/1 (freshmen)	
6/1 (transfer)	

Students

Percentage of male / female students:	85% / 15%
Percentage of students from out of state:	92%
Percentage of students graduating in 4 years / 6 years:	82% / 85%

Money

Total endowment:	—
Total tuition:	—
Total cost with fees & expenses:	—
Average financial aid package:	—
Percentage of students who sought aid and received it:	—
Percentage of students receiving financial aid:	—

Also Check Out

Carnegie Mellon University

Harvard University

United States Air Force Academy

United States Coast Guard Academy

United States Naval Academy–Annapolis

Yale University

United States Naval Academy–Annapolis

121 Blake Road
Annapolis, MD 21402

(410) 293-1000
http://www.usna.edu/

 **BIG BRAIN**

 BIG JOB

 **BIG PLAN**

Anchors aweigh!

5 REASONS IT'S COOL

1. Admissions are rigorous, but the **education is free**, and graduates become commissioned officers.

2. The Trident Scholars program allows select seniors to conduct **independent research under faculty supervision.**

3. The Academy's Foreign Affairs Conference allows students from around the globe to meet and **discuss contemporary international issues with world leaders.**

4. **Cadets are trained** to fire weapons, lead brigades, commandeer sailboats, and handle the high seas.

5. **Midshipmen develop a close camaraderie** as they eat, sleep, study, and drill together.

The Basics

Public / private: public federal
Total enrollment / undergrads: 4,479 / 4,479
Campus setting: small town
Students call it: The Naval Academy, Annapolis
Students are called: Cadets, midshipmen, mids, plebes (as freshmen are better known)
Notable alums: Charles Bolden (astronaut), Jimmy Carter (U.S. president), Wendy Lawrence (astronaut), John McCain (senator), General Peter Pace (chairman, Joint Chiefs of Staff), Alan Shepard (astronaut), Roger Staubach (pro football player)

Sea, Air, and Master's Degrees

The Naval Academy's commitment to academics is captured by its motto: "From knowledge, seapower." Admissions are rigorous, and core requirements include courses in engineering, science, the humanities, and social sciences. Additional classes on topics such as leadership and military training acquaint cadets with the naval officer's life. Midshipmen choose from twenty-one majors, including engineering, architecture, and Arabic. Honors programs also allow students to conduct research in areas such as literature and economics. Humanities majors are capped at 30 percent, and because of the technical requirements of the curriculum, everyone graduates with a bachelor of science degree. Classes average fewer than eighteen students, and faculty include both doctorate-holding civilians and military personnel. Among the nation's service academies, the Navel Academy gives its students the most postgraduate

Getting Their Goat

Legend has it that when a much-beloved goat died aboard a Navy vessel, two midshipmen decided to get it stuffed. On their way to the taxidermist's, the sailors stopped to catch a football game at their alma mater. At halftime, one of the officers donned the goat skin and began cavorting around the sidelines. Navy won the game, and the goat became the school's mascot.

employment options, including positions working on ballistic missile submarines, conducting surface warfare, and operating fighter jets. The Voluntary Graduate Education Program allows seniors to work toward a master's at a nearby university and earn their grad degrees within seven months of completing their bachelor's.

Running a Tight Ship

From the start, a midshipman's days are filled with required duties. Training begins the summer before freshman year, known as Plebe Summer, during which recruits complete a seven-week boot camp. Days start before sunrise and last until 10 P.M., with no breaks or free time. The strict regimen continues into freshmen year, when new cadets are barred from listening to music or watching movies. Freedoms increase for upperclassmen, and mids can participate in over ninety extracurricular activities ranging from community service to art clubs, as well as popular varsity and extracurricular sports. The party scene is virtually nonexistent, and drinking and dating rules are strict. The school sponsors several social events, the most significant of which involves class rings, which are designed by committees formed during plebe year and presented at the junior year Ring Dance. Before they are worn, the rings are dipped in water from the seven seas.

By the Bay Is Where I'll Stay

The academy makes its home on the Severn River, a tributary of the Chesapeake Bay. The founders selected this spot for its distance from large, potentially distracting cities. Although not as vast as that of other military academies, the 338-acre campus—known as the Yard—is a National Historic Landmark and lays claim to several historic monuments and stately buildings. The Renaissance-style Bancroft Hall, with its imposing granite exterior, high ceilings, and gold-lined rotunda, houses all four classes of cadets. Bancroft connects to Memorial Hall, which honors academy graduates killed in action or awarded medals for bravery. Luce Hall houses simulation rooms where mids train on virtual-reality equipment. The surrounding town of Annapolis offers a picturesque main street flanked with boutiques and restaurants.

Admissions

Average high school GPA:	—
Average freshman SAT verbal / math score:	648 / 670
Average freshman ACT score:	—
Application fee:	—
Application deadlines:	
1/31 (freshmen)	
— (transfer)	
Total applicants:	10,747
Total accepted:	1,228 (11%)
Total accepted who enrolled:	1,191
Notification dates:	
4/15 (freshmen)	
— (transfer)	

Students

Percentage of male / female students:	81% / 19%
Percentage of students from out of state:	96%
Percentage of students graduating in 4 years / 6 years:	86% / 86%

Money

Total endowment:	$126,000,000
Total tuition:	—
Total cost with fees & expenses:	—
Average financial aid package:	—
Percentage of students who sought aid and received it:	—
Percentage of students receiving financial aid:	—

Also Check Out

Duke University

Massachusetts Institute of Technology

The Pennsylvania State University–University Park

United States Air Force Academy

United States Coast Guard Academy

United States Military Academy–West Point

University of Alabama–Tuscaloosa

Box 870132
Tuscaloosa, AL 35487

(205) 348-6010
http://www.ua.edu/

BIG CHOICE

Sweet home Alabama

5 REASONS IT'S COOL

1. UA's New College offers students a **unique opportunity to shape their own academic futures.**

2. The College of Communication and Information Sciences is **among the nation's best.**

3. Thanks to a recent building boom, students have a number of **new residence halls to choose from.**

4. Spirits rise with **Crimson Tide football.**

5. Tuscaloosa offers students a mix of **down-home barbeque and uptown culture.**

The Basics

Public / private: public state
Total enrollment / undergrads: 23,838 / 19,471
Campus setting: suburban
Students call it: Alabama, UA, 'Bama, The Capstone
Students are called: The Crimson Tide
Notable alums: Shaun Alexander (pro football player), Mel Allen (sportscaster), Samuel DiPiazza (CEO, PricewaterhouseCoopers), Forrest Gump (businessman, recreational runner, American hero), Timothy Leary (psychologist), Harper Lee (attended; novelist), Joe Namath (pro football player), Gay Talese (journalist), E. O. Wilson (entomologist)

Turning the Tide

Administrators have worked hard to change UA's rep from *football and party powerhouse* to *leading flagship institution.* Among the many strong programs, humanities and arts draw the most students. Programs in music and dance are particularly well regarded. Education, engineering, and environmental studies are also strong, and the College of Commerce and Business, with its popular finance and accounting majors, is among the school's best. Aspiring journalists get a terrific education at the nationally recognized College of Communication and Information Sciences. The honors college offers challenging coursework in separate computer-based, university, and international programs of study. For a more intimate experience, the selective New College provides an interdisciplinary liberal arts curriculum that allows students to create their curricula around the humanities, social sciences, and natural sciences. New College

Showing Segregation the Door

Civil rights history was made at UA on June 11, 1963, when two African American students tried to enroll. Governor George Wallace himself tried to block the admissions office door. Persuaded by federal marshals, he relented, and one of the students, Vivian Malone, went on to become the school's first black female graduate. In 2000, the UA bestowed on her a doctorate of humane letters.

Admissions

Average high school GPA:	3.4
Average freshman SAT verbal / math score:	571 / 570
Average freshman ACT score:	23
Application fee:	$35
Application deadlines:	—
Total applicants:	12,513
Total accepted:	8,766 (70%)
Total accepted who enrolled:	4,359
Notification dates:	— (freshmen) continuous (transfer)

students also have numerous research and direct study opportunities. In general, professors are praised for being accessible and challenging.

Welcome to the Machine

UA students live and die by Crimson Tide football. Students and locals alike party hard for each game, especially against rival Auburn. But a raucous atmosphere is the norm across the campus and especially on fraternity row. The Greek system, often referred to as the Machine, has the run of campus life and student government, and students admit that non-Greeks and nonpartiers are left out of many social occasions. The school hosts events such as movies, music, theater, and dance, along with art galleries and lectures. The Student Recreation Center has an indoor and outdoor pool, various ball courts, and a rock-climbing wall. Campus housing rates highly among the 25 percent of students who live in it. Several new residence halls have sprung up thanks to a recent building boom, and living-learning communities are available for students with shared interests. A large majority of students are homegrown Alabamans. Compared to other southern flagships, the school is fairly diverse in regard to ethnicity.

Life at 'Bama: You'll Cotton to It

Tuscaloosa, home to roughly 85,000 residents, gets mixed ratings from UA students. Some see it as the perfect balance of southern charm and urban bustle, while others find it to be slow and lifeless. Students have easy access to a busy downtown, courtesy of the streetcar service that runs from campus. Most students head to the Strip, a stretch of road that contains several shops, bars, and restaurants, where they indulge in the nightlife and plates of barbeque. UA's beautiful thousand-acre campus mixes classical and revival-style buildings with more modern structures. Denny Chimes, the school's bell tower, rings out the time throughout the day. That iconic structure sits around the main greenery, called the Quad, alongside the president's mansion and the main campus library. Other campus highlights include the Moody Music building, home to the Tuscaloosa Symphony Orchestra, and an arboretum, which houses a unique collection of native flora.

Students

Percentage of male / female students:	47% / 53%
Percentage of students from out of state:	24%
Percentage of students graduating in 4 years / 6 years:	35% / 63%

Money

Total endowment:	$504,244,635
Total in-state tuition, fees & expenses:	$11,608
Total out-of-state tuition, fees & expenses:	$21,624
Average financial aid package:	$8,542
Percentage of students who sought aid and received it:	67%
Percentage of students receiving financial aid:	28%

Also Check Out

Auburn University

Florida State University

University of Georgia

The University of Mississippi

The University of Tennessee

University of Alaska–Fairbanks

PO Box 757500
Fairbanks, AK 99775

(907) 474-7211
http://www.uaf.edu/

 **BIG CHOICE**

 **BIG RESEARCH**

Staying warm on the last frontier

5 REASONS IT'S COOL

1. If you're interested in arctic culture, climate, engineering, or wildlife, UAF is the place to be.

2. **Mix and mingle:** About half the student body at this midsized school is from out of state.

3. Explore the **stunning natural beauty** of the last frontier in your own 360-million-acre classroom!

4. For in- and out-of-staters alike, **tuition at this research institution is a steal.**

5. **Midnight sunshine and northern lights**—life is magical this far north.

The Basics

Public / private: public state
Total enrollment / undergrads: 8,341 / 7,274
Campus setting: small town
Students call it: UAF
Students are called: Nanooks
Notable alums: Bob Bartlett (senator), Flora Jane Harper (first Alaska native graduate), Eileen Panigeo MacLean (noted educator, state representative)

Uniquely Alaska

There are 161 degree options at UAF, but it's the unique programs of study that are most notable. Wildlife biology, Alaska native studies, and northern studies are just some of the programs that take advantage of UAF's inimitable natural and cultural surroundings. Founded as an agricultural and mining school in 1917, the Mining and Geological Engineering Department is still going strong. Tuition is a steal for native Alaskans, and even out-of-state students will find it affordable. If you're from a qualifying western state, look into the Western Undergraduate Exchange program, which offers discounted nonresident tuition. UAF is the state's largest research institution and has centers focused on large animal wildlife, native Alaskan languages, arctic climate, and supercomputing. The International Arctic Research Center is on campus, as is the architecturally stunning Museum of the North. All this research doesn't distract professors from their students: UAF has a 13:1 student-to-faculty ratio and keeps most classes to thirty students or fewer.

How Cold Is It, Really?

Out-of-state students are sometimes shocked by the frigidity of typical Alaskan winters. Biting cold is the norm. In fact, students say it has to be 50 degrees below zero before the university will cancel classes. On campus, the predominately snow-white buildings might fool you into thinking it's winter year round!

Embrace the Frontier

The university's Outdoor Adventures program takes students into the wild for an affordable price. If you couldn't be paid—much less pay—to go winter camping, there are over a hundred student organizations on campus, all of which offer (relatively) well-heated activities. Nanook ice hockey is a fan favorite, especially when the team plays longtime rival the University of Alaska at Anchorage. Native Alaskans/Native Americans are the most represented minority on campus, making up nearly 20 percent of the student body, and students hail from all fifty states. For those living on campus, the options include traditional residence halls, two First Year Experience Halls, and a house aimed at helping native or rural Alaskans transition into college. After freshman year, most students move to the affordable housing surrounding campus. But even those who strike out on their own are easily lured back by a drink and a brat at the Pub in the William Ransom Wood Campus Center, a favorite hangout for the over-21 crowd.

Into the Wild

UAF is located in Fairbanks, Alaska's second largest city. Just two hundred miles from the Arctic Circle, UAF is a prime spot to watch the northern lights, experience late-night sun (there are almost twenty-two hours of sunshine during the Summer Solstice!), and enjoy the unique beauty of Alaska. Fairbanks is about five hours from Anchorage and about a two-hour drive from Denali National Park, but you don't have to go that far to experience the Alaskan wilderness. Miles of trails are accessible from campus. Summers can be lovely, with temperatures in the seventies, but winters are long and cold, so make sure you bring a warm coat!

Admissions

Average high school GPA:	3.19
Average freshman SAT verbal / math score:	535 / 522
Average freshman ACT score:	21
Application fee:	$40
Application deadlines:	
7/1 (freshmen)	
7/1 (transfer)	
Total applicants:	1,743
Total accepted:	1,283 (74%)
Total accepted who enrolled:	750
Notification dates:	
continuous (freshmen)	
continuous (transfer)	

Students

Percentage of male / female students:	48% / 52%
Percentage of students from out of state:	15%
Percentage of students graduating in 4 years / 6 years:	6% / 23%

Money

Total endowment:	—
Total in-state tuition, fees & expenses:	$10,338
Total out-of-state tuition, fees & expenses:	$18,708
Average financial aid package:	$8,905
Percentage of students who sought aid and received it:	67%
Percentage of students receiving financial aid:	17%

Also Check Out

Seattle University

The University of Montana–Missoula

University of Oregon

University of Puget Sound

University of Washington

The University of Arizona

| PO Box 210040 | (520) 621-2211 |
| Tucson, AZ 85721 | http://www.arizona.edu/ |

 **BIG CHOICE**    **BIG RESEARCH**

To study, to tan, or to party? Decisions, decisions!

5 REASONS IT'S COOL

1. A first-rate Astronomy Department is just one of the **strong science programs.**

2. Art galleries, game rooms, restaurants, movie theaters—**the student center is one of the largest in the country.**

3. At UA, cheer your head off for **Wildcat basketball,** which has reached the NCAA Tournament twenty-three years in a row.

4. 350 is your lucky number: Enjoy **350 days of Arizona sunshine** on the 350-acre campus.

5. Don't be fooled by the relaxed atmosphere on campus: **Wildcats shift into high gear when it comes time to party.**

The Basics

Public / private: public state
Total enrollment / undergrads: 36,805 / 28,442
Campus setting: urban
Students call it: UA
Students are called: Wildcats
Notable alums: Jerry Bruckheimer (filmmaker), Sean Elliott (pro basketball player), Greg Kinnear (actor), Gordon Lish (writer, editor), David Foster Wallace (writer)

Large and In Charge

Pre-professional programs and the sciences are UA's calling cards, but with eighteen colleges, twelve schools, and 150 degree programs, students have a wealth of options. "Space-y" students can take advantage of the top-notch Astronomy Department, and future Einsteins have the opportunity to study under renowned astrophysicist Fang Lizhi. UA's largest college, Social and Behavioral Sciences, has strong programs in anthropology and philosophy. The research facilities are excellent, and students can also choose from an array of research programs, including participation in NASA's Phoenix Mars Mission or study at Biosphere 2. In the popular Eller College of Management, students can explore fields such as entrepreneurship or management information systems. And for those with a hop in their step, the dance program is one of the best in the nation. About 15 percent of each incoming class is chosen for the esteemed Honors Program, which provides access to smaller classes and priority registration. While attending a large research institution

Bear Down

In 1926, the UA lost popular student body president and star quarterback John Sutton in a car crash. His final message to his teammates before he died was, "Tell them ... tell the team to bear down." The team honored his wish, playing their hearts out, and UA adopted "Bear Down" as its motto.

Admissions

Average high school GPA:	3.44
Average freshman SAT verbal / math score:	550 / 566
Average freshman ACT score:	23
Application fee:	$25

Application deadlines:
4/1 (freshmen)
6/1 (transfer)

Total applicants:	16,609
Total accepted:	13,353 (80%)
Total accepted who enrolled:	5,788

Notification dates:
continuous (freshmen)
— (transfer)

---

has incredible advantages, class size is often in the hundreds. Students give their professors good reviews, although some complain about the number of TA-taught courses. In general, you'll thrive in your studies at UA if you're motivated and disciplined.

Got Sunscreen?

"Fun in the sun" could be UA's unofficial motto. It's not unusual to see members of the fit, attractive student body tanning on the Main Mall, an expansive palm-lined lawn at the center of campus. If you're craving shade, the student center is a popular hangout. And watch out for the Freshmen Fifteen—students rave about the UA food, which ranges from Panda Express to Chipotle. The limited on-campus housing is primarily used by freshmen. Most upperclassmen take advantage of affordable off-campus housing options after their first year. Greek life is a significant presence; about 15 percent of students join one of forty-nine different fraternities and sororities. Greek or not, Wildcats are partiers. The bars and clubs of Fourth Ave. offer alternatives to the frat scene, and committed (underage) students drive an hour to Nogales, Mexico, where there is no drinking age. Although there are nearly thirty thousand undergrads at UA, most students find a niche. There are hundreds of clubs on campus, some of the most popular of which are ethnic organizations. Wildcats' sense of community is solidified by the immense school spirit surrounding their basketball team. The Division I Wildcats unite students and townspeople alike, though competition for tickets to home games is fierce.

City, Desert, Mountains—and Southwestern Charm

The redbrick architecture of the large UA campus is inspired by Old Main, the first building on campus. More modern facilities have been constructed in recent years, including the underground Integrated Learning Center and a plethora of high-tech science labs. Campus is just minutes away from downtown Tucson, a pleasant, sunny town. Surrounded by the Sonoran Desert and the Catalina Mountains, Tucson provides both nightlife and easy access to nature. Nearby Mt. Lemmon has skiing, climbing, biking, and hiking trails.

Students

Percentage of male / female students:	47% / 53%
Percentage of students from out of state:	33%
Percentage of students graduating in 4 years / 6 years:	32% / 58%

Money

Total endowment:	$348,343,000
Total in-state tuition, fees & expenses:	$13,432
Total out-of-state tuition, fees & expenses:	$23,638
Average financial aid package:	$8,078
Percentage of students who sought aid and received it:	64%
Percentage of students receiving financial aid:	34%

Also Check Out

University of California–Irvine

University of California–Los Angeles

University of California–Santa Barbara

University of Colorado at Boulder

University of Washington

University of Arkansas–Fayetteville

800 Hotz Hall
Fayetteville, AR 72701

(479) 575-2000
http://www.uark.edu/

BIG CHOICE

"Wooooooo, Pig! Sooie!"

5 REASONS IT'S COOL

1. The Sam Walton School of Business, named for the founder of Wal-Mart, **trains the next generation of business entrepreneurs.**

2. If farm livin' is the life for you, check out the **Dale Bumpers College of Agricultural, Food, and Life Sciences.**

3. A UA education is super-**affordable**, especially for in-state students.

4. **Razorbacks football** will have you "calling the hogs" (the university's trademark cheer) with thousands of other excited fans.

5. Fayetteville's cool main drag, Dickson Street, puts **plenty of clubs, bars, and eateries right at students' front doors.**

The Basics

Public / private: public state
Total enrollment / undergrads: 17,926 / 14,350
Campus setting: suburban
Students call it: Arkansas, UA, the Hill
Students are called: Razorbacks, Hogs
Notable alums: Veronica Campbell (Olympic sprinter), John Daly (pro golfer), William T. Dillard (founder, Dillard's Department Stores), J. William Fulbright (senator), E. Lynn Harris (novelist), Jimmy Johnson (pro football coach), Jerry Jones (owner, Dallas Cowboys), Edward Durell Stone (architect), Pat Summerall (sportscaster)

Razorback to the Future

UA has recently been busy improving a number of its programs, thanks in large part to a generous financial gift from Wal-Mart founder (and Arkansas son) Sam Walton. The university offers a huge selection of majors, many of which are geared toward preparing students for professional careers. The aptly named Sam Walton College of Business offers three of the university's strongest programs: marketing, management, and finance. Future teachers benefit from a solid education program, and programs in architecture and engineering are also competitive. UA's roots are in agriculture, and the College of Agricultural, Food, and Life Sciences offers several strong programs, particularly in the poultry sciences. Newly added majors include landscape architecture, public service, and biomedical engineering. The university also offers a competitive Honors College. As is the case at many large public universities,

Callin' the Hogs

Pig calling and pigskin go hand-in-hand at UA. Legend has it that a group of farmers attending a Razorbacks football game back in the 1920s first cheered on the team with the enthusiastic call "Wooooooo, Pig! Sooie!" A tradition was born, and to this day enthusiastic fans can be heard "calling the hogs" at football games.

Admissions

Average high school GPA:	3.58
Average freshman SAT verbal / math score:	580 / 576
Average freshman ACT score:	24
Application fee:	$40

Application deadlines:
8/15 (freshmen)
8/15 (transfer)
11/15 (early action)

Total applicants:	8,443
Total accepted:	5,770 (68%)
Total accepted who enrolled:	2,726

Notification dates:
10/1 (freshmen)
continuous (transfer)
12/15 (early action)

Acceptance rate for early action applicants:	—

---

student-faculty relations vary widely, depending on the specific situation: Some professors are wrapped up in their research, while others make free time for students. The overall academic climate isn't terribly competitive, and most students find that schoolwork doesn't encroach on their leisure time.

Hog Heaven

Because of UA's remote location in northwestern Arkansas, most students stick close to the campus and its environs. The Greek scene tends to dominate, and, come weekends or a Razorback football or basketball game, the beer flows freely. Over 30 percent of students, including all freshmen, reside on campus, where the vibe is friendly and free-spirited. Close to three hundred student groups cater to a range of interests. Intramural sports are also widely popular and include unusual offerings like dominoes, putt-putt, and trivia. Students tend to be conservative and native to Arkansas, and diversity isn't terribly high: Fewer than 15 percent of students are minorities. But most Hogs are respectful of differences and happy to hoist a few pints in the name of school spirit.

Pastoral Idyll

Among Fayetteville's cultural attractions are drive-in movies, a solid independent music scene, and the Walton Arts Center, which hosts fine arts exhibits and touring Broadway shows. Dickson Street, the town's main drag, is lined with student-friendly bars and restaurants. UA's campus itself is a scenic stretch of lakes and rivers nestled in the hills of the Ozark Mountains. The architecture ranges from Depression-era structures, many of which are listed as national historic buildings, to more modern facilities. Students can enjoy hiking, biking, and camping in the nearby mountains, but for urban excitement, they'll have to drive a bit farther: Kansas City, Memphis, and Oklahoma City, the nearest big cities, are quite a ways away.

Students

Percentage of male / female students:	50% / 50%
Percentage of students from out of state:	21%
Percentage of students graduating in 4 years / 6 years:	30% / 56%

Money

Total endowment:	$763,000,000
Total in-state tuition, fees & expenses:	$13,286
Total out-of-state tuition, fees & expenses:	$21,420
Average financial aid package:	$8,068
Percentage of students who sought aid and received it:	73%
Percentage of students receiving financial aid:	30%

Also Check Out

Louisiana State University–Baton Rouge

Texas A&M University–College Station

University of Alabama–Tuscaloosa

The University of Mississippi

The University of Tennessee

University of California–Berkeley

110 Sproul Hall #5800
Berkeley, CA 94720

(510) 642-6000
http://www.berkeley.edu/

 **BIG BRAIN**

 **BIG CHOICE**

 **BIG RESEARCH**

Looking for a "radically" good education?

5 REASONS IT'S COOL

1. Berkeley is the oldest university in the University of California system and **one of the nation's most prestigious public universities.**

2. It's all about **academic balance**: Berkeley has produced as many leaders in the humanities as it has leaders in science and technology.

3. **Hard work is a way of life** for students in all disciplines.

4. Since its activist heyday in the sixties, the campus has been a **home to radical activism and a force for social change.**

5. What's not to love about the Bay Area, with its combination of **natural beauty and urban activities?**

The Basics

Public / private: public state
Total enrollment / undergrads: 33,933 / 23,863
Campus setting: urban
Students call it: UC Berkeley, Berkeley, Cal, UCB
Students are called: Golden Bears
Notable alums: Beverly Cleary (author), Natalie Coughlin (Olympic swimmer), Joan Didion (writer), Clark Kerr (educator), Glenn T. Seaborg (Nobel Laureate, Chemistry), Steve Wozniak (cofounder, Apple), Alice Waters (restaurateur)

The Cal Challenge

Berkeley is arguably the most prestigious public research university in the nation, and it enjoys the rep of being the best and most selective of the ten universities in the University of California system. Admitted students can expect to encounter tough academics (and tough grading), diverse areas of study, and professors who have reached the tops of their fields. Students select their majors from within the College of Chemistry, the College of Engineering, the College of Environmental Design, the College of Letters and Science, the College of Natural Resources, and the Haas School of Business (open only to juniors). Popular majors include biology, psychology, electrical engineering and computer science, and those in the physical sciences. Many students go abroad with the UC Education Abroad Program, work on independent research projects, or join the projects of their professors.

Give 'Em the Axe

Each year, the winner of the Big Game (the annual football game between die-hard rivals Berkley and Stanford) gets the axe—not in the getting-fired sense. It's an actual axe that originally belonged to Stanford over one hundred years ago and was used as part of their cheering section. In 1899, after a basketball game between the two schools, Berkeley students stole the axe from Stanford, whose students finally stole it back in 1930. A few years later, both schools agreed to make the Axe into a symbol of football victory, and it's passed back and forth as the schools continue their rivalry.

From Hipsters to Hippies

The atmosphere at Berkeley might be described as a combination of contemporary counterculture, hippie vibes (which have long found a home on this campus), and serious studiousness. The extent to which students fall into a single category varies widely, and there are certainly students at Berkeley who defy categorization. The campus and its surroundings are constantly buzzing with activity. The focal point is Telegraph Avenue, which has quick eats, shopping, and lots of those hippie vibes. Parties (frat, apartment, co-op, and otherwise) are in abundance, but many students choose to keep it low key. Dorm life and dining options vary greatly, and if you're planning to live in an apartment, you may face quite a hunt when it comes to finding reasonably priced housing options. The Cal Golden Bears' rivalry with the Stanford Cardinals peaks during the Big Game between the schools' two football teams. Rallies of the political and sports-oriented variety prove that Berkeley students, as antiestablishment as they can be, also thrive on tradition.

The Best of the Bay Area

Berkeley's lovely campus offers a distinct urban yet natural feel, with lots of trees and creeks, and a combination of early twentieth-century architecture mixed with more modern buildings. Natural beauty also surrounds the campus: The Berkeley Rose Garden, home to over 250 varieties of roses, and the woodsy Tilden Regional Park are just short walks away. Redwoods, Marin County, and some of the state's most beautiful shores can easily be reached by car. On campus, the campanile (or Sather Tower) and Sather Gate are the most recognizable landmarks; it's worth a trip up the campanile to take beautiful views of the Bay Area. San Francisco has all of the nightlife, arts, and diversions that a college student could want, and BART (Bay Area Rapid Transit) is an economical (if slightly unreliable) way to get around.

Admissions

Average high school GPA:	3.89
Average freshman SAT writing / math / critical reading score:	652 / 674 / 644
Average freshman ACT score:	—
Application fee:	$60

Application deadlines:
11/30 (freshmen)
11/30 (transfer)

Total applicants:	41,750
Total accepted:	9,944 (24%)
Total accepted who enrolled:	4,138

Notification dates:
3/31 (freshmen)
4/30 (transfer)

Students

Percentage of male / female students:	46% / 54%
Percentage of students from out of state:	11%
Percentage of students graduating in 4 years / 6 years:	58% / 87%

Money

Total endowment:	$2,494,763
Total in-state tuition, fees & expenses:	$21,054
Total out-of-state tuition, fees & expenses:	$39,738
Average financial aid package:	$15,710
Percentage of students who sought aid and received it:	89%
Percentage of students receiving financial aid:	47%

Also Check Out

Northwestern University

The Pennsylvania State University–University Park

Stanford University

University of California–Los Angeles

University of Michigan–Ann Arbor

University of North Carolina at Chapel Hill

University of California–Davis

One Shields Avenue
Davis, CA 95616

(530) 752-1011
http://www.ucdavis.edu/

 **BIG CHOICE**

 **BIG RESEARCH**

Studying until the cows come home

5 REASONS IT'S COOL

1. Students flock to UC–Davis for its **top-ranked programs in the biological sciences,** including agriculture and veterinary science.

2. This is top research school offers **big-time research opportunities** for students.

3. At 5,500 acres, the university's **sprawling, rural campus** is the largest in the University of California system.

4. The **performing arts thrive** at the new **Mondavi Center,** home to the university's Symphony Orchestra.

5. Bikes are the preferred method of transportation. The city of Davis, in fact, is home to approximately forty thousand bikes, the highest per capita of any U.S. city.

The Basics

Public / private: public state
Total enrollment / undergrads: 29,628 / 23,458
Campus setting: suburban
Students call it: UC Davis, Davis, UCD
Students are called: Aggies
Notable alums: Anna Escobedo Cabral (U.S. treasurer), Steve Robinson (astronaut), DJ Shadow (hip hop DJ)

A Learning Environment

UC–Davis has four undergraduate colleges: Agricultural and Environmental Sciences, Biological Sciences, Engineering, and Letters and Science. Over one hundred majors are offered, the most popular of which are psychology, biological sciences, economics, and communications. The university boasts major research opportunities for undergrads and sponsors summer-, semester-, and yearlong projects. Undergrads apply for awards and grants to help subsidize their costs and are encouraged to present their work formally during the annual Davis Undergraduate Research Conference. Various honors programs for ambitious students include the Davis Honors Challenge, the freshman Integrated Studies Honors Program, and the Chemical Engineering and Biochemical Engineering Honors Program. As students reach upper-division courses, large lectures tend to give way to smaller class sizes, and it's easier to get face time with professors. Students who seek out professors and research projects find that there are ample opportunities to advance their prospects for grad school and their careers.

A Perfect Day for a Picnic

Over fifty thousand people gather at the UC–Davis campus every year to check out Picnic Day, the student-run open house that's the biggest event of its kind in the nation. Students orchestrate over 150 events, including hamster ball races, a parade, cow and goat milking, departmental displays, and sporting events. The Chemistry Department's magic show, in particular, is always a real crowd pleaser. Picnic Day has been canceled only four times in its nearly one-hundred-year history. One of those times was in 1924, when there was an outbreak of hoof-and-mouth disease among the local cowherds.

Large and Laid-Back

UC–Davis's student body is pretty darn big—we're talking twenty thousand students. Students tend to be a conservative though laid-back bunch, as befitting the laid-lack lifestyle of the university's hometown of Davis. Fraternity and sorority life has a strong presence (one sorority was even featured on the MTV reality show *Sorority Life*). On-campus parties are easy to come by on Thursdays, but many students buckle down and study or just take it easy on the weekends. Most freshmen live on campus, while most upperclassmen move off campus, where affordable apartments are plentiful. The new Mondavi Center for the Performing Arts (named for wine magnate Robert Mondavi) has become a showcase for a variety of world-class performances. The university's athletics program has recently transitioned from NCAA Division II to I-AA. Football games are popular, spirit-filled events. The Aggie Pack, the nation's largest student-run spirit organization, leads the crowd in cheering, while Band-Uh!, the university's official marching band, provides ear-splitting musical accompaniment.

Let's Take This Outside

Because of the campus's huge size—5,500acres, and all of it flat—bikes are the favored mode of transportation for most UC–Davis students. Davis itself is a laid-back college town that's known for its environmental friendliness. Students have access to free or low-cost public transportation, including a fleet of London-style double-decker buses. Nature lovers will have a field day, every day: The UCñDavis Arboretum is home to more than four thousand species of trees and plants, and the bucolic fields and forests of the area also function as living laboratories. The city of Sacramento is eleven miles away, and San Francisco and the Sierra Nevada are also easy to reach by car.

Admissions

Average high school GPA:	3.7
Average freshman SAT writing / math / critical reading score:	566 / 602 / 561
Average freshman ACT score:	—
Application fee:	$60
Application deadlines: 11/30 (freshmen) 11/30 (transfer)	
Total applicants:	32,635
Total accepted:	22,142 (68%)
Total accepted who enrolled:	5,526
Notification dates: 3/15 (freshmen) 3/15 (transfer)	

Students

Percentage of male / female students:	44% / 56%
Percentage of students from out of state:	2%
Percentage of students graduating in 4 years / 6 years:	42% / 80%

Money

Total endowment:	$95,925,000
Total in-state tuition, fees & expenses:	$20,460
Total out-of-state tuition, fees & expenses:	$38,628
Average financial aid package:	$11,697
Percentage of students who sought aid and received it:	75%
Percentage of students receiving financial aid:	42%

Also Check Out

California Polytechnic State University–San Luis Obispo

University of California–Irvine

University of California–San Diego

University of California–Santa Cruz

University of Southern California

University of Washington

University of California–Irvine

204 Aldrich Hall
Irvine, CA 92697

(949) 824-5011
http://www.uci.edu/

 **BIG CHOICE**

 **BIG RESEARCH**

Local school makes good!

5 REASONS IT'S COOL

1. "So Cal" to the core, UCI is **a great option for California residents** who want to stay close to home and get a first-rate education at public university prices.

2. Got extra ambition? Take advantage of **the top-notch honors track**, called the Campuswide Honors Program.

3. UCI has **science and engineering** in spades.

4. Got a way with words? The unique **literary journalism major** will help you put pen to paper.

5. **Swimming, tanning, body boarding.** What's not to like about the campus's prime location bordering world-famous Newport Beach?

The Basics

Public / private: public state
Total enrollment / undergrads: 25,229 / 20,719
Campus setting: suburban
Students call it: UC Irvine, Irvine, UCI
Students are called: Anteaters
Notable alums: Zach de la Rocha (musician), Roy Fielding (computer scientist), Greg Louganis (Olympic diver), Jon Lovitz (actor), Joseph McGinty Nichol (creator, The O.C.)

Local Favorite with a National Reputation

UCI's Henry Samueli School of Engineering, an academic powerhouse, is one of the university's twelve strong academic divisions. Popular majors include engineering, biological sciences, economics, computer science, and psychology; also of note are the music, art, and literary journalism programs. UCI's impressive roster of professors and researchers includes Nobel Prize laureates, Pulitzer Prize winners, National Academy of Sciences members, and bestselling authors. The Campuswide Honors Program (CHP) offers a decidedly intense program: 90 percent of CHP grads go on to earn graduate and professional degrees. CHP also recently launched an independent, interdisciplinary study program that allows students to design their own majors. Ninety-seven percent of UCI's undergraduates hail from California: With these programs, it's no wonder UCI attracts so many highly capable California students.

Spooky San Joaquin

The San Joaquin Freshwater Marsh Reserve, adjacent to UCI, offers students the chance to study and restore its rich ecosystem, which is home to more than 250 species of birds. And rumor has it that it's haunted. Whether that's true is up for debate, but the spooky wetland weather can make you wonder what's really out there.

From Rush Lines to Tan Lines

Campus life at UCI is a mixed bag. Many students are commuters, so the weekends tend to lack the energy you'll find on campus during the week. Less than 40 percent of all undergrads live on campus. But at a university this large, there is always something for everyone, and dedicated students can still have a ball. Those interested in rushing a fraternity or sorority will be pleased to find an active Greek scene. Dining plans offer a combo of meals and flex dollars. Late-night munchies used to be hard to satisfy on campus, but now some on-campus eateries, including Starbucks, stay open until 11:00 P.M. or midnight. The nearby cities of Newport Beach and Laguna Beach are shopping havens, and there are plenty of gorgeous beaches just a short drive away for the typically laid-back Anteaters who want to soak up the sun.

A Safe Haven

UCI was founded as the centerpiece of a planned community created by the Irvine Company, which donated the land for the campus to the University of California and which still owns a large portion of land in the county. Because of its 1960s heritage, UCI's futurist-style buildings and the surrounding suburban architecture don't have the same "wow" factor as some of the other UC campuses, but the campus does have quite a lot of natural beauty. The mile-long Ring Road creates the center of this circular campus and connects important buildings. According to the FBI, Irvine is the safest large city in the United States, and has been for the last several years.

Admissions

Average high school GPA:	3.7
Average freshman SAT verbal / math score:	583 / 620
Average freshman ACT score:	—
Application fee:	$60
Application deadlines:	
11/30 (freshmen)	
11/30 (transfer)	
Total applicants:	38,466
Total accepted:	23,174 (60%)
Total accepted who enrolled:	4,819
Notification dates:	
3/31 (freshmen)	
5/31 (transfer)	

Students

Percentage of male / female students:	49% / 51%
Percentage of students from out of state:	3%
Percentage of students graduating in 4 years / 6 years:	42% / 80%

Money

Total endowment:	—
Total in-state tuition, fees & expenses:	$15,956
Total out-of-state tuition, fees & expenses:	$34,640
Average financial aid package:	$13,221
Percentage of students who sought aid and received it:	84%
Percentage of students receiving financial aid:	45%

Also Check Out

California Polytechnic State University–San Luis Obispo

Harvey Mudd College

University of California–Berkeley

University of California–Los Angeles

University of California–San Diego

University of California–Los Angeles

405 Hilgard Avenue
Los Angeles, CA 90095

(310) 825-4321
http://www.ucla.edu/

 **BIG CHOICE**

 **BIG RESEARCH**

Big school, big options

5 REASONS IT'S COOL

1. **Want to conduct research?** Two undergraduate research centers and the West Coast's finest medical center are on campus.

2. UCLA offers **more than 130 undergraduate majors** and eight-hundred-plus student clubs and organizations.

3. **On-campus housing is guaranteed** for three years for incoming freshmen and one year for transfer students—quite the deal considering how pricey L.A. can be.

4. A Pac 10 school, UCLA was the first to win **one hundred NCAA championships**.

5. Enjoy the fun, sun, and Hollywood stars **in lovely L.A.**

The Basics

Public / private: public state
Total enrollment / undergrads: 38,218 / 25,432
Campus setting: urban
Students call it: UCLA
Students are called: Bruins
Notable alums: Tom Anderson (founder, MySpace), Carol Burnett (actor), John Williams (composer), Kareem Abdul-Jabbar (pro basketball player), Jackie Robinson (pro baseball player), Francis Ford Coppola (film director)

Mix, Match, and Make It Your Own

UCLA students may find that the onus is on them to seek out the programs, pals, and professors who can help them make the most of their time at this large public university. Programs such as College Honors, *Fiat Lux*, and Freshman Clusters help to take the sting out of the school's size, but students still encounter frequent lecture-style classes clocking in at over three hundred students (with smaller TA-taught discussions). UCLA students choose from academic divisions including the College of Letters and Science, the School of the Arts and Architecture, the Henry Samueli School of Engineering and Applied Science, the School of Nursing, and the School of Theater, Film, and Television, each with its own set of core requirements. The most popular majors are business economics, psychology, biology, and sociology (all in the College of Letters and Science. The UC Education Abroad Program takes globally minded Bruins to all corners of the map.

Don't Even Think About Waking It Up

During Blue and Gold Week, the week preceding the annual football game against rival USC, the bronze Bruin statue in UCLA's Ackerman Plaza gets some extra TLC. To protect it from USC Trojan hijinks, students cover up the beloved Bruin, forcing it into a sort of hibernation. Die-hard fans watch it round the clock, while others students host a blood drive and traditional bonfire rally. Meanwhile, over at USC, Tommy Trojan gets the same protective treatment.

Welcome to the Bruin's Den

The old "study hard, party harder" adage applies to student life at UCLA. Perhaps this is because the university is on the quarter system, which means that the first day of class turns into midterms and then to finals in the blink of an eye. To strike that essential studying/socializing balance, many students find that creating smaller communities is key, whether it's their dorm floor, a Greek organization, or one of the many popular club sports team. On most Thursday nights, students head over to Gayley Avenue, home to fraternity and apartment parties. For culture vultures, UCLA offers the Fowler Museum (world arts), the Hammer Museum (contemporary art), and UCLA Live (performing arts). All-campus events like Spring Sing (where melodious students compete for prizes) and the amazing athletics games bring all Bruins together. And there's nothing like the long-lived cross-town rivalry with the USC Trojans during Blue and Gold Week to bring even the most studious Bruins out of hibernation.

Westwood, Ho!

The iconic Royce Hall anchors the beautiful UCLA campus. Older buildings on campus share Royce's Romanesque architectural style, but they're outnumbered by newer buildings that are decidedly more modern, including the certified-green La Kretz Hall and the new I. M. Pei–designed Ronald Reagan UCLA Medical Center. Students live comfortably in the new and newly refurbished on-campus housing "on the hill." Surrounding the south end of campus is Westwood Village, home to theaters where many movies premiere (and star sightings abound), lots of tasty eateries, and shopping. The beach is about fifteen minutes away, and all of L.A. boasts oodles of activities—that is, if you have a car. Buses and the Metro can only get you so far in L.A.

Admissions

Average high school GPA:	4.0
Average freshman SAT writing / math / critical reading score:	646 / 668 / 635
Average freshman ACT score:	25
Application fee:	$60

Application deadlines:
11/30 (freshmen)
11/30 (transfer)

Total applicants:	47,317
Total accepted:	12,189 (26%)
Total accepted who enrolled:	4,713

Notification dates:
3/15 (freshmen)
4/30 (transfer)

Students

Percentage of male / female students:	43% / 57%
Percentage of students from out of state:	2%
Percentage of students graduating in 4 years / 6 years:	57% / 87%

Money

Total endowment:	—
Total in-state tuition, fees & expenses:	$19,838
Total out-of-state tuition, fees & expenses:	$38,665
Average financial aid package:	$14,329
Percentage of students who sought aid and received it:	82%
Percentage of students receiving financial aid:	48%

Also Check Out

Stanford University

University of California–Berkeley

University of California–San Diego

University of Michigan–Ann Arbor

University of Southern California

University of Washington

University of California–San Diego

9500 Gilman Drive
La Jolla, CA 92093

(858) 534-2230
http://www.ucsd.edu/

 **BIG CHOICE**

 **BIG RESEARCH**

Beekers, brains, and beaches

5 REASONS IT'S COOL

1. UCSD's **six residential colleges** provide students with the comforts, amenities, and sense of community that you'd expect from a much smaller school.

2. Calling all bio nerds! **Biotech and bioengineering** are big business on this campus.

3. The campus is an **active, academically challenging place** where social butterflies and bookworms are equally welcome.

4. With San Diego so close by, there's no shortage of **urban enjoyment, zoological wonders, and tasty seafood.**

5. **Live near the beach.** 'Nuff said!

The Basics

Public / private: public state
Total enrollment / undergrads: 26,465 / 21,369
Campus setting: suburban
Students call it: UC San Diego, UCSD
Students are called: Tritons
Notable alums: Mark Allen (triathlete), James Avery (actor), Rex Pickett (writer), Kim Stanley Robinson (author), Philip Rosedale (creator, Second Life), Craig Venter (biologist)

Six Colleges in One

All incoming UCSD students choose from one of six residential colleges. Each college in this unique system has its own core curriculum and themes: Marshall emphasizes social responsibility; Muir students focus on individual choices and the environment; Revelle provides a solid liberal arts education; Roosevelt students are international and interdisciplinary; Warren students are citizen-scholars with scholastic diversity; and Sixth emphasizes global awareness and action. UCSD students are free to major in any of the subjects available at the university, regardless of their residential college. The university is best known for its science and engineering programs, including the popular and highly ranked Department of Bioengineering, and UCSD grads populate the biotech firms in the San Diego area. Ambitious incoming students can apply for the eight-year, combined bachelor/MD UCSD Medical Scholars programs. The faculty includes eight Nobel laureates, and the overall student-faculty ratio is 19:1.

All Hail the Sun God!

The Sun God Festival is the highlight of student life at UCSD. During this annual music festival, popular bands (including Busta Rhymes, My Chemical Romance, and Ludacris in recent years) rock the usually calm campus. Held right after midterms in the spring semester, the Sun God Festival was inspired by the arrival of Nikki de Saint Phalle's colorful sculpture of the same name in 1983. Students have given the statue several costume changes over the years, including sunglasses, a cap and gown, a birds' nest, and headphones.

Watch Out for Falling Food!

As is the case at many larger schools, UCSD students must take the initiative when it comes to finding fun ways to keep busy. Greek life is lively, and certain colleges, like Muir, are known for their parties. While there can be tension on campus between studious students and their more social peers, UCSD will satisfy students on either end of the social spectrum. The university's many on-campus activities include a TV station, a hip radio station, and several student publications. For some reason, students here have a thing for dropping food out of buildings— so keep your eyes peeled for falling food, especially during the annual Pumpkin Drop at Muir and the Watermelon Drop at Revelle. There's lots of choice when it comes to where, when, and what to eat, and the "Dining Dollars" student dining plan is required for all on-campus residents. Triton athletics are split between NCAA Division I and Division II, but the real sports highlight is the club-level surfing team, which has won multiple national titles.

Lovely La Jolla

UCSD is located right along the beach in beautiful La Jolla—some dorm rooms in Muir college even offer ocean views. If you're a surfer, you can easily catch a few waves in the morning before hitting the books or attending class. Besides recreational advantages, the university's location offers research opportunities. Just south of the main campus is the world-renowned Scripps Institute of Oceanography and the Steven Birch Aquarium and Museum. The campus itself is a bit spread out, but the residential colleges, each with its own architectural style, provide students with a comfortable home base. Students frequently travel beyond wealthy La Jolla to San Diego fifteen minutes to the south, where there's that famous zoo in beautiful Balboa Park, Sea World, shopping and dining in the Gaslamp Quarter, and all sorts of urban and beachfront delights. For some south-of-the-border fun, Tijuana, Mexico, is just about an hour from campus.

Admissions

Average high school GPA:	3.93
Average freshman SAT verbal / math score:	605 / 653
Average freshman ACT score:	24
Application fee:	$60

Application deadlines:
11/30 (freshmen)
11/30 (transfer)

Total applicants:	40,418
Total accepted:	17,866 (44%)
Total accepted who enrolled:	4,589

Notification dates:
3/31 (freshmen)
5/1 (transfer)

Students

Percentage of male / female students:	48% / 52%
Percentage of students from out of state:	3%
Percentage of students graduating in 4 years / 6 years:	50% / 78%

Money

Total endowment:	—
Total in-state tuition, fees & expenses:	$17,845
Total out-of-state tuition, fees & expenses:	$36,529
Average financial aid package:	$13,745
Percentage of students who sought aid and received it:	83%
Percentage of students receiving financial aid:	48%

Also Check Out

Stanford University

University of California—Berkeley

University of California—Irvine

University of California—Los Angeles

University of California—Santa Cruz

University of California–Santa Barbara

1234 Cheadle Hall
Santa Barbara, CA 93106

(805) 893-8000
http://www.ucsb.edu/

 **BIG CHOICE**

 **BIG RESEARCH**

Soak up knowledge and sun at the same time.

5 REASONS IT'S COOL

1. UCSB more than earns its reputation as **one of the nation's top research institutions**.

2. **The College of Creative Studies**, unique to UCSB, offers students a more creative, project-oriented alternative to regular ole academics.

3. The campus is just **steps away from the beach**, and many dorm rooms have ocean views.

4. We're talking paradise: Students **live, study, and party in Isla Vista**, a cool beachside neighborhood adjacent to campus.

5. Go Gauchos! UCSB's **nineteen varsity athletic teams** give sports fans plenty to cheer about.

The Basics

Public / private: public state
Total enrollment / undergrads: 21,062 / 18,212
Campus setting: suburban
Students call it: UC Santa Barbara, UCSB
Students are called: Gauchos
Notable alums: Robert Ballard (oceanographer), Michael Douglas (actor), Jack Johnson (singer-songwriter), Brian Shaw (pro basketball player), Joseph Wilson (ambassador)

Lush Pickings

UCSB is all about choices. The pickings are so lush, in fact, that students choose from more than 1,800 classes each quarter. Of the university's three undergraduate colleges, the College of Letters & Science is the largest, offering eighty different majors. The most popular majors include communications, business economics, biology, and psychology. The College of Engineering is second in size and offers engineering students a huge variety of research opportunities. Unique to UCSB, the College of Creative Studies offers tutorials, studio courses, and faculty-directed seminar classes in eight areas of study. All Creative Studies courses are small, intense, and designed to push students beyond their own creative boundaries. Students also receive personal faculty advising and participate in a wealth of self-directed research and artistic projects, exposing them to graduate-level work without paying the extra tuition costs. Santa Barbara employs heavily laurelled professors, including Nobel Prize winners and American Academy of Arts and Sciences members.

Always Fair Weather

UCSB's student newspaper, the *Daily Nexus*, does not contain a traditional weather section—apparently, there's no need for a weather report when the sun shines every day. Instead, an anonymous writer known to readers as the "Weatherhuman" provides humorous commentary on current events, ranging from important to the truly trivial.

The twelve national centers and institutes at UCSB include the California NanoSystems Institute—a partnership with sister campus UCLA.

Life's a Beach

Over ten thousand UCSB students live in Isla Vista, or IV, the student community that lies just beyond the university's campus. IV is home to cool restaurants, a post office, grocery stores, university-owned apartment buildings, and, best of all, the beach, where students gather every day to swim, surf, and study. UCSB offers 250 students organizations, ranging from the Academy of Film Geeks to the Zen Sitting Group. Bikes are almost mandatory on campus, where there are over fourteen miles of bike paths. Pedestrians beware: Cyclists have the right of way. Nontraditional intramural sports, like inner-tube water polo, Ultimate Frisbee, and kickball are popular. Most Gaucho teams compete in the Big West Conference, and the women's basketball team dominated the conference for nine years through 2005. The surf team also makes waves, and with this much coastline, it's easy to understand why.

Year-Round Vacation

Let out a sigh as you look up at 175-foot Storke Tower and then down at its reflection in the UCSB campus's private lagoon. It really doesn't get more stunning than this. Santa Barbara has been dubbed the American Riviera because of the similarity of its gorgeous coastline to Southern France and Italy. UCSB is about a twenty-minute drive from downtown Santa Barbara, and students with a valid student ID can ride the bus there for free. Downtown Santa Barbara's State Street has many shops, restaurants, and theaters, and it's a prime location for people- (and even celebrity-) watching. Swimming, surfing, and sun-tanning are all right at hand, and the nearby Santa Ynez Mountains offer great spots for hiking, mountain-biking, and wine tasting. Los Angeles is just about an hour south, and beaches stretch in both directions.

Admissions

Average high school GPA:	3.74
Average freshman SAT verbal / math score:	590 / 602
Average freshman ACT score:	—
Application fee:	$60
Application deadlines: 11/30 (freshmen) 11/30 (transfer)	
Total applicants:	39,854
Total accepted:	21,281 (53%)
Total accepted who enrolled:	4,089
Notification dates: 3/15 (freshmen) 5/1 (transfer)	

Students

Percentage of male / female students:	45% / 55%
Percentage of students from out of state:	4%
Percentage of students graduating in 4 years / 6 years:	62% / 84%

Money

Total endowment:	$80,336
Total in-state tuition, fees & expenses:	$19,960
Total out-of-state tuition, fees & expenses:	$38,644
Average financial aid package:	$13,437
Percentage of students who sought aid and received it:	82%
Percentage of students receiving financial aid:	42%

Also Check Out

California Polytechnic State University–San Luis Obispo

University of California–Los Angeles

University of California–San Diego

University of California–Santa Cruz

University of Washington

University of California–Santa Cruz

1156 High Street
Santa Cruz, CA 95064

(831) 459-0111
http://www.ucsc.edu/

 **BIG CHOICE**

 **BIG HAND**

 **BIG RESEARCH**

Science, surfing, and slugs

5 REASONS IT'S COOL

1. Love the physical sciences? UCSC has **top-ranked programs in astronomy, astrophysics, and physics**.

2. The university's **ten residential colleges** provide students with small-school comforts galore.

3. Bring your bike and a pair of hiking boots: UCSC's 2,000-plus-acre campus is a **woodsy outdoor paradise.**

4. It's all about the good vibes: The relaxed atmosphere on campus typifies the **Northern California lifestyle**.

5. Know it, love it, squish it: The UCSC banana slug is the **most creative mascot in the country.**

The Basics

Public / private: public state
Total enrollment / undergrads: 15,364 / 13,961
Campus setting: small town
Students call it: UCSC, UC Santa Cruz, Santa Cruz
Students are called: Slugs
Notable alums: Joseph DeRisi (molecular biologist), Laurie Garrett (writer, journalist), Kent Nagano (musician), Huey P. Newton (founder, Black Panthers), Marc Okrand (linguist), Rebecca Romijn (actress), Maya Rudoloph (writer, comedienne), Andy Samberg (writer, comedian)

Take 10

Up until 1997, UCSC was a grade-free zone: Profs gave students narrative evaluations along with grades of "pass" and "no pass." However, those glory days are over, and now students receive letter grades along with their evaluations. The university assigns all first-year students to one of ten residential colleges, each with its own academic support systems, extracurricular and social activities, living themes, scholarship opportunities, and small set of core courses. Students across all academic disciplines live, eat, learn, and have fun together. Professors, whose ranks include ten members of the National Academy of Sciences, two members of the Institute of Medicine, and nineteen fellows of the American Academy of Arts and Sciences, are generally affiliated with one of the ten colleges. UCSC stands out as an innovator in scientific research, especially in physics. The most popular majors are psychology, business management, economics, art, and literature; students can also go their own ways

Feeling Sluggish?

Most colleges and universities cheer on mascots that are decidedly run-of-the-mill: Tigers or Wolves, anyone? But students at UCSC are anything but ordinary. About twenty years ago, students voted to replace their previous mascot, the sea lion, with the university's long-time unofficial mascot, the banana slug. Why the slithery creature? The banana slug idea wasn't just pulled out of thin air; the yellow, shell-less mollusks reside in the campus's indigenous redwood trees, growing up to ten inches long.

with creative, interdisciplinary majors. All UC students have a chance to study abroad through the UC Education Abroad Program, which offers 150 programs in thirty-five countries.

Come One, Come All

The defining aspect of student life at UCSC is the university's residential college system and the close-knit communities it provides for students. About half of students live on campus, either in their residential college or in one of several other housing options, such as the RV Camper Park located in the Redwood forest at the northern end of the campus. The diverse student body has liberal and progressive leanings but welcomes students of all persuasions, political or otherwise. If the whole hippie, Northern California vibe isn't your thing, you'll still find a great group of friends. Greek life and athletics both have sizeable followings on campus. Parties prevail, especially the small, impromptu kind, and students choose from many cool hangouts and eateries in Santa Cruz. The lovely shoreline offers superb surfing—just be sure to wear a wetsuit and watch out for sharks.

Is This Summer Camp?

At UCSC, you may find yourself wondering if you should head off to archery practice or noodle-necklace-making rather than your physics lecture—the campus, a nature lover's paradise, just has that summer camp feeling. Redwoods groves, creeks, footbridges, meadows, rare Mima Mounds, and caves are all familiar sites on this 2,000-acre campus. Sitting pretty on the Pacific Ocean, the city of Santa Cruz calls surfers to its shores and students to its bars. The Santa Cruz Beach Boardwalk and the Monterey Bay Aquarium in Monterey are nearby attractions, and the midsized city is less than two hours south of San Francisco. But who needs the city when there's this much natural beauty to enjoy?

Admissions

Average high school GPA:	3.51
Average freshman SAT writing / math / critical reading score:	567 / 580 / 569
Average freshman ACT score:	23
Application fee:	$60

Application deadlines:
11/30 (freshmen)
11/30 (transfer)

Total applicants:	24,534
Total accepted:	19,687 (80%)
Total accepted who enrolled:	3,313

Notification dates:
3/15 (freshmen)
4/30 (transfer)

Students

Percentage of male / female students:	47% / 53%
Percentage of students from out of state:	3%
Percentage of students graduating in 4 years / 6 years:	48% / 70%

Money

Total endowment:	$96,200,000
Total in-state tuition, fees & expenses:	$21,162
Total out-of-state tuition, fees & expenses:	$39,330
Average financial aid package:	$14,422
Percentage of students who sought aid and received it:	87%
Percentage of students receiving financial aid:	44%

Also Check Out

University of California–Davis

University of California–San Diego

University of California–Santa Barbara

University of Oregon

University of Washington

University of Central Florida

4000 Central Florida Boulevard
Orlando, FL 32816

(407) 823-2000
http://www.ucf.edu/

 **BIG CHOICE**

 **BIG JOB**

High-tech hospitality

5 REASONS IT'S COOL

1. This young university has some of **the newest and most high-tech amenities** of any state institution in the country.

2. The College of Hospitality Management gives future managers and concierges on-the-job experience in Orlando.

3. Engineering students enjoy the enviable perk of **working with the nice folks at the Kennedy Space Center.**

4. Central Florida's long summers and mild winters allow students to **lead an outdoorsy, laid-back lifestyle.**

5. Students make the most of **Orlando's bustling vibe and theme park distractions.**

The Basics

Public / private: public state
Total enrollment / undergrads: 46,719 / 39,545
Campus setting: suburban
Students call it: Central Florida, UCF
Students are called: Knights
Notable alums: Michelle Akers (pro soccer player), John Bersia (journalist), Daunte Culpepper (pro football player), Cheryl Hines (actress), Daniel Myrick (filmmaker)

Forty Going on Forty Thousand

UCF has quickly grown from a tiny new tech school to the largest undergrad institution in the state, drawing its share of students away from the older mainstays, Florida and Florida State. In the process, it has become more selective and raised its standards and academic reputation. Students interested in professional disciplines and hard sciences will find tons of great options here. The College of Engineering and Computer Science provides solid, hands-on training thanks to its relationship to the Kennedy Space Center and other industry partners. The hospitality management program benefits from the school's convenient Orlando location. Business programs are perennial favorites and provide students with internships and partnerships in the corporate world. Education and health are also popular programs. The humanities, while they attract many students, lack the resources of the school's other top programs. Academic life generally favors the ambitious and career driven, although students aren't cutthroat. The academic resource

Smells like Steeped Spirit

Young UCF already boasts a unique homecoming tradition, Spirit Splash, in which students show their school spirit by plunging into the campus Reflection Pool. A pep rally and various festivities follow the annual autumnal dunking.

center provides tutoring in any subject, and large classes are made friendlier by experienced upperclassmen who are available to help.

Boogie Knights

The newness of the UCF campus has its pros and cons. You won't find Gothic buildings here, and the constant construction at Under Construction Forever (as UCF is lovingly called) is distracting and unsightly. On the other hand, most residence halls come equipped with modern amenities, including cable and Internet. The new Towers at Golden Knights Plaza provides residents with easy access to the school's arena and stadium, as well as numerous chain restaurants, shops, and a Barnes & Noble. State-of-the-art technology is everywhere, and students have online access to the library's many resources. The new Recreation and Wellness Center comes with the best in modern equipment, along with multiple pools and a rock-climbing wall. The massive student body chooses from hundreds of organizations, including a slew of intramural sports, fine and performing arts, and academic, cultural, political, and religious groups. Spectator sports are big, and the football team brings in students, if not wins. Student government is very energetic, and a strong current of activism also runs through the student body. The population is fairly diverse, with minority students representing 30 percent. Nearly 95 percent of students are Florida grown.

Orlando Furioso

UCF's meteoric rise over the years is matched only by the rise of its home city, Orlando. Although the campus social scene is often dominated by the Greeks, the city offers plenty of alternatives to the frathouse kegger. Civic distractions include the many big-name theme parks, shopping, movies, museums, and public parks, as well as an NBA team. Students also praise the dining and nightlife. The large Latino population has influenced the city's musical and cultural trends. UCF's campus offers a number of recreational options of its own. Student can make use of tennis and volleyball courts, several public pools, and Lake Claire, with canoes, kayaks, and paddle boats free for use.

Admissions

Average high school GPA:	3.57
Average freshman SAT writing / math / critical reading score:	550 / 591 / 575
Average freshman ACT score:	24
Application fee:	$30

Application deadlines:
3/1 (freshmen)
5/1 (transfer)

Total applicants:	24,345
Total accepted:	12,552 (52%)
Total accepted who enrolled:	6,408

Notification dates:
continuous (freshmen)
continuous (transfer)

Students

Percentage of male / female students:	45% / 55%
Percentage of students from out of state:	5%
Percentage of students graduating in 4 years / 6 years:	30% / 57%

Money

Total endowment:	$95,580,670
Total in-state tuition, fees & expenses:	$12,380
Total out-of-state tuition, fees & expenses:	$25,905
Average financial aid package:	$6,068
Percentage of students who sought aid and received it:	54%
Percentage of students receiving financial aid:	36%

Also Check Out

Florida State University

University of Florida

The University of Miami

University of South Florida

Virginia Polytechnic Institute and State University

University of Chicago

5801 Ellis Avenue
Chicago, IL 60637

(773) 702-1234
http://www.uchicago.edu/

 **BIG BRAIN**

 **BIG PERSPECTIVE**

 **BIG RESEARCH**

Serious academics wanted. Must have warm coats.

5 REASONS IT'S COOL

1. **History is made at Chicago.** The academic discipline of sociology was pioneered here, and the university has educated or employed more than seventy-five Nobel laureates.

2. **The alumni hall of fame puts all others to shame.** Chicago grads and past professors include Carl Sagan, Milton Friedman, Saul Bellow, Kurt Vonnegut, and Edwin Hubble.

3. Love a heated debate? Chicago's **super-intellectual atmosphere** means stimulating conversations.

4. Chicago's got an impressive **6:1 student-to-faculty ratio**.

5. Chicago awards **twenty full-tuition College Honor Scholarships**.

The Basics

Public / private: private nonprofit
Total enrollment / undergrads: 11,730 / 4,807
Campus setting: urban
Students call it: Chicago, U of C, UChicago, UC
Students are called: Maroons
Notable alums: Philip Glass (composer), Philip Roth (novelist), Susan Sontag (critic), John Paul Stevens (U.S. Supreme Court justice), Kurt Vonnegut (novelist)

The Intellectual Capital of the World

The University of Chicago isn't for the faint of heart. Students here are incredibly driven and able to endure academic pressure. The university's core curriculum stresses interdisciplinary thinking and different perspectives and requires students to complete classes in the humanities, civilizations, mathematics, art, natural sciences, and social sciences. Students find that this foundation helps immensely when taking upper-level courses, as well as the many graduate-level classes that are open to undergrads. The university operates on a quarter system. Professors are demanding and aren't apt to spoon-feed students—nor are they likely to inflate grades. That said, Chicago professors are the best of the best and include some of the world's most influential scholars (including a number of Nobel laureates). While sleep is a rare commodity on this campus, Chicago students can at least rest easy knowing they're receiving one of the very best educations around. Students seem to be up for the challenge: 98 percent of freshmen return for their sophomore years.

Winter Blues? Not Here

Faced with long, cold winters every year, Chicago students have devised some pretty creative ways to keep their spirits, if not their bodies, warm. Each January, students celebrate a festival called Kuviasungnerk (or "Kuvia" for short), an Eskimo word that means "pursuit of happiness." The festivities include ice sculpting, hot chocolate drinking, a dance marathon, musical performances, and fireside discussions with the faculty. There's also an early morning exercise routine called kangeiko, a Japanese tradition that's performed outside and concludes with a yoga-inspired sun salutation.

Caution: Intensity Ahead

If we had to summarize Chicago students in one word, it would be *intense*. Maroons work hard, and at any given moment you'll find a high concentration of them whiling away the hours at the campus's Regenstein Library (or "The Reg" as students call it). When they're not studying, students blow off steam by playing intramural sports, which are very popular on campus. Many students also get involved with one or more of the university's four hundred student organizations, including the Mock Trial Team, the Model UN Team, and the College Bowl Team, all of which are among the most competitive in the country. Students also attend guest lectures hosted by the Chicago Society, performances by the ever-popular University Theater, and film screenings and occasional question-and-answer sessions with filmmakers sponsored by Doc Films. And every Wednesday, students flock to the Reynolds Club for Shake Day, when milkshakes cost just $1.

Winter Wonderland

Chicago's breathtaking Gothic-style architecture, complete with gargoyles galore, will make you forget that you're in the middle of a major city. Just a few blocks from Lake Michigan, the campus is gorgeous year round, featuring flowers in the spring, colorful foliage in the fall, and an ice-skating rink in the winter. The university is located in Hyde Park, a predominantly African American neighborhood on Chicago's south side. While the neighborhood isn't particularly student-friendly, there are a number of restaurant options as well as the University of Chicago Seminary Bookstore and Powell's bookstore, two independent favorites. Downtown Chicago can be reached in about fifteen minutes by train or about twenty-five minutes by bus. In the winter months, when the temperature hovers around zero degrees, students often prefer the warmth of campus environs to making the trek downtown.

Admissions

Average high school GPA:	3.89
Average freshman SAT verbal / math score:	703 / 699
Average freshman ACT score:	26
Application fee:	$60
Application deadlines:	
1/2 (freshmen)	
4/1 (transfer)	
11/1 (early action)	
Total applicants:	9,538
Total accepted:	3,670 (38%)
Total accepted who enrolled:	1,259
Notification dates:	
4/1 (freshmen)	
5/15 (transfer)	
12/15 (early action)	
Acceptance rate for early action applicants:	49%

Students

Percentage of male / female students:	50% / 50%
Percentage of students from out of state:	78%
Percentage of students graduating in 4 years / 6 years:	85% / 91%

Money

Total endowment:	$4,294,967,295
Total tuition:	$33,336
Total cost with fees & expenses:	$47,442
Average financial aid package:	—
Percentage of students who sought aid and received it:	—
Percentage of students receiving financial aid:	—

Also Check Out

Columbia University

Cornell University

Grinnell College

Northwestern University

Tufts University

University of Cincinnati

2624 Clifton Avenue
Cincinnati, OH 45221

(513) 556-6000
http://www.uc.edu/

BIG CHOICE

BIG JOB

Co-ops galore!

5 REASONS IT'S COOL

1. Interested in **getting paid to practice your major?** UC is where college co-op programs were born.

2. International co-ops allow you to **earn credit—and money**—while working in Germany, Japan, or Chile.

3. You'll find **all student services**, including financial aid, registration, and a visitor center, housed in one convenient building: the University Pavilion.

4. Much of the **new construction on campus is unique and modern.** The Steger Student Life Center, for example, is only forty feet wide!

5. **MainStreet**, the main drag on campus, brings students together.

The Basics

Public / private: public state
Total enrollment / undergrads: 27,932 / 19,512
Campus setting: urban
Students call it: UC
Students are called: Bearcats
Notable alums: Cris Collinsworth (pro football player, sports analyst), Michael Graves (architect), George Rieveschl Jr. (inventor, Benadryl), William Howard Taft (U.S. president), Myron Ullman III (CEO, JC Penney)

Earn While You Learn

Don't worry if you can't settle on one of the hundred-plus majors—this school views indecision as an opportunity for growth. The Center for Exploratory Studies will pair you with an advisor who will conduct a career assessment and direct you to students or alumni you can grill with career questions. UC follows its own advice: It's currently undergoing an exploration process of its own. UC21, the name given to the acatdemic development plan, addresses topics such as how to attract outstanding faculty, how to teach diversity, and how to increase the ever-popular co-op offerings. CU invented co-op education, and its program is large and well managed. The colleges of Design, Architecture, Art, and Planning (DAAP), Engineering, and Applied Science are particularly strong at UC, and most majors within them require co-op experience. However, co-op opportunities are available to all students. Students can end up alternating between classroom study and paid time at companies such as the Aveda Corporation, Procter & Gamble, and Fossil, among others.

What's a Bearcat?

Technically, *bearcat* is another word for panda. But when UC adopted the bearcat mascot, it wasn't thinking of a cute bamboo-chomping animal. In the early 1900s, a football player named "Teddy" Baehr helped Cincinnati win an important game against the Kentucky Wild*cats*. A cheerleader's chant for the "Baehr-Cats" eventually turned into "Bearcats," and thus a mascot was born.

CU = Construction Underway

CU's commitment to increasing the student body's tolerance, understanding, and respect for a variety of cultures is clear. Several programs on campus promote diversity education, including the African-American Cultural and Research Center (AACRC), the Racial Awareness Program (RAPP), and OutReach. The student body itself is fairly diverse, especially in terms of student interests. Jocks, geeks, hippies, artsy types—all are present on this campus. More than 80 percent are from Ohio, and a fair number commute to school. Construction is the norm on campus these days, although a number of architecturally impressive buildings have already been completed, including the Stegner Student Life Center, Sigma Sigma Commons, and the Engineering Research Center, just to name a few. Upperclassmen get the pick of the university's newest dorms, including Campus Recreation Center housing and Schneider Hall. Or join one of the thirty-one Greek chapters on campus and call the Greek house home.

MainStreet, UC

One of the most unifying additions to campus is MainStreet, which has attractions including a bookstore, student union, computer lab, and convenience store, not to mention lots of green space and an impressive new recreation center. Can't motivate yourself to exercise? Lose your excuse to skip the gym by living in new housing right in the rec center building. The university is expanding with new buildings that are unique and modern, as befits an urban university. Campus abuts downtown Cincinnati; greater Cincinnati includes parts of northern Kentucky and southeastern Indiana. Graduates tend to stay in the city after earning a degree. About half of the school's alumni live in the area.

Admissions

Average high school GPA:	3.35
Average freshman SAT verbal / math score:	561 / 573
Average freshman ACT score:	23
Application fee:	$40
Application deadlines: continuous (freshmen) continuous (transfer)	
Total applicants:	11,813
Total accepted:	8,975 (76%)
Total accepted who enrolled:	3,863
Notification dates: 11/1 (freshmen) continuous (transfer)	

Students

Percentage of male / female students:	53% / 47%
Percentage of students from out of state:	10%
Percentage of students graduating in 4 years / 6 years:	17% / 50%

Money

Total endowment:	$1,031,408,791
Total in-state tuition, fees & expenses:	$19,830
Total out-of-state tuition, fees & expenses:	$34,353
Average financial aid package:	$7,787
Percentage of students who sought aid and received it:	59%
Percentage of students receiving financial aid:	43%

Also Check Out

The Ohio State University

University of Connecticut

University of Notre Dame

The University of Pittsburgh

West Virginia University

University of Colorado at Boulder

Regent Administrative Center 125, 552 UCB
Boulder, CO 80309

(303) 492-1411
http://www.colorado.edu/

BIG CHOICE

BIG RESEARCH

Healthy bodies, healthy minds

5 REASONS IT'S COOL

1. Four Nobel laureates in Physics, hi-tech labs for engineers, exciting projects in space exploration—suffice to say, **the sciences at CU are strong**.

2. The Undergraduate Research Opportunities Program is just one of the **academic enrichment opportunities** at this large research institution.

3. The **large Tuscan-style campus** is one of the loveliest in the country.

4. If you're **fun-loving, laid-back, and love the outdoors**, you'll feel right at home.

5. Bars, restaurants, live music, and theater festivals are just some of the attractions in **Boulder, the ideal college city.**

The Basics

Public/private: public state
Total enrollment/undergrads: 31,399 / 26,163
Campus setting: suburban
Students call it: CU, Colorado
Students are called: Buffaloes
Notable alums: Chauncey Billups (pro basketball player), Judy Collins (musician), Alan Kay (computer scientist), Glenn Miller (band leader), Kenneth Miller (biologist), Trey Parker and Matt Stone (creators, *South Park*), Jack Swigert (astronaut)

Are You a Future Astronaut?

Don't let the laid-back approach to academics fool you: These students have plenty of ways to expand their intellects. Freshmen enroll in the College of Arts & Sciences, Architecture & Planning, Engineering and Applied Science, Music, or the Leeds School of Business. Future teachers or journalists can apply to the Schools of Journalism or Education after their first year. Psychology, integrative physiology, and English are the most popular majors, but CU's strengths are in the sciences. Students in the Engineering School have access to state-of-the-art equipment in the Discovery Learning Center, while future astronauts or rocket builders (of which CU has produced eighteen) will benefit from the huge amount of funding CU receives from NASA. CU has had several Nobel laureates in Physics. The rigor of classes and the skill of profs depends largely on the major, and some students can coast—or ski—by with minimal effort. Still, the majority of classes are

Home, Home on the Football Field

What weighs 1,300 pounds, runs twenty-five miles an hour, lives in a confidential location, and can trample a man? That would be the live CU mascot, Ralphie the Buffalo. Ralphie runs a loop around the football field at every home game. The current Ralphie has refused to run only twice, both before games against long-time rival Nebraska. CU lost both games.

challenging, and students are fulfilled by the myriad opportunities at their fingertips.

Parties and Powder Turns

Why are CU students so relaxed and happy? Is it because they live in a picturesque college town at the foot of the Rocky Mountains, or because they attend classes on one of the prettiest campuses in the country, or because there's always a party and the slopes are thirty minutes away? For most kids, the answer is "all of the above." More than half the students come from upper-middle-class Centennial State families. They like to party, but also like to stay healthy and active. Club sports are hugely popular, as are skiing and snowboarding. Boulder Freeride, the ski and snowboard club, has more members than the Greek system! Frats and sororities still draw about 15 percent of the student body, but the administration has cracked down on underage drinking and keeps a close watch on the party scene. This hasn't diminished the fun at the Pearl Street Mall or on the Hill, an area adjacent to campus teeming with bars, restaurants, and off-campus housing. The University Memorial Center, a hub of student activity on campus, also hosts live music and lectures. The 210,000-square-foot Student Recreation Center is a busy spot.

Boulder Is Bomber!

The 786-acre campus, located just one mile south of downtown, is characterized by rural Italian-style architecture. The Buff Bus, a free student shuttle, takes students to and from campus. Boulder is also very bike friendly. There are tons of outdoor activities in the surrounding areas, from hiking beneath the Flatirons to climbing in Eldorado Canyon to skiing at Breckenridge, Aspen, or nearby Eldora. Life in the small city of Boulder is equally pleasant. The Fox and Boulder theaters have great live music, and there are tons of bars and restaurants lining the Pearl Street Mall. Film festivals, museums, and the annual Colorado Shakespeare Festival offer cultural enrichment, while anyone searching for inspiration need only look to the Rocky Mountains.

Admissions

Average high school GPA:	3.52
Average freshman SAT verbal / math score:	579 / 596
Average freshman ACT score:	24
Application fee:	$50
Application deadlines: 1/15 (freshmen) 4/1 (transfer)	
Total applicants:	18,173
Total accepted:	15,971 (88%)
Total accepted who enrolled:	5,603
Notification dates: continuous (freshmen) continuous (transfer)	

Students

Percentage of male / female students:	53% / 47%
Percentage of students from out of state:	31%
Percentage of students graduating in 4 years / 6 years:	38% / 66%

Money

Total endowment:	$290,700,000
Total in-state tuition, fees & expenses:	$13,943
Total out-of-state tuition, fees & expenses:	$31,839
Average financial aid package:	$10,362
Percentage of students who sought aid and received it:	92%
Percentage of students receiving financial aid:	30%

Also Check Out

Colorado State University–Fort Collins

University of California–Santa Cruz

University of Denver

University of Oregon

University of Vermont

University of Connecticut

2131 Hillside Road, Unit 3088 Storrs, CT 06269	(860) 486-2000 http://www.uconn.edu/

BIG CHOICE

An Ivy League education at a state school price

5 REASONS IT'S COOL

1. UConn, ranked among the **nation's top public universities**, is the only public university in New England with its own law school, social work school, and medicine/dentistry schools.

2. The low price tag means you'll graduate with a **prestigious degree without breaking the bank.**

3. **More than one hundred majors** are offered through ten undergraduate colleges.

4. **Husky fever reigns supreme**, especially during basketball season, when fans go doggone crazy.

5. UConn's **picture-perfect New England setting** offers bucolic scenery and cows, lots of cows.

The Basics

Public / private: public state
Total enrollment / undergrads: 23,557 / 16,347
Campus setting: rural
Students call it: UConn
Students are called: Huskies
Notable alums: Tate George (pro basketball player), Robert D. Kaplan (author, journalist), Bobbie Ann Mason (writer), Richard Mastracchio (astronaut), Peter Niedmann (composer), Emeka Okafor (pro basketball player), Les Payne (journalist), Brian Schulz (cinematographer)

Get More Bang for Your Buck

UConn is often ranked among the nation's top public universities and is cited as a "public Ivy," a school that offers an Ivy League–caliber education at a public university price. The university offers 105 majors and 64 minors in its ten undergraduate colleges, which include colleges of liberal arts and sciences, agriculture, education, business, allied health, engineering, and business—to name just a few. Ninety percent of professors hold terminal degrees in their fields. The campus library has over 2.5 million print volumes and access to more than 35,000 online journals and 250 electronic databases. The university's Institute for Student Success (ISS), meanwhile, features a number of programs designed to help UConn students maximize their educational experience, such as peer education programs, academic advising, and first-year mentoring programs. The popular study-abroad office sends students to over sixty-five countries on six continents, including South Africa, China, and Mexico.

Jonathan the Husky

When Connecticut Agricultural College changed its name to Connecticut State College (before settling on University of Connecticut), it no longer made sense for the college's athletic teams to be called "Aggies." The top choice for a new mascot was the Husky dog. A student contest resulted in naming the dog "Jonathan" for Jonathan Trumbull, Connecticut's Revolutionary War–era governor. While the first Jonathan (the dog, not the man) was brown and white, later mascots have been all white. UConn's current mascot is Jonathan XII. Students commemorate their long line of beloved Jonathans with a statue of a Husky, which has a well-worn nose from repeated rubbings by those seeking good luck.

Basketball Is Just the Beginning

UConn sponsors many campus events throughout the year and oversees more than three hundred student organizations—from musical, religious, and political groups to cultural and community service clubs. Student-run media opportunities include the *Daily Campus*, the largest student newspaper in Connecticut, WHUS, the campus radio station, and UCTV, the cable television station. Greek life is popular, and students choose from twenty-seven fraternities and sororities. UConn's numerous athletic teams, meanwhile, enjoy a solid reputation both on the field and in the classroom; in fact, last year's football team outperformed 80 percent of all other students on campus, just one of several teams in the country to do so. Huskies basketball, however, holds a special place in students' hearts. The men's and women's teams have been perennial contenders for the national championship for years.

Not Just Another Pretty Face

UConn's main campus lies in the picturesque Connecticut town of Storrs, roughly thirty minutes from state capital Hartford. Students craving a night on the town would be best advised to avoid Hartford, though, and head for the brighter lights of Boston or New York, both of which are between two and three hours away. The university provides free bus service to local venues and also arranges frequent bus trips to these cities as well as the Connecticut shore. While Storrs lacks a nightlife, it makes up for the absence of a bar scene with its ample scenic beauty, particularly in autumn when the leaves turn their famous red, yellow, and orange colors. UConn's recent decision to invest $2.8 billion in campus buildings and infrastructures over the next twenty years suggests that the university will keep its academic reputation as well as its New England charm in the years ahead.

Admissions

Average high school GPA:	—
Average freshman SAT writing / math / critical reading score:	591 / 614 / 591
Average freshman ACT score:	24
Application fee:	$70

Application deadlines:
2/1 (freshmen)
4/1 (transfer)
12/1 (early action)

Total applicants:	19,778
Total accepted:	10,102 (51%)
Total accepted who enrolled:	3,229

Notification dates:
1/1 (freshmen)   7/1 (transfer)
1/1 (early action)

Acceptance rate for early action applicants:	69%

Students

Percentage of male / female students:	48% / 52%
Percentage of students from out of state:	23%
Percentage of students graduating in 4 years / 6 years:	50% / 72%

Money

Total endowment:	$300,000,000
Total in-state tuition, fees & expenses:	$17,692
Total out-of-state tuition, fees & expenses:	$31,636
Average financial aid package:	$10,507
Percentage of students who sought aid and received it:	72%
Percentage of students receiving financial aid:	45%

Also Check Out

The Pennsylvania State University–University Park

University of Maine–Orono

University of Massachusetts Amherst

University of New Hampshire

University of Virginia

University of Dallas

1845 East Northgate Drive
Irving, TX 75062

(972) 721-5000
http://www.udallas.edu/

 BIG PERSPECTIVE

 BIG WORLD

CAUTION: inquisitive minds ahead

5 REASONS IT'S COOL

1. Nearly 95 percent of students receive **merit-based scholarships or need-based awards**.

2. **A semester abroad in Rome** is a typical rite: More than 80 percent of students study art and history at the university's Rome campus.

3. Read any **Great Books** lately? The curriculum focuses on original texts from ancient scholars like Homer and Euripides, all the way up to Elie Wiesel.

4. Students enjoy a close-knit campus and **personal attention from professors**.

5. Incoming freshmen boast the **third highest SAT scores among schools in Texas**, right behind Rice and Trinity.

The Basics

Public / private: private religious
Total enrollment / undergrads: 2,941 / 1,188
Campus setting: suburban
Students call it: UD
Students are called: Crusaders
Notable alums: Arthur L. Boyer (radiologist), Peter MacNicol (actor), Trish Murphy (singer-songwriter)

When in Rome . . .

UD's core curriculum teaches Western civilization directly from those who created it. Students take small, seminar courses in literature, philosophy, history, and theology and read writers both ancient and modern, from Plato and Aristotle to Dostoevsky and Nietzsche. The university also requires students to fulfill science, math, fine arts, theology, and foreign language requirements outside of the Great Books program. Almost all students spend a semester during their sophomore year at the university's campus in Rome, where they study the art and history of Western civilization right in the center of the ancient world. UD offers twenty-three majors, and English, biology, and theology are the most popular. A five-year BA/MBA program allows business-minded students to get on the fast track to their graduate degrees. Over 80 percent of students go on to grad school, and high numbers of pre-law and pre-medical students get into their first choice of professional schools. The student-to-faculty ratio of 11:1 and average class size of twenty ensure that students get plenty of face time with professors.

This Jailhouse Rocks

UD juniors kick of the fall with the annual Charity Week, a wild seven-day, campuswide extravaganza. The highpoint of festivities comes when students and professors pay to throw each other in a makeshift jail. Not only do the imprisoned have to miss class, but all penal proceeds go to student-selected charities.

Campus Is Where the Sacre Coeur Is

UD students have a reputation for being conservative and Catholic, although non-Catholics do feel welcome. Thanks to a requirement that everyone live on campus, students enjoy a close-knit community. There are no fraternities or sororities, and any parties tend to be controlled affairs that are largely free of drugs and binge drinking. The university sponsors nearly fifty student clubs, including the Jane Austen Society, the Investment Club, and several service organizations. Guest speakers, plays, dances, religious services, free movies, and other social events are also provided. While sports don't turn students out in high numbers as they do at other Texas schools, Crusader teams are competitive, particularly in basketball, baseball, and soccer. Intramural sports, especially the weekend rugby games, are also popular. Unique bonding traditions include karaoke night, Thank Goodness It's Thursday concerts, and annual music and Groundhog festivals.

Nothing to Complain About

In a way, UD's suburban Dallas location offers the best of both worlds. Sitting atop the highest point in Dallas County, students are treated to one of the best views of the metro skyline. But they also get the perks of a self-contained, suburban campus. While the campus may leave much to be desired in terms of architecture and landscaping, all the necessities are there, including a sanctuary, residence halls, food, performance spaces, and athletic facilities. The best of Dallas's restaurants, nightclubs, bars, professional sporting events, and shopping, not to mention hundreds of other college students, are also available to students with cars.

Admissions

Average high school GPA:	3.6
Average freshman SAT writing / math / critical reading score:	609 / 597 / 628
Average freshman ACT score:	25
Application fee:	$40

Application deadlines:
8/1 (freshmen)
7/1 (transfer)
11/1 (early action)

Total applicants:	876
Total accepted:	743 (85%)
Total accepted who enrolled:	315

Notification dates:
continuous (freshmen)
continuous (transfer)
1/15 (early action)

Acceptance rate for early action applicants:	94%

Students

Percentage of male / female students:	44% / 56%
Percentage of students from out of state:	44%
Percentage of students graduating in 4 years / 6 years:	70% / 74%

Money

Total endowment:	$45,592,500
Total tuition:	$21,819
Total cost with fees & expenses:	$30,882
Average financial aid package:	$17,668
Percentage of students who sought aid and received it:	82%
Percentage of students receiving financial aid:	53%

Also Check Out

Austin College

Baylor University

Southwestern University

Trinity University

University of Houston

University of Delaware

116 Hullihen Hall
Newark, DE 19716

(302) 831-2000
http://www.udel.edu/

 **BIG CHOICE**

 **BIG WORLD**

Rich in tradition and reputation

5 REASONS IT'S COOL

1. It's the largest school in Delaware, and one of the **oldest and most established schools** in the nation.

2. If you know you want to **study art conservation**, this is the place for you: UD is one of only four North American schools to offer a major in the field.

3. UD was **the first in America to institute a study-abroad program,** and travel remains a priority.

4. It doesn't get more patriotic than this: The first graduating class included **three signers of the Declaration of Independence.**

5. Who wouldn't want to be a **Fightin' Blue Hen?**

The Basics

Public / private: public state-related
Total enrollment / undergrads: 19,742 / 16,296
Campus setting: small town
Students call it: Delaware, UD
Students are called: Blue hens
Notable alums: Mike Adams (pro football player), Joseph Biden (senator), Thomas Clayton (senator), Susan Stroman (film/theater director, performer), George Thorogood (musician)

Study Abroad or at Home

Appropriately enough for a school located in Delaware, which is home to the nation's chemical and pharmaceutical industries, UD features great business, chemical engineering, chemistry, and biochemistry programs. UD also has extensive degree offerings in arts and sciences, human services, and marine and earth studies. The University Honors Program is open to students of all majors who want a rigorous academic experience with additional opportunities for interdisciplinary research. True to its pioneering roots, the renowned program now encompasses over seventy programs of study across more than forty subject areas in thirty-five countries on all seven continents. Undergraduates may study in another country for a unique five-week winter session or for a semester. In Sydney, Australia, a program connects business students interested in international marketing with some of Sydney's top companies. UD is also home to the Disaster Research Center, where researchers study everything from tornadoes to riots.

The Curse of Poe?

One winter evening in 1843, Edgar Allen Poe was lecturing at what was then called the Academy (later the University). One story has it that he slipped and fell in the mud outside a nearby tavern and angrily cursed the building. The bar, which had stood since 1747, burned down a few years later.

Sing, Play, or Cheer

The lovely campus has recently been improved further by big-league construction projects. UD offers twenty-three varsity sports as a member of the Colonial Athletic Association. Delaware's football teams have won six national titles, including the NCAA Division I-AA championship in 2003. The university also has a rich musical tradition, featuring one of the best marching bands on the East Coast, an early music ensemble, several concert ensembles, choral ensembles, and even a steel drum band. The one student newspaper at UD, the *Review*, has a print circulation of twelve thousand copies. The student-run radio station broadcasts noncommercial, educational content twenty-four hours a day. Roughly 15 percent of UD undergraduates belong to one of nineteen fraternities and fifteen sororities. Whether you want to go Greek or not, there will be ample social opportunities for you to take advantage of.

Close to Everything

Newark is a lively town that derives much of its energy and attitude from the university. The city is focusing on creating shopping and housing opportunities for a broader segment of the local population, rather than for the students alone. Still, UD undergrads have a noticeable and mostly positive influence on the town. Main Street, in particular, has long been a popular student hangout. Newark is roughly halfway between Washington, D.C. and New York City. The railroad station near campus is serviced by both Amtrak and SEPTA, which makes getting up and down the Eastern Seaboard a snap.

Admissions

Average high school GPA:	3.6
Average freshman SAT writing / math / critical reading score:	592 / 613 / 591
Average freshman ACT score:	25
Application fee:	$60

Application deadlines:
1/15 (freshmen)   5/1 (transfer)
specific (early decision)

Total applicants:	21,930
Total accepted:	10,373 (47%)
Total accepted who enrolled:	3,151

Notification dates:
3/15 (freshmen)
continuous (transfer)
specific (early decision)

Acceptance rate for early decision applicants:	38%

Students

Percentage of male / female students:	42% / 58%
Percentage of students from out of state:	60%
Percentage of students graduating in 4 years / 6 years:	62% / 76%

Money

Total endowment:	$1,223,200,000
Total in-state tuition, fees & expenses:	$15,906
Total out-of-state tuition, fees & expenses:	$26,616
Average financial aid package:	$9,891
Percentage of students who sought aid and received it:	79%
Percentage of students receiving financial aid:	31%

Also Check Out

The Pennsylvania State University–University Park

University of Connecticut

University of Maine–Orono

University of Maryland–College Park

University of New Hampshire

niversity of Denver

2199 South University Park Boulevard	(303) 871-2000
Denver, CO 80208	http://www.du.edu/

 **BIG PERSPECTIVE**  **BIG WORLD**

Skiing + Studying = DU

5 REASONS IT'S COOL

1. The Partners in Scholarship Program, which funds undergrad research projects, is just one of **DU's special academic programs.**

2. With a 10:1 student-to-faculty ratio, small classes, and a mentoring program for freshman, students get **a lot of attention.**

3. Almost **70 percent of students participate in study-abroad programs.**

4. If you enjoy **winter sports**, you'll be in good company. Campus empties out on winter weekends as students hit the slopes.

5. **Campus is within minutes of downtown Denver** and less than an hour from the Rockies.

The Basics

Public/private: private nonprofit
Total enrollment/undergrads: 10,374 / 4,877
Campus setting: suburban
Students call it: DU
Students are called: Pioneers
Notable alums: George Casey Jr. (chief of staff, U.S. Army), Peter Coors (CEO, Coors Brewing Company), James Cox Kennedy (CEO, Cox Communications), Gale Norton (U.S. secretary of the interior), Condoleezza Rice (U.S. secretary of state)

Going Global

DU is one of the few midsized private liberal arts school in the western region. It runs on the quarter system, which allows students more time to take advantage of cool course offerings such as The Science of Poker or Video Game Development. The core requirements are fairly extensive, but most students appreciate the exposure to diverse areas of study. Small class sizes and attentive professors also win accolades. The well-respected Daniels College of Business draws quite a few undergrads and offers majors in marketing, real estate, and hotel, restaurant, and tourism management, among others. Other popular majors include psychology, communications, music, and biology. The prestigious Pioneer Leadership Program and the Honors Program both offer living/learning communities, and the Partners in Scholarship Program distributes grants to undergrads to support research and faculty-student collaboration. Last year, the International Service

Are You Afraid of Ghosts?

Legend has it that one of the great benefactors of DU, Mary Reed, haunts the building of her namesake. The ghostly figure has been spotted perusing books in what used to be the DuPont Reading Room. Once a bookworm, always a bookworm!

Learning Program sent students to Bosnia, India, and South Africa, where they taught English, worked in a group home for teens, and ran a summer school.

Doers, Not Viewers

The dreaded Freshman Fifteen is a mere fable at DU, which has one of the most fit student bodies in the country. The 125-acre, bike-friendly campus has recently enjoyed many additions and renovations. The Coors Fitness Center is home to the only Olympic-sized swimming pool in Denver. Intramural and club sports are popular, as is writing for the *Clarion* (the school newspaper). Although DU has been trying to downplay its rep as a ski school, students still live it up on the slopes every winter weekend. Back on campus, students watch free movies at Sturm, attend plays, or bask in the Denver sunshine. Students must live on campus for two years, a requirement that fosters a strong sense of community. Freshmen choose between Johnson-McFarlane Hall (J-Mac) or Centennial Hall. The former caters to more studious types. Some upperclassmen remain on campus in apartment-style living arrangements, but most opt for off-campus housing or move into their fraternities or sororities. About 20 percent of the student body goes Greek. For the most part, DU students would rather be doing than viewing, so varsity sports don't garner much attention. The exception is ice hockey, especially when rival Colorado College is in town.

High Altitude Livin'

Located in a residential neighborhood close to downtown Denver, DU offers the best of both worlds. A ride on the light rail (DU students ride for free) leads to art museums, live music venues, or LoDo, the downtown Denver spot for nightlife. And when students need a taste of mountain air, the Rockies are only thirty minutes away. From Breckenridge to Winter Park, there are enough ski resorts nearby to make a snow bunny giddy. No matter what, the Denver climate guarantees students three hundred days of sunshine.

Admissions

Average high school GPA:	3.57
Average freshman SAT verbal / math score:	583 / 592
Average freshman ACT score:	24
Application fee:	$50
Application deadlines: 1/15 (freshmen) continuous (transfer) 11/1 (early action)	
Total applicants:	4,038
Total accepted:	3,304 (82%)
Total accepted who enrolled:	1,090
Notification dates: 3/15 (freshmen) continuous (transfer) 1/15 (early action)	
Acceptance rate for early action applicants:	—

Students

Percentage of male / female students:	47% / 53%
Percentage of students from out of state:	50%
Percentage of students graduating in 4 years / 6 years:	52% / 69%

Money

Total endowment:	$194,427,134
Total tuition:	$29,628
Total cost with fees & expenses:	$40,906
Average financial aid package:	$20,757
Percentage of students who sought aid and received it:	69%
Percentage of students receiving financial aid:	39%

Also Check Out

Boston College

Colorado College

Colorado State University–Fort Collins

University of Colorado at Boulder

University of Puget Sound

University of Florida

201 Criser Hall, PO Box 114000
Gainesville, FL 32611

(352) 392-3261
http://www.ufl.edu/

BIG CHOICE

BIG RESEARCH

College, Gator style

5 REASONS IT'S COOL

1. UF's "public Ivy" status means you can get a dynamite education at a low cost.

2. With more than thirty-five thousand undergrads, UF is the **third-largest university in the nation.**

3. The massive library network provides students with access to **the largest information resource system in Florida.**

4. **Gator pride soars during football season** and reaches its zenith at Gator Growl, the gigantic homecoming week pep rally.

5. Students are treated to **year-round sunshine** and a famously relaxed campus vibe.

The Basics

Public / private: public state
Total enrollment / undergrads: 50,822 / 35,110
Campus setting: suburban
Students call it: Florida, UF
Students are called: Gators
Notable alums: Kiki Carter (activist, singer-songwriter), Michael Connelly (author), David Finkel (journalist), Bob Graham (governor, Florida), Robert Grubbs (Nobel Laureate, Chemistry), Frances Mayes (writer), Emmitt Smith (pro football player), Steve Spurrier (college football coach), Bob Vila (TV host)

Options Galore

Despite its party school rep and its size, UF ranks among the most selective public universities. And with thirty thousand undergrads, it also ranks among the biggest. The university offers more than a hundred majors through its sixteen undergraduate colleges, which include colleges of liberal arts and sciences, business, education, engineering, nursing, and architecture. Pre-professional majors attract the highest numbers of students, and programs in healthcare, engineering, communications, and pharmacy are especially notable. Internship, volunteer, and study-abroad programs are plentiful, and students benefit from the wide range of research activities on campus, including those in neurology, biotechnology, and citrus production (this is Florida, after all). As can be expected given the university's size, students are likely to face their fair share of large lecture halls and TA-taught courses.

Aide for the Gators

In 1965, professor of medicine J. Robert Cade, along with two other colleagues, concocted an energy drink to help the Gator football players stay at the top of their game. The drink, which was dubbed Gator-ade, worked like a charm and may have contributed to the team's first Orange Bowl win.

The student to faculty to ratio is 23:1. And while students voice the usual complaints about frustrating administrative workings, most agree that the self-motivated will find no lack of stimulation.

Shiny, Happy People

Gators like to party. The university's huge Greek system is the primary partying engine, and Gainesville offers plenty of bars and nightclubs that cater to most tastes. Students tend to be politically conservative, and more than 90 percent are native to Florida. But what students lack in regional diversity they more than make up for in ethnic diversity, and a host of student organizations and events celebrate the campus's multiculturalism. Less than a quarter of students live on campus. Residence halls are largely clean and serviceable, if unremarkable, but many upperclassmen skip the housing lottery and seek digs in the surrounding neighborhoods. UF offers more than 650 student organizations, ranging from service and religious organizations to the *Alligator*, the student newspaper. Students also enjoy the campus's huge permanent art and natural history collections, as well as the more than two thousand annual on-campus cultural and athletic events. Cheering on Gators sports, especially during football (where students inhabit The Swamp) and basketball seasons, takes a bite out of most students' schedules.

A Lot to Gain in Gainesville

Gainesville is located in north central Florida, midway between the Atlantic Ocean and the Gulf of Mexico. UF's 2,000-acre campus features Gothic-style buildings, many of which are national historic landmarks, as well as a certified Audubon Cooperative Sanctuary that houses environmental and wildlife management, conservation, and outreach programs. Gainesville offers a notable independent music scene and a number of student-friendly bars, restaurants, and shopping options. Mild winters allow students to enjoy outdoor activities throughout most of the year. UF-owned Lake Alice is popular for water sports, and equipment is available free of charge. Beaches are easily reached by car, but drivers be forewarned: Parking at UF is such a crapshoot that students often bring bikes in for the week and leave their cars in the lot.

Admissions

Average high school GPA:	3.8
Average freshman SAT verbal / math score:	615 / 634
Average freshman ACT score:	25
Application fee:	$30

Application deadlines:
1/17 (freshmen) — (transfer)
10/1 (early decision)

Total applicants:	22,093
Total accepted:	10,652 (48%)
Total accepted who enrolled:	6,641

Notification dates:
continuous (freshmen)
— (transfer)
12/1 (early decision)

Acceptance rate for early decision applicants:	63%

Students

Percentage of male / female students:	46% / 54%
Percentage of students from out of state:	5%
Percentage of students graduating in 4 years / 6 years:	51% / 78%

Money

Total endowment:	$996,244,638
Total in-state tuition, fees & expenses:	$10,726
Total out-of-state tuition, fees & expenses:	$25,310
Average financial aid package:	$10,653
Percentage of students who sought aid and received it:	81%
Percentage of students receiving financial aid:	35%

Also Check Out

Florida State University

University of Central Florida

University of Georgia

The University of Miami

University of North Carolina at Chapel Hill

University of Georgia

Terrell Hall, The University of Georgia
Athens, GA 30602

(706) 542-3000
http://www.uga.edu/

 **BIG CHOICE**

 **BIG RESEARCH**

It's a peach.

5 REASONS IT'S COOL

1. The lotto-backed HOPE Scholarship has **raised academic standards and increased selectivity**.

2. **More than 20 percent of students study abroad** in ninety-plus programs.

3. The College of Environmental Design has **a well-regarded landscape architecture program**, the largest of its kind.

4. First-year students jump into UGA life at **Dawg Camp**, a summer program of arts and entertainment, community service, and outdoor activities.

5. The city of Athens has a **historically hip music and art scene**, thanks in part to its close relationship with the university.

The Basics

Public / private: public state
Total enrollment / undergrads: 33,959 / 25,437
Campus setting: suburban
Students call it: UGA, Georgia
Students are called: Bulldogs, Dawgs
Notable alums: Kim Basinger (actress), Maxine Clark (founder, Build-A-Bear Workshop), Cathy Cox (Georgia secretary of state), Deborah Norville (journalist), Sonny Perdue (governor, Georgia), Deborah Roberts (producer, ABC News)

Old Dawgs *Can* Learn New Tricks

UGA, the nation's oldest state university, is raising its profile from agriculture and party school to premier flagship institution. The HOPE Scholarship has helped by bringing in the state's best and brightest, tuition-free. The UGA Honors Program is a good fit for smarties, and about 10 percent of undergrads enroll in it. The honors program caps classes at eighteen, a big perk at this large university. Despite the large number of students at the school, UGA tries to keep class sizes manageable. While large lectures are common, most classes are forty students or fewer, and the student-to-faculty ratio is 14:1. Another perk is the sheer number of offerings students have to choose from in terms of schools, programs, and course selection. The university offers 170 undergraduate programs. New state-of-the-art facilities, such as the Complex Carbohydrate Research Center, present exciting research and learning opportunities for undergrads. Students at the School of Public

Freshmen, Beware the Arch!

The columns pictured on the University of Georgia logo are from the arched entrance to university and represent three ideals every college student should aspire to: moderation, justice, and wisdom. It's odd, then, that according to superstition, those who walk underneath the arch will never graduate.

and International Affairs can take advantage of the internship, outreach, and fellowship programs through the Center for International Trade and Security. Speaking of international affairs, students at UGA are eager to study abroad. Twenty percent do so, in locations as varied as Tanzania, Croatia, China, and France.

Corrupting the Youth of Athens

UGA has a party school rep, but the increasingly demanding curriculum has led many students to strike a balance between boozing and books. The many cultural attractions of Athens provide an alternative to the school's potent Greek scene, as do the five hundred student organizations and clubs. Popular options include volunteer organizations, political and cultural clubs, and several intramural sports. The Ramsey Center, one of the largest student recreational facilities in the country, offers the latest in fitness and athletic equipment. Loyalty to Bulldog football is fierce. Residence halls are comfortable, particularly the new Russell and McWhorter Halls, and the school's fixed-rate all-you-can-eat meal plan is popular enough to keep juniors and seniors coming back for more. Nearly 80 percent of full-time undergrads are Georgia-born, helped along by the HOPE program. Minorities make up only around 5 percent of the population, a number that administrators would like to see increase.

College Town Extraordinaire

Athens, Georgia, is the quintessential college town, with plenty to keep the UGA student happy. Athens's music scene is legendary, with rock veterans REM, The B-52s, and Widespread Panic having had their start there, and recent indie darlings like Of Montreal among the local up-and-comers. This ultimate college town has hip clubs, bars, restaurants, and shops that cater to the tastes of the student population. The campus is an attractive mix of nineteenth-century architecture and landscaping sprinkled around manicured lawns and wooded areas. Housed on the grounds are the State Botanical Garden, State Museum of Art, and State Museum of Natural History, along with the Georgia Writers Hall of Fame. For a quick getaway, the college-friendly metropolis of Atlanta lies just an hour away.

Admissions

Average high school GPA:	3.76
Average freshman SAT writing / math / critical reading score:	605 / 621 / 616
Average freshman ACT score:	25
Application fee:	$50

Application deadlines:
1/15 (freshmen)   4/1 (transfer)
10/15 (early action)

Total applicants:	15,924
Total accepted:	9,214 (58%)
Total accepted who enrolled:	5,055

Notification dates:
12/15 (freshmen)
continuous (transfer)
12/15 (early action)

Acceptance rate for early action applicants: —

Students

Percentage of male / female students:	43% / 57%
Percentage of students from out of state:	15%
Percentage of students graduating in 4 years / 6 years:	41% / 74%

Money

Total endowment:	$574,576,000
Total in-state tuition, fees & expenses:	$12,612
Total out-of-state tuition, fees & expenses:	$25,688
Average financial aid package:	$7,767
Percentage of students who sought aid and received it:	72%
Percentage of students receiving financial aid:	24%

Also Check Out

University of Florida

University of Kentucky

The University of Mississippi

The University of South Carolina–Columbia

Vanderbilt University

University of Hawaii at Manoa

2500 Campus Road
Honolulu, HI 96822

(808) 956-8III
http://www.uhm.hawaii.edu/

 **BIG CHOICE**

 **BIG RESEARCH**

A rainbow of diversity—and tropical majors too

5 REASONS IT'S COOL

1. UH offers **an astounding variety of majors**, Division I athletics, and more than a hundred undergraduate organizations.

2. Got a thing for coral, sharks, and giant squids? The university's **oceanography programs are top-notch**.

3. **More foreign languages** are offered here than at any other public college in the United States.

4. There's a wide range of ethnic organizations on campus—not surprising considering the **diverse makeup of the student body**.

5. It's Hawaii—need we say **more?** One thing's for sure: You won't have any trouble convincing people to visit you!

The Basics

Public / private: public state
Total enrollment / undergrads: 20,357 / 14,037
Campus setting: urban
Students call it: UH, Manoa
Students are called: Rainbow Warriors (men)/Wahine (women)
Notable alums: Beau Bridges (actor), Hiram Fong (senator), Bette Midler (singer, actress), Kenneth P. Moritsugu (U.S. surgeon general), Andre S. Tatibouet (founder, Aston Hotels & Resorts)

Study a Language ... or Ten

Of the ten campuses in the University of Hawaii System, the University at Manoa is the flagship. It's a great place to study the travel industry, oceanography, or tropical environments. Hawaii's eighty-seven undergraduate majors include all the programs you might expect to find at a large state university, such as social work, business, and engineering. But at UH, you'll also find a host of unique majors, including Hawaiian studies, travel industry management, and global environmental science. For students studying oceanography, the university uses a 222-foot ship, a three-person submarine, and a research vessel. Students in Hawaii's Honors Program work hard and in return are given priority registration, access to graduate-level courses, and their own floor in the freshmen dorms. The university's student-to-faculty ratio is 15:1, and an average freshman or sophomore class runs about thirty-three. Students who want even more personal attention can enroll in freshmen seminars, TA-led courses capped at ten. More languages are

Aloha, Hawaii!

Students at Hawaii are exposed to some uniquely Hawaiian customs. Travel industry management students study Hawaii's hospitality culture, known as *ho'okipa*. Graduates can request that their diploma be written in Hawaiian. At graduation, you'll notice a marshal carrying a *ko'o*, a Hawaiian staff. And don't forget the distinctly Hawaiian clubs on campus, including hula, Hawaiian chorus, and traditional Hawaiian music.

offered than at any other public university in the country, and it's the only one that offers majors in Hawaiian or Filipino. The language lineup includes Japanese, Korean, Chinese, Russian, French, Spanish, Italian, German, Hawaiian, Hindi, and Vietnamese—to name just a few.

Diversity Reigns with the Rainbows

To match the diverse course offerings, you'll find a diverse mix of ethnicities on UH's campus. The 20,400 students—14,000 of them undergrads—come from all fifty states and over eighty countries. Asians make up the bulk of the study body, at 41 percent, while Caucasians account for 26 percent. Native Hawaiians, Pacific Islanders, and those of mixed race make up the rest of the population. Hawaii is part of the Western Undergraduate Exchange program, which discounts tuition to about half the usual nonresident rate for residents of most western states. There are more than a hundred clubs on campus, including ethnic organizations that span the globe. UH also has strong Division I sports teams that compete in the Western Athletic Conference. Students aren't required to live on campus, but most freshmen apply for residential housing nonetheless. Freshmen typically reside in Hale Aloha Hall, but the new Mary Dillingham Frear Hall, with its two interconnected twelve-story towers, offers additional housing.

I'm Dreaming of Hawaii

Anyone dreaming of a tropical vacation is, in essence, dreaming of Hawaii. Attending class on the gorgeous UH campus combines learning with stunning views, perfect weather, and gorgeous flora and fauna. The campus is in the Manoa Valley, three miles from Honolulu and on the island of Oahu. You won't have to go far to stick your toes in the sand—the beaches of Ala Moana and Waikiki are only one mile away. Honolulu is a large city with plenty to do, from theater in the Arts District to shopping in Kakaako. Getting to campus from the continental United States isn't the simplest endeavor, but once you've made it to the Honolulu International Airport, the university is only ten miles away.

Admissions

Average high school GPA:	3.41
Average freshman SAT writing / math / critical reading score:	527 / 570 / 536
Average freshman ACT score:	23
Application fee:	$50

Application deadlines:
5/1 (freshmen)
5/1 (transfer)

Total applicants:	6,167
Total accepted:	4,208 (68%)
Total accepted who enrolled:	1,713

Notification dates:
continuous (freshmen)
continuous (transfer)

Students

Percentage of male / female students:	45% / 55%
Percentage of students from out of state:	26%
Percentage of students graduating in 4 years / 6 years:	12% / 56%

Money

Total endowment:	$207,325,567
Total in-state tuition, fees & expenses:	$12,575
Total out-of-state tuition, fees & expenses:	$21,839
Average financial aid package:	$7,573
Percentage of students who sought aid and received it:	68%
Percentage of students receiving financial aid:	27%

Also Check Out

Arizona State University

University of California–Los Angeles

University of Oregon

The University of South Florida

University of Washington

University of Houston

4800 Calhoun Road
Houston, TX 77204

(713) 743-1000
http://www.uh.edu/

 **BIG CHOICE**

 **BIG RESEARCH**

A Texas-sized university

5 REASONS IT'S COOL

1. The **College of Hotel and Restaurant Management** is the only school of its kind in Texas and has been ranked third in the nation.

2. The Bauer College of Business has **430 corporate partners and over 1,400 companies looking to recruit** its students.

3. When they say it's diverse, they *really* mean it: **Racial and ethnic minorities make up the majority of the student body.**

4. The **prestigious Honors College** features small, rigorous classes taught by illustrious professors.

5. **More than three hundred student organizations** provide endless ways for students to unwind.

The Basics

Public / private: public state
Total enrollment / undergrads: 34,334 / 27,400
Campus setting: urban
Students call it: Houston, UH, U of H
Students are called: Cougars
Notable alums: Fred Couples (pro golfer), Tom Delay (U.S. congressman), Neil Denari (architect), Clyde Drexler (pro basketball player), Bernard A. Harris Jr. (astronaut), Carl Lewis (Olympic track and field athlete), Shannon Miller (Olympic gymnast), Pauline Oliveros (musician, composer), Julian Schnabel (artist, filmmaker), Margaret Spellings (U.S. secretary of education)

Texas-Sized Academics

With more than 27,000 undergrads, twelve academic colleges, and over a hundred majors, UH proves that things really are bigger in Texas. The university has an excellent program in hotel and restaurant management, while undergraduate programs in engineering, pre-pharmacy, and music also earn high marks. The most popular majors include business/commerce, engineering, and psychology. Research opportunities, many of which are tied to local industry, are available in every department, with notable work being conducted in superconductivity, biomedical engineering, and virtual technology. The university's forty-two-hour core curriculum includes a wide range of classes and ensures that students master basic skills such as writing, speaking, and computer literacy. While students may encounter large lectures and TA

A Springtime Arriba!

Every spring, UH hosts a Texas-sized festival called Frontier Fiesta. An entire section of campus is sectioned off and rechristened "Fiesta City," and for three days, students enjoy carnival rides, variety shows, multicultural performances, and a barbeque cook-off. All proceeds from the student-run festival go to scholarships.

teaching, especially in lower-level classes, most upper-level classes have fewer than thirty students. To supplement classroom studies, UH offers a host of internship and fieldwork opportunities in the local area.

A Friendly State of Mind

Two words describe most UH students: friendly and Texan (or *Houstonian*, to be more specific). Students range from eighteen-year-olds to adult professionals and represent all ethnic and socioeconomic backgrounds. This wide assortment makes for a welcoming campus vibe where students are eager to get to know each other and learn from their different backgrounds. The campus is largely a commuter population, with less than 10 percent of students living in on-campus housing. Greek life is healthy: Around 10 percent of students join one of the university's twenty-one fraternities and eighteen sororities. Extracurricular activities include more than three hundred registered organizations catering to a range of interests, whether it's student publications, ceramic and fine arts, anime, or religious and ethnic groups. The intramural sports program is popular, offering everything from soccer and bowling to roller hockey. Spirits run high for Cougar athletics, especially for the storied football and basketball programs.

Huge City, Huge Options

UH is located in the middle of Houston, the nation's fourth largest city. The university's location just off the interstate gives students easy access to theaters, restaurants, bars, clubs, museums, parks, and several professional sports franchises. Few destinations, however, are within walking distance of campus, and the sprawling city and less-than-convenient public transportation make having a car helpful, if not essential. The campus itself offers plenty of entertainment options, including a film series, athletic events, concerts, guest lectures, theater, and everything in between. The beaches of the Gulf Coast and the hills of Texas Hill Country are all within an easy drive.

Admissions

Average high school GPA:	3.35
Average freshman SAT verbal / math score:	527 / 556
Average freshman ACT score:	21
Application fee:	$50

Application deadlines:
4/1 (freshmen)
5/1 (transfer)

Total applicants:	9,935
Total accepted:	7,403 (75%)
Total accepted who enrolled:	3,218

Notification dates:
continuous (freshmen)
continuous (transfer)

Students

Percentage of male / female students:	48% / 52%
Percentage of students from out of state:	2%
Percentage of students graduating in 4 years / 6 years:	10% / 40%

Money

Total endowment:	$470,357,206
Total in-state tuition, fees & expenses:	$14,377
Total out-of-state tuition, fees & expenses:	$22,627
Average financial aid package:	$11,340
Percentage of students who sought aid and received it:	80%
Percentage of students receiving financial aid:	38%

Also Check Out

Baylor University

Texas A&M University–College Station

Texas Tech University

The University of Arizona

The University of Texas at Austin

University of Idaho

875 Perimeter Drive, PO Box 442282
Moscow, ID 83844

(208) 885-6111
http://www.uidaho.edu/

 **BIG CHOICE**

 **BIG RESEARCH**

Vandals, Greeks, and happy hellos

5 REASONS IT'S COOL

1. With eight colleges, 140 majors, and a wide range of classes, you've got **all the choices of a large state school, without the anonymity**.

2. As part of the Western Undergraduate Exchange program, residents from other western states can attend UI for a **reduced out-of-state cost**.

3. Take advantage of the many **research, internship, and work-study opportunities** at this research institution.

4. If you dream in Greek, you'll feel right at home: **Fraternities and sororities dominate** the social scene.

5. The small town of Moscow is the typical **cozy college town**.

The Basics

Public / private: public state
Total enrollment / undergrads: 11,739 / 9,127
Campus setting: small town
Students call it: UI, U of I
Students are called: Joe Vandals
Notable alums: William Agee (CEO, Bendix), Jeffery Ashby (astronaut), Carol Ryrie Brink (writer), W. Mark Felt ("Deep Throat"), Michelle Kwan (figure skater), Sarah Palin (governor, Alaska)

Middle of the Road

Neither too large nor too small, U of I offers students all the perks of a research institution without the anonymity of an ultra-large state school—and for a bargain-basement price. Students have an array of course options but can register without competing with masses. Professors are accessible and caring, and the academic atmosphere on campus is intimate and friendly. Undergrads can major in anything from agribusiness to zoology. The engineering program is strong, and students studying business can get hands-on experience managing portfolios and assessing risk in a high-tech trading room. Research and work-study opportunities are common; students in the College of Agricultural and Life Sciences (CALS), for example, give back to the state through research aimed at solving regional issues. Select students may gain admission to the Honors Program, where they are offered a diverse array of seminars, as well as free tickets to cultural activities such as film and music festivals. In general, the university accommodates

Bonjour, Hola, Guten Tag. . .

Being friendly is no problem for U of I students—in fact, it's all part of a long tradition. The so-called Hello Walk across the Administration Lawn has friends and strangers alike greeting each other with . . . you guessed it—"Hello!"

slackers and overachievers alike—students need only choose their courses accordingly. No Vandal can escape CORE requirements, which span the disciplines. The Idaho Commons lends out free laptops to students, and the library is the largest in the state.

Greeks Take Over Moscow!

Vandals live up to their party-hearty reputation, helped along by the heavy Greek presence on campus. Almost half the student body joins one of the nineteen fraternities or nine sororities, and some incoming freshmen rush the summer after their senior year of high school. Greek housing is on one side of campus and dorms are on the other. Ninety percent of freshmen live in dorms, however, so initial friendships can transcend Greek affiliation. Upperclassmen who stay on campus can opt for residence halls, apartment-style Living Learning Communities, or co-ops. Off-campus housing is available, but is a bit far away from campus. There are over 150 student organizations and a range of campus events, including concerts, film festivals, plays, and seminars. The Outdoor Program hosts a variety of instructional trips from sea kayaking on Lake Coeur d'Alene to ice climbing on Kokanee Glacier. The Palouse region is great for hiking and rafting. Plenty of students are content to hang out at the Recreation Center on campus, which houses an indoor roller-hockey rink and the tallest climbing wall in the nation. For those who are drawn to team sports, intramurals are popular, and Kibbie Dome always draws a crowd for Division I sporting events.

More than Potatoes

Most U of I students are residents of the lovely state of Idaho, so they're already familiar with the natural beauty of the place. The campus meshes well with the surrounding countryside while also offering students modern facilities such as the Idaho Commons, the heart of campus. Moscow, a tiny town of 21,000, caters entirely to the university. Bucer's Coffeehouse and Gambino's Pizza are typically filled with students, as is the local movie theater. Though it's easy to get around town without a car, most students prefer to have one for road trips. Spokane is an hour away, Seattle is five, and there are plenty of outdoor activities in close proximity to town.

Admissions

Average high school GPA:	3.36
Average freshman SAT writing / math / critical reading score:	520 / 559 / 546
Average freshman ACT score:	22
Application fee:	$40
Application deadlines: 8/1 (freshmen) continuous (transfer)	
Total applicants:	6,495
Total accepted:	3,460 (53%)
Total accepted who enrolled:	1,575
Notification dates: continuous (freshmen) continuous (transfer)	

Students

Percentage of male / female students:	55% / 45%
Percentage of students from out of state:	26%
Percentage of students graduating in 4 years / 6 years:	20% / 54%

Money

Total endowment:	$186,858,700
Total in-state tuition, fees & expenses:	$11,284
Total out-of-state tuition, fees & expenses:	$20,884
Average financial aid package:	$9,471
Percentage of students who sought aid and received it:	75%
Percentage of students receiving financial aid:	54%

Also Check Out

The University of Montana–Missoula

University of Utah

University of Wyoming

University of Illinois at Urbana-Champaign

601 East John Street
Champaign, IL 61820

(217) 333-1000
http://www.uiuc.edu/

 **BIG CHOICE**

 **BIG RESEARCH**

Big, bold, and beautiful

5 REASONS IT'S COOL

1. Illinois provides the **classic, big state school experience**.

2. Just how big is it? **Let the numbers speak for themselves: 40,000** classes, 31,000 students, 2,000 tenured faculty members, 1,000 student organizations, 270 campus buildings, and 150 majors.

3. The university enjoys a reputation for **top-notch academics, tough admissions standards, and cutting-edge research.**

4. Eighteen Pulitzer winners, eleven Nobel laureates, and six NASA astronauts can be counted among **Illinois's illustrious alumni.**

5. It's all Greek to them: Illinois is home to **the largest Greek system** in the nation.

The Basics

Public / private: public state
Total enrollment / undergrads: 42,728 / 31,472
Campus setting: urban
Students call it: Illinois, U of I, UIUC, Illini
Students are called: Fighting Illini
Notable alums: Roger Ebert (journalist), Dave Eggers (writer), Gene Hackman (actor), Hugh Heffner (entrepreneur), Ang Lee (filmmaker), Suze Orman (financial advisor, TV personality)

Super-Sized Academics

The sheer magnitude of choices puts Illinois in a league of its own. The university offers over forty thousand classes at a given time, along with 150 distinct majors. Students select their majors from among the university's undergraduate colleges, including the colleges of Liberal Arts and Sciences (the biggest), Agriculture, Applied Health Sciences, Aviation, Business, Communications, Education, Engineering, and Fine and Applied Arts. The most popular majors are engineering, business/marketing, and the social sciences. The university's top-ranked programs in agriculture draw in students wishing to cultivate careers in agriculture or the environmental sciences. Illinois's faculty members are about as illustrious a group as you're likely to find anywhere. Many have Nobel and Pulitzer prizes. The student-to-faculty ratio is 17:1. Teaching assistants are in charge of a quarter to a third of classes, and the discussions and labs they teach tend to be smaller than average-sized classes. More than a hundred study-abroad options are available, along with a vast array of research opportunities.

Quad Day

Held annually just before the fall semester begins, Quad Day brings out Illinois students in full force. Thousands of students gather on campus to survey the booths belonging to the university's thousand-plus student organizations—and to collect the free pens and Frisbees that the organizations ply them with in an attempt to entice new members. At around noon, the crowds turn toward Foellinger Auditorium for a rousing performance by the Marching Illini marching band.

Illinois's Brightest

Illinois students represent all fifty states, but the vast majority of students come from Illinois. While it's true that most students are locally produced, the campus still showcases a huge amount of diversity, and the admissions office's tough standards ensure that students are Illinois's best and brightest. Greek life is huge—in fact, Illinois is home to the nation's largest community of Greek-letter organizations, numbering ninety-six total. Over 20 percent of students participate. Greek parties tend to dominate the social scene, but the campus scene is varied enough that independent students still find plenty of social options. The university offers more than one thousand organizations, ranging from WPGU, the student radio station, to the Marching Illini, the university marching band. Sports are a big deal at this Big Ten school, arousing considerable passion during Fighting Illini football and basketball games. After all, the tradition of the homecoming football game was invented by Illinois students back in 1910.

Chambana

The Illinois campus is located in between the two cities of Champaign and Urbana, a cornfield-laden area that many students refer to simply as "Chambana." The university's sprawling main campus has 272 buildings, including the third largest university library and Assembly Hall, the world's largest edge-supported dome (and home of Fighting Illini basketball). The Siebel Center for Computer Science opened in 2004 and is packed with sensors and surveillance devices used to study communication and computation. Students head to Green Street, near campus, for shopping and a variety of dining options, while Chicago is easy three-hour's drive to the north.

Admissions

Average high school GPA:	—
Average freshman SAT verbal / math score:	608 / 678
Average freshman ACT score:	25
Application fee:	$40

Application deadlines:
1/2 (freshmen)
3/1 (transfer)

Total applicants:	22,367
Total accepted:	14,438 (65%)
Total accepted who enrolled:	7,161

Notification dates:
continuous (freshmen)
continuous (transfer)

Students

Percentage of male / female students:	53% / 47%
Percentage of students from out of state:	7%
Percentage of students graduating in 4 years / 6 years:	58% / 80%

Money

Total endowment:	$872,695,592
Total in-state tuition, fees & expenses:	$19,326
Total out-of-state tuition, fees & expenses:	$33,412
Average financial aid package:	$10,180
Percentage of students who sought aid and received it:	87%
Percentage of students receiving financial aid:	37%

Also Check Out

Northwestern University

University of Chicago

The University of Iowa

University of Michigan–Ann Arbor

University of Nebraska–Lincoln

University of Wisconsin–Madison

The University of Iowa

107 Calvin Hall, The University of Iowa
Iowa City, IA 52242

(319) 335-3500
http://www.uiowa.edu/

 **BIG CHOICE**

 **BIG RESEARCH**

Writers, scientists, athletes—keepin' 'em all happy!

5 REASONS IT'S COOL

1. **Big school. Big options. Big value.**

2. Talk about balanced: UI excels in both the sciences and the creative arts.

3. If you're an Iowa resident who ranks in the top half of your high school class, you could **qualify for guaranteed admission.**

4. Engineering students who want to start their own businesses can earn a **Technological Entrepreneurship Certificate.**

5. Go Hawkeyes! UI is a member of the **Big Ten** athletic conference.

The Basics

Public / private: public state
Total enrollment / undergrads: 28,816 / 20,738
Campus setting: small town
Students call it: UI
Students are called: Hawkeyes
Notable alums: Max A. Collins Jr. (comic strip illustrator), Rita Dove (U.S. poet laureate), George Gallup (inventor, the Gallup Poll)

Big School, Low Cost, Lotsa Choices!

From the eleven colleges at UI, close to 80 percent of students enroll in the College of Arts & Sciences, where they can choose from over a hundred majors. Psychology, communication studies, and English are among the most popular, but there are a host of well-regarded programs, including printmaking, rehabilitation counseling, speech-language pathology, and creative writing. UI comes with all the benefits and drawbacks of a large research institution. Students have unique opportunities to work with faculty on cutting-edge projects but must also expect large lectures and a certain amount of anonymity. The university has several programs in place to support students in this regard, including a course on transitioning to college and "Courses in Common," which places groups of freshmen together in the same courses. In addition, Iowa's Four-Year Graduation Plan Agreement promises that if you stay on track academically, the college will make sure to provide the classes you need to graduate. All in all, low tuition costs and stellar programs make this school a great deal.

Here's the Suit—Pass It On!

When Larry Herb, one of the early Herky the Hawkeye mascots, was dismissed from school, he passed on his Herky suit to one of his fraternity brothers and asked him to take over the mascot duties. Little did Herb know that he was starting a tradition among the Delta Tau Delta fraternity. All the brothers jumped on the privilege, and a built-in mascot pool was born. Herky (short for "Hercules") is now always portrayed by the Delta Tau Delta men.

Sports Come "First"

UI has a rich history of "firsts": It was among the first public universities to give as much attention to the arts as to scientific research, to admit male and female students equally, and to recognize a gay student union. Although UI isn't particularly diverse—minorities represent around 10 percent of the student body—increasing diversity is one of the university's top goals. About 85 percent of students are either from Iowa or from adjoining states. Students describe the atmosphere on campus as friendly, tolerant, and active—there are more than four hundred clubs on campus that cater to any interest. UI is a Big Ten school, and sports generate a lot of excitement on campus, especially football and wrestling. Intramural sports teams are also a popular option for those who want to get off the sidelines. Club sports include sailing, waterskiing, and rugby. Thirty-four fraternities and sororities draw about 1,900 students, a good showing but not enough to completely hijack campus social life.

Old Capitol in a Small City

UI is located in Iowa City, a small city of about 100,000. The lovely campus is home to the original state capitol building, built back in the days when Iowa City was the state capital. The historic center of the campus is the Pentacrest, a central green space featuring five of the university's main buildings. While UI is the smallest of the Big Ten group of public universities, plans for growth are in the works. Buildings devoted to liberal arts and public health are slated for construction, and work on a new, much-needed campus recreation center is nearing completion. And students can now cheer in style—renovation was recently completed on Kinnick Stadium, home of the Hawkeyes. Cedar Rapids, Iowa's second largest city, lies about twenty miles north.

Admissions

Average high school GPA:	3.56
Average freshman SAT verbal / math score:	584 / 607
Average freshman ACT score:	24
Application fee:	$40
Application deadlines:	
4/1 (freshmen)	
4/1 (transfer)	
Total applicants:	14,350
Total accepted:	11,880 (83%)
Total accepted who enrolled:	4,256
Notification dates:	
continuous (freshmen)	
continuous (transfer)	

Students

Percentage of male / female students:	47% / 53%
Percentage of students from out of state:	32%
Percentage of students graduating in 4 years / 6 years:	38% / 66%

Money

Total endowment:	$343,142,494
Total in-state tuition, fees & expenses:	$6,293
Total out-of-state tuition, fees & expenses:	$19,465
Average financial aid package:	$7,480
Percentage of students who sought aid and received it:	97%
Percentage of students receiving financial aid:	45%

Also Check Out

The Ohio State University

Texas A&M University–College Station

University of Kansas

University of Missouri–Columbia

University of Kansas

KU Visitor Center, I502 Iowa
Lawrence, KS 66045

(785) 864-2700
http://www.ku.edu

 **BIG CHOICE**

 **BIG RESEARCH**

Beautiful setting, top-notch academics, bargain-basement price

5 REASONS IT'S COOL

1. You'll be at the top of the world, *literally*. KU's **campus is perched high atop Mt. Oread.** Sure it's a hike to get to, but students know it's worth it.

2. With eleven colleges and 190 majors, you'll have academic choices galore.

3. What a steal: KU pairs **low tuition costs with top-notch academics.**

4. **"Rock chalk, Jayhawk, KU!"** The university's chant is one of the country's most famous college yells.

5. There's a reason the **Division I basketball team is so good:** The school's first basketball coach was James A. Naismith—the inventor of the game.

The Basics

Public / private: public state
Total enrollment / undergrads: 28,924 / 21,353
Campus setting: suburban
Students call it: KU, Kansas
Call the students: Jayhawks
Notable alums: Etta Moten Barnett (actress, singer), Wilt Chamberlain (pro basketball player), David Dillon (CEO, Kroger Co.), Bob Dole (senator), Nancy Landon Kassebaum (governor, Kansas), Paul Rudd (actor)

Any of These 190 Majors Will Do

With eleven colleges and 190 majors, KU students have plenty of options. Architecture, engineering, fine arts, and social welfare are some of the strongest programs, but academics get high marks across the board. Classes can be large, but most are kept under forty students, especially at the upper level. Students have nothing but praise for the dynamic and knowledgeable faculty. Students in the top-notch Honors Program work hard and get to enjoy perks like priority registration and small classes. Incoming students can apply directly to the school of their choice, though it isn't required. Most enroll in the College of Liberal Arts & Sciences and must complete a fairly hefty set of core requirements, including courses in both Western and non-Western civilization. KU is a major research institution, and the Lawrence campus teems with research activity. Teamed with faculty mentors, undergraduates have the chance to participate in trailblazing research.

How to Become a Jayhawk

If you have family who went to KU, you might be asked to receive the symbolic "torch of knowledge" on Traditions Night at the start of your freshman year. During this annual event, upperclassmen pass the symbolic torch of knowledge to a group of freshmen representatives, at least one of whom tends to have a long family legacy at KU. The torch passing is just one aspect of Traditions Night, when new KU students are indoctrinated into all things Jayhawk.

Big in Every Way

Lots of things are "big" at KU: most notably, basketball. Students at this Big 12 school go crazy for the Division I Jayhawks, shouting the famous Rock Chalk chant, much to the dismay of opposing teams. Also big are the fraternities and sororities—more than 3,500 students participate in forty Greek organizations. If you want a close-knit group without going Greek, look into Scholarship Halls, KU's unique cooperative living programs. Each "school hall" houses around fifty students and offers organized social activities, a unique identity, and experience living in a cooperative environment. In all, students are happy, healthy, and full of love for their school. While there's a decent-sized international population on campus, the university isn't known for its diversity. One-fourth of Jayhawks take flight in search of other cultures—KU encourages overseas study and has study-abroad programs in over sixty countries.

Isn't Kansas Supposed to Be Flat?

Lawrence, KU's home, is a small, welcoming city that caters to college students. Students flock to the restaurants, music venues, and coffee shops lining Massachusetts Avenue, also known as "Mass." One of the first things you'll learn at KU is that not *all* of Kansas is flat. The university sits atop Mount Oread, which overlooks the Kansas and Wakarusa rivers. The campus's stately, red-roofed buildings are spread over a thousand acres on or around Mt. Oread. A number of architectural beauties grace the campus, including the Campanile, a bell tower that honors those lost in World War II. And don't be fooled if someone asks you to hang out on "the beach." They're likely referring to the plaza outside Wescoe Hall, not the banks of nearby Clinton Lake. Travel to and from Lawrence is easy—the airport in Kansas City is an hour drive, and Topeka is only thirty minutes away.

Admissions

Average high school GPA:	3.43
Average freshman SAT verbal / math score:	— / —
Average freshman ACT score:	24
Application fee:	$30
Application deadlines:	
4/1 (freshmen)	
5/1 (transfer)	
Total applicants:	10,240
Total accepted:	7,874 (77%)
Total accepted who enrolled:	4,094
Notification dates:	
continuous (freshmen)	
continuous (transfer)	

Students

Percentage of male / female students:	50% / 50%
Percentage of students from out of state:	26%
Percentage of students graduating in 4 years / 6 years:	26% / 57%

Money

Total endowment:	$1,400,000,000
Total in-state tuition, fees & expenses:	$12,650
Total out-of-state tuition, fees & expenses:	$21,620
Average financial aid package:	$7,594
Percentage of students who sought aid and received it:	70%
Percentage of students receiving financial aid:	33%

Also Check Out

University of Illinois at Urbana–Champaign

The University of Iowa

University of Missouri–Columbia

University of Nebraska–Lincoln

University of Oklahoma

University of Kentucky

100 W.D. Funkhouser Building, University of Kentucky	(859) 257-9000
Lexington, KY 40506	http://www.uky.edu/

BIG CHOICE

See blue in everything you do.

5 REASONS IT'S COOL

1. Looking for that **big public university** experience? Have we got a school for you.

2. The **academic choices are astounding**: We're talking ten different undergraduate colleges and ninety-three majors.

3. After a **$58 million renovation,** the library stacks up well.

4. Go Blue! **Sports and school spirit** are the names of the game here.

5. Like horses? Lexington is a midsized city in the heart of **Kentucky's Bluegrass Region**, which means plenty equestrian activities.

The Basics

Public / private: public state
Total enrollment / undergrads: 26,382 / 19,292
Campus setting: urban
Students call it: UK
Call the students: Wildcats
Notable alums: Sam Abell (photographer), J. B. Holmes (pro golfer), Ashley Judd (actress), William Lipscomb (Nobel Laureate, Chemistry)

Eyes on the Future

UK is a big school, and classes—especially introductory courses—tend to run on the large side. Still, the university makes an effort to keep class sizes manageable, and the average size overall is twenty-four students. The university offers over ninety majors through its ten undergraduate colleges. These colleges include those of arts and sciences, business, communications, education, engineering, social work, fine arts, public health, health sciences, and design. The Discovery Seminar Program provides small, entry-level courses for freshmen. The university offers a number of summer enrichment opportunities, including Bucks for Brains, a program that provides students with hands-on-experience *and* a stipend. During Winter Intersession, a short period between fall and spring semester, students have the opportunity to study one topic intensively. The recently completed James W. Stuckert Career Center is a popular destination for soon-to-be-grads; its new database connects students to more than 4.5 million jobs.

A Little More Bacon, Please

Every finals week, exhausted and hungry students head over to Memorial Coliseum for UK's annual Crunch Brunch. On one night only from 9 P.M. to midnight, professors and administrators serve students a free late-night breakfast. The event also includes massages, games, and other activities to help ease students' stress.

Frats R Us

If you're looking for a large state school with a strong Greek system, school spirit, and a love of the game, UK fits the bill. The university is Kentucky's largest, and the vast majority of students are Kentucky born and bred. Greeks are top dogs here, and about one-fifth of students join one of the twenty-five fraternities and seventeen sororities. While partying is a popular pastime, it's worth mentioning that UK is one of just a handful of universities whose Greek houses are officially dry. For those who opt out of the Greek scene, the university offers more than twenty dorms, as well as living-learning communities that connect students with shared interests. The Wildcats are intense about their basketball and football teams, and fans turn "blue" in support. But you won't see a live mascot at any of the games: The real UK wildcat, a bobcat, lives exclusively at the campus's Salato Wildlife Education Center.

Big Blue Barn Art

The UK campus is made up of the North, South, and Central campuses. North campus is home to classroom buildings and provides easy access to downtown Lexington, South campus is close to athletic facilities, and Central campus houses the dining hall, the K-Lair Grill. Lexington is a midsized city with a vibrant downtown that's also home to neighboring Transylvania University. The larger cities of Cincinnati and Louisville are each about an hour and a half away. While driving, you may notice that Wildcat loyalty runs true blue throughout central Kentucky: Just look for the UK logo and messages like "Go Big Blue!" painted on barns and silos throughout the region.

Admissions

Average high school GPA:	3.48
Average freshman SAT verbal / math score:	560 / 574
Average freshman ACT score:	24
Application fee:	$40
Application deadlines: 2/15 (freshmen) 8/1 (transfer)	
Total applicants:	10,024
Total accepted:	8,073 (81%)
Total accepted who enrolled:	4,118
Notification dates: continuous (freshmen) continuous (transfer)	

Students

Percentage of male / female students:	48% / 52%
Percentage of students from out of state:	17%
Percentage of students graduating in 4 years / 6 years:	29% / 60%

Money

Total endowment:	$538,384,000
Total in-state tuition, fees & expenses:	$15,066
Total out-of-state tuition, fees & expenses:	$22,866
Average financial aid package:	$7,861
Percentage of students who sought aid and received it:	81%
Percentage of students receiving financial aid:	34%

Also Check Out

Indiana University–Bloomington

University of Alabama–Tuscaloosa

University of Florida

University of Georgia

The University of Mississippi

The University of Tennessee

University of Maine–Orono

5713 Chadbourne Hall
Orono, ME 04469

(207) 581-1110
http://www.umaine.edu/

 **BIG CHOICE**

 **BIG RESEARCH**

Ready for Maine's main event?

5 REASONS IT'S COOL

1. UMaine is known as **one of the best deals in higher education.**

2. The university boasts **top-rated programs in engineering and business** (just to name a few).

3. Students take advantage of **250 student organizations,** forty honor societies, eighty-eight majors, and the state's largest library.

4. Outdoorsy types choose from **programs in agriculture and forestry.** And when they're not studying, there are plenty of outdoor opportunities.

5. **Stephen King went here.** And his writing professors are still scared stiff.

The Basics

Public / private: public state
Total enrollment / undergrads: 11,435 / 9,179
Campus setting: small town
Students call it: UMaine, UM Orono
Students are called: Black Bears
Notable alums: Stephen King (novelist), John Baldacci (governor, Maine), Lawrence Bender (filmmaker), Olympia Snowe (senator)

Calling All Stephen King Wannabees!

UMaine is Maine's best deal in higher education. The university's eighty-eight majors are distributed across five undergraduate colleges of liberal arts and sciences; engineering; education; business, public policy, and health; and natural sciences, forestry, and agriculture. The most popular majors include business administration, engineering, education, forestry, and agriculture. There are also a number of more specialized academic offerings, including programs in wood science, aquaculture, and sustainable agriculture. The university's engineering school has long been a standout in environmental engineering research and training, and the business school provides a full range of business majors, including management, marketing, accounting, and international business. The university's Fogler Library is the largest in Maine. In addition to its millions of books and periodicals, the library is home to the collected papers of Stephen King.

Rockin' the Charts

The official song of UMaine, the "Stein Song," holds an unusual distinction: It is the only college fight song to have reached the number one spot on the pop charts. The song achieved this distinction in 1930 when it was recorded by the popular singer Rudy Vallee, who attended Maine from 1921 to 1922.

Maine-centric

UMaine is a pretty Maine-centric place: About 85 percent of students hail from Maine, and the majority of those who don't come from other states in the Northeast. The university offers more than 250 student organizations, including student government, Outing Club, Volunteers in Community Efforts (VOICE), Circle K, and the student-run newspaper and radio station. Greek life is a popular (though not dominating) presence on campus, and fewer than 10 percent of students participate in the university's twenty-two fraternities and sororities. The newest center of student life is the 87,000-square-foot recreation center, which features basketball, volleyball, and racquetball courts, a fitness center, pool, and more. The university offers seventeen Division I varsity sports teams, including a popular men's hockey program.

Bangor, Bogs, and More

UMaine, the flagship of the seven-member University of Maine system, is located in the town of Orono, about eight miles north of Bangor. The university's 660-acre main campus is home to more than two hundred buildings. The Bangor City Forest and other nearby parks, forests, and waterways offer outdoorsy types endless opportunities for hiking, sailing, canoeing, hunting, fishing, skiing, and snowmobiling. The Orono Bog Boardwalk, located near the campus, is a regional destination for nature lovers. Bangor, the third-largest city in the state, is situated about 250 miles north of Boston and 300 miles from Montreal. The city offers attractions such as the Bangor Symphony Orchestra, free summer concerts by the Bangor Band, and the historic Bangor Opera House.

Admissions

Average high school GPA:	3.25
Average freshman SAT verbal / math score:	548 / 553
Average freshman ACT score:	22
Application fee:	$40
Application deadlines: continuous (freshmen) continuous (transfer)	
Total applicants:	5,702
Total accepted:	4,580 (80%)
Total accepted who enrolled:	1,736
Notification dates: continuous (freshmen) 1/15 (transfer)	

Students

Percentage of male / female students:	51% / 49%
Percentage of students from out of state:	13%
Percentage of students graduating in 4 years / 6 years:	28% / 53%

Money

Total endowment:	$159,576,000
Total in-state tuition, fees & expenses:	$14,589
Total out-of-state tuition, fees & expenses:	$25,539
Average financial aid package:	$10,946
Percentage of students who sought aid and received it:	89%
Percentage of students receiving financial aid:	54%

Also Check Out

University of Connecticut

University of Delaware

University of Massachusetts Amherst

University of New Hampshire

University of Vermont

University of Maryland–College Park

Mitchell Building
College Park, MD 20742

(301) 405-1000
http://www.maryland.edu/

 **BIG CHOICE**

 **BIG RESEARCH**

Good school, good times, good location

5 REASONS IT'S COOL

1. **Big school, big diversity, big choices:** There's something for everyone at Maryland.

2. Dream of breaking the next big story for the *Washington Post*? Maryland's top-ranked Philip Merrill College of Journalism is a **perfect training ground for aspiring journalists.**

3. Get some **personal attention through several honors programs.**

4. **Sports fever runs high** on this super-spirited campus, where football games are so popular that fans get tickets by lottery.

5. Maryland's just a short **train ride away from Washington, D.C.**

The Basics

Public / private: public state
Total enrollment / undergrads: 35,300 / 25,373
Campus setting: suburban
Students call it: Maryland, UM
Students are called: Terrapins
Notable alums: Connie Chung (news anchor), Jim Henson (creator, the Muppets), Steny Hoyer (congressman), Kathleen Turner (actress)

Lots of People, Lots of Classes

Maryland is a big school, and the wide range of classes offered reflects its immense size. Classes run the gamut from interdisciplinary programs in soil, water, and land resources to lesbian, gay, bisexual, and transgender studies—and just about every subject in between. Maryland's core requirement means that students devote about one-third of all classes to fulfilling general requirements in areas such as writing, math, and cultural diversity. Engineering, business, and journalism are among the most well-regarded and popular majors. While minors aren't offered, many students choose two majors and pick up a certificate along the way. Students can complement their classes with internships in nearby cities or study abroad through Maryland's programs in places such as Australia, Denmark, and Sweden. With 22,000 undergraduate students and lots of large lecture classes, it can be easy to go unnoticed. For the extra-high achievers, there's an invitational Gemstone program, which allows students to conduct four-year science, technology, or societal research projects that culminate in a team thesis defense before a panel of experts.

On the Lines of Fire

In 1912, a fire started in the administration building, swept through campus, and went on to destroy most of Maryland's academic buildings. Students insisted on continuing classes. Today, a large brick compass marks the remains of the former campus, with lines indicating the old buildings. A campus legend has it that if a student steps on the intersecting lines, he or she won't graduate within four years.

Good Sports

Sports are a big deal at Maryland, and most students channel their school spirit into cheering on the Terps's Division I football and basketball teams. The university's athletic facilities are top-notch: The campus pools are heated, and underwater speakers play music from local radio stations. Dining halls are open late and provide a variety of options, both healthy and decidedly less so. Although less than 35 percent of undergrads live on campus, demand is high for on-campus rooms and only freshman are guaranteed a spot. There's a healthy Greek scene, with around 11 percent of men and women joining frats and sororities, but it doesn't shape the tenor of social life. Maryland also hosts popular yearly events such as Art Attack, which brings local artists to campus to perform and display their work. This daylong event includes moon bounces and performances from top bands such as the Black Eyed Peas and Outkast.

Good Ole College Park

Entering the main archway onto the central grounds of Maryland's campus, one passes a huge M made up of flowers (pansies in the fall, annuals in the spring) atop a grassy knoll. This is the center of campus, where recreational fields and oak trees set off stately redbrick Georgian architecture. A newly renovated student union building (complete with pool hall, bowling alley, and movie theater) is just a short walk from the main campus library, McKeldin. The campus's tree-lined mall is the largest college mall in the nation. Although students find the surrounding College Park area slightly sketchy at times, most appreciate the shops, bars, and restaurants along the main road, Route 1. Other universities, including Johns Hopkins (in Baltimore) and Georgetown and George Washington (in Washington, D.C.), are short train rides away.

Admissions

Average high school GPA:	3.86
Average freshman SAT verbal / math score:	628 / 655
Average freshman ACT score:	—
Application fee:	$55
Application deadlines: 1/20 (freshmen) 7/1 (transfer) 12/1 (early action)	
Total applicants:	22,428
Total accepted:	11,002 (49%)
Total accepted who enrolled:	4,198
Notification dates: 4/1 (freshmen) continuous (transfer) 2/15 (early action)	
Acceptance rate for early action applicants:	55%

Students

Percentage of male / female students:	51% / 49%
Percentage of students from out of state:	24%
Percentage of students graduating in 4 years / 6 years:	50% / 76%

Money

Total endowment:	$329,359,567
Total in-state tuition, fees & expenses:	$17,237
Total out-of-state tuition, fees & expenses:	$30,676
Average financial aid package:	$10,722
Percentage of students who sought aid and received it:	67%
Percentage of students receiving financial aid:	34%

Also Check Out

The Pennsylvania State University–University Park

Towson University

University of Delaware

Virginia Polytechnic Institute and State University

University of Massachusetts Amherst

Mather Building, 37 Mather Drive
Amherst, MA 01003

(413) 545-0111
http://www.umass.edu/

 **BIG CHOICE**

 **BIG RESEARCH**

Where size *does* matter

5 REASONS IT'S COOL

1. *Enormous* doesn't even begin to describe UMass. We're talking twenty thousand students, eighty-plus majors, and research facilities that rake in more than $100 million.

2. As part of the **Five Colleges Consortium**, UMass students can enroll in classes at nearby colleges for no extra charge.

3. They don't call it "ZooMass" for nothing. **Students here love to have a good time.**

4. The campus's W. E. B. DuBois library is the **tallest library building in the United States.**

5. Amherst is a **charming college town** that offers plenty of outdoorsy activities.

The Basics

Public / private: public state
Total enrollment / undergrads: 25,593 / 19,823
Campus setting: small town
Students call it: UMass, UMass Amherst, ZooMass
Students are called: Minutemen
Notable alums: Rob Corddry (comedian, writer), Julius "Dr. J" Erving (pro basketball player), Fardeen Khan (actress), Taj Mahal (musician), Jeff Taylor (founder, Monster.com), Paul Theroux (writer), Jack Welch (CEO, General Electric)

Endless Options, Endless Opportunities

UMass Amherst is the flagship university in the the University of Massachusetts system. With more than nineteen thousand undergraduates, it's also the largest university in the state. The university offers more than eighty majors through nine undergraduate colleges of humanities, natural sciences and mathematics, agriculture, environment, management, engineering, public health, social and behavioral sciences, and nursing. The most prestigious and popular majors include psychology, communications, business, and music. Students also have the option of taking classes for no extra cost at neighboring colleges Amherst, Hampshire, Mount Holyoke, and Smith through the Five Colleges Consortium. The university's top-rated honors college, Commonwealth College (ComCol), offers smaller, more intensive classes and other small-college benefits to qualifying students. The study-abroad office offers opportunities on six continents,

Leading Research by a Nose

UMass is home to some of the country's most cutting-edge research. The research projects currently taking shape on campus include investigating the Geobacter microbe, developing new and improved methods of using articifial intelligence, and constructing the world's most sensitive radio telescope. One research team has recently developed a molecular nose that can detect the malformed proteins made by cancer cells. Now that's nothing to sniff at!

including far-flung destinations such as China, Ecuador, Egypt, and Senegal.

Living Large

UMass has earned the nickname "ZooMass" for its many parties. And while parties are a big deal (aided in no small part by the thirty-plus fraternities and sororities), the university is large enough that non-partiers will also find a place in the social scene. The university offers a huge array of student organizations, including the Student Government Association (SGA), the Minuteman Marching Band, and student-interest groups ranging from a chapter of the Audio Engineering Society to a club for gaming enthusiasts. The *Daily Collegian*, the student-run university newspaper, is known for its editorial independence from the university's administration. UMass is an NCAA Division I institution and a member of the NCAA's Atlantic Ten Conference (except for ice hockey, which plays in the Hockey East Association, and football, which plays in the Colonial Athletic Association). Athletes choose from ten men's and ten women's intercollegiate sports and a wide selection of club sports.

Lovely Western Mass

UMass is located in the town of Amherst in western Massachusetts. The university's huge campus sprawls across 1,450 acres. The *New York Times* has called Amherst one of the country's "ten best college towns." The area offers film, dance, theater, music venues, and art galleries, along with plenty of opportunities for hiking, skiing, and camping in the nearby Berkshires and Green mountains. An extensive free bus service allows students to easily travel to and from nearby colleges in the Five Colleges Consortium. Amherst is situated about 20 miles from Springfield, less than 100 miles from Boston, 175 miles from New York City, and about 30 miles form the Vermont and New Hampshire state lines.

Admissions

Average high school GPA:	3.46
Average freshman SAT verbal / math score:	570 / 586
Average freshman ACT score:	—
Application fee:	$40

Application deadlines:
1/15 (freshmen)
4/15 (transfer)
11/1 (early action)

Total applicants:	22,451
Total accepted:	15,941 (71%)
Total accepted who enrolled:	4,230

Notification dates:
continuous (freshmen)
continuous (transfer)
12/15 (early action)

Acceptance rate for early action applicants:	—

Students

Percentage of male / female students:	51% / 49%
Percentage of students from out of state:	18%
Percentage of students graduating in 4 years / 6 years:	45% / 66%

Money

Total endowment:	$91,248,247
Total in-state tuition, fees & expenses:	$17,584
Total out-of-state tuition, fees & expenses:	$25,807
Average financial aid package:	$11,265
Percentage of students who sought aid and received it:	87%
Percentage of students receiving financial aid:	45%

Also Check Out

University of Connecticut

University of Delaware

University of New Hampshire

University of Pennsylvania

University of Vermont

The University of Miami

PO Box 248025
Coral Gables, FL 33124

(305) 284-2211
http://www.miami.edu/

 **BIG CHOICE**

 **BIG RESEARCH**

Head down to Hurricane central!

5 REASONS IT'S COOL

1. UM has an **embarrassment of academic riches**: Students choose from 180 majors, 250 student organizations, and $270 million in sponsored research projects.

2. Future entrepreneurs and corporate types learn the ropes at the first-rate **School of Business Administration.**

3. Future oceanographers get their feet wet at the renowned **Rosenstiel School of Marine and Atmospheric Science.**

4. Students' passions for **Hurricanes sports teams** often reach Category Five.

5. It's in **Miami.** OK, technically it's right outside of Miami. But you get the idea.

The Basics

Public / private: private nonprofit
Total enrollment / undergrads: 15,670 / 10,509
Campus setting: suburban
Students call it: Miami, UM
Students are called: 'Canes
Notable alums: Vincent Bugliosi (author, attorney), Gloria Estefan (singer), Ben Folds (singer-songwriter), Enrique Iglesias (singer), Duane "The Rock" Johnson (actor, pro wrestler), Sylvester Stallone (actor)

Workin' Your Tan Off

Slackers and beach bums may be in for an unpleasant surprise: UM enjoys a reputation as a top-flight academic institution. The university offers 180 majors in its eight undergraduate colleges of arts and sciences, business, education, nursing, architecture, music, communication, and engineering. Pre-professional tracks are very popular here, and the excellent undergraduate marine science program benefits from close proximity to the ocean. Dual undergraduate/graduate degree programs are offered in a number of areas, including medicine, law, business, physical therapy, and biomedical engineering. UM's Music Department offers a quality jazz program and a unique music engineering major, and the business and communication schools have benefited from recent investments in facilities. Students can take advantage of a wide range of internships, study-abroad options, and other out-side-of-the-classroom opportunities. UM professors come armed with awards from institutions like the National Science Foundation and the

Secret Agent Orange

UM's campus may appear to be the very picture of the relaxed south Florida lifestyle, but there's actually much more to it than meets the eye. A certain building on the university's south campus, about twelve miles away from the main campus, once served as an important CIA base for covert operations to overthrow Fidel Castro's administration. The station was the largest employer of agents outside of CIA headquarters in Virginia.

American Academy for Arts and Sciences. The student-to-faculty ratio is 13:1, although larger departments offer less personal attention.

Tropical Matters

UM's student body is the picture of diversity. Hispanic enrollment hovers near 30 percent, while African Americans and Asians also make up sizeable percentages. The university also enjoys a considerable amount of geographic diversity, with nearly 50 percent of students coming from out of state. Designer labels and high-end beachwear are common sights on this always-sunny campus. Freshmen are assigned to one of five coed residential colleges, where they join senior faculty members for regular events and a monthly dinner. Upperclassmen may choose to live in the new University Village apartment complex. 'Canes football reigns supreme when it comes to athletics, though baseball, basketball, tennis, and track and field are also popular. The state-of-the-art Wellness Center recently received a $14 million facelift, all the better to help students stay in beach-worthy shape.

Miami Vices

UM is located in Coral Gables, a suburb that's within easy reach of downtown Miami, club-hub South Beach, and the retail-mecca Coconut Grove. UM's 230-acre campus is home to palm-lined walkways and attractive buildings including the Lowe Art Museum and Gusman Concert Hall. Nature lovers can explore the campus's Ibis Nature Walk and Lake Osceola. Just a few blocks away lies Sunset Place, a popular dining and shopping strip. Nearby attractions include the Everglades National Park, a coral reef, and world-famous zoos and aquariums.

Admissions

Average high school GPA:	—
Average freshman SAT writing / math / critical reading score:	605 / 647 / 629
Average freshman ACT score:	26
Application fee:	$65

Application deadlines:
2/1 (freshmen)	11/1 (early decision)
3/1 (transfer)	11/1 (early action)

Total applicants:	19,037
Total accepted:	7,709 (40%)
Total accepted who enrolled:	2,047

Notification dates:
4/15 (freshmen)
4/15 (transfer)
12/15 (early decision)
2/1 (early action)

Acceptance rate for early action/early decision applicants:	62% / 47%

Students

Percentage of male / female students:	45% / 55%
Percentage of students from out of state:	48%
Percentage of students graduating in 4 years / 6 years:	56% / 71%

Money

Total endowment:	$620,500,000
Total tuition:	$32,422
Total cost with fees & expenses:	$42,676
Average financial aid package:	$25,088
Percentage of students who sought aid and received it:	79%
Percentage of students receiving financial aid:	46%

Also Check Out

Boston University

Duke University

New York University

University of Florida

University of Southern California

University of Michigan– Ann Arbor

1220 Student Activities Building
515 E. Jefferson
Ann Arbor, MI 48109

(734) 764-1817
http://www.umich.edu/

 **BIG CHOICE**

 **BIG RESEARCH**

We're talking big—*really* big.

5 REASONS IT'S COOL

1. **The academic options are practically unlimited:** We're talking 225 undergraduate majors with additional specialized concentrations.

2. Got a passion for all things Persian? Always wanted a degree in Armenian? Michigan offers lots of **rare and specialized majors.**

3. Michigan boasts **one of the most diverse student populations in the nation.**

4. This school is **big on sports.** The university's stadium, appropriately named the Big House, holds over 107,000 fans and is the largest football stadium in the country.

5. You'll never be bored in Ann Arbor, one of the country's **truly great college towns.**

The Basics

Public / private: public state
Total enrollment / undergrads: 40,025 / 25,555
Campus setting: suburban
Students call it: Michigan, U of M, UM
Students are called: Wolverines
Notable alums: Dan Dierdorf (pro football player), Gerald Ford (U.S. president), Lucy Liu (actor), Arthur Miller (playwright), Gilda Radner (actor)

From African Studies to Zoology

One of the most prestigious public universities in the country, Michigan comprises eleven undergraduate schools, including the College of Literature, Science, and the Arts (LSA), the College of Engineering, and the School of Music. Core requirements for all students are sprinkled across the foreign languages, natural and social sciences, English, and the humanities, while LSA students have additional requirements in quantitative reasoning and a class in race or ethnicity. Popular majors include economics, English, and mechanical engineering. Students interested in interdisciplinary topics should look into the Residential College program, in which groups of about fifteen students live together, take smaller, seminar-style classes, and enjoy active and engaged learning. All students are eligible for the university's Undergraduate Research Opportunities Program, which provides summer fellowships, faculty and peer mentors, and residential learning community options for students with a drive to create their own projects. Michigan boasts funding and facilities for original research in

Watch Your Step

The bronze-plated M seal surrounded by a circle at the center of the Diag is touchy territory. Student legend has it that walking over the seal on the way to an exam dooms your chances of passing.

the areas of computer science, math, and engineering, and it also has special grants designed for those in the arts and social sciences.

Big Ten Living

Michigan is a member of the Big Ten, the oldest Division I athletic conference. Sports are a big deal for many students, and school spirit runs high. Greek life is also healthy, attracting around 15 percent of the student body, but the scene can be exclusive: Only fraternity or sorority members may attend Greek parties unless arrangements are made beforehand. The campus's Hill Auditorium hosts a huge variety of performances, including groups and entertainers such as the Vienna Philharmonic, the Lincoln Center Jazz Orchestra, and Yo-Yo Ma. The university and the surrounding town enjoy a good relationship, and the majority of Michigan students live off campus in surrounding neighborhoods. The ten dining halls on campus offer everything edible under the sun, including Kosher and vegetarian options. Minority students now make up a quarter of the total undergraduate enrollment, and students hail from far and wide, including every corner of the country and over 100 foreign countries.

Diagonal Dreams

Michigan's campus is split into two main parts, the Central Campus and the North Campus. The latter includes the engineering, art, music, and architecture schools, while the rest of campus life tends to center around the Central Campus. The Diag, which earns its nickname because of its many diagonal pathways, is a large open space surrounded by classroom buildings. It's the most popular daytime hangout on campus and a prime congregation spot for campus demonstrations. The oldest buildings on the Central Campus are predominately classical or Gothic in style, and the North Campus trends toward the modern, although Michigan is home to more than five hundred major buildings representing a cross-section of architectural styles. Bell towers on each division of campus mirror the contrasting architectural styles. Detroit is the closest big city at forty miles away, and Cincinnati, Chicago, and Toronto are all within four hours.

Admissions

Average high school GPA:	3.75
Average freshman SAT verbal / math score:	637 / 677
Average freshman ACT score:	26
Application fee:	$40
Application deadlines:	
2/1 (freshmen)	
3/1 (transfer)	
Total applicants:	25,806
Total accepted:	12,246 (47%)
Total accepted who enrolled:	5,033
Notification dates:	
4/1 (freshmen)	
4/1 (transfer)	

Students

Percentage of male / female students:	50% / 50%
Percentage of students from out of state:	31%
Percentage of students graduating in 4 years / 6 years:	67% / 87%

Money

Total endowment:	$4,294,967,295
Total in-state tuition, fees & expenses:	$18,638
Total out-of-state tuition, fees & expenses:	$37,410
Average financial aid package:	$11,111
Percentage of students who sought aid and received it:	90%
Percentage of students receiving financial aid:	45%

Also Check Out

Duke University

Michigan State University

New York University

Northwestern University

University of Wisconsin–Madison

Washington University in St. Louis

University of Minnesota– Twin Cities

100 Church Street, SE
Minneapolis, MN 55455

(612) 625-5000
http://www.umn.edu/tc/

 **BIG CHOICE**

 **BIG RESEARCH**

Big, cold, and sporty

5 REASONS IT'S COOL

1. You'll be **spoiled for choice:** U of M has 148 majors, six hundred student groups, and fourteen libraries.

2. The **Undergraduate Research Opportunities Program** provides research funding to about five hundred undergrads.

3. **Service learning courses** are offered by forty academic departments, and students can receive academic recognition for public service through the new Community Engagement Scholars Program.

4. U of M is a Big Ten school, which means **big time fun for sports fans.**

5. Sure it's cold, but the Twin Cities are **home to a cool culture scene.**

The Basics

Public / private: public state
Total enrollment / undergrads: 50,402 / 32,113
Campus setting: urban
Students call it: U of M
Students are called: Golden Gophers
Notable alums: Norman Borlaug (Nobel Laureate, Peace), Garrison Keillor (writer, humorist), Walter Mondale (U.S. vice president), Patricia Schroeder (congresswoman)

A Behemoth by Any Standard

With almost 32,000 undergraduates and a number of top-ranked departments, the University of Minnesota is a behemoth by any standard—its students make up the fourth-largest student body in the United States. The university comprises sixteen colleges and offers 148 majors. Three new colleges of agriculture, design, and education help meet the growing demand for multidisciplinary research. All U of M students must fulfill of a set of core requirements, which generally include twenty-nine credits in the sciences, humanities, social sciences, and diversity, along with extra writing courses completed within a student's major. Social sciences, engineering, and business are the most popular majors, and some unique offerings include youth studies, sports studies, and mortuary science, to name just a few. The university is known for its commitment to research, and faculty members have done groundbreaking work, including developing the K ration and performing the first bone marrow transplant.

Yay, Rah-Rah, Gophers!

U of M is known around the world for important contributions in various fields of research, but the university's most important contribution may well be in an entirely different type of field. In 1898, U of M student Johnny Campbell invented cheerleading. Campbell, inspired by a university newspaper article lamenting the lack of enthusiasm at games, organized "yell leaders" to guide and organize the crowd cheers during a game against Northwestern. Minnesota won the game, and the rest is history.

Getting to Snow Each Other Better

While generalizing about a student population this huge is difficult, it's safe to say that U and M students are by and large a friendly bunch. The overwhelming majority of students are white, but economic diversity and an international student population mix things up considerably. Between 10 and 20 percent of students go Greek. Cheering the Gophers sports teams, especially the hockey, basketball, and football teams, is probably the most popular campus pastime. On-campus freshman housing (guaranteed for those who apply by the deadline) goes a long way toward making the university seem smaller than it actually is, and dorms provide all the amenities—including computer labs, pool tables, kitchens, and videogame systems. After freshman year, most students move off campus into the surrounding neighborhoods, where there are plenty of housing options. As befitting the local climate, "Snow Week" is a popular six-day campus event packed with dog-sledding rides, ice sculpting, cross-country skiing, and other wintry events.

A River Runs Through It

The U of M campus stretches far and wide, covering almost three thousand acres of land around the state's capital city, St. Paul, and its sister city, Minneapolis. The Mississippi River flows through the campus, dividing the main area of campus, the East Bank, from the other section, the West Bank. Students travel between the two sections either by the free shuttle service or on foot. Because weather conditions can get pretty rough in the winter months, the campus's major academic buildings are linked by underground tunnels, and the East and West Banks are joined by an enclosed walkway on the Washington Avenue Bridge. Architectural styles run the gamut from Pillsbury Hall, the second-oldest building on campus complete with decorative gargoyles, to the sleek, Frank Gehry–designed Weisman Art Museum. Off-campus activities are plentiful in this major metropolis and include the Guthrie Theatre and the Minneapolis Institute of Art.

Admissions

Average high school GPA:	—
Average freshman SAT verbal / math score:	605 / 637
Average freshman ACT score:	24
Application fee:	$45
Application deadlines:	
continuous (freshmen)	
continuous (transfer)	
Total applicants:	24,660
Total accepted:	14,165 (57%)
Total accepted who enrolled:	5,424
Notification dates:	
continuous (freshmen)	
continuous (transfer)	

Students

Percentage of male / female students:	47% / 53%
Percentage of students from out of state:	27%
Percentage of students graduating in 4 years / 6 years:	32% / 61%

Money

Total endowment:	—
Total in-state tuition, fees & expenses:	$17,069
Total out-of-state tuition, fees & expenses:	$28,699
Average financial aid package:	$11,969
Percentage of students who sought aid and received it:	85%
Percentage of students receiving financial aid:	39%

Also Check Out

Northwestern University

University of Michigan–Ann Arbor

University of Wisconsin–Madison

The University of Mississippi

145 Martindale University, MS 38677	(662) 915-7211 http://www.olemiss.edu/

 **BIG CHOICE**    **BIG RESEARCH**

Ole-school southern sophistication

5 REASONS IT'S COOL

1. Ole Miss **ranks among the nation's leading research institutions.**

2. Campus attractions include **the largest blues archive in the United States**, a cannabis research facility, and Rowan Oak, an estate that once belong to writer William Faulkner.

3. The acclaimed Sally McDonnell-Barksdale Honors College offers **extra-challenging classes** to a select group.

4. Pack your togas: The **Greek scene reigns supreme**.

5. **Pre-football game picnics** at Ole Miss are lavish affairs: Think of them as tops-and-tails-gating.

The Basics

Public / private: public state
Total enrollment / undergrads: 15,220 / 12,661
Campus setting: small town
Students call it: Ole Miss
Students are called: Rebels
Notable Alum: Larry Brown (author), Trent Lott (senator), Archie Manning (pro football player), Eli Manning (pro football player), Shepard Smith (news broadcaster)

Learning's Where You Find It

Ole Miss is probably known as much for its lively students, storied athletic programs, and rich history as it is for its academics. But this top-ranked research university's strong academic programs stand apart. A wide range of majors are offered through the seven undergraduate colleges of liberal arts, business, education, engineering, applied sciences, pharmacy, and accountancy. The highly touted Honors College provides students with a challenging liberal arts education, along with ample study-abroad and service learning opportunities. Acoustics, business, computer science, engineering, law, pharmacy, and southern studies are among the popular programs or divisions. Two institutes on campus, the Lott Leadership Institute and the Croft Institute of International Studies, help groom the next generation of politicians and international policy experts. Most students find the faculty to be friendly and accessible, which is fortunate given the high student-to-faculty ratio of 20:1. Overall, Ole Miss offers something for everyone:

Good Thing He Didn't Wear Number 1!

Throughout the Ole Miss campus, the official speed limit on all streets is 18 miles per hour. Why 18? This curious speed limit was established as a tribute to Archie Manning, the revered Rebel quarterback and later NFL great, whose uniform number during his Ole Miss days was 18.

Serious students will find a rich and challenging academic atmosphere, and more laid-back students will enjoy a fun collegiate experience.

Rebel Y'all

The centerpiece of campus life at Ole Miss is Rebels football. Home games are celebrated all over campus, nowhere more so than in the Grove, a lush fifteen-acre lawn where fans tailgate in sumptuous southern elegance. Football's only rival for campus dominance is another Ole Miss tradition: fraternities and sororities. Greek organizations exert near total control of the university's party scene. The generally raucous atmosphere has led to some problems related to abuse and harassment, although administrators are working to address these issues. Campus facilities vary in terms of quality. Dorms receive low marks, and many students choose to live off campus after sophomore year. The Turner Recreation Center fares better in student estimations. A sizeable percentage of the largely preppy student body hails from the upper echelons of southern society. Regional and ethnic diversity is low, and left-leaning political activism is rare. Still, students are generally friendly, and the overall vibe is an easygoing one.

Southern Fried Somnolence

Ole Miss lies just outside of Oxford, a small, sleepy town where awkward sidewalk encounters with professors are common. What the town lacks in size, it more than makes up for in student-friendly charm. Oxford's centerpiece is the Square, home to several bars, restaurants, and shops. Square Books is one of the country's best independent bookstores and has been the part-time employer of many an English major over the years. The town has a rich artistic history and is (or has been in the past) the home of many artistic and literary luminaries, including William Faulkner, Willie Morris, Glennray Tutor, Jere Allen, and John Grisham, among others. Students who long for city lights will find that Memphis, Nashville, and New Orleans are all within driving distance.

Admissions

Average high school GPA:	—
Average freshman SAT verbal / math score:	529 / 531
Average freshman ACT score:	22
Application fee:	$25
Application deadlines: 7/20 (freshmen) 7/24 (transfer)	
Total applicants:	7,849
Total accepted:	6,587 (84%)
Total accepted who enrolled:	2,527
Notification dates: 8/16 (freshmen) 8/16 (transfer)	

Students

Percentage of male / female students:	48% / 52%
Percentage of students from out of state:	32%
Percentage of students graduating in 4 years / 6 years:	33% / 54%

Money

Total endowment:	$421,400,000
Total in-state tuition, fees & expenses:	$11,494
Total out-of-state tuition, fees & expenses:	$17,440
Average financial aid package:	$8,549
Percentage of students who sought aid and received it:	65%
Percentage of students receiving financial aid:	35%

Also Check Out

University of Alabama–Tuscaloosa

University of Florida

University of Kentucky

The University of Tennessee

University of Missouri– Columbia

230 Jesse Hall
Columbia, MO 65211

(573) 882-2121
http://www.missouri.edu/

 **BIG CHOICE**

 **BIG RESEARCH**

Show me the MO.

5 REASONS IT'S COOL

1. Academics are strong across the board, especially the **top-notch engineering and business programs.**

2. **MU's journalism school was the world's first,** and it's consistently ranked as one of the best in the country.

3. The new **recreation center is state-of-the-art** and includes an outdoor pool, a lazy river, climbing walls, and big-screen TVs.

4. "Mizzou-Rah!" UM is a member of the Big 12, and the **football team is a university-wide obsession.**

5. The gorgeous campus is within walking distance of downtown Columbia, a great college town.

The Basics

Public / private: public state
Total enrollment / undergrads: 28,253 / 21,551
Campus setting: suburban
Students call it: Mizzou, MU
Call the students: Tigers
Notable alums: George Caleb Bingham (artist), Sheryl Crow (musician), William Least Heat-Moon (author), Sam Walton (founder, Wal-Mart and Sam's Club)

Journalism, Right?

UM is home to the world's first journalism school, the nationally ranked Missouri School of Journalism. Students come from all over the country to write for the *Columbia Missourian*, the student newspaper, or to get anchoring and reporting experience at KOMU, the college-run NBC affiliate TV station. The university offers more than 260 majors, which are distributed across fourteen different undergraduate colleges and schools. The most popular majors include education, engineering, and business. High-performing students in medicine, law, nursing, and other pre-professional fields are offered guaranteed admission to the university's graduate programs. UM is a major research university, and research opportunities are widely available to undergrads. The popular study-abroad program sends students to more than fifty countries. Professors are generally available for office hours and support, but make sure you're proactive about seeing your academic adviser. With 21,000 students, it's easy to get lost in the crowd.

Tiger Traditions

When UM students pass through the archway at the school of journalism, they rub the noses of the 600-year-old Chinese stone lions for good luck. Freshmen celebrate the start of college with a walk through the campus's famous columns (all that remain of a building that burned down long ago) and a dish of Tiger Stripe ice cream.
And don't forget to remove or tip your hat when walking through the Memorial Union arch in honor of Mizzou's fallen war heroes.

Mizzou ... Rah!

On football weekends, Faurot Field swells with college students and locals alike, all chanting "Mizzou-Rah!" Mizzou is a member of the Big 12, and football games are huge—especially when the team plays rival University of Kansas. Greek life plays a big part in weekend life too. Although most students embrace these two pillars of the social scene, it's still possible to have a social life without either. Columbia offers more than enough coffee shops, cafés, and nature trails to keep students' caffeinated, fed, and healthy. The university also has a competitive intramural sports scene. The dining halls win high marks, and all conveniently accept students' EZ Charge cards (which can also be used across the campus for other purchases such as school supplies and clothes). From barhopping to float trips, most students are pleased with Columbia, a pleasant town that caters to the huge student population. Quite a few students are probably familiar with the area already—the vast majority of the student body is from Missouri.

College Town, USA

Columbia is a quintessential college town that enjoys a good relationship with the university. Students cite Columbia's friendly atmosphere, fun bars, various restaurants, and ample shopping as perks. MU's campus can be divided into three parts: White Campus, home to the sciences; Red Campus, home to the liberal arts and social sciences; and a third part that's currently under construction. New additions include a Life Sciences Center, a state-of-the-art recreation center, and the Donald W. Reynolds Journalism Institute. St. Louis and Kansas City, both favorite weekend destinations, are two hours away, though in opposite directions.

Admissions

Average high school GPA:	—
Average freshman SAT verbal / math score:	—/—
Average freshman ACT score:	24
Application fee:	$45
Application deadlines: continuous (freshmen) continuous (transfer)	
Total applicants:	13,102
Total accepted:	10,228 (78%)
Total accepted who enrolled:	4,786
Notification dates: continuous (freshmen) continuous (transfer)	

Students

Percentage of male / female students:	49% / 51%
Percentage of students from out of state:	14%
Percentage of students graduating in 4 years / 6 years:	38% / 68%

Money

Total endowment:	$500,272,029
Total in-state tuition, fees & expenses:	$14,285
Total out-of-state tuition, fees & expenses:	$23,867
Average financial aid package:	$11,452
Percentage of students who sought aid and received it:	86%
Percentage of students receiving financial aid:	40%

Also Check Out

Northwestern University

University of Illinois at Urbana-Champaign

University of Kansas

University of Nebraska–Lincoln

The University of Montana–Missoula

Lommasson Center, 2nd Floor
Missoula, MT 59812

(406) 243-0211
http://www.umt.edu/

 **BIG CHOICE**

Big love for Big Sky Country

5 REASONS IT'S COOL

1. Students love UM's size— not too big, not too small.

2. **Forestry and creative writing** are just two of the strong programs on offer.

3. Take advantage of the many **study-abroad and student-exchange** programs.

4. Grizzlies in the wild are dangerous, but on this campus **they're as friendly as can be.**

5. Missoula is a **great college town** that's close to stellar skiing, climbing, kayaking, and other outdoor activities.

The Basics

Public / private: public state
Total enrollment / undergrads: 13,558 / 11,431
Campus setting: urban
Students call it: UM
Students are called: Grizzlies
Notable alums: Dave Dickenson (pro football player), Mike Mansfield (senator), Carroll J. O'Conner (actor), Jeannette Rankin (first female member of Congress)

To Study or to Ski?

UM is a medium-sized university composed of three colleges: Arts & Science, Forestry and Conservation, and Technology. Within these colleges are six professional schools, including the schools of Fine Arts, Physical Therapy, Education, and Business Administration. The creative writing program is exceptional. Physical Therapy and Journalism are also strong. The impressive forestry programs benefit from the wealth of research opportunities nearby. Academically, students reap what they sow. Some Grizzlies would rather snowboard than attend class, but hard workers can get a stellar education at a rock-bottom price. Freshman can ease the transition to college by joining First-Year Interest Groups, which help them develop a schedule arranged around themes. There are also Freshman Seminars and the First-Year Reading Experience, essentially a large book club that culminates in a visit by the author. Students accepted to the Davidson Honors College have access to small, challenging courses, priority registration, and personalized

Cowboy Up!

Get in touch with your inner pioneer at the Forrester's Ball: Every year, UM-ers don their best cowboy attire and spend the night two-stepping in a faux mining town.

advising. TAs teach some of the introductory courses, but professors are friendly and accessible. Study-abroad opportunities abound, as the university has programs in thirty-eight different countries and gives students the option of constructing their own study-abroad experience.

Who Says Grizzlies Aren't Cuddly?

While there is no typical UM student, a love of the outdoors unites most undergrads. Sixty-eight percent come from Montana and are predisposed to adore the rugged mountain landscape. Those from out of state should brace themselves for a long winter and take advantage of the Outdoor Program's classes and trips. The slopes, only thirty minutes away, are a popular weekend destination. In the warmer months, hiking, rafting, and other outdoor Big Sky Country activities beckon. Grizzlies like to let loose at house parties, fraternities (although the Greek scene isn't very strong), and bars. Students adore Missoula, which has a lively food and arts scene and affordable off-campus housing. There's also a variety of on-campus housing options, including nine residence halls and three apartment complexes. Environmental, political, and musical groups are popular, as are club and intramural sports. There's an interesting hippie-meets-logger dynamic on campus, but UMers are laid-back and don't segregate into cliques. Everyone comes together to support Griz football, especially when the two-time Division I-AA National Champs are up against rival Montana State.

The Ultimate Outdoor Adventure College Town

The heart of the 156-acre campus is the Oval, a large expanse of lawn that, come spring, is covered with students studying, playing Frisbee, and generally enjoying life. Recent renovations include the state-of-the-art Recreation Center and a new student union. Campus is bike friendly—a cruiser co-op allows students to borrow bikes for free—and the shops, restaurants, bars, and theaters of downtown Missoula are only five minutes away. The small, friendly city sits on the banks on the Clark Fork River and is at the heart of the Northern Rockies.

Admissions

Average high school GPA:	—
Average freshman SAT verbal / math score:	—/—
Average freshman ACT score:	—
Application fee:	$30
Application deadlines: continuous (freshmen) continuous (transfer)	
Total applicants:	4,452
Total accepted:	4,133 (93%)
Total accepted who enrolled:	—
Notification dates: continuous (freshmen) continuous (transfer)	

Students

Percentage of male / female students:	48% / 52%
Percentage of students from out of state:	23%
Percentage of students graduating in 4 years / 6 years:	20% / 44%

Money

Total endowment:	$78,300,000
Total in-state tuition, fees & expenses:	$11,687
Total out-of-state tuition, fees & expenses:	$21,194
Average financial aid package:	$7,866
Percentage of students who sought aid and received it:	75%
Percentage of students receiving financial aid:	52%

Also Check Out

University of Idaho

University of Oregon

University of Washington

University of Wyoming

University of Nebraska–Lincoln

14th and R Streets	(402) 472-7211
Lincoln, NE 68588	http://www.unl.edu/

BIG CHOICE

All that and an ear of corn

5 REASONS IT'S COOL

1. **Big school, big savings.** UNL offers tons of majors at the low cost you'd expect from a public university.

2. Sure, it's a large school. But UNL has special programs aimed to take the sting out of the size by building small campus communities, including the **University Learning Communities program for freshmen.**

3. Their **top-notch agriculture programs** are some of the strongest around.

4. **Big Red football:** Know it, live it, love it.

5. Lincoln, Nebraska's second biggest city, offers **plenty of student-friendly attractions.** Plus, it's just down the road from Omaha, the state's *biggest* city.

The Basics

Public / private: public state
Total enrollment / undergrads: 22,106 / 17,371
Campus setting: urban **Students call it:** UNL
Students are called: Huskers, Cornhuskers
Notable alums: George W. Beadle (Nobel Laureate, Genetics), Warren Buffet (billionaire investor), Johnny Carson (talk show host), Willa Cather (novelist), Aaron Douglas (artist), Bob Kerrey (governor, Nebraska)

Growing Great Minds

Originally founded as a land-grant university to teach farming and mechanical trades, UNL has long since outgrown its agricultural beginnings. The university offers more than 150 majors, including popular programs in business, engineering, journalism, and education. The wide variety of agriculture classes are still among the university's strongest, and unusual and/or specialized majors such as professional golf management and the Great Plains Studies Program are also offered. UNL's eight undergraduate colleges include colleges of arts and science, agriculture, business administration, architecture, education, engineering, journalism, and fine and performing arts. Freshmen can elect to take part in the University Learning Communities, which are small groups of students that live and take classes together and receive special support from faculty members. The university operates a prestigious honors college that admits a select number of students every year who are rewarded with small classes, numerous research opportunities, and personal attention from top faculty members. The student-to-faculty ratio is 19:1, and while

If You Build It, They Will Come

Talk about box office gold. Since November 3, 1962, every single football game held at UNL's Memorial Stadium has been sold out. Not many schools can boast an attendance record like that.

the situation varies depending on the major, large lecture-style classes tend to dominate.

Must Love Football

Football is serious business in these parts. UNL students are proud to be called Huskers, and the football team receives the lion's share of their school spirit. Every year during the "Big Red Welcome," freshmen accompany the football team as they walk through the tunnel and onto the field at Memorial Stadium, where they are welcomed by cheering throngs. The university provides a wide range of on-campus housing, and freshmen are required to live on campus. About 40 percent of students remain in the dorms throughout their ensuing four years. With twenty-eight fraternities and fourteen sororities, UNL's Greek scene monopolizes much of the social scene. However, the campus is officially dry, so parties take place off campus. The overwhelming majority of the student body hails from Nebraska and tends to be conservative, but the common love of being a Husker overrides most political differences.

Lively in Lincoln

UNL is divided into two campuses, which are about two miles apart from each other. The City Campus is located in the heart of downtown Lincoln and houses most undergraduate academic departments, while the East Campus, home to the agricultural program, is situated farther out to the northeast. The city of Lincoln has plenty of bars and nightlife options, and the Historic Haymarket District nearby has specialty shops, restaurants, and student-friendly establishments. Lincoln's most distinguished building is its gold-domed capitol building, which is the second tallest in the country. UNL students often head up to the larger city of Omaha, an easy forty-five-minute drive.

Admissions

Average high school GPA:	—
Average freshman SAT verbal / math score:	584 / 600
Average freshman ACT score:	23
Application fee:	$45
Application deadlines: 5/1 (freshmen) 6/30 (transfer)	
Total applicants:	7,993
Total accepted:	5,858 (73%)
Total accepted who enrolled:	3,831
Notification dates: continuous (freshmen) continuous (transfer)	

Students

Percentage of male / female students:	53% / 47%
Percentage of students from out of state:	14%
Percentage of students graduating in 4 years / 6 years:	22% / 63%

Money

Total endowment:	$185,473,654
Total in-state tuition, fees & expenses:	$12,930
Total out-of-state tuition, fees & expenses:	$22,380
Average financial aid package:	$8,245
Percentage of students who sought aid and received it:	85%
Percentage of students receiving financial aid:	42%

Also Check Out

Indiana University–Bloomington

University of Illinois at Urbana–Champaign

University of Kansas

University of Michigan–Ann Arbor

University of Wisconsin–Madison

University of Nevada–Las Vegas

4505 Maryland Parkway
Las Vegas, NV 89154

(702) 895-3011
http://www.unlv.edu/

BIG CHOICE

Viva Las Vegas!

5 REASONS IT'S COOL

1. The university's **Good Neighbor Policy** extends discounted tuition to select counties in states adjacent to Nevada.

2. **Hotel administration** is a four-star program here.

3. The **new Moyer Student Union** is a great focal point on campus.

4. Students bet on scarlet and gray, the colors of their **beloved Rebels sports teams.**

5. Vegas, baby, Vegas!

The Basics

Public / private: public state
Total enrollment / undergrads: 27,933 / 21,853
Campus setting: urban
Students call it: UNLV
Students are called: Rebels
Notable alums: Guy Fieri (celebrity chef), Ashlyn Gere (adult film actress), Suge Knight (CEO, Death Row Records), Jimmy Kimmel (TV personality), Kenny Mayne (sports journalist)

Beating the House

Academics at UNLV are something of a crapshoot. Some classes are excellent, and others suffer from indifferent professors or dull course matter. The large enrollment also means that students should prepare themselves for big lecture courses, as well as the occasional smaller course taught by a completely baffled TA. Such hazards are par for the course at most large state schools, though, and with a little initiative, you'll be able to extract a perfectly serviceable university education from UNLV. The William F. Harrah College of Hotel Administration leads the pack among campus programs and is very popular. The College of Education also stands out. Its elementary education program is particularly good. Those who incline toward the social sciences can pursue a degree in psychology or history, two solid and popular majors.

A Wolf in Offensive Clothing

Beauregard, the school's original mascot, was a wolf dressed as a Confederate soldier, garb that was intended to symbolize UNLV's rebellion against its northern oppressor, the University of Nevada–Reno. This lupine mascot was retired in the '70s.

What Happens at UNLV, Stays at UNLV

Campus is just a stone's throw from the Vegas strip, which means casinos and nightclubs are a constant temptation. Students who are over twenty-one—or who own excellent fake IDs—find that the world is their oyster. Underage and ID-less students have campus and the Greek scene, and that's about it. The high ratio of commuters further dampens the possibility for a vibrant on-campus social life; nearly 75 percent of students are Nevadans, of whom some 95 percent hail from the university's home county of Clark. The university is notably diverse, with a student body that is only 48 percent white. UNLV's Good Neighbor Policy, which offers discounted tuition rates to students hailing from certain counties in neighboring states, makes it an attractive option for young people in the area. Known more for its location than for its scholastic community, UNLV will thrill certain students and disappoint others.

Playaz Paradise

As a Sunbelt city "on the grow," Vegas now offers far more than casinos, gender-ambiguous German magicians, and scantily clad showgirls. Like the city in which it's located, UNLV is a study in glittery postmodern grandeur. The Lied Library is the campus's largest and most remarkable structure. Thanks to a recent fundraising campaign called Invent the Future, the school has recently added a new student union and a recreation center. The class of 2011 is the first to enjoy these, as the new facilities opened in summer 2007. Dorm life at UNLV has its own attractions. Tonopah, the school's oldest residence hall, is the place to meet up or to hook up, students report. Some undergrads prefer the quieter environs of Dayton Hall. Regardless of where they live, freshmen should be prepared to plunk down over a grand for a compulsory meal plan.

Admissions

Average high school GPA:	3.28
Average freshman SAT verbal / math score:	505 / 524
Average freshman ACT score:	21
Application fee:	$60

Application deadlines:
2/1 (freshmen)
4/1 (transfer)

Total applicants:	5,903
Total accepted:	4,403 (75%)
Total accepted who enrolled:	2,510

Notification dates:
continuous (freshmen)
continuous (transfer)

Students

Percentage of male / female students:	44% / 56%
Percentage of students from out of state:	21%
Percentage of students graduating in 4 years / 6 years:	14% / 41%

Money

Total endowment:	$121,177,316
Total in-state tuition, fees & expenses:	$13,024
Total out-of-state tuition, fees & expenses:	$23,834
Average financial aid package:	$6,416
Percentage of students who sought aid and received it:	70%
Percentage of students receiving financial aid:	30%

Also Check Out

California State University–Chico

Northern Arizona University

University of Central Florida

University of Utah

University of Wyoming

University of New Hampshire

4 Garrison Avenue
Durham, NH 03824

(603) 862-1234
http://www.unh.edu/

 **BIG CHOICE**

 **BIG RESEARCH**

An intellectual hot spot by the sea

5 REASONS IT'S COOL

1. UNH is one of just nine **land, sea, and space grant institutions** in the nation.

2. The university offers **more than 100 majors**, 2,000 courses, and more research opportunities than you can shake a stick at.

3. Looking to get involved in research? The **Undergraduate Research Opportunities Program** will hook you up.

4. Outdoor enthusiasts rejoice: **the Atlantic Ocean and the White Mountains** are both within easy reach of campus.

5. Marine biology students get their feet wet (literally) at the university's **living labs**.

The Basics

Public / private: public state
Total enrollment / undergrads: 14,848 / 11,971
Campus setting: small town
Students call it: UNH
Students are called: Wildcats
Notable alums: Jerry Azumah (pro football player), Marcy Carsey (TV producer), John Irving (novelist), Carol Shea-Porter (congresswoman)

Research Opportunities and Expense Accounts

UNH offers more than 100 majors through its six undergraduate colleges and schools of liberal arts, business, engineering, life sciences and agriculture, health and human services, and applied science. The most popular majors include English, psychology, business, and hospitality management. The university also has strong programs in marine biology and oceanography, along with access to two living laboratories on the nearby Atlantic coast. Writing skills are emphasized across the curriculum, and all students must complete courses in core areas including quantitative reasoning, history, and foreign cultures. The Undergraduate Research Opportunities Program, open to all majors, puts students in charge of a self-directed research project and gives them an expense account, a salary, and sometimes a travel stipend. Students learn not only the basics of conducting and presenting research but also how to manage their time and money. More than twenty study-abroad programs are offered on several continents, and UNH also accepts credit from over 300 approved programs

Picture This

In the old days, UNH sophomores delighted in hassling freshmen. One traditional way of getting under freshmen's skin: preventing them from showing up for their own class picture. In 1904, sophomores boarded the train the frosh were taking to the photographer's studio, smashing windows and absconding with three first-year students. Police had to escort the remaining freshmen to the photographer's studio.

administered by other colleges and universities. Roughly five percent of students study abroad.

Wild About the Wildcats

UNH frequently shows up on lists of top party schools, but even teetotaling students will find plenty of social outlets. The university offers thirteen Greek organizations, and about six percent of students participate. Around 60 percent of students live on campus in one of three dormitory areas on the 300-acre "campus core," where the majority of administrative and academic buildings are located. There are more than 160 student organizations that cater to a wide variety of academic, cultural, and special interests. Popular groups include WUNH, the campus radio station, *The New Hampshire*, the student newspaper, the Outing Club, and the Student Environmental Action Coalition. The campus's Memorial Union Building (MUB) is a popular spot that is home to two movie theaters, a food court, student government offices, and many other student organizations. The university offers fifteen varsity Wildcats sports teams, most of which compete at the NCAA Division I level, along with a huge variety of club sports.

New England Charm

UNH's 1,100-acre campus is located in the small town of Durham in New Hampshire's seacoast region. The town itself offers plenty of student-friendly bars and restaurants, along with plenty of New England charm, and the region offers skiing, hiking, kayaking and other diversions for nature lovers. New Hampshire's White Mountains are about an hour away, and frequent trips to the region are organized through the university's popular Outing Club. Boston is about an hour away, and Portsmouth can be reached in about 20 minutes.

Admissions

Average high school GPA:	—
Average freshman SAT verbal / math score:	546 / 566
Average freshman ACT score:	—
Application fee:	$45

Application deadlines:
2/1 (freshmen)
3/1 (transfer)
12/1 (early action)

Total applicants:	13,991
Total accepted:	9,363 (67%)
Total accepted who enrolled:	3,078

Notification dates:
4/15 (freshmen)
4/15 (transfer)
1/15 (early action)

Acceptance rate for early action applicants:	74%

Students

Percentage of male / female students:	43% / 57%
Percentage of students from out of state:	43%
Percentage of students graduating in 4 years / 6 years:	53% / 72%

Money

Total endowment:	$211,643,146
Total in-state tuition, fees & expenses:	$17,985
Total out-of-state tuition, fees & expenses:	$30,435
Average financial aid package:	$15,688
Percentage of students who sought aid and received it:	80%
Percentage of students receiving financial aid:	49%

Also Check Out

University of Connecticut

University of Delaware

University of Pennsylvania

University of Vermont

University of New Mexico

University of New Mexico
Albuquerque, NM 87131

(505) 277-0111
http://www.unm.edu/

BIG CHOICE

BIG RESEARCH

A great education served with a side of green chile sauce

5 REASONS IT'S COOL

1. **Diversity rules:** UNM is home to many nontraditional students and sizeable Latin and Native American populations.

2. Night owls and working students benefit from the **many evening and weekend classes**.

3. The campus's **cool Pueblo architecture** highlights the rich cultural heritage of the Southwest.

4. Albuquerque is packed with student-friendly nightspots and great restaurants specializing in southwestern cuisine. Plus, there's **proximity to skiing, hiking, and biking in the nearby mountains**.

5. The best part: It all comes at a **super-low price**.

The Basics

Public / private: public state
Total enrollment / undergrads: 26,172 / 18,725
Campus setting: urban
Students call it: UNM
Students are called: Lobos
Notable alums: Rudolfo Anaya (novelist), Michael Cooper (pro basketball coach), Robert Creeley (poet), Tony Hillerman (novelist), Katie Hnida (first woman to score in a DI-A football game), Brian Urlacher (pro football player)

U 'N' Me

UNM offers an exceptionally good deal for New Mexico state residents. The university has over ninety majors distributed across eleven undergraduate colleges and two independent divisions, including colleges and schools of Arts and Sciences, Management, Fine Arts, Nursing, Architecture and Planning, Engineering, and Education. Some of the more widely praised majors include psychology, Latin American and Southwest Hispanic studies, photography, and anthropology and archeology. Many students take advantage of the bachelor's of university studies program, in which they can create their own interdisciplinary major while fulfilling core requirements. UNM has many commuter and adult learner students, and, to accommodate them, offers over a thousand classes in the evenings or on weekends. Students report that some initiative may be required to break through the professor-student barrier. The academic environment is serious without begin super-competitive.

Deck the Campus with Bags of Candles

UNM students really know how to get in the holiday spirit. Every December, students celebrate with the annual "Hanging of the Greens," thought to be the oldest continuing tradition on campus. Thousands of luminaria—small, sand-filled paper bags containing lit candles—are placed all over campus. A caroling tour sets the mood, and the magical event culminates with the presentation of a holiday wreath to the university president.

Come One, Come All

UNM is a diverse place. More than 30 percent of students are Hispanic, and 6 percent are Native American. Students tend to be older as well (the median student age is about twenty-four). The vast majority of students live off campus and come and go depending on their class schedules. The unusual campus layout offers several spots for students to hang out and unwind, such as the charming Duck Pond and recently renovated Student Union. UNM hosts a number of sporting and cultural events, and nearly four hundred student groups cater to a wide array of interests. Every fall, Lobos spirit soars high around the time of the big football game with rival New Mexico State University. This is especially true on the night of the Red Rally, the traditional bonfire that takes place on the Thursday before the big game. Men's and women's basketball games also draw huge crowds to the Pit, as University Arena is commonly called.

ABQ OK

Many of the buildings on the UNM campus are built in a modern Pueblo style, befitting the university's location in the heart of the Southwest. The 600-acre main campus is home to the Maxwell Museum of Anthropology and its impressive collection of cultural artifacts from the Southwest and beyond. The nondenominational Alumni Memorial Chapel, built in the Franciscan mission style, is another distinctive structure. Albuquerque is a sprawling city of roughly a half million residents. Local entertainment options are plentiful and include a host of student-friendly bars and restaurants. The annual International Balloon Fiesta, when hundreds of colorful hot air balloons fill the skies, occurs every October and is quite a sight. The Albuquerque region offers incredible natural beauty, including a pleasant desert climate and the gorgeous Sandias Mountains, which rise just beyond the city. Bikers and hikers rave about the many nearby trails, and in the winter, skiers and snowboarders can hit the slopes at Sandia Peak or neighboring Taos.

Admissions

Average high school GPA:	3.34
Average freshman SAT verbal / math score:	545 / 536
Average freshman ACT score:	22
Application fee:	$20
Application deadlines:	6/15 (freshmen) 6/15 (transfer)
Total applicants:	6,981
Total accepted:	5,123 (73%)
Total accepted who enrolled:	3,016
Notification dates:	continuous (freshmen) continuous (transfer)

Students

Percentage of male / female students:	42% / 58%
Percentage of students from out of state:	11%
Percentage of students graduating in 4 years / 6 years:	— / —

Money

Total endowment:	$245,234,064
Total in-state tuition, fees & expenses:	$11,016
Total out-of-state tuition, fees & expenses:	$20,857
Average financial aid package:	$7,829
Percentage of students who sought aid and received it:	75%
Percentage of students receiving financial aid:	34%

Also Check Out

Arizona State University

San Diego State University

The University of Arizona

University of Colorado at Boulder

The University of Texas at Austin

University of North Carolina at Chapel Hill

CB #2200, Jackson Hall
Chapel Hill, NC 27599

(919) 962-2211
http://www.unc.edu/

BIG CHOICE

BIG RESEARCH

Southern hospitality with all the trimmings

5 REASONS IT'S COOL

1. UNC has one of the **top undergraduate journalism schools in the country.**

2. **Research opportunities abound**, from supervised honors theses to grants of up to $6,000 to pursue specific interests.

3. A **unique Womentoring program pairs women faculty and staff** members with undergrad women to develop leadership skills.

4. With its charming tree-lined lawns and historic nineteenth century buildings, **UNC's campus is one of the most beautiful in the country.**

5. **One of the country's coolest college towns**, Chapel Hill offers student-friendly restaurants, bars, and shops.

The Basics

Public / private: public state
Total enrollment / undergrads: 27,717 / 17,124
Campus setting: suburban
Students call it: UNC, Carolina
Call students: Tar Heels
Notable alums: Frank Bruni (journalist), Andy Griffith (actor), William B. Harrison Jr. (CEO, JP Morgan Chase), Michael Jordan (attended; pro basketball player), James K. Polk (U.S. president), Paul Wellstone (senator)

Public Ivy

Not only is UNC the oldest public university in the country, but it was also among the first state universities to attain public Ivy status for excellence in academics. The university requires all students to fulfill general requirements in two categories: basic skills (including writing, foreign languages, and math) and perspectives (encompassing philosophy, comparative studies, science, and art). During their freshman year, students meet in small seminars as part of a freshman seminar program. Sixty-nine majors are offered, including popular choices such as sociology, mass communications, and classics and pre-professional programs such as pharmacy and sports science. There's also the option of a self-designed major. Class size varies between small seminars and large lecture halls that hold as many as four hundred. Students interested in busting out of campus have multiple opportunities to do so by taking advantage of UNC's 230 study-abroad programs, including three in Africa, a number in Latin America, and a six-week summer program

A Ram-tastic Mascot

UNC has been the breeding ground for athletes ranging from Michael Jordan to Marion Jones to Mia Hamm. Back in 1924, it was UNC athlete Jack "Battering Ram" Merrit, a popular fullback on the football team, who inspired the team manager to acquire a live ram as the team's mascot. The ram was purchased before a UNC-VMI game, and when UNC won, fans credited the ram for the team's victory. Ever since that fateful game, "Ramses the Ram" has been UNC's official mascot.

in Russia. Students can also gain academic credit through service learning and mentoring courses called APPLES (Assisting People in Planning Learning Experiences in Service).

Something for Everyone

"Something for everyone" aptly describes the many social options at UNC. The Greek scene is relatively small, attracting less than 20 percent of the student body, but frat parties are abundant and it can sometimes feel like the Greek presence on campus is bigger than the numbers indicate. Sports are a big deal year round, and fans go especially nuts during basketball season. The UNC Sport Club program caters to sporty students, offering over fifty clubs for activities such as bodybuilding, golf, and waterskiing. Students stay active politically too, and a popular spot for demonstrations and fundraising campaigns is the Pit, the campus's brick-paved courtyard, which serves as the epicenter of student life. While most students are North Carolina born and bred, the study body is a moderately diverse bunch. African Americans make up 11 percent, Asian Americans account for 6 percent, and Hispanics 3 percent of the student body.

All's Well

Vast stretches of open lawns and charming colonial buildings define UNC's lovely campus. One of the campus's oldest and most famous landmarks is the Old Well, a small columned rotunda with a water fountain at its center surrounded by benches and trees. Another campus landmark is the Morehead Planetarium and Science Center, the nation's first university-owned planetarium. UNC's larger, modern South campus is home to mostly medical and sports venues, although new plans have attempted to make this campus more integral to the rest. Bordering campus is the ever-hopping Franklin Street, Chapel Hill's main thoroughfare, packed with cool record stores, bars, clubs, coffee shops, and other student haunts. Chapel Hill's close proximity to nearby universities Duke and NC State helps make it an ideal college town.

Admissions

Average high school GPA:	4.0
Average freshman SAT verbal / math score:	643 / 660
Average freshman ACT score:	25
Application fee:	$70

Application deadlines:
1/15 (freshmen)
3/1 (transfer)
11/1 (early action)

Total applicants:	19,728
Total accepted:	6,737 (34%)
Total accepted who enrolled:	3,800

Notification dates:
3/31 (freshmen)
4/15 (transfer)
1/31 (early action)

Acceptance rate for early action applicants:	46%

Students

Percentage of male / female students:	41% / 59%
Percentage of students from out of state:	17%
Percentage of students graduating in 4 years / 6 years:	71% / 84%

Money

Total endowment:	$1,687,838,091
Total in-state tuition, fees & expenses:	$12,879
Total out-of-state tuition, fees & expenses:	$27,527
Average financial aid package:	$10,575
Percentage of students who sought aid and received it:	100%
Percentage of students receiving financial aid:	30%

Also Check Out

Duke University

University of Florida

University of Georgia

University of Virginia

Wake Forest University

University of North Dakota

100 Carnegie Hall, 250 Centennial Dr., Stop 8135
Grand Forks, ND 58202

(701) 777-2011
http://www.und.nodak.edu/

BIG CHOICE

The sky's the limit.

5 REASONS IT'S COOL

1. **UND is the oldest and largest school in North Dakota.** Not surprisingly, the campus's main library, with over 1.4 million volumes, is the state's biggest library.

2. Students with an interest in **professional or specialized programs** will find exactly what they're looking for.

3. Up, up, and away . . . UND is home to one of the **country's largest flight schools.**

4. Hit the ice, ladies! It's **all about hockey** here, with Division I men's *and* women's hockey teams.

5. **Grand Forks city buses are free for students**, and the Cab Crawler will give you a ride home for just a buck.

The Basics

Public / private: public state
Total enrollment / undergrads: 12,834 / 10,376
Campus setting: urban
Students call it: UND
Call the students: The Fighting Sioux
Notable alums: Maxwell Anderson (playwright), Bennett Brien (sculptor), Chuck Klosterman (journalist, author), Nicole Linkletter (*America's Next Top Model* winner), Sally Smith (CEO, Buffalo Wild Wings), Jim Kleinsasser (pro football player)

Take to the Skies

UND has all the resources of a major university, but with an enrollment of just ten thousand, students find it to be a manageable size. The university offers more than 190 majors and is home to a renowned aviation program. Students enrolled in the Odegard School of Aerospace Sciences choose from degree options including airport management, commercial aviation, air traffic control, atmospheric science, and flight education. The university also has a fleet of more than 120 aircraft at the Grand Forks International Airport, making it one of the world's largest flight training facilities. Although the aviation-related majors are among the most popular at UND, there are a host of other notable programs, including elementary education, communications, psychology, and nursing. Approximately 90 percent of faculty members hold the highest degrees in their fields. Students choose from a wide range of study-abroad programs in unique locations, including Cameroon, Iceland, Norway, and India.

A Flood of Construction

In the spring of 1997, a massive flood in the Red River valley devastated the Grand Forks area. As you make your way through Grand Forks today, you may notice a lot of fairly recent construction. Much of that is the result of the rebuilding that took place after the flood.

Hockey's Huge Home

Hockey is the most popular sport at UND, and most students devote quite a bit of time to rooting for the men and women's Division I teams in the Ralph Engelstad Arena. The truly devoted can join the Sioux Crew, green-shirted fans who lead the cheers at home games. UND aims to raise all of its sports teams to the Division I level, instead of just the hockey teams, a move that should be complete by 2012. About half of students hail from North Dakota, and the campus itself is fairly homogenous, with the largest minority group being Native American students. The university offers thirteen fraternities and seven sororities, more than two hundred student organizations, and cultural centers for Native American students and international students, among other groups. About three thousand students live on campus in one of the university's fifteen residence halls.

Grand Forks

UND's 550-acre campus is located in the city of Grand Forks, home to a population of about fifty thousand. The campus has expanded in recent years, and new additions include the American Indian Center and the Student Wellness Center, a recreation facility with fitness classes, state-of-the-art equipment, and a climbing wall. Athletic teams have also benefited from new facilities, including the Ralph Engelstad Arena, the Alerus Center, and the Betty Engelstad Sioux Center, home of the basketball and volleyball teams. Hiking, fishing, and camping opportunities are all available in the surrounding region, and Fargo and Winnepeg, Canada are 70 miles away and 150 miles away, respectively.

Admissions

Average high school GPA:	3.37
Average freshman SAT verbal / math score:	— / —
Average freshman ACT score:	23
Application fee:	$35
Application deadlines: — (freshmen) continuous (transfer)	
Total applicants:	3,698
Total accepted:	2,725 (74%)
Total accepted who enrolled:	1,879
Notification dates: — (freshmen) continuous (transfer)	

Students

Percentage of male / female students:	54% / 46%
Percentage of students from out of state:	49%
Percentage of students graduating in 4 years / 6 years:	22% / 54%

Money

Total endowment:	$9,734,821
Total in-state tuition, fees & expenses:	$11,677
Total out-of-state tuition, fees & expenses:	$19,671
Average financial aid package:	$7,032
Percentage of students who sought aid and received it:	32%
Percentage of students receiving financial aid:	51%

Also Check Out

Purdue University

University of Minnesota–Twin Cities

University of Nebraska–Lincoln

The University of South Dakota

University of Notre Dame

220 Main Building
Notre Dame, IN 46556

(574) 631-5000
http://www.nd.edu/

 **BIG BRAIN**

 **BIG CHOICE**

Faith and football

5 REASONS IT'S COOL

1. The *Fighting* Irish? Try the *Ambitious* Irish, the *Competitive* Irish, or maybe even the *Overachieving* Irish. **Academics here are top-notch.**

2. **Successful Notre Dame alums** include college presidents, CEOs, television producers, public defenders, and Nobel, Pulitzer, and Emmy winners.

3. More than a hundred masses are offered weekly at this **Roman Catholic university.**

4. **Dorm loyalty is fierce.** Expect inter-hall rivalry and lots of fun events.

5. **Notre Dame football rocks.** The team is one of college football's most famous and winning ever.

The Basics

Public / private: private religious
Total enrollment / undergrads: 11,603 / 8,352
Campus setting: suburban
Students call it: Notre Dame
Students are called: Fighting Irish
Notable alums: Paul Charron (CEO, Liz Claiborne), Phil Donahue (talk show host), Francis Harvey (U.S. secretary of the Army), Joe Montana (pro football player), Regis Philbin (TV personality), Tim Ryan (sportscaster)

It's Not All Football, People!

While the sports teams are beloved by students, the top-notch academics are Notre Dame's biggest draw. Over 95 percent of students ranked in the top quarter of their high school classes, and competition for admission is stiff. The university welcomes students of all faiths, but students should know that academics are infused with Catholic intellectual and cultural teachings and values. Freshmen are admitted into the First Year of Studies program, which includes small seminar courses, a plan for completing general education requirements, and major advising. Students then enroll in one of five colleges: Arts & Letters, Business, Science, Engineering, or Architecture. The university offers a number of unique majors, including Africana studies, gender studies, Irish language and literature, and public service. The Undergraduate Research and Teaching Program (UROP) offers students the chance to work closely with faculty members to design innovative research projects, some of which are published or presented at

Running with Underwear

On the mornings of home games during football season, members of the Morrissey Manor dorm rise early and run through campus in their boxers. Their goal? To wake up sleeping dorm dwellers and get them excited for the day's game. Keep in mind, these sprints take place at 7:15 A.M. Saturday—now that's dedication!

conferences. The university offers twenty-eight international study programs, and more than half of students take part.

The Glory of the Game

School spirit runs high at Notre Dame, to put it mildly. The football team is one of college football's most legendary, and students devote many a weekend to spectating or playing in the marching band, the oldest in the country. The university offers a total of twenty-five NCAA sports teams. Most students live on campus all four years of college—in fact, many students stick with their freshman dorm. Each dorm is a tight community, throwing fundraisers and events throughout the year. Dorm loyalty replaces the definitive absence of Greek life on campus. The university is Roman Catholic, and this religious affiliation is more than a backdrop. Clergy have a visible presence on campus, dorms come complete with their own chapels, and students must respect certain rules of decorum. This includes strict regulations regarding dorm visitation from the opposite sex.

Go Gothic

Notre Dame's 1,250-acre campus is located in the small community of Notre Dame, just outside of the city of South Bend. The stunning campus boasts manicured lawns, state-of-the-art new facilities, and beautiful Gothic buildings, many of which are currently under renovation. The campus is also home to two dining halls, two lakes, an array of sports complexes, and twenty-seven residence halls. Students share the town with two other colleges: Saint Mary's College and Holy Cross College are both adjacent to the Notre Dame campus. The airport at South Bend is about fifteen minutes away, and Chicago, the nearest big city, is about two hours away.

Admissions

Average high school GPA:	—
Average freshman SAT verbal / math score:	678 / 700
Average freshman ACT score:	24
Application fee:	$50
Application deadlines:	
12/31 (freshmen)	
4/15 (transfer)	
11/1 (early action)	
Total applicants:	12,796
Total accepted:	3,492 (27%)
Total accepted who enrolled:	2,037
Notification dates:	
4/10 (freshmen)	
7/15 (transfer)	
12/20 (early action)	
Acceptance rate for early action applicants:	49%

Students

Percentage of male / female students:	53% / 47%
Percentage of students from out of state:	92%
Percentage of students graduating in 4 years / 6 years:	88% / 96%

Money

Total endowment:	$4,294,967,295
Total tuition:	$34,680
Total cost with fees & expenses:	$44,477
Average financial aid package:	$28,373
Percentage of students who sought aid and received it:	99%
Percentage of students receiving financial aid:	47%

Also Check Out

Georgetown University

Indiana University–Bloomington

University of Cincinnati

University of Illinois at Urbana-Champaign

University of Oklahoma

660 Parrington Oval
Norman, OK 73019

(405) 325-0311
http://www.ou.edu/

 **BIG CHOICE**

 **BIG RESEARCH**

Oklahoma, OK!

5 REASONS IT'S COOL

1. OU currently enrolls **more first-year National Merit Scholars** than any other public university and ranks among the top five public universities for graduating Rhodes Scholars.

2. **Livin' large:** The university offers 147 undergraduate degrees, 143 student exchange programs, and the largest, most comprehensive library in the state.

3. OU offers a **major and more courses in Native American studies** than any other place.

4. The orientation program Camp Crimson **helps freshmen make the adjustment** to Sooner life.

5. Prepare to rally! **Sooner sports get everyone in town cheering.**

The Basics

Public / private: public state
Total enrollment / undergrads: 26,002 / 19,600
Campus setting: suburban
Students call it: OU
Call the students: Sooners
Notable alums: Larry Drake (actor), Fred Haise (astronaut), Brad Henry (governor, Oklahoma), Shannon Lucid (astronaut), Steve Owens (pro football player)

Oh, the Okie Choices!

OU offers more than 150 majors through its fifteen undergraduate colleges. To help narrow down the many academic choices, all freshmen start off in the University College, where they take small seminars or intro-to-college classes. Notable majors include petroleum engineering, geography, and dance. The renowned Native American Studies Department offers language courses in Cherokee, Creek, Choctaw, and Kiowa. Meteorology students take advantage of resources such as the National Weather Research Center, the largest center of its kind in the nation. OU's Honors College draws about 10 percent of the student body and is one of the largest honors colleges at any public university. High-achieving students can also apply to the Scholarship-Leadership Enrichment Program, which awards credit for attending additional seminars and lectures. Overall, OU is distancing itself from its former rep as a football school. The proof is in the numbers: OU has six hundred National Merit Scholars, one of the highest concentrations anywhere in the nation.

Shots Heard All Around Campus

At home football games, you might see a group of red-shirted guys walk into OU's stadium with 12-gauge shotguns. No need to call for security. They're members of RUF/NEKs ("rough necks"), the university's all-male athletic spirit group. The modified red-and-white shotguns fire gunpowder, not bullets.

Sooner (than Later) Football

Frat parties largely define the social scene at OU. The university offers forty Greek organizations, and many students participate. The university is proud of its commitment to diversity; minorities make up more than 20 percent of the student body, and a sizeable percentage of these include Native American students. On-campus dorms get average marks, and the majority of students move off campus after freshman year. There are more than twenty-two dining locations scattered around the campus. Many students take advantage of study-abroad options through the university's 171 international exchange agreements, which offer opportunities in sixty countries. Sooners football is a focal point of student life: Plan to spend game days cheering on the team with the help of the Pride of Oklahoma, the university's stellar marching band.

Daily Forecast: Bright and Sunny

Students love the town of Norman, a great college town with a cozy vibe. The tree-lined campus isn't so bad either. It's home to state-of-the art facilities galore, including the new National Weather Center building and the Gaylord Family Oklahoma Stadium, one of the fifteen largest college stadiums in the nation. The Bizzell Memorial Library, located at the center of campus, is one of ten libraries that make up the UO Libraries system, the largest in the state. Norman is a welcoming town with plenty of arts, culture, and nightlife to keep a college student happy. Quite a few students have cars, but the CART bus system allows for easy transportation to and from campus, and is free for students.

Admissions

Average high school GPA:	3.6
Average freshman SAT verbal / math score:	—/—
Average freshman ACT score:	24
Application fee:	$40
Application deadlines: 4/1 (freshmen) 4/1 (transfer)	
Total applicants:	7,471
Total accepted:	6,822 (91%)
Total accepted who enrolled:	3,303
Notification dates: continuous (freshmen) continuous (transfer)	

Students

Percentage of male / female students:	51% / 49%
Percentage of students from out of state:	24%
Percentage of students graduating in 4 years / 6 years:	19% / 56%

Money

Total endowment:	$585,402,624
Total in-state tuition, fees & expenses:	$13,072
Total out-of-state tuition, fees & expenses:	$21,361
Average financial aid package:	$9,316
Percentage of students who sought aid and received it:	87%
Percentage of students receiving financial aid:	43%

Also Check Out

University of Kansas

University of Missouri–Columbia

The University of South Dakota

The University of Texas at Austin

University of Tulsa

University of Oregon

127 University of Oregon
Eugene, OR 97403

(541) 346-3111
http://www.uoregon.edu/

 **BIG CHOICE**

 **BIG RESEARCH**

Where minds move mountains

5 REASONS IT'S COOL

1. From science labs to residence halls to recreation centers, this campus has **some of the finest facilities in the country**.

2. A **friendly, caring, and knowledgeable faculty** makes a point of being accessible to undergrads.

3. An open mind is required on this **liberal, easygoing school**.

4. **Everyone loves Ducks football**, top contenders in the Pac-10 Conference.

5. The small city of **Eugene is a fun, friendly place** located in the heart of the lush Willamette Valley.

The Basics

Public / private: public state
Total enrollment / undergrads: 20,348 / 16,529
Campus setting: urban
Students call it: UO
Students are called: Ducks
Notable alums: Ann Bancroft (first woman to reach the North Pole), Douglas Hofstadter (scholar, author), Ken Kesey (writer), Phil Knight (cofounder, Nike), Chuck Palahniuk (writer), Steve Prefontaine (runner)

Which Mountain Do You Want to Move?

Don't be surprised if your faculty mentor asks you this question in earnest: Commitment, service, and big ideas are taken seriously at this public research institution. The general academic atmosphere is cozy, and students praise their professors for being attentive, accessible, and interesting. UO offers degree programs in eight schools, with pre-professional programs such as business, education, and journalism being among the best. The School of Architecture and Allied Arts is nationally recognized, and Professor G. Z. Brown recently garnered acclaim for his work on sustainable design using sunlight. Music, dance, psychology, and English are also quite strong, as are programs in the sciences—in fact, the "green chemistry" program is the first of its kind. Academically, students are laid-back, though students in the highly competitive Clark Honors College are forced to step it up a notch. Registration gives priority to upperclassmen, but newbies have access to some of most popular professors through freshmen seminars.

I Declare This Duck Territory!

Pioneer Statue, a bronzed, bearded trapper, was unveiled on campus in 1919 and has been the subject of much love—and speculation—ever since. Students decorate "Father Pioneer" with everything from tie-dyes to graduation caps, and rumor has it that the statue inspired the fictional Jebediah Springfield pioneer statue in *The Simpsons*.

Hippies, Jocks, Greeks, and Granolas

Stand at the corner of 13th and University, the center of campus, and you'll see an eclectic array of students pass by. Tattoos, khakis, dreadlocks, sweatpants—anything goes in this liberal, open-minded environment. UO's reputation as a hippie paradise shouldn't scare away the jocks, as most feel that everyone finds a niche. The Greek scene balances out the alternative crowd. School spirit runs high when the Ducks take on Oregon State on the football field, and the Pit Crew, a die-hard basketball fan club, keep McArthur Court cheering—loudly. Club and intramural sports are popular, as are outings to nearby beaches, mountains, and rivers with the Outdoor Club. This is an eco-friendly bunch, and many students are committed to community service or activism. There are a number of popular and sometimes controversial student-run publications, as well as a competitive debate team. The majority of freshmen live on campus, while most upperclassmen move to apartments or houses nearby.

Hippiesville, U.S.A.

On campus, constant construction and renovation have produced several new centers in recent years, including the eco-friendly Lillis Business Complex, the Jordan Schnitzer Museum of Art, and the Living-Learning Center, which includes a residence hall, performance space, classrooms, and meeting rooms. UO's lovely 295-acre campus is a short bike ride away from downtown Eugene, a small, friendly city with a liberal bent. Eugene is cozy, but there are still plenty of coffee shops, restaurants, bars, galleries, museums, music venues, and farmer's markets every Saturday. Hiking, climbing, rafting, kayaking, and surfing are all within easy reach of campus, though a raincoat is necessary on your expeditions. When students feel a need to explore beyond "Hippiesville, USA," Portland is two hours away, and the snow and surf of the Cascade Mountains and the Pacific Ocean are just one.

Admissions

Average high school GPA:	3.5
Average freshman SAT verbal / math score:	552 / 561
Average freshman ACT score:	—
Application fee:	$50
Application deadlines: 1/15 (freshmen) 5/15 (transfer)	
Total applicants:	10,821
Total accepted:	9,531 (88%)
Total accepted who enrolled:	3,352
Notification dates: 4/1 (freshmen) continuous (transfer)	

Students

Percentage of male / female students:	47% / 53%
Percentage of students from out of state:	25%
Percentage of students graduating in 4 years / 6 years:	39% / 65%

Money

Total endowment:	$365,859,000
Total in-state tuition, fees & expenses:	$14,565
Total out-of-state tuition, fees & expenses:	$26,979
Average financial aid package:	$7,671
Percentage of students who sought aid and received it:	64%
Percentage of students receiving financial aid:	35%

Also Check Out

Oregon State University

University of California–Davis

University of California–Santa Cruz

University of Colorado at Boulder

University of Washington

University of Pennsylvania

3451 Walnut Street
Philadelphia, PA 19104

(215) 898-5000
http://www.upenn.edu/

 **BIG BRAIN**

 **BIG PERSPECTIVE**

Be a part of Ben Franklin's legacy.

5 REASONS IT'S COOL

1. **Ben Franklin founded Penn,** and his spirit is alive and well on campus today.

2. The **top-ranked Wharton School for Business** is the oldest school of its kind and its graduates represent a who's who of global business.

3. Penn is the place to be for **career-oriented students** who nonetheless appreciate a broad liberal arts curriculum.

4. **Volunteer opportunities abound**, ranging from Big Brother/Big Sister mentoring programs to once-a-week tutoring.

5. The parklike campus is just minutes away from the **myriad entertainment** in Philly.

The Basics

Public / private: private nonprofit
Total enrollment / undergrads: 18,809 / 9,730
Campus setting: urban
Students call it: Penn, U Penn
Students are called: Quakers
Notable alumni: William J. Brennan, Jr. (U.S. Supreme Court justice), Noam Chomsky (author), Maury Povich (TV host), Donald Trump (business leader, entrepreneur)

Pre-Professional Drive with an Ivied Twist

Penn students choose from four undergraduate colleges of arts and sciences, engineering, nursing, and business. There are more than 80 undergraduate major options, and students can also choose a major of their own design. Most students enroll in the College of Arts and Sciences, where they are required to complete courses in a broad mix of subjects ranging from math to history. Penn's Wharton School of Business is the only undergraduate business college in the Ivy League, and its graduates include thousands of business leaders, from Warren Buffet and Ron Perelman to Donald Trump. The university encourages interdisciplinary learning, and students are given lots of freedom to chart their own academic courses. Dual degree programs, such as the Computer and Cognitive Science Program from the arts and sciences and engineering colleges, allow students to attain degrees from more than one of Penn's colleges. Students may also take classes in Penn's graduate schools or at local colleges Swarthmore, Bryn Mawr, and Haverford at no extra cost.

Feeling Toasty

Back when the legal drinking age was 18 (oh, those were the days!), Penn students would raise a glass during the third quarter of football games and sing, "Here's a toast to dear old Penn." Now that the drinking age is 21, students have taken to dumping toast (as in toasted bread) onto the field. This has forced the athletics department to invest in toast sweepers to clean the field so the games can continue.

Fun in Philly

Frats and sororities dominate the social scene at Penn. And while Greek parties rule, it's not hard for students to find non-Greek social alternatives. After all, this campus enjoys a prime location just minutes from downtown Philadelphia. Basketball and football are popular sporting events on campus, and the atmosphere gets especially spirited when the football team plays Harvard. About 35 percent of students choose to live off campus, where housing is generally more affordable. The dorm options are many, and include apartment-style housing in high-rise buildings and themed houses for those with common interests. Dining halls offer flexible meal plans with kosher options. Penn students are a notably diverse bunch: Around ten percent come from overseas, with 18 percent Asian American, 6 percent Asian, and 6 percent Hispanic, respectively. Popular clubs include *The Daily Pennsylvanian*, the award-winning college paper; UTV13, the campus televisions station; a glee club; and an all-male musical comedy group called the Mask and Wig Club, which has performed since 1889.

West Is Best

Penn's campus lies in West Philadelphia, near the Schuylkill River. Gothic-style buildings, many covered in ivy, lend the 230-acre campus an aura of grandeur that's in keeping with the university's august academic reputation. Locust Walk is a brick-lined footpath that connects the campus buildings. The university's oldest building, College Hall, inspired the Addams Family creator (Penn alumnus Charles Addams) when he designed his famously spooky Addams mansion. Listed on the National Register of Historic Places, College Hall is notable for its rich Gothic beauty, set off by prominent spires stretching high above lancet windows set in green, serpentine stone. For those seeking the pulse of city life, Philadelphia's Center City, with bars, clubs, and restaurants, is just a 20-block walk or intercity bus ride. Many students, however, particularly underclassmen, prefer the quiet and safer setting of the campus.

Admissions

Average high school GPA:	3.83
Average freshman SAT writing / math / critical reading score:	696 / 712 / 692
Average freshman ACT score:	26
Application fee:	$70

Application deadlines:
1/1 (freshmen)
3/15 (transfer)
11/1 (early decision)

Total applicants:	20,483
Total accepted:	3,613 (18%)
Total accepted who enrolled:	2,373

Notification dates:
4/1 (freshmen)
continuous (transfer)
12/15 (early decision)

Acceptance rate for early decision applicants:	34%

Students

Percentage of male / female students:	50% / 50%
Percentage of students from out of state:	80%
Percentage of students graduating in 4 years / 6 years:	87% / 94%

Money

Total endowment:	$4,294,967,295
Total tuition:	$30,598
Total cost with fees & expenses:	$44,790
Average financial aid package:	$28,633
Percentage of students who sought aid and received it:	100%
Percentage of students receiving financial aid:	43%

Also Check Out

Brown University

Columbia University

Cornell University

Harvard University

Stanford University

The University of Pittsburgh

4200 Fifth Avenue
Pittsburgh, PA 15260

(412) 624-4141
http://www.pitt.edu/

 **BIG CHOICE**

 **BIG RESEARCH**

Tall buildings, taller aspirations

5 REASONS IT'S COOL

1. Pitt holds the record for **the tallest academic building in the western hemisphere**. The campus's Cathedral of Learning is an amazing, forty-two-story behemoth.

2. You'll never be lonely. Pitt is home to **seventeen thousand diverse undergrads**.

3. This university has a long tradition of producing **cutting-edge research**, including the first polio vaccine.

4. Like sports? Students here love to **cheer on the Division I athletic teams**.

5. **Pittsburgh is a cool, low-cost city** with tons of student-friendly things to see and do—and universities like Carnegie Mellon and Duquesne.

The Basics

Public / private: public state-related
Total enrollment / undergrads: 26,860 / 17,246
Campus setting: urban
Students call it: Pitt
Students are called: Panthers
Notable alums: Michael Chabon (novelist), Gene Kelly (actor), Dan Marino (pro football player), Andrew Mellon (financier), Jonas Salk (vaccine pioneer)

Researching High and Low

Pitt sets the bar when it comes to research. The university is rated among the top schools in total research expenditures, and it rakes in over $430 million a year for biomedical and health science research alone. What does all this research mean for undergrads? Well, first and foremost, lots of research opportunities. Students and faculty push scientific progress to the next level in fields like nanotechnology, stem cell research, complex computer modeling (of molecular interactions, for instance, or of the stock market), and quantum computing. Students consider what science *is* at the Philosophy Department's Center for the Philosophy of Science, which attracts visiting scholars and lecturers from around the world. Pitt students take advantage of a wide selection of programs and opportunities; international culture and regional studies, engineering, and philosophy are all popular choices. Although many classes take place in large lecture halls, students still report that they receive plenty of attention from professors, and more than half of Pitt's classes have fewer than thirty students.

Girl Power, Circa 1898

Pitt's class of 1898 put it to a vote, and the results were undisputed: No women would be admitted to the university. Pitt's administration, however, had other ideas. Eager to boost student enrollment, they overrode the student's vote. The first women admitted were Margaret and Stella Stein. They graduated with the class of 1898, tied for class valedictorians.

Not Just Lab Coats and Bunsen Burners

Pitt students—all seventeen thousand of them—are an incredibly diverse, energetic bunch. Students often unite around a common love of sports, and lots of hours are clocked cheering on one of Pitt's seventy varsity teams, especially the football and men's basketball squads. The university offers more than three hundred student organizations, including the Blue and Gold Society, the student-alumni liaison group, and the Pitt Pathfinders, which conducts campus tours and hosts prospective students. Various student-run media outlets are popular options, including WPTS, the student-run radio station; the *Pitt News*, the campus newspaper; UPTV, the television station; and the three journals published on campus. Popular traditions abound, such as the Forbes Field Home Plate Slide for good luck on midterms and finals, and Lantern Night, which helps induct incoming freshmen.

Crossing Bridges

Located in the heart of Pittsburgh's Oakland neighborhood, the Pitt campus is dominated by the soaring Cathedral of Learning. This Gothic-style, forty-two-story tower contains classrooms, administrative offices, and a series of themed rooms representing different countries and cultures from around the world. The Pitt campus is located just a stone's throw away from several major cultural attractions, including the Carnegie Museums of Art and Natural History. Other local attractions include the Carnegie Science Center, the Andy Warhol Museum, the Pittsburgh Zoo, and the PPG Aquarium. Pittsburgh itself is a safe, cool, and affordable city that's home to tons of students and a whole lot of bridges (more than 450 total—they don't call Pittsburgh "The City of Bridges" for nothing!).

Admissions

Average high school GPA:	—
Average freshman SAT verbal / math score:	618 / 625
Average freshman ACT score:	25
Application fee:	$35
Application deadlines:	
continuous (freshmen)	
continuous (transfer)	
Total applicants:	18,195
Total accepted:	10,160 (56%)
Total accepted who enrolled:	3,390
Notification dates:	
continuous (freshmen)	
continuous (transfer)	

Students

Percentage of male / female students:	49% / 51%
Percentage of students from out of state:	15%
Percentage of students graduating in 4 years / 6 years:	44% / 67%

Money

Total endowment:	$1,819,295,000
Total in-state tuition, fees & expenses:	$20,938
Total out-of-state tuition, fees & expenses:	$30,256
Average financial aid package:	$9,087
Percentage of students who sought aid and received it:	79%
Percentage of students receiving financial aid:	50%

Also Check Out

The George Washington University

The Pennsylvania State University–University Park

University of Delaware

University of Maryland–College Park

University of Virginia

University of Puget Sound

1500 North Warner Street Tacoma, WA 98416	(253) 879-3100 http://www.ups.edu/

BIG PERSPECTIVE

To the heights

5 REASONS IT'S COOL

1. The academic approach bridges the gap between **traditional and innovative**.

2. Take advantage of **the strong Asian studies program** and you might be selected for a sponsored trip to eight Far East nations.

3. The **small class size and 11:1 student-to-faculty ratio** puts you on a first-name basis with your professors.

4. The **lush, forested, Tudor-style campus** is within minutes of downtown Tacoma.

5. The **Pacific Northwest** is a lively and laid-back region of art, music, and outdoor activity.

The Basics

Public / private: private nonprofit
Total enrollment / undergrads: 2,819 / 2,539
Campus setting: suburban
Students call it: UPS
Students are called: Loggers
Notable alums: Bill Baarsma (mayor, Tacoma, WA), George Obiozor (Nigerian ambassador), Jeff Smith (host, *The Frugal Gourmet*), Richard Wiley (writer)

Traditional with a Twist

Tucked away in the residential area of North Tacoma, the University of Puget Sound, affectionately known as UPS, is gradually gaining nation-wide recognition for its rigorous academics. UPS has all the standard (and impressive) trappings of the classic small, private liberal arts institution: little classes, no TAs, and an 11:1 student-to-faculty ratio, for example. But it also offers students such academic opportunities as a stellar Asian studies program, an undergraduate business degree, and the notable School of Music. Select students can take part in the Honors Program; the Business Leadership Program, which sets up mentorships between students and business owners in the community; and the popular Pacific Rim/Asia Study Travel Program, which sponsors a group of students to travel to eight Asian nations. These innovative programs can be paired with interdisciplinary or traditional majors. Every student must complete an extensive core curriculum that covers Argument and Inquiry, Five Approaches to Knowing, and Connections, a course

The Disappearing Hatchet

In 1908, a group of UPS students were helping tear down an old barn when they unearthed a hatchet. Now an unofficial mascot, the hatchet has been the victim of prank thefts. It reappeared in 1998 after a twelve-year absence, only to be stolen from the secure glass case in which it was housed. Its whereabouts are currently unknown.

Admissions

Average high school GPA:	3.55
Average freshman SAT writing / math / critical reading score:	610 / 618 / 638
Average freshman ACT score:	25
Application fee:	$40

Application deadlines:
2/1 (freshmen)
7/1 (transfer)
11/15 (early decision)

Total applicants:	5,231
Total accepted:	3,388 (65%)
Total accepted who enrolled:	678

Notification dates:
4/1 (freshmen)
continuous (transfer)
12/15 (early decision)

Acceptance rate for early decision applicants:	92%

Students

Percentage of male / female students:	42% / 58%
Percentage of students from out of state:	70%
Percentage of students graduating in 4 years / 6 years:	65% / 73%

Money

Total endowment:	$222,688,000
Total tuition:	$29,870
Total cost with fees & expenses:	$38,530
Average financial aid package:	$22,740
Percentage of students who sought aid and received it:	82%
Percentage of students receiving financial aid:	59%

Also Check Out

Colorado College

Lewis & Clark College

Reed College

Whitman College

taken senior year that underscores the interrelatedness of disciplines. Writing skills are stressed for all students. In contrast to undergrads at other schools, students here love the gen-ed requirements and introductory seminars.

The Art of a Healthy Balance

Students here tend to be hardworking but not cutthroat. Academics are a priority, but students get involved in a host of other activities, such as clubs, intramural sports, and community service (many students go on to join the Peace Corps). Students are not allowed to rush fraternities and sororities until the second semester of freshman year, and though 20 percent eventually join, Greek life doesn't dominate the social scene. The North End of Tacoma doesn't have much nightlife, but students make do with house parties, movies, or road trips to nearby national parks or ski slopes. A few annual traditions get everyone revved up, including the Rail, a set of parties around Halloween, and "Foolish Pleasures," a student-run short-film festival. The administration has made increasing diversity a priority. The lovely fir-dotted campus has undergone some recent renovations, and plans are in the works to greatly expand on-campus housing. As is, dorms get high marks for spacious rooms and great upkeep. Freshmen live in one of eight residence halls, while upperclassmen can opt for on-campus apartments or theme houses. Other campus facilities are also praised, especially Harbed Hall, a "green" classroom building.

East Coast Digs, West Coast Rain

The ivy-covered, Tudor-Gothic-style buildings on the ninety-seven-acre campus sit among manicured lawns and gardens, an arboretum, and a concert hall. You might think you were at an East Coast prep school were it not for the Pacific Northwest weather. On clear days, Mt. Rainer looks close enough to touch (it's actually an hour-and-a-half drive away). Tacoma, a growing city, has a good relationship with the university. Fifteen miles north of Olympia and thirty miles south of Seattle, the city also has great access to parks, coastal beaches, and ski resorts.

University of Redlands

1200 East Colton Avenue, PO Box 3080
Redlands, CA 92373

(909) 793-2121
http://www.redlands.edu/

 **BIG IDEA**

 **BIG PERSPECTIVE**

 **BIG WORLD**

Come together, right now!

5 REASONS IT'S COOL

1. Students in the **Johnston Center for Integrative Studies** take no set courses, have no set majors, and get no grades.

2. Looking for **something more traditional**? Redlands has such majors as accounting, managerial studies, pre-med, and pre-law.

3. There's always music playing at the **under-graduate School of Music.**

4. The May term offers **a month-long window for students to dig deeper** into research, study abroad, or complete an internship.

5. The **two tallest mountains in Southern California** are visible from campus. And Los Angeles is a just an hour away.

The Basics

Public / private: private nonprofit
Total enrollment / undergrads: 2,407 / 2,313
Campus setting: small town
Students call it: Redlands
Students are called: Bulldogs
Notable alums: Glen and Les Charles (TV writers, producers), John Raitt (actor), Alan Shugart (cofounder, Seagate Technology), James Q. Wilson (author, scholar)

Have It Your Way

Progressive is a good way to describe the academic programs at Redlands. The College of Arts and Sciences houses the Johnson Center for Integrative Studies, a unique, highly selective program limited to about two hundred students. Integrative studies students don't take required classes, nor do they receive grades. Instead, they design their own majors and receive written feedback from professors. Each semester, students and faculty advisors draw up specialized learning contracts that list activities and study plans. Students enrolled in the College of Arts and Sciences choose from a wide selection of more than forty majors, including global business, accounting, English, and history. Students take at least one Community Service Activity course—Into the Streets, for example, pairs students with agencies around Southern California. The month-long May term gives students a chance to focus more intensively on one subject, study abroad, or complete an intern-ship. Study-abroad options include a yearlong program in Hong Kong

Everybody Now, "Och Tamale, Gazolly Gazump!"

If there were an award for the silliest student cheer, Redlands would win it hands down. Penned by a student back in the early twentieth century, the "Och Tamale" cheer can be heard at all Bulldogs games. It's a rite of passage to memorize the utterly nonsensical ditty, which includes memorable includes lines like: "Och Tamale, Gazolly Gazump, Deyump Deyatty Yahoo!"

and a music-intensive program in Germany, among others. Redlands is also home to the conservatory-style School of Music, which trains a small number of undergrads and offers performances throughout the year.

We're All in This Together

About 75 percent of Redlands students live on campus in one of twelve residence halls. Bekins and Holt house students in a coed complex that also includes faculty offices and a coffeehouse. Freshmen live off of Frosh Quad, in the doubles and triples of Williams and the carpeted East Halls. The active campus community stays connected by eating together at the Hunsaker University Center's dining halls. Students slurp smoothies at the Plaza Café, or enjoy special sit-down meals at the University Club (which is so popular that reservations are often needed). As the Bulldogs, students compete across nineteen Division III varsity teams, and they're particularly strong in men's and women's water polo. There are five fraternities and five sororities; about 30 percent of students go Greek. Other Redlands student groups include the a cappella group Those Guys, Wilderness Connections, and the Car Club.

Valley Low, Mountain High

Redlands 160-acre campus is located in the small city of Redlands in the San Bernardino Valley. Majestic mountains—the tallest in Southern California—can be seen from campus. The campus's most iconic structure is its administration building, which was dedicated in 1910. A trolley links the university to the city's downtown, home to shops, restaurants, and stately nineteenth-century Victorian houses. Every Thursday, downtown Redland hosts Market Night, with entertainment, food, and a farmers' market, along historic State Street. Palm Springs and the Joshua Tree National Park are close by, and the beaches, malls, and nightlife of Los Angeles are about an hour away.

Admissions

Average high school GPA:	3.58
Average freshman SAT verbal / math score:	582 / 575
Average freshman ACT score:	23
Application fee:	$45
Application deadlines: 3/1 (freshmen) 5/1 (transfer)	
Total applicants:	3,480
Total accepted:	2,272 (65%)
Total accepted who enrolled:	613
Notification dates: continuous (freshmen) continuous (transfer)	

Students

Percentage of male / female students:	43% / 57%
Percentage of students from out of state:	32%
Percentage of students graduating in 4 years / 6 years:	52% / 59%

Money

Total endowment:	$110,928,960
Total tuition:	$28,476
Total cost with fees & expenses:	$39,386
Average financial aid package:	$25,693
Percentage of students who sought aid and received it:	91%
Percentage of students receiving financial aid:	68%

Also Check Out

Claremont McKenna College

Pitzer College

University of California–Irvine

University of California–Los Angeles

University of San Diego

University of Rhode Island

14 Upper College Road
Kingston, RI 02881

(401) 874-1000
http://www.uri.edu

BIG CHOICE

Study the ocean, inside or outside the classroom.

5 REASONS IT'S COOL

1. **Would-be lawyers can get their JDs** through a cooperative program with Roger Williams University School of Law.

2. **URI helps you get a job** by bringing more than five hundred recruiters to campus every year.

3. Put the nearby beaches to use by getting a degree in **aquaculture and fishery technology**.

4. If you like to play dirty, you'll enjoy the **annual mud volleyball game**.

5. Kingston is near **ski mountains, the ocean, Boston, and New York**, meaning there's plenty for city and country mice alike.

The Basics

Public / private: public state
Total enrollment / undergrads: 15,062 / 11,875
Campus setting: small town
Students call it: URI, Rhody
Students are called: Rams
Notable alums: Christiane Amanpour (journalist), Robert Ballard (oceanographer, discoverer of the *Titanic*), Robert Crandall (president and CEO, American Airlines), Steve Furness (pro football player), Robert Weygand (congressman)

An Emphasis on Excellence

URI makes a real effort to ensure that its new students succeed. The University College advising program, which is mandatory for all entering freshmen, helps students understand the rigors and requirements of the degree they choose to purse. There are over a hundred undergraduate majors on offer, some of the most popular of which are business, engineering, and the environmental sciences. URI's Honors Program automatically enrolls admitted students who graduated in the top 10 percent of their classes. So long as they maintain a GPA of at least 3.2, these students may remain in the Honors Program throughout their undergrad careers, enjoying access to top-notch faculty and seminars, and completing a capstone research project in cooperation with a faculty advisor.

A Not-So-Loose Cannon

Major-General Benjamin F. Butler was a controversial military leader who earned a reputation as a loose cannon during his tenure as military governor of New Orleans, which he captured from the Confederacy during the Civil War. Fittingly, the cannon that stands on URI's quad is nicknamed "Ben Butler."

Right on Down the Line

More than a hundred clubs, twenty-two NCAA Division I varsity teams, seventeen club teams, and a passel of intramural sports compete for students' attention outside the classroom. First-years can live in one of thirteen dormitories, some of which have themes. Fraternities and sororities have houses of their own. Many upperclassmen choose to live "down the line," a reference to an old bus line that ran from the campus to downtown Kingston, in apartments and rented houses in and around nearby resort areas. Upperclassmen are eligible to participate in internships and get a foot in the door with over ninety potential employers, including museums, congressional offices, coastal management agencies, and the attorney general's office. Students who need a change of scenery can spend a semester or year at any of eighty participating institutions without losing their status or financial aid at URI, or visit one of more than forty countries through the university's study-abroad office.

All That New England Has to Offer

URI's flagship campus is in Kingston, situated on 1,200 acres of woods and sprawling green space, just six miles from some of New England's best beaches. Kingston is also thirty miles south of Providence, and within easy reach of Newport (a half-hour drive away), Boston (an hour and a half), and New York City (three and a half hours). Kingston offers an unusual blend of seaside rural surroundings and easy access to the cultural and social outlets of nearby major metropolitan areas. URI's three other campuses are also integral to the university. The Providence campus houses the College of Continuing Education (for nontraditional students) and several other department; the Narragansett Bay campus is home to the Graduate School of Oceanography; and the 2,300-acre Alton Jones campus, west of Providence, is home to the National Center for Environmental Education.

Admissions

Average high school GPA:	—
Average freshman SAT verbal / math score:	545 / 562
Average freshman ACT score:	—
Application fee:	$50

Application deadlines:
2/1 (freshmen)
5/1 (transfer)
12/15 (early action)

Total applicants:	13,497
Total accepted:	9,968 (74%)
Total accepted who enrolled:	2,735

Notification dates:
continuous (freshmen)
continuous (transfer)
1/15 (early action)

Acceptance rate for early action applicants:	—

Students

Percentage of male / female students:	44% / 56%
Percentage of students from out of state:	39%
Percentage of students graduating in 4 years / 6 years:	36% / 56%

Money

Total endowment:	$68,000,000
Total in-state tuition, fees & expenses:	$16,990
Total out-of-state tuition, fees & expenses:	$30,690
Average financial aid package:	$12,707
Percentage of students who sought aid and received it:	63%
Percentage of students receiving financial aid:	43%

Also Check Out

James Madison University

University of Connecticut

University of New Hampshire

University of Vermont

University of Virginia

University of Richmond

28 Westhampton Way
University of Richmond, VA 23173

(804) 289-8000
http://www.richmond.edu/

BIG PERSPECTIVE

Elite academics, the Southern way

5 REASONS IT'S COOL

1. The highly selective Jepson School for Leadership Studies **teaches its students to serve society.**

2. Biologists and physicists alike should be pleased with the plans for a $35 million expansion of the Gottwald Science Center.

3. Over half the student body participates in one of **seventy-five study-abroad programs.**

4. With gothic architecture, manicured lawns, and lovely Westhampton Lake, UR has **the quintessential college campus.**

5. From the debutante Ring Ball to the freshmen Investiture and Proclamation Night, the university **honors both tradition and fun.**

The Basics

Public / private: private nonprofit
Total enrollment / undergrads: 3,554 / 2,857
Campus setting: suburban
Students call it: Richmond, UR
Students are called: Spiders
Notable alums: Leslie M. Baker Jr. (president and CEO, Wachovia Corp.), Sam Beam (musician), Sean Casey (pro baseball player), Virgil H. Goode Jr. (congressman), Mary Sue Terry (attorney general, Virginia)

Where Pre-Professionals Meet Liberal Artists

Don't be fooled by the southern ambiance—academics at this elite liberal arts institution are rigorous. They are also interdisciplinary in nature. The Richmond Quest, for example, is a program in which students tackle issues facing society and academia. Winners see their proposals implemented into UR curriculum and collect a $25,000 prize—useful, given Richmond's hefty tuition. Of UR's five undergrad schools, the Robins School of Business draws the most students. Its graduates do very well on the job market and are accepted to grad school in high numbers. The Jepson School of Leadership Studies, which was established in 1992 and is the first school of its kind in the nation, teaches students about the history, theory, and ethics of leadership. English, biology, and political science are just a few of the other strong programs. Small class sizes and a 10:1 student-to-faculty ratio guarantee stimulating discussions and personal attention in every discipline. Spiders tend to be motivated multitaskers, and professors are dedicated

Put On Your Ball Gown

The Ring Dance, one of the many traditions at UR, is a special event for the women of the junior class. If you've ever wondered what life was like for Scarlett O'Hara, this night at the ritzy Jefferson Hotel will give you a hint.

to helping them grow intellectually. Study abroad and research opportunities abound, and UR's proximity to the state capital provides plentiful corporate and governmental internship opportunities.

For the Love of Tradition

Academic buildings are clustered around lovely Westhampton Lake, which originally divided the women's Westhampton College from the men's Richmond College. Times have changed—sort of. Male and female students now live, eat, and study together, but the men and women's colleges have separate student governments, dean's offices, and residence-life staffs. Although the majority of students are from out of state, Spiders are a pretty homogenous group. Most could be described as preppy, wealthy, and fun. The huge Greek system absorbs over 30 percent of men and almost 50 percent of women. There's also a lively bar scene in downtown Richmond, as well as a variety of on-campus events. Over 275 clubs on the UR campus keep the student body active and engaged. Student government and judicial societies are popular, as are a cappella groups and volunteer organizations. It doesn't take much to unify this tight-knit group, but the Division I basketball team is a special source of pride. Over ninety percent of students live on campus all four years, adding to the sense of community. Dorms are well-maintained. The University Forest Apartments offers particularly spacious accommodations. Truth be told, Richmond is a place for tradition hounds, not radicals, which is good news for seniors who graduate with a wide web of alumni support.

The Spider Bubble and Beyond

Although ten minutes from downtown Richmond, UR's 350-acre campus feels worlds away. The trendy, eclectic neighborhood of Carytown is popular for shopping, eating, or catching a movie at the historic Byrd Theater. Brown's Inland, an outdoor venue on the James River, hosts live music in the spring, and Byrd and Maymont Parks are great places to relax and take in the natural surroundings. The Blue Ridge Mountains and Virginia Beach are close by, and D.C. is just two hours away.

Admissions

Average high school GPA:	3.48
Average freshman SAT writing / math / critical reading score:	639 / 644 / 633
Average freshman ACT score:	26
Application fee:	$50

Application deadlines:
1/15 (freshmen)
2/15 (transfer)
11/15 (early decision)

Total applicants:	5,414
Total accepted:	2,473 (46%)
Total accepted who enrolled:	757

Notification dates:
4/1 (freshmen)
4/15 (transfer)
12/15 (early decision)

Acceptance rate for early decision applicants:	47%

Students

Percentage of male / female students:	49% / 51%
Percentage of students from out of state:	84%
Percentage of students graduating in 4 years / 6 years:	78% / 84%

Money

Total endowment:	$1,387,834,000
Total tuition:	$37,610
Total cost with fees & expenses:	$44,810
Average financial aid package:	$27,205
Percentage of students who sought aid and received it:	100%
Percentage of students receiving financial aid:	36%

Also Check Out

College of William & Mary

University of North Carolina at Chapel Hill

University of Virginia

Vanderbilt University

Washington & Lee University

University of San Diego

5998 Alcala Park
San Diego, CA 92110

(619) 260-4600
http://www.sandiego.edu/

BIG WORLD

Grab a towel and sunscreen—and oh yeah, your books.

5 REASONS IT'S COOL

1. USD may be a young university, but it is **growing in popularity and prestige**.

2. The undergraduate school of business is consistently ranked among **the West Coast's strongest business programs**.

3. **A multitude of service-learning programs** connect students to the community.

4. **The perfect study break awaits:** The beautiful campus is just a stone's throw from the beach.

5. The USD campus is located in **the heart of sunny, relaxed San Diego**. And for more exotic adventures, students head south of the border, literally—Mexico is just minutes away.

The Basics

Public / private: private religious
Total enrollment / undergrads: 7,483 / 4,962
Campus setting: urban
Students call it: USD
Students are called: Toreros
Notable alums: Maggie Dixon (college basketball coach), Theo Epstein (general manager, Boston Red Sox), Andrew Firestone (star, *The Bachelor*), Lowell C. McAdam (CEO, Verizon), John Redmond (president and CEO, MGM Grand Resorts)

Getting Down to Business

USD's academic reputation is on the rise. This prestigious Catholic university is known for preparing professionals for career fields such as business, education, and the social sciences. The most popular majors are business, marketing, and management, while programs in engineering and science, psychology, communication, nursing, accountancy, and political science are also notable. The university also offers nontraditional majors such as peace and justice studies and interdisciplinary humanities. USD recently opened the Kroc School of Peace Studies, following a generous donation from Joan B. Kroc, the widow of Ray Kroc, long-time CEO of McDonalds. The center gives students a wide range of opportunities to study social justice and human rights issues. Student-faculty relations are notably amicable, helped by small class sizes and a manageable student-to-faculty ratio of 15:1. Service learning is strongly encouraged, due to both the curriculum and the university's religious

San Diego-go-go-go

While strolling along the west end of the USD campus's Colachis Plaza, students may hear some strange noises. That's because that side of the plaza is home to an echo spot. When students stand on, or cross over, a certain spot on the concrete, their voices bounce off a curved wall at the other end of the plaza and come back to them in the form of an eerie echo.

tradition. A program for freshmen includes small courses taught by faculty advisors, as well as a residential life component.

Toreros, Olé!

More than half of USD students identify as Catholic, and religious and ethical pursuits are at the core of student life. Community service, administered through the university's Center for Community Service-Learning, is very popular: About 70 percent of students take part. The campus offers a number of fitness and recreational facilities and spectator sports venues, including the new multipurpose Jenny Craig Pavilion. The administration strictly prohibits drinking on campus, for even students who are over age 21. Predictably, this means that many students head off campus on weekend nights. Students gravitate to the nearby Pacific Beach (or PB), to San Diego's historic Gaslamp Quarter and its many hot spots and shops, or to Tijuana, Mexico, which is just a short drive away.

Alcalá Park, a.k.a. Paradise

USD's 180-acre campus is perched atop a mesa, offering views of Mission Bay on one side and mountain peaks on the other. The location is pretty spectacular. And not surprisingly, most students choose to live on campus. The campus grounds are known as Alcalá Park, partly because the campus's Spanish Renaissance–style architecture is based on that of Spain's University of Alcalá. A slate of new buildings have recently been added to the campus, including the Donald P. Shiley Center for Science and Technology, home to labs, classrooms, an astronomy deck, and an aquarium, among other facilities. The university sits just north of downtown San Diego. Students benefit from the ideal location, enjoying the beaches, parks, and many cultural attractions that San Diego has to offer.

Admissions

Average high school GPA:	3.74
Average freshman SAT verbal / math score:	581 / 600
Average freshman ACT score:	24
Application fee:	$55

Application deadlines:
1/15 (freshmen)
3/1 (transfer)
11/15 (early action)

Total applicants:	10,048
Total accepted:	4,630 (46%)
Total accepted who enrolled:	1,106

Notification dates:
4/15 (freshmen)
7/15 (transfer)
1/31 (early action)

Acceptance rate for early action applicants:	—

Students

Percentage of male / female students:	40% / 60%
Percentage of students from out of state:	36%
Percentage of students graduating in 4 years / 6 years:	62% / 73%

Money

Total endowment:	$172,090,000
Total tuition:	$32,300
Total cost with fees & expenses:	$43,524
Average financial aid package:	$20,558
Percentage of students who sought aid and received it:	71%
Percentage of students receiving financial aid:	45%

Also Check Out

Gonzaga University

Loyola Marymount University

San Diego State University

Santa Clara University

University of California–San Diego

The University of South Carolina–Columbia

902 Sumter Street Access
Columbia, SC 29208

(803) 777-7000
http://www.sc.edu/

 **BIG CHOICE**

 **BIG RESEARCH**

Gamecocks o' the walk

5 REASONS IT'S COOL

1. **International wheeler-dealers** can learn the tricks of the global business trade at USC's renowned Moore School of Business.

2. USC's prestigious honors college offers **small, extra-challenging classes** and prime campus housing to a select group of high achieving students.

3. The campus's new state-of-the-art recreational center is the perfect place to get physical.

4. Gamecocks sports get everyone crowing—especially when rival Clemson's in the house.

5. The nearby shopping districts of Five Points and the Congaree Vista are favorite student hangouts.

The Basics

Public / private: public state
Total enrollment / undergrads: 27,390 / 18,648
Campus setting: urban
Students call it: USC, SC, Carolina
Students are called: Gamecocks
Notable alums: Lee Atwater (political strategist), Aleen Bailey (Olympic sprinter), Charles Frazier (author), Jim Hoagland (journalist), Jasper Johns (painter), Larry Kellner (CEO, Continental Airlines), David King (director, NASA), Sterling Sharpe (pro football player)

Eco-Friendly and Academically Loaded

While UNC–Chapel Hill grabs the headlines as the premier public university of the Carolinas, USC has quietly been building its own flagship reputation. USC excels in a wide variety of academic areas and offers serious bang for the tuition buck. The business school boasts a well-respected international business program, and programs in English, criminal justice, journalism, and marine science are also strong. The most popular majors include biology, psychology, nursing, and political science. USC is also a top research institution, particularly in the areas of biomedical, health, and environmental studies. The university recently opened the "green dorm," the world's largest environmentally sustainable residence hall complex. All students are required to complete core requirements, which include courses in English, math, natural science, liberal arts, and a foreign language. For a select group of high-achieving students, the university's prestigious Honors College

Kiss Me, I'm Southern?

Every March, USC students throw an epic St. Patrick's Day bash in Five Points, the shopping district located close to campus. In addition to the requisite drinking, students celebrate all things Irish with a parade and games for children. And, to really get in the Irish mood, they dye the water in the Five Points fountain a bright Irish green.

offers extra-challenging classes, along with prime on-campus housing arrangements.

I Tappa Kegga

Drinking is a popular pastime at USC, due in large part to the university's significant Greek scene, which draws about 15 percent of students. While ethnic diversity is notable, regional diversity is not. The typical student profile is that of the laid-back, outgoing, conservative southerner. That said, Yankees needn't fear: They're also welcomed on this friendly campus. The university turns a blind eye to the campus's widespread alcohol consumption, as long as students keep it under control. Student groups such as Gamecocks Advocating the Mature Management of Alcohol (GAMMA) provide a range of alcohol-free events and other safe alternatives to typical keg parties. USC offers more than three hundred students clubs, as well as a full schedule of theater and music performances and other cultural events. Students rally around their beloved Gamecocks sports teams, particularly the resurgent football program. The rivalry against nearby Clemson inspires a special fervor, but school spirit runs consistently high.

Diggin' Dixie

Situated in the large city of Columbia, the state capital, USC offers a pleasant mix of city excitement and country delights. Popular destinations in the city include Five Points, a cool retail and restaurant district, and the Congaree Vista, another happening shopping spot. The Horseshoe, a cluster of 200-year-old buildings, forms the historic heart of the USC campus and also provides the choicest (and costliest) on-campus accommodations. Wherever students end up living, they're within easy reach of the student union, as well as the new, state-of-the-art Strom Thurmond Wellness and Recreation Center.

Admissions

Average high school GPA:	3.86
Average freshman SAT verbal / math score:	583 / 601
Average freshman ACT score:	24
Application fee:	$50

Application deadlines:
12/1 (freshmen)
8/1 (transfer)

Total applicants:	13,946
Total accepted:	8,782 (63%)
Total accepted who enrolled:	3,646

Notification dates:
10/1 (freshmen)
10/1 (transfer)

Students

Percentage of male / female students:	45% / 55%
Percentage of students from out of state:	11%
Percentage of students graduating in 4 years / 6 years:	41% / 65%

Money

Total endowment:	—
Total in-state tuition, fees & expenses:	$15,110
Total out-of-state tuition, fees & expenses:	$27,538
Average financial aid package:	$9,840
Percentage of students who sought aid and received it:	73%
Percentage of students receiving financial aid:	41%

Also Check Out

Duke University

Clemson University

University of Florida

University of Georgia

University of North Carolina at Chapel Hill

The University of South Dakota

414 East Clark Street
Vermillion, SD 57069

(605) 677-5011
http://www.usd.edu/

 **BIG CHOICE**

 **BIG PERSPECTIVE**

Big choice. Big value. Cute coyote.

5 REASONS IT'S COOL

1. USD is South Dakota's **only public liberal arts university.**

2. The icing on the cake: It's **extremely affordable,** even for students from out of state.

3. USD has produced nine Rhodes Scholars—and **Tom Brokaw.**

4. Check out the **unique "signature programs":** the IdEA program, First Year Experience program, Honors Program, and Undergraduate Research and Creative Activity.

5. Home of the Coyotes, the **DakotaDome** features a pool, track, racquetball and basketball courts, and more.

The Basics

Public / private: public state
Total enrollment / undergrads: 8,746 / 6,468
Campus setting: small town
Students call it: The U, USD
Call the students: Coyotes
Notable alums: Dorothy Cooper Foote (writer), Ken Bode (journalist), Tom Brokaw (news anchor), Joe Foss (governor, South Dakota), Al Neuharth (founder, *USA Today*)

Sounds like a Good IdEA

USD offers more than 110 majors through its six colleges of arts and sciences, fine arts, business, education, law, and health sciences. Notable majors include American Indian studies, business, education, and psychology. Regardless of their major, all students are required to take part in the Interdisciplinary Education and Action Program (IdEA). Through IdEA, in-depth investigation of an issue (such as global health or leadership) is combined with community service, research, or a creative activity. The U offers several other "signature programs," including the First Year Experience, the Honors Program, and the Undergraduate Research and Creative Activity. All signature programs aim to broaden perspectives, with the additional benefit of giving students' resumes a boost. Classes sizes are manageable: Many have fewer than forty students, and the majority have fewer than twenty.

Where the Coyotes Roam

USD fans love Charlie, the lovable costumed coyote that gets the crowd revved up at football games. But the university's mascot wasn't always so cute and cuddly. Back in the 1960s, an *actual* coyote named Snoopy graced football games. The move away from the live coyote was a good one, not only for wary spectators, but also for the students who audition to wear the Charlie costume every year.

Home Sweet Dorm

Three-quarters of USD students are from South Dakota, and most of the remaining students hail from someplace else in the Midwest. Cultural diversity isn't one of the university's calling cards, but there are several organizations for minority students, and Native American students make up about 2 percent of the population. Greek life enjoys a healthy presence on campus, and the university is home to twelve fraternities and sororities. All students are required to live on campus for the first two years, unless they're living with parents or in a Greek house. All told, more than 80 percent of students live on campus. DakotaDome, USD's sports complex, caters to a range of athletic interests and is the site of many intramural competitions. And when you're heading to a Coyotes football game during the cold winter months, you'll be happy to know that you won't freeze: The DakotaDome is an enclosed field.

Vermillion, How I Love Thee

There's nothing but love between USD and its host town, Vermillion. Support for USD is everywhere, from banners for the football team to discounts for students at local shops. Students often take to the road on the weekends, driving the hour to Sioux Falls, Sioux City, IA, or just heading home. Vermillion, though small (population 10,000), has a wide selection of student-friendly coffee shops and bars, as well as a movie theater. If hunting, fishing, or camping sound appealing, the Missouri River and surrounding countryside offer a wealth of possibilities. The campus has seen quite a bit of construction recently, including a new student center, an addition to the Beacon School of Business, and a 1,500-seat performing arts center.

Admissions

Average high school GPA:	3.27
Average freshman SAT verbal / math score:	533 / 545
Average freshman ACT score:	23
Application fee:	$20
Application deadlines:	
continuous (freshmen)	
continuous (transfer)	
Total applicants:	3,044
Total accepted:	2,619 (86%)
Total accepted who enrolled:	1,021
Notification dates:	
continuous (freshmen)	
continuous (transfer)	

Students

Percentage of male / female students:	43% / 57%
Percentage of students from out of state:	26%
Percentage of students graduating in 4 years / 6 years:	21% / 46%

Money

Total endowment:	$102,128,218
Total in-state tuition, fees & expenses:	$11,093
Total out-of-state tuition, fees & expenses:	$15,972
Average financial aid package:	$5,500
Percentage of students who sought aid and received it:	73%
Percentage of students receiving financial aid:	41%

Also Check Out

The University of Iowa

University of Minnesota–Twin Cities

University of Nebraska–Lincoln

University of North Dakota

The University of South Florida

4202 East Fowler Avenue
Tampa, FL 33620

(813) 974-2011
http://www.usf.edu

 **BIG CHOICE**

 **BIG RESEARCH**

A bullish outlook

5 REASONS IT'S COOL

1. My, how it's grown: USF is the **second-largest university in the Southeast** and among the top 20 largest in the nation.

2. You'll find **the next generation of corporate movers and shakers** at USF's top-notch College of Business.

3. The successful **Bulls sports program** is horning in on the attention previously reserved for Florida's other hometown favorites, the Gators and the 'Noles.

4. **Movies on the Lawn** is always a good time—and it's free!

5. With the beach so close to campus, students frequently have **toes in the sand and drinks in their hands.**

The Basics

Public / private: public state
Total enrollment / undergrads: 43,636 / 34,438
Campus setting: urban
Students call it: USF
Students are called: Bulls
Notable alums: Chucky Atkins (pro basketball player), Leo Gallagher (comedian), Tony La Russa (pro baseball manager), Ann Ligouri (sports broadcaster), Lobo (musician), Kerry Sanders (news correspondent), Kurt Wimmer (filmmaker)

History in the Making

Founded in 1956, USF is a relatively new institution that has worked hard to establish itself alongside its more prominent neighbors Florida State University and the University of Florida. The university offers more than two hundred majors through its ten undergraduate colleges. Popular programs include health sciences, education, architecture, engineering, business, psychology, communication, and environmental science. A strong marine science program is housed on the St. Petersburg campus, just 20 minutes away. A cool $250 million in sponsored research grants and contracts, brought in by on-campus researchers every year, only adds to the number of learning opportunities available to undergrads. The university also offers a competitive Honors College; study-abroad opportunities in countries such as Spain, South Korea, and South Africa; and workplace programs with eight hundred companies worldwide. Although the student body is

Alma Matters

Any respectable institution needs a school song, and USF wasted no time in getting one. In 1960, when the university was in its fourth year, then-professor of music Wayne Hugoboom entered his original composition in a university-sponsored songwriting competition. Legend has it that the tune was inspired by good food and drink at a faculty party. Hugoboom's song took the prize, becoming the USF Alma Mater, and Hugoboom walked away with $250, which he allegedly used to buy a riding lawn mower.

huge and class sizes average in the twenties, the faculty tends to be open and accessible. There's no getting around bureaucratic snarls and limited class availability, but students find the great education at low cost well worth it.

"See Ya Monday!"

USF is primarily a commuter campus. Though more than 90 percent of students are Floridians, the university is quite diverse: Students hail from all fifty states and many foreign countries, and nearly a third of students represent minority groups such as African Americans and Hispanics. The healthy Greek scene, which includes seventeen fraternities and thirteen sororities, contributes to the lively social scene. The university offers more than three hundred student organizations, including the *Oracle*, a daily student newspaper, and campus radio and television stations. A full slate of on-campus concerts, performances, movies, and other events further encourages a sense of community to counter the commuter campus blues. Bulls athletics are a growing point of pride. The campus's new athletic facilities are excellent, the sailing team is nationally recognized, and recent successes have also shot the football team to national prominence.

Tampa

USF is located in an area of Tampa best known for its sprawl of houses, condos, and strip malls. And while the local vibe is, according to some students, "suburban blah," local bright spots include popular watering holes like the Greenery Pub and Peabody's. The Ybor City neighborhood also offers a lively nightlife for those over 21, and the nearby beaches on the Gulf of Mexico are student favorites. USF's campus offers many creature comforts. For the few on-campus residents, the dorms are reportedly livable; the university-owned Magnolia Apartments are the pick of the litter. The university's deluxe student center provides excellent new fitness and recreation facilities.

Admissions

Average high school GPA:	3.61
Average freshman SAT writing / math / critical reading score:	528 / 569 / 558
Average freshman ACT score:	23
Application fee:	$30
Application deadlines:	
4/15 (freshmen)	
4/15 (transfer)	
Total applicants:	22,462
Total accepted:	11,509 (51%)
Total accepted who enrolled:	4,253
Notification dates:	
continuous (freshmen)	
continuous (transfer)	

Students

Percentage of male / female students:	41% / 59%
Percentage of students from out of state:	3%
Percentage of students graduating in 4 years / 6 years:	21% / 47%

Money

Total endowment:	$298,240,000
Total in-state tuition, fees & expenses:	$11,470
Total out-of-state tuition, fees & expenses:	$24,169
Average financial aid package:	$9,025
Percentage of students who sought aid and received it:	26%
Percentage of students receiving financial aid:	32%

Also Check Out

Florida State University

University of Central Florida

University of Florida

The University of Miami

University of Southern California

University Park Campus Los Angeles, CA 90089	(213) 740-2311 http://www.usc.edu/

BIG CHOICE

BIG RESEARCH

Trojan scholars and urban warriors

5 REASONS IT'S COOL

1. The **oldest private research university in the West,** USC also has the oldest schools of medicine and pharmacy in Southern California.

2. The **impressive range of professional majors** includes business, cinema, music, and architecture, and many students double-major.

3. **USC means movies.** Grads such as George Lucas have created some of the greatest movies of all time.

4. Students' **love of leadership and spirit of volunteerism** make a positive impact on the surrounding community.

5. The **third most-winning athletics program in the nation** brings the campus together.

The Basics

Public / private: private nonprofit
Total enrollment / undergrads: 33,389 / 16,729
Campus setting: urban
Students call it: USC
Students are called: Trojans
Notable alums: William French Anderson (geneticist), Neil Armstrong (astronaut), Will Ferrell (actor), Ron Howard (filmmaker), Lisa Ling (journalist), George Lucas (filmmaker), Sol Price (businessman)

Yeah, We're Good at That—and That, and That, and That

A leader in many research and professional fields, USC is on the rise in the academic community and can offer ambitious students the chance to branch out intellectually and creatively. The College of Letters, Arts, and Sciences and the seventeen professional schools at USC offer a staggering 150-plus majors and almost as many minors. The first year, during which students complete the required six-course core curriculum, can be less challenging than years two through four. For those who want to up the intellectual ante, there are the Freshman Seminars and the Thematic Option, general education honors programs that replace the core. The student-to-faculty ratio is 14:1, class sizes average twenty-six, and TAs often lead discussion sections and labs. Undergrads are encouraged to spend a year abroad; USC has several overseas centers and partners with other programs to send students to all corners of the globe.

The Essence of Troy

So how did a So Cal school get tangled up with ancient Troy? In 1912, a *Los Angeles Times* sportswriter compared USC's athletes to legendary Trojan warriors, and the moniker stuck. A large stone from the city of Troy, a gift from the Republic of Turkey, sits near Taper Hall on campus, and the bronze Tommy Trojan sculpture is the embodiment of the Trojan spirit.

Strike Up the Fun

Trojan athletics make up a huge part of campus life: The Spirit of Troy, the USC marching band, leads the way to football games past the statue of Tommy Trojan and to the historic Coliseum across the street. Another athletic nucleus is the brand new Galen Center, home of basketball and volleyball games. Nearly half of USC's undergraduates come from out of state. For some, USC life equals Greek life, but the great majority of students don't rush. Students can pick from over six hundred campus clubs. They can also (and many do) spend time volunteering in the community or working on a creative project, big business idea, or the latest scientific innovation. Classes, libraries, and tasty food are never far away no matter where students are on the compact University Park campus. The city's excitement draws many students out on the weekends, but there are still plenty of movie screenings and events on campus to keep life interesting.

It's a Brick House

You don't see lots of brick in earthquake-prone Los Angeles, but the Romanesque buildings on USC's University Park campus are an exception, and their beauty makes the risk worth it. More modern and contemporary buildings also incorporate brick, but the lines are cleaner and less ornate. Recent renovations to the urban campus have brought more green space, adding tranquility to this big-city campus. Downtown is nearby, decreasingly sketchy Exposition Park is across the street, and still-sketchy neighborhoods are beyond. The original University Park campus is still at the heart of USC, but the university itself has major buildings and facilities throughout Los Angeles, including Los Angeles County–USC Medical Center and Children's Hospital Los Angeles, and down into Orange County.

Admissions

Average high school GPA:	3.71
Average freshman SAT writing / math / critical reading score:	686 / 693 / 674
Average freshman ACT score:	26
Application fee:	$65

Application deadlines:
1/10 (freshmen)
2/1 (transfer)

Total applicants:	33,979
Total accepted:	8,634 (25%)
Total accepted who enrolled:	2,759

Notification dates:
4/1 (freshmen)
6/1 (transfer)

Students

Percentage of male / female students:	49% / 51%
Percentage of students from out of state:	39%
Percentage of students graduating in 4 years / 6 years:	61% / 83%

Money

Total endowment:	$3,065,935,000
Total tuition:	$33,314
Total cost with fees & expenses:	$44,786
Average financial aid package:	$29,641
Percentage of students who sought aid and received it:	99%
Percentage of students receiving financial aid:	41%

Also Check Out

New York University

Northwestern University

University of California–Berkeley

University of California–Los Angeles

University of Pennsylvania

The University of Tennessee

320 Student Services Building
Knoxville, TN 37996

(865) 974-1000
http://www.tennessee.edu/

 **BIG CHOICE**

 **BIG RESEARCH**

The big orange

5 REASONS IT'S COOL

1. This large research institution boasts **strong pre-professional programs** in business, architecture, and engineering.

2. Ample academic opportunities allow you to get **a top-notch education at a rock-bottom price**.

3. UT's program with the Oak Ridge Laboratory provides **endless research possibilities**.

4. You haven't felt school pride until you've heard the **Pride of the Southland Band play "Rocky Top" before a football game**.

5. If you like a packed social calendar, you'll feel right at home at **this notorious party school**.

The Basics

Public / private: public state
Total enrollment / undergrads: 28,901 / 20,619
Campus setting: urban
Students call it: UT
Students are called: Volunteers, Vols
Notable alums: Howard Baker (senator, ambassador, White House chief of staff), James Denton (actor), Allan Houston (pro basketball player), Johnny Majors (college football coach), Peyton Manning (pro football player), Margaret Rhea Seddon (astronaut)

Driven—or Just Cruising?

With eleven colleges and three hundred degree programs, this large research institution, Tennessee's only major public university, has something to satisfy all brands of intellectual curiosity. Most UT students gravitate toward the College of Arts & Sciences, which offers fourteen interdisciplinary programs. The strong engineering program will soon be housed in a state-of-the-art building, and the business program is well regarded, especially in the specialty area of supply-chain management. A partnership with the Battelle Memorial Institute to manage the Department of Energy's Oak Ridge National Laboratory has led to some unique research opportunities for undergrads. And the Honors Program is a good option for those looking for a more rigorous course of study. To get the most out of UT academics, students need to take some initiative. Personalized advising is hard to come by, lecture classes routinely pack students in by the hundreds, and discussion

Sign 'Em Up

The nickname "Volunteers" originated from the Tennesseans' penchant for volunteer military service. During the Mexican-American War, Governor Aaron Brown requested the services of 2,800 men—and got 30,000!

sections are often led by TAs. Still, the 15:1 faculty-to-student ratio is lower than the ratio at many like-sized state schools.

Fight, Vols, Fight!

UT's social atmosphere can be captured in one word: football. The frenzy surrounding home games infects all of Knoxville. Basketball also draws a good deal of student interest; the Lady Vols are consistently among the nation's best women's teams. Not surprisingly, sports mania overflows into a strong intramural program. For the less athletically inclined, over 450 student organizations cater to a wide variety of religious, political, and social interests. Although the administration is trying to combat UT's party school rep, the joint continues to jump. The popular Greek scene hosts a variety of events, from formals to the annual All-Sing featuring a band and fiddle contest. Freshmen are required to live on campus, and most wind up in the dorms around Presidential Court. Most upperclassmen take advantage of the affordable off-campus housing options. School loyalty and tradition, from homecoming to the freshmen initiation ritual of Torch Night, are important. And with nearly 90 percent of the student body hailing from Tennessee, Vols are just dripping in state pride.

Friendly City with a Bluesy Bent

A big city with a small-town vibe, Knoxville is neither stifling nor overwhelming, which makes it a great place for a college student. The university shares a close bond with the city, and students and townspeople band together to support Volunteer sports. The Strip, a row of restaurants and coffee shops, is a popular haunt near campus. The city also boasts a dedicated arts community and a music history rich in bluegrass and country lore and noted for its current contributions to the indie rock scene. Thursday nights feature the Sundown in the City outdoor music series. Blue Cats and Bijou are great music venues, and dance troupes and theater companies create a lively cultural atmosphere. Atlanta and Nashville are each three-hour drives away, and the Smokey Mountains are only one hour away.

Admissions

Average high school GPA:	3.59
Average freshman SAT verbal / math score:	581 / 592
Average freshman ACT score:	25
Application fee:	$30

Application deadlines:
2/1 (freshmen)
6/1 (transfer)
11/1 (early action)

Total applicants:	12,372
Total accepted:	9,132 (74%)
Total accepted who enrolled:	4,219

Notification dates:
continuous (freshmen)
continuous (transfer)
12/15 (early action)

Acceptance rate for early action applicants: —

Students

Percentage of male / female students:	49% / 51%
Percentage of students from out of state:	14%
Percentage of students graduating in 4 years / 6 years:	29% / 55%

Money

Total endowment:	$585,445,000
Total in-state tuition, fees & expenses:	$12,222
Total out-of-state tuition, fees & expenses:	$23,788
Average financial aid package:	$8,804
Percentage of students who sought aid and received it:	71%
Percentage of students receiving financial aid:	39%

Also Check Out

Auburn University

Emory University

University of Alabama–Tuscaloosa

University of Georgia

University of Kentucky

The University of Texas at Austin

PO Box 8058 Austin, TX 78712	(512) 471-3434 http://www.utexas.edu/

 **BIG CHOICE**    **BIG RESEARCH**    **BIG WORLD**

Sometimes bigger really is better.

5 REASONS IT'S COOL

1. With **nine hundred organizations and dozens of majors in twelve different colleges**, the hardest part about attending UT Austin is deciding what *not* to do.

2. Students get a great education **without acquiring tons of debt**.

3. How's this for great service: Roughly **75 percent of students volunteer to serve the community** at least once a year.

4. **Go Longhorns!** UT Austin's basketball, baseball, and football teams are among the best in the country.

5. Austin is known as the **"Live Music Capital of the World"**—and that includes far more than just country music.

The Basics

Public / private: public state
Total enrollment / undergrads: 49,697 / 37,037
Campus setting: urban
Students call it: UT Austin, The University of Texas, Texas, UT
Students are called: Longhorns
Notable alums: Wes Anderson (filmmaker), J. M. Coetzee (writer), Walter Cronkite (news anchor), Michael Dell (founder, Dell, Inc.), Marcia Gay Harden (actress), Matthew McConaughey (actor), Bill Moyers (author, journalist), Mary Lou Retton (Olympic gymnast), Ann Richards (governor, Texas), Vince Young (pro football player), Chris Ware (cartoonist), Renee Zellweger (actress)

One Size Fits All

UT Austin truly fits the mold of the "public Ivy." The university's eleven undergraduate colleges offer more than 120 majors. The most popular majors include economics and political science, along with education, engineering, and the sciences. The university attracts prominent faculty members in just about every field, and about 90 percent of professors hold PhDs. Introductory-level classes are known to hold up to several hundred students, but most classes average between twenty and thirty. Some classes, especially labs and lower-level foreign language classes, are taught by teaching assistants. Even the administration garners few complaints—quite a feat, given that they're contending with upwards of 37,000 undergrad (not to mention an additional 12,000 grad students!).

"Hook 'Em, Horns!"

"Hook 'em, Horns!" is the unofficial UT Austin motto. You'll hear it whenever Longhorns greet each other, say goodbye, or cheer for a Longhorns sports team. This expression is generally accompanied by a hand gesture resembling the head and horns of Bevo, the original "Longhorn." Thousands of hands flash this symbol during football games when the Longhorn Band plays "The Eyes of Texas," the school song, or when cheerleaders lead a chorus of "Texas Fight," the school fight song. One surefire way to offend any Longhorn faithful? Flip the Hook-'em sign upside down.

Big Pond, Big Possibilities

There's something for everyone at UT Austin. Students choose from more than nine hundred registered organizations, including religious groups, student publications, student-run radio and TV stations, service organizations, and intramural sports teams. The university is reputed to be a big party school, and about 20 percent of students participate in the more than fifty Greek organizations. The university does not require students to live on campus, and nearly 80 percent of students opt for private apartments, co-ops, or privately run dorms. High-rise apartments have been sprouting up throughout West Campus neighborhoods, ensuring that students will have plenty of housing options. Close proximity to campus can be a blessing and a curse during football season, when rabid fans tailgate and fill Daryl K. Royal Memorial Stadium, the home of Longhorn football. UT Austin's athletic teams are perennial national championship contenders, and even the least sporty students get swept up in Longhorn fever.

Where Weird Is Cool

The slogan "Keep Austin Weird" suits Austin perfectly. An indie spirit pervades all parts of the city, including the restaurant, political, film, and fashion worlds. UT students frequent the many bars and music venues on Austin's famed Sixth Street, where music spills out onto the streets nightly—this is where Austin earns its reputation as the live music capital of the world. Any time the sun's out, students can be found walking down the Drag, a retail strip that runs parallel to campus, or sunbathing on one of the campus's several quads. Students also make use of the plentiful hiking and biking trails in Austin's many city parks. Love for Austin is so intense, in fact, that many students never leave. And because so many city residents are UT alums, the university enjoys a healthy camaraderie with the local populace.

Admissions

Average high school GPA:	—
Average freshman SAT writing / math / critical reading score:	591 / 638 / 605
Average freshman ACT score:	24
Application fee:	$60
Application deadlines: 2/1 (freshmen) 3/1 (transfer)	
Total applicants:	23,502
Total accepted:	13,307 (57%)
Total accepted who enrolled:	7,369
Notification dates: continuous (freshmen) continuous (transfer)	

Students

Percentage of male / female students:	47% / 53%
Percentage of students from out of state:	4%
Percentage of students graduating in 4 years / 6 years:	42% / 75%

Money

Total endowment:	$2,445,624,180
Total in-state tuition, fees & expenses:	$16,606
Total out-of-state tuition, fees & expenses:	$29,340
Average financial aid package:	$10,900
Percentage of students who sought aid and received it:	90%
Percentage of students receiving financial aid:	48%

Also Check Out

Rice University

Texas Tech University

Tulane University

University of California–Berkeley

University of Michigan–Ann Arbor

University of Tulsa

600 South College Avenue
Tulsa, OK 74104

(918) 631-2000
http://www.utulsa.edu/

BIG CHOICE

Challenging academics in an intimate setting

5 REASONS IT'S COOL

1. The sciences are strong here, especially the **excellent engineering program**.

2. Approximately 10 percent of students are **National Merit Finalists**.

3. Like research? Students who take part in the **Tulsa Undergraduate Research Challenge** get stipends to perform original studies.

4. Although historically tied to the Presbyterian Church, TU is proud of its **cultural and religious diversity**.

5. TU is the smallest college (with about 2,880 undergrads) to have a **Division I football team**.

The Basics

Public / private: private religious
Total enrollment / undergrads: 4,125 / 2,882
Campus setting: urban
Students call it: TU
Students are called: Golden Hurricanes
Notable alums: Bob Brown (TV news correspondent), Steve Largent (pro football player, Hall of Famer), Rue McClanahan (actress), Drew Pearson (pro football player), Mark Radcliffe (film producer)

You Won't Be the Only Smart One

Academics are taken seriously at TU, and students wouldn't have it any other way. After all, one in ten is a National Merit Finalist, and more than a fair share go on to receive Goldwater or Truman scholarships. And although the atmosphere is studious, it's more collaborative than competitive. The university offers a wide range of majors through its three undergraduate colleges of arts and sciences, business administration, and engineering and natural sciences. Finance, psychology, and history are all strong programs, while the science programs, including engineering and computer science, are particularly renowned. The Tulsa Undergraduate Research Challenge (TURC) gives students money to do all sorts of independent projects, from working in a laboratory to writing an original musical score. The average class size is nineteen, and the student-to-faculty ratio is 11:1. The many study-abroad opportunities include language classes in Spain and Russia, law programs in Ireland and Argentina, and a nursing program in France.

Going to the John?

The all-male residence hall on Tulsa's campus is named after its benefactor, John E. Mabee. Leave it to the guys to shorten their hall's name to "The John." Soon after opening its doors in 1950, The John's men began hosting the annual Toilet Bowl, a spirited game of flag football. Girls, don't think you're off the hook—the Toilet Bowl Queen is crowned at halftime, and everyone joins in the festivities at the Toilet Ball after the game.

Sports and Spades

TU students of all stripes hang out on the U, the grassy area at the center of campus, and at the Allen Chapman Activity Center (known as Ack Ack). Nearly 30 percent of students are international or belong to a minority group, making for an extremely diverse population. But the campus bonds over sports: Just about everyone cheers on the Golden Hurricanes, particularly the football and basketball teams. There are eighteen Division I athletic teams in all, as well as a host of intramurals, from flag football to spades. The university offers more than three hundred student organizations, ranging from the Angolan Student Association to the TU Ballroom Dancers to Trio Tulsa, a chamber music group. Fraternities and sororities also play a large role in social life, with over 20 percent of students participating. As freshmen, students choose from one of four residence halls, and many opt to move to off-campus apartments as upperclassmen. And though students at this Presbyterian university aren't required to attend church services, many enjoy stopping by the lovely Sharp Chapel, which has graced campus since 2004.

Tulsa

TU is located in Tulsa, the second-largest city in Oklahoma. Nearby Cherry Street offers shops, galleries, and such restaurants as Atomic Burrito and Panera Bread Co. At night, students head to the Brookside entertainment district to play pool at Sharky's or grab a bite at Garlic Rose. Among Tulsa's other attractions are the Oklahoma Jazz Hall of Fame, the Brady Arts District, the Tulsa Zoo, and River Parks, more than twenty miles of shoreline alongside the Arkansas River. Home to the Myriad Botanical Gardens and the Frontier City Theme Park, Oklahoma City is just about ninety minutes away.

Admissions

Average high school GPA:	3.7
Average freshman SAT verbal / math score:	613 / 614
Average freshman ACT score:	24
Application fee:	$35
Application deadlines: continuous (freshmen) continuous (transfer)	
Total applicants:	2,720
Total accepted:	2,058 (76%)
Total accepted who enrolled:	656
Notification dates: continuous (freshmen) continuous (transfer)	

Students

Percentage of male / female students:	51% / 49%
Percentage of students from out of state:	36%
Percentage of students graduating in 4 years / 6 years:	43% / 60%

Money

Total endowment:	$817,517,000
Total tuition:	$21,690
Total cost with fees & expenses:	$29,174
Average financial aid package:	$22,586
Percentage of students who sought aid and received it:	87%
Percentage of students receiving financial aid:	41%

Also Check Out

Rice University

Tulane University

University of Oklahoma

Vanderbilt University

University of Utah

20I South University Street	(80I) 58I-7200
Salt Lake City, UT 84II2	http://www.utah.edu/

 **BIG CHOICE**

 **BIG RESEARCH**

The A through Z of the U of U

5 REASONS IT'S COOL

1. There are strong science programs, research opportunities, and internships at this **nationally recognized research institution.**

2. Live where the athletes did! Built for the 2002 Winter Olympics, **the dorms are some of the nicest in the nation.**

3. Enjoy a unique setting that offers **the perks of city life and the beauty of nature.**

4. Hit the slopes: The **world-class skiing** of Alta and Snowbird is less than an hour away.

5. Cheer on the **great sports teams**, especially when they're up against longtime rival Brigham Young University.

The Basics

Public / private: public state
Total enrollment / undergrads: 28,619 / 22,155
Campus setting: urban
Students call it: The U, U of U
Students are called: Swoops, Utes
Notable alums: Jamal Anderson (pro football player), Orson Scott Card (writer), Edwin Catmull (cofounder, Pixar), Tom Chambers (pro basketball player), David Neeleman (founder, JetBlue), Wallace Stegner (writer)

Getting What You Want Out of the U

U of U, the state's oldest and largest university, provides a more secular alternative to nearby Brigham Young. Primarily a commuter school, it has plentiful course offerings, many in the form of large lecture classes. Several programs foster scholastic community among students. Students enrolled in LEAP courses, for example, take a sequence of classes with the same students and professor for the entire year. The Honors Program places select students in smaller, more demanding courses. Students agree that you get out of the U what you put in. Intellectual stimulation varies from class to class, as does the workload and accessibility of the professor, but overall, students are satisfied. The U is a nationally recognized research institution, so there are a wealth of resources and internship opportunities available. The Undergraduate Research Opportunities Program provides semester grants to students who work alongside faculty. In addition to study-abroad programs, there is a National Student Exchange, which allows Utes to study at

Do the Math

The U was founded in 1850 as the University of Deseret (*deseret* means *honeybee* in the Book of Mormon, and today, a beehive decorates the Utah state flag). But wait, Utah wasn't admitted into the union as a state until 1896! That's right: The university came *before* the state.

participating universities all over the United States without paying the high cost of out-of-state tuition. There are over one hundred majors and especially strong programs in the sciences. Popular majors include economics, political science, and mass communications.

City, Mountains, and Utes, Oh My!

Situated at the base of the Wasatch Mountains, the U combines the benefits of an urban environment with the quiet beauty of the mountains. Since the university is a commuter school, there can be a tepid sense of community. For those who are interested, it's easy to get involved in one of the many clubs and organizations. And the 7 percent of students who do choose to live on campus enjoy some of the spiffiest dorms in the United States: Heritage Commons, built to house athletes during the 2002 Winter Olympics, which have spacious rooms, high-speed Internet connections, cable TV access, and dining facilities. Students can also opt for Living Learning communities. Seventy-nine percent of Utes are from Utah, and while they come from diverse economic backgrounds, they are racially and ethnically homogenous. They are also homogenous in their love for their football team.

Free to Ski

The tree-lined campus is located five minutes from downtown Salt Lake City, easily accessed by the light-rail called the Trax. The school, which is one of the largest employers in Utah, has a strong relationship with this safe, clean city. Students can take advantage of the museums, shops, restaurants, and dance and theater companies nearby. Those with an interest in outdoor pursuits couldn't ask for a better location. Some of the nation's best mountain biking, rock climbing, and kayaking are here, and there's plenty of hiking within minutes of campus. The world-class skiing of Alta and Snowbird are just forty-five minutes away—and a bus will drop you slope-side right from campus!

Admissions

Average high school GPA:	3.52
Average freshman SAT verbal / math score:	572 / 576
Average freshman ACT score:	23
Application fee:	$35
Application deadlines: 4/1 (freshmen) 4/1 (transfer)	
Total applicants:	6,770
Total accepted:	5,711 (84%)
Total accepted who enrolled:	2,463
Notification dates: — (freshman) — (transfer)	

Students

Percentage of male / female students:	56% / 44%
Percentage of students from out of state:	16%
Percentage of students graduating in 4 years / 6 years:	16% / 45%

Money

Total endowment:	$382,764,000
Total in-state tuition, fees & expenses:	$11,591
Total out-of-state tuition, fees & expenses:	$21,521
Average financial aid package:	$8,526
Percentage of students who sought aid and received it:	56%
Percentage of students receiving financial aid:	26%

Also Check Out

Brigham Young University

University of Idaho

The University of Montana–Missoula

University of Wyoming

University of Vermont

194 S. Prospect St.
Burlington, VT 05405

(802) 656-3131
http://www.uvm.edu/

 **BIG CHOICE**

 **BIG RESEARCH**

Green Mountains, green school

5 REASONS IT'S COOL

1. UVM's **commitment to saving the environment** is hard to beat—campus life and many classes here are all about the green.

2. And speaking of green stuff, UVM is consistently ranked among the **best buys in higher education**.

3. Want to make a difference? This university has tons of **student community service organizations**.

4. UVM's **majestic lakeside location** will take your breath away. You'd be hard-pressed to find a more beautiful place.

5. We can't offer enough kudos to the city of Burlington for being a cool town and **a great place to live and work**.

The Basics

Public / private: public state
Total enrollment / undergrads: 11,870 / 10,082
Campus setting: suburban
Students call it: UVM
Students are called: Catamounts
Notable alums: John Dewey (educator), Annie Proulx (novelist), Gail Sheehy (author), Kerr Smith (actor)

A Green Giant (Academically Speaking)

UVM comprises seven undergraduate colleges: the College of Arts and Sciences, the College of Engineering and Mathematics, the College of Education and Social Services, the College of Agricultural and Life Sciences, the College of Nursing and Health Sciences, the School of Business Administration, and the Rubenstein School of Environment and Natural Resources. The university's highly selective Honors College admitted just one hundred students its first year (2004); students enrolled in the college are granted a more intense academic experience along with access to visiting scholars, research projects, and other special opportunities. UVM is home to more than eighty-five undergraduate majors and the largest library in Vermont. In a state full of private liberal arts schools, UVM also offers what none other in the state can—a leading research university that receives copious funding from such clients as the Department of Defense, the National Cancer Institute, NASA, and the National Science Foundation. Studying abroad is a popular option: The Office of International Education offers

Shouldn't It Be UV?

Ever wonder where the *M* comes from in UVM? Ira Allen, one of the leaders of the Green Mountain Boys and brother of American Revolutionary leader Ethan Allen, founded the university with the name of the University of the Green Mountains. In Latin, this translates to *Universitas Viridis Montis*, or UVM. In 1865, the university was joined with the Vermont Agricultural College and the official name remains the University of Vermont and State Agricultural College.

programs on six continents, and additional opportunities are available in conjunction with other institutions.

Bring Your Birkenstocks

A laid-back, hippy vibe is pervasive on the UVM campus, and a good chunk of the student body tends to be left-leaning, environmentally conscious, and Birkenstock wearing. More than a hundred clubs keep students busy outside of the classroom and the campus abuzz with activity. The largest student organization is one dedicated to public outreach and community service. From raising food for needy families to teaching kids about global warming, students give back to the Burlington area through a multitude of service programs, internships, and service learning courses throughout the curriculum. Twenty varsity teams compete in NCAA Division I athletics, and intramural and club sports from sailing to horseshoes to whiffle ball keep the fans cheering and the pulses racing.

Lakeside Living

UVM's campus sits on the shores of Lake Champlain, just up the hill from Burlington's city center. The Burlington metro area has a population of 146,000 and is just a stone's throw from hiking, biking, camping, and cultural venues galore. Skiers will find countless opportunities to hit the slopes, including nearby Sugarbush and Smuggler's Notch. Students can eat a picnic lunch overlooking the lake or jog the seven-mile trail along the lake's shore and still make it back to campus in time for afternoon classes. Burlington's just a hundred miles from Montreal, so students can practice speaking French with the *Quebecoises* in the world's second-largest French-speaking city.

Admissions

Average high school GPA:	—
Average freshman SAT verbal / math score:	589 / 592
Average freshman ACT score:	24
Application fee:	$45

Application deadlines:
1/15 (freshmen)
4/1 (transfer)
11/1 (early action)

Total applicants:	17,731
Total accepted:	11,531 (65%)
Total accepted who enrolled:	2,178

Notification dates:
3/31 (freshmen)
continuous (transfer)
12/15 (early action)

Acceptance rate for early action applicants:	86%

Students

Percentage of male / female students:	45% / 55%
Percentage of students from out of state:	64%
Percentage of students graduating in 4 years / 6 years:	49% / 65%

Money

Total endowment:	$261,485,000
Total in-state tuition, fees & expenses:	$19,831
Total out-of-state tuition, fees & expenses:	$34,815
Average financial aid package:	$15,408
Percentage of students who sought aid and received it:	78%
Percentage of students receiving financial aid:	46%

Also Check Out

Middlebury College

Mount Holyoke College

Northeastern University

University of Connecticut

University of New Hampshire

University of Virginia

PO Box 400160
Charlottesville, VA 22903

(434) 924-0311
http://www.virginia.edu/

 **BIG CHOICE**

 **BIG RESEARCH**

C'mon down to Mr. Jefferson's University!

5 REASONS IT'S COOL

1. Get a **top-notch education at a state school price**.

2. Classes are taught by **professors who are tops in their fields**.

3. **School spirit is infectious** at UVA. You'll feel like you are part of history when you take part in the university's many traditions.

4. Colonial architecture graces this lovely campus, the original parts of which were **designed by founder Thomas Jefferson**.

5. **UVA kids like to party**, whether they're hangin' at the frats on Rugby Road or at the bars at the Corner.

The Basics

Public / private: public state
Total enrollment / undergrads: 24,068 / 14,676
Campus setting: suburban
Students call it: UVA, UV, "Mr. Jefferson's University"
Students are called: Cavaliers
Notable alums: Tiki and Ronde Barber (identical-twin pro football players), Francis S. Collins (director, the Human Genome Project), Claudia Emerson (poet), Tina Fey (writer, comedienne), Stephen Malkmus (musician), Edgar Allan Poe (attended; writer), John Snow (U.S. secretary of the treasury), Woodrow Wilson (U.S. president)

Mr. Jefferson's "Academical Community"

Since its 1819 founding by Thomas Jefferson, UVA has enjoyed a reputation as a prestigious university that offers a lot of bang for the buck. If you're a Virginia native, as close to 70 percent of the students here are, you'll take advantage of low tuition costs, but all students in state or otherwise benefit from the high level of learning. Renowned scholars populate UVA's faculty, including political science guru Larry Sabato and civil rights activist Julian Bond. The "E" and "Comm" are purportedly the toughest and most competitive schools, and English, history, and economics are the most popular majors. While advising is minimal, professors are friendly and eager to help. Students must complete a core curriculum, but there are plenty of interesting courses that satisfy the requirements. Tradition pervades all aspects of campus life, including academics.

Shhh, It's a Secret!

Wondering about the strange white lettering covering the steps and buildings all over the UVA campus? They're the markings of the university's secret societies. One of them, the Seven Society, chooses members at convocation and doesn't reveal their identities until they die, at which time the bells in the campus's Rotunda toll seven times. Will you be among the chosen?

All the Hoos Down in Hoo-ville . . .

UVA's official mascot might be the Cavalier, but its unofficial mascot is the Wahoo, a fish that can drink more than twice its weight. Point being? UVA kids like to party. Thirty percent of the student body joins fraternities and sororities, and Greek life dominates the social scene, especially among first-year students. There's also a lively bar scene at the Corner, a strip adjacent to campus. Athletics are a big deal, and students show their heartfelt school spirit by swaying to a chorus of "The Good Ole Song" after touchdowns during football games. Freshmen are required to live on campus in either Old or New dorms (Old dorms are the more social option). They can then move to residence halls, language houses, or off campus. Many students choose the latter option, settling in the frats and sororities that line Rugby Road or one of the many houses and apartments around 14th Street. Khakis and baseball caps are the dominant look on campus, and although there's some diversity, students lament that there isn't more. Notable traditions at this tradition-happy school include the Foxfield Races, Mid-Winters, Fourth-Year-Fifth, and streaking the lawn to kiss the statue of Homer on the bottom. Pucker up!

The Perfect College Town?

UVA's architecture is a testament to the lasting traditions of the school. The Rotunda, a model of the Roman Pantheon designed by Jefferson himself, overlooks the Lawn, which is usually filled with students lounging on the grass, studying, or playing Frisbee. Surrounded by the rolling hills of the Blue Ridge Mountains, the small city of Charlottesville might be the quintessential college town. There's a lively local music scene, tons of great restaurants, and plenty of shops and bars on the Corner (the Corner Meal plan even allows students to substitute restaurant fare for dining halls). Come springtime, students and locals alike flock to the downtown's outdoor pedestrian mall for the live music, cafés, and art galleries. And if you feel the itch for city life, Richmond and Washington, D.C. are an hour and two-hour drive away, respectively.

Admissions

Average high school GPA:	4.0
Average freshman SAT writing / math / critical reading score:	663 / 674 / 656
Average freshman ACT score:	25
Application fee:	$60

Application deadlines:
1/2 (freshmen)   11/1 (early decision)
3/1 (transfer)

Total applicants:	16,086
Total accepted:	6,019 (37%)
Total accepted who enrolled:	3,079

Notification dates:
4/1 (freshmen)   12/1 (early decision)
4/15 (transfer)

Acceptance rate for early decision applicants:	39%

Students

Percentage of male / female students:	45% / 55%
Percentage of students from out of state:	28%
Percentage of students graduating in 4 years / 6 years:	84% / 93%

Money

Total endowment:	$2,482,000,000
Total in-state tuition, fees & expenses:	$15,754
Total out-of-state tuition, fees & expenses:	$33,854
Average financial aid package:	$15,687
Percentage of students who sought aid and received it:	100%
Percentage of students receiving financial aid:	21%

Also Check Out

College of William & Mary

Duke University

University of North Carolina at Chapel Hill

University of Pennsylvania

Virginia Polytechnic and State University

University of Washington

320 Schmitz Hall
Seattle, WA 98195

(206) 543-2100
http://www.washington.edu/

BIG CHOICE

BIG RESEARCH

The freedom to choose

The Basics

Public / private: public state
Total enrollment / undergrads: 39,524 / 27,836
Campus setting: urban
Students call it: UW, U-Dub
Students are called: Huskies, U-Dubbers
Notable alums: Michael P. Anderson (astronaut), Linda B. Buck (Nobel Laureate, Biology), Chuck Close (artist), Timoth Egan (journalist, author), Bruce Lee (actor, martial arts expert), Warren Moon (pro football player), Irv Robbin (cofounder, Baskin & Robbins), Tom Robbins (author), Orin C. Smith (CEO, Starbucks), Minoru Yamasaki (architect)

The Big Picture

With 1,800 courses, 140 possible majors, and 60 study-abroad programs to choose from, UW students have options—*lots* of options. Science programs such as biology, engineering, fisheries, and computer science earn especially high marks, and research opportunities abound. Other popular majors include business and pre-med, where students benefit from excellent faculty and hospital facilities. However, no department is weak, and faculty members across all departments include Nobel laureates and National Academy members. The university's huge size can result in some frustrations for students. For example, personalized advising can be hard to come by, registration is often difficult, and students often must take the initiative to get the most from classes and professors. The university offers several programs to help students navigate the many academic options. The University Honors

Wet Frosh

One fateful day in 1909, a group of UW sophomores decided to assert their seniority by chasing a group of hapless freshmen into Geyser Basin, a pond located on the campus. This little prank became an enduring tradition, and Geyser Basin was thereafter known as Frosh Pond. Nowadays, UW freshmen throw themselves in as a rite of passage. Go figure.

Program places select students in smaller, more rigorous courses, and the Freshman Interest Group (FIG) program gathers small groups of freshmen with similar interests into clusters of courses. The university's sixteen libraries house over 6 million volumes.

Something for Everyone

UW students are often characterized as laid-back hipsters with left-leaning sensibilities. While this stereotype certainly describes many UW students, the student body is large enough that every student is sure to find his or her niche. The typical Husky tends to be active and eager to take advantage of Seattle's many outdoor activities. More than 550 student organizations cater to every possible interest. The renovated Intramurals Activities Building boasts a swimming pool, climbing wall, martial arts classes, and tons of fitness equipment. The university's Division I sports program arouses considerable passion in students and Seattleites alike. While students aren't required to live on campus, many find that living in the dorms helps create a stronger sense of community. The university's nine residence halls each have distinct a feel, ranging from party-hearty McMahon to quieter Hansee.

Gateway to the Emerald City

UW's large campus is contained within its own 643-acre park. Campus focal points include Red Square with its many libraries and the Quad, a large cherry blossom-lined lawn. Trails winding from campus into Seattle make biking safe and easy, though buses are also available. U-District, with its shopping centers and mainstream stores, and the Ave, with its strip of shops and restaurants, are both very close to campus, and quirkier neighborhoods like Wallingford and Fremont are a bit farther away. Seattle has plenty to offer college students, including scenic waterfront pavilions, a zoo, and ubiquitous coffee shops. Come winter, students can hit the slopes for skiing and snowboarding, and in the spring, there's hiking, biking, climbing, and kayaking. And on clear days, Mt. Rainer provides an impressive backdrop.

Admissions

Average high school GPA:	3.67
Average freshman SAT verbal / math score:	588 / 618
Average freshman ACT score:	24
Application fee:	$50
Application deadlines: 1/15 (freshmen) 2/15 (transfer)	
Total applicants:	16,571
Total accepted:	11,339 (68%)
Total accepted who enrolled:	5,392
Notification dates: continuous (freshmen) continuous (transfer)	

Students

Percentage of male / female students:	48% / 52%
Percentage of students from out of state:	14%
Percentage of students graduating in 4 years / 6 years:	46% / 74%

Money

Total endowment:	$963,000,000
Total in-state tuition, fees & expenses:	$13,494
Total out-of-state tuition, fees & expenses:	$28,792
Average financial aid package:	$12,000
Percentage of students who sought aid and received it:	86%
Percentage of students receiving financial aid:	31%

Also Check Out

University of Michigan–Ann Arbor

University of Oregon

University of Washington

University of Wisconsin–Madison

niversity of Wisconsin–Madison

| 500 Lincoln Drive | (608) 262-1234 |
| Madison, WI 53706 | http://www.wisc.edu/ |

 **BIG CHOICE**

 **BIG RESEARCH**

The cheese stands alone.

5 REASONS IT'S COOL

1. Its **"public Ivy"** status makes UW an attractive choice for high achievers with limited funds.

2. The **Honors Program** allows the cleverest Badgers to steer clear of typical big-school pitfalls.

3. Students can pursue **the life aquatic** on the two lakes bordering Madison.

4. **Two campus recreation centers** let students work off all that beer and cheese.

5. **Badgers football** has fans baring their claws at the competition.

The Basics

Public / private: public state
Total enrollment / undergrads: 41,466 / 30,055
Campus setting: urban
Students call it: UW
Students are called: Badgers
Notable alums: Lynne Cheney (author, wife of Vice President Dick Cheney), Charles Lindbergh (aviator), John Muir (founder, the Sierra Club), Greta Van Susteren (journalist), Eudora Welty (writer), Frank Lloyd Wright (architect)

The Cream of the Crop

UW is not for the faint of heart. Massive enrollment and high academic standards combine to present challenges you won't find at many other state institutions. Among the dizzying number of choices awaiting new Badgers are well-regarded programs in economics, political science, and psychology. There is also a whole slew of nationally recognized programs in the agricultural, biological, and physical sciences. Humanists and literature lovers also have reason to celebrate; English and history rank among UW's best programs. Not everything is milk and honey in America's Dairyland, however. The school has been accused of grade inflation in recent years, and there are also the familiar huge-school headaches of remote professors, gigantic lecture courses, and perplexing bureaucracy. Easing these difficulties, at least for UW's best and brightest, is the Honors Program, which seeks to strike a balance between granting its members improved access to faculty and administration

Boo-hoo!

The annual State Street Halloween party has drawn as many as 100,000 partygoers in years past. Recently, in response to vandalism, the police have been clamping down. For the 2006 observance, Madison officials implemented an age-old capitalist remedy: charging admission to the party. Incidences of vandalism declined, but complaints skyrocketed. After all, the easiest way to take away a poor college student's fun is to make him pay for it!

and keeping them cordoned off from the hoi polloi. Those capable of steering their own ship will succeed, even flourish, in this academic powerhouse, and those who want an Ivy-quality education at a fraction of the cost will be hard-pressed to find a better option.

Binging Badgers

This university offers something for everyone, from tree-huggers to beer-chuggers. The latter group certainly doesn't hurt for entertainment. It's no secret that UW is a nationally recognized party school. Administrators fret over this reputation, but students say it's way overblown. The party scene on campus is about what you'd expect at an enormous state school, but the frat-boy fetes are easily avoided at a place this big. Partiers and straightedgers are united in their love of Badgers' sports: Home games always inspire hearty celebration, especially when the visitors are Big Ten rivals. The student body is itself somewhat atypical for a state school; because of its public Ivy status, UW draws nearly 30 percent of its students from out of state.

The People's Republic of Wisconsin

The city of Madison has natural beauty in spades. Although it's centered on an isthmus between two lakes, Mendota and Monona, this capital city has a political tradition that leans decidedly left. Madison consistently rates as one of the nation's most livable midsized cities. In many ways, it's the very picture of a college town. State Street, which runs adjacent to the UW campus, is home to wonderful cafés, bookshops, and restaurants, and the UW campus offers plenty of delights of its own. The Student Union has a lovely view of Lake Mendota and offers Badgers many recreational options. When it comes to living on campus, Badgers recommend finagling a room in the Chadbourne Residential College; it offers the best in comfort, lifestyle, and amenities. Regardless of what dorm you end up in, you won't be far from workout facilities, since the university has two student recreation centers. In less virtuous moods, try the homemade ice cream in Babcock Hall.

Admissions

Average high school GPA:	3.67
Average freshman SAT writing / math / critical reading score:	623 / 659 / 614
Average freshman ACT score:	26
Application fee:	$35
Application deadlines:	
2/1 (freshmen)	
2/1 (transfer)	
Total applicants:	22,816
Total accepted:	13,322 (58%)
Total accepted who enrolled:	5,633
Notification dates:	
continuous (freshmen)	
continuous (transfer)	

Students

Percentage of male / female students:	47% / 53%
Percentage of students from out of state:	31%
Percentage of students graduating in 4 years / 6 years:	43% / 78%

Money

Total endowment:	$1,022,600,000
Total in-state tuition, fees & expenses:	$14,536
Total out-of-state tuition, fees & expenses:	$28,536
Average financial aid package:	$11,818
Percentage of students who sought aid and received it:	—
Percentage of students receiving financial aid:	27%

Also Check Out

Northwestern University

The Ohio State University

The University of Arizona

University of Illinois at Urbana-Champaign

University of Michigan–Ann Arbor

University of Wyoming

3435 1000 E. University Ave.
Laramie, WY 82070

(307) 766-1121
http://www.uwyo.edu/

 **BIG CHOICE**

 **BIG RESEARCH**

Ride 'em, cowboys!

5 REASONS IT'S COOL

1. Get a first-rate education at a bargain-basement price at this research institution.

2. The earth system science and environment and natural resources majors are just two of the **unique interdisciplinary offerings**.

3. Students love the size: small enough for real prof-student interaction, but big enough for interesting internship and research opportunities.

4. Ever **dream of being a cowboy**? Learn from the Pokes, many of whom are no stranger to rodeos.

5. Climbing, skiing, hunting, fishing—the two mountain ranges offer **countless outdoor activities**.

The Basics

Public / private: public state
Total enrollment / undergrads: 13,203 / 9,468
Campus setting: small town
Students call it: UW
Students are called: Cowboys
Notable alums: Jerry Buss (owner, L.A. Lakers), Dick Cheney (U.S. vice president), Stephen Nicholas (founder, Internatinal Children's Center for children with HIV/AIDS), General Peter Schoomaker (Army chief of staff), Mark Spragg (writer)

Cowboys in the Library

UW, the only four-year college in the state, conveys the benefits of a research institution at a remarkably affordable price. Science programs are especially strong and give students have a variety of options, from the standard biology and chemistry to the more specific rangeland ecology and watershed management majors. Engineering, known as one of the most challenging departments, offers a new intercollegiate, interdisciplinary earth system science major. The Helga Otto Haub School of Environment and Natural Resources also emphasizes an interdisciplinary approach to environmental issues and offers work-study opportunities through the affiliate Wyoming Conservation Corps. Motivated students have an array of research resources at their disposal but must seek them out. Profs get high marks for their dedication to undergraduate learning. The 16:1 student-to-faculty ratio is lower than that of many other research institutions, and the school prides itself on an average

Giddy Up!

The UW logo honors a historical horse named Steamboat. The first time he was ever ridden, he bucked so hard he landed on his nose and broke his septum. From then on, his snorts sounded like the squeal of a river steamboat (hence his name). Quite a few cowboys tried to stay on Steamboat, but only one ever succeeded.

class size of twenty-nine. These smaller classes are more common at the higher level; freshmen shouldn't be surprised to find themselves in lectures with three hundred other students. In general, the intellectually ambitious will fare best here.

Pastures, Parties, and Pokes

It's still legal to graze your horse on Prexy's Pasture, the large grassy lawn that is the heart of campus. Although no one actually brings their steed to school, a uniquely Western attitude prevails on campus. The majority of students are from Wyoming and represent the culture of the Cowboy State. There are six residence halls on campus and apartments available for families. Upperclassmen tend to move off campus. The administration is vigilant about underage drinking, so most partying takes place at fraternities or off-campus houses. Friday Night Fever organizes movie screenings, casino nights, and stand-up comedy. Arena Auditorium gets a wide range of musical acts, and the Dance and Theater departments put on excellent performances, including vertical ballet productions at the nearby Vedauwoo cliffs. The Centennial Singers, the university's musical ambassadors, tour around the United States during school breaks, and the Speech and Debate Team has won several national championships. The men and women's ski teams have won national championships in recent years, and it wouldn't be Wyoming without a strong Rodeo Club and Rifle Team.

Big Sky and Beyond

Laramie isn't much of a college town, but there are plenty of restaurants and great cowboy bars like The Buckhorn, The Cowboy, and The Ranger. Laramie doubles in size during the school year, teeming with a mix of rancher types and outdoor enthusiasts. The latter group has plenty to be excited about: Twenty minutes to the east are the Medicine Bow Mountains, which offer stellar rock climbing at Vedauwoo, as well as cross-country skiing and mountain biking at Happy Jack; thirty minutes to the west is the Snowy Range, which has excellent hunting, hiking, and fishing and a small ski area; and Steamboat Springs, for skiing enthusiasts, is two hours away. Denver is three hours away, and Fort Collins, home to Colorado State, is only two.

Admissions

Average high school GPA:	3.43
Average freshman SAT verbal / math score:	— / 550
Average freshman ACT score:	23
Application fee:	$40

Application deadlines:
8/10 (freshmen)
8/10 (transfer)

Total applicants:	—
Total accepted:	—(—)
Total accepted who enrolled:	1,553

Notification dates:
continuous (freshmen)
continuous (transfer)

Students

Percentage of male / female students:	51% / 49%
Percentage of students from out of state:	27%
Percentage of students graduating in 4 years / 6 years:	25% / 55%

Money

Total endowment:	$259,773,000
Total in-state tuition, fees & expenses:	$10,828
Total out-of-state tuition, fees & expenses:	$17,668
Average financial aid package:	$7,012
Percentage of students who sought aid and received it:	76%
Percentage of students receiving financial aid:	43%

Also Check Out

Colorado State University–Fort Collins

University of Idaho

The University of Montana–Missoula

University of Nevada–Las Vegas

University of Utah

West Virginia University

Ursinus College

Box 1000, Main Street
Collegeville, PA 19426

(610) 409-3000
http://www.ursinus.edu/

 **BIG HAND**

 BIG JOB

 **BIG PERSPECTIVE**

Preparing the leaders of tomorrow

5 REASONS IT'S COOL

1. Students love their **passionate and accessible professors.**

2. Seventy-five scholarships are available to self-motivated students who want to **conduct their own research** over the summer.

3. The Independent Learning Experience provides **real-world work experience** through internships, independent research, and student teaching.

4. The unique Residential Village housing system groups students together in **cozy, charming Victorian houses** just minutes from campus.

5. **Free laptops:** Every Ursinus student receives one.

The Basics

Public / private: private nonprofit
Total enrollment / undergrads: 1,589 / 1,589
Campus setting: suburban
Students call it: Ursinus
Students are called: Bears
Notable alums: Gerald Edelman (Nobel Laureate, Medicine), Sam Keen (author, scholar), Joseph Melrose (ambassador), J. D. Salinger (novelist), James F. Scott II (director, NASA), Robert M. Yerkes (psychologist)

Up-Close and Personal

Every freshman at Ursinus is required to take the Common Intellectual Experience (CIE), which pushes students to think critically and speak their minds. In addition to debating some of life's biggest questions—love, God, happiness, death, and nature, just to name a few—the small CIE courses give students the opportunity to get to know their professors and each other. Of course, Ursinus students also get a lot of personal attention in their other courses too, and the school boasts a 12:1 faculty-to-student ratio across all twenty-seven different majors. Ursinus students must also complete an Independent Learning Experience (ILE) requirement, where they apply their liberal arts education in the working world through internships, research, and student teaching. It's no surprise, then, that Ursinus gets high marks from students and employers alike for producing top-notch graduates who are well prepared for graduate studies and the working world.

Where Poet Wannabes Rule

Each spring, this literary-minded college hosts a one-of-a-kind poetry event called Poempalooza, where students read their own poems aloud and faculty impersonate their favorite dead poets. There's even a team poetry slam, which pits teams of two student poets against each other. At the end of the evening, the audience votes for the best poets—and poet wannabes.

Let's Get to Know Each Other Better, Shall We?

Ursinus has a tight-knit community where students are welcoming and excited about where they are and what they're learning. While the college lacks huge numbers of minorities, students find that their peers bring an array of interests and ideas to campus. Most are hardworking and ambitious, but they're also well rounded and live active lives outside of the library. Just about everyone participates in at least one of the college's nearly one hundred different clubs. Over 95 percent of students live on campus, about one-third of them pledge a fraternity or sorority, and nearly everyone else attends their parties, which are the center of campus social life. And when the parties die down, the college also offers movies, concerts, lectures, and twenty-six Division III intercollegiate varsity sports teams.

Little Campus in the Big Woods

There are many colleges in Philly, but few are as beautiful as Ursinus. Walking to and from class, students and professors take in the trees and flowers lining the campus's brick walkways. Ursinus also has a thirty-five-acre forest known as the Hunsberger Woods, which offers students abundant opportunities to run, walk, swim, or just hang when the weather's nice. For students seeking some artistic inspiration, the Philip and Muriel Berman Museum of Art on campus features a beautiful sculpture garden where many go to clear their heads when studying gets to be too much. And when even the sculptures aren't doing the trick, students take the thirty-minute bus ride to Philly, which is one of the nation's biggest cultural hubs, with museums, concerts, sports games, restaurants, and shopping galore.

Admissions

Average high school GPA:	—
Average freshman SAT verbal / math score:	605 / 609
Average freshman ACT score:	23
Application fee:	$50

Application deadlines:
2/15 (freshmen)
8/1 (transfer)
1/15 (early decision)

Total applicants:	4,408
Total accepted:	2,056 (47%)
Total accepted who enrolled:	405

Notification dates:
4/1 (freshmen)
9/1 (transfer)
2/1 (early decision)

Acceptance rate for early decision applicants:	80%

Students

Percentage of male / female students:	48% / 52%
Percentage of students from out of state:	38%
Percentage of students graduating in 4 years / 6 years:	72% / 76%

Money

Total endowment:	$115,000
Total tuition:	$33,200
Total cost with fees & expenses:	$41,550
Average financial aid package:	$24,109
Percentage of students who sought aid and received it:	80%
Percentage of students receiving financial aid:	78%

Also Check Out

Bennington College

Bucknell University

Oberlin College

Villanova University

Whitman College

Utica College

1600 Burrstone Road
Utica, NY 13502

(315) 792-3111
http://www.utica.edu/

BIG PERSPECTIVE

Big college degree in a small college setting

5 REASONS IT'S COOL

1. Utica was founded by Syracuse University, and though students get degrees from Syracuse, they also get a **small, cozy, student-focused education.**

2. Students receive a liberal arts training with a **career-ready focus.**

3. **CSI fans, listen up:** Between the on-campus Economic Crime Investigation Institute and the Computer Forensics Research Development Center, forensics students have access to crime labs, internships, and more.

4. Students are encouraged to get **internship, clinical, or co-op experience.**

5. The **Strebel Student Center is open to students 24/7.**

The Basics

Public / private: private nonprofit
Total enrollment / undergrads: 2,952 / 2,429
Campus setting: suburban
Students call it: UC
Students are called: Pioneers
Notable alums: Sherwood Boehlert (congressman), John M. McHugh (congressman), Frank Lentricchia (scholar), Larry Platt (magazine editor, author)

Two Degrees in One!

Founded by Syracuse University in 1946, Utica became a legally and financially independent college in 1995. Students earn a Syracuse degree but get to enjoy the intimate setting of a smaller school. The college specializes in providing a solid liberal arts education with a career focus, and internships and other experiential learning opportunities are encouraged for all students. The most popular programs include nursing, journalism, biology, occupational and physical therapy, public relations, and criminal justice. Some more unusual programs include economic crime investigation, cybersecurity and information assurance, and therapeutic recreation. Students are happy with the college's 17:1 student-to-faculty ratio, average class size of twenty-two, and close student-professor relationships. Utica offers study-abroad opportunities in locations such as Wales, Finland, Hungary, Italy, and Ireland. Students searching for careers after graduation can take advantage of Syracuse's plentiful career services.

Freshly Independent

Utica didn't become a fully independent college until 1995. When it was founded in 1946, it offered extension courses through Syracuse, and nothing else. And while a lot has changed since those early days, the Syracuse-Utica tie is still present, as students actually graduate with a Syracuse degree.

Game On

Sports play a big role in campus life at Utica. The college offers more than twenty NCAA Division III sports teams. The men's hockey team draws a particularly big crowd, even earning the record for the most highly attended home games in the nation for Division III teams in 2007. The team has a student fan club, the Pioneer Posse, to lead their cheers. Nearly 70 percent of students participate in intramurals, choosing from a huge selection that includes unique offerings like whiffle ball, pool, and snow softball. Fraternities and sororities draw some students, and more than eighty student organizations are offered, including a student newspaper, campus radio station, and literary magazine. Students have access to the UC Daysheet, an online record of the daily events and activities on campus. Three dorms have recently been built, including Ben Hall, a five-story hall with mostly single rooms. In addition, four other residence halls offer a variety of living arrangements, from apartments to suites.

A Central Location

Utica is a small city in central New York. The college is relatively new, and it's growing. The newly built F. Eugene Romano Hall has state-of-the-art labs, clinical spaces, and science and technology classrooms. Having a car on campus is helpful but not necessary. The Student Senate Van makes daily rounds to the local grocery store and downtown Utica. The area is packed with other college students, as both Mohawk Valley Community College and SUNY IT are nearby. Adirondack State Park is a short drive away, offering plenty of hiking and camping opportunities—just expect to encounter cold temperatures and plentiful snow, and dress accordingly. Major cities such as Boston, New York, and Montreal are all within a four hours' drive.

Admissions

Average high school GPA:	2.98
Average freshman SAT writing / math / critical reading score:	467 / 495 / 475
Average freshman ACT score:	21
Application fee:	$40
Application deadlines: continuous (freshmen) continuous (transfer)	
Total applicants:	2,335
Total accepted:	1,807 (77%)
Total accepted who enrolled:	495
Notification dates: 9/1 (freshmen) continuous (transfer)	

Students

Percentage of male / female students:	40% / 60%
Percentage of students from out of state:	16%
Percentage of students graduating in 4 years / 6 years:	40% / 57%

Money

Total endowment:	$16,834,326
Total tuition:	$23,130
Total cost with fees & expenses:	$33,820
Average financial aid package:	$18,190
Percentage of students who sought aid and received it:	73%
Percentage of students receiving financial aid:	71%

Also Check Out

Connecticut College

Northeastern University

SUNY–Binghamton University

Syracuse University

Trinity College

Valparaiso University

1700 Chapel Drive
Valparaiso, IN 46383

(219) 464-5000
http://www.valpo.edu/

 **BIG PERSPECTIVE**

Values, variety, and victory

5 REASONS IT'S COOL

1. Valpo offers **pre-professional training** in career-ready fields such as nursing, engineering, and business.

2. Students enrolled in **Valpo's Honors College** receive extra attention—along with extra-challenging coursework.

3. **New construction on campus** has resulted in a renovated student center and facilities for meteorology students.

4. The Valpo Core **introduces freshmen to the human experience.**

5. Students balance Lutheran values with an **overall campus vibe of inclusiveness.**

The Basics

Public / private: private religious
Total enrollment / undergrads: 3,868 / 2,960
Campus setting: small town
Students call it: Valparaiso, Valpo
Students are called: Crusaders
Notable alums: Lowell Thomas (journalist, author), Donald Fites (CEO, Caterpillar), Jacki Lyden (news correspondent), William March (author), David Ruprecht (actor, game show host)

Know Where You're Going

Valpo offers over seventy majors through a unique blend of pre-professional and liberal arts programs in the arts, sciences, business, nursing, and engineering. The most popular majors include communication, biology, business, engineering, and nursing, with many students opting for a double major. An honors program administered through Christ College offers small, interdisciplinary courses to a select group of high-achieving students. For the rest of the undergrad population, higher education starts with the Valpo Core: a two-semester, interdisciplinary course that introduces students to the human experience and offers practical instruction in writing, research, and service. Class time is supplemented by for-credit activities such as plays, films, and concerts. Across all departments, the ratio student-to-faculty is 13:1 and the average class size is twenty-two. Valpo's accessible and friendly professors are known to go out of their way to help students and sometimes even host dinner parties that take class discussions outside of the classroom.

You Can Ring My Bell

For the past fifty years, athletic victories at Valpo have been celebrated with a traditional ringing of the Victory Bell, located in the campus's student union. Regular upkeep of the bell is performed by the Valparaiso Alumni Undergrad Leadership Team.

In the Eye of the Storm

Valparaiso sits near the Indiana-Illinois border, but while many students hail from the Midwest, the student body is quite geographically diverse. The university's Lutheran affiliation and strong Catholic presence mix to create a dominantly conservative vibe. Nearly three-quarters of students attend some form of religious service, and the campus's Chapel of the Resurrection is a popular spot for churchgoing. The university offers more than a hundred student groups, many of which reflect the university's emphasis on all things pre-professional and religious. Meteorology students join the Storm Intercept Team, a group of severe-weather watchers, while religious students take up a variety of ethical and moral causes. Partying does take place, but the campus is officially dry, and crackdowns have been more frequent of late. Even so, the university's sixteen Greek organization chapters absorb much of student life. Athletics are also popular: Around 15 percent of students participate in eighteen NCAA Division I teams, and about half participate in intramurals.

All That and a Bag of Popcorn

Valpo's 320-acre campus is a short jaunt from Lake Michigan and the Indiana Dunes National Lakeshore. The campus's new Kallay-Christopher Hall houses the Department of Geography and Meteorology and includes a state-of-the-art weather center. The recently opened Christopher Center Library has been praised as a great leap forward into the information age, and the multifaced Chapel of the Resurrection is among the more striking buildings on campus. The midsized town of Valparaiso has Midwestern charm to spare. Big events include the annual Popcorn Festival, which honors former town resident and popcorn guru Orville Redenbacher. The festival features the usual carnival fare and boasts the nation's first popcorn parade, with floats decorated with, of course, popcorn. For big-city entertainment, students make the hour drive to Chicago.

Admissions

Average high school GPA:	3.43
Average freshman SAT writing / math / critical reading score:	558 / 586 / 571
Average freshman ACT score:	24
Application fee:	$30

Application deadlines:
8/15 (freshmen)
— (transfer)
11/1 (early action)

Total applicants:	3,785
Total accepted:	3,381 (89%)
Total accepted who enrolled:	760

Notification dates:
— (freshmen)
continuous (transfer)
12/1 (early action)

Acceptance rate for early action applicants:	90%

Students

Percentage of male / female students:	48% / 52%
Percentage of students from out of state:	64%
Percentage of students graduating in 4 years / 6 years:	59% / 71%

Money

Total endowment:	$166,851,715
Total tuition:	$23,200
Total cost with fees & expenses:	$31,640
Average financial aid package:	$18,608
Percentage of students who sought aid and received it:	85%
Percentage of students receiving financial aid:	47%

Also Check Out

Creighton University

Hope College

Indiana University–Bloomington

Purdue University

University of Notre Dame

Vanderbilt University

2305 West End Ave.
Nashville, TN 37240

(615) 322-7311
http://www.vanderbilt.edu/

 **BIG BRAIN**

 **BIG PERSPECTIVE**

Be a Nashville star without singing a note.

5 REASONS IT'S COOL

1. Vanderbilt is home to exceptional academics and caring, supportive faculty members.

2. **Cool immersion courses and travel opportunities abound** during Vanderbilt's unique May session.

3. The Commons, the **all-new housing community for first-year students and** resident faculty, includes a food court and dining hall, café, fitness center, and wireless service.

4. **Commodores athletics,** especially basketball, breed big-time school spirit.

5. **Downtown Nashville,** home base for the biggest acts in country music, provides ample opportunities for students to unwind.

The Basics

Public / private: private nonprofit
Total enrollment / undergrads: 11,607 / 6,378
Campus setting: urban
Students call it: Vanderbilt, VU, Vandy
Students are called: Commodores
Notable alums: Lamar Alexander (senator), Roy Blount Jr. (writer), Rosanne Cash (singer-songwriter), Al Gore (attended; U.S. vice president; Nobel Laureate, Peace), Amy Grant (singer), Dinah Shore (singer, actress), Fred Thompson (actor, senator), Robert Penn Warren (poet, author), Muhammad Yunus (Nobel Laureate, Economics)

Vandy's Dandy

Before classes start, Vanderbilt freshmen sign the honor code, which is displayed prominently in the campus's Sarratt Student Center. Such pomp and circumstance underscores how committed Vanderbilt students are to academic success. Students take courses from any of the university's four undergraduate colleges of arts and sciences, engineering, education, and music. Economics, political science, English, psychology, and Spanish top the list of popular majors. Vanderbilt is also a major research center with ties to several neighboring private institutions that conduct research in medicine, political and social sciences, and astronomy, among other fields. About 30 percent of students study abroad; the university offers a total of fifty programs in twenty countries. Students with clear professional or academic goals can choose from multiple 4+1 BA/MA degree programs. Vanderbilt professors are

Walk of Fame

Before home games, Vanderbilt football players take a walk, literally. Team members walk from the McGugin Center down Jess Nelly Drive all the way to Vanderbilt Stadium, in an event known as Star Walk. Students, many dressed in blazers, wave gold pom-poms, and the Spirit of Gold marching band plays peppy tunes as the players pass by on their way (maybe) to a Vanderbilt victory.

top-notch across the board and are committed to spending time with students outside of the classroom. Class sizes average about nineteen, and the student-to-faculty ratio is 9:1.

Opening 'Dores

Vanderbilt made waves recently when the university dissolved its Athletic Department and rolled athletics into the student life office in an effort to better integrate athletes and the student population. Men's and women's basketball and women's bowling just won championships in their conferences, and tennis and golf are always competitive. Vanderbilt offers about four hundred students groups, including eight print publications and student radio and television stations. The university also hosts numerous events, including concerts that bring big-name acts to campus. And as the originators of service-oriented Alternative Spring Break, Vanderbilt students have long valued community service. Over 80 percent of students live in dorms, townhouses, or themed living/learning communities on campus. Greek life is fairly large, drawing in over 40 percent of students. Southern traditions abound, but the university's reputation as a bastion of preppiness is starting to fade due to gradually increasing ethnic and geographic diversity. About 20 percent of students are minorities, and more than half come from outside the South.

The House That Vanderbilt

Vanderbilt's historic and handsome campus is located in Nashville. The main campus features a walkable collection of art and sculptures scattered among the buildings. The campus itself doubles as a registered arboretum, complete with more than three hundred species of trees. Nashville, a.k.a. Music City USA, is home to the Country Music Hall of Fame, the Grand Ole Opry, and Music Row, where honky-tonk crooners get their big breaks. Downtown Nashville lies just a short walk from campus, and students can take in as much music and nightlife as they can handle.

Admissions

Average high school GPA:	—
Average freshman SAT writing / math / critical reading score:	673 / 688 / 672
Average freshman ACT score:	26
Application fee:	$50

Application deadlines:
1/3 (freshmen)
3/1 (transfer)
11/1 (early decision)

Total applicants:	12,189
Total accepted:	4,128 (34%)
Total accepted who enrolled:	1,590

Notification dates:
4/1 (freshmen)
4/15 (transfer)
12/15 (early decision)

Acceptance rate for early decision applicants:	41%

Students

Percentage of male / female students:	48% / 52%
Percentage of students from out of state:	83%
Percentage of students graduating in 4 years / 6 years:	83% / 88%

Money

Total endowment:	$2,600,000,000
Total tuition:	$32,620
Total cost with fees & expenses:	$45,434
Average financial aid package:	$33,896
Percentage of students who sought aid and received it:	99%
Percentage of students receiving financial aid:	41%

Also Check Out

Cornell University

Duke University

Emory University

Georgetown University

Rice University

Vassar College

124 Raymond Avenue
Poughkeepsie, NY 12604

(845) 437-7000
http://www.vassar.edu/

 **BIG PERSPECTIVE**

Liberal arts, liberal living

5 REASONS IT'S COOL

1. Formerly considered the most liberal of the Seven Sisters, Vassar is still **big on tolerance, diversity, and quirkiness**.

2. The Undergraduate Research Summer Institute (URSI) offers stipends to students **conducting original scientific research**.

3. Vassar has one of the best music libraries, each dorm has a Steinway, and **there is a concert almost every night**.

4. **The campus is a designated arboretum** and is home to over 200 kinds of trees, meandering streams, shimmering lakes, and grassy paths.

5. **The bright lights of New York City are just an hour away.**

The Basics

Public / private: private nonprofit
Total enrollment / undergrads: 2,424 / 2,424
Campus setting: suburban
Students call it: Vassar
Students are called: Brewers
Notable alums: Noah Baumbach (filmmaker), Ruth Benedict (anthropologist), Elizabeth Bishop (poet), Caterina Fake (cofounder, Flickr), Nancy Graves (artist), Geraldine Laybourne (founder and CEO, Oxygen Media), Rick Lazio (congressman), Edna St. Vincent Millay (poet), Judith Regan (editor), Vera Rubin (astronomer), Meryl Streep (actress), Nina Zagat (cofounder, Zagat Survey)

Creative to the Core

No graduate population means undergrads get full access to professors. Classes tend to average around seventeen students, with many upper-level classes having fewer than ten. The close attention isn't limited to the classroom: at least two faculty members live in each student dorm, and professors often invite students to their homes. With no core curriculum or general education requirements, students enjoy a generous amount of academic flexibility. But there are some requirements: foreign language proficiency (either by exam or in one of the eighteen languages offered) and one quantitative class, along with a small freshman seminar to strengthen communication skills. Students also must take a quarter of their classes outside their major to promote creative thinking. Popular majors include English, psychology, and political science,

A Sing Thing

The many Vassar traditions include the annual Serenading festivities. To kick off each year, upper classes welcome incoming first years in each house with song. Upper-class students serenade the freshmen, the freshmen serenade back, and a winner is chosen in the end.

though many students choose to pursue interdisciplinary or multidisciplinary majors, such as cognitive science, urban studies, or the design-it-yourself Independent Program. Vassar also offers an eclectic array of study-abroad programs in far-flung locations like Morocco, Ireland, and Russia, and exchange programs in Japan, Turkey, England, and France.

More Aesthetic Than Athletic

Though no longer a women's only college, Vassar maintains a love of tradition. Each May marks the Founder's Day festival, started in 1866 to celebrate founder Matthew Vassar's birthday, which consists of rides on a Ferris wheel, fireworks, and live music. The school hosts over 100 student organizations, including an active Queer Coalition, animal rights groups, Madrigal singers, and even a Pagan Study Group for the discussion of marginalized religious beliefs. An on-campus dance club called Matthew's Mug is a hot spot for the 21-and-older crowd. Art enthusiasts can appreciate the Frances Lehman Loeb Art Center, whose 13,500-work collection includes art by Pablo Picasso and Georgia O'Keefe. Vassar has no Greek system, and varsity sports go relatively unnoticed. Intramural sports are popular, thanks in part to a new athletic center and nine-hole golf course at the edge of campus. Vassar dorms aren't segregated by level, so freshmen, sophomores, and juniors all live together. Seniors are treated to exclusive apartment-style housing.

Seeing the Forest for the Trees

The architecture at Vassar runs the gamut from neo-Gothic to modern. Perhaps the most imposing monument is the Thompson Memorial Library, with its cathedral-like circular towers, gigantic stained-glass window, and crenellations lining the top. Tom Hanks and Samuel Jackson helped inaugurate the equally impressive Vogelstein Center for Drama and Film, which contains a Broadway-size theater, state-of-the-art multimedia equipment, and costume and prop shops. The architectural beauty is matched only by the campus' natural splendors, celebrated annually when each class either adopts or plants a tree. Internship and fieldwork opportunities are plentiful for students.

Admissions

Average high school GPA:	3.7
Average freshman SAT verbal / math score:	697 / 683
Average freshman ACT score:	—
Application fee:	$60

Application deadlines:
1/1 (freshmen)
4/1 (transfer)
11/15 (early decision)

Total applicants:	6,075
Total accepted:	1,829 (30%)
Total accepted who enrolled:	668

Notification dates:
4/1 (freshmen)
5/10 (transfer)
12/15 (early decision)

Acceptance rate for early decision applicants:	44%

Students

Percentage of male / female students:	40% / 60%
Percentage of students from out of state:	73%
Percentage of students graduating in 4 years / 6 years:	86% / 91%

Money

Total endowment:	$741,655,000
Total tuition:	$35,520
Total cost with fees & expenses:	$45,000
Average financial aid package:	$27,982
Percentage of students who sought aid and received it:	100%
Percentage of students receiving financial aid:	51%

Also Check Out

Brown University

Columbia University

New York University

Tufts University

Wesleyan University

Villanova University

800 Lancaster Avenue
Villanova, PA 19085

(610) 519-4500
http://www.villanova.edu/

 **BIG CHOICE**

Professional training, partying, and prayer

5 REASONS IT'S COOL

1. Pre-professional programs in **engineering, business, and nursing are tops** with students.

2. **Community service is popular** with the civic-minded, from building houses for Habitat for Humanity to serving on mission trips to foreign countries over breaks.

3. The lovely chapel is a campus landmark at this Catholic university, though **all faiths are welcome.**

4. Wildcats are truly ferocious about their winning **NCAA Division I basketball team.**

5. The lush, suburban campus is an easy twelve miles from the **big-city bars of Philly.**

The Basics

Public / private: private religious
Total enrollment / undergrads: 10,456 / 7,254
Campus setting: suburban
Students call it: Villanova, VU, 'Nova
Students are called: Novans, Wildcats
Notable alums: Andrew Allen (astronaut), John G. Drosdick (CEO, Sunoco), James O'Connor (division president, Ford), Diana Sugg (journalist), Vincent Trosino (president, State Farm)

Pre-professional Training with a Spiritual Bent

Students at this Catholic university enroll in one of four colleges: the College of Liberal Arts, the College of Nursing, the College of Engineering, or the Villanova School of Business. VU offers forty majors, including theology and religious studies, communication, political science, and biology. A wide range of interdisciplinary concentrations is also available, such as Africana studies, Arab and Islamic studies, Irish studies, and naval science. Students can take advantage of accelerated bachelor's/master's degree programs in engineering, accountancy, finance, Hispanic studies, and psychology, among others, where they shave time (and money) from grad school. All freshmen must take two semesters of the Augustine and Culture Villanova Seminar, a series of reading- and writing-intensive seminars that focus on the Bible, Augustine's writings, and more modern works. Students in the Honors Program attend challenging seminars with top professors

Sister Bell

When Philadelphia's famed Liberty Bell cracked, city officials commissioned a new one to replace it. The new "Sister Bell" hung at Independence Hall alongside the original bell and took over the former's hourly ringing duties. Eventually, the Sister Bell was retired and sold when Independence Hall was renovated. Today, it is proudly housed at VU's Falvey Memorial Library.

and can apply for the Connelly-Delouvrier International Scholarship, which covers tuition during study abroad. Honors or not, group work is encouraged, and the 13:1 student-to-faculty ratio ensures that class sizes are manageable across the board. About a third of students study abroad in locations such as Greece, Spain, Israel, Russia and China.

Sainthood or Revelry? Or Both!

Founded in 1842 by the Friars of the Order of St. Augustine, VU still attracts mostly Catholic students, though all faiths are welcome. Community service is popular with students. VEMS, Villanova's volunteer emergency medical service, is completely student run, and the annual Special Olympics' Fall Festival, the largest event of its kind in the world, is made possible thanks to the participation of more than 2,500 student volunteers. Volunteerism isn't the only common interest among these tight-knit students: They share an equally spirited interest in partying. Greek life is a huge part of the social scene, and students also like to hop on the train to hit up the bars in Philly. There is a strong sense of community on campus, but there's also some truth to the stereotype that VU students tend to be preppy rich kids. Basketball is the sport of choice here, and students go nuts cheering on the Wildcats, their winning NCAA Division I men's basketball team.

Meet You at the Oreo

VU is located in Villanova, a wealthy suburban town just twelve miles west of Philadelphia. Trains on either side of campus, as well as a weekend shuttle, make it easy to pop into the city for the culture, bars, or just for a change of scenery. The university's tree-lined campus, an officially designated arboretum, is dotted with pretty stone buildings, including the newer West Campus apartments. Students love St. Thomas of Villanova Church, the pride and focal point of campus. And if a Wildcat tells you to meet at the Oreo, don't show up bringing cookies. It refers to *The Oreo*, a black-and-white circular sculpture on a main campus walkway.

Admissions

Average high school GPA:	3.72
Average freshman SAT verbal / math score:	624 / 656
Average freshman ACT score:	26
Application fee:	$70

Application deadlines:
1/7 (freshmen)
6/1 (transfer)
11/1 (early action)

Total applicants:	12,913
Total accepted:	5,511 (43%)
Total accepted who enrolled:	1,634

Notification dates:
4/1 (freshmen)
continuous (transfer)
12/20 (early action)

Acceptance rate for early action applicants:	63%

Students

Percentage of male / female students:	49% / 51%
Percentage of students from out of state:	67%
Percentage of students graduating in 4 years / 6 years:	79% / 85%

Money

Total endowment:	$278,643,000
Total tuition:	$30,430
Total cost with fees & expenses:	$40,790
Average financial aid package:	$20,503
Percentage of students who sought aid and received it:	78%
Percentage of students receiving financial aid:	39%

Also Check Out

Boston College

Colgate University

Georgetown University

Lehigh University

University of Notre Dame

Virginia Polytechnic Institute and State University

201 Burruss Hall
Blacksburg, VA 24061

(540) 231-6000
http://www.vt.edu/

 **BIG CHOICE**

 **BIG RESEARCH**

Who you callin' a Hokie?

5 REASONS IT'S COOL

1. From engineering to forestry, **sciences are top-notch** at this large research institution.

2. At Virginia's largest university, the **Tech community is close-knit and nurturing**.

3. Tech students have over **six hundred clubs and organizations** and tons of recreational sports options to choose from.

4. **Hokie football packs fans into Lane Stadium**, one of the loudest sports venues in the country.

5. Got a free Sunday afternoon? **Go tubing down the New River, hike along the Appalachian Trail, or just enjoy a quiet day in rural Blacksburg**.

The Basics

Public / private: public state
Total enrollment / undergrads: 28,470 / 21,997
Campus setting: small town
Students call it: Virginia Tech, VT, Tech
Students are called: Hokies
Notable alums: Frank Beamer (college football coach), Donaldson Brown (business executive, DuPont GM), Jim Buckmaster (CEO, Craigslist), Charlie Byrd (jazz guitarist), Chet Culver (governor, Iowa), Kylene Hibbard (Miss America), Sharyn McCrumb (novelist), Bruce Smith (pro football player)

Not to Get All Technical, But . . .

Tech offers majors in everything from traditional liberal arts to specialized, pre-professional majors. Freshmen enroll in one of eight colleges or choose the University Studies program, which gives them more time to decide which track suits them best. The prestigious College of Engineering consistently draws the biggest crowds, and each of its thirteen areas of study doles out a hefty workload. The Pamplin College of Business offers internships, semesters abroad, and a five-year dual BA/MBA degree. The College of Architecture & Urban Studies has been rated one of the nation's best. Tech also boasts plenty of high-tech labs and opportunities to conduct research alongside faculty members. Oversized intro lecture classes and a high number of TAs across the board have led to complaints from students. But overall, students that take the initiative are quite satisfied with their academic experience.

Skipper Goes Boom!

One of the many traditions surrounding Hokie football is the firing of the cannon following every score. During World War II, the university was left cannonless when it donated its cannon for scrap to aid the war effort. Rival Virginia Military Institute, which still possessed a cannon, took to gloating. Tired of hearing the "Where's your cannon?" chant, a group of Tech cadets constructed a replacement cannon in secret. Skipper, as the cannon is affectionately called, first sounded off at the '64 Thanksgiving home game against VMI, and it's been booming ever since.

Happy to Be Hokie

School spirit runs high on the Tech campus. Hokies like to have fun, and apartment parties and the local off-campus bar scene figure prominently in the nightlife. The universal passion, however, is football. Students can often be seen playing an impromptu game on the Drillfield, a large expanse of lawn that serves as a reminder of Tech's military past. And fans clad in maroon and orange pack Lane Stadium to cheer on their team at every home game, especially those played against rival UVA for the Commonwealth Cup. With over six hundred clubs and organizations and fifty-four club and intramural sports teams, there are plenty of opportunities for students to get involved. Tech is also home to the Corps of Cadets, one of only two full-time military and leadership training units housed on a university campus, and a distinctive presence here. Freshmen are required to live in one of twenty-five residence halls, which tend to have fairly cramped rooms. Most upperclassmen move to larger apartments off campus, and about 10 percent go Greek.

Small Town Charm

The small town of Blacksburg, located in Virginia's New River valley, doubles in size with the arrival of Tech students each fall. The university and town share a strong connection, which was demonstrated by the warm outpouring of civic support following 2007's campus shooting. The rolling countryside, mountain lakes, and rushing rivers are undeniably beautiful and offer plenty of options for nature lovers. Popular activities range from hiking in the Blue Ridge Mountains to tubing down the James River. The downtown bars, restaurants, and shops are only a short walk from campus. West Virginia, North Carolina, Kentucky, and Tennessee are all within driving distance.

Admissions

Average high school GPA:	3.74
Average freshman SAT verbal / math score:	590 / 623
Average freshman ACT score:	24
Application fee:	$50

Application deadlines:
1/15 (freshmen)
2/15 (transfer)
11/1 (early decision)

Total applicants:	19,032
Total accepted:	12,595 (66%)
Total accepted who enrolled:	5,082

Notification dates:
4/1 (freshmen)
5/1 (transfer)
12/15 (early decision)

Acceptance rate for early decision applicants:	55%

Students

Percentage of male / female students:	58% / 42%
Percentage of students from out of state:	27%
Percentage of students graduating in 4 years / 6 years:	47% / 76%

Money

Total endowment:	$447,400,000
Total in-state tuition, fees & expenses:	$12,573
Total out-of-state tuition, fees & expenses:	$24,529
Average financial aid package:	$8,171
Percentage of students who sought aid and received it:	68%
Percentage of students receiving financial aid:	34%

Also Check Out

George Mason University

James Madison University

North Carolina State University

The Pennsylvania State University–University Park

University of Virginia

Wabash College

PO Box 352
Crawfordsville, IN 47933

(765) 361-6100
http://www.wabash.edu/

BIG PERSPECTIVE

Just for men

5 REASONS IT'S COOL

1. Wabash professors are great teachers, helpful advisors, and often close friends.

2. The **Malcolm X Institute of Black Studies** is not only an excellent academic resource but a terrific example of Wabash's commitment to diversity.

3. Wallies **take their gentleman's code seriously** and treat each other with respect.

4. The **generous financial aid program** is kept afloat by one of the thirty largest per capita college endowments in America.

5. Crawfordsville is **a small and peaceful town**, with a handful of larger (and coed!) universities close by.

The Basics

Public / private: private nonprofit
Total enrollment / undergrads: 874 / 874
Campus setting: small town
Students call it: Wabash
Students are called: Wallies
Notable alums: Robert Allen (CEO, AT&T), Dick Brams (inventor, Happy Meal®), John Coburn (congressman), Mitsuya Goto (general manager, Nissan International), Dean Jagger (actor), Andrea James (filmmaker, activist), Tom Ostrom (pioneering social psychologist, educator), Lawrence Sanders (author), Allen Saunders (cartoonist), Max Wright (actor)

Welcome to Your New Home: The Library

Students and professors alike take academics seriously at Wabash, a fact confirmed by the following statistics: 95 percent of professors have terminal degrees, and 75 percent of students go on to postgrad education. The college's most popular majors are English, history, and psychology. Programs in biology and chemistry are particularly strong and benefit from new, state-of-the-art facilities. Wabash's core curriculum is rooted in the liberal arts and includes required classes in fine arts, composition, foreign language, history, humanities, math, philosophy, natural science, and social science. Students are also required to take at least two courses in an area called "Cultures and Traditions." Classes are small, and professors are attentive and friendly. Intercollegiate study opportunities are available through the Great Lakes Colleges Association, and the

West of the Alleghenies, You Say?

Wabash students really know how to get in the spirit. Members of the Sphinx Club, the college's unusual cheerleading squad, wear candy-striped overalls and white beanies while leading cheers during football games. School spirit is particularly high during the Monon Bell classic. This annual football game against rival DePauw is touted as the "oldest annually contested small college football rivalry west of the Allegheny Mountains."

college's study-abroad program presents such options as studying classics in Athens or biology in the Galapagos. The 3-3 and 3-2 programs connect future lawyers and engineers with other institutions, and a ninth-semester education program is available for prospective teachers.

Kicking Back, Wally Style

The Wabash student body is small, predominantly Indianan, and all male—three factors that define campus life. Students enjoy a generous amount of personal freedom, and the administration tends to let them do as they please, within reason. The hands-off approach results in an encouraging amount of camaraderie and maturity among students, who take an active involvement in their student government. About 90 percent of students live on campus, either in dorms or Greek houses. Extracurriculars are popular, particularly sports, with 40 percent of students playing on intercollegiate teams and 80 percent joining intramural leagues. Wabash's ten fraternities claim nearly 70 percent of the student body, and are responsible for much of the campus's social life, including recruiting females from nearby coed institutions for weekend visits. Although Greek parties are generally open to everyone, independent students may occasionally feel left out.

Where?

Wabash's sixty-acre campus makes its home in Crawfordsville, a town of fifteen thousand located forty-five minutes northwest of Indianapolis. While the town is far less diverse than Wabash itself, and economic misfortunes have plagued the citizens of late, Wallies say the community is safe and welcoming. It's also fairly boring, leading many students to venture to the many coed colleges close by. Purdue is thirty minutes down the road, and Indiana, DePauw, and Illinois at Urbana-Champagne are all popular road-trip destinations. Nearby state parks also provide plentiful opportunities for outdoorsy activities.

Admissions

Average high school GPA:	3.58
Average freshman SAT writing / math / critical reading score:	558 / 607 / 579
Average freshman ACT score:	24
Application fee:	$30

Application deadlines:
continuous (freshmen)
3/15 (transfer)
11/15 (early decision)
12/15 (early action)

Total applicants:	1,319
Total accepted:	678 (51%)
Total accepted who enrolled:	268

Notification dates:
continuous (freshmen)
4/1 (transfer)
12/15 (early decision)
1/31 (early action)

Acceptance rate for early decision applicants:	75%

Students

Percentage of male / female students:	100% / —
Percentage of students from out of state:	26%
Percentage of students graduating in 4 years / 6 years:	66% / 70%

Money

Total endowment:	$348,000,000
Total tuition:	$24,342
Total cost with fees & expenses:	$32,856
Average financial aid package:	$20,607
Percentage of students who sought aid and received it:	100%
Percentage of students receiving financial aid:	72%

Also Check Out

DePauw University

Hamilton College

Indiana University–Bloomington

University of Notre Dame

Wake Forest University

Reynolda Station
Winston-Salem, NC 27109

(336) 758-5000
http://www.wfu.edu/

Rigorous academics, parties aplenty, and school spirit to boot!

5 REASONS IT'S COOL

1. Wake has the resources of a large research university, but its small size fosters **close relationships between professors and students.**

2. As the school motto ("In Service to Humanity") attests, **volunteerism is big.**

3. **More than 50 percent of students study abroad** at study centers in Venice, London, and Vienna, and through summer programs in China, Mexico, and Vietnam, among others.

4. Wake issues **free laptops and printers** to all incoming undergrads—and upgrades them junior year.

5. Students have a reputation for **showing their spirit at basketball and football games.**

The Basics

Public / private: private nonprofit
Total enrollment / undergrads: 6,739 / 4,332
Campus setting: suburban
Students call it: Wake Forest, Wake
Students are called: Demon Deacons
Notable alums: A. R. Ammons (poet, scholar), Marc Blucas (actor), Muggsy Bogues (pro basketball player), Jesse Helms (senator), Maria Henson (journalist), Al Hunt (journalist), Arnold Palmer (pro golfer)

Work Forest

The workload at Wake is intense, and grade inflation is practically non-existent. But students help each other, professors are accessible, and individual attention makes the experience bearable. Typical class size is around twenty students, with large lectures rarely topping 100 students. Undergraduate research in collaboration with faculty is encouraged through various scholarships and grants, including the Richter Scholarship and Environmental Studies Grants. These programs often include living stipends for summer or international research. Incoming freshman enter either the School of Arts and Sciences or the Wayne Calloway School of Business and Accountancy, where a five-year B.A./M.A. program in Accountancy can prepare majors to take the CPA exam. The expansive core curriculum includes twelve classes in subjects ranging from fine arts and history to the social sciences, as well as courses in health and fitness and a cultural diversity class reflecting the school's global attitude. Business, communications, and political science are

Let the Good Times Roll

Major celebrations, including athletic victories, inspire the unfurling of dozens of toilet paper rolls upon the ash trees lining the quad. The tradition of "Rolling the Quad" has come under fire for its environmental consequences. But the tradition, which started in the 1960s, has at least some administration approval. When the school hosted a 2000 presidential debate, spirited red, white, and blue streamers replaced toilet paper as the garnish of choice.

among the most popular major, and newer offerings include East Asian languages and a music performance track.

Color Me Greek

Greek life is the glue that holds life at Wake together, taking in more than half of the female students and a third of the males. But the integrated living quarters, with Greek "houses" limited to sections of school dorms, help to generate a generally active and social campus atmosphere. Evidence of this kinship can be seen in one Greek tradition that requires new pledges to run around campus kissing passersby and tallying their achievements in notebooks. Intramural sports are popular and include water polo and bowling along with the standard fare. Budding comedians and their prey will appreciate the campus's nationally recognized comedy troupe, the Lilting Banshees. Another popular event is Shag on the Mag, where students shag dance under a large tent covering the Magnolia Quad. The student body is largely conservative and wealthy, although recent trends have seen a leftward tug and a growing gay and lesbian population.

Demons in Paradise

Resting on the edge of the Blue Ridge Mountains in North Carolina's Piedmont region, Wake Forest's campus encompasses 340 acres of blossoming magnolias, well-trimmed lawns, and elm-tree-lined paths. Stately limestone and brick buildings dominate, though more modern edifices such as the large Fine Arts Building populate the outer edges. The campus also boasts a nine-hole golf course and the Reynolda Gardens, home to a woodland preserve and a unique collection of Japanese cherry trees. Wake is constantly updating its campus facilities, including an expansion to the cafeteria at Reynolda Hall. For those who grow tired of this gated community—which is closed off to non-students after 10 P.M.—the surrounding town of Winston-Salem provides cultural attractions, including art museums, live music venues, and shopping boutiques. The outdoor adventures of hiking, camping, and beaches and the indoor adventures of UNC–Chapel Hill, Duke, and North Carolina State are all less than two hours away.

Admissions

Average high school GPA:	—
Average freshman SAT verbal / math score:	653 / 669
Average freshman ACT score:	—
Application fee:	$50
Application deadlines:	
1/15 (freshmen)	
— (transfer)	
11/15 (early decision)	
Total applicants:	7,431
Total accepted:	3,130 (42%)
Total accepted who enrolled:	1,121
Notification dates:	
4/1 (freshmen)	
— (transfer)	
12/15 (early decision)	
Acceptance rate for early decision applicants:	53%

Students

Percentage of male / female students:	49% / 51%
Percentage of students from out of state:	74%
Percentage of students graduating in 4 years / 6 years:	78% / 88%

Money

Total endowment:	$906,803,000
Total tuition:	$34,230
Total cost with fees & expenses:	$43,830
Average financial aid package:	$24,745
Percentage of students who sought aid and received it:	86%
Percentage of students receiving financial aid:	37%

Also Check Out

Emory University

University of North Carolina at Chapel Hill

University of Richmond

University of Virginia

Vanderbilt University

Warren Wilson College

PO Box 9000
Asheville, NC 28815

(828) 298-3325
http://www.warren-wilson.edu/

 **BIG IDEA**

 **BIG WORLD**

Not your ordinary school

5 REASONS IT'S COOL

1. Warren Wilson's **unique Triad curriculum** combines labor, learning, and volunteerism.

2. All students are required to **work on campus to offset tuition costs**. And we mean *real* work: Students join one of more than 110 work crews, ranging from the campus auto shop to Admissions Office.

3. **Professors put teaching first** and make themselves accessible to their students.

4. Students enjoy **a real campus community**, with 90 percent living on campus.

5. **Surrounded by the Blue Ridge Mountains**, the location is a nature-lover's dream.

The Basics

Public / private: private religious
Total enrollment / undergrads: 908 / 841
Campus setting: small town
Students call it: Warren Wilson, WWC
Students are called: Owls
Notable alums: Tony Earley (novelist), Meghan O'Rourke (editor), Billy Edd Wheeler (musician), David Wilcox (musician)

Working Hard ...

Warren Wilson's Triad Program encourages students to lead a balanced life of work, learning, and service. Students take two courses during each eight-week term and have a broad choice of twenty-one different majors, including traditional offering such as biology and English as well as more unusual disciplines such as outdoor leadership and environmental studies. Students are also required to put in fifteen hours of work each week on their assigned work crew, which may involve removing trash from hiking trails, painting, blacksmithing, farming, or even scrubbing toilets to learn the necessity of responsibility. Finally, all students must devote at least twenty-five hours a term to supporting a single cause or community group. Some students choose to volunteer in the community, while some trek halfway around the world to serve in another country. Not surprisingly, the demands of the Triad leave students with little downtime, which has prompted some students to complain that WWC really stands for "We Work Constantly."

Country Living

As if Warren Wilson students needed a reminder that they exist in a bubble apart from the rest of the world, the college throws a big country party twice a year. Known as the "Bubba," the faculty- and staff-chaperoned event takes place around a roaring bonfire in the middle of a cow pasture. To help foot the bill for the kegs, the staff sells T-shirts. Underage partygoers might not get to drink the beer, but Bubba organizers make sure that there are more than enough nonalcoholic refreshments to go around.

... or Hardly Working?

If you love to watch or play football, or you want to join a fraternity or sorority, WWC is not the school for you: The college offers neither football nor Greeks. Instead, students focus their energies on sports such as mountain biking, swimming, canoeing, kayaking, and USCAA basketball. While most students tend to be very liberal and environmentally conscious, overall they can be tough to categorize. All students, whether they're the sporting type or not, tend to be pretty health conscious, and yoga and helping out at the student-run food co-op are popular pastimes. Students also love the outdoors, and they aren't afraid to come to class covered in dirt. Each spring on Work Day, students, faculty, and staff put aside their regular duties and help beautify the campus. Roughly 90 percent of students live on campus in one of thirteen residence halls, including the new EcoDorm, which features an energy-efficient design. Poetry readings, campus forums, and the Student Caucus are also very popular.

Just like Heaven

Warren Wilson has a stunning and unique campus. Surrounded by the Blue Ridge Mountains, the 1,100-acre campus features its own river with a whitewater kayaking course, a 300-acre farm, a 700-acre forest, and twenty-five miles of hiking trails. Suffice it to say, Warren Wilson is a nature lover's dream. Offering four distinct seasons, the region features vibrant foliage in the fall, a combination of natural and machine-made snow for snow sports in the winter, and mild temperatures for hiking and swimming in the spring and summer. To help students make the most of the area, Warren Wilson also partners with the North Carolina Outward Bound School. And when students want to get off campus, they can make the twenty-five-mile drive to Asheville, where arts events, good restaurants and bars, and even more outdoor activities abound.

Admissions

Average high school GPA:	3.21
Average freshman SAT verbal / math score:	612 / 567
Average freshman ACT score:	24
Application fee:	—
Application deadlines:	
3/15 (freshmen)	
3/15 (transfer)	
11/15 (early decision)	
Total applicants:	840
Total accepted:	622 (74%)
Total accepted who enrolled:	221
Notification dates:	
continuous (freshmen)	
4/1 (transfer)	
12/1 (early decision)	
Acceptance rate for early decision applicants:	95%

Students

Percentage of male / female students:	40% / 60%
Percentage of students from out of state:	85%
Percentage of students graduating in 4 years / 6 years:	37% / 48%

Money

Total endowment:	$31,860,000
Total tuition:	$21,084
Total cost with fees & expenses:	$27,784
Average financial aid package:	$14,705
Percentage of students who sought aid and received it:	73%
Percentage of students receiving financial aid:	58%

Also Check Out

Bard College

Bennington College

Hampshire College

University of North Carolina at Chapel Hill

Washington & Lee University

204 West Washington St.
Lexington, VA 24450

(540) 458-8400
http://www.wlu.edu/

 **BIG BRAIN**

 **BIG PERSPECTIVE**

Southern tradition meets serious academics.

5 REASONS IT'S COOL

1. Think you can handle heaps of homework? **Academics are tough**, but super-motivated W & L students thrive under pressure.

2. No hiding! **W & L classes are small**, taught by professors, and emphasize group discussions.

3. The honor system, which dates back to former W & L president Robert E. Lee, fills the campus with **a sense of communal trust**.

4. **Greek life is huge.** Enormous. Gigantic. And lots of fun.

5. This is the South, y'all. **Southern history, charm, and traditions** are defining aspects of the W & L experience.

The Basics

Public / private: private nonprofit
Total enrollment / undergrads: 2,148 / 1,752
Campus setting: small town
Students call it: W & L
Students are called: Generals
Notable alums: Meriwether Lewis (explorer), Roger H. Mudd (journalist), Lewis Powell Jr. (U.S. Supreme Court justice), Pat Robertson (televangelist), Cy Twombly (artist), John Warner (secretary of the Navy, senator), Tom Wolfe (writer)

No Free Passes

W & L classes are tough and demanding across the board. Students are required to complete coursework in a foreign language, humanities, math, physical education, natural sciences, and social sciences and demonstrate proficiency in writing and computers. W & L's most popular majors are business, economics, and history, and programs in the sciences are also strong. The lab facilities, which include a scanning electron microscope, are excellent. The university runs on a trimester system, which includes two twelve-week terms and a shortened, six-week-long spring term. During this latter term, students usually enroll in just two classes and focus more intently on a narrower spectrum of subjects. The student-to-professor ratio is 10:1, and as a result, classes are small and tend to involve (often lively) discussions. Professors demand that all students keep up with their heavy reading lists and be ready to contribute to class debates. In return, office doors are open

A Proud Tradition Begins

George William Crump was a student at Washington College, as W & L used to be known, when, in 1804, he was arrested for running naked through the streets of Lexington. The stunt, the very first recorded act of streaking in American history, got Crump suspended for a semester. He was later elected to the United States Congress.

and professors make every effort to help students. Cozy relations between students and teachers are reinforced by the honor code, which prohibits cheating and academic dishonesty.

Which Frat Are You In?

There's a southern twist to life at W & L. Most everyone dresses nicely, formal events are popular, and stodgy-sounding terms like *honor* and *personal responsibility* are used unironically. Greek life rules the day: Over 80 percent of men join one of fourteen fraternities, and around 75 percent of women join one of seven sororities. Independent students, while few and far between, still find plenty of ways to keep busy. W & L offers about ninety student organizations. Varsity sports don't hit the radar too often, although students find that big games are a great excuse to throw tailgate parties. Intramural sports are also popular options. Campus facilities are mostly keeping pace with the times. A new exercise facility was recently completed, and the $30 million student commons is a popular spot for study and relaxation. An enormous new music and arts building has recently been completed.

Pretty and Pretty Dull

Strolling around the W & L campus can feel like taking a trip back in time. Historical highlights include the Colonnade, a row of brick buildings that have been designated a National Historic Landmark, and Lee Chapel, where students can pay their respects to Robert E. Lee himself by visiting the Lee family crypt. W & L's campus directly adjoins the campus of the Virginia Military Institute. The town of Lexington, located in the Shenandoah Valley, is postcard-pretty but offers very little by way of nightlife. The surrounding area, however, is an outdoors-lover's dream, offering plenty of hiking and other sporty activities in the nearby mountains.

Admissions

Average high school GPA:	—
Average freshman SAT verbal / math score:	692 / 695
Average freshman ACT score:	27
Application fee:	$50

Application deadlines:
1/15 (freshmen)
4/1 (transfer)
11/15 (early decision)

Total applicants:	4,215
Total accepted:	1,158 (27%)
Total accepted who enrolled:	450

Notification dates:
4/1 (freshmen)
continuous (transfer)
12/22 (early decision)

Acceptance rate for early decision applicants:	48%

Students

Percentage of male / female students:	51% / 49%
Percentage of students from out of state:	85%
Percentage of students graduating in 4 years / 6 years:	84% / 87%

Money

Total endowment:	$586,968,000
Total tuition:	$31,175
Total cost with fees & expenses:	$42,345
Average financial aid package:	$27,934
Percentage of students who sought aid and received it:	99%
Percentage of students receiving financial aid:	34%

Also Check Out

College of William & Mary

Davidson College

Duke University

Georgetown University

University of Richmond

University of Virginia

Washington University in St. Louis

1 Brookings Drive
St. Louis, MO 63130

(314) 935-5000
http://www.wustl.edu/

BIG BRAIN

BIG RESEARCH

An academic star that's right in the middle of things.

5 REASONS IT'S COOL

1. Wash U's **academic star is on the rise**, drawing students from all over who might otherwise attend Ivy League universities.

2. **Freedom and flexibility** are hallmarks of the undergraduate experience, and many students double major or design their own.

3. Wash U's top-notch **undergraduate architecture program** trains the next generation of Frank Gehrys.

4. **The campus is gorgeous**, and comes complete with stately Gothic buildings and peaceful quads.

5. **St. Louis has lots of attractions**—ride to the top of the Arch! catch a Cardinals game!—and the Loop is just a short walk.

The Basics

Public / private: private nonprofit
Total enrollment / undergrads: 13,355 / 7,386
Campus setting: suburban
Students call it: Wash U, WUSTL
Students are called: Bears
Notable alums: Anita Diamant (novelist), Johnny Kastl (actor), David Merrick (theater producer), Harold Ramis (actor, filmmaker), Peter Sarsgaard (actor), Tennessee Williams (attended; playwright)

The Major, Remixed

You would be hard pressed to find a mediocre major at Wash U. The university's academic reputation is on the rise, and has been for quite some time now. Academics are distributed across the five undergraduate colleges of arts & science, architecture, art, business, and engineering. Many Wash U students choose to go the pre-med route, while others take advantage of other specialized programs in engineering and architecture. A high degree of flexibility makes it easy for students to minor, double major, or design their own courses of study. Students with clearly defined career goals may apply to the University Scholars Program, where they can work toward a graduate degree in a field such as medicine or architecture concurrently with their undergraduate work. Most Wash U classes are fewer than twenty-five students. Faculty and teaching assistants are highly accessible, and the advising system is very helpful. Wash U sates students' wanderlust by sending them to over forty countries for a semester, summer, or year.

Goin' Wild!

Wash U students really know how to go wild. WILD stands for Walk In Lay Down, the annual concert program on campus that draw big name acts like Guster, Sugarhill Gang, and Ben Folds. Held at the beginning of the fall semester and the end of the spring semester, this huge music event evolved from an outdoor movie screening in 1973, and it's still free to Wash U students. WILD got its name because students used to bring couches and blankets to take in the movies and music from a supine position.

All's Fairs

While Wash U students are known to hit the books pretty hard, they still find time for fun. The student body is notably diverse and includes students from every corner of the country and many foreign countries. Students pull out all of the stops for popular cultural events, like Diwali, the Indian Festival of Light held every fall, and the Chinese Lunar Near Year Festival in early winter. The university's annual Thurtene Carnival, the largest and oldest student-run fair in the country, draws massive crowds of up to 100,000 and directs proceeds to local charities. Freshmen are required to live in on-campus housing or residential colleges, each of which has its own themed activities and programs. Most residence halls are located in the South 40 section of campus, named for its location at the south end of campus and its size of forty acres. The dorms here are posh and include places to eat, shoot hoops, and even develop photos. Other housing options include on-campus apartments and eleven fraternity houses. There are fifteen eateries, which offer a wide range of dining options, including vegan, vegetarian, and Kosher fare.

Collegiate Comfort

Wash U's Gothic-style campus is located next to Forest Park, St. Louis's large urban park and the former site of the 1904 World's Fair. The park's nearly 1,300 acres contain grassy knolls and lots of trees, as well as museums, a zoo, the Muny Opera, and other natural and cultural attractions. New campus buildings, including the Laboratory Sciences Building and the Earth and Planetary Sciences Building, have recently brought a new wave of up-to-date technology and equipment to campus. The new building for the Sam Fox School of Design & Visual Arts has a sleek, contemporary style. The Loop is a cool, student-friendly area within walking distance that features boutiques, book and record shops, and inexpensive eateries. Many students choose to live off campus in this area for its proximity and vibe.

Admissions

Average high school GPA:	—
Average freshman SAT verbal / math score:	708 / 725
Average freshman ACT score:	27
Application fee:	$55

Application deadlines:
1/15 (freshmen)
4/15 (transfer)
11/15 (early decision)

Total applicants:	22,251
Total accepted:	4,634 (21%)
Total accepted who enrolled:	1,461

Notification dates:
4/1 (freshmen)
continuous (transfer)
12/15 (early decision)

Acceptance rate for early action applicants:	—

Students

Percentage of male / female students:	50% / 50%
Percentage of students from out of state:	89%
Percentage of students graduating in 4 years / 6 years:	83% / 91%

Money

Total endowment:	$4,294,967,295
Total tuition:	$34,500
Total cost with fees & expenses:	$46,776
Average financial aid package:	$27,310
Percentage of students who sought aid and received it:	100%
Percentage of students receiving financial aid:	36%

Also Check Out

Duke University

Harvard University

Northwestern University

Stanford University

University of Pennsylvania

Wellesley College

106 Central Street
Wellesley, MA 02481

(781) 283-1000
http://www.wellesley.edu/

**BIG
BRAIN**

**BIG
PERSPECTIVE**

We are women, watch us soar!

5 REASONS IT'S COOL

1. Uh, in case you haven't heard . . . **this Seven Sisters school is all women.** And most alums say they wouldn't trade their experience for the world.

2. What do **Hillary Clinton, Madeleine Albright, and Diane Sawyer** have in common?

3. Talk about connected: **Wellesley's alumni network** is active and committed to making sure grads continue to lead every field.

4. The three S's: **Small classes, stellar professors, and a supportive community.**

5. Need a break from the all-girl campus? Wellesley is just **minutes away from downtown Boston.**

The Basics

Public / private: private nonprofit
Total enrollment / undergrads: 2,318 / 2,318
Campus setting: suburban
Student call it: Wellesley
Students are called: Sisters
Notable alums: Hillary Clinton (senator), Nora Ephron (filmmaker), Cokie Roberts (broadcast journalist), Diane Sawyer (broadcast journalist), Madeleine Albright (U.S. secretary of state, ambassador)

The Feminine Mystique

Young women from all social, economic, cultural, and academic backgrounds converge at Wellesley because of its well-deserved reputation for stellar academics in a supportive, all-female environment. The college provides a list of majors that act as guidelines rather than regimented programs. Students are free—no, expected—to supplement their coursework with long-term research projects (sometimes with a stipend courtesy of the college), add courses from other departments, or rewrite their majors entirely according to individual goals. All fifty-three of the college's majors command respect from employers and graduate schools. Popular majors include economics, hard sciences, political science, psychology, and English. Twenty percent of every graduating class goes on to pursue medical degrees. An unwritten honor code governs all academic endeavors, allowing students to take unproctored exams whenever they choose. Classes are small: An average classroom has twenty seats, and the overall student-faculty ratio is

9:1. Wellesley students rave about their professors: *brilliant* and *friendly* are typical adjectives used to describe faculty members. For budding scientists, the campus science center features electron microscopes, NMR spectrometers, and ultracentrifuges; plus, nearby MIT offers full cross-registration privileges.

Diverse Women

The only demographic missing from Wellesley's student body is, well, men. Students here are a diverse bunch: 26 percent of students are Asian American, 6 percent are African American, and 7 percent are Hispanic American. All fifty states and seventy-five foreign countries are represented. Wellesley students pride themselves on packing their schedules with extracurricular commitments. There are 160 campus organizations to choose from, including choral groups, dance troupes, literary magazines, and a radio station. Art and literature societies are also enduring traditions at Wellesley; at the beginning of the spring semester, members are selected through the so-called tea process, which resembles a rush process, only featuring a different choice of beverage. Attitudes vary when it comes to sports: Wellesley's lacrosse and tennis teams have strong records, and excitement on campus rises whenever teams play rival Smith, but the Boston Marathon is cited by many students as the best spectator sport available.

Quiet and Safe

Wellesley's campus is gorgeous, its five hundred acres encompassing gentle hills, an arboretum, and a botanical garden. Amid the older Gothic buildings are newer facilities for science and athletics, plus an art gallery, movie theater, and commuter rail station. The town of Wellesley is pleasant, quiet, and safe, but it's also alcohol free and usually quiet by 9 P.M. Boston, of course, is just a quick train ride away, and Wellesley operates an hourly shuttle to and from Harvard Square in nearby Cambridge. Beaches in Cape Cod and skiing in other parts of New England are all within reasonable driving distance.

Admissions

Average high school GPA: —

Average freshman SAT writing / math / critical reading score: 700 / 688 / 701

Average freshman ACT score: 27

Application fee: $50

Application deadlines:
1/15 (freshmen)
2/10 (transfer)
11/1 (early decision)

Total applicants: 3,974

Total accepted: 1,434 (36%)

Total accepted who enrolled: 586

Notification dates:
4/1 (freshmen)
4/1 (transfer)
12/15 (early decision)

Acceptance rate for early decision applicants: 74%

Students

Percentage of male / female students: — / 100%

Percentage of students from out of state: 89%

Percentage of students graduating in 4 years / 6 years: 88% / 93%

Money

Total endowment: $1,412,410,000

Total tuition: $32,384

Total cost with fees & expenses: $45,288

Average financial aid package: $29,797

Percentage of students who sought aid and received it: 100%

Percentage of students receiving financial aid: 57%

Also Check Out

Amherst College

Barnard College

Brown University

Bryn Mawr College

Vassar College

Wesleyan University

70 Wyllys Ave
Middletown, CT 06459

(860) 685-2000
http://www.wesleyan.edu/

 **BIG BRAIN**

 **BIG IDEA**

 **BIG PERSPECTIVE**

Smart thinking, any way you want it

5 REASONS IT'S COOL

1. **Open-minded, adventurous, and creative** just begins to describe the students at Wesleyan. Oh, and did we mention smart?

2. Goldilocks would like it here: Wesleyan is **neither tiny nor huge**, offering the advantages of both small and large schools.

3. Wesleyan has that ever-appealing trifecta of **small classes, fantastic professors, and unique courses.**

4. Wesleyan students are a **passionate bunch**, and they get equally revved up about chemistry, Frisbee, and campus protests.

5. There's a social scene for **every taste alike:** party animals and teetotalers.

The Basics

Public / private: private nonprofit
Total enrollment / undergrads: 3,220 / 2,813
Campus setting: small town
Students call it: Wesleyan
Students are called: Cardinals
Notable alums: Eric Asimov (wine critic), Michael Bay (film director), Amy Bloom (novelist), Bradley Whitford (actor), Bill Belichick (pro football coach)

May We Suggest . . .

Wesleyan has no traditional distribution requirements. Instead, the university provides students with a set of academic expectations, which are basically just distribution "suggestions" covering different areas of the liberal arts, such as humanities, social science, science, and math. To put it another way, Wesleyan students have a lot of freedom when it comes to planning their courses. Academic programs are strong across the board, and students choose from over nine hundred courses in thirty-nine departments. Outside-the-box thinking is encouraged: Students can participate in one of ten interdisciplinary programs. Professors are tough and have a tendency to concoct merciless reading lists, but Wesleyan students are up for the challenge. Fortunately, when they need face time with their professors, they'll most likely get it. The student-faculty ratio is 9:1. Half of students study abroad, and a quarter of those students venture to countries other than those in Western Europe, including Botswana, Nepal, and Israel.

Pardon me, have you seen my cannon?

Back in the 1860s, an annual contest positioned members of the freshmen class, who tried to set off the Douglas cannon, against members of the sophomore class, who tried to stop their efforts. For obvious reasons, the bit about firing a cannon onto a crowded college campus was eventually phased out. By the mid-twentieth century, the challenge was to *steal* the cannon. According to Wesleyan, the stolen cannon has seen many adventures: It has been presented to magazine editors, U.S. presidents, and the Russian delegation to the UN. It has even been baked into a cake.

Get Active

Wesleyan is known for its politically inclined students. But even students who prefer sitting on couches to attending sit-in protests will feel at home on this super-diverse campus. Not surprisingly, volunteer work is very popular, and Wesleyan is among the top five Peace Corps volunteer–producing schools in the country. Other popular activities include WESU-FM, the oldest continually broadcasting college radio station in the country, and athletics, which about 70 percent of students are involved with in some way or another. Six fraternities and two sororities claim only 5 percent of the student body, and most parties take place in the campus dorms or apartments. On-campus housing is guaranteed for four all years. Some of this housing is very new, and renovations are happening all the time.

Small City Lights

Wesleyan's picturesque campus is a smorgasbord of architectural styles. The athletic facilities are excellent, and a new dining center opened in 2007. The world immediately beyond campus, though, offers little by way of excitement, and most students tend to entertain themselves within the confines of campus. Middletown offers a few good restaurants, movie theaters, and arts venues. Fortunately, more exciting places are all within reach: New Haven, home to Yale, is just forty-five minutes down the road. And a couple hours' more driving will have you in New York, Boston, or the wilds of New England.

Admissions

Average high school GPA:	3.95
Average freshman SAT writing / math / critical reading score:	686 / 691 / 692
Average freshman ACT score:	26
Application fee:	$55

Application deadlines:
1/1 (freshmen)
3/15 (transfer)
11/15 (early decision)

Total applicants:	7,242
Total accepted:	2,012 (28%)
Total accepted who enrolled:	720

Notification dates:
4/1 (freshmen)
5/15 (transfer)
12/15 (early decision)

Acceptance rate for early decision applicants:	48%

Students

Percentage of male / female students:	50% / 50%
Percentage of students from out of state:	95%
Percentage of students graduating in 4 years / 6 years:	83% / 90%

Money

Total endowment:	$619,800,000
Total tuition:	$34,844
Total cost with fees & expenses:	$46,994
Average financial aid package:	$29,465
Percentage of students who sought aid and received it:	100%
Percentage of students receiving financial aid:	47%

Also Check Out

Amherst College

Brown University

Skidmore College

Tufts University

Williams College

West Virginia University

University Avenue
Morgantown, WV 26506

(304) 293-0111
http://www.wvu.edu/

BIG CHOICE

Mountaineer spirit and Morgantown charm

5 REASONS IT'S COOL

1. Learn how CSI is *really* done in **WVU's forensic science program.**

2. **Rock-bottom prices** mean that just about everyone can take advantage of top-notch programs in engineering, business, and health sciences.

3. **Old meets new on the Downtown campus,** where nineteenth-century buildings blend with state-of-the-art facilities.

4. Don't miss the chance to cheer on the football squad at **legendary Mountaineer Field.**

5. Small-towns don't get more **charming** than Morgantown.

The Basics

Public / private: public state
Total enrollment / undergrads: 27,115 / 20,590
Campus setting: small town
Students call it: WVU
Students are called: Mountaineers, Mounties
Notable alums: Maggie Anderson (poet), Tommy Bowden (college football coach), Stephen Coonts (novelist), Marc Bulger (pro football player), Don Knotts (actor), Jon McBride (astronaut), Asra Nomani (author, activist), Brad Paisley (musician), Jerry West (pro basketball player)

From Forensics to Physical Therapy

WVU boasts thirteen undergraduate schools and over 180 majors that span the disciplines. The College of Arts & Sciences, with popular English and psychology programs, attracts the most students. Engineering, journalism, physical therapy, nursing, business, and communications are also strong. WVU has one of the few accredited forensic science programs in the country, making it a leader in CSI (crime scene investigation) studies. There's no getting around large class sizes, and students often grumble about the limited availability of classes come registration time. Although professors are described as warm and caring, some initiative is required on the part of the students. Operation Jump-Start and the Resident Faculty Leaders Program are just two of the programs underway to engage incoming freshmen. Expansive internship and study-abroad programs provide students with additional opportunities. Overall, academics at this major research institution are as challenging

Can You Fiddle? Or Grow a Beard?

School spirit is on full display during **Mountaineer Week**, WVU's annual celebration of **West Virginian** and **Appalachian** culture that culminates in a home football game. Fiddling, clogging, and beard-growing competitions put students in touch with some good ole **Mountaineer** heritage. **Mountaineer Idol**, a new addition to the festivities, tests out their singing skills.

as students make them, and the level of commitment among students hits both ends of the spectrum. For every Rhodes or Truman Scholar, there's a seven-year student or two . . . or three . . .

Almost Heaven, West Virginia . . .

To quote John Denver's song "Take Me Home Country Roads" (as students do at every home football game), West Virginia is "almost heaven." Mountie pride peaks during football season, although basketball games are also widely attended. Intramural and club sports are popular, and students love the new Recreation Center. The Mountainlair Student Union houses a food court, bowling alley, pool hall, video arcade, movie theater, and study areas. WVU deserves its party school rep, and students aren't afraid to toss back a few any night of the week. The administration has been cracking down on underage drinking, however, and has instituted WVUp All Night, a weekly program including everything from movies (both watched and made) to performances to video-game competitions, as a popular alternative to the party scene. Most freshmen live in the Towers, a high-rise dorm on the Evansdale campus, while upperclassmen often seek housing off campus.

Mountaineer Mama

With eight experimental farms, four research forests, and a 4-H Camp, WVU extends far and wide. The campus is divided into two locations—Evansdale and downtown—which are one and a half miles apart, or a five-minute ride on the PRT (personal rapid transit), the public transportation system. Morgantown, a quintessential college town, is inextricably linked to WVU and has experienced a boom coinciding with the university's recent growth. The main downtown campus sits within walking distance of numerous bars, shops, and restaurants. While the mountainous terrain makes for a tiring walk to class, it also provides a wealth of activities for the many outdoors enthusiasts among the student body. For those desiring more cosmopolitan entertainment, Pittsburgh is just over an hour away, and Washington, D.C., is just over three.

Admissions

Average high school GPA:	3.0
Average freshman SAT verbal / math score:	518 / 536
Average freshman ACT score:	23
Application fee:	$25

Application deadlines:
8/1 (freshmen)
8/1 (transfer)

Total applicants:	12,047
Total accepted:	11,040 (92%)
Total accepted who enrolled:	4,787

Notification dates:
— (freshmen)
continuous (transfer)

Students

Percentage of male / female students:	55% / 45%
Percentage of students from out of state:	43%
Percentage of students graduating in 4 years / 6 years:	25% / 54%

Money

Total endowment:	$420,100,000
Total in-state tuition, fees & expenses:	$12,006
Total out-of-state tuition, fees & expenses:	$21,370
Average financial aid package:	$5,977
Percentage of students who sought aid and received it:	87%
Percentage of students receiving financial aid:	60%

Also Check Out

James Madison University

The Pennsylvania State University–University Park

The University of Pittsburgh

Virginia Polytechnic and State University

Wheaton College

East Main Street	(508) 285-7722
Norton, MA 02766	http://www.wheatoncollege.edu/

 **BIG PERSPECTIVE**

Laid-back *and* intense

5 REASONS IT'S COOL

1. **Give a little, get a lot.** Professors will do just about anything for students who show a passion for learning.

2. **Interdisciplinary work** is emphasized.

3. As a member of the 12 College Consortium, Wheaton students can do an **exchange program with another school** in the area.

4. The Filene Center for Work and Learning gets high marks for helping students find internships and plan their first **postcollege career move.**

5. There's excitement in two directions: The college is nestled between **two of New England's major cities.**

The Basics

Public / private: private nonprofit
Total enrollment / undergrads: 1,561 / 1,561
Campus setting: small town
Students call it: Wheaton
Students are called: Wheaties
Notable alums: Catherine Keener (actress), Jean Fritz (author), Alexandra Marshall (writer), Esther Newberg (cocreator, ICM), Lesley Stahl (TV journalist), Christine Todd Whitman (governor, New Jersey), Amanda Urban (literary agent)

Evening Things Out

Wheaties devote widely disparate amounts of time to their class work. Some put the pedal to the metal from their first day on campus; others note, proudly, that it's possible to hide in the larger introductory classes for your first two years without doing much reading. That said, there's very little grade inflation, and professors have a reputation for being tough. They are also encouraging and accessible; the average class size is fifteen, and the student-to-faculty ratio is 12:1. The most popular majors are English, psychology, and economics, and the strongest programs are in the social sciences and humanities. The education program is also demanding, as it requires a double major and student-teaching experience. In recent years, the administration has been working to raise the profile of the natural science programs. This effort is reflected in a construction plan that aims to have all science buildings rebuilt by 2014. The fine arts facilities are also getting a polish; a

We've Got That

For a small school, Wheaton has an impressive list of extracurricular clubs and activities. In addition to the standards you'd expect, there are a number of eclectic, occasionally ironic, student groups, including the Cooking Consortium, Colleges Against Cancer, Model Arab League, Norton Youth Theater, the Gentlemen Callers, the Grilling Society, and Voices United to Jam.

$20 million refurbishment was recently completed. As for distribution requirements, students must take English, math, a foreign language, and one class with a non-Western focus. There's also a required first-year seminar that hones writing and critical-thinking skills.

Going to Town

Wheaton only became coed in 1988, and, as a result, the gender numbers have yet to reach perfect equilibrium; over 60 percent of the students are female. Most students are from middle- or upper-class communities in the Northeast, but only 30 percent are from Massachusetts. Although it's in the Bay State, Wheaton is actually closer to Providence than it is to Boston, and both cities play an important role in the social life of many students. On certain weekends, the Boston and Providence Connections programs give Wheaties a chance to grab dinner and catch a show for five dollars. For homebodies, the campus bar, Loft, provides an ID-lenient, if expensive, place to get drinks. The administration tends to go easy on drinkers. Athletes are frequent party throwers, though their impact on campus life is otherwise limited. Norton's relative blandness tends to unify the student body. This is the kind of place where it's not considered an assault on social etiquette to strike up a conversation with a stranger. There are sixty campus organizations, and a cappella groups are particularly popular. They often serve as hubs of friendship—important at a school without fraternities or sororities.

Meet the Neighbors

An optimistic take on Norton, Massachusetts, would be that it doesn't provide many distractions from schoolwork. Another perspective? It's a boring town whose residents don't like Wheaton students. The truth is somewhere in between. Providence is twenty minutes away, Boston twice as far. A shuttle bus takes students to the commuter rail station near campus every half hour. Speaking of campus, it's pretty: 358 acres, with the expected critical mass of brick and ivy, plus a heated duck pond.

Admissions

Average high school GPA:	3.5
Average freshman SAT verbal / math score:	640 / 621
Average freshman ACT score:	26
Application fee:	$55

Application deadlines:
1/15 (first year)
4/1 (transfer)
11/15 (early decision)

Total applicants:	3,614
Total accepted:	1,464 (41%)
Total accepted who enrolled:	410

Notification dates:
4/1 (first year)
5/15 (transfer)
12/15 (early decision)

Acceptance rate for early decision applicants:	86%

Students

Percentage of male / female students:	38% / 62%
Percentage of students from out of state:	67%
Percentage of students graduating in 4 years / 6 years:	70% / 75%

Money

Total endowment:	$173,000,000
Total tuition:	$34,365
Total cost with fees & expenses:	$52,160
Average financial aid package:	$25,229
Percentage of students who sought aid and received it:	98%
Percentage of students receiving financial aid:	53%

Also Check Out

Bates College

Clark University

Northeastern University

Tufts University

Wellesley College

Whitman College

345 Boyer Avenue
Walla Walla, WA 99362

(509) 527-5III
http://www.whitman.edu/

BIG PERSPECTIVE

Where academics are eco-friendly

5 REASONS IT'S COOL

1. **Small class size and a IO:I student-to-faculty ratio** ensure lively classroom discussions and lots of personal attention.

2. Don't be fooled by the laid-back atmosphere; **academics are challenging and rigorous.**

3. Study, research, and publish with a **dedicated, friendly faculty.**

4. The **outdoorsy, eco-conscious students** are a tight-knit bunch.

5. The **cute town of Walla Walla** is surrounded by golden hills, evergreens, and the Columbia River.

The Basics

Public / private: private nonprofit
Total enrollment / undergrads: 1,455 / 1,455
Campus setting: small town
Students call it: Whitman
Students are called: Whitties
Notable alums: Ryan Crocker (ambassador), William O. Douglas (U.S. Supreme Court justice), John Markoff (journalist), John Stanton (founder, Western Wireless), Adam West (actor, original Batman)

Study, Laugh, Lounge—The Whittie Way

Small and studious, Whitman College offers one the strongest liberal arts educations in the Northwest. The Summer Reading program, in which incoming freshmen read and then come together to discuss a book chosen by the president, is typical of the Whittie approach to academics. Students can frequently be found lounging on Ankeny Field, continuing scholarly debates post-class. Seniors must take comprehensive exams in their major field to graduate. Despite the rigor of academics here, students are easygoing and not at all competitive. Perhaps they are bonded by the experience of "Antiquity and Modernity," a notorious year-long course that is part of the First Year Core. English, biology, psychology, and politics are among the strongest and most popular majors. Professors are praised as knowledgeable, dedicated, and friendly, and there are many research and internship opportunities available. Semester in the West, a unique field-study program in environmental studies, is popular, as are urban semesters in Chicago and

Be Green!

The Whitman campus is keen on green. From the student-run organic garden to the vegan options in the dining hall, this is an eco-friendly environment.

Philadelphia. Whitman also offers a number of combined study programs, among them a 3-2 forestry and environmental management program with Duke and a 3-2 engineering program with schools such as Caltech and Columbia. About 40 percent of the student body studies abroad in countries including Botswana, Costa Rica, and Taiwan.

Laid-Back and Outdoorsy

If you had to choose one word to describe the typical Whitman student, it would have to be *outdoorsy*. Whitties love their surroundings, from the hills around Walla Walla to the streams they pass on their way to class. Ankeny Field is the heart of this small campus and the site of many an intramural sports game, as well as the annual Beer Mile, an event that basically involves running and drinking. Reid Campus Center houses the Center for Community Service, the popular Outdoor Program, and a coffee shop where the president of the college can be found holding office hours. Students are required to live on campus for two years. Upperclassmen tend to move off campus, but those who stay can live in apartment-style residences. Prentiss, the all-female residence, houses four sororities, and there are also a number of Interest Houses. A third of the student body goes Greek; students insist, however, that the stereotypical frat scene is toned down here. Clubs and organizations run the gamut from the Peace Coalition to the Juggling Club, and this passionate student body is always forming new groups.

Walla Squared

Known as "the town so nice they named it twice," Walla Walla is a historic town situated in an arid region of southern Washington. The small seventy-seven-acre campus is only three blocks from downtown, but aside from a bowling alley, movie theater, and some restaurants and coffee places, there's not too much to entertain a college student. Some cite Walla Walla's sleepiness as a drawback, while others believe it's the reason campus life is so active. For outdoor enthusiasts, there's plenty to do in the surrounding area, including skiing, hiking, and boating. When they tire of wheat fields and sweet onions, students can get to Portland and Seattle in four hours, and Spokane in less than three.

Admissions

Average high school GPA:	3.82
Average freshman SAT writing / math / critical reading score:	657 / 657 / 664
Average freshman ACT score:	26
Application fee:	$45

Application deadlines:
1/15 (freshmen)
1/15 (transfer)
11/15 (early decision)

Total applicants:	2,740
Total accepted:	1,292 (47%)
Total accepted who enrolled:	366

Notification dates:
4/1 (freshmen)
4/1 (transfer)
12/15 (early decision)

Acceptance rate for early decision applicants:	76%

Students

Percentage of male / female students:	46% / 54%
Percentage of students from out of state:	59%
Percentage of students graduating in 4 years / 6 years:	78% / 86%

Money

Total endowment:	$340,803,000
Total tuition:	$30,530
Total cost with fees & expenses:	$39,896
Average financial aid package:	$22,300
Percentage of students who sought aid and received it:	91%
Percentage of students receiving financial aid:	44%

Also Check Out

Colgate University

Colorado College

Reed College

University of Puget Sound

Williams College

PO Box 687
Williamstown, MA 01267

(413) 597-3131
http://www.williams.edu/

 BIG BRAIN

 BIG PERSPECTIVE

Sitting on top of the world

5 REASONS IT'S COOL

1. Williams students are smart, motivated, well-rounded, ambitious, fun-loving, hard-working, and diverse. In other words, they're **the cream of the high school crop**.

2. The student-faculty ratio is 7:1. **Your professors** *will* **know your name.**

3. **Williams will meet your demonstrated financial need for all four years.**

4. Yes, the location is rural and middle-of-nowhere. But that just means that students pull out all the stops to make theirs **a fun and lively campus.**

5. Two words: fall foliage. The **leafy Berkshire mountains** nearby are breathtaking come autumn.

The Basics

Public / private: private nonprofit
Total enrollment / undergrads: 2,049 / 2,003
Campus setting: small town
Students call it: Williams
Students are called: Ephs (after Ephraim Williams, the college's founder)
Notable alums: Steve Case (CEO, AOL), Robert F. Engle (Nobel Laureate, Economics), Elia Kazan (filmmaker), James Garfield (U.S. president), Stephen Sondheim (composer)

Breadth and Depth

Williams encourages academic breadth and depth in its students, who are cut from the same super-intellectual cloth. All students must complete three courses in each of three categories: arts and humanities, social science, and natural science and math. Also required is a course focused on non-Western subject matter. Williams runs a 4-1-4 schedule, which means that students take four classes in the fall and spring, sandwiching one in-depth short-term class in January. This Winter Study allows students to complete an independent project, travel abroad, volunteer, or work one-on-one with professors on special projects. The faculty members at Williams are highly regarded, not only as talented teachers but also as scholars. Workloads can be intense, and professors occasionally assign reading lists that defy realistic expectations. About a third of students double major, and a third study abroad. Among Williams's exclusive offerings are programs in Oxford and New York City and an oceanography program in Connecticut.

School's Out for . . . Autumn

One Friday morning every October, Williams's president decides that Mountain Day has arrived. Bells are rung to communicate the decision to students, and all classes are cancelled. The Williams community—well, those who want to, anyway—hikes to the top of nearby **Mount Greylock**, enjoys a free lunch, and takes in the area's spectacular fall foliage.

One Small Happy Family

The Williams community is a close-knit one, which may be the product of necessity, given the college's remote location. There are no fraternities, sororities, or even special-interest housing, as the administration is committed to maintaining a social atmosphere that enables mixing and openness. Parties are generally low-key events in the dorms, although things get considerably more spirited when a game against rival Amherst has just finished or is about to start. Only seniors may live off campus, which is where the lion's share of social life occurs. Williams is a Division III athletic powerhouse, and even students who aren't into organized sports take advantage of the many opportunities for staying fit on the hiking and bike trails throughout the Berkshires. Williams offers around 120 student clubs, including singing groups and the *Record* newspaper. Students represent all sides of the political spectrum, and fully one-third of the student body identify as people of color.

Sure Is Quiet out Here

Williams is located in the far northwest corner of Massachusetts, just a few miles from both the New York and Vermont borders. The small size, isolation, and rural character of Williamstown are causes for either complaint or celebration, depending on your taste. The campus is home to many first-rate facilities, including the Museum of Art, which contains paintings by Pisarro and Chagall, an observatory, a theater, and four libraries. The Berkshires offer plenty of outdoor activities, including hiking and nature watching galore. The nearest big cities are Boston, which is 145 miles away, and New York City, which is 165 miles.

Admissions

Average high school GPA:	—
Average freshman SAT verbal / math score:	703 / 704
Average freshman ACT score:	26
Application fee:	$60

Application deadlines:
1/1 (freshmen)
3/1 (transfer)
11/10 (early decision)

Total applicants:	5,999
Total accepted:	1,146 (19%)
Total accepted who enrolled:	534

Notification dates:
4/1 (freshmen)
5/1 (transfer)
12/15 (early decision)

Acceptance rate for early decision applicants:	38%

Students

Percentage of male / female students:	49% / 51%
Percentage of students from out of state:	83%
Percentage of students graduating in 4 years / 6 years:	90% / 95%

Money

Total endowment:	$1,334,402,000
Total tuition:	$33,478
Total cost with fees & expenses:	$43,450
Average financial aid package:	$32,979
Percentage of students who sought aid and received it:	100%
Percentage of students receiving financial aid:	43%

Also Check Out

Amherst College

Bowdoin College

Dartmouth College

Wesleyan University

Yale University

Wofford College

429 North Church Street Spartanburg, SC 29303	(864) 597-4000 http://www.wofford.ed

BIG PERSPECTIVE

A great education never looked this good.

5 REASONS IT'S COOL

1. **Students are known by their names**, not by their student ID numbers.

2. The one-month Interim Period allows students to **learn in nontraditional ways** by traveling, taking unusual classes, or designing their own course of study.

3. Study the environment or just relax in the gardenlike setting of the **150-acre Wofford Arboretum**, which features more than 4,500 different species.

4. **Professors are a friendly and accessible bunch** who make sure students get the attention they need to succeed.

5. **Southern hospitality and friendliness** is served up (with a side of corn bread!).

The Basics

Public/private: private religious
Total enrollment/undergrads: 1,240 / 1,240
Campus setting: urban
Students call it: Wofford
Students are called: Terriers
Notable alums: Paul S. Atkins (commissioner, Securities and Exchange Commission), Olin D. Johnston (governor, South Carolina), Jerry Richardson (owner, Carolina Panthers)

This Liberal Arts College Means Serious Business

Students love Wofford because they know they'll be pushed to succeed, no matter their major. The college boasts a high admittance rate to professional schools, and many students choose to major in pre-professional subjects such as business, political science, and theology. Wofford also has a strong track record in putting its students into top medical and dental schools. Students get a well-earned academic break and change of pace during the month-long January term known as the Interim Period. This is when students get to mix things up a bit by taking offbeat courses such as The Politics of Hip-Hop, The History of Mapmaking, and The Study of America's Food Culture. Other students use the time to intern, go abroad on university-sponsored trips, or pursue their own academic interests in independent study courses. Study abroad is popular, and opportunities are available in fifty-nine different countries.

Ride Your Pride

Sports are a big deal at Wofford, but it isn't just the school's Division I athletic teams that draw big crowds. Each May, academic departments and student organizations decorate golf carts and race them around campus in an event known as Terrio. Each cart is decorated in a way that represents the department or organization sponsoring it, and the riders wear matching uniforms. Prizes are given for the fastest and best-decorated carts. In 2007, the French Department took the design prize for a cart clad in mustaches, striped shirts, berets, bread, and wine.

Students of All Stripes

With dozens of extracurricular activities, movies, concerts, seventeen Division I athletic teams, and social clubs, Wofford has something to offer everyone. Students of all stripes show their Wofford colors when they paint their faces to cheer on the men's basketball team. More than half of students go Greek, choosing from eight fraternities and six sororities. And while Wofford has traditionally attracted a conservative study body, the current administration is working hard to recruit more people from all ethnic and socioeconomic backgrounds. In recent years, the college has also launched living-learning communities, where students live among students with similar interests who are enrolled in the same classes. These communities have themes, such as race relations or the arts.

A Little Piece of Heaven

When the NFL's Carolina Panthers held their training camp at Wofford in 2007, *Sports Illustrated*'s Tim Layden referred to the college as "Training Camp Heaven." But the school isn't just heavenly for jocks and sports enthusiasts. With its own arboretum spanning more than 150 acres and touting almost 4,500 trees, Wofford is a nature lover's dream come true. Even those who aren't into hiking and exploring find the campus to be a great place to study. The campus also features several theaters, free movie rentals, concerts, and guest lectures. The local restaurants and shops leave much to be desired, which is why most students head down to nearby Greenville for shopping, eating, concerts, and pub-crawling.

Admissions

Average high school GPA:	4.0
Average freshman SAT writing / math / critical reading score:	601 / 637 / 617
Average freshman ACT score:	24
Application fee:	$40

Application deadlines:
2/1 (freshmen)
continuous (transfer)
11/15 (early decision)

Total applicants:	2,089
Total accepted:	1,201 (57%)
Total accepted who enrolled:	378

Notification dates:
3/15 (freshmen)
continuous (transfer)
12/1 (early decision)

Acceptance rate for early decision applicants:	69%

Students

Percentage of male / female students:	52% / 48%
Percentage of students from out of state:	38%
Percentage of students graduating in 4 years / 6 years:	74% / 78%

Money

Total endowment:	$132,000,000
Total tuition:	$26,110
Total cost with fees & expenses:	$34,255
Average financial aid package:	$22,401
Percentage of students who sought aid and received it:	89%
Percentage of students receiving financial aid:	48%

Also Check Out

Sewanee: The University of the South

University of Georgia

The University of South Carolina–Columbia

Vanderbilt University

Wake Forest University

Yale University

38 Hillhouse Ave
New Haven, CT 06520

(203) 432-4771
http://www.yale.edu/

 **BIG BRAIN**

 **BIG PERSPECTIVE**

 **BIG RESEARCH**

Who wants to be the next POTUS?

5 REASONS IT'S COOL

1. An array of **special academic programs** for freshmen enhances the already-amazing curricula.

2. Despite their stellar achievements, **faculty members are there for students**, at a ratio of 6:1 in the classroom and as members of students' residential colleges.

3. The **dazzling alumni roster** includes U.S. presidents and leaders in every field.

4. **Arts and culture** are at the heart of student life, with world-class museums and theater right on campus.

5. Super hush-hush **secret societies** dot Yale's social and architectural landscape.

The Basics

Public / private: private nonprofit
Total enrollment / undergrads: 11,416 / 5,333
Campus setting: urban
Students call it: Yale
Students are called: Bulldogs, Yalies
Notable alums: George W. Bush (U.S. president), George H. W. Bush (U.S. president), Michiko Kakutani (book critic), William Howard Taft (U.S. president), Cole Porter (composer), Benjamin Spock (child psychologist), Wendy Wasserstein (playwright), Noah Webster (author of the first dictionary of American English), Eli Whitney (inventor, cotton gin), Naomi Wolf (author), Bob Woodward (journalist)

Undergrads First

Professors teach all undergraduate classes at Yale, and the student-faculty ratio is an astonishing 6:1. Yale College brings together undergraduates of all majors and offers them exceptional programs of study. Students must apply for admission to some special programs, including Directed Studies, which focuses on Western civilization, and Perspectives on Science, a supplemental lecture and discussion series. Freshman seminars, which are open to all, have an enrollment limit of fifteen to eighteen students. There is no core curriculum and no required courses. The most popular majors are economics, history, and political science. Exceptional programs in the arts and architecture enrich the academic diversity at Yale.

Can You Keep a Secret?

Yale has a number of secret societies housed on campus, from Wolf's Head to Scroll and Key. The most infamous, though, is the Skull and Bones Society. Several Supreme Court justices and captains of industry were Bonesmen; so were President George W. Bush and his 2004 rival, John Kerry, both of whom have declined to discuss the group.

College Collage

Students of all stripes tend to feel welcome at Yale. There's a spirit of camaraderie and support that is often lacking at the nation's other top schools. Like its English peers, Yale has residential colleges around which student life revolves. Students compete on behalf of their colleges in intramural sports, adding to the distinct personality of each. The twelve residential colleges have affiliated faculty members who support students and help sort out any life or academic issues that come up. Masters of each college host Master's Teas, at which renowned guest speakers meet with students. Close to 90 percent of students live in university housing, which attests both to the appeal of the Yale campus and to the less-than-desirable nature of New Haven. New Haven's social scene is not great, but Yale's is terrific. Among its slew of major arts and culture venues are the Yale Repertory Theater, where Meryl Streep strutted her stuff, and the Peabody Museum of Natural History, which boasts the nation's second-largest collection of dinosaur fossils. Singers will find a cappella groups aplenty at this musical school.

New Haven Gothic

Yale's stately collegiate Gothic architecture reinforces its storied history and towering reputation. Modern exceptions to older styles dot the campus. The unusual Ingalls Rink, for example, features tensile architecture and suggests the shape of a whale. Since the early 2000s, big renovation projects throughout campus have brought the residential colleges up to date. Each college has a unique look, which strengthens the students' sense that their particular college is its own small community. In contrast to campus, surrounding New Haven has an urban feel. New York City is about two hours away, and cars and trains make getting to the city a breeze.

Admissions

Average high school GPA:	—
Average freshman SAT writing / math / critical reading score:	722 / 721 / 723
Average freshman ACT score:	—
Application fee:	$75

Application deadlines:
12/31 (freshmen)
3/1 (transfer)
11/1 (early action)

Total applicants:	21,101
Total accepted:	1,878 (9%)
Total accepted who enrolled:	1,315

Notification dates:
4/1 (freshmen)
5/4 (transfer)
12/15 (early action)

Acceptance rate for early action applicants:	17%

Students

Percentage of male / female students:	51% / 49%
Percentage of students from out of state:	92%
Percentage of students graduating in 4 years / 6 years:	88% / 96%

Money

Total endowment:	$4,294,967,295
Total tuition:	$33,030
Total cost with fees & expenses:	$44,050
Average financial aid package:	$32,533
Percentage of students who sought aid and received it:	100%
Percentage of students receiving financial aid:	43%

Also Check Out

Brown University

Harvard University

Massachusetts Institute of Technology

Princeton University

Stanford University

Schools by Category

BIG BRAIN

BIG CHOICE

BIG HAND

BIG IDEA

BIG JOB

BIG PERSPECTIVE

SCHOOLS BY CATEGORY

BIG PLAN

BIG RESEARCH

SCHOOLS BY CATEGORY

BIG WORLD

Schools by Region

NORTHEAST

SOUTHEAST

MIDWEST

SOUTHWEST

NORTHWEST